TADATOSHI FUJIMAKI

Whenever I go out to eat, I can't bear to order the same dish as anyone else in my party. No matter how much I want it, I'll always just change my order. I know it's pointless, but this is a rule I can never break.

—2010

Tadatoshi Fujimaki was born on June 9, 1982, in Tokyo. He made his debut in 2007 in *Akamaru Jump* with *Kuroko's Basketball*, which was later serialized in *Weekly Shonen Jump*. *Kuroko's Basketball* quickly gained popularity and became an anime in Japan in 2012.

BASKETBALL

5 & 6

SHONEN JUMP Manga Edition
BY TADATOSHI FUJIMAKI

Translation/Caleb Cook
Touch-Up Art & Lettering/Mark McMurray
Design/Sam Elzway
Editor/John Bae

KUROKO NO BASUKE © 2008 by Tadatoshi Fujimaki
All rights reserved.
First published in Japan in 2008 by SHUEISHA Inc., Tokyo.
English translation rights arranged by SHUEISHA Inc.

The stories, characters and incidents mentioned in this
publication are entirely fictional.

Printed in the U.S.A.

Published by VIZ Media, LLC
P.O. Box 77010
San Francisco, CA 94107

10 9 8 7 6 5 4 3 2 1
First printing, December 2016

www.viz.com

THE WORLD'S
MOST POPULAR MANGA

www.shonenjump.com

SHONEN JUMP MANGA

I KNEW IT 5

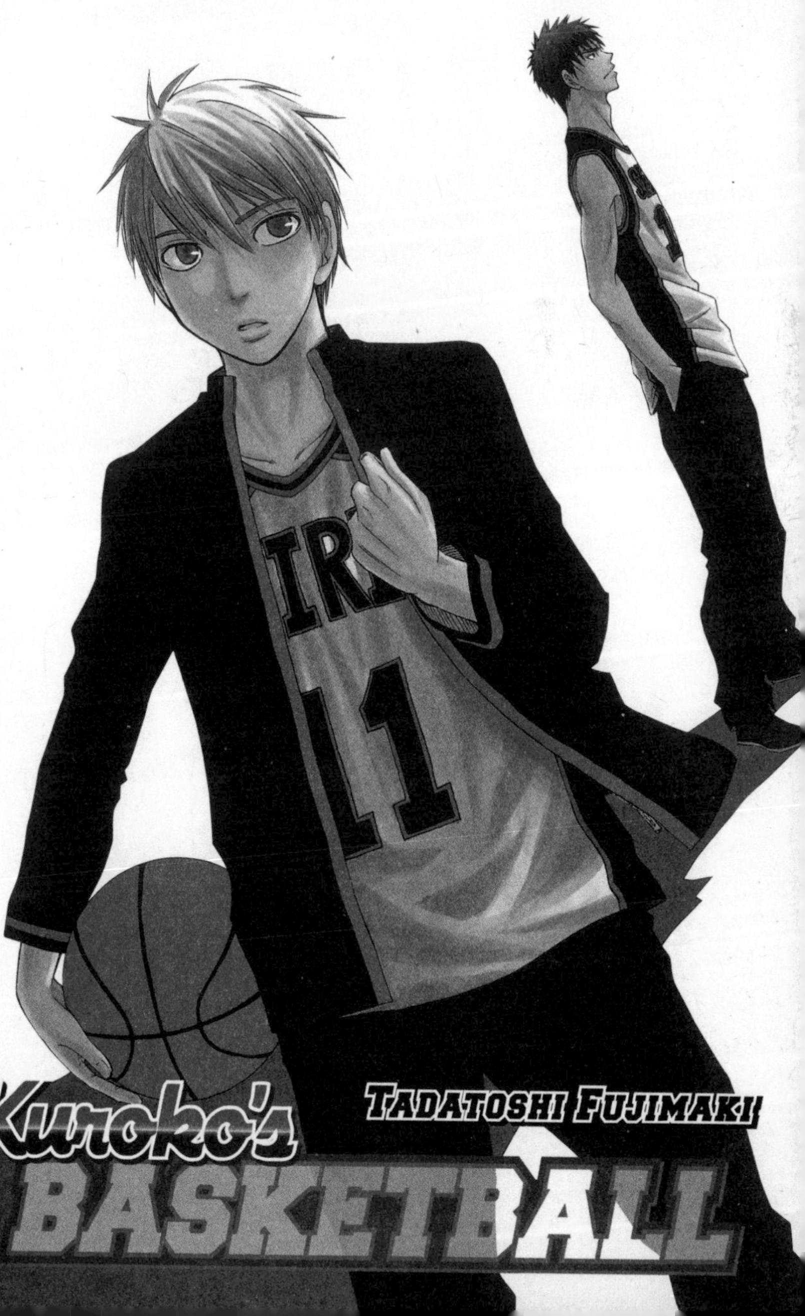

Kuroko's BASKETBALL

TADATOSHI FUJIMAKI

Characters

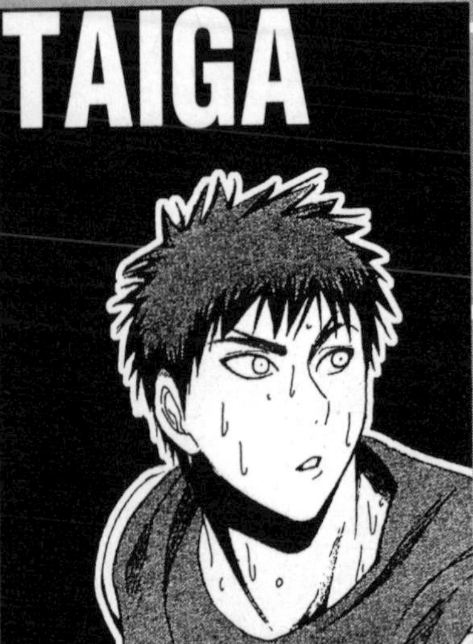
TAIGA
KAGAMI

A first-year on Seirin High's basketball team. Though he's rough around the edges, he's a gifted player with a lot of potential. His goal is to beat the Miracle Generation.

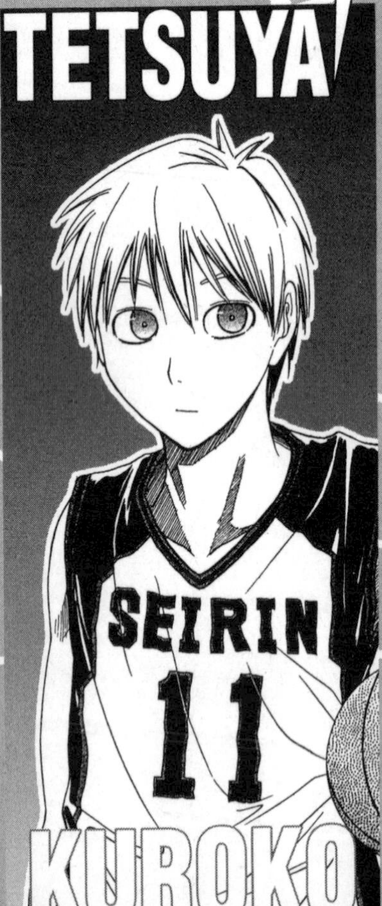
TETSUYA
SEIRIN
11
KUROKO

A first-year on Seirin High's basketball team. Gifted with a natural lack of presence, he utilizes misdirection on the court to make nearly invisible passes.

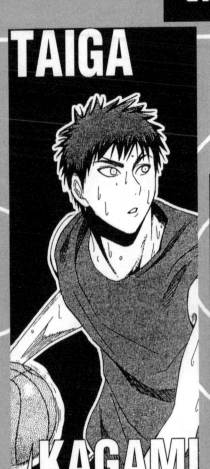

KUROKO'S BASKETBALL

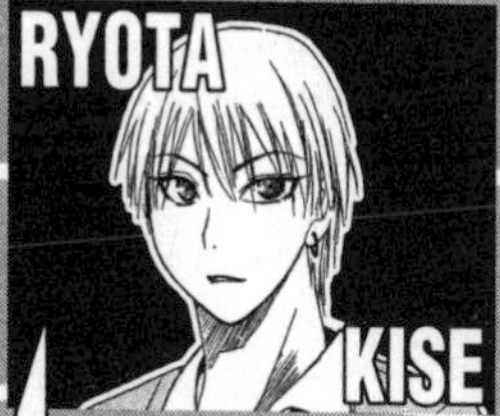
RYOTA
KISE

One of the Miracle Generation. Any basketball move he sees, he can mimic in an instant.

A second-year on Seirin High's basketball team. As captain, he led his team to the Finals League last year despite only playing first-year players.

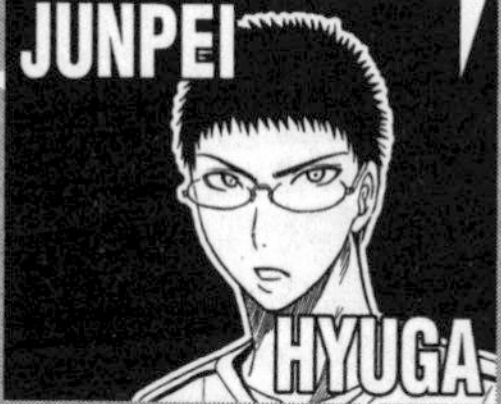
JUNPEI
HYUGA

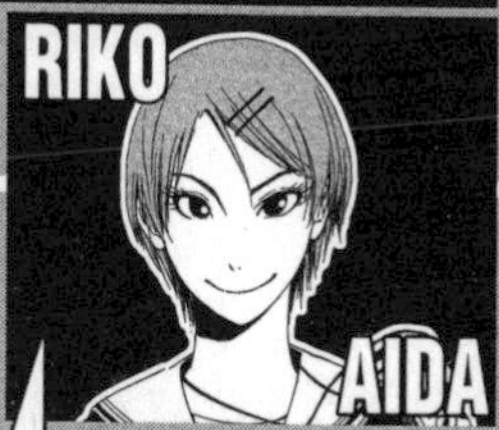
RIKO
AIDA

A second-year who's the coach of Seirin High's basketball team.

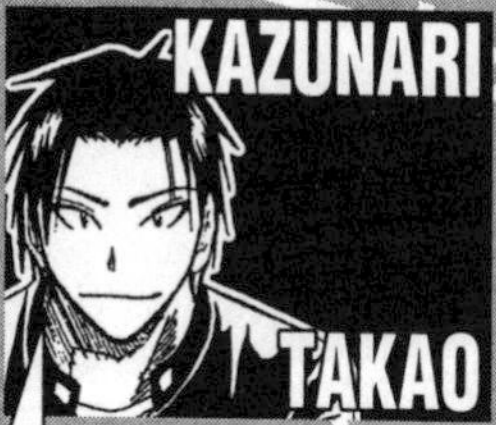
KAZUNARI
TAKAO

A first-year on Shutoku High's basketball team. He carts Midorima around in a rickshaw. His abilities are unclear at this point.

The top shooter of the Miracle Generation. He plans everything according to his horoscope.

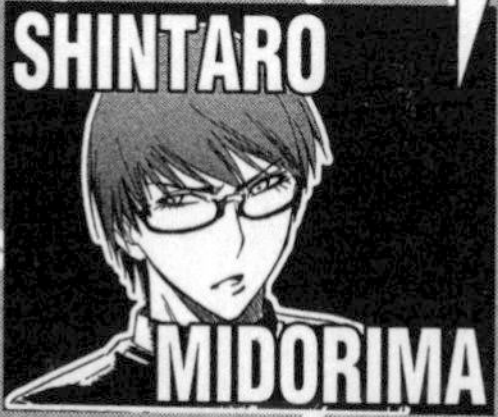
SHINTARO
MIDORIMA

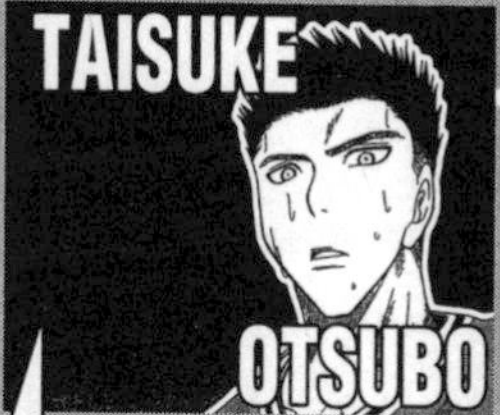
TAISUKE
OTSUBO

A third-year on Shutoku High's basketball team. As captain, he helped crush Seirin High in last year's Finals League.

Teiko Middle School is an elite championship school whose basketball team once fielded five prodigies collectively known as "the Miracle Generation." But supporting those five was a phantom sixth man—Tetsuya Kuroko. Kuroko's now a first-year high school student with zero presence who joins Seirin High's basketball club. Though his physical abilities and stats are well below average, Kuroko thrives on the court by making passes his opponents can't detect!

Seirin's aiming to qualify for Inter-High. So far, they've made their way through the qualifiers, taking down the North King, Seiho. Now, in the final qualifier game against the East King, Shutoku, Seirin is struggling against the Miracle Generation's number one shooter, Midorima, and his devastating three-pointers. Seirin pulls off a stunning comeback at the end, but Midorima might still be able to turn the tables on them in the final seconds!

STORY THUS FAR

TABLE OF CONTENTS

35TH QUARTER: I KNEW IT

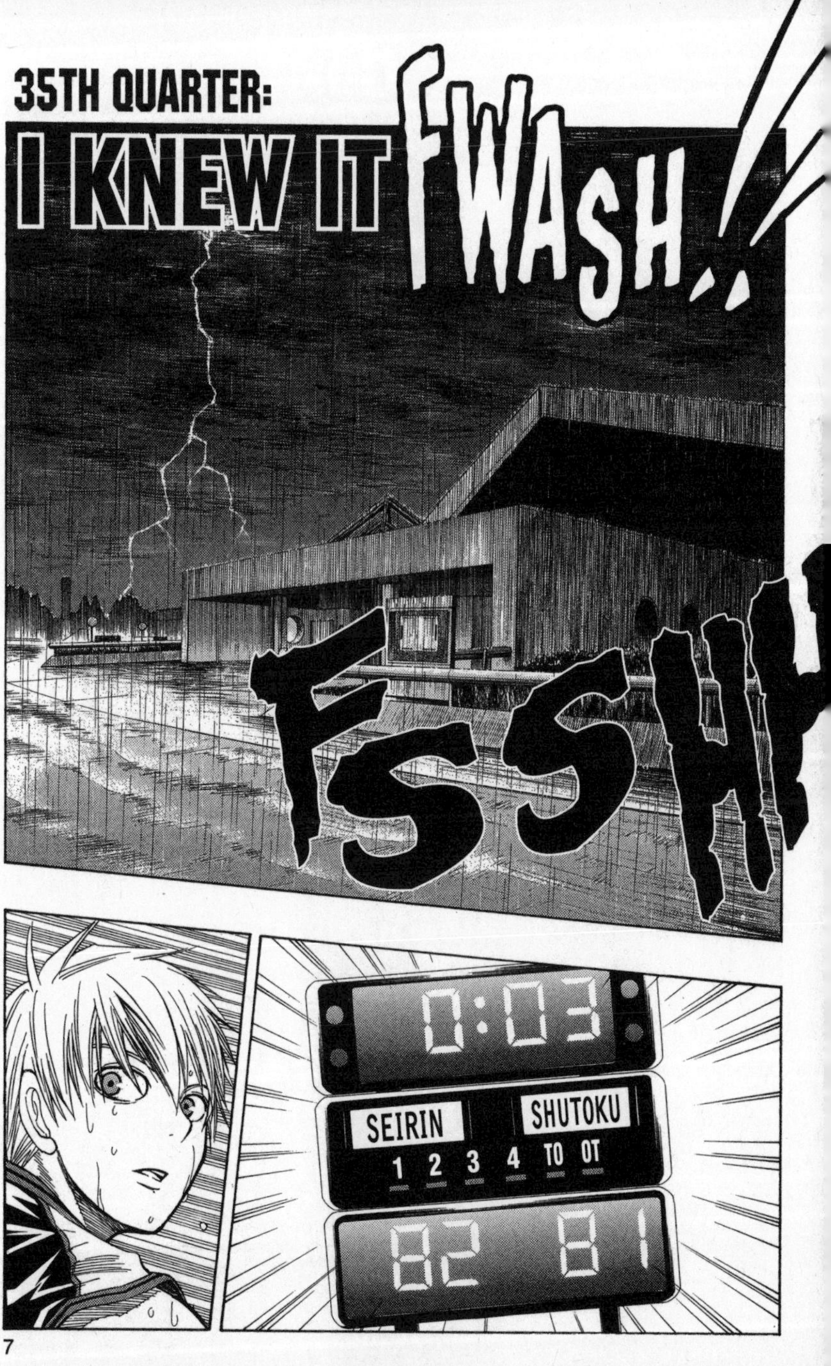
FWASH!!
FSSH
0:03
SEIRIN
SHUTOKU
1 2 3 4 TO OT
82 81

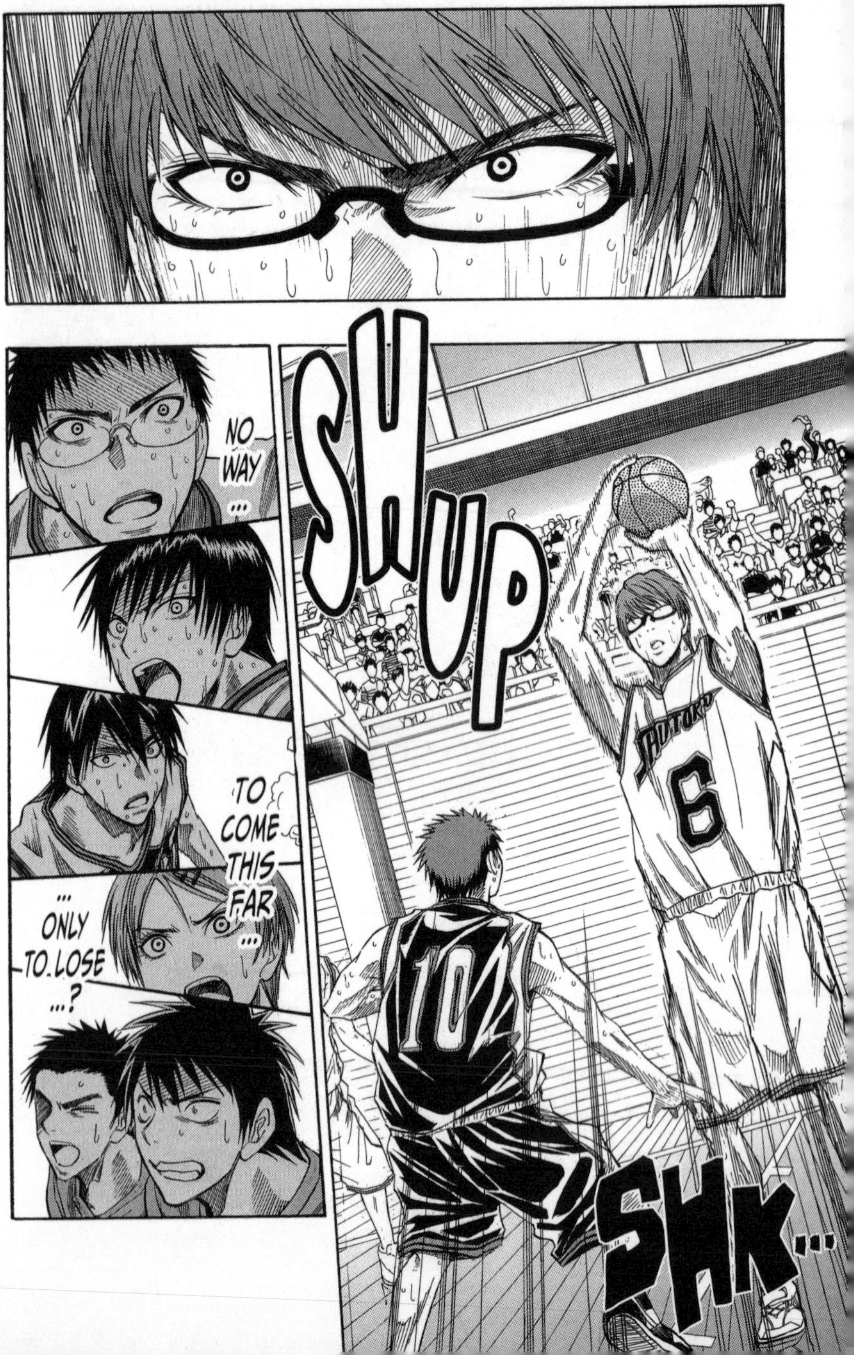
SHUP
SHK...
NO WAY ...
TO COME THIS FAR ...
... ONLY TO LOSE ...?

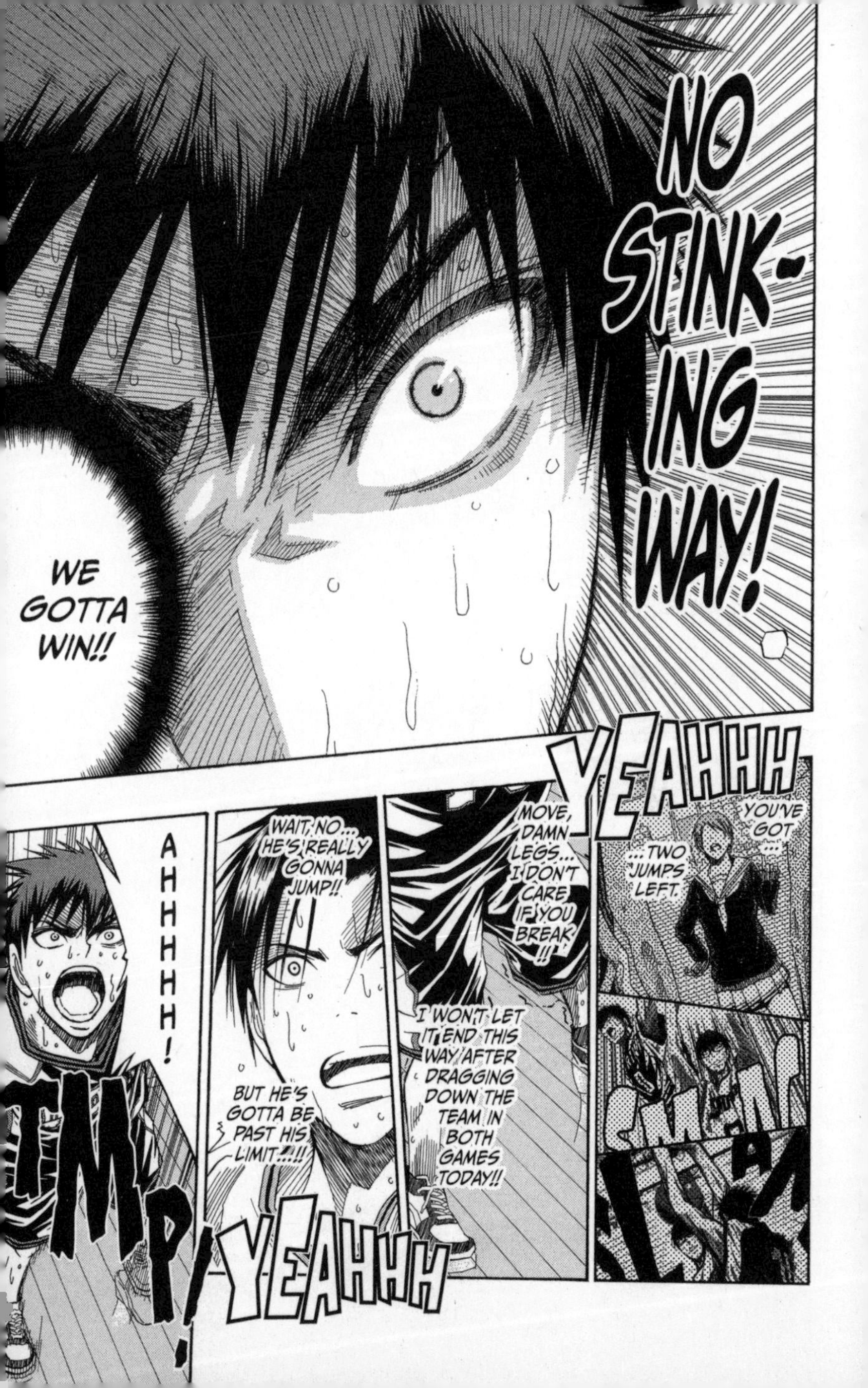
NO STINK-ING WAY!
WE GOTTA WIN!!
YEAHHH
YOU'VE GOT...
...TWO JUMPS LEFT.
MOVE, DAMN LEGS... I DON'T CARE IF YOU BREAK!!
I WON'T LET IT END THIS WAY AFTER DRAGGING DOWN THE TEAM IN BOTH GAMES TODAY!!
WAIT, NO... HE'S REALLY GONNA JUMP!!
BUT HE'S GOTTA BE PAST HIS LIMIT...!!
AHHHHHH!
TMP!
YEAHHH

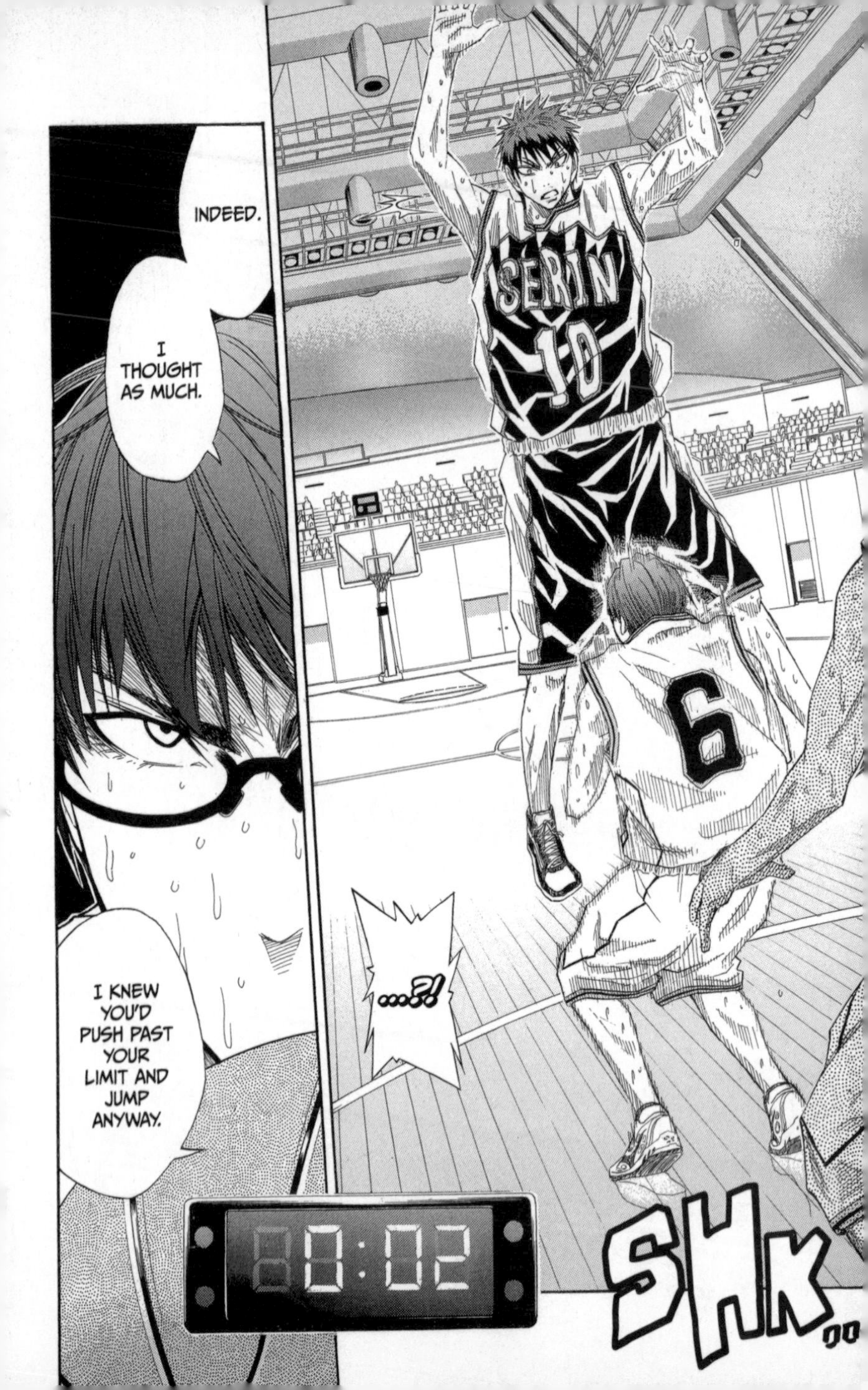
SERIN
10
6
...?!
SHK
INDEED.
I THOUGHT AS MUCH.
I KNEW YOU'D PUSH PAST YOUR LIMIT AND JUMP ANYWAY.
0:02

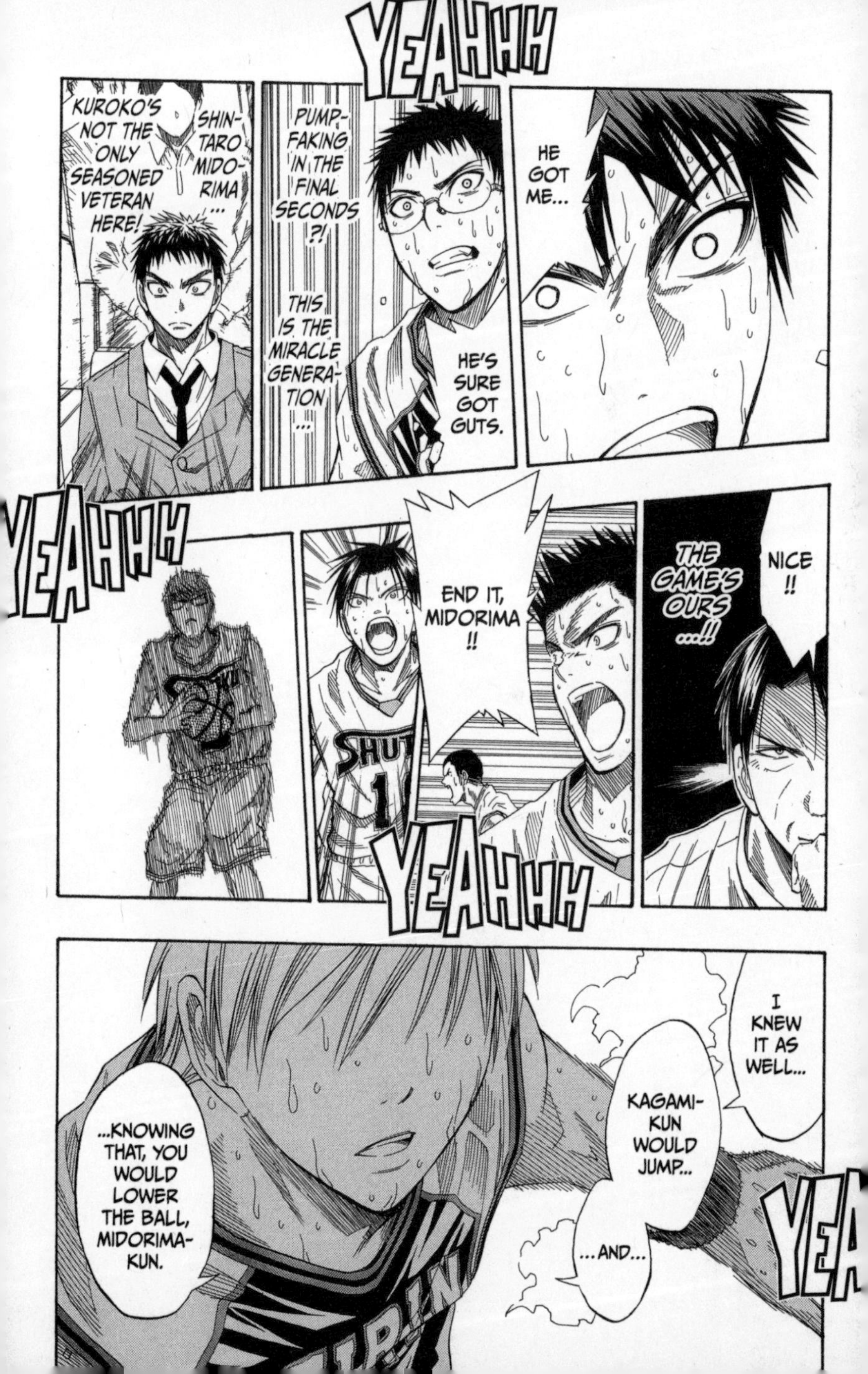
YEAHHH
HE GOT ME...
PUMP-FAKING IN THE FINAL SECONDS ?!
THIS IS THE MIRACLE GENERATION ...
HE'S SURE GOT GUTS.
SHINTARO MIDORIMA ...
KUROKO'S NOT THE ONLY SEASONED VETERAN HERE!
NICE !!
THE GAME'S OURS ...!!
END IT, MIDORIMA !!
YEAHHH
YEAHHH
I KNEW IT AS WELL...
KAGAMI-KUN WOULD JUMP...
...AND...
...KNOWING THAT, YOU WOULD LOWER THE BALL, MIDORIMA-KUN.
YEA

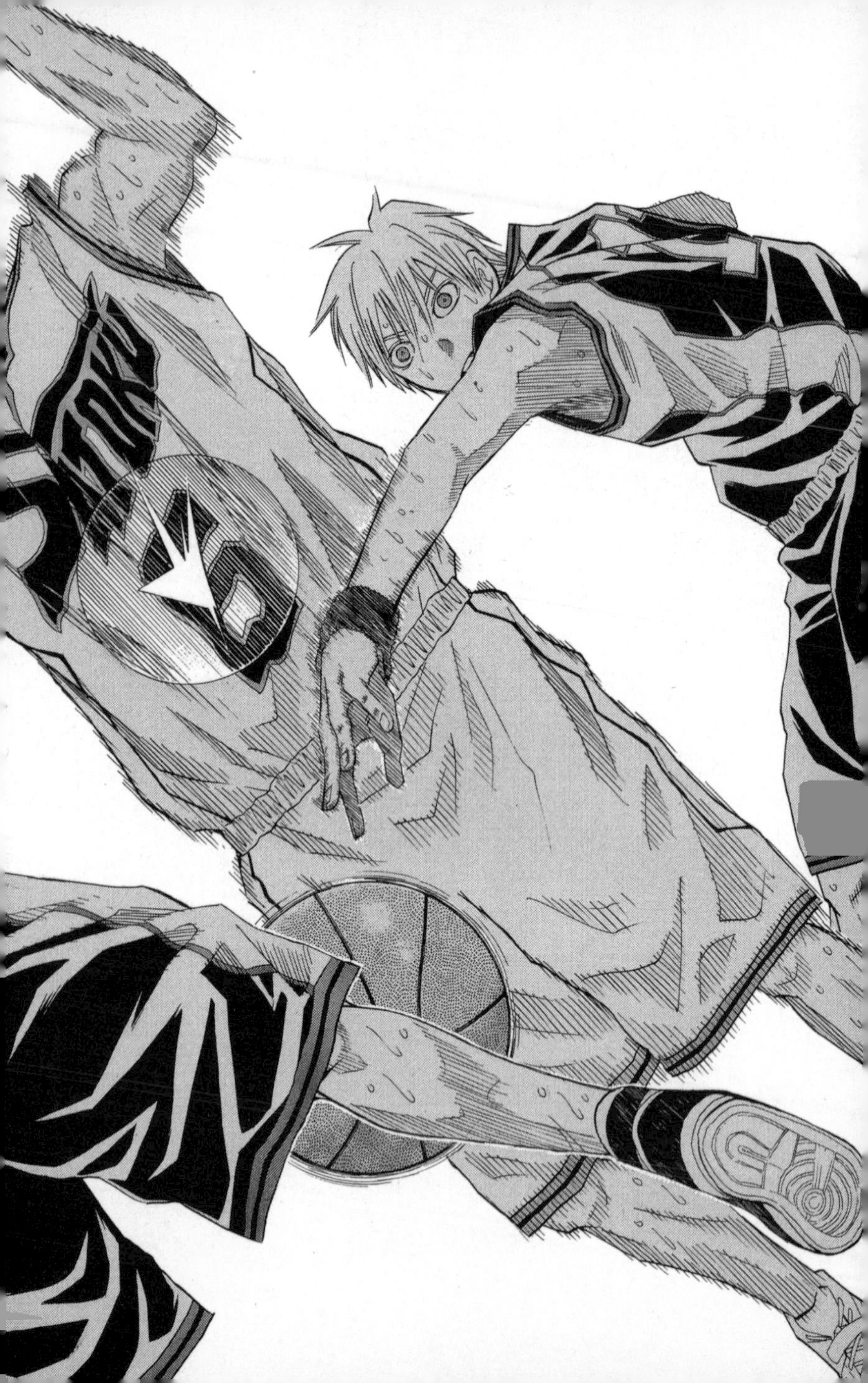

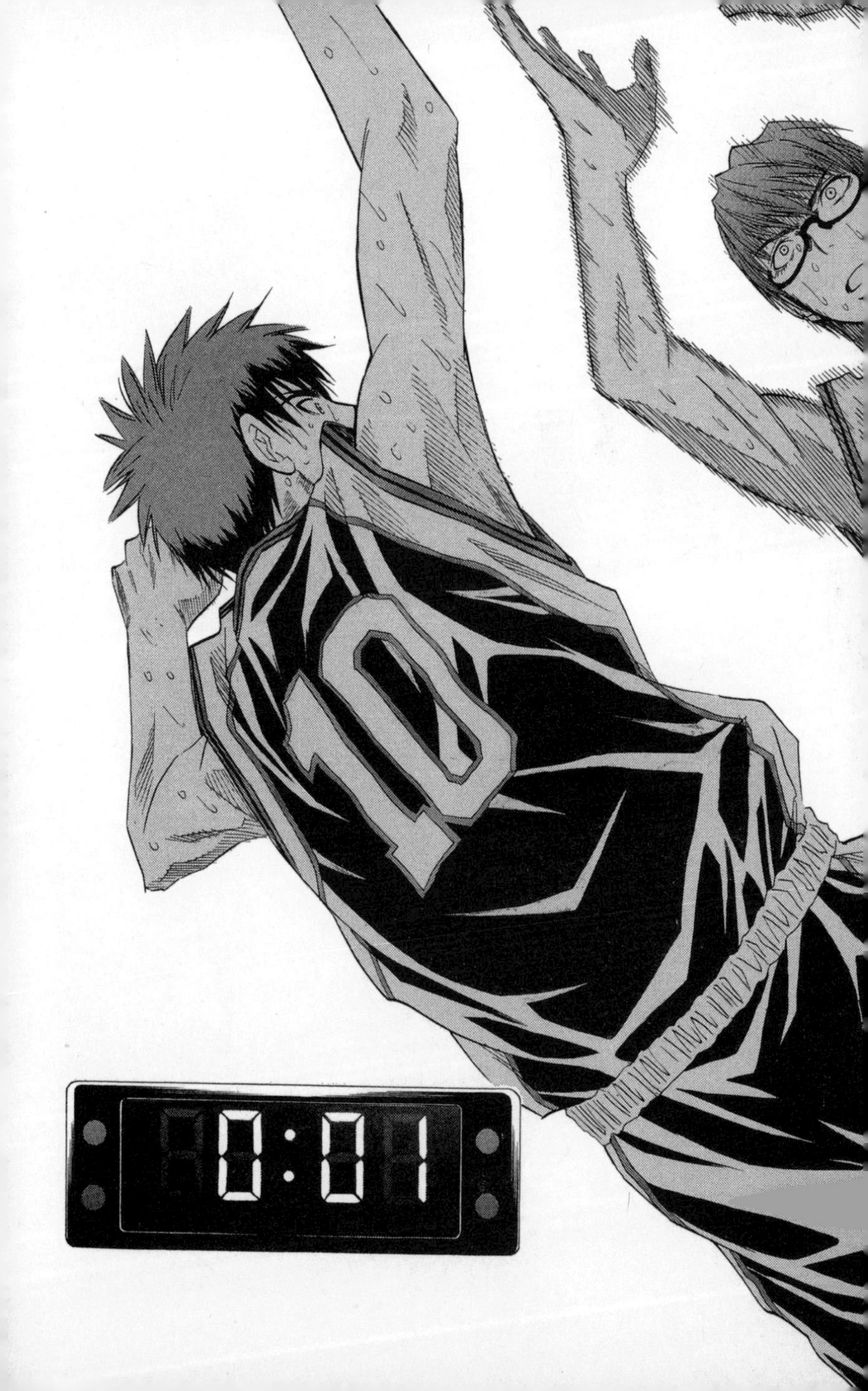
0:01

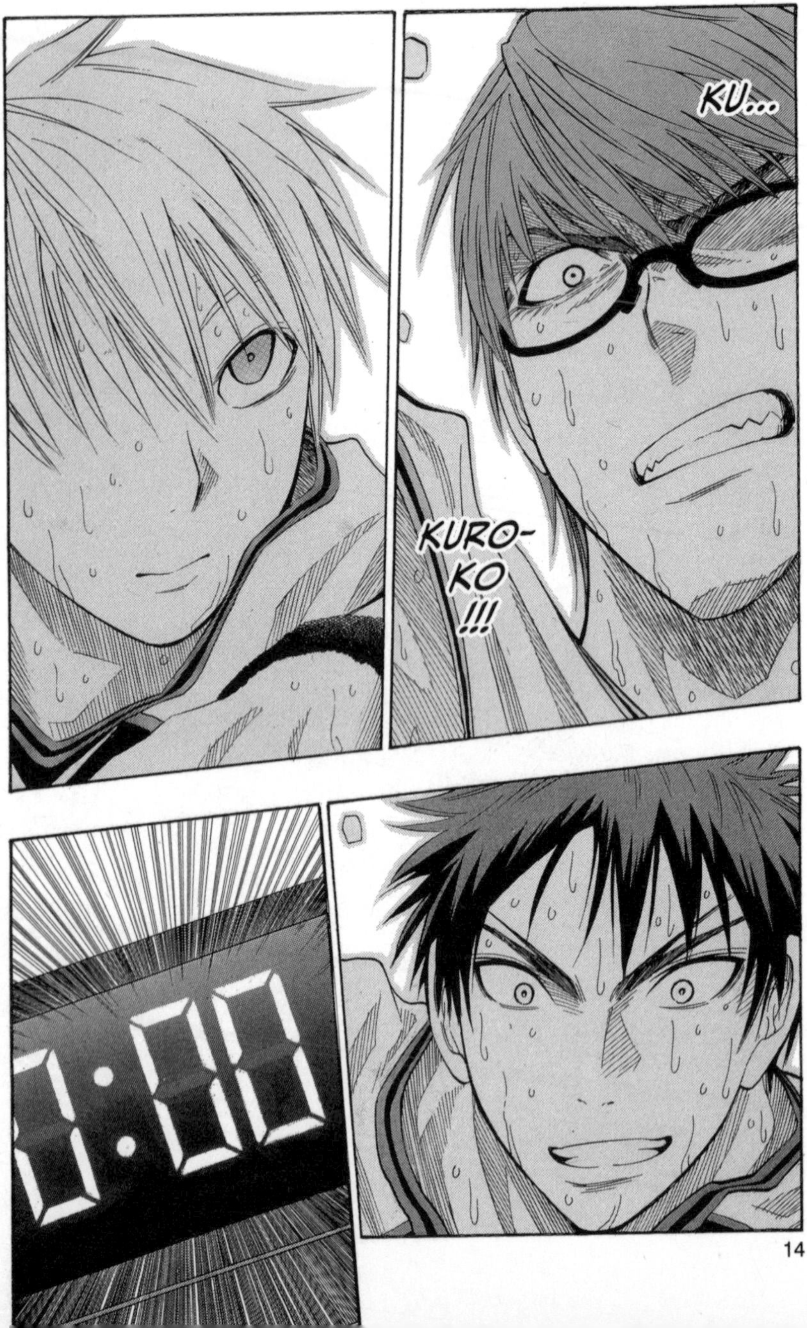
KU...
KURO-
KO
!!!

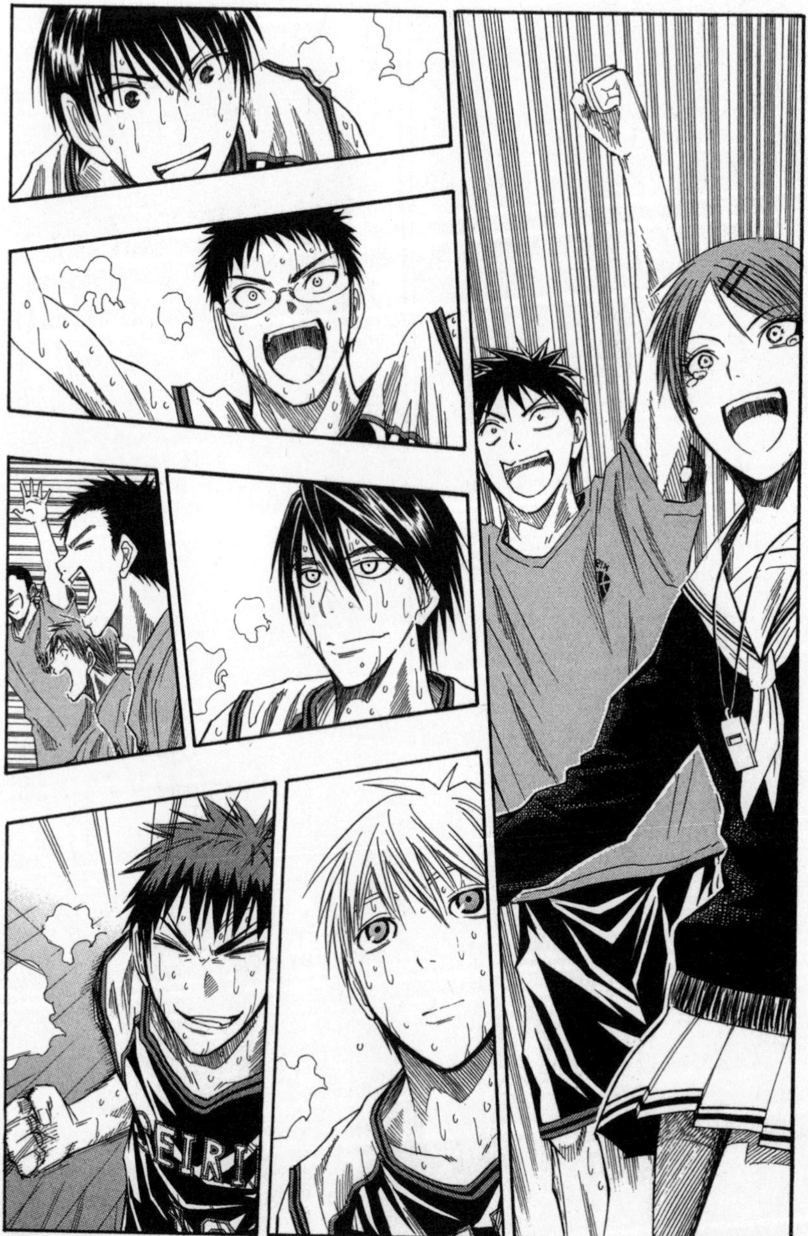

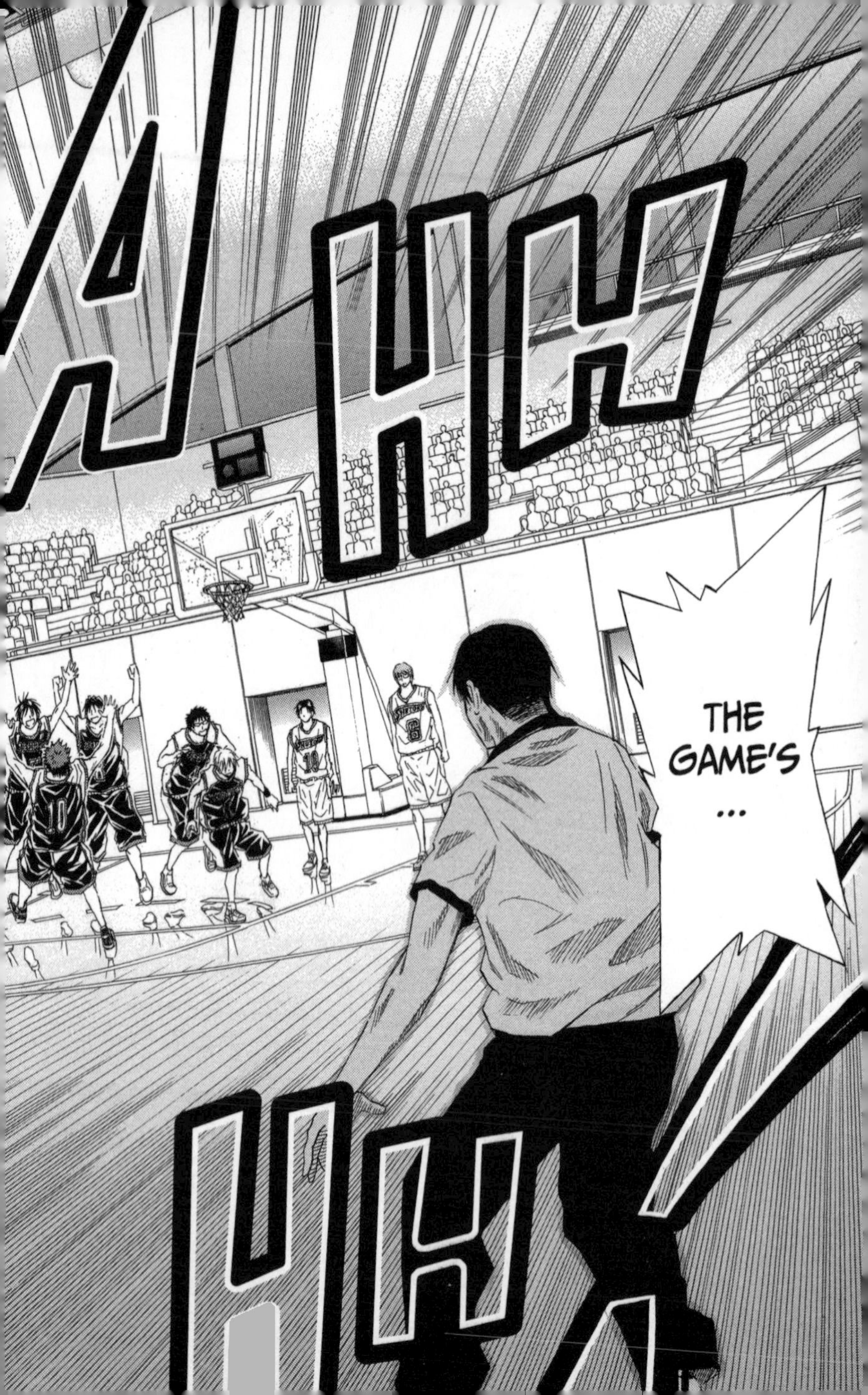
AHH
THE GAME'S ...
HHH

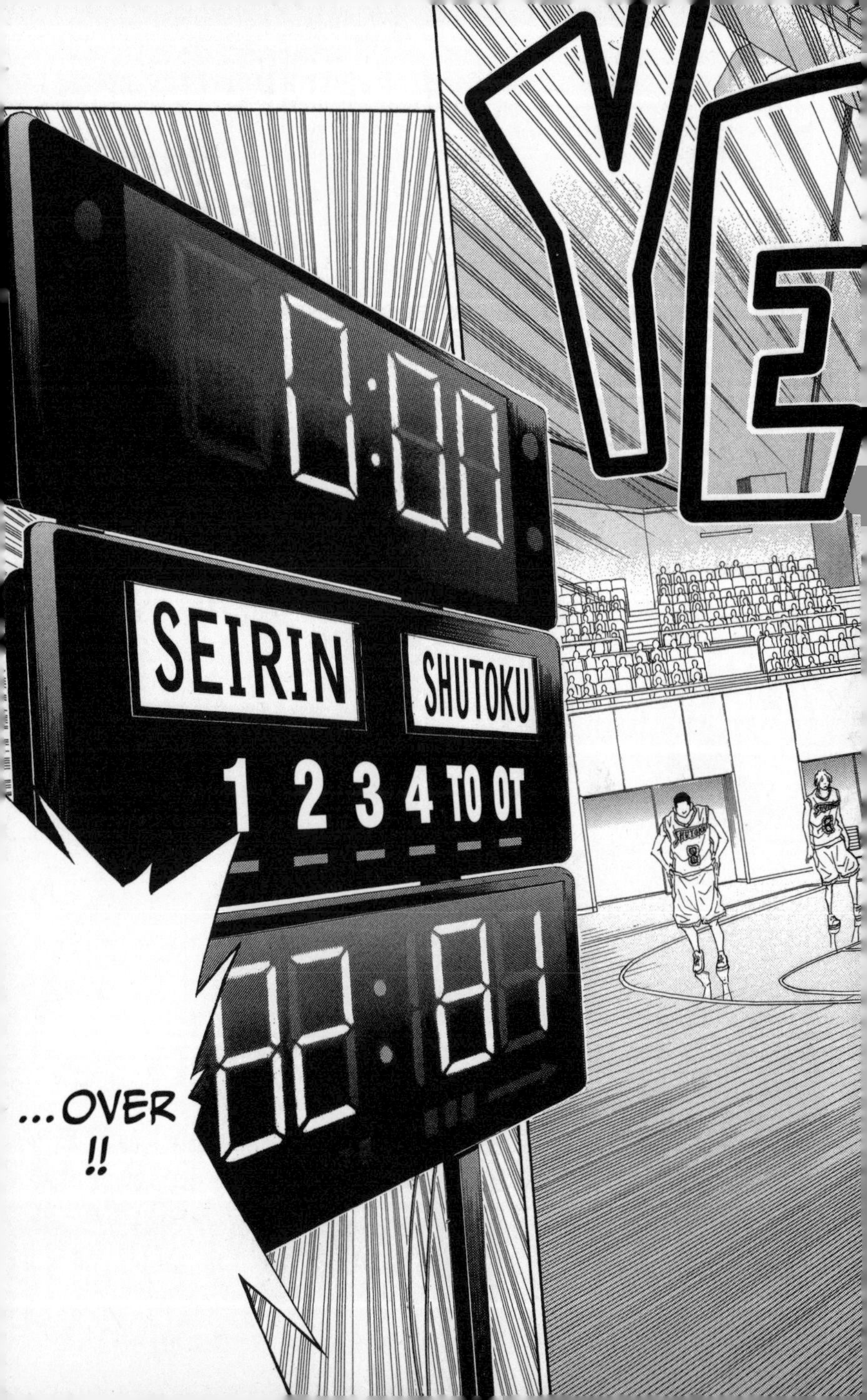
YE
SEIRIN
SHUTOKU
1 2 3 4 TO OT
...OVER !!

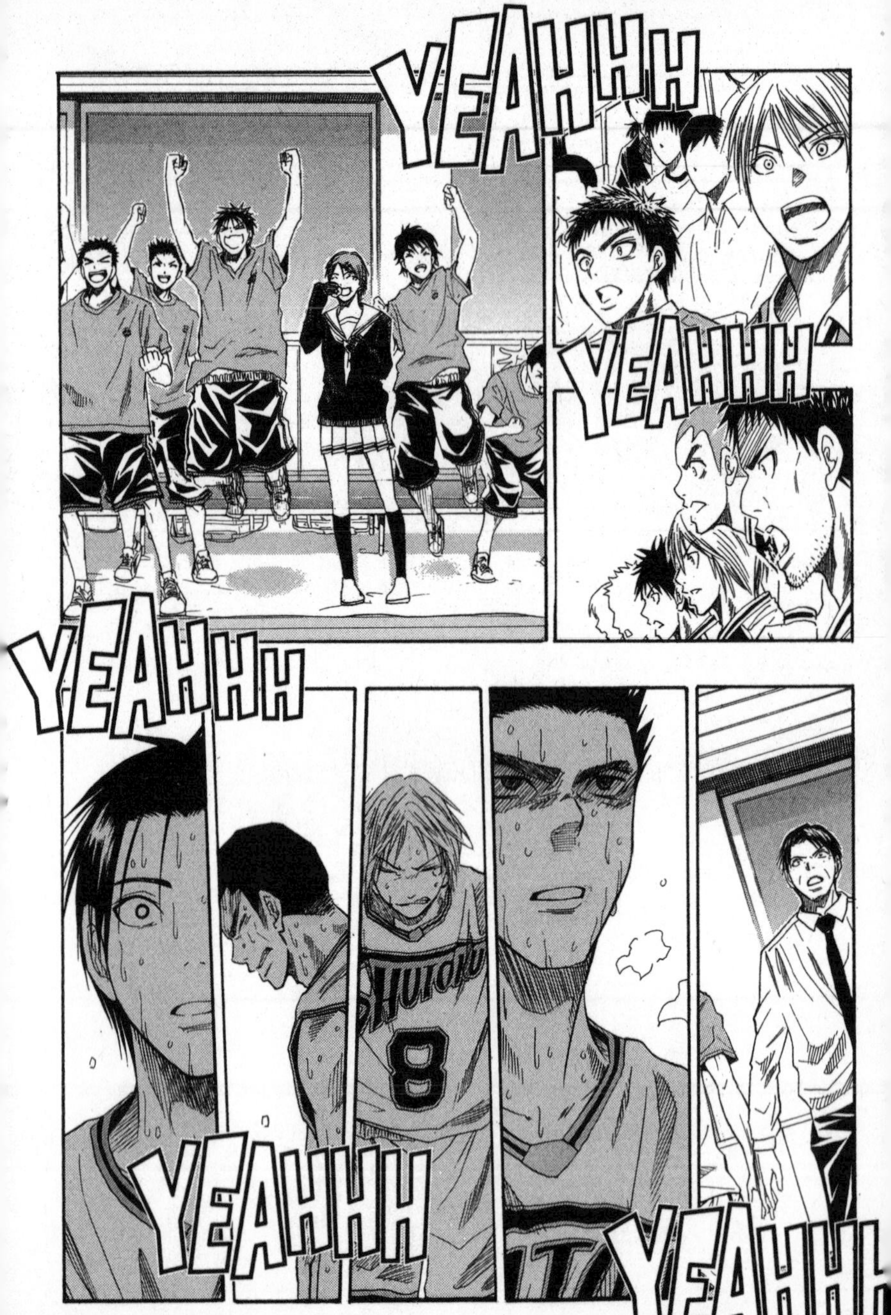
YEAHHH
YEAHHH
YEAHHH
YEAHHH
SHUTOKU
8
YEAHHH

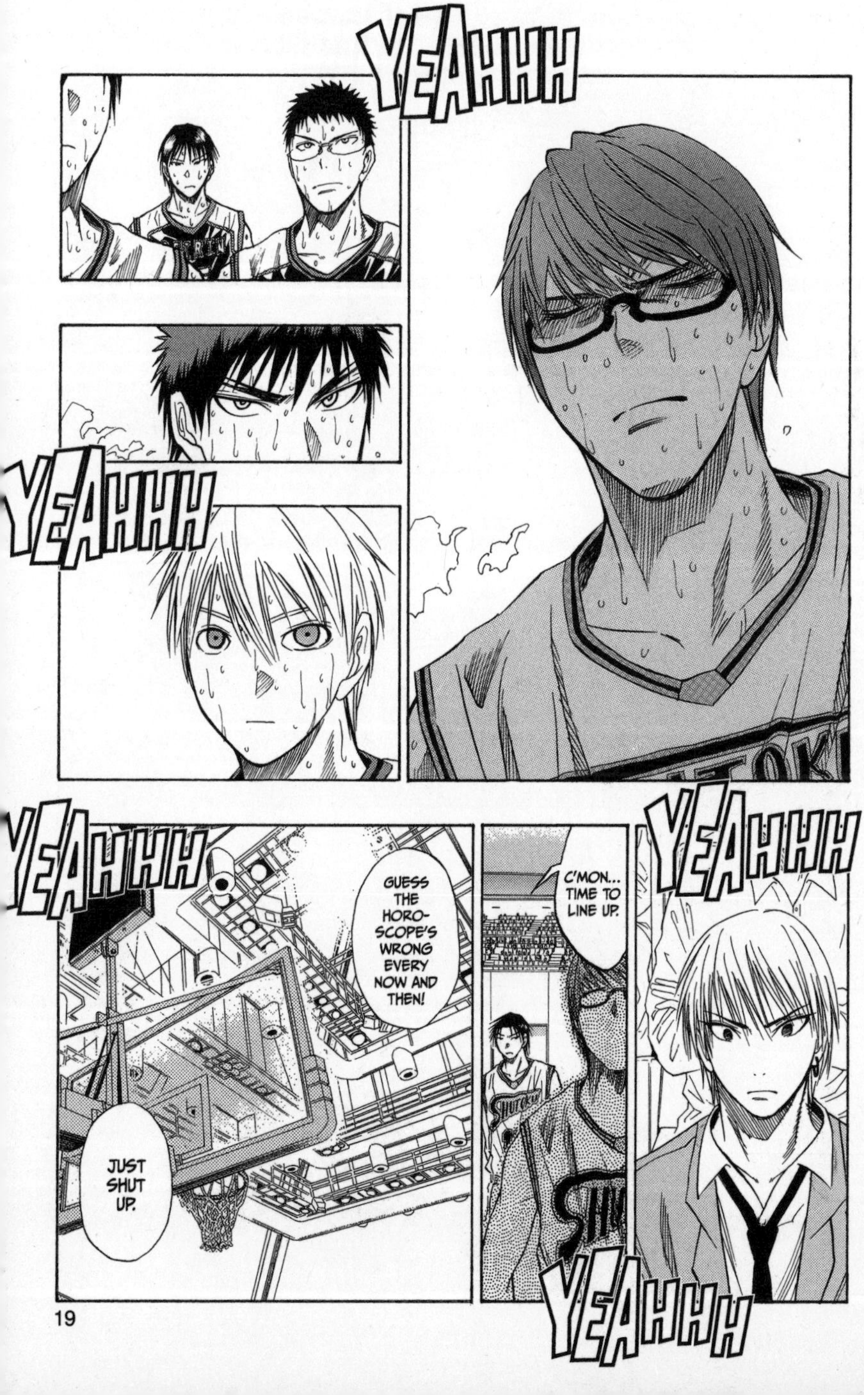
YEAHHH
YEAHHH
YEAHHH
C'MON... TIME TO LINE UP.
YEAHHH
GUESS THE HORO-SCOPE'S WRONG EVERY NOW AND THEN!
JUST SHUT UP.
YEAHHH

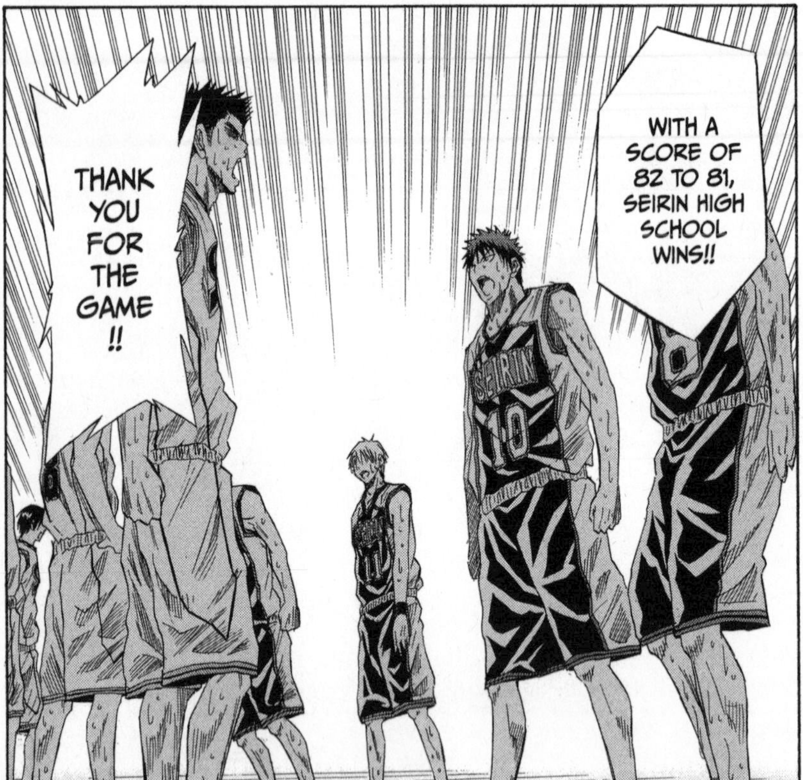
WITH A SCORE OF 82 TO 81, SEIRIN HIGH SCHOOL WINS!!
THANK YOU FOR THE GAME !!

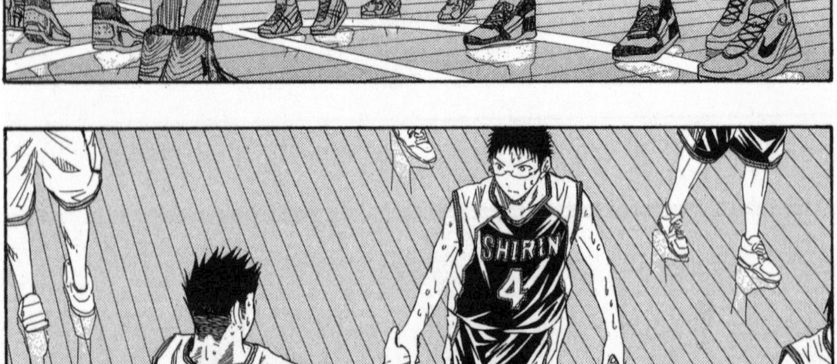

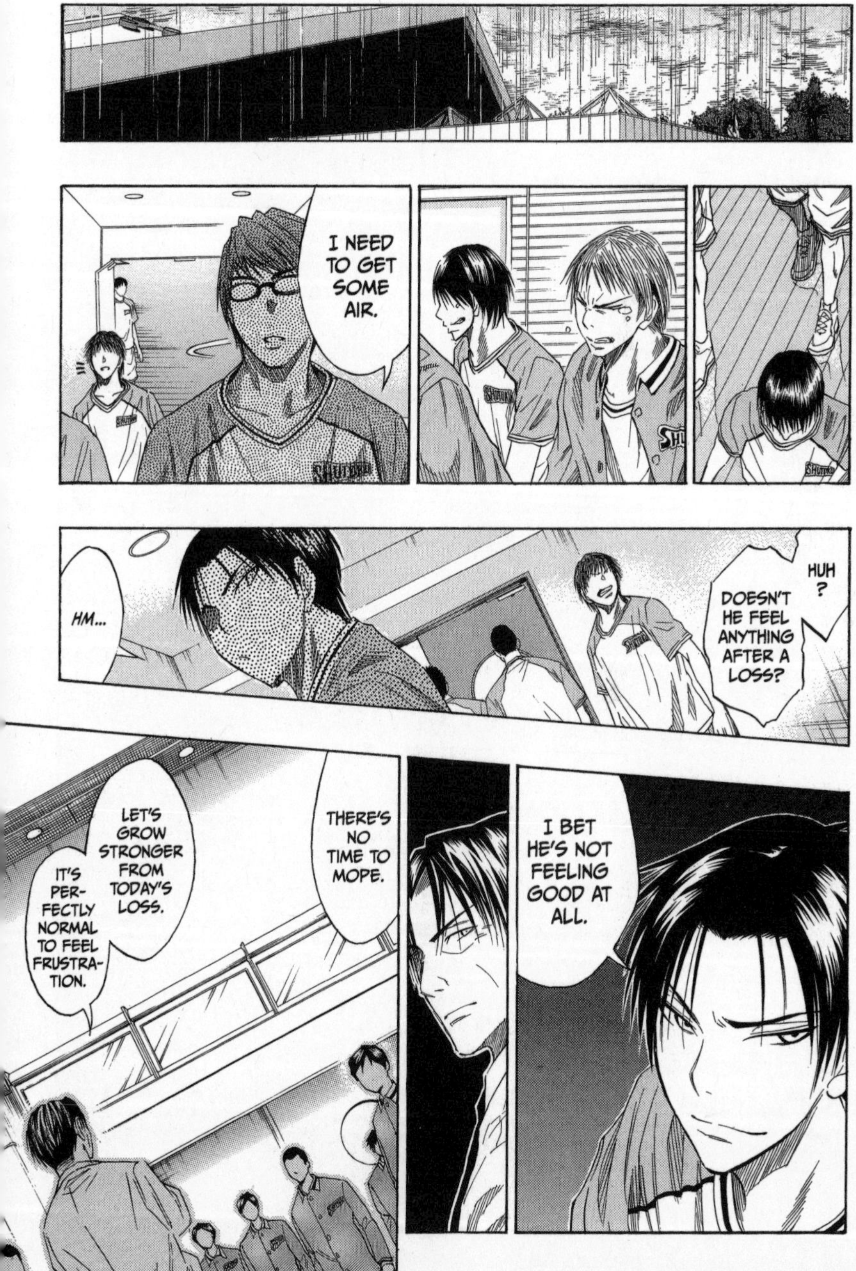
I NEED TO GET SOME AIR.
HUH?
DOESN'T HE FEEL ANYTHING AFTER A LOSS?
HM...
I BET HE'S NOT FEELING GOOD AT ALL.
THERE'S NO TIME TO MOPE.
LET'S GROW STRONGER FROM TODAY'S LOSS.
IT'S PER-FECTLY NORMAL TO FEEL FRUSTRA-TION.

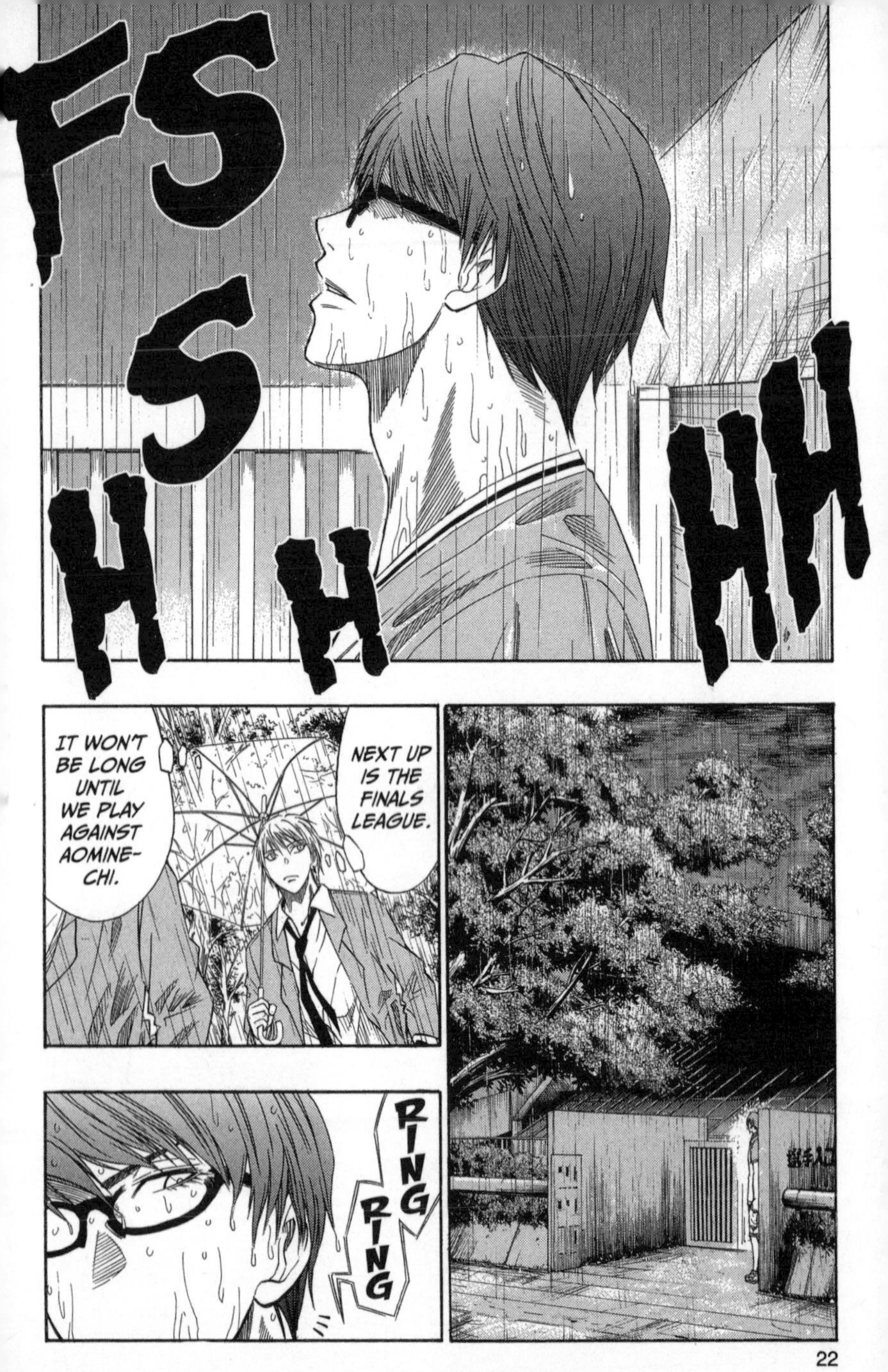
FSSHHHH
NEXT UP IS THE FINALS LEAGUE.
IT WON'T BE LONG UNTIL WE PLAY AGAINST AOMINE-CHI.
RING RING
RING RING

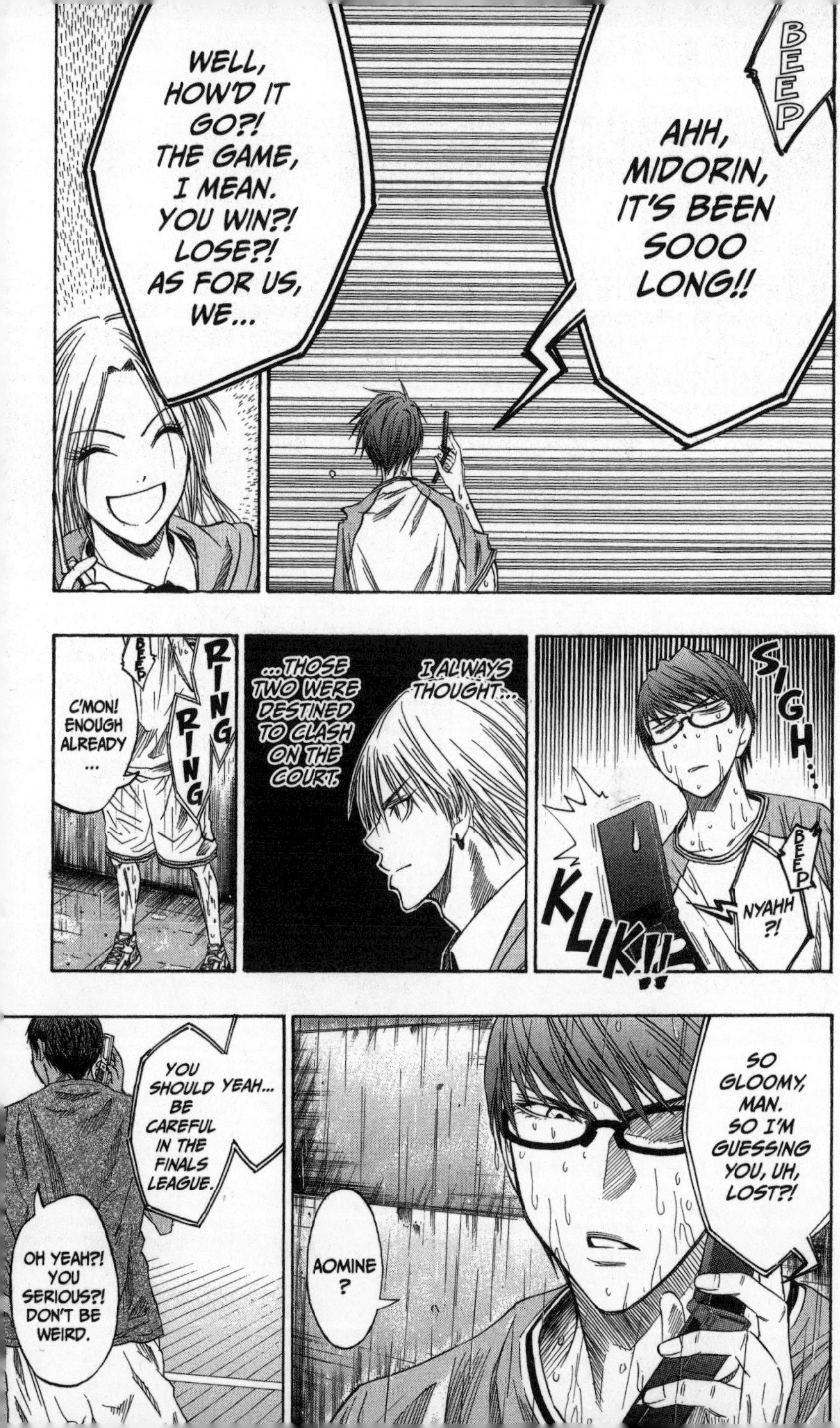
BEEP
AHH, MIDORIN, IT'S BEEN SOOO LONG!!
WELL, HOW'D IT GO?! THE GAME, I MEAN. YOU WIN?! LOSE?! AS FOR US, WE...
SIGH..
BEEP
NYAHH ?!
KLIK!!
I ALWAYS THOUGHT...
...THOSE TWO WERE DESTINED TO CLASH ON THE COURT.
BEEP
RING
RING
RING
C'MON! ENOUGH ALREADY ...
SO GLOOMY, MAN. SO I'M GUESSING YOU, UH, LOST?!
AOMINE ?
YEAH...
YOU SHOULD BE CAREFUL IN THE FINALS LEAGUE.
OH YEAH?! YOU SERIOUS?! DON'T BE WEIRD.

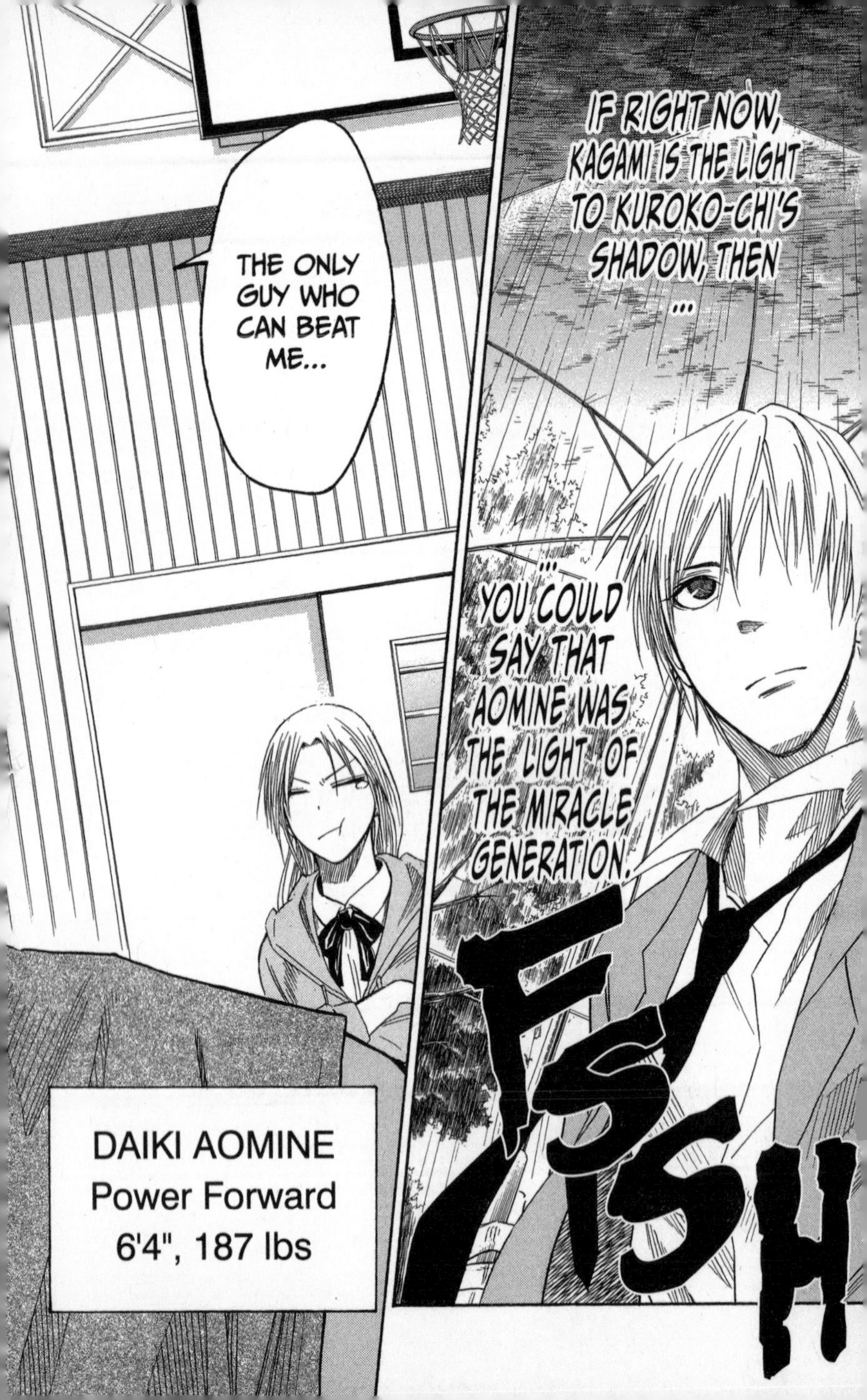
IF RIGHT NOW, KAGAMI IS THE LIGHT TO KUROKO-CHI'S SHADOW, THEN ...
... YOU COULD SAY THAT AOMINE WAS THE LIGHT OF THE MIRACLE GENERATION.
FSSH
THE ONLY GUY WHO CAN BEAT ME...
DAIKI AOMINE
Power Forward
6'4", 187 lbs

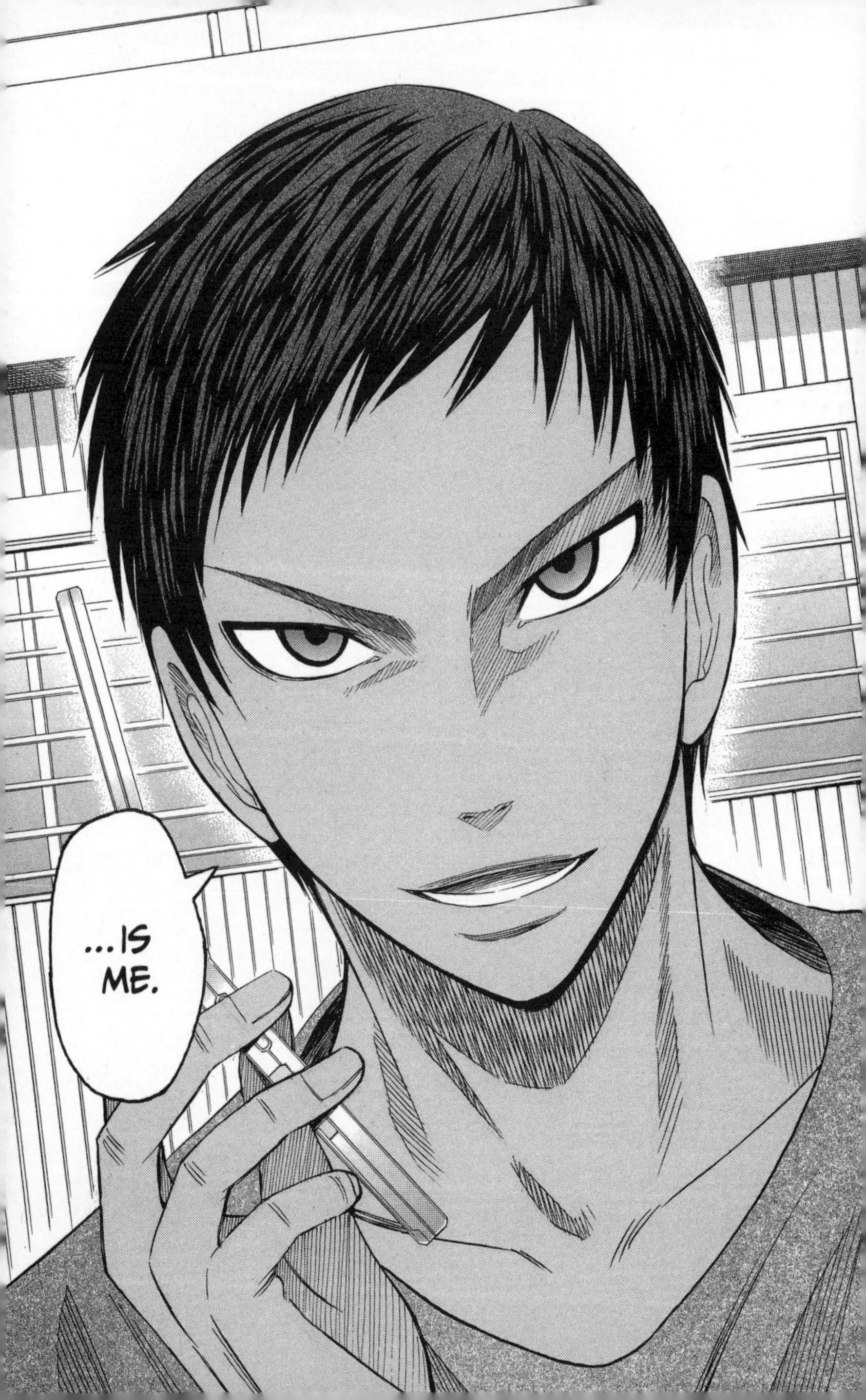
...IS ME.

KUROKO'S BASKETBALL BLOOPERS

TAKE 12

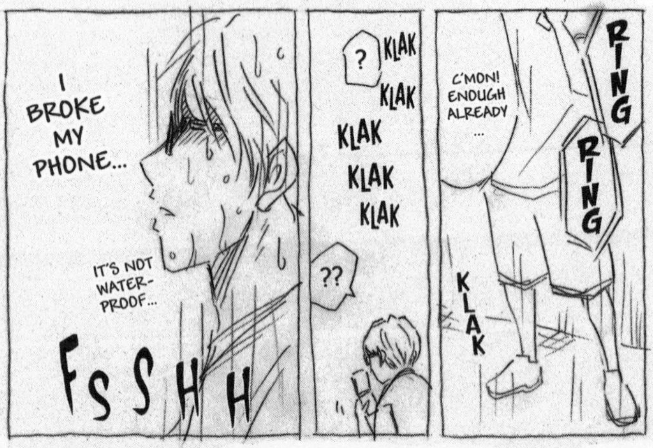
RING
RING RING
C'MON! ENOUGH ALREADY ...
KLAK KLAK
?
KLAK
KLAK
KLAK
KLAK
KLAK
??
I BROKE MY PHONE...
IT'S NOT WATER-PROOF...
FSSHH

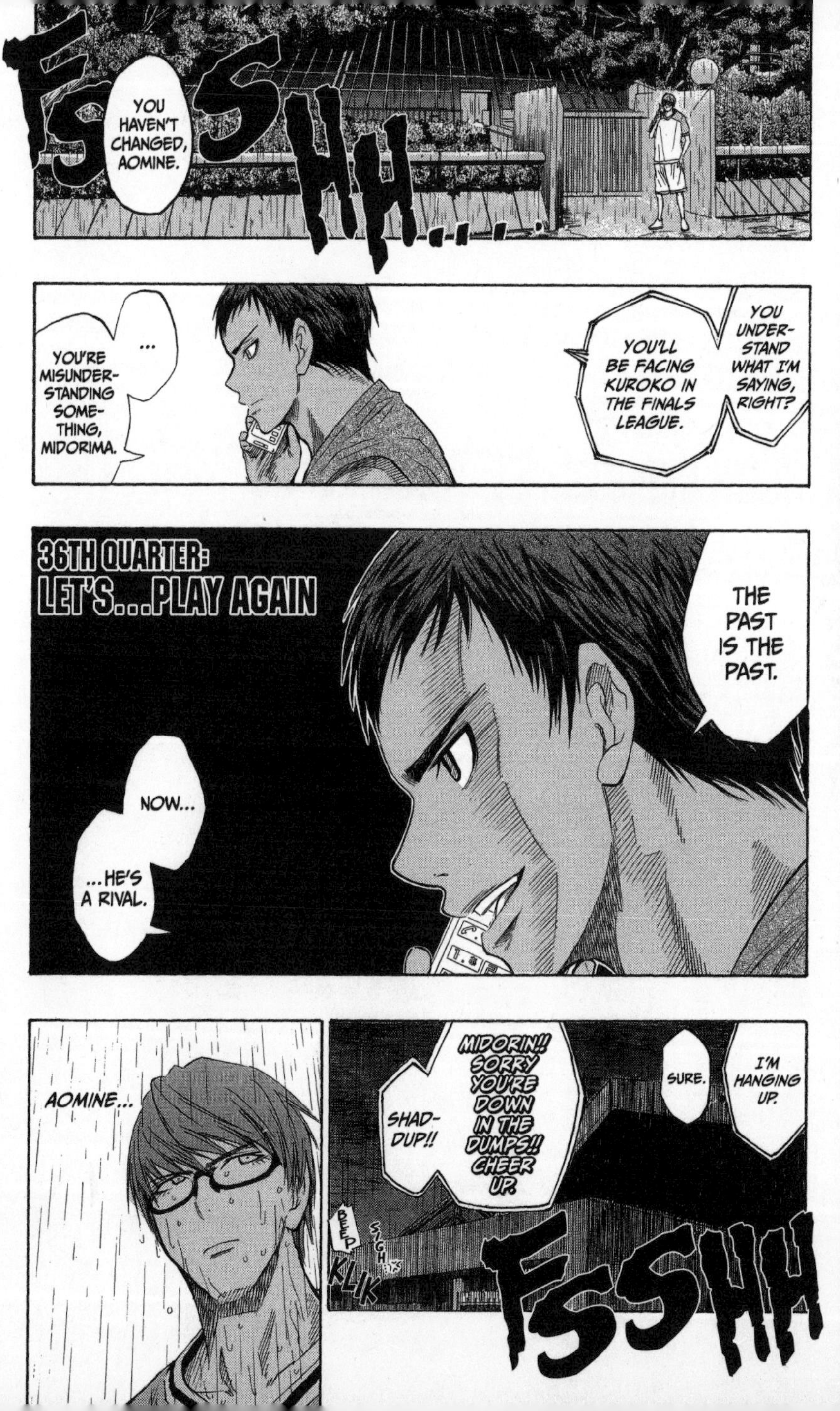
FSSHH.....
YOU HAVEN'T CHANGED, AOMINE.
YOU UNDERSTAND WHAT I'M SAYING, RIGHT?
YOU'LL BE FACING KUROKO IN THE FINALS LEAGUE.
...
YOU'RE MISUNDERSTANDING SOMETHING, MIDORIMA.
36TH QUARTER:
LET'S...PLAY AGAIN
THE PAST IS THE PAST.
NOW...
...HE'S A RIVAL.
I'M HANGING UP.
SURE.
MIDORIN!! SORRY YOU'RE DOWN IN THE DUMPS!! CHEER UP.
SHAD-DUP!!
BEEP
SIGH
KLIK
FSSHH
AOMINE...

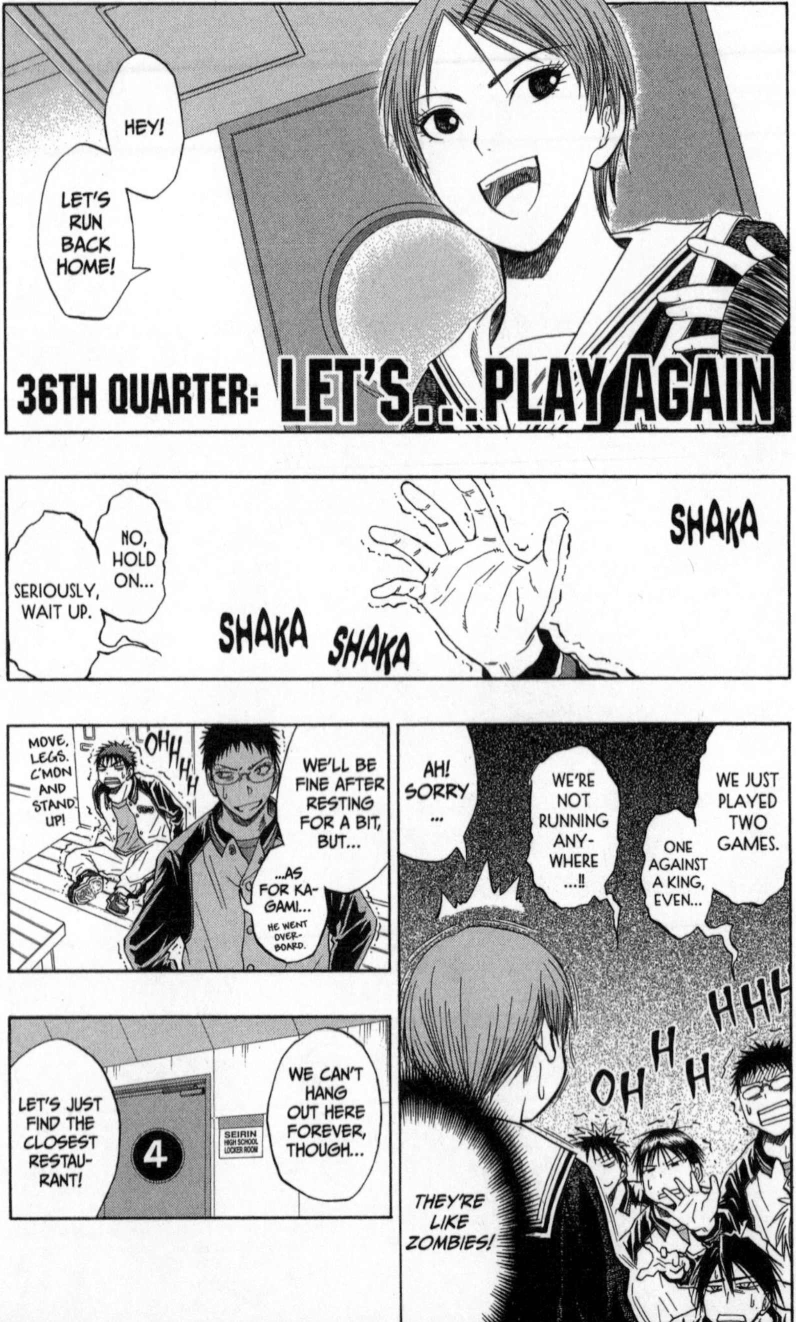
HEY!
LET'S RUN BACK HOME!
36TH QUARTER: LET'S...PLAY AGAIN
SHAKA
SHAKA SHAKA
NO, HOLD ON...
SERIOUSLY, WAIT UP.
WE JUST PLAYED TWO GAMES.
ONE AGAINST A KING, EVEN...
WE'RE NOT RUNNING ANYWHERE...!!
AH! SORRY...
OHHHHHH
THEY'RE LIKE ZOMBIES!
WE'LL BE FINE AFTER RESTING FOR A BIT, BUT...
...AS FOR KAGAMI...
HE WENT OVERBOARD.
OHHHHH
MOVE, LEGS. C'MON AND STAND UP!
WE CAN'T HANG OUT HERE FOREVER, THOUGH...
SEIRIN HIGH SCHOOL LOCKER ROOM
4
LET'S JUST FIND THE CLOSEST RESTAURANT!

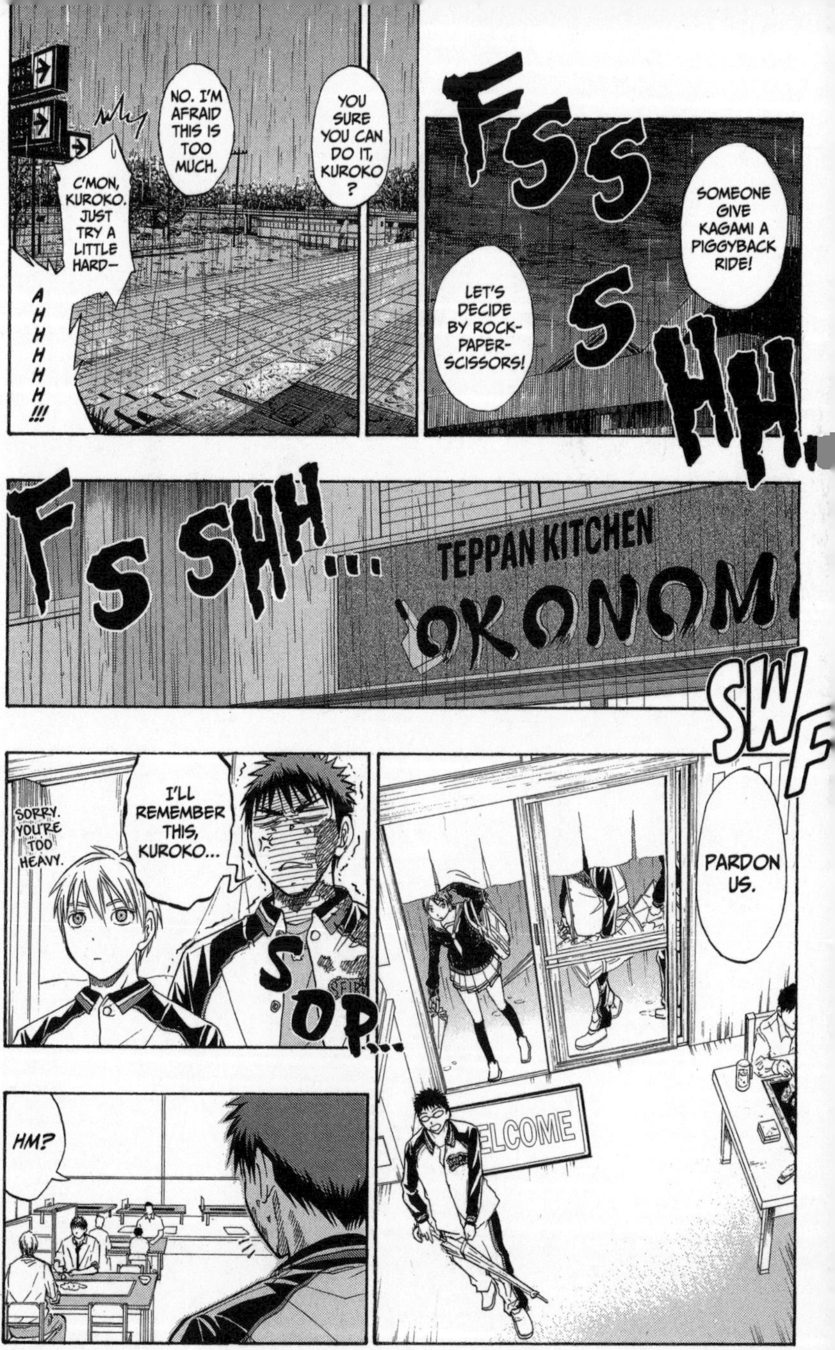
FSS S SHH...
SOMEONE GIVE KAGAMI A PIGGYBACK RIDE!
LET'S DECIDE BY ROCK-PAPER-SCISSORS!
YOU SURE YOU CAN DO IT, KUROKO?
NO. I'M AFRAID THIS IS TOO MUCH.
C'MON, KUROKO. JUST TRY A LITTLE HARD—
AHHHHHH!!!
F S SHH...
TEPPAN KITCHEN
OKONOMI
SWF
PARDON US.
ELCOME
I'LL REMEMBER THIS, KUROKO...
SORRY. YOU'RE TOO HEAVY.
SOP...
HM?

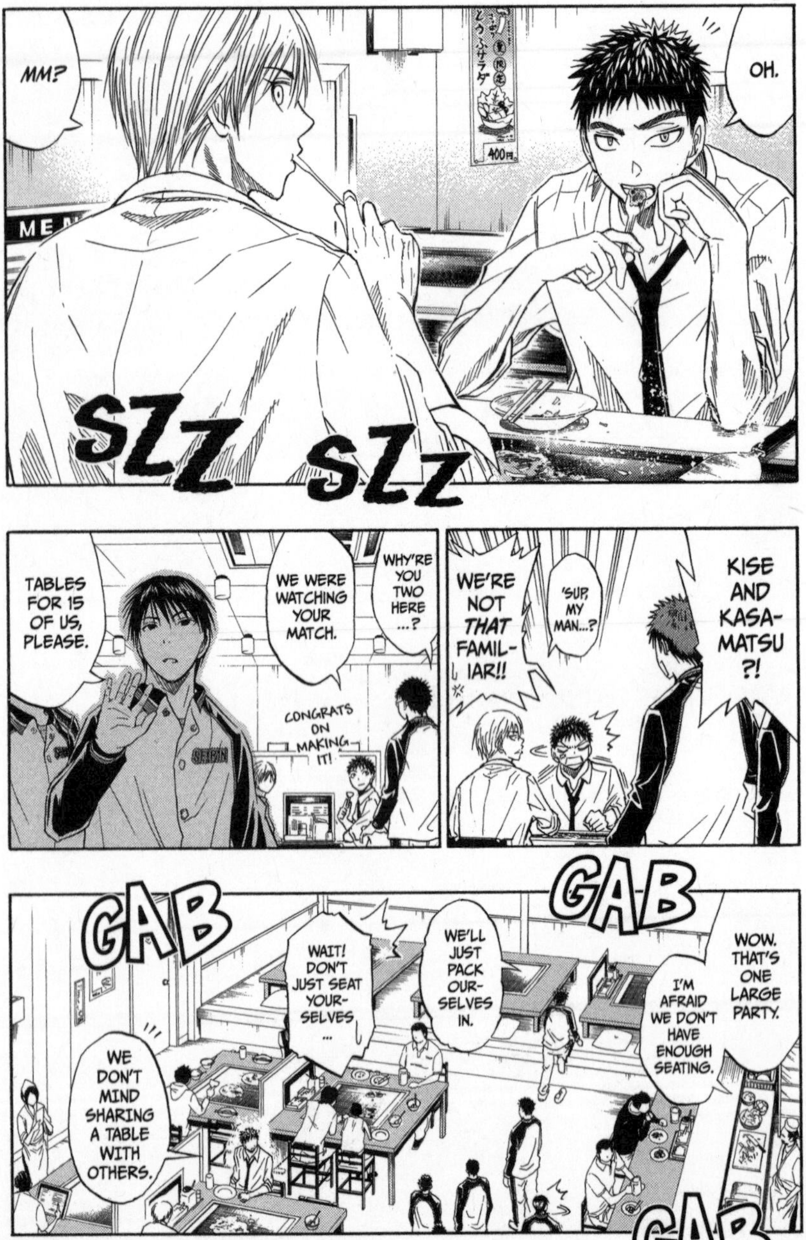
OH.
MM?
SZZ
SZZ
KISE AND KASA-MATSU?!
'SUP, MY MAN...?
WE'RE NOT *THAT* FAMIL-IAR!!
WHY'RE YOU TWO HERE...?
WE WERE WATCHING YOUR MATCH.
CONGRATS ON MAKING IT!
TABLES FOR 15 OF US, PLEASE.
GAB
GAB
WOW. THAT'S ONE LARGE PARTY.
I'M AFRAID WE DON'T HAVE ENOUGH SEATING.
WE'LL JUST PACK OUR-SELVES IN.
WAIT! DON'T JUST SEAT YOUR-SELVES...
WE DON'T MIND SHARING A TABLE WITH OTHERS.
GAB

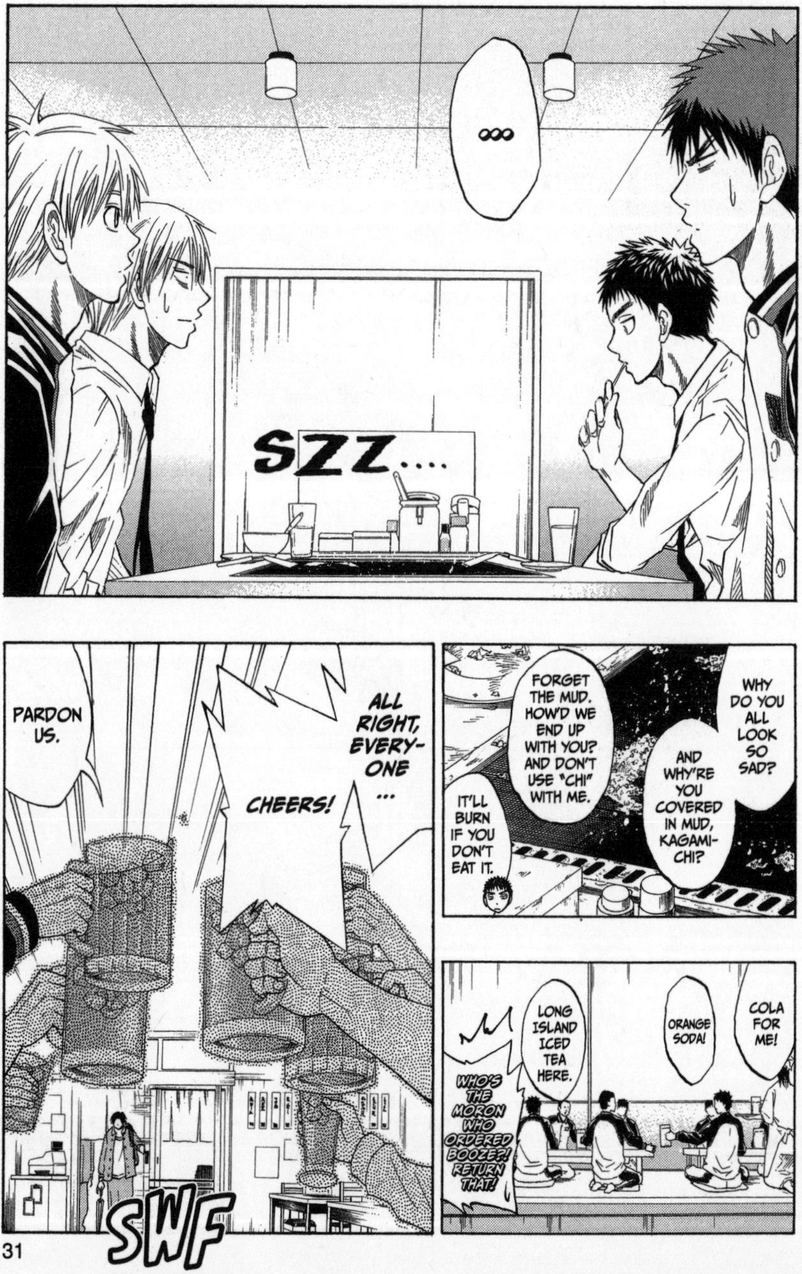
...
SZZ....
WHY DO YOU ALL LOOK SO SAD?
AND WHY'RE YOU COVERED IN MUD, KAGAMI-CHI?
FORGET THE MUD. HOW'D WE END UP WITH YOU? AND DON'T USE "CHI" WITH ME.
IT'LL BURN IF YOU DON'T EAT IT.
COLA FOR ME!
ORANGE SODA!
LONG ISLAND ICED TEA HERE.
WHO'S THE MORON WHO ORDERED BOOZE?! RETURN THAT!
ALL RIGHT, EVERYONE...
CHEERS!
PARDON US.
SWF

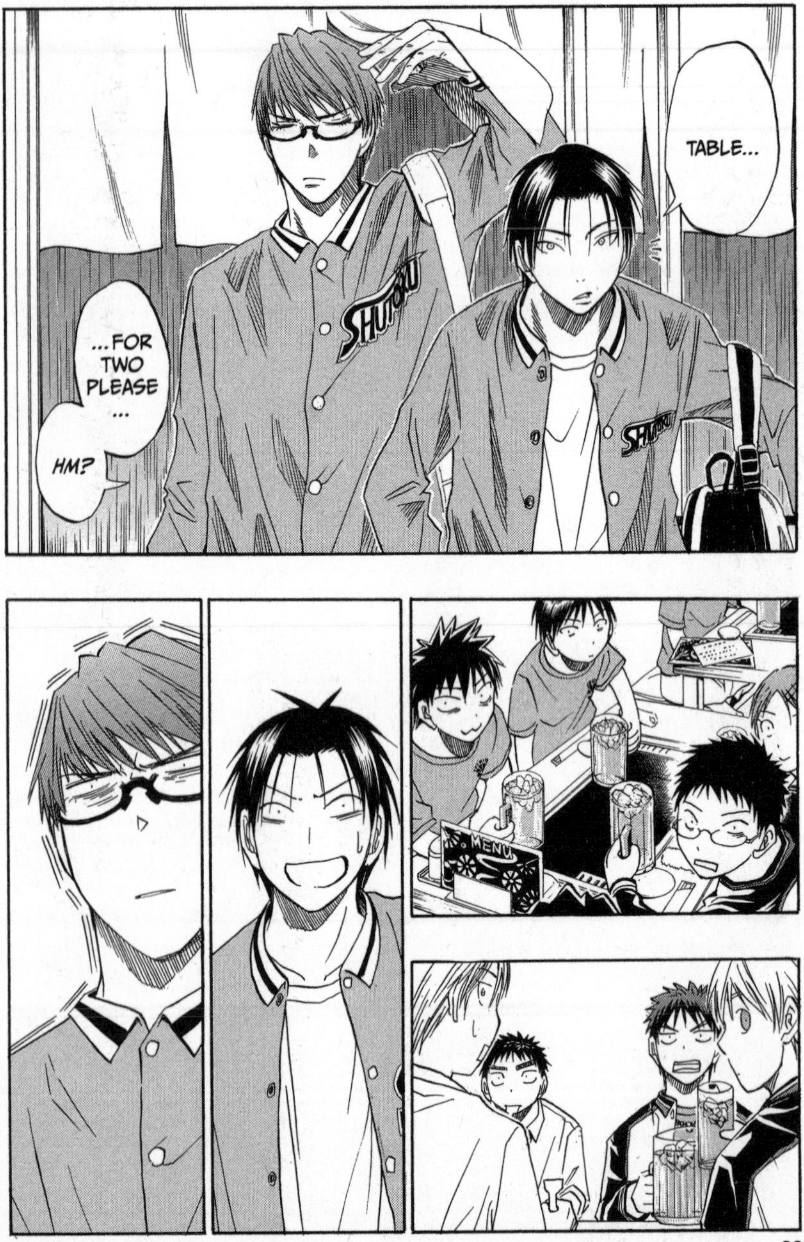
TABLE...
...FOR TWO PLEASE ...
HM?

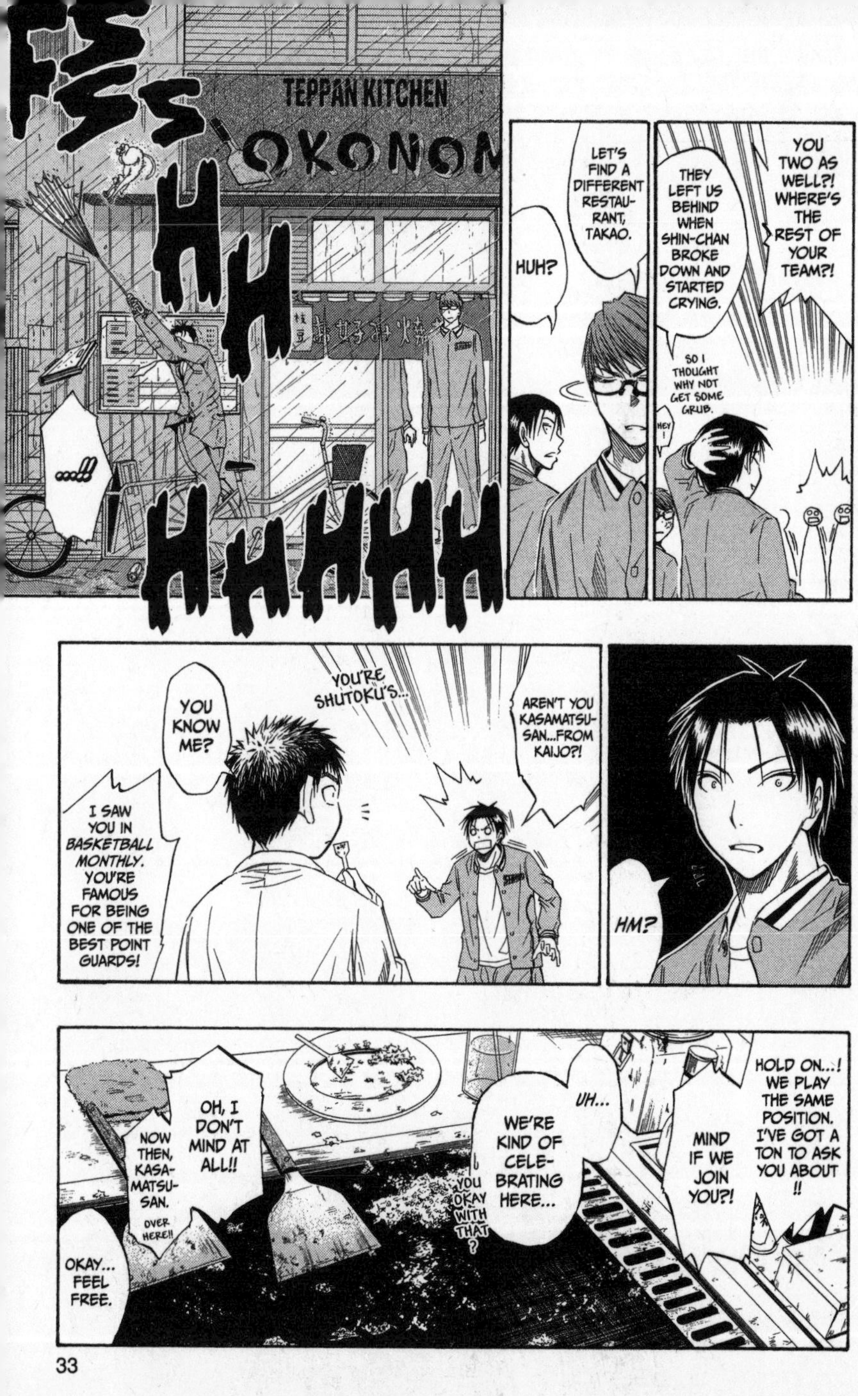
YOU TWO AS WELL?! WHERE'S THE REST OF YOUR TEAM?!
THEY LEFT US BEHIND WHEN SHIN-CHAN BROKE DOWN AND STARTED CRYING.
SO I THOUGHT WHY NOT GET SOME GRUB.
HEY!
LET'S FIND A DIFFERENT RESTAURANT, TAKAO.
HUH?
TEPPAN KITCHEN
OKONOM
FSS
HH
HHHHHH
...!!
HM?
AREN'T YOU KASAMATSU-SAN...FROM KAIJO?!
YOU'RE SHUTOKU'S...
YOU KNOW ME?
I SAW YOU IN *BASKETBALL MONTHLY*. YOU'RE FAMOUS FOR BEING ONE OF THE BEST POINT GUARDS!
HOLD ON...! WE PLAY THE SAME POSITION. I'VE GOT A TON TO ASK YOU ABOUT!!
MIND IF WE JOIN YOU?!
UH...
WE'RE KIND OF CELEBRATING HERE...
YOU OKAY WITH THAT?
OH, I DON'T MIND AT ALL!!
NOW THEN, KASAMATSU-SAN.
OVER HERE!!
OKAY... FEEL FREE.

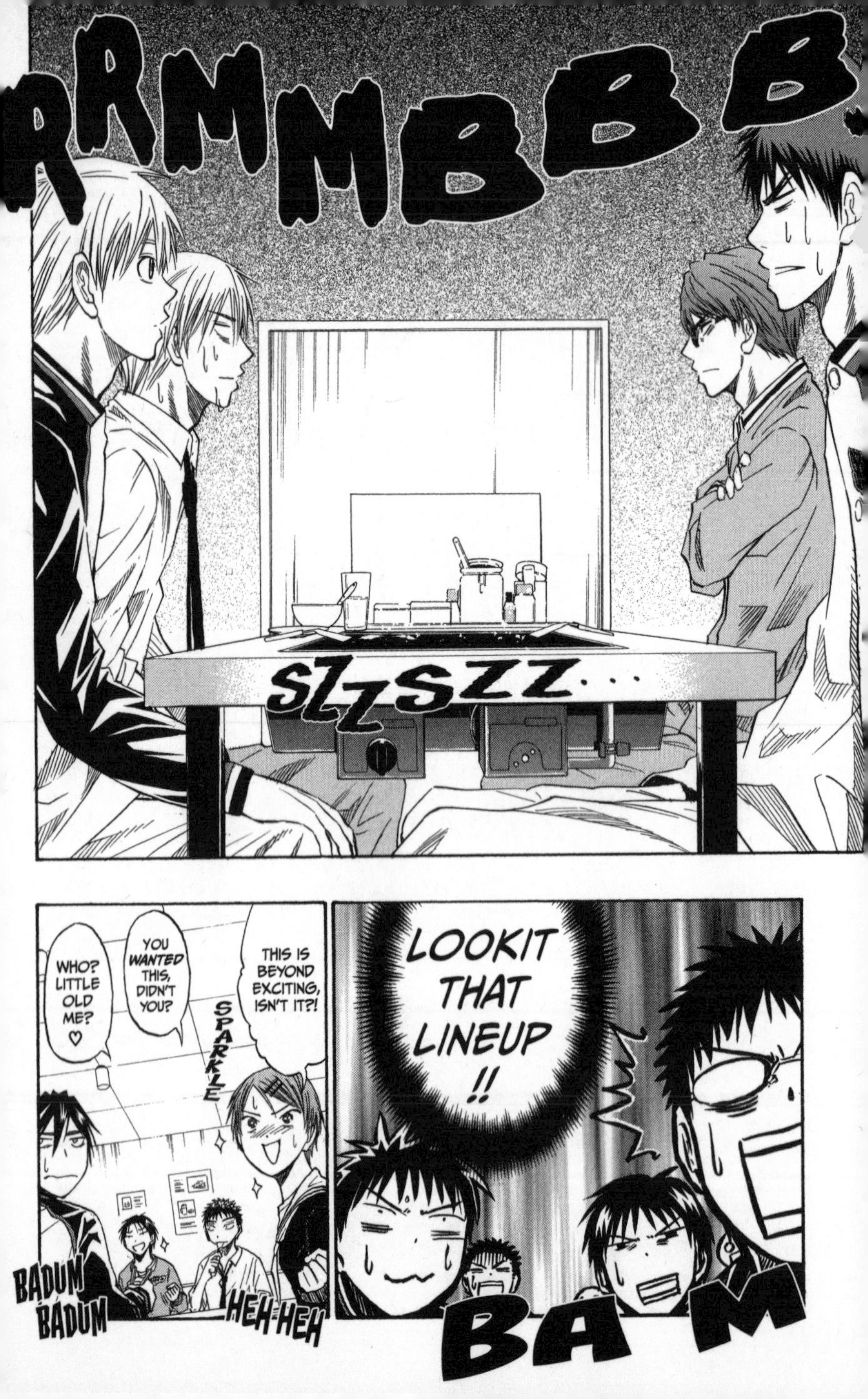
RRMMBBB
SZZSZZ...
LOOKIT THAT LINEUP!!
BAM
THIS IS BEYOND EXCITING, ISN'T IT?!
SPARKLE
YOU *WANTED* THIS, DIDN'T YOU?
WHO? LITTLE OLD ME? ♡
HEH HEH
BADUM BADUM

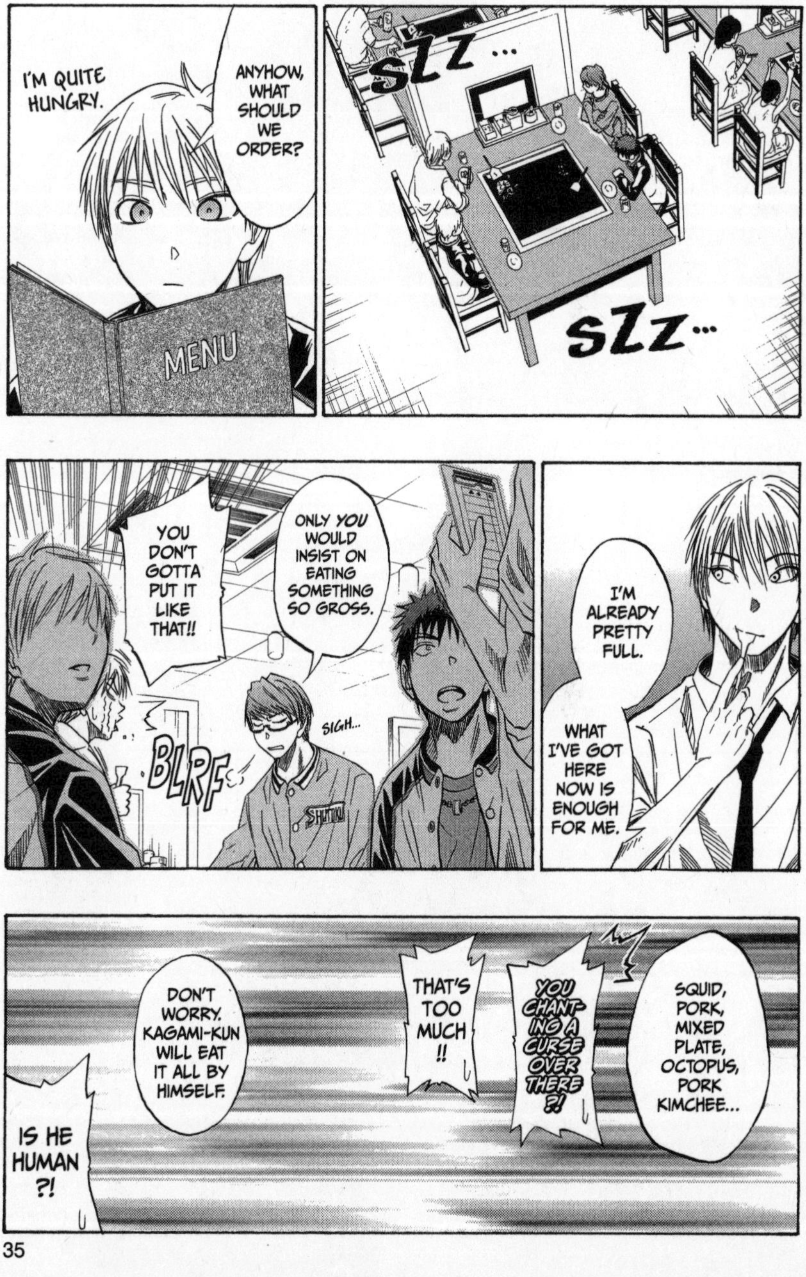
SZZ...
SZZ...
ANYHOW, WHAT SHOULD WE ORDER?
I'M QUITE HUNGRY.
MENU
I'M ALREADY PRETTY FULL.
WHAT I'VE GOT HERE NOW IS ENOUGH FOR ME.
ONLY YOU WOULD INSIST ON EATING SOMETHING SO GROSS.
SIGH...
YOU DON'T GOTTA PUT IT LIKE THAT!!
BLRF
SQUID, PORK, MIXED PLATE, OCTOPUS, PORK KIMCHEE...
YOU CHANTING A CURSE OVER THERE?!
THAT'S TOO MUCH!!
DON'T WORRY. KAGAMI-KUN WILL EAT IT ALL BY HIMSELF.
IS HE HUMAN?!

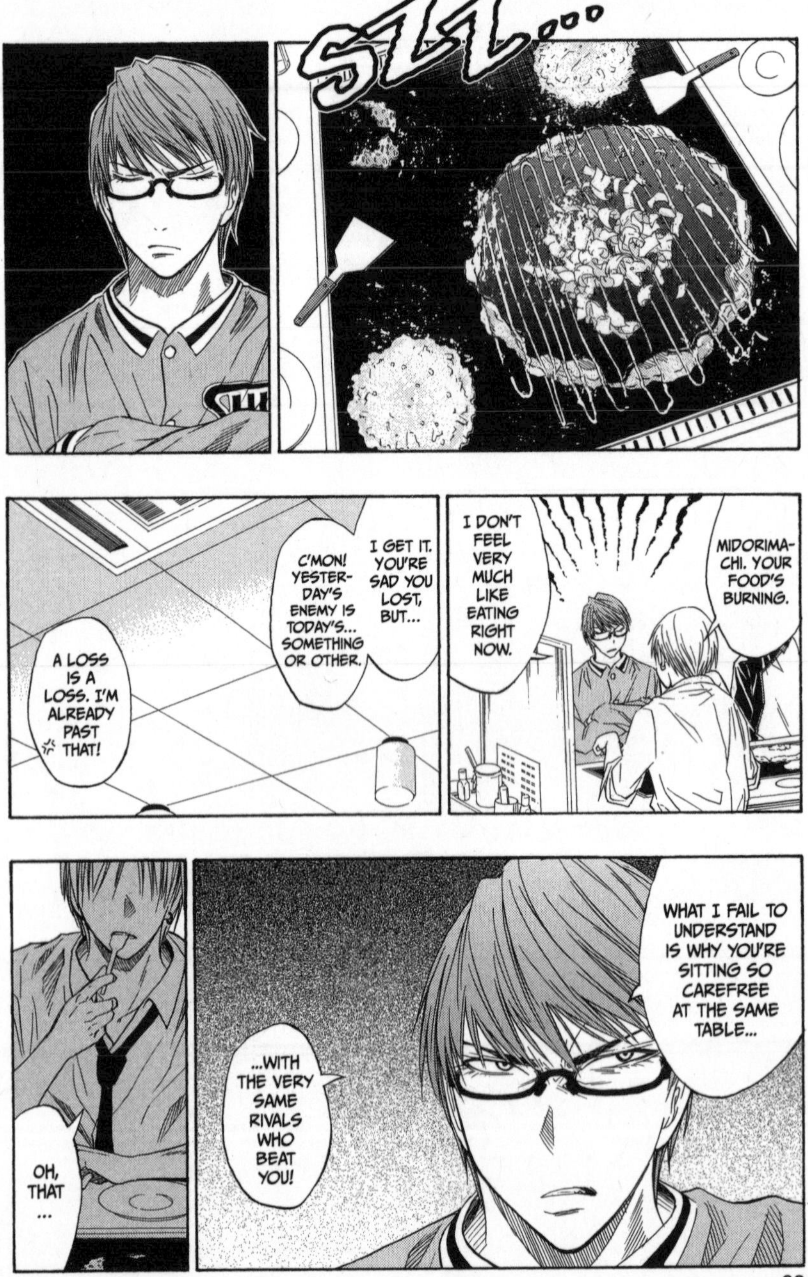
SZZ...
MIDORIMA-CHI. YOUR FOOD'S BURNING.
I DON'T FEEL VERY MUCH LIKE EATING RIGHT NOW.
I GET IT. YOU'RE SAD YOU LOST, BUT...
C'MON! YESTER-DAY'S ENEMY IS TODAY'S... SOMETHING OR OTHER.
A LOSS IS A LOSS. I'M ALREADY PAST THAT!
WHAT I FAIL TO UNDERSTAND IS WHY YOU'RE SITTING SO CAREFREE AT THE SAME TABLE...
...WITH THE VERY SAME RIVALS WHO BEAT YOU!
OH, THAT ...

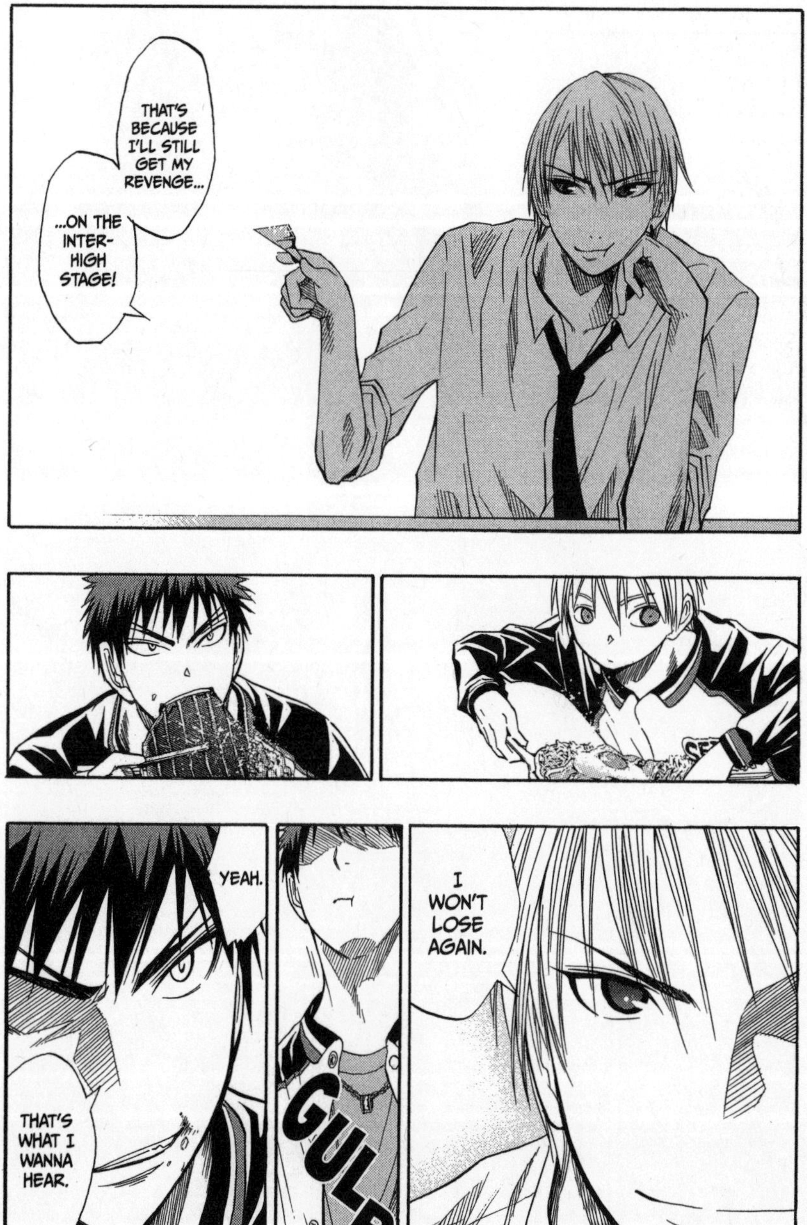

THAT'S BECAUSE I'LL STILL GET MY REVENGE...
...ON THE INTER-HIGH STAGE!
I WON'T LOSE AGAIN.
GULP
YEAH.
THAT'S WHAT I WANNA HEAR.

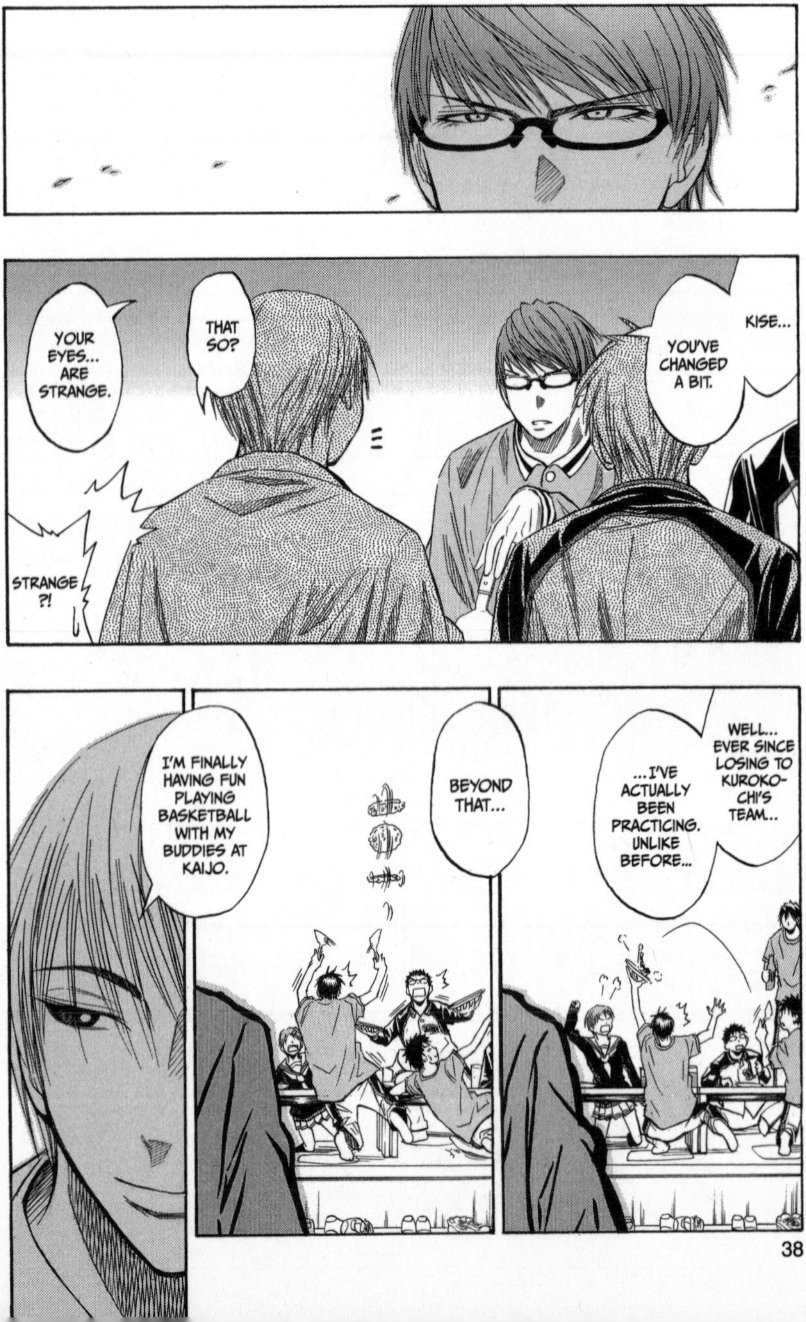
KISE...
YOU'VE CHANGED A BIT.
THAT SO?
YOUR EYES... ARE STRANGE.
STRANGE?!
WELL... EVER SINCE LOSING TO KUROKO-CHI'S TEAM...
...I'VE ACTUALLY BEEN PRACTICING. UNLIKE BEFORE...
BEYOND THAT...
I'M FINALLY HAVING FUN PLAYING BASKETBALL WITH MY BUDDIES AT KAIJO.

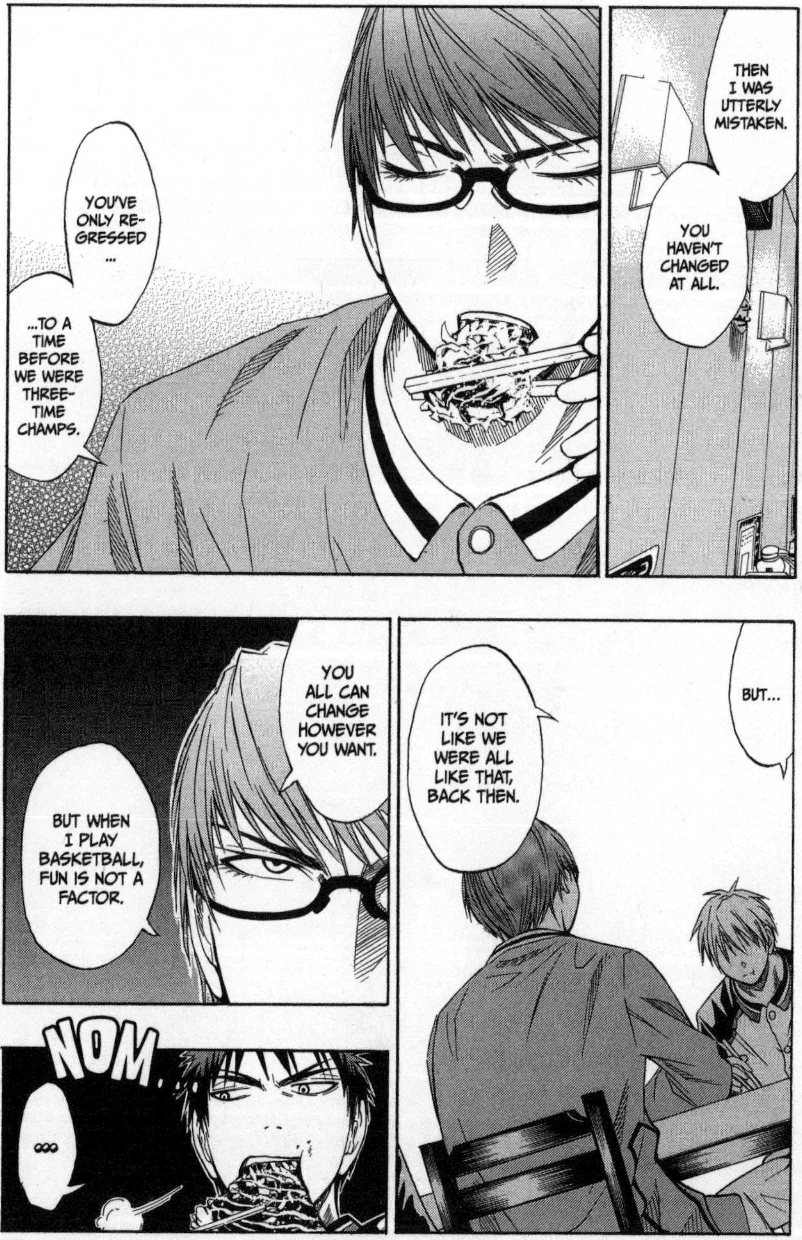
THEN I WAS UTTERLY MISTAKEN.
YOU HAVEN'T CHANGED AT ALL.
YOU'VE ONLY RE-GRESSED ...
...TO A TIME BEFORE WE WERE THREE-TIME CHAMPS.
BUT...
IT'S NOT LIKE WE WERE ALL LIKE THAT, BACK THEN.
YOU ALL CAN CHANGE HOWEVER YOU WANT.
BUT WHEN I PLAY BASKETBALL, FUN IS NOT A FACTOR.
NOM.
...

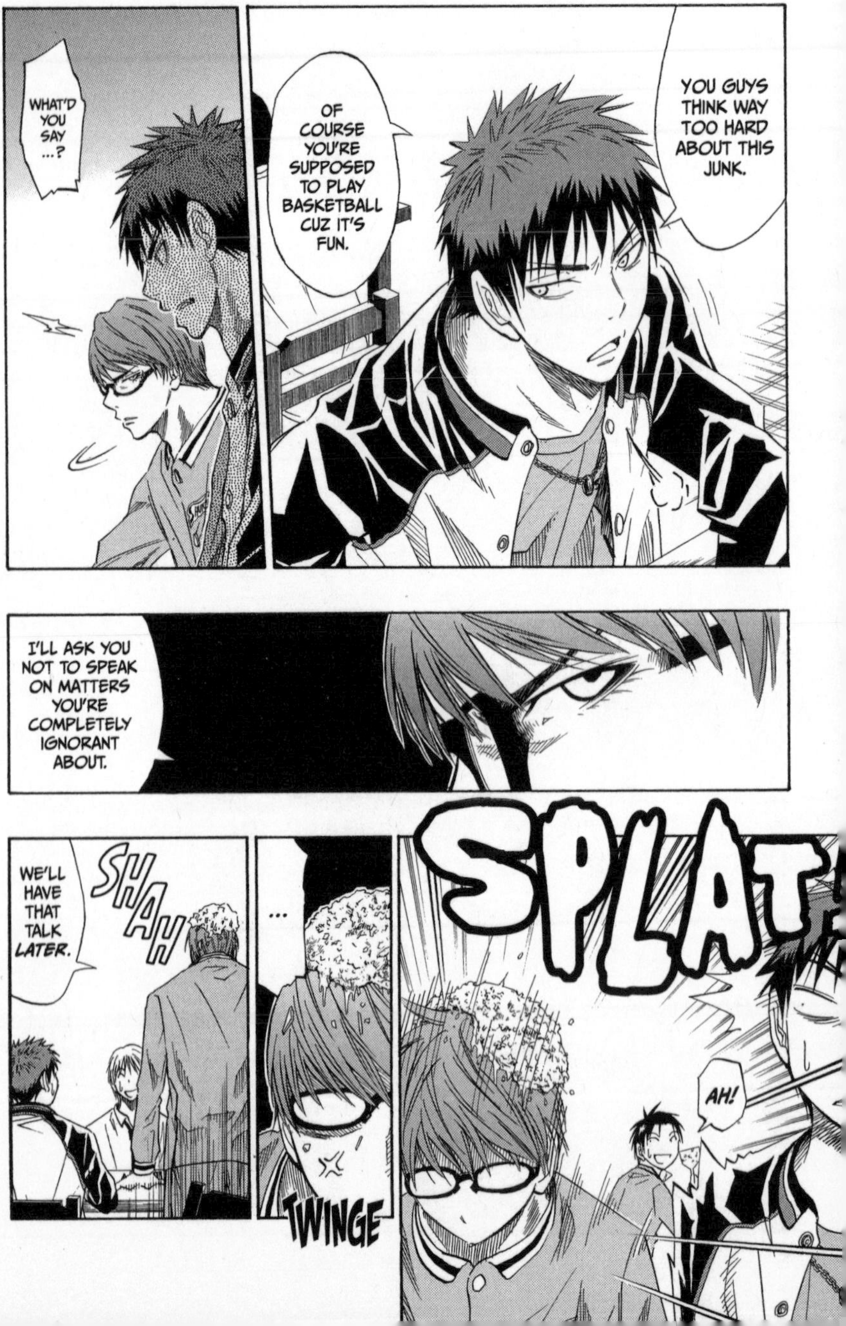
YOU GUYS THINK WAY TOO HARD ABOUT THIS JUNK.
OF COURSE YOU'RE SUPPOSED TO PLAY BASKETBALL CUZ IT'S FUN.
WHAT'D YOU SAY ...?
I'LL ASK YOU NOT TO SPEAK ON MATTERS YOU'RE COMPLETELY IGNORANT ABOUT.
SPLAT
AH!
...
TWINGE
SHAH
WE'LL HAVE THAT TALK LATER.

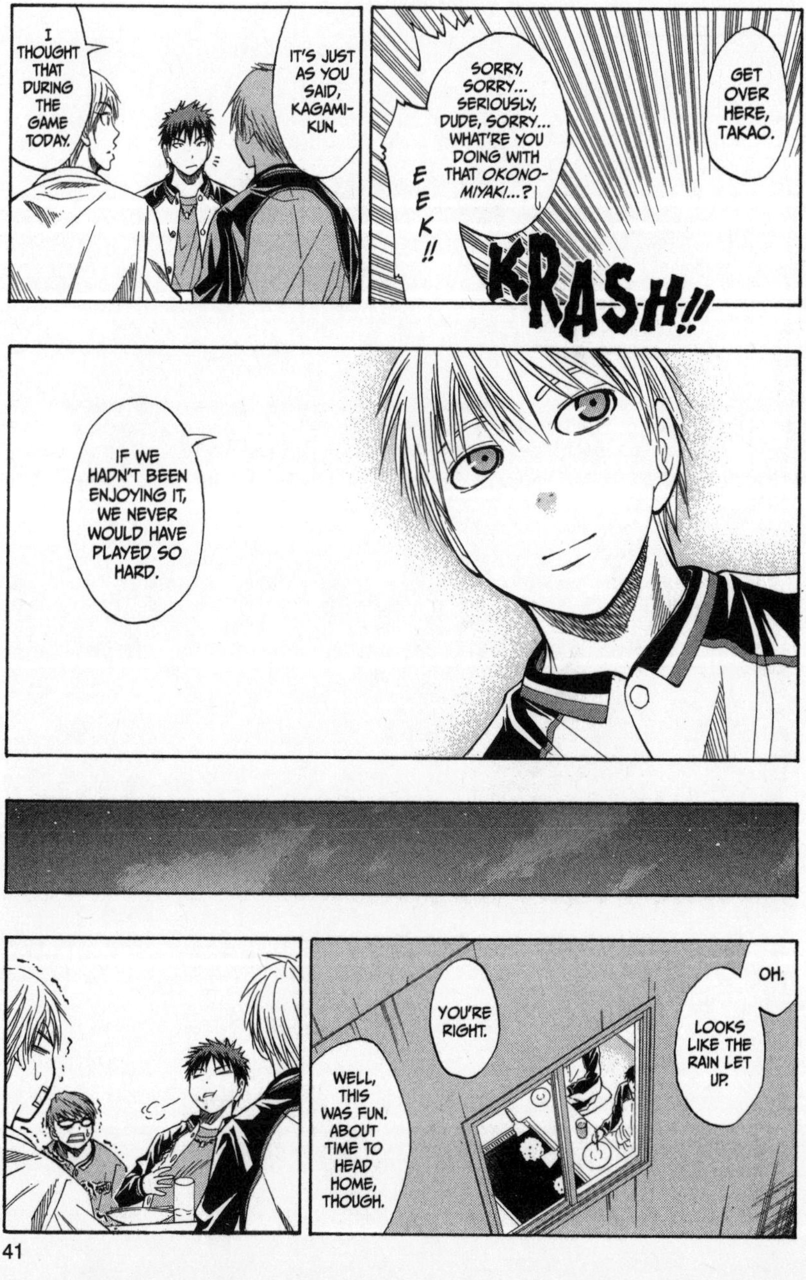
GET OVER HERE, TAKAO.
SORRY, SORRY... SERIOUSLY, DUDE, SORRY... WHAT'RE YOU DOING WITH THAT OKONOMIYAKI...?
EEK!!
KRASH!!
IT'S JUST AS YOU SAID, KAGAMI-KUN.
I THOUGHT THAT DURING THE GAME TODAY.
IF WE HADN'T BEEN ENJOYING IT, WE NEVER WOULD HAVE PLAYED SO HARD.
OH.
LOOKS LIKE THE RAIN LET UP.
YOU'RE RIGHT.
WELL, THIS WAS FUN. ABOUT TIME TO HEAD HOME, THOUGH.

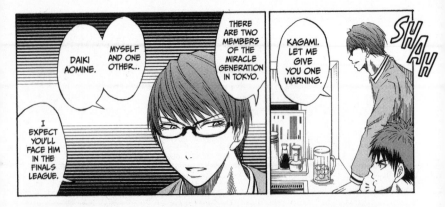

SHAH
KAGAMI. LET ME GIVE YOU ONE WARNING.
THERE ARE TWO MEMBERS OF THE MIRACLE GENERATION IN TOKYO.
MYSELF AND ONE OTHER...
DAIKI AOMINE.
I EXPECT YOU'LL FACE HIM IN THE FINALS LEAGUE.
YOU SHOULD KNOW ...
...THAT HE'S THE SAME TYPE OF PLAYER AS YOU.
HUH?
THE HELL'S THAT S'POSED TO MEAN ...?
YOU'RE BASICALLY JUST SAYING HE'S GOOD?

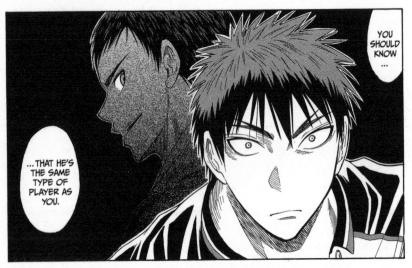

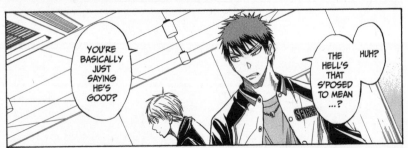

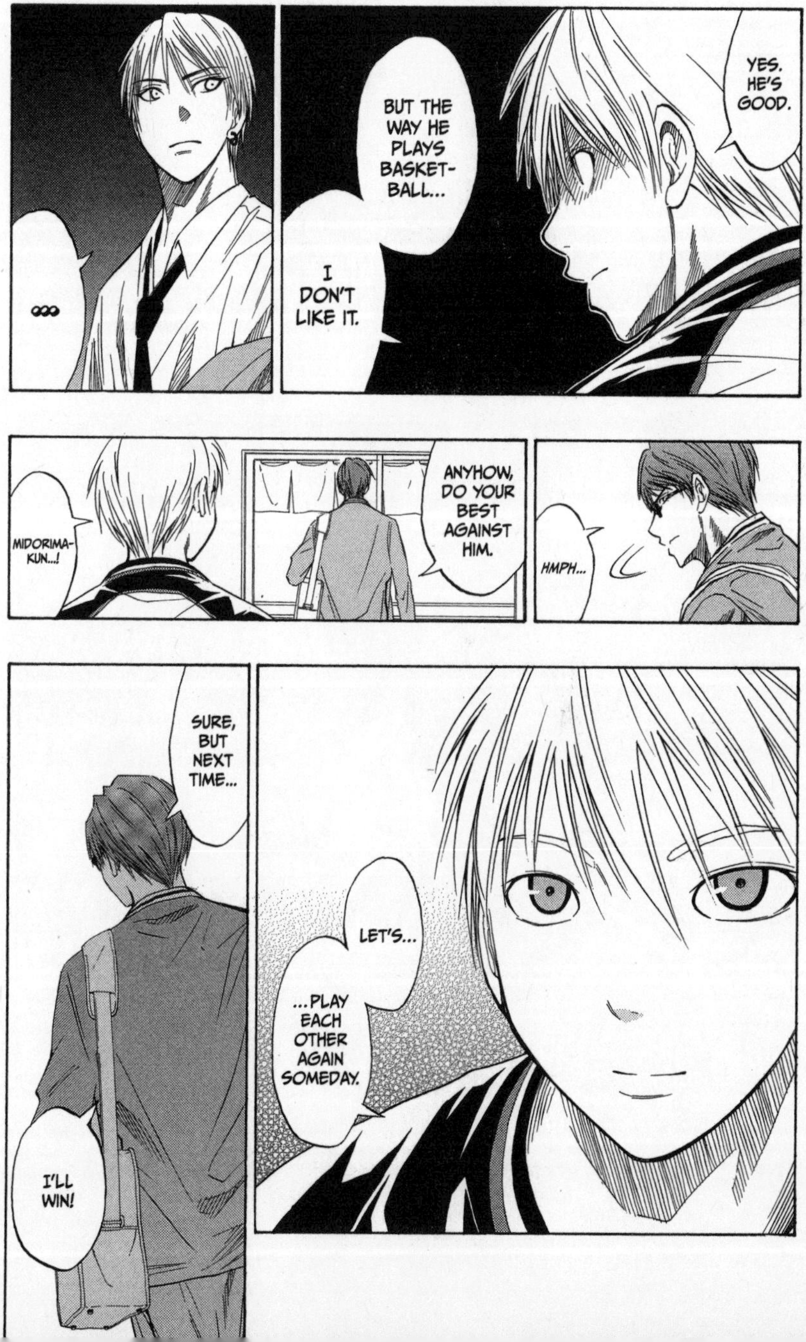
YES. HE'S GOOD.
BUT THE WAY HE PLAYS BASKET-BALL...
I DON'T LIKE IT.
...
HMPH...
ANYHOW, DO YOUR BEST AGAINST HIM.
MIDORIMA-KUN...!
LET'S...
...PLAY EACH OTHER AGAIN SOMEDAY.
SURE, BUT NEXT TIME...
I'LL WIN!

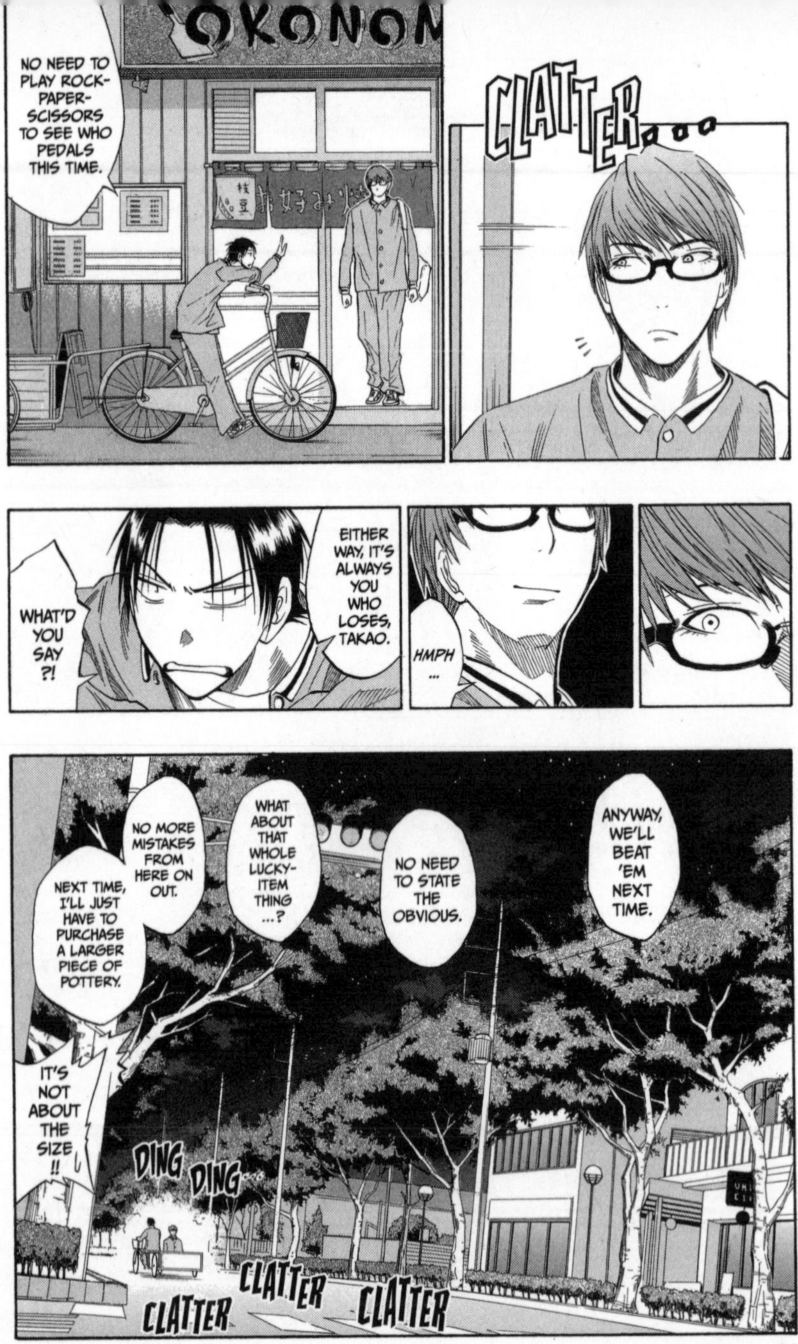
CLATTER...
OKONOM
お好み焼
NO NEED TO PLAY ROCK-PAPER-SCISSORS TO SEE WHO PEDALS THIS TIME.
HMPH...
EITHER WAY, IT'S ALWAYS YOU WHO LOSES, TAKAO.
WHAT'D YOU SAY?!
ANYWAY, WE'LL BEAT 'EM NEXT TIME.
NO NEED TO STATE THE OBVIOUS.
WHAT ABOUT THAT WHOLE LUCKY-ITEM THING...?
NO MORE MISTAKES FROM HERE ON OUT.
NEXT TIME, I'LL JUST HAVE TO PURCHASE A LARGER PIECE OF POTTERY.
IT'S NOT ABOUT THE SIZE!!
DING DING...
CLATTER
CLATTER
CLATTER

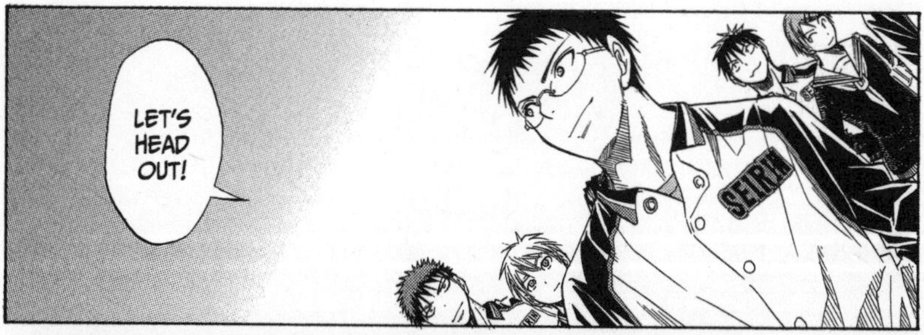
LET'S HEAD OUT!

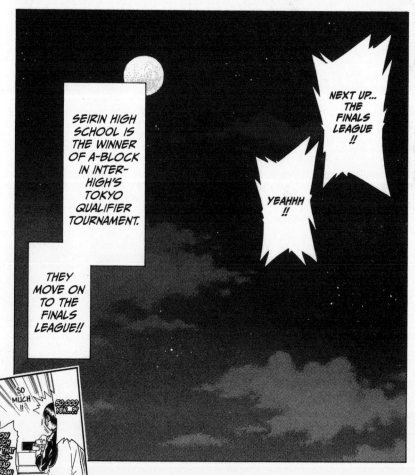

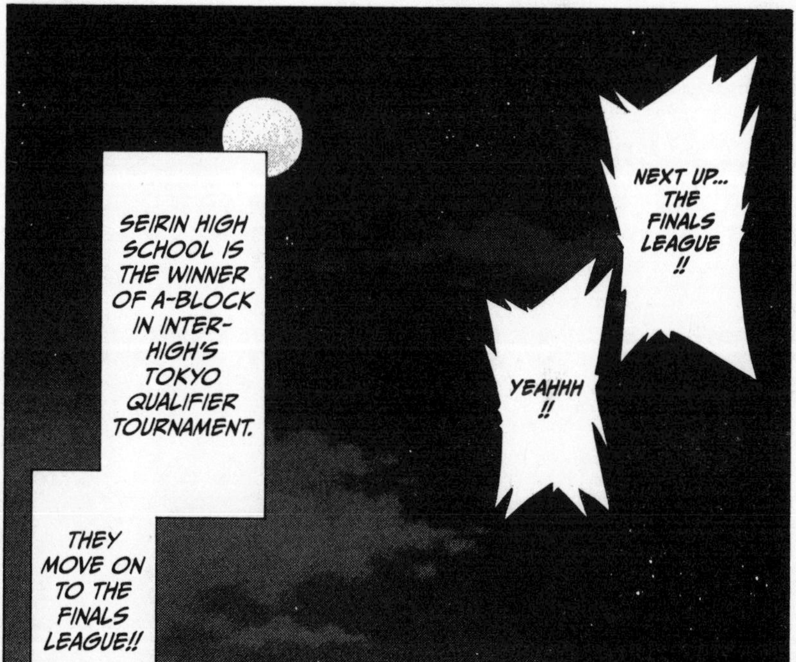
NEXT UP... THE FINALS LEAGUE!!
YEAHHH!!
SEIRIN HIGH SCHOOL IS THE WINNER OF A-BLOCK IN INTER-HIGH'S TOKYO QUALIFIER TOURNAMENT.
THEY MOVE ON TO THE FINALS LEAGUE!!

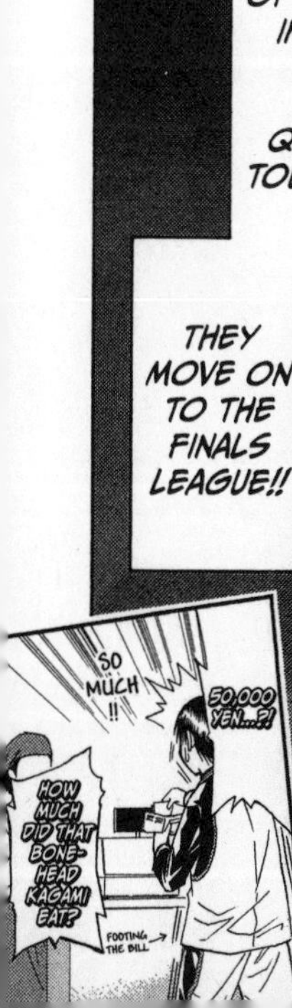
SO MUCH!!
50,000 YEN...?!
HOW MUCH DID THAT BONE-HEAD KAGAMI EAT?
FOOTING THE BILL

KUROKO'S BASKETBALL BLOOPERS
TAKE 3

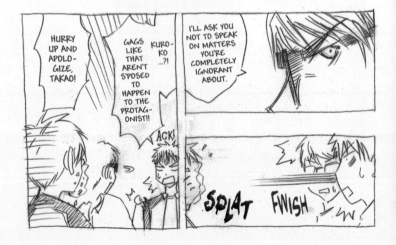

I'LL ASK YOU NOT TO SPEAK ON MATTERS YOU'RE COMPLETELY IGNORANT ABOUT.
FWISH
SPLAT
KURO-KO ...?!
GAGS LIKE THAT AREN'T S'POSED TO HAPPEN TO THE PROTAG-ONIST!!
HURRY UP AND APOLO-GIZE, TAKAO!
ACK!

37TH QUARTER: IDIOTS WON'T WIN!

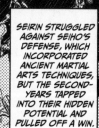

ON THE FINAL DAY OF THE INTER-HIGH QUALIFIERS TOURNAMENT, A-BLOCK ...
SEIRIN'S SEMI-FINAL MATCH WAS AGAINST SEIHO HIGH, THE NORTH KING.
SEIRIN STRUGGLED AGAINST SEIHO'S DEFENSE, WHICH INCORPORATED ANCIENT MARTIAL ARTS TECHNIQUES, BUT THE SECOND-YEARS TAPPED INTO THEIR HIDDEN POTENTIAL AND PULLED OFF A WIN.
SHK

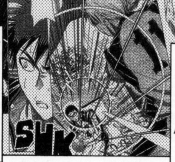

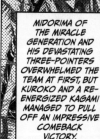

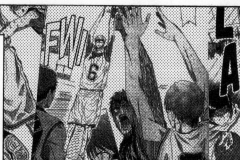

THE FINAL MATCH WAS AGAINST SHUTOKU HIGH, THE EAST KING.
FWI
MIDORIMA OF THE MIRACLE GENERATION AND HIS DEVASTATING THREE-POINTERS OVERWHELMED THE TEAM AT FIRST, BUT KUROKO AND A RE-ENERGIZED KAGAMI MANAGED TO PULL OFF AN IMPRESSIVE COMEBACK VICTORY.

SEIRIN FACED AN UPHILL BATTLE BY PLAYING TWO OF THE THREE KINGS, TOKYO'S ELITE SCHOOLS, IN ONE DAY. HOWEVER, THEY EMERGED AS THE WINNERS OF THE TOURNAMENT'S A-BLOCK.

TOKYO INTER-HIGH QUALIFIERS FINALS LEAGUE

		SEIRIN	B-BLOCK WINNER	C-BLOCK WINNER	D-BLOCK WINNER
A-BLOCK WINNER	SEIRIN				
B-BLOCK WINNER	?				
C-BLOCK WINNER	?				
D-BLOCK WINNER	?				

*THE TOP THREE OF FOUR MOVE ON TO INTER-HIGH.

SEIRIN HAS REACHED THE FINALS LEAGUE, THE LAST BATTLE STANDING BETWEEN THEM AND INTER-HIGH.

HOW-EVER ...

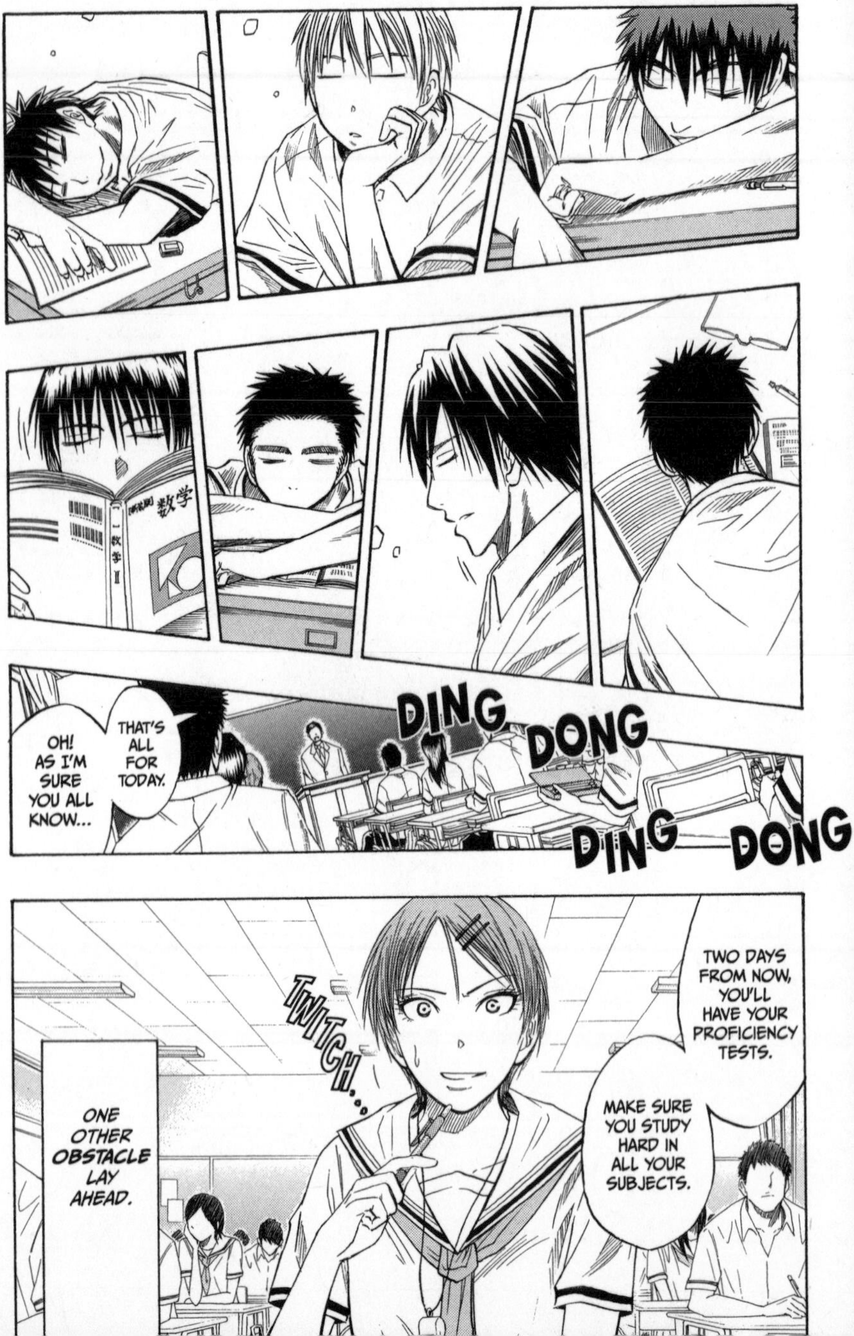
DING DONG
DING DONG
THAT'S ALL FOR TODAY.
OH! AS I'M SURE YOU ALL KNOW...
TWO DAYS FROM NOW, YOU'LL HAVE YOUR PROFICIENCY TESTS.
MAKE SURE YOU STUDY HARD IN ALL YOUR SUBJECTS.
TWITCH...
ONE OTHER OBSTACLE LAY AHEAD.

37TH QUARTER: IDIOTS WON'T WIN!

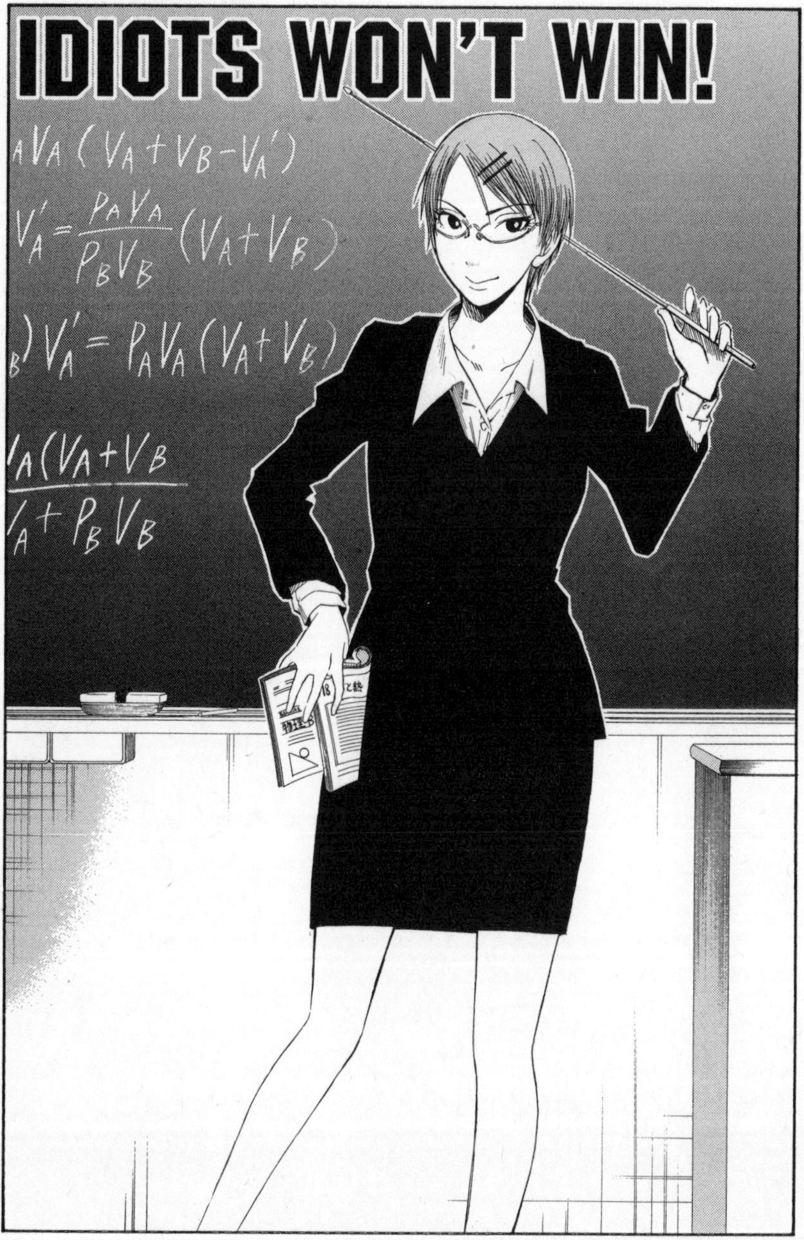

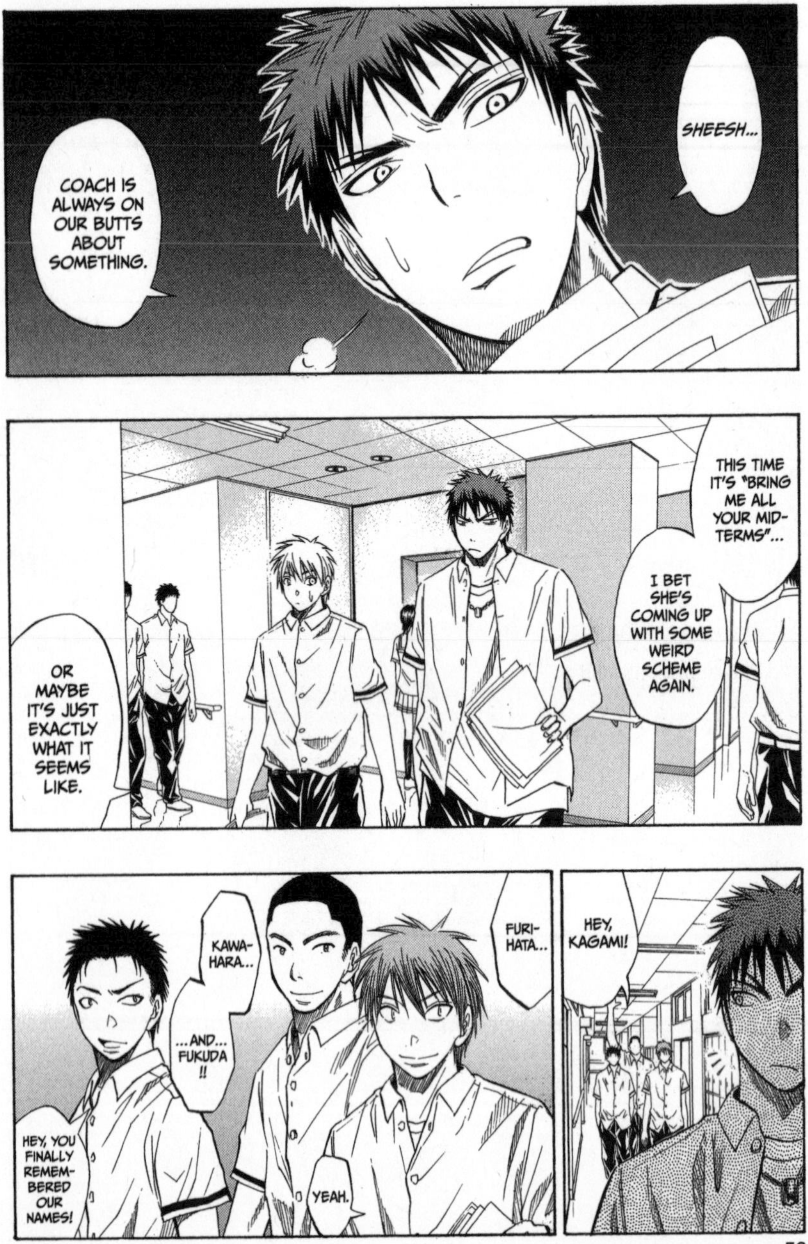
SHEESH...
COACH IS ALWAYS ON OUR BUTTS ABOUT SOMETHING.
THIS TIME IT'S "BRING ME ALL YOUR MID-TERMS"...
I BET SHE'S COMING UP WITH SOME WEIRD SCHEME AGAIN.
OR MAYBE IT'S JUST EXACTLY WHAT IT SEEMS LIKE.
HEY, KAGAMI!
FURIHATA...
KAWAHARA...
...AND... FUKUDA!!
YEAH.
HEY, YOU FINALLY REMEMBERED OUR NAMES!

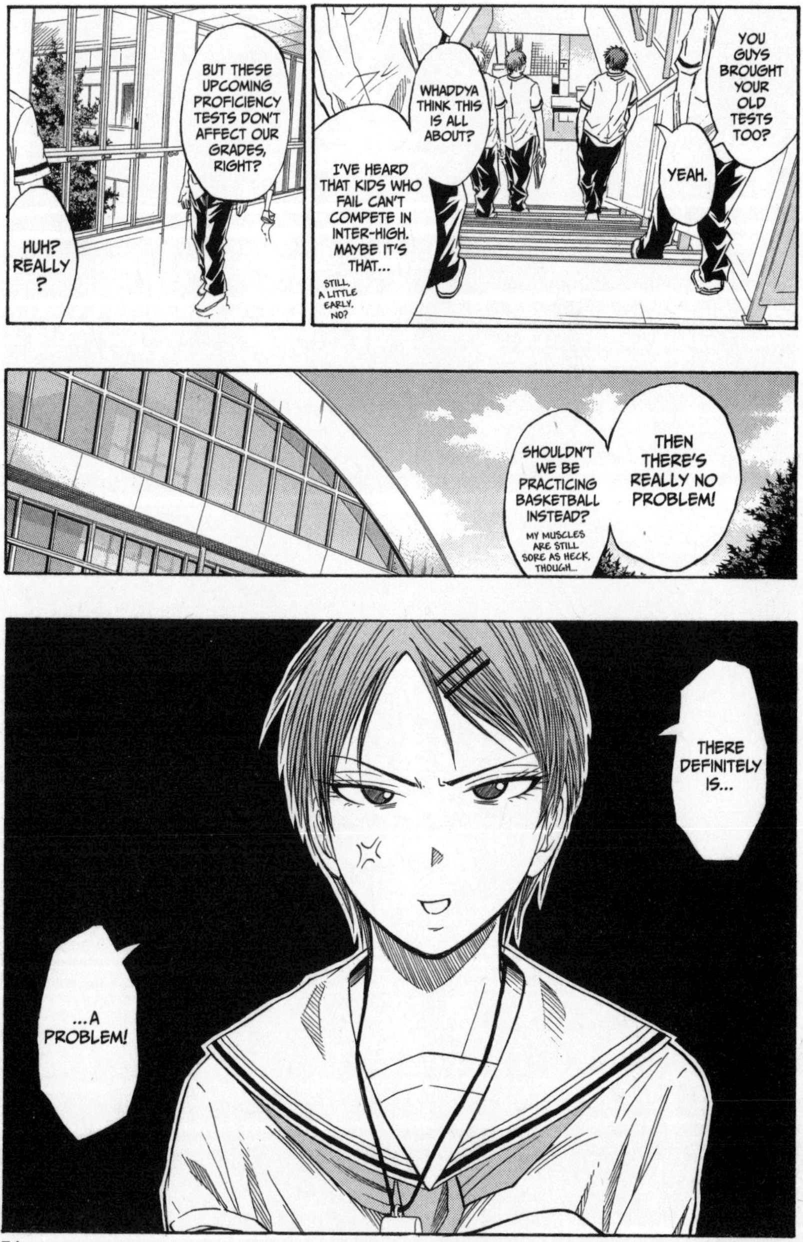
YOU GUYS BROUGHT YOUR OLD TESTS TOO?
YEAH.
WHADDYA THINK THIS IS ALL ABOUT?
I'VE HEARD THAT KIDS WHO FAIL CAN'T COMPETE IN INTER-HIGH. MAYBE IT'S THAT...
STILL, A LITTLE EARLY, NO?
BUT THESE UPCOMING PROFICIENCY TESTS DON'T AFFECT OUR GRADES, RIGHT?
HUH? REALLY?
THEN THERE'S REALLY NO PROBLEM!
SHOULDN'T WE BE PRACTICING BASKETBALL INSTEAD?
MY MUSCLES ARE STILL SORE AS HECK, THOUGH...
THERE DEFINITELY IS...
...A PROBLEM!

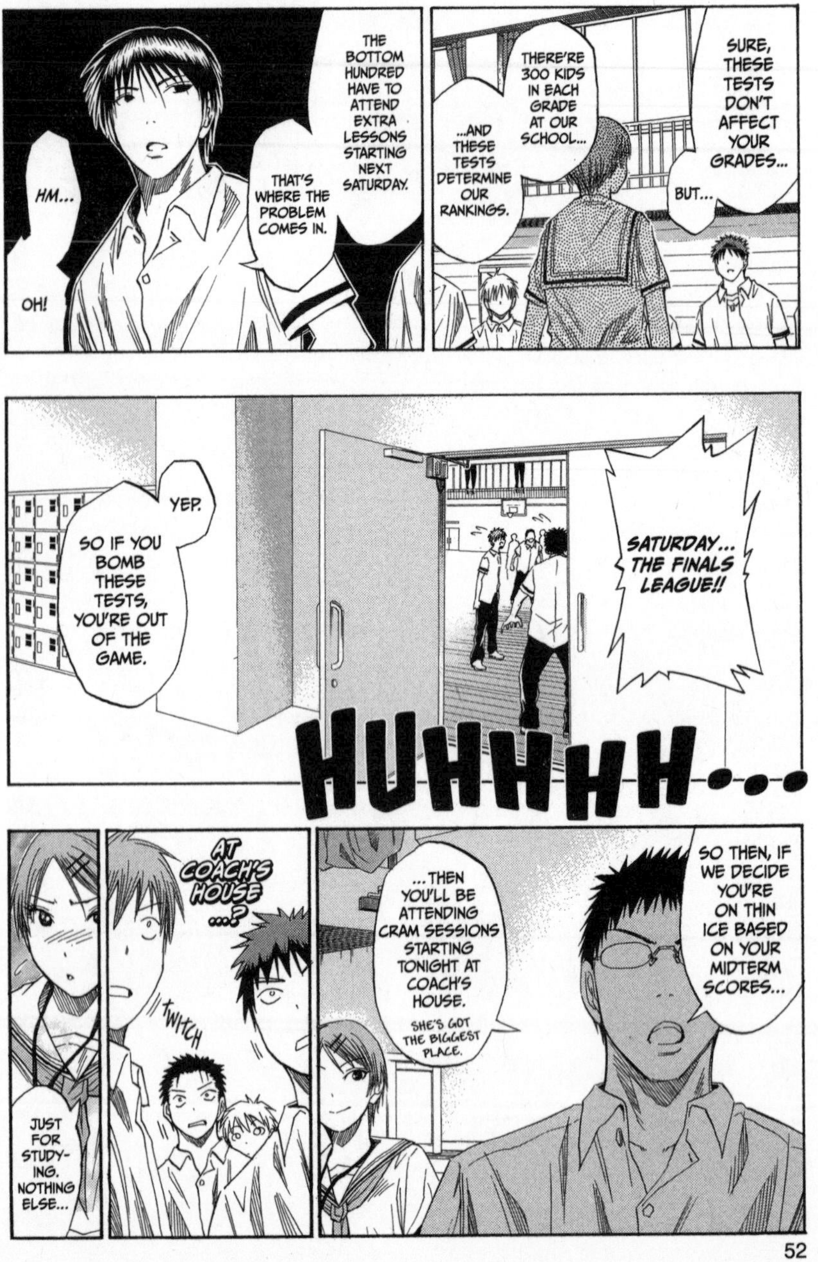
SURE, THESE TESTS DON'T AFFECT YOUR GRADES...
BUT...
THERE'RE 300 KIDS IN EACH GRADE AT OUR SCHOOL...
...AND THESE TESTS DETERMINE OUR RANKINGS.
THE BOTTOM HUNDRED HAVE TO ATTEND EXTRA LESSONS STARTING NEXT SATURDAY.
THAT'S WHERE THE PROBLEM COMES IN.
HM...
OH!
SATURDAY... THE FINALS LEAGUE!!
YEP.
SO IF YOU BOMB THESE TESTS, YOU'RE OUT OF THE GAME.
HUHHHH...
SO THEN, IF WE DECIDE YOU'RE ON THIN ICE BASED ON YOUR MIDTERM SCORES...
...THEN YOU'LL BE ATTENDING CRAM SESSIONS STARTING TONIGHT AT COACH'S HOUSE.
SHE'S GOT THE BIGGEST PLACE.
AT COACH'S HOUSE ...?
TWITCH
JUST FOR STUDYING. NOTHING ELSE...

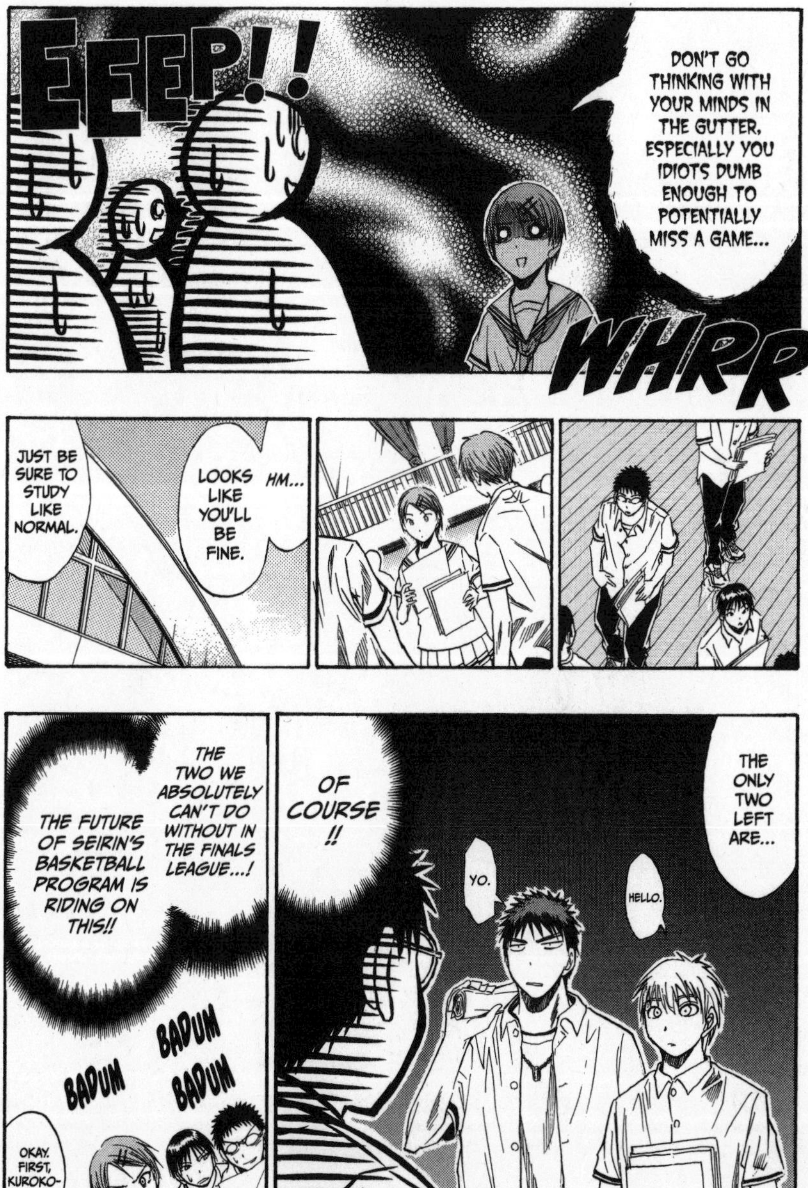
DON'T GO THINKING WITH YOUR MINDS IN THE GUTTER, ESPECIALLY YOU IDIOTS DUMB ENOUGH TO POTENTIALLY MISS A GAME...
EEEP!!
WHRR
HM...
LOOKS LIKE YOU'LL BE FINE.
JUST BE SURE TO STUDY LIKE NORMAL.
THE ONLY TWO LEFT ARE...
OF COURSE!!
HELLO.
YO.
THE TWO WE ABSOLUTELY CAN'T DO WITHOUT IN THE FINALS LEAGUE...!
THE FUTURE OF SEIRIN'S BASKETBALL PROGRAM IS RIDING ON THIS!!
BADUM
BADUM
BADUM
OKAY. FIRST, KUROKO-KUN.

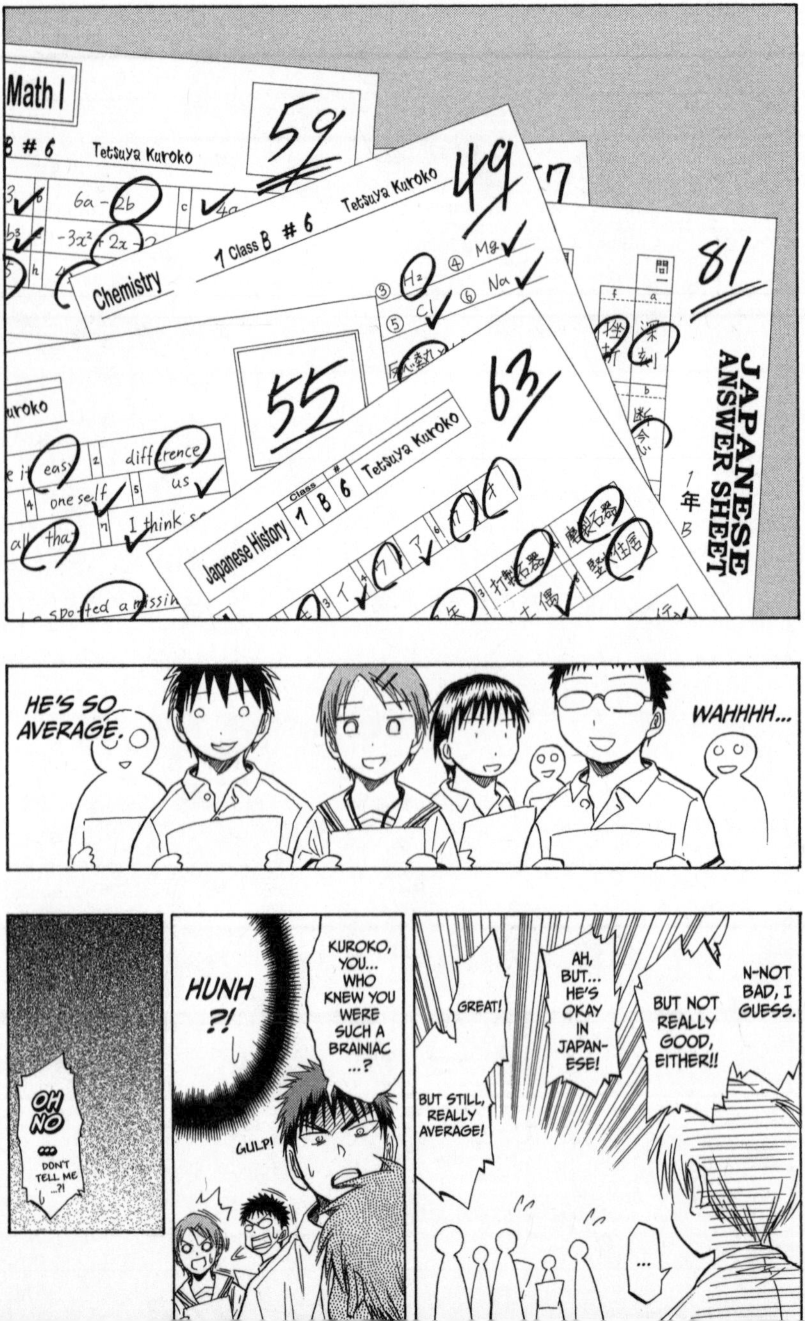
Math I
59
Tetsuya Kuroko
49
Chemistry
1 Class B # 6
Tetsuya Kuroko
81
JAPANESE ANSWER SHEET
55
63
Japanese History
Class 1 B 6
Tetsuya Kuroko
WAHHHH...
HE'S SO AVERAGE.
N-NOT BAD, I GUESS.
BUT NOT REALLY GOOD, EITHER!!
AH, BUT... HE'S OKAY IN JAPANESE!
GREAT!
BUT STILL, REALLY AVERAGE!
...
KUROKO, YOU... WHO KNEW YOU WERE SUCH A BRAINIAC...?
HUNH ?!
GULP!
OH NO
... DON'T TELL ME ...?!

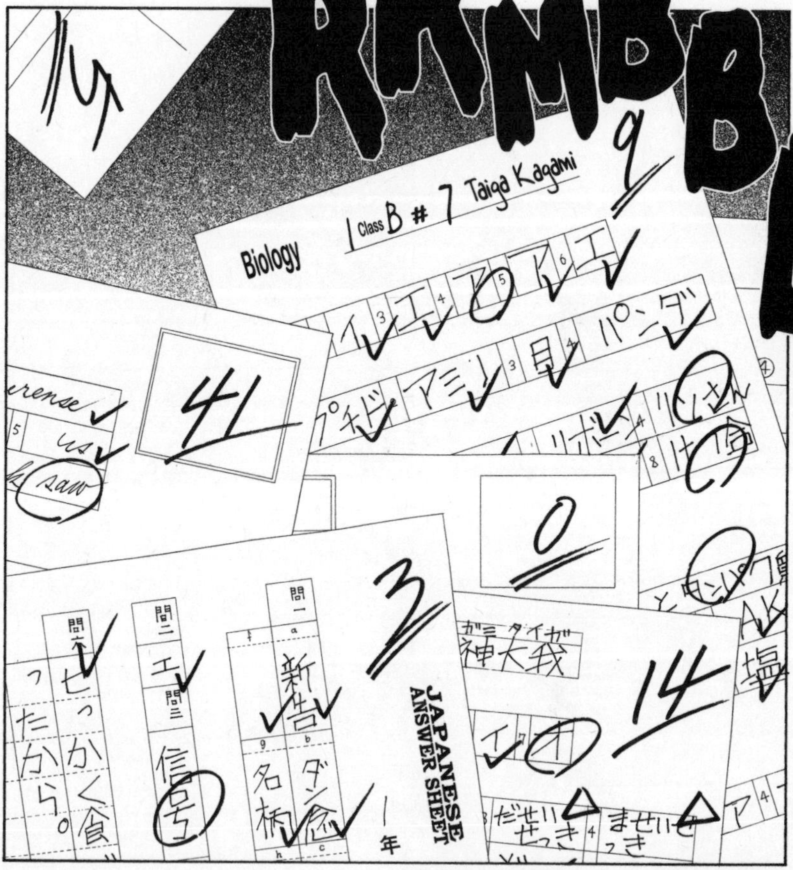
RRMBBB
Biology
1 Class B # 7 Taiga Kagami
41
0
3
14
JAPANESE ANSWER SHEET

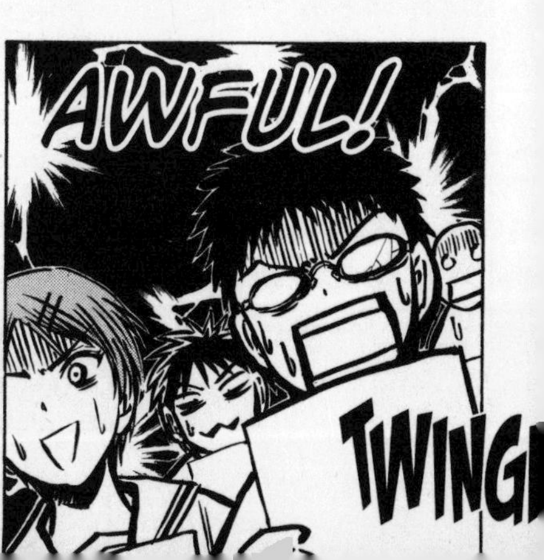
AWFUL!
TWINGE

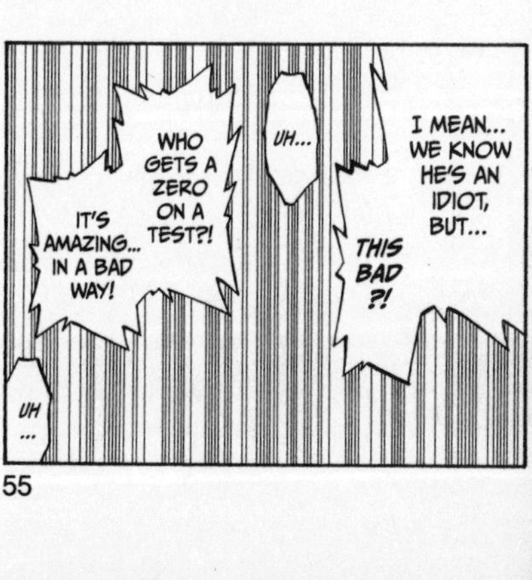
I MEAN... WE KNOW HE'S AN IDIOT, BUT...
THIS BAD?!
UH...
WHO GETS A ZERO ON A TEST?!
IT'S AMAZING... IN A BAD WAY!
UH...

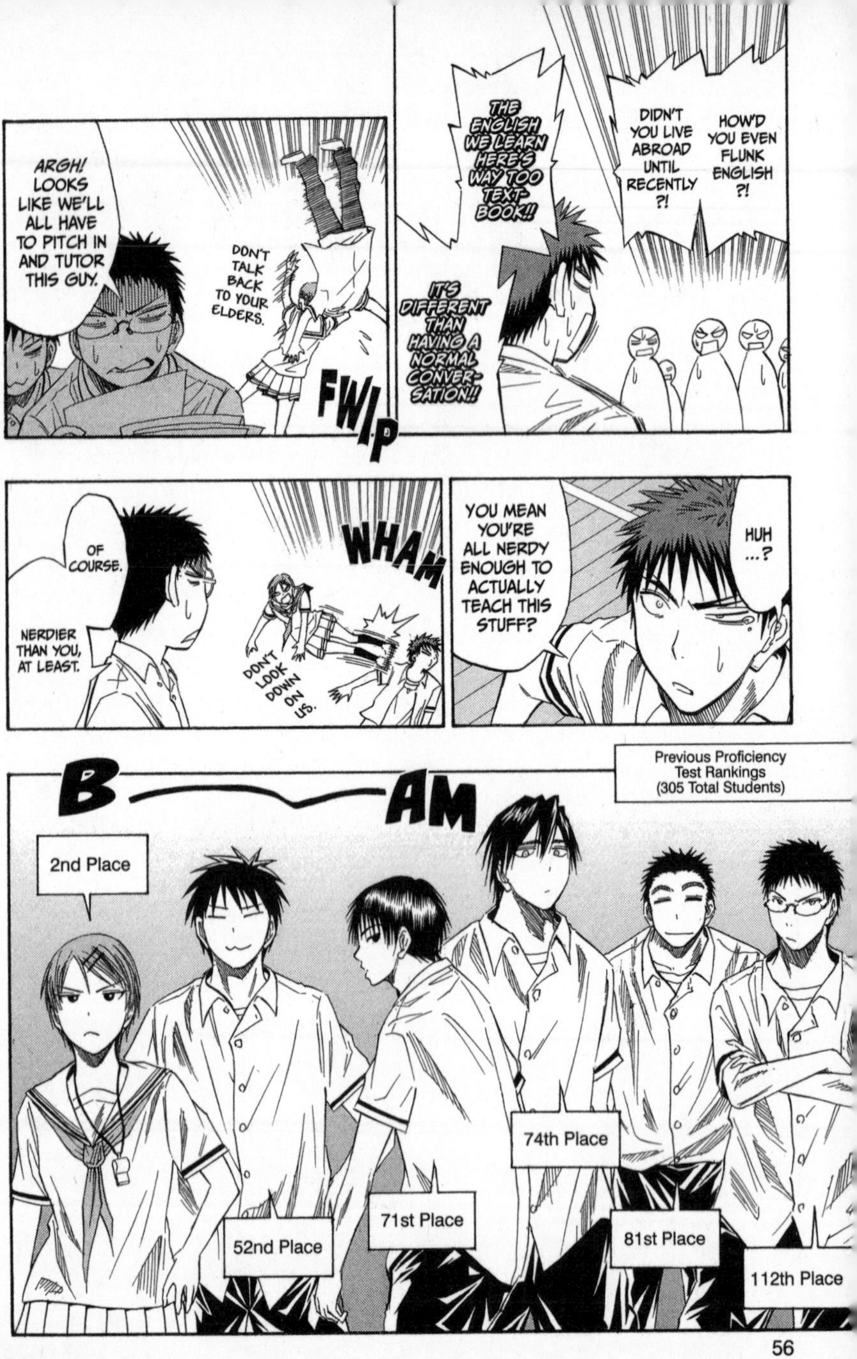
HOW'D YOU EVEN FLUNK ENGLISH ?!
DIDN'T YOU LIVE ABROAD UNTIL RECENTLY ?!
THE ENGLISH WE LEARN HERE'S WAY TOO TEXT-BOOK!!
IT'S DIFFERENT THAN HAVING A NORMAL CONVER-SATION!!
ARGH! LOOKS LIKE WE'LL ALL HAVE TO PITCH IN AND TUTOR THIS GUY.
DON'T TALK BACK TO YOUR ELDERS.
FWIP
HUH ...?
YOU MEAN YOU'RE ALL NERDY ENOUGH TO ACTUALLY TEACH THIS STUFF?
WHAM
OF COURSE.
NERDIER THAN YOU, AT LEAST.
DON'T LOOK DOWN ON US.
Previous Proficiency Test Rankings (305 Total Students)
B——AM
112th Place
81st Place
74th Place
71st Place
52nd Place
2nd Place

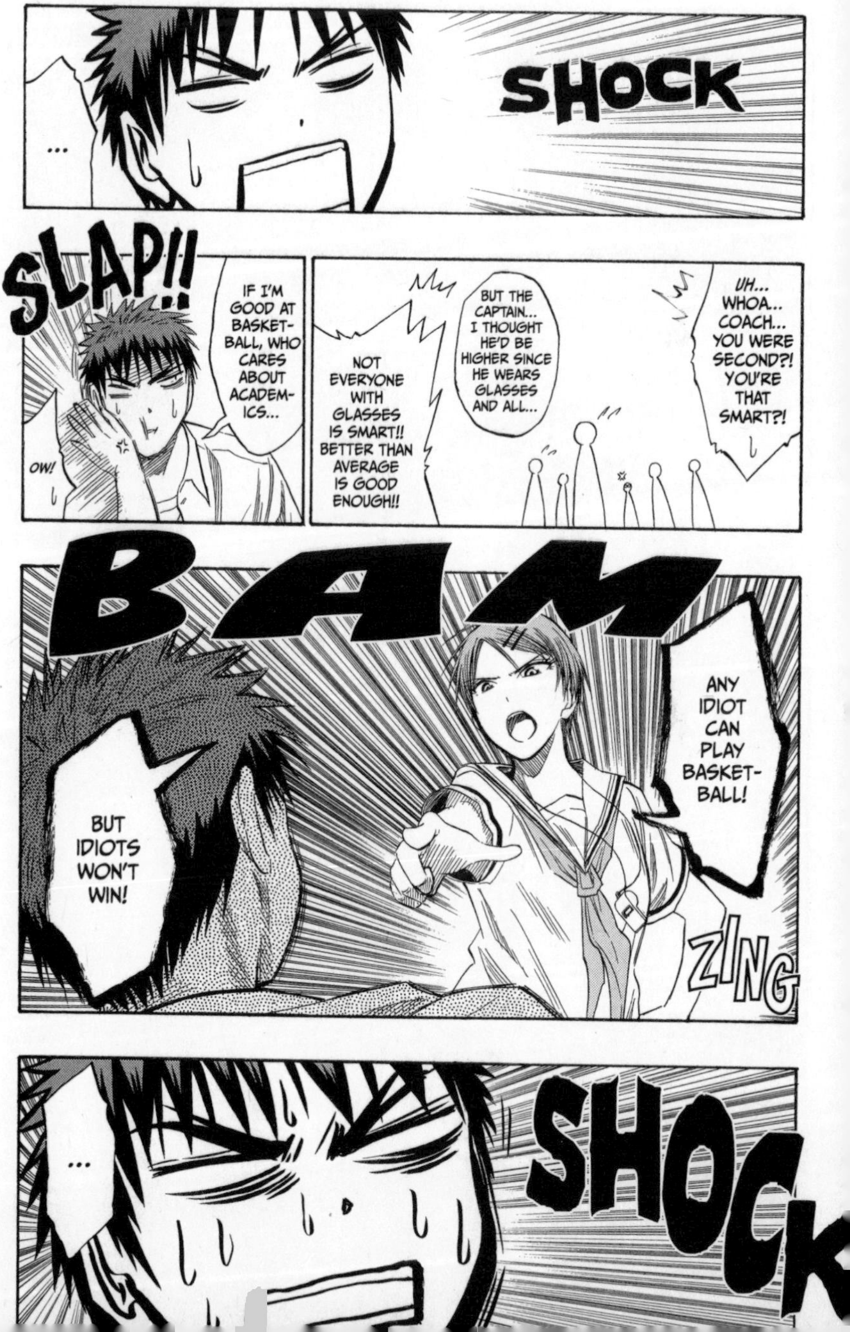
SHOCK
...
UH... WHOA... COACH... YOU WERE SECOND?! YOU'RE THAT SMART?!
BUT THE CAPTAIN... I THOUGHT HE'D BE HIGHER SINCE HE WEARS GLASSES AND ALL...
NOT EVERYONE WITH GLASSES IS SMART!! BETTER THAN AVERAGE IS GOOD ENOUGH!!
SLAP!!
IF I'M GOOD AT BASKETBALL, WHO CARES ABOUT ACADEMICS...
OW!
BAM
ANY IDIOT CAN PLAY BASKETBALL!
BUT IDIOTS WON'T WIN!
ZING
SHOCK
...

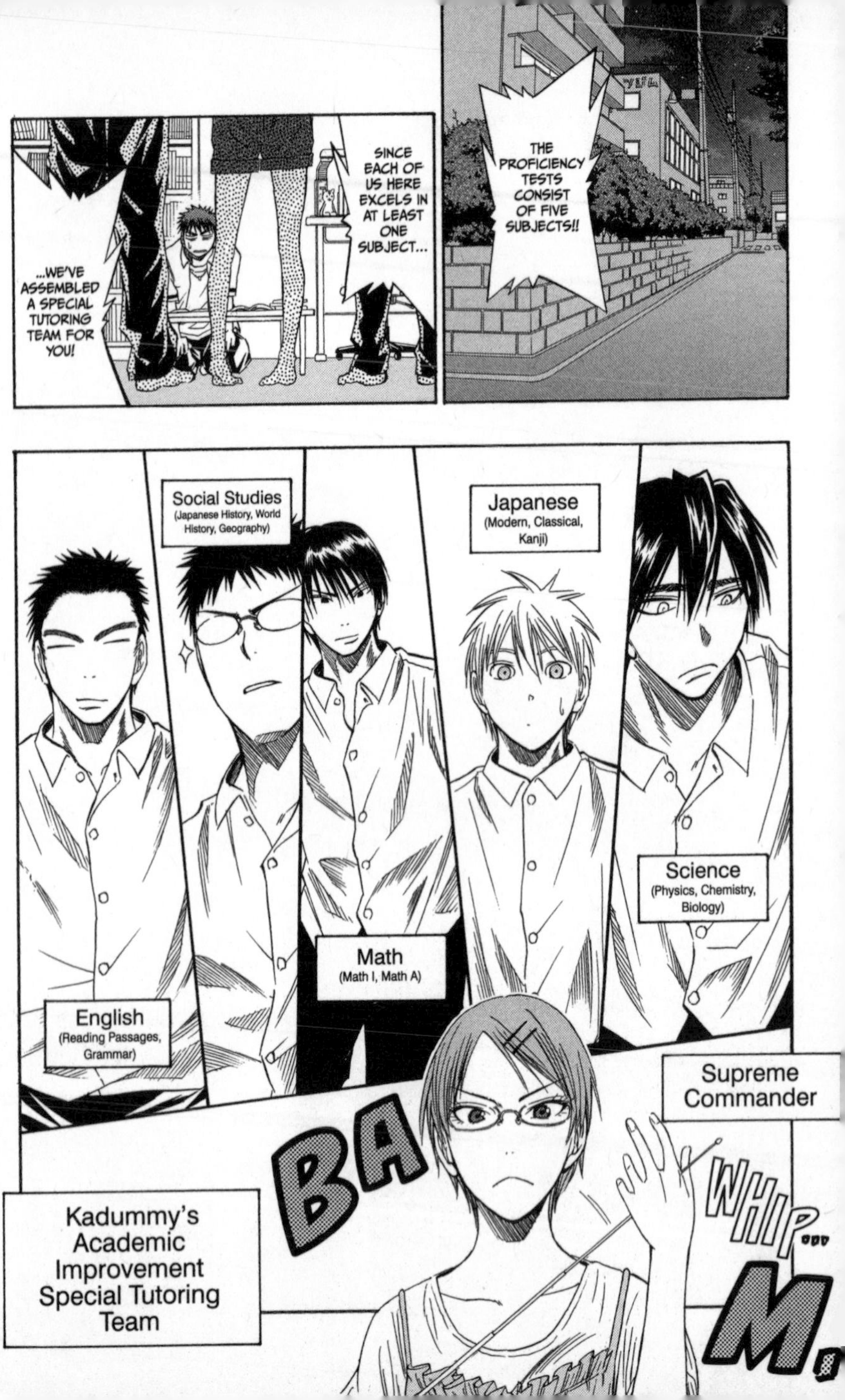
THE PROFICIENCY TESTS CONSIST OF FIVE SUBJECTS!!
SINCE EACH OF US HERE EXCELS IN AT LEAST ONE SUBJECT...
...WE'VE ASSEMBLED A SPECIAL TUTORING TEAM FOR YOU!
Japanese (Modern, Classical, Kanji)
Social Studies (Japanese History, World History, Geography)
Science (Physics, Chemistry, Biology)
Math (Math I, Math A)
English (Reading Passages, Grammar)
Supreme Commander
WHIP...
BA
M,
Kadummy's Academic Improvement Special Tutoring Team

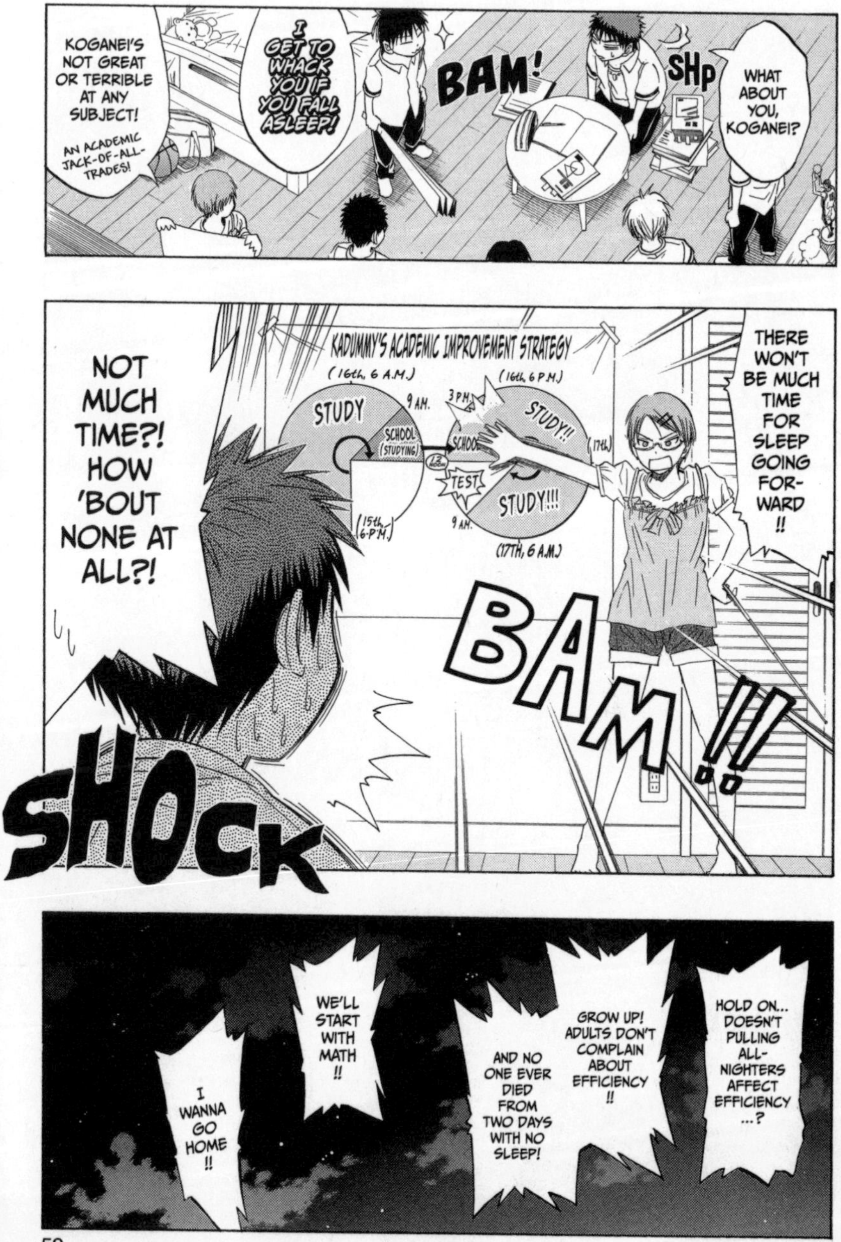
WHAT ABOUT YOU, KOGANEI!?
SHp
BAM!
I GET TO WHACK YOU IF YOU FALL ASLEEP!
KOGANEI'S NOT GREAT OR TERRIBLE AT ANY SUBJECT!
AN ACADEMIC JACK-OF-ALL-TRADES!
THERE WON'T BE MUCH TIME FOR SLEEP GOING FORWARD!!
KADUMMY'S ACADEMIC IMPROVEMENT STRATEGY
(16th, 6 A.M.)
STUDY
9 A.M.
SCHOOL (STUDYING)
(15th, 6 P.M.)
(16th, 6 P.M.)
3 P.M.
SCHOOL
STUDY!!
(17th)
TEST
STUDY!!!
9 A.M.
(17TH, 6 A.M.)
BAM!!
NOT MUCH TIME?! HOW 'BOUT NONE AT ALL?!
SHOCK
HOLD ON... DOESN'T PULLING ALL-NIGHTERS AFFECT EFFICIENCY...?
GROW UP! ADULTS DON'T COMPLAIN ABOUT EFFICIENCY!!
AND NO ONE EVER DIED FROM TWO DAYS WITH NO SLEEP!
WE'LL START WITH MATH!!
I WANNA GO HOME!!

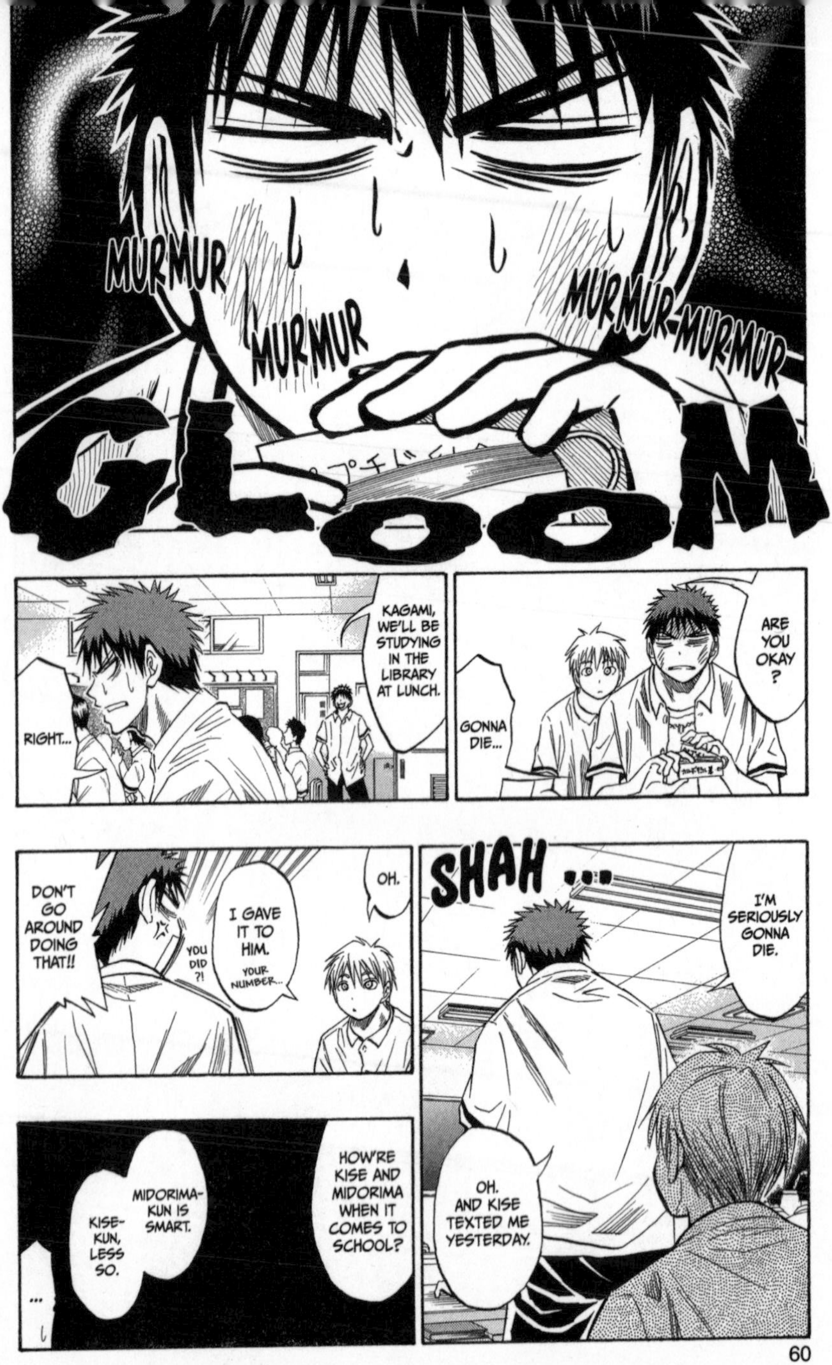
MURMUR-MURMUR
MURMUR
MURMUR
GLOOM
ARE YOU OKAY?
GONNA DIE...
KAGAMI, WE'LL BE STUDYING IN THE LIBRARY AT LUNCH.
RIGHT...
SHAH...
I'M SERIOUSLY GONNA DIE.
OH. AND KISE TEXTED ME YESTERDAY.
OH.
I GAVE IT TO HIM. YOUR NUMBER...
YOU DID?!
DON'T GO AROUND DOING THAT!!
HOW'RE KISE AND MIDORIMA WHEN IT COMES TO SCHOOL?
MIDORIMA-KUN IS SMART.
KISE-KUN, LESS SO.
...

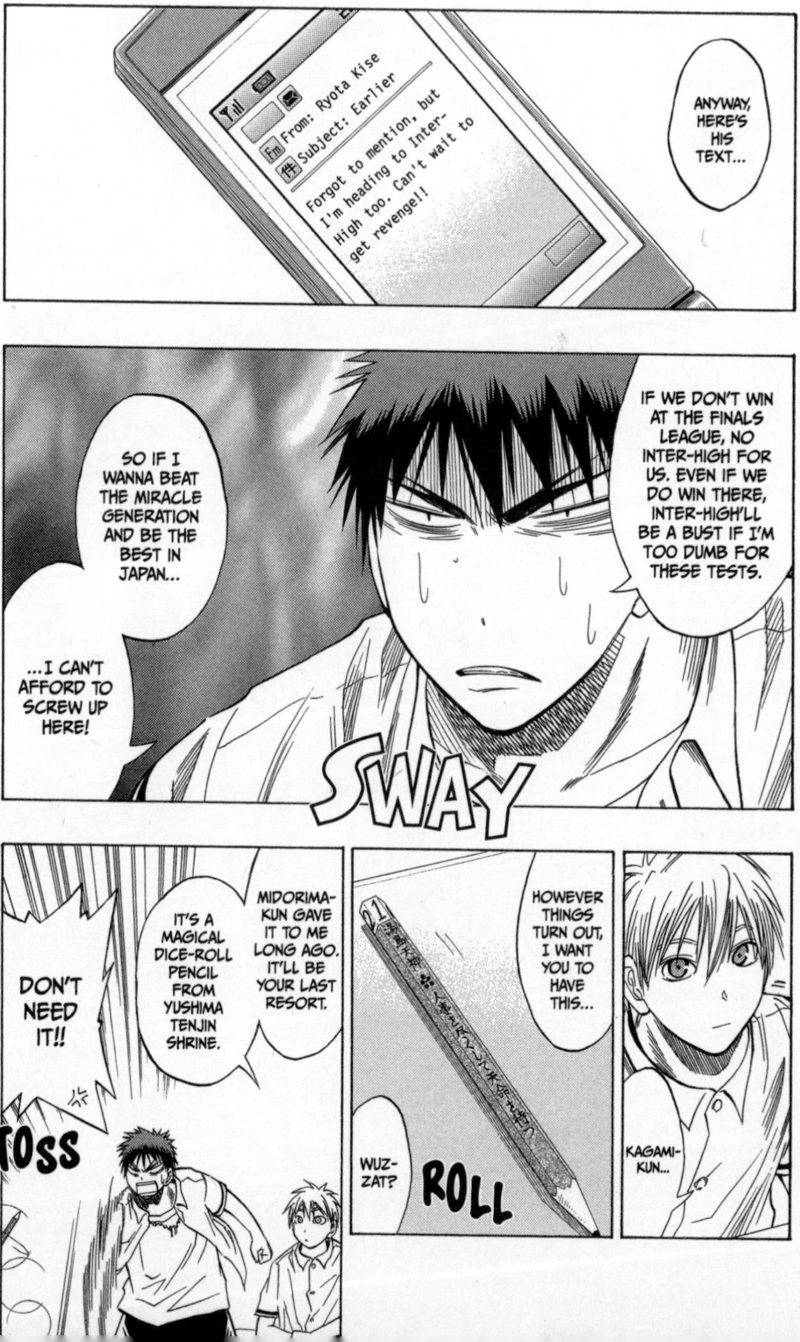
ANYWAY, HERE'S HIS TEXT...
From: Ryota Kise
Subject: Earlier
Forgot to mention, but I'm heading to Inter-High too. Can't wait to get revenge!!
IF WE DON'T WIN AT THE FINALS LEAGUE, NO INTER-HIGH FOR US. EVEN IF WE DO WIN THERE, INTER-HIGH'LL BE A BUST IF I'M TOO DUMB FOR THESE TESTS.
SO IF I WANNA BEAT THE MIRACLE GENERATION AND BE THE BEST IN JAPAN...
...I CAN'T AFFORD TO SCREW UP HERE!
SWAY
KAGAMI-KUN...
HOWEVER THINGS TURN OUT, I WANT YOU TO HAVE THIS...
WUZ-ZAT?
ROLL
MIDORIMA-KUN GAVE IT TO ME LONG AGO. IT'LL BE YOUR LAST RESORT.
IT'S A MAGICAL DICE-ROLL PENCIL FROM YUSHIMA TENJIN SHRINE.
DON'T NEED IT!!
TOSS

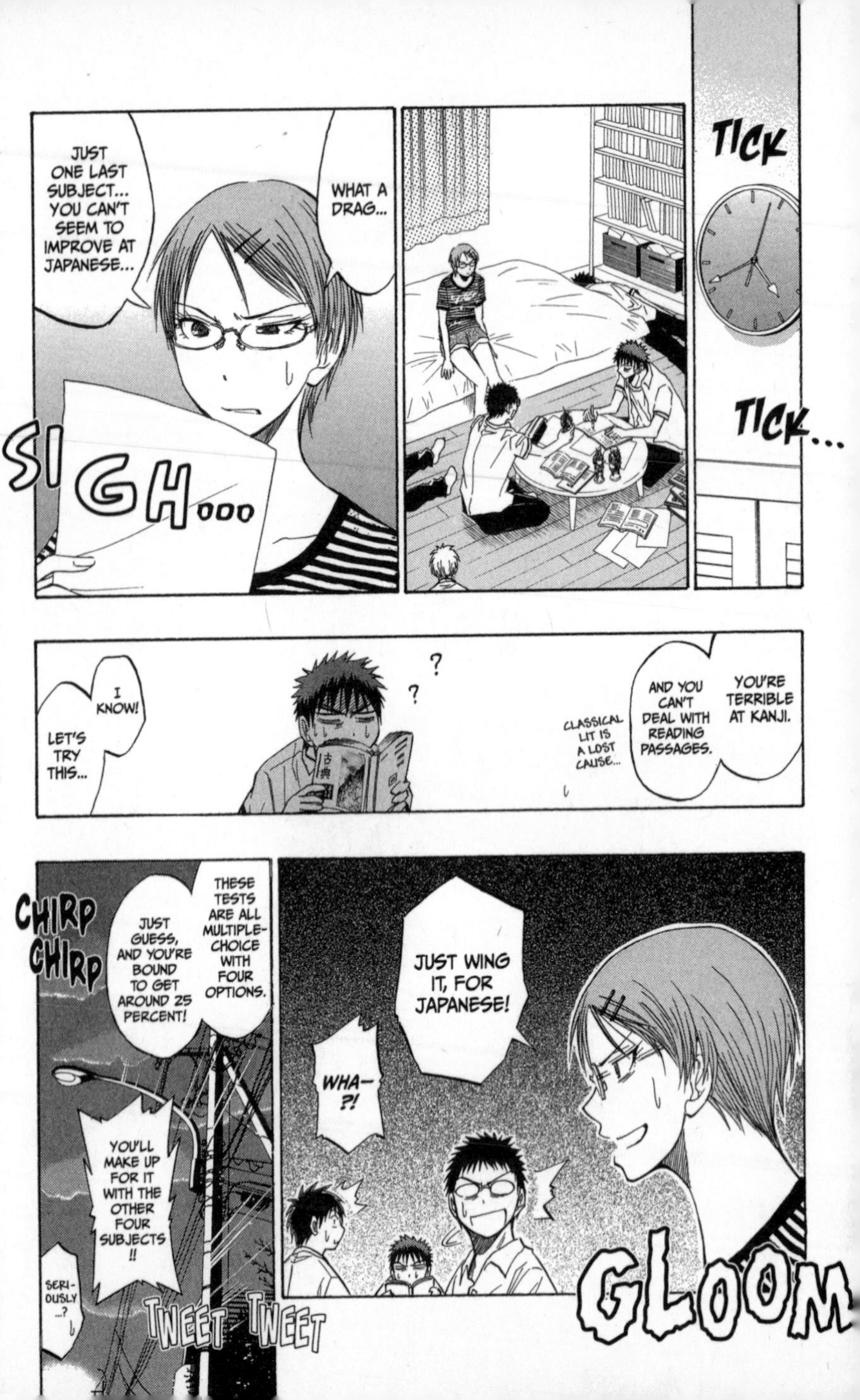
TICK
TICK...
WHAT A DRAG...
JUST ONE LAST SUBJECT... YOU CAN'T SEEM TO IMPROVE AT JAPANESE...
SIGH...
YOU'RE TERRIBLE AT KANJI.
AND YOU CAN'T DEAL WITH READING PASSAGES.
CLASSICAL LIT IS A LOST CAUSE...
?
?
I KNOW!
LET'S TRY THIS...
JUST WING IT, FOR JAPANESE!
WHA-?!
GLOOM
THESE TESTS ARE ALL MULTIPLE-CHOICE WITH FOUR OPTIONS.
JUST GUESS, AND YOU'RE BOUND TO GET AROUND 25 PERCENT!
CHIRP CHIRP
YOU'LL MAKE UP FOR IT WITH THE OTHER FOUR SUBJECTS!!
SERI-OUSLY...?
TWEET TWEET

JUST LIKE I THOUGHT...

SKRITCH
SKRITCH
SKRITCH
SKRITCH

SKRITCH
SKRITCH
SKRITCH
SKRITCH
SKRITCH

I'M NOT GONNA PASS IN ANY OF THESE SUBJECTS!

FORGET SACRIFICING ONE SUBJECT

GLoooom

I CAN DO IT!

BAM

NO! AFTER ALL THAT STUDYING, I CAN'T GIVE UP!

SKRITCH SKRITCH

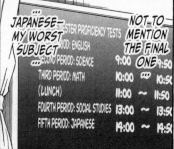

...JAPANESE—MY WORST SUBJECT...

...NOT TO MENTION THE FINAL ONE.

SEMESTER PROFICIENCY TESTS

FIRST PERIOD: ENGLISH	9:00	~	9:50
SECOND PERIOD: SCIENCE	10:00	~	10:50
THIRD PERIOD: MATH	11:00	~	11:50
(LUNCH)			
FOURTH PERIOD: SOCIAL STUDIES	13:00	~	13:50
FIFTH PERIOD: JAPANESE	14:00	~	14:50

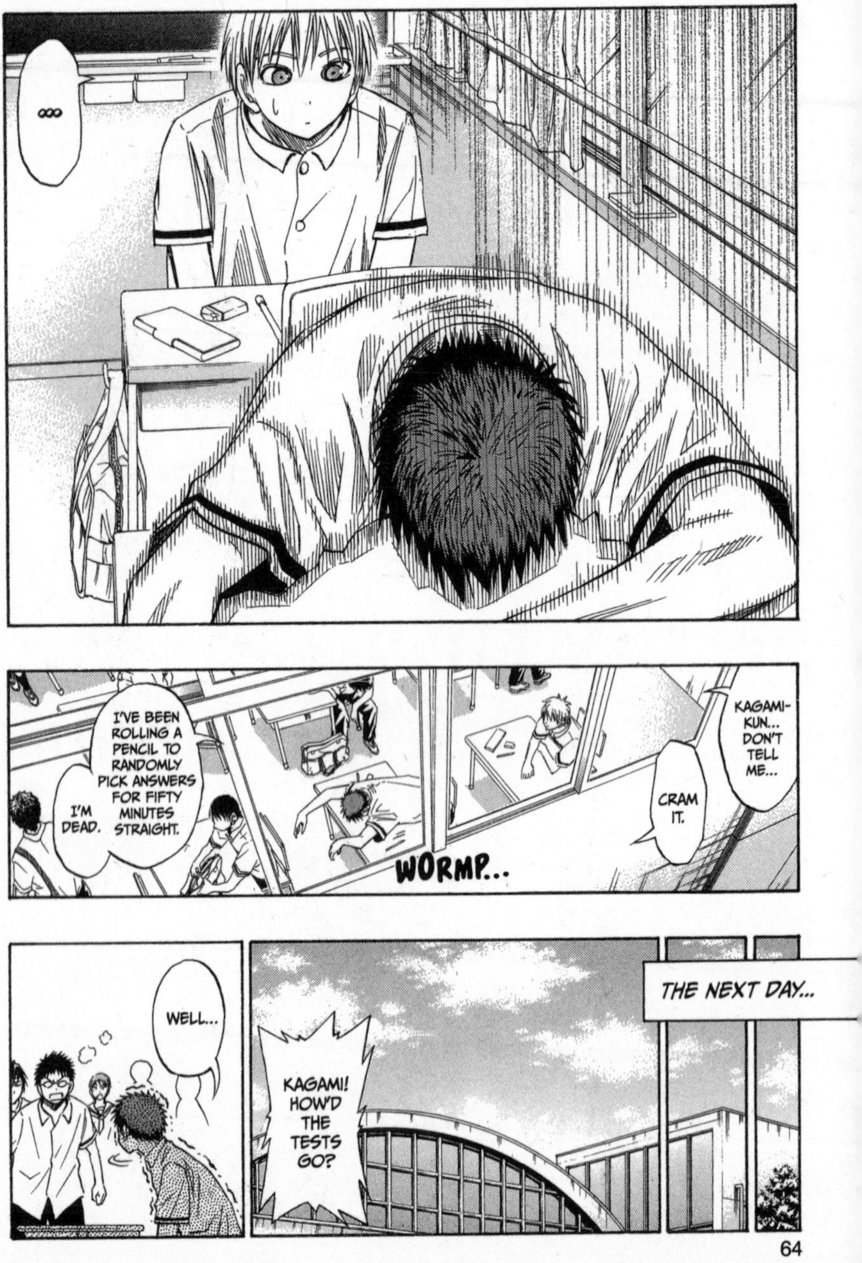
...
KAGAMI-KUN... DON'T TELL ME...
CRAM IT.
I'VE BEEN ROLLING A PENCIL TO RANDOMLY PICK ANSWERS FOR FIFTY MINUTES STRAIGHT.
I'M DEAD.
WORMP...
THE NEXT DAY...
KAGAMI! HOW'D THE TESTS GO?
WELL...

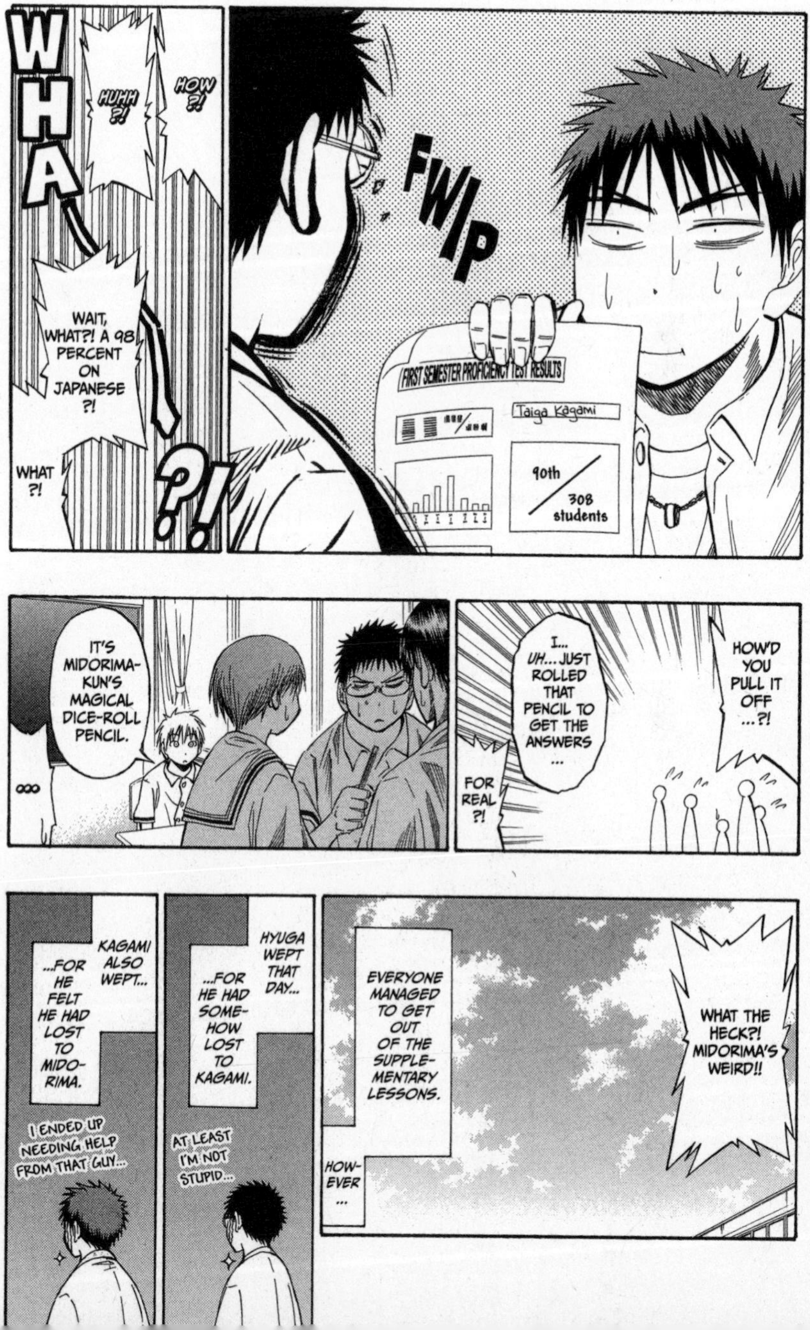
FWIP
FIRST SEMESTER PROFICIENCY TEST RESULTS
Taiga Kagami
90th / 308 students
HOW ?!
HUHH ?!
WHA
WAIT, WHAT?! A 98 PERCENT ON JAPANESE ?!
?!
WHAT ?!
HOW'D YOU PULL IT OFF ...?!
I... UH... JUST ROLLED THAT PENCIL TO GET THE ANSWERS ...
FOR REAL ?!
IT'S MIDORIMA-KUN'S MAGICAL DICE-ROLL PENCIL.
WHAT THE HECK?! MIDORIMA'S WEIRD!!
EVERYONE MANAGED TO GET OUT OF THE SUPPLE-MENTARY LESSONS.
HOW-EVER ...
HYUGA WEPT THAT DAY...
...FOR HE HAD SOME-HOW LOST TO KAGAMI.
AT LEAST I'M NOT STUPID...
KAGAMI ALSO WEPT...
...FOR HE FELT HE HAD LOST TO MIDO-RIMA.
I ENDED UP NEEDING HELP FROM THAT GUY...

KUROKO'S BASKETBALL BLOOPERS

TAKE 1

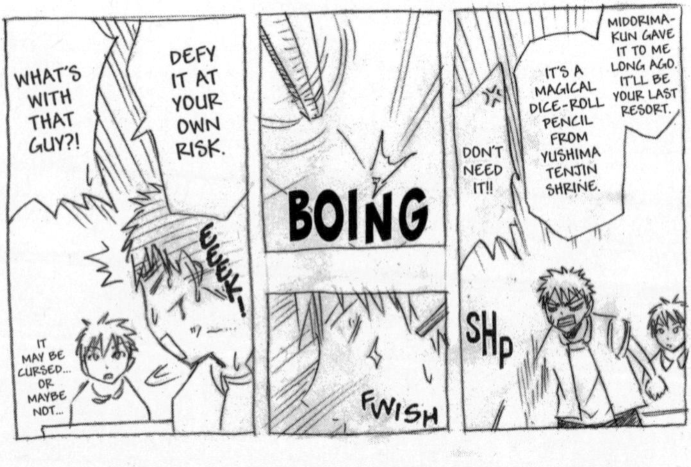
MIDORIMA-KUN GAVE IT TO ME LONG AGO. IT'LL BE YOUR LAST RESORT.
IT'S A MAGICAL DICE-ROLL PENCIL FROM YUSHIMA TENJIN SHRINE.
DON'T NEED IT!!
SHP
BOING
FWISH
DEFY IT AT YOUR OWN RISK.
WHAT'S WITH THAT GUY?!
EEEK!
IT MAY BE CURSED... OR MAYBE NOT...

38TH QUARTER: COULDN'T WAIT

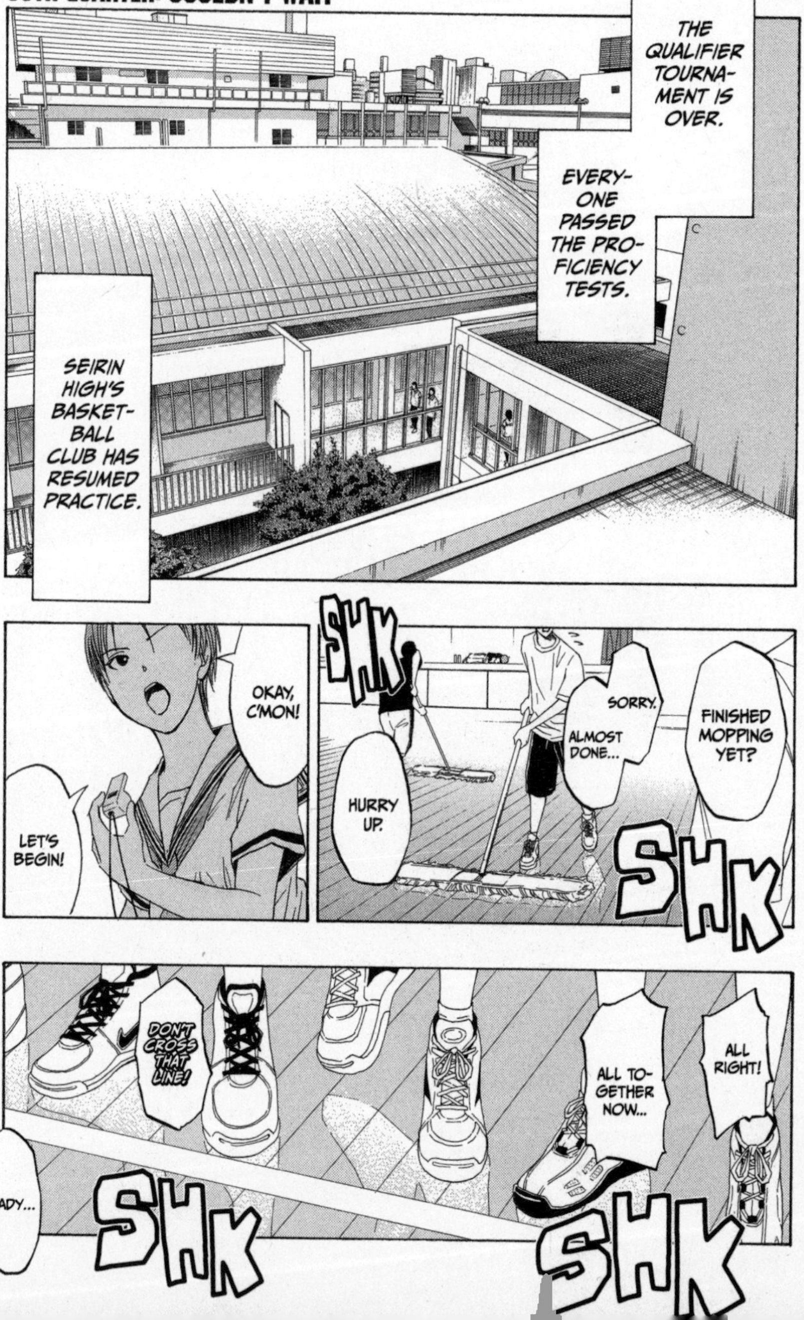
THE QUALIFIER TOURNAMENT IS OVER.
EVERYONE PASSED THE PROFICIENCY TESTS.
SEIRIN HIGH'S BASKETBALL CLUB HAS RESUMED PRACTICE.
FINISHED MOPPING YET?
SORRY. ALMOST DONE...
SHK
HURRY UP.
SHK
OKAY, C'MON!
LET'S BEGIN!
ALL RIGHT!
ALL TOGETHER NOW...
SHK
DON'T CROSS THAT LINE!
SHK
READY...

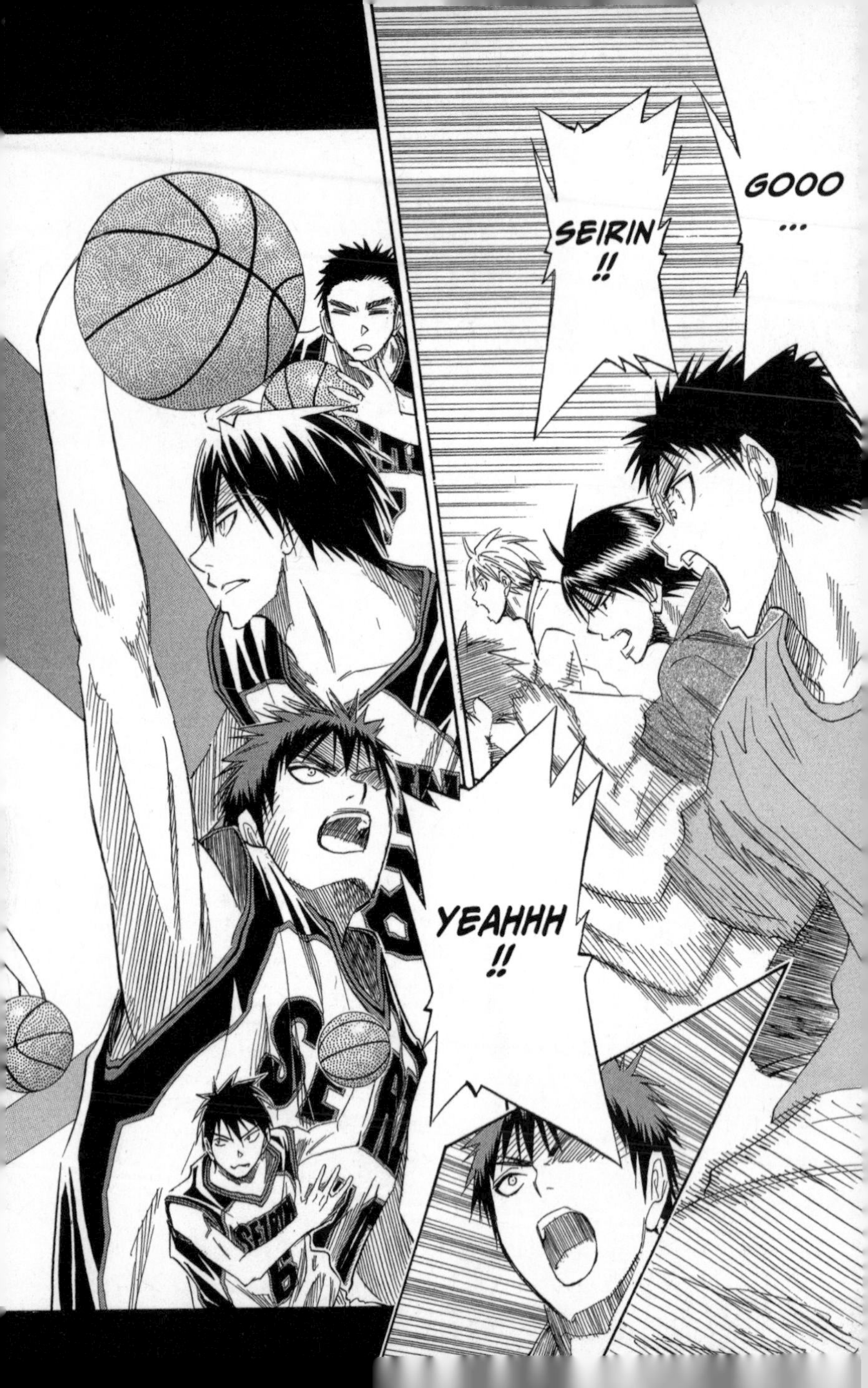
GOOO ...
SEIRIN !!
YEAHHH !!

38TH QUARTER: COULDN'T WAIT

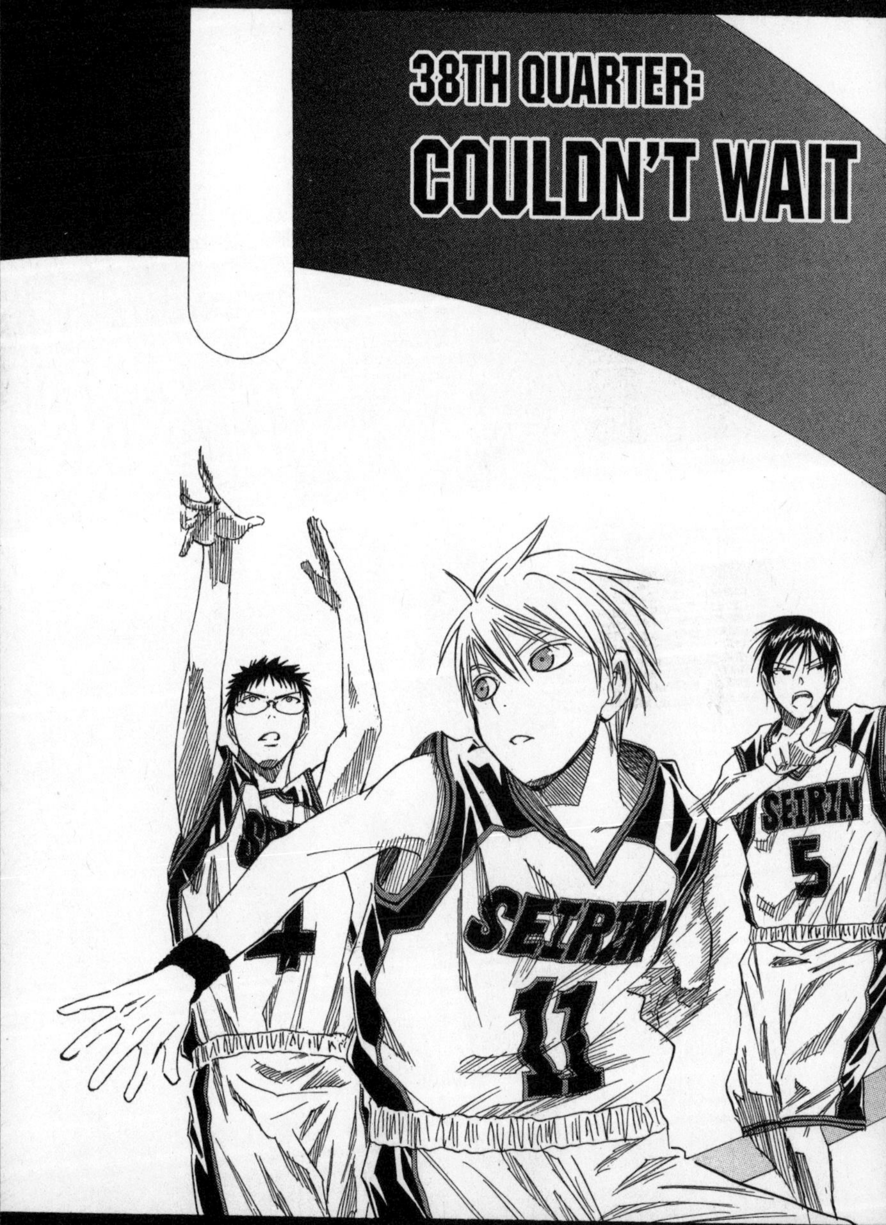
SEIRIN
5
SEIRIN
11

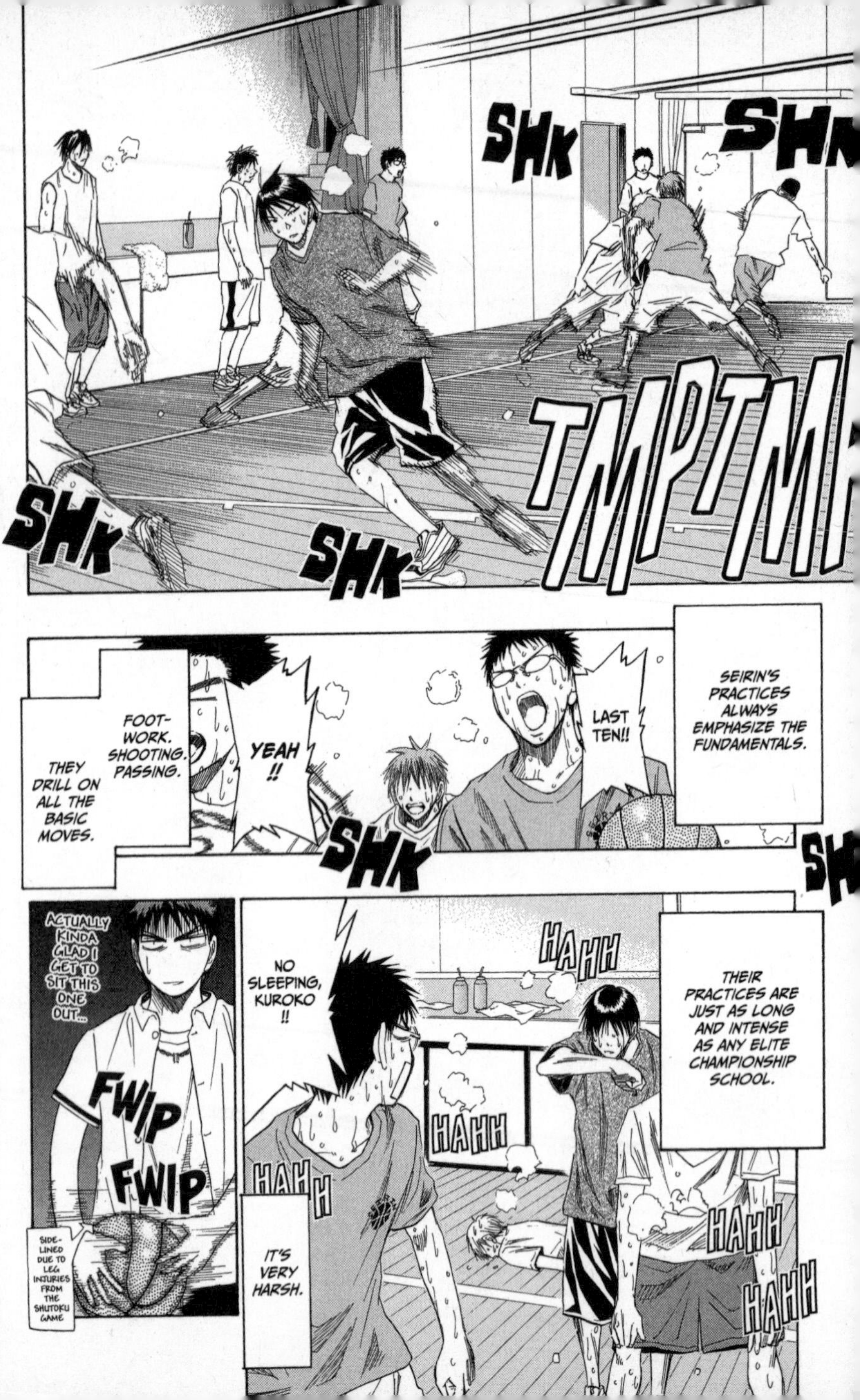
SHK
SHK
SHK
SEIRIN'S PRACTICES ALWAYS EMPHASIZE THE FUNDAMENTALS.
LAST TEN!!
YEAH !!
SHK
FOOT-WORK. SHOOTING. PASSING.
THEY DRILL ON ALL THE BASIC MOVES.
THEIR PRACTICES ARE JUST AS LONG AND INTENSE AS ANY ELITE CHAMPIONSHIP SCHOOL.
HAHH
HAHH
HAHH
HAHH
NO SLEEPING, KUROKO !!
HAHH
IT'S VERY HARSH.
ACTUALLY KINDA GLAD I GET TO SIT THIS ONE OUT...
FWIP
FWIP
SIDE-LINED DUE TO LEG INJURIES FROM THE SHUTOKU GAME

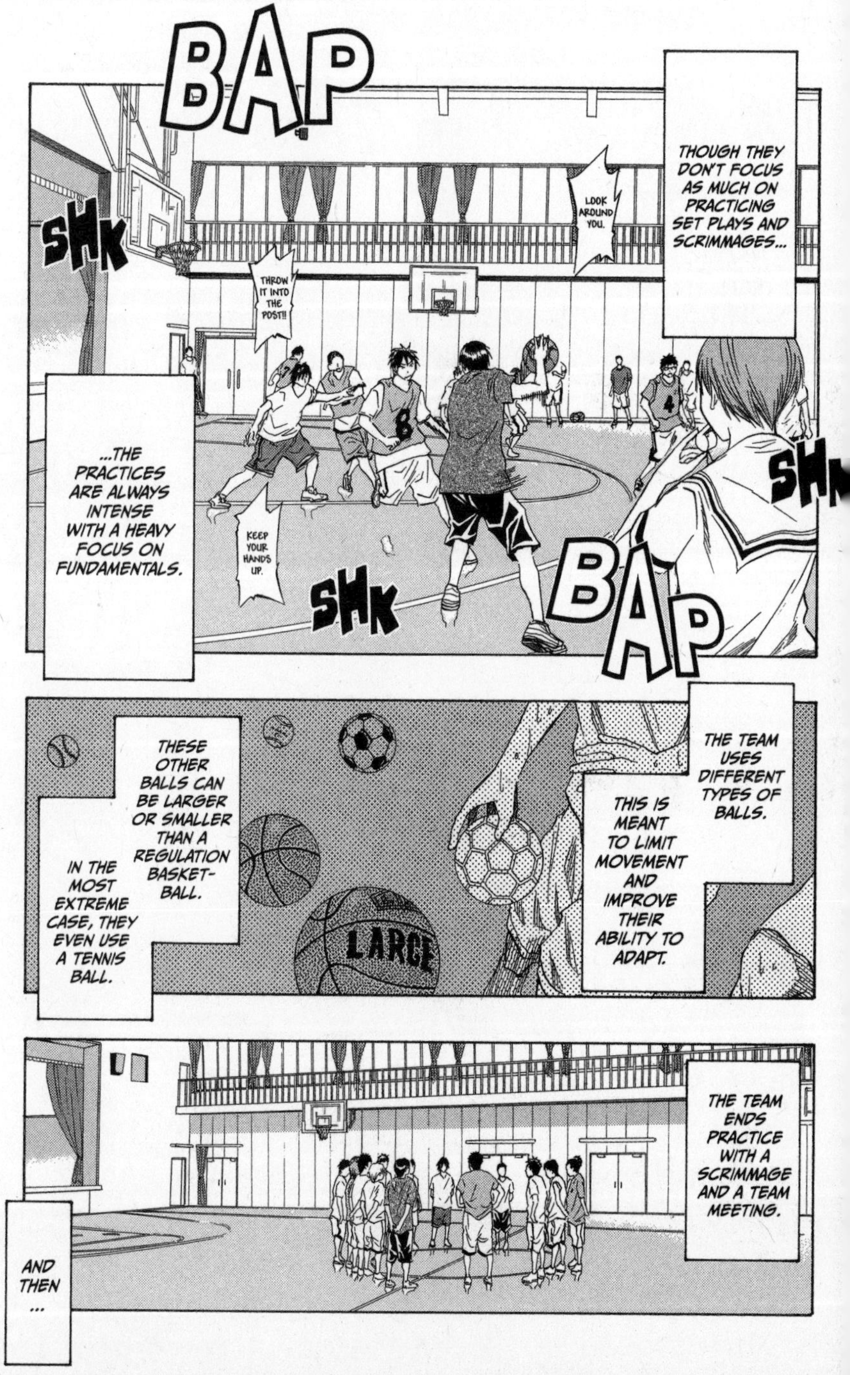
THOUGH THEY DON'T FOCUS AS MUCH ON PRACTICING SET PLAYS AND SCRIMMAGES...
LOOK AROUND YOU.
THROW IT INTO THE POST!!
BAP
SHK
SH
...THE PRACTICES ARE ALWAYS INTENSE WITH A HEAVY FOCUS ON FUNDAMENTALS.
BAP
KEEP YOUR HANDS UP.
SHK
THE TEAM USES DIFFERENT TYPES OF BALLS.
THIS IS MEANT TO LIMIT MOVEMENT AND IMPROVE THEIR ABILITY TO ADAPT.
THESE OTHER BALLS CAN BE LARGER OR SMALLER THAN A REGULATION BASKET-BALL.
IN THE MOST EXTREME CASE, THEY EVEN USE A TENNIS BALL.
LARGE
THE TEAM ENDS PRACTICE WITH A SCRIMMAGE AND A TEAM MEETING.
AND THEN ...

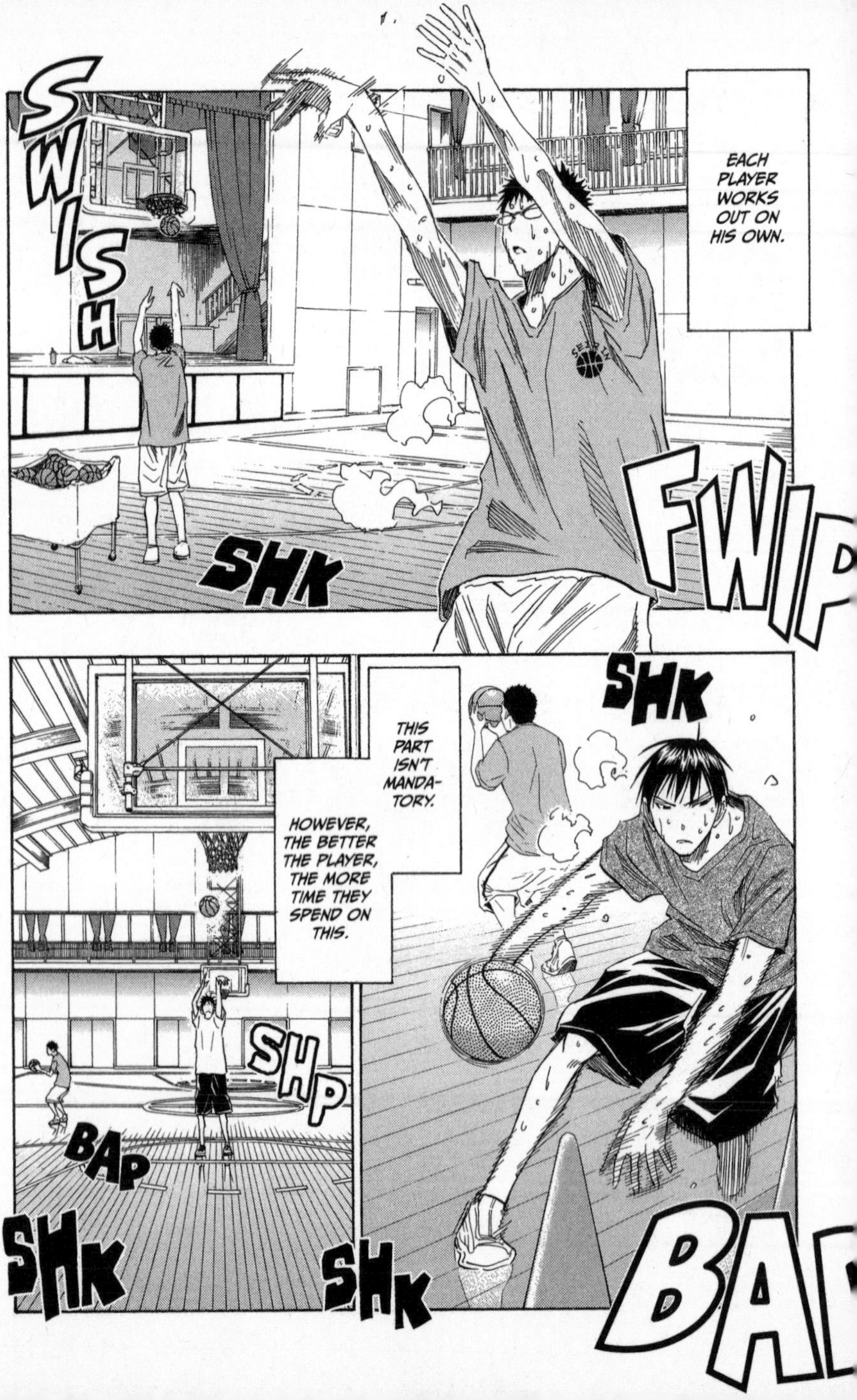

EACH PLAYER WORKS OUT ON HIS OWN.
FWIP
SWISH
SHK
SHK
BAP
SHK
THIS PART ISN'T MANDATORY.
HOWEVER, THE BETTER THE PLAYER, THE MORE TIME THEY SPEND ON THIS.
SHP
BAP
SHK

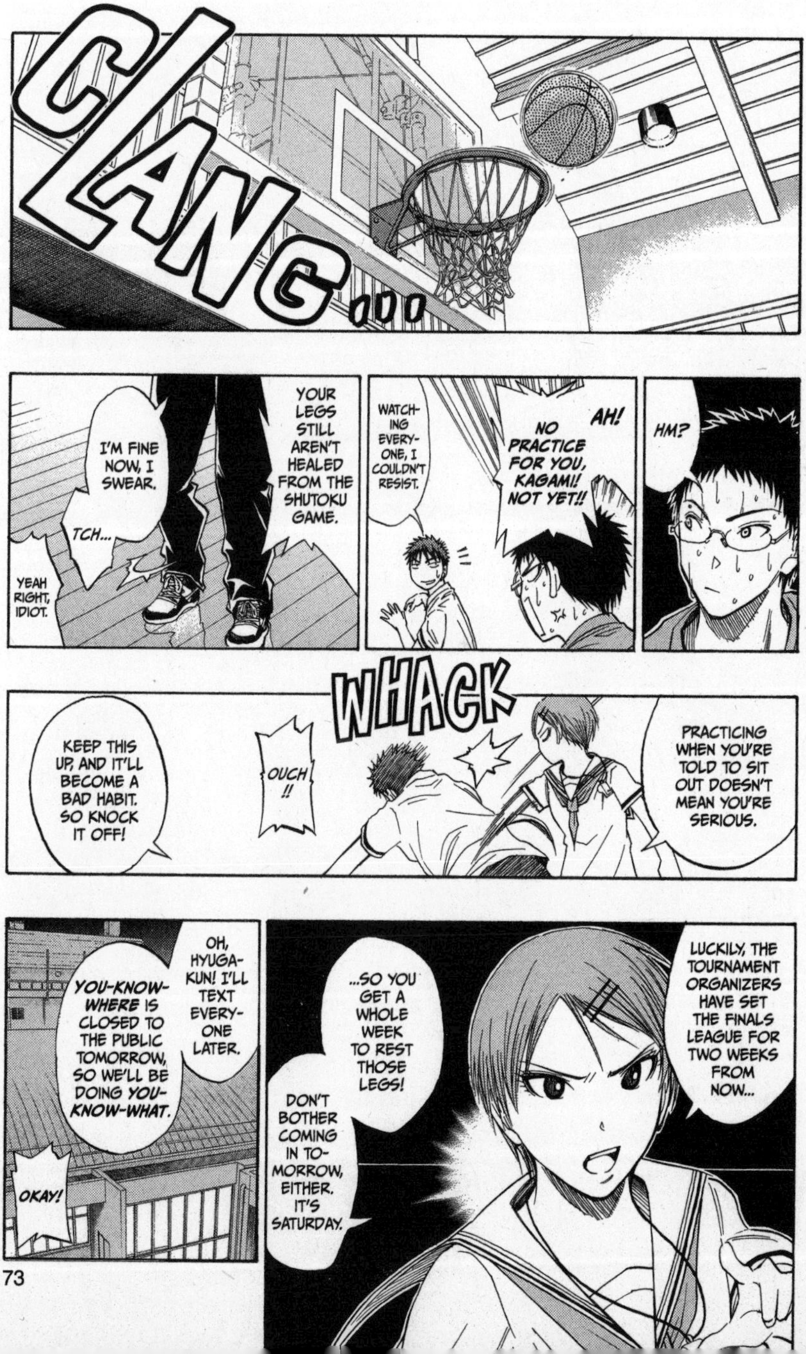
CLANG...
HM?
AH!
NO PRACTICE FOR YOU, KAGAMI! NOT YET!!
WATCHING EVERYONE, I COULDN'T RESIST.
YOUR LEGS STILL AREN'T HEALED FROM THE SHUTOKU GAME.
I'M FINE NOW, I SWEAR.
TCH...
YEAH RIGHT, IDIOT.
WHACK
PRACTICING WHEN YOU'RE TOLD TO SIT OUT DOESN'T MEAN YOU'RE SERIOUS.
OUCH!!
KEEP THIS UP, AND IT'LL BECOME A BAD HABIT. SO KNOCK IT OFF!
LUCKILY, THE TOURNAMENT ORGANIZERS HAVE SET THE FINALS LEAGUE FOR TWO WEEKS FROM NOW...
...SO YOU GET A WHOLE WEEK TO REST THOSE LEGS!
DON'T BOTHER COMING IN TOMORROW, EITHER. IT'S SATURDAY.
OH, HYUGA-KUN! I'LL TEXT EVERYONE LATER.
YOU-KNOW-WHERE IS CLOSED TO THE PUBLIC TOMORROW, SO WE'LL BE DOING YOU-KNOW-WHAT.
OKAY!

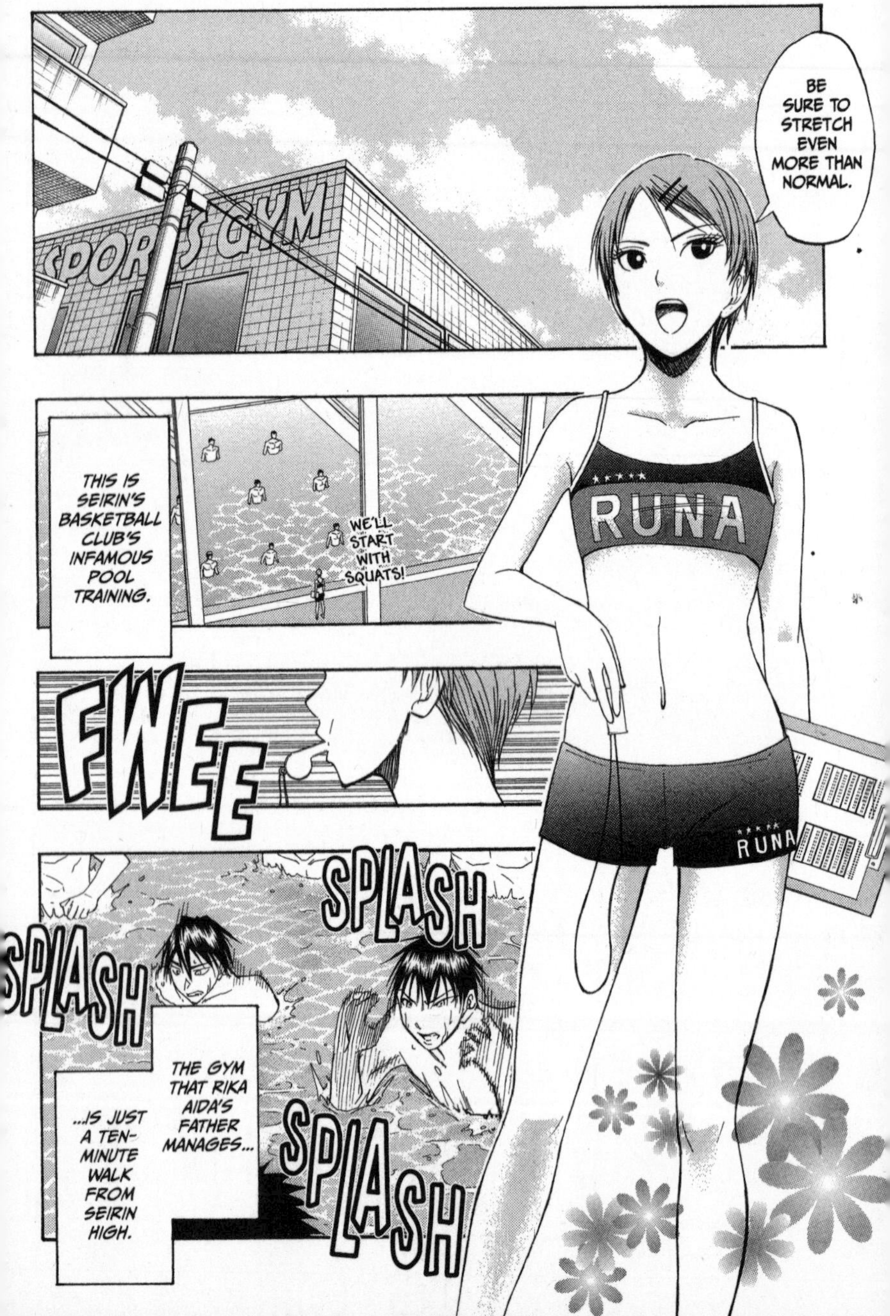
BE SURE TO STRETCH EVEN MORE THAN NORMAL.
RUNA
THIS IS SEIRIN'S BASKETBALL CLUB'S INFAMOUS POOL TRAINING.
WE'LL START WITH SQUATS!
FWEE
SPLASH
SPLASH
SPLASH
THE GYM THAT RIKA AIDA'S FATHER MANAGES...
...IS JUST A TEN-MINUTE WALK FROM SEIRIN HIGH.

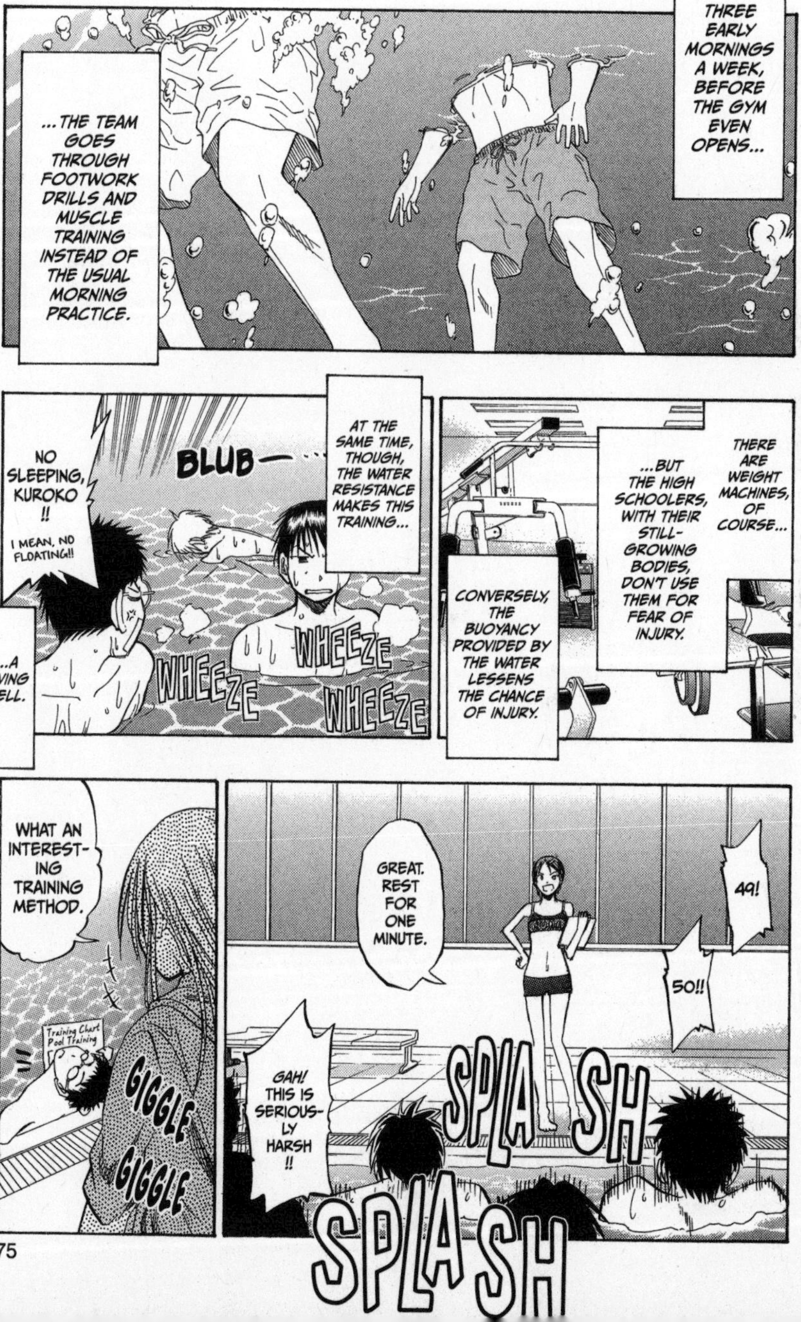
THREE EARLY MORNINGS A WEEK, BEFORE THE GYM EVEN OPENS...
...THE TEAM GOES THROUGH FOOTWORK DRILLS AND MUSCLE TRAINING INSTEAD OF THE USUAL MORNING PRACTICE.
THERE ARE WEIGHT MACHINES, OF COURSE...
...BUT THE HIGH SCHOOLERS, WITH THEIR STILL-GROWING BODIES, DON'T USE THEM FOR FEAR OF INJURY.
CONVERSELY, THE BUOYANCY PROVIDED BY THE WATER LESSENS THE CHANCE OF INJURY.
AT THE SAME TIME, THOUGH, THE WATER RESISTANCE MAKES THIS TRAINING...
BLUB—...
NO SLEEPING, KUROKO!!
I MEAN, NO FLOATING!!
WHEEZE
WHEEZE
WHEEZE
...A LIVING HELL.
49!
50!!
GREAT. REST FOR ONE MINUTE.
SPLASH
GAH! THIS IS SERIOUSLY HARSH!!
SPLASH
WHAT AN INTERESTING TRAINING METHOD.
Training Chart
Pool Training
GIGGLE
GIGGLE

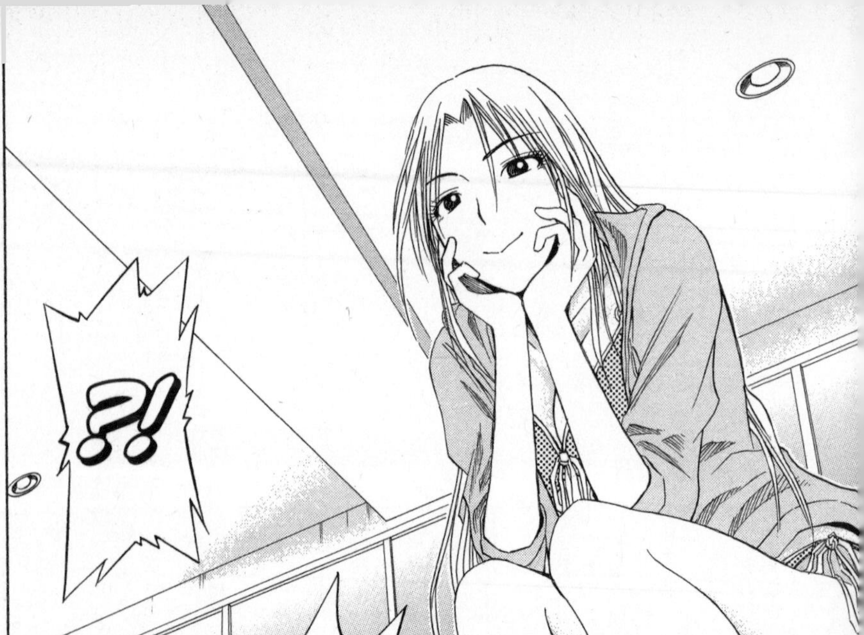
?!
BUH?!!

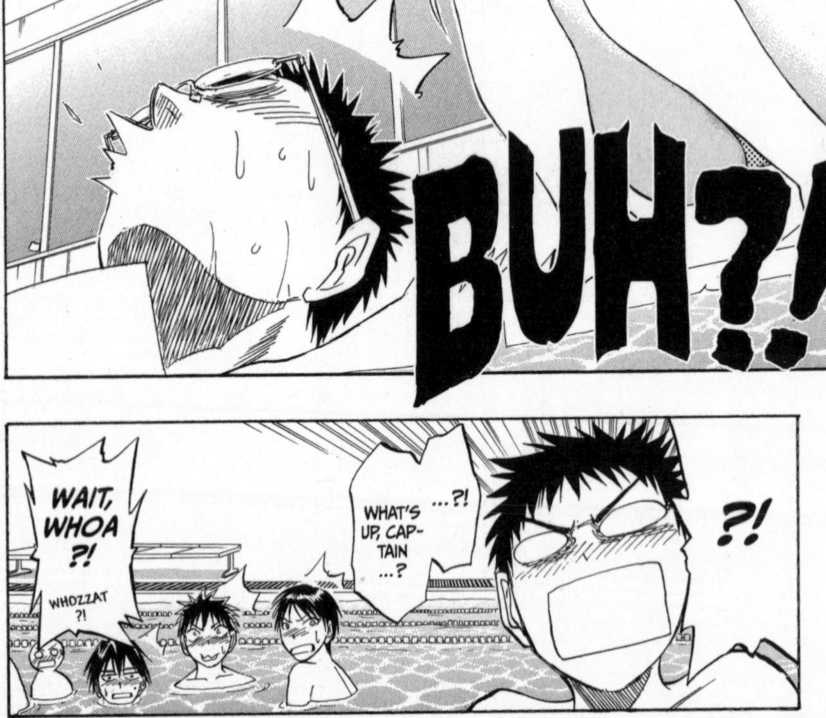
?!
...?!
WHAT'S UP, CAP-TAIN ...?
WAIT, WHOA ?!
WHOZZAT ?!

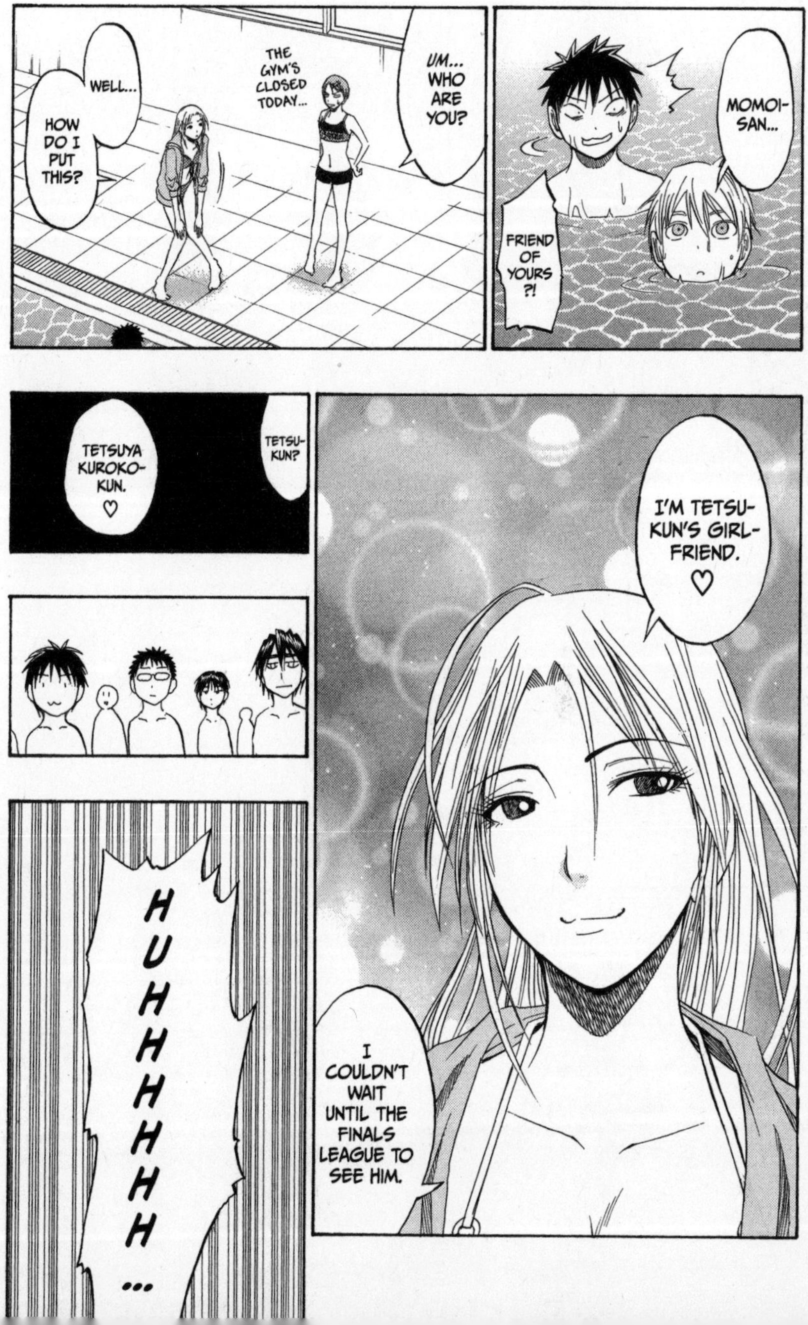
MOMOI-SAN...
FRIEND OF YOURS ?!
UM... WHO ARE YOU?
THE GYM'S CLOSED TODAY...
WELL...
HOW DO I PUT THIS?
I'M TETSU-KUN'S GIRL-FRIEND. ♡
I COULDN'T WAIT UNTIL THE FINALS LEAGUE TO SEE HIM.
TETSU-KUN?
TETSUYA KUROKO-KUN. ♡
HUHHHHHHH...

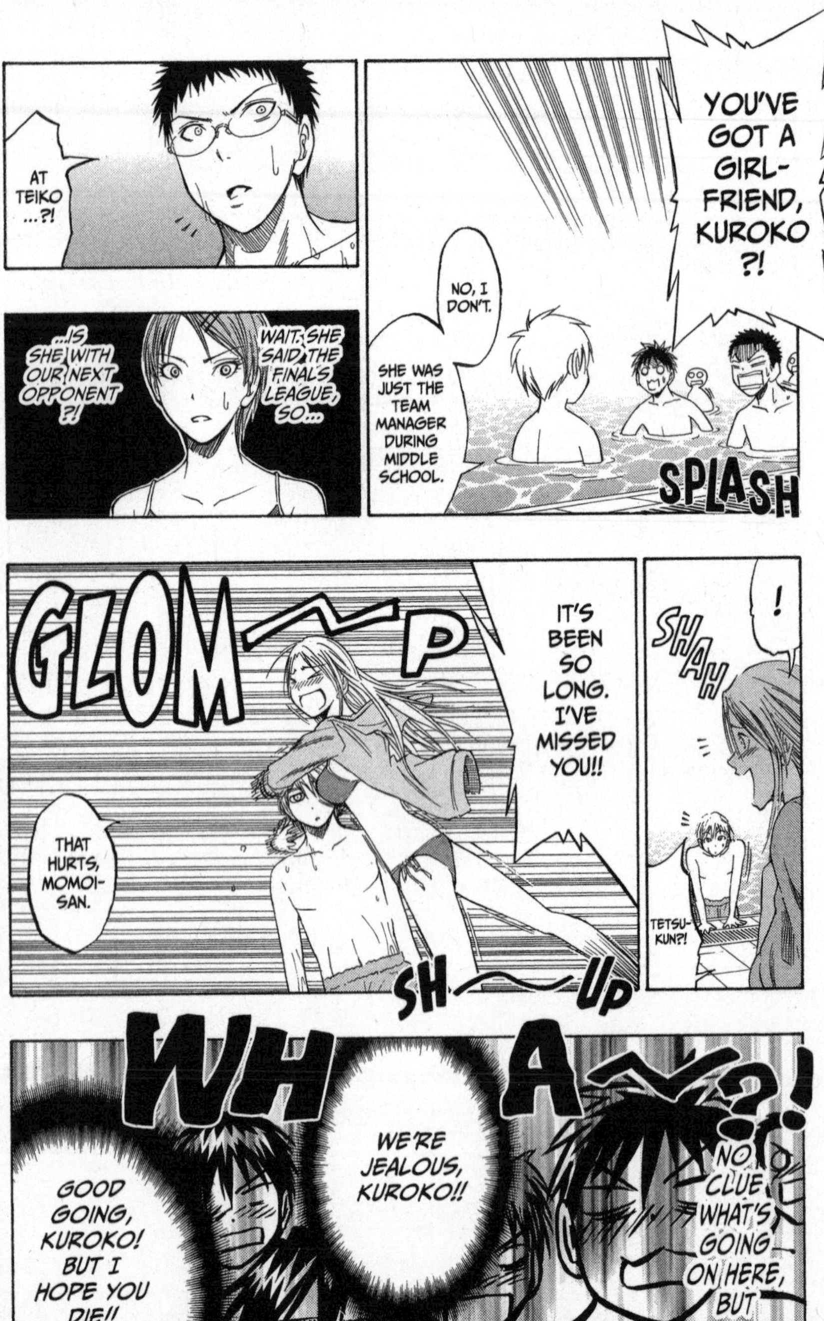
YOU'VE GOT A GIRL-FRIEND, KUROKO?!
NO, I DON'T.
SHE WAS JUST THE TEAM MANAGER DURING MIDDLE SCHOOL.
SPLASH
AT TEIKO ...?!
WAIT. SHE SAID THE FINALS LEAGUE, SO...
...IS SHE WITH OUR NEXT OPPONENT?!
!
SHAH
TETSU-KUN?!
GLOM—P
IT'S BEEN SO LONG. I'VE MISSED YOU!!
THAT HURTS, MOMOI-SAN.
SH—UP
WH A~Y?!
NO CLUE WHAT'S GOING ON HERE, BUT...
WE'RE JEALOUS, KUROKO!!
GOOD GOING, KUROKO! BUT I HOPE YOU DIE!!

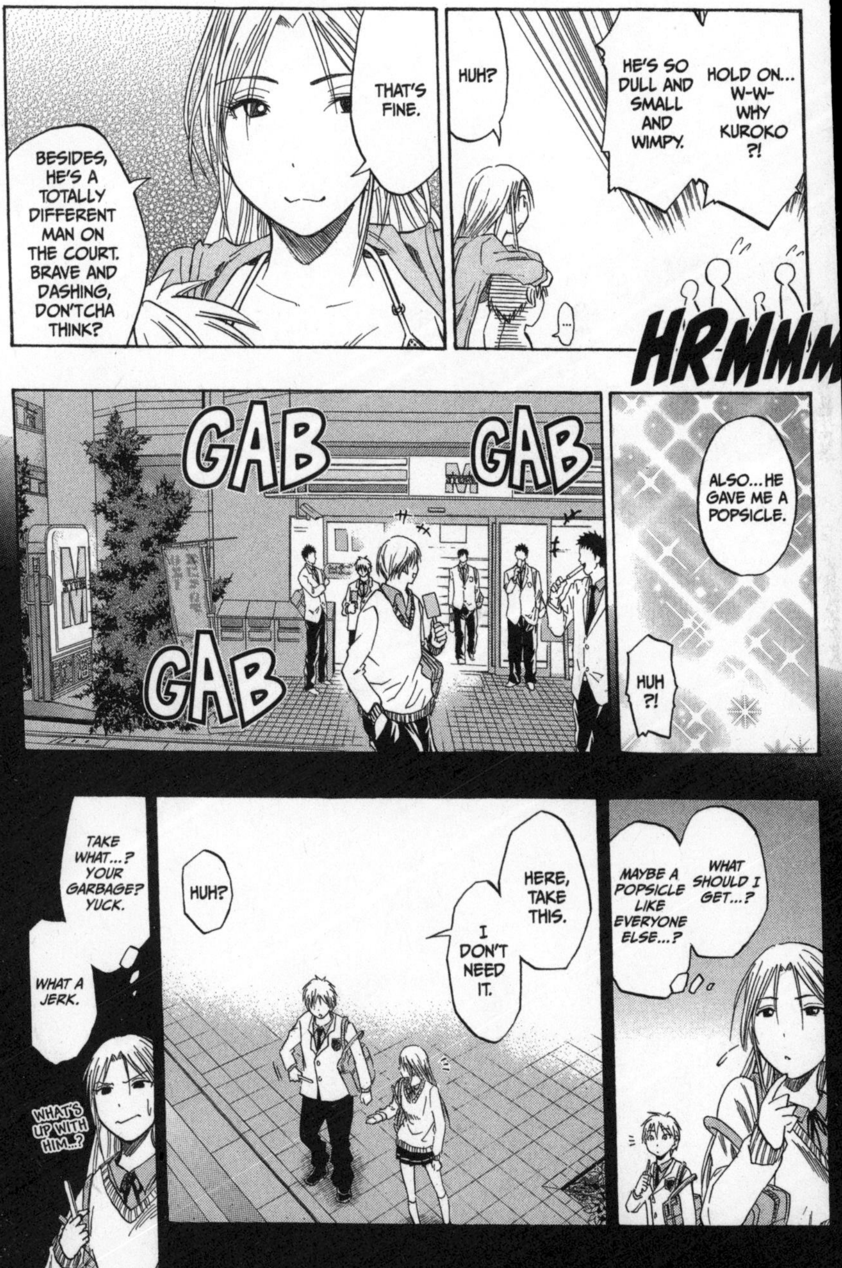
HOLD ON... W-W-WHY KUROKO?!
HE'S SO DULL AND SMALL AND WIMPY.
HUH?
...
HRMMM
THAT'S FINE.
BESIDES, HE'S A TOTALLY DIFFERENT MAN ON THE COURT. BRAVE AND DASHING, DON'TCHA THINK?
ALSO... HE GAVE ME A POPSICLE.
HUH?!
GAB
GAB
GAB
WHAT SHOULD I GET...?
MAYBE A POPSICLE LIKE EVERYONE ELSE...?
HERE, TAKE THIS.
I DON'T NEED IT.
HUH?
TAKE WHAT...? YOUR GARBAGE? YUCK.
WHAT A JERK.
WHAT'S UP WITH HIM...?

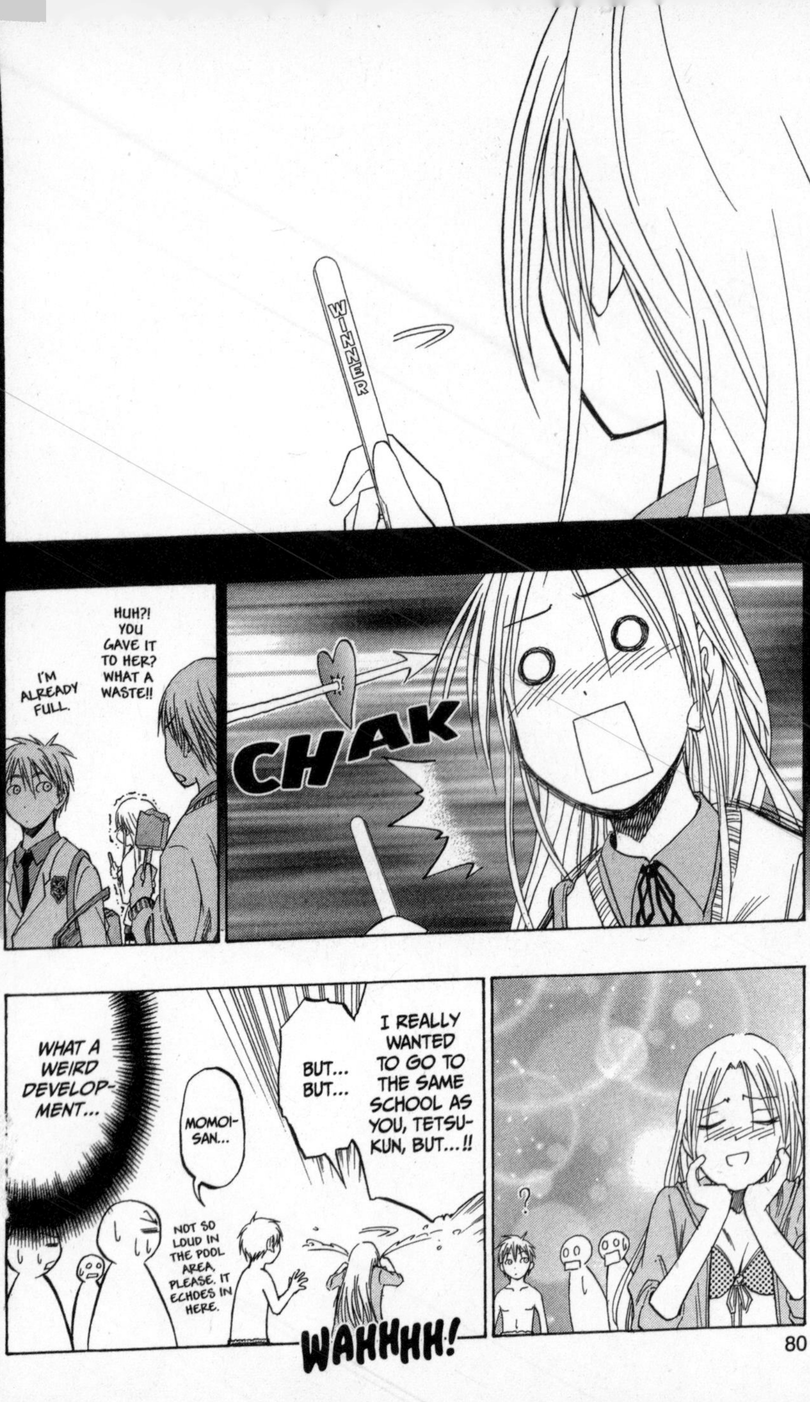
WINNER
CHAK
HUH?! YOU GAVE IT TO HER? WHAT A WASTE!!
I'M ALREADY FULL.
?
I REALLY WANTED TO GO TO THE SAME SCHOOL AS YOU, TETSU-KUN, BUT...!!
BUT... BUT...
MOMOI-SAN...
WHAT A WEIRD DEVELOPMENT...
NOT SO LOUD IN THE POOL AREA, PLEASE. IT ECHOES IN HERE.
WAHHHH!

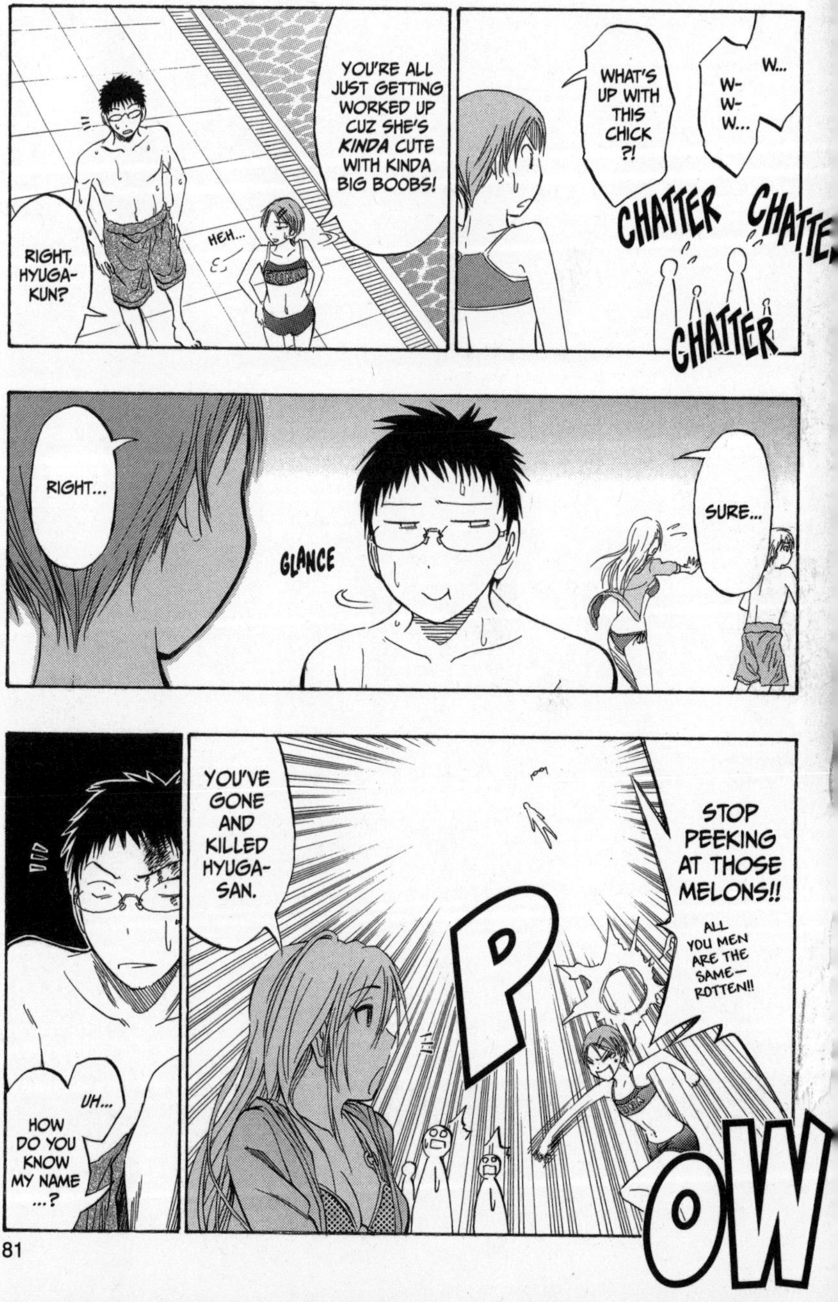
W... W- W- W...
WHAT'S UP WITH THIS CHICK ?!
CHATTER
CHATTE
CHATTER
YOU'RE ALL JUST GETTING WORKED UP CUZ SHE'S KINDA CUTE WITH KINDA BIG BOOBS!
HEH...
RIGHT, HYUGA-KUN?
SURE...
GLANCE
RIGHT...
STOP PEEKING AT THOSE MELONS!!
ALL YOU MEN ARE THE SAME—ROTTEN!!
POW
YOU'VE GONE AND KILLED HYUGA-SAN.
UH...
HOW DO YOU KNOW MY NAME ...?

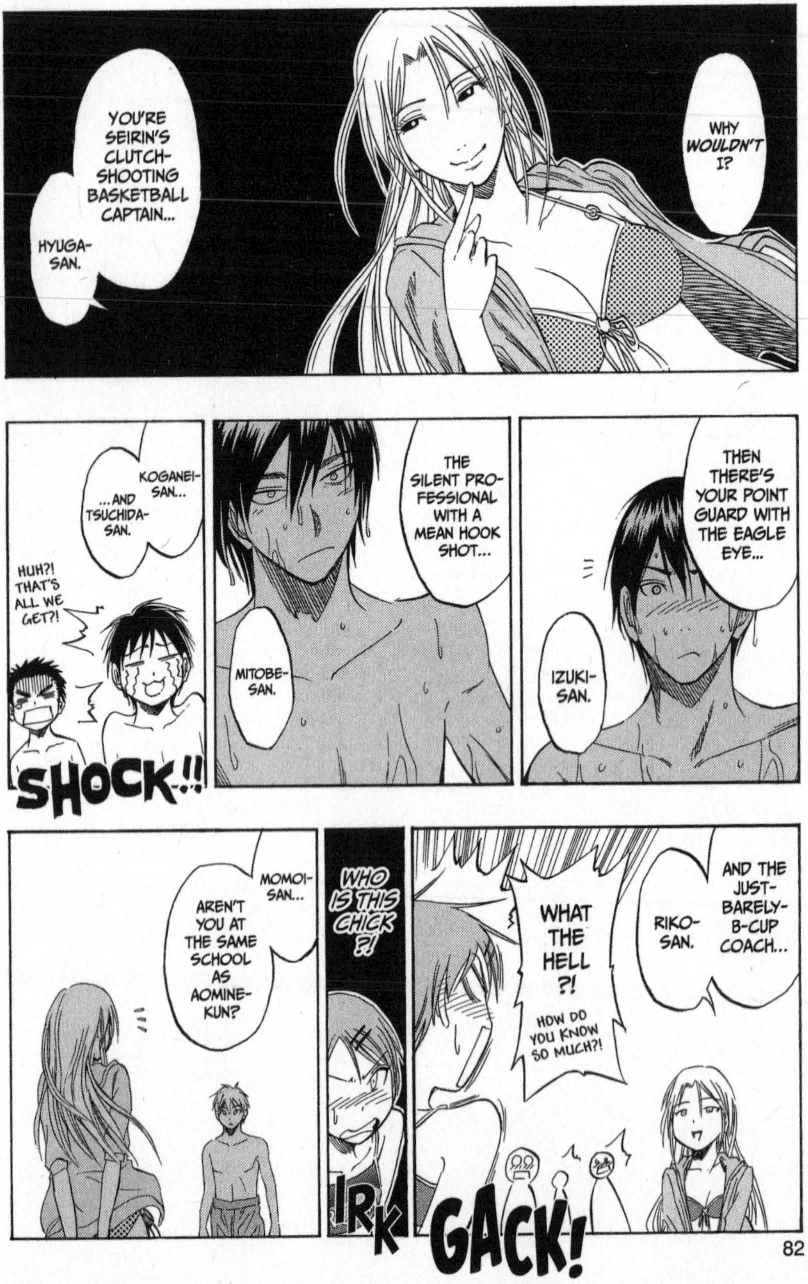
WHY WOULDN'T I?
YOU'RE SEIRIN'S CLUTCH-SHOOTING BASKETBALL CAPTAIN...
HYUGA-SAN.
THEN THERE'S YOUR POINT GUARD WITH THE EAGLE EYE...
IZUKI-SAN.
THE SILENT PRO-FESSIONAL WITH A MEAN HOOK SHOT...
MITOBE-SAN.
KOGANEI-SAN...
...AND TSUCHIDA-SAN.
HUH?! THAT'S ALL WE GET?!
SHOCK!!
AND THE JUST-BARELY-B-CUP COACH...
RIKO-SAN.
WHAT THE HELL?!
HOW DO YOU KNOW SO MUCH?!
GACK!
WHO IS THIS CHICK?!
IRK
MOMOI-SAN...
AREN'T YOU AT THE SAME SCHOOL AS AOMINE-KUN?

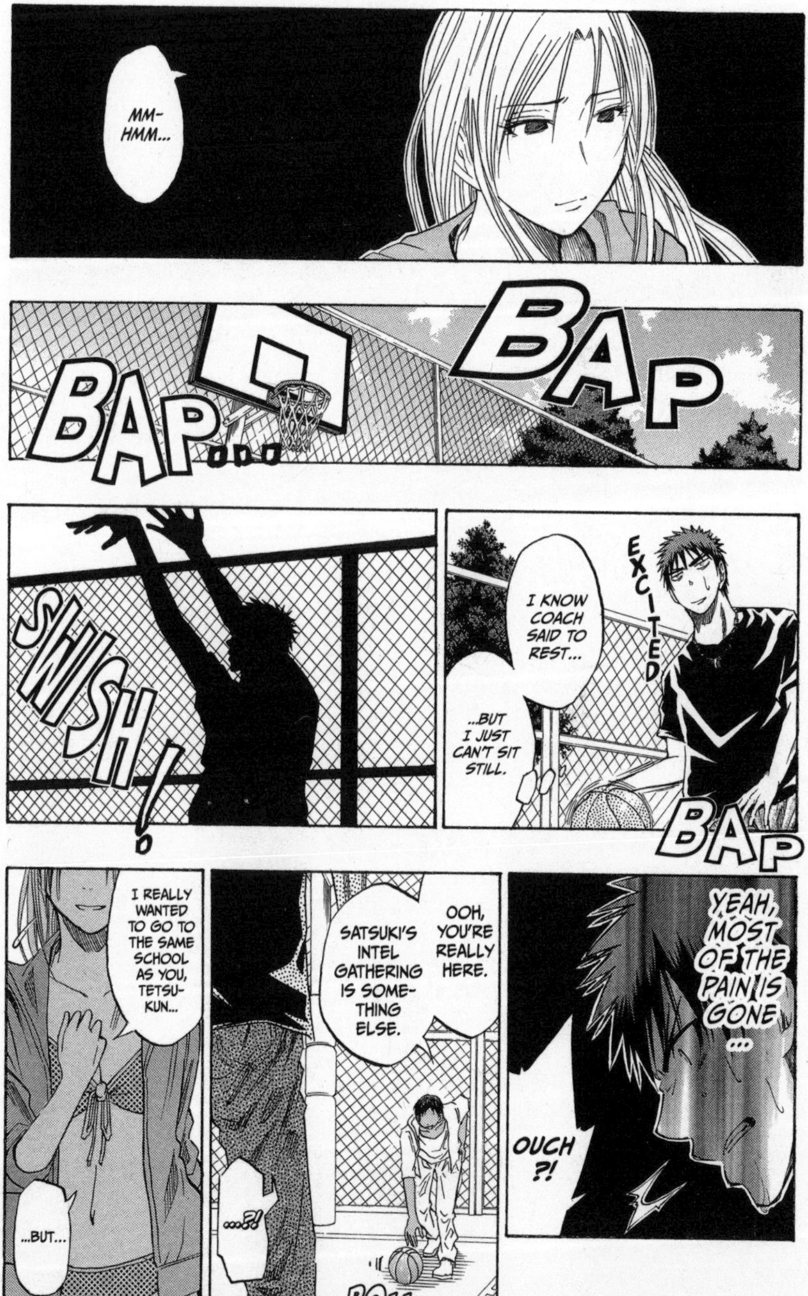
MM-HMM...
BAP
BAP...
EXCITED
I KNOW COACH SAID TO REST...
...BUT I JUST CAN'T SIT STILL.
BAP
SWISH!
YEAH, MOST OF THE PAIN IS GONE...
OUCH?!
OOH, YOU'RE REALLY HERE.
SATSUKI'S INTEL GATHERING IS SOME-THING ELSE.
...?!
ROLL
I REALLY WANTED TO GO TO THE SAME SCHOOL AS YOU, TETSU-KUN...
...BUT...

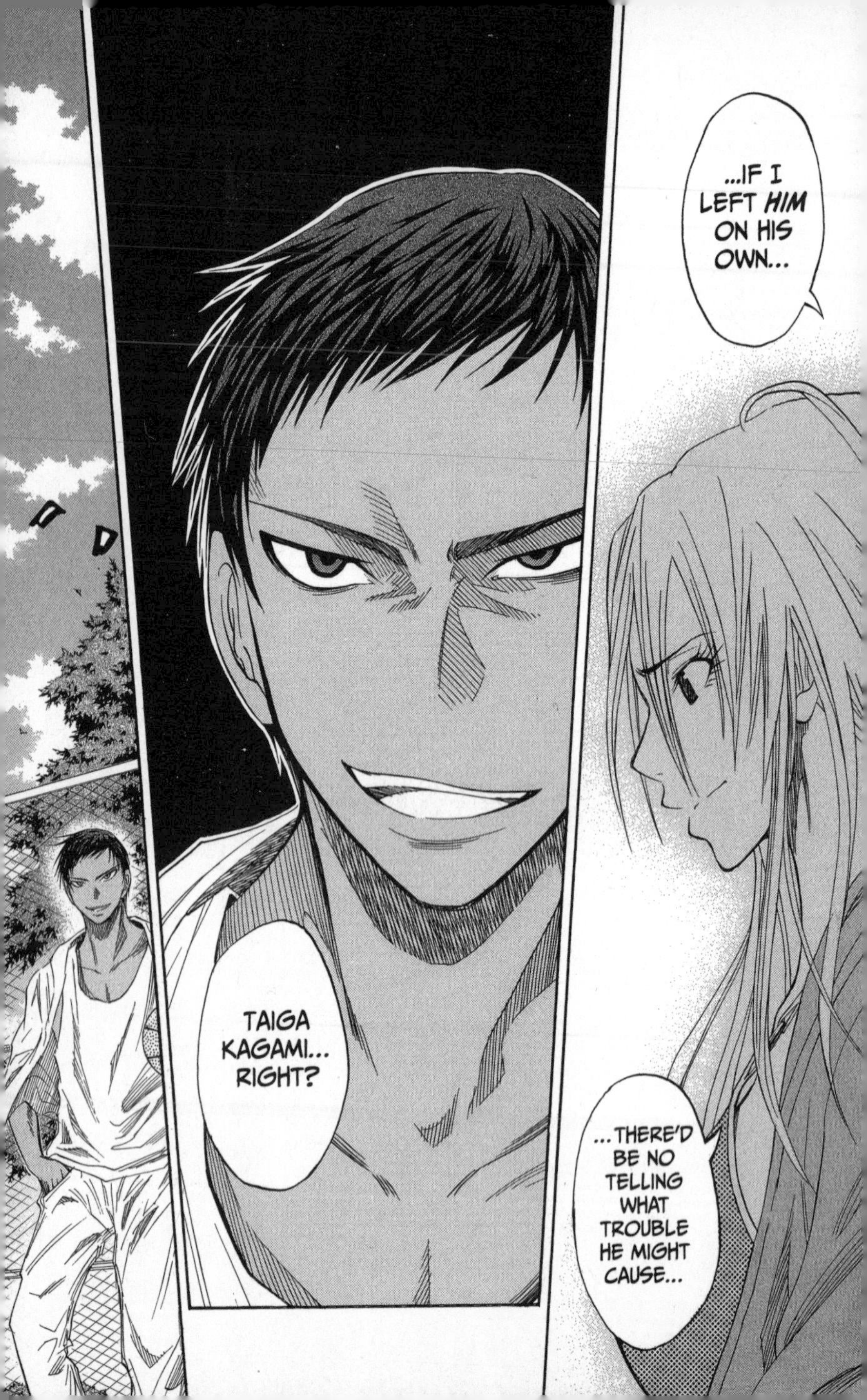
...IF I LEFT *HIM* ON HIS OWN...
...THERE'D BE NO TELLING WHAT TROUBLE HE MIGHT CAUSE...
TAIGA KAGAMI... RIGHT?

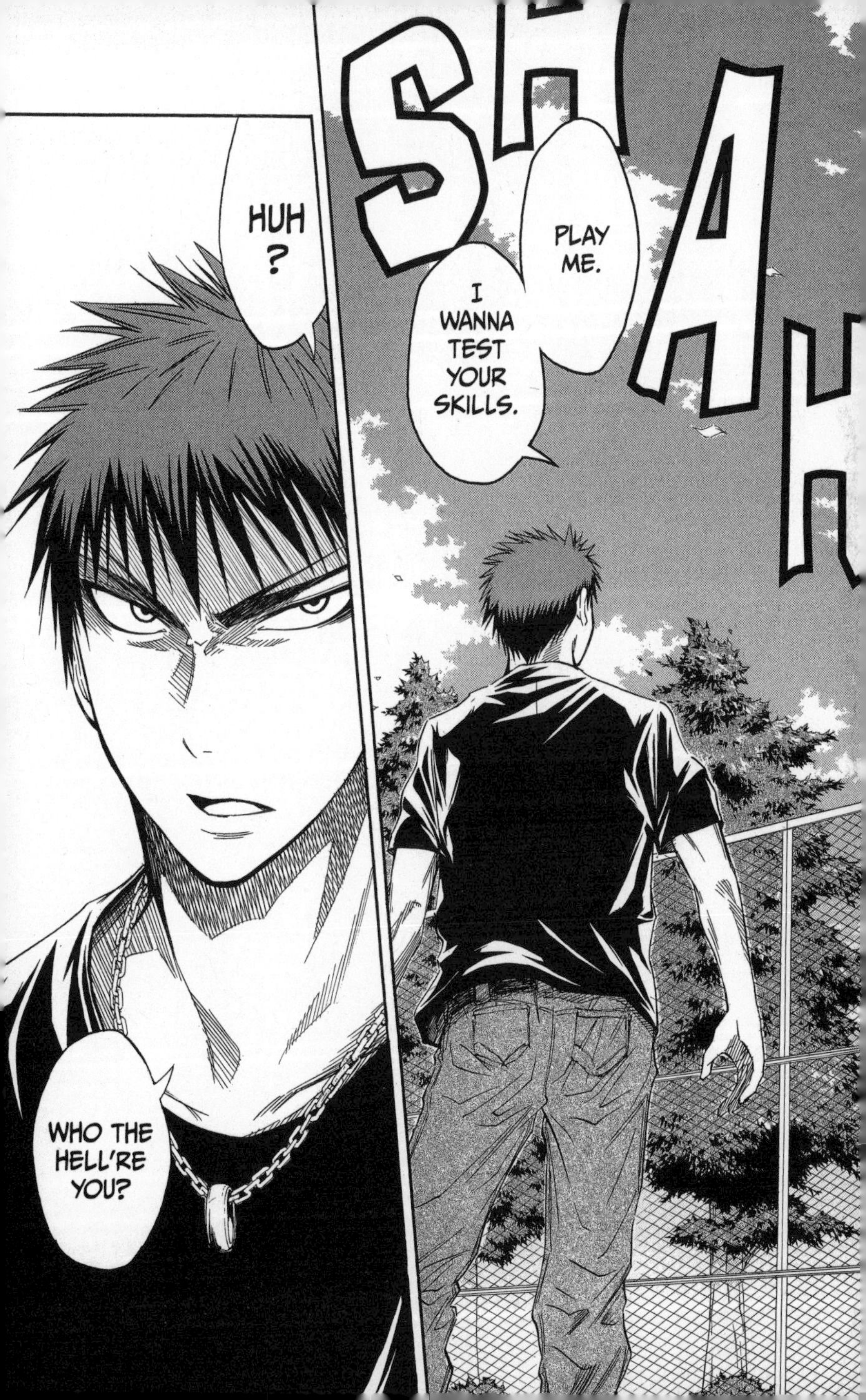
SHAH
PLAY ME.
I WANNA TEST YOUR SKILLS.
HUH?
WHO THE HELL'RE YOU?

KUROKO'S BASKETBALL BLOOPERS
TAKE 2

TAKE WHAT...? YOUR GARBAGE? YUCK.
WHAT A JERK.
WHAT'S UP WITH HIM...?
IT REALLY IS GARBAGE!!
OUCH! WHY ME?!
SORRY, I MUSTVE BEEN MISTAKEN.
SMACK
TOSS!!

39TH QUARTER: SPITTING IMAGE

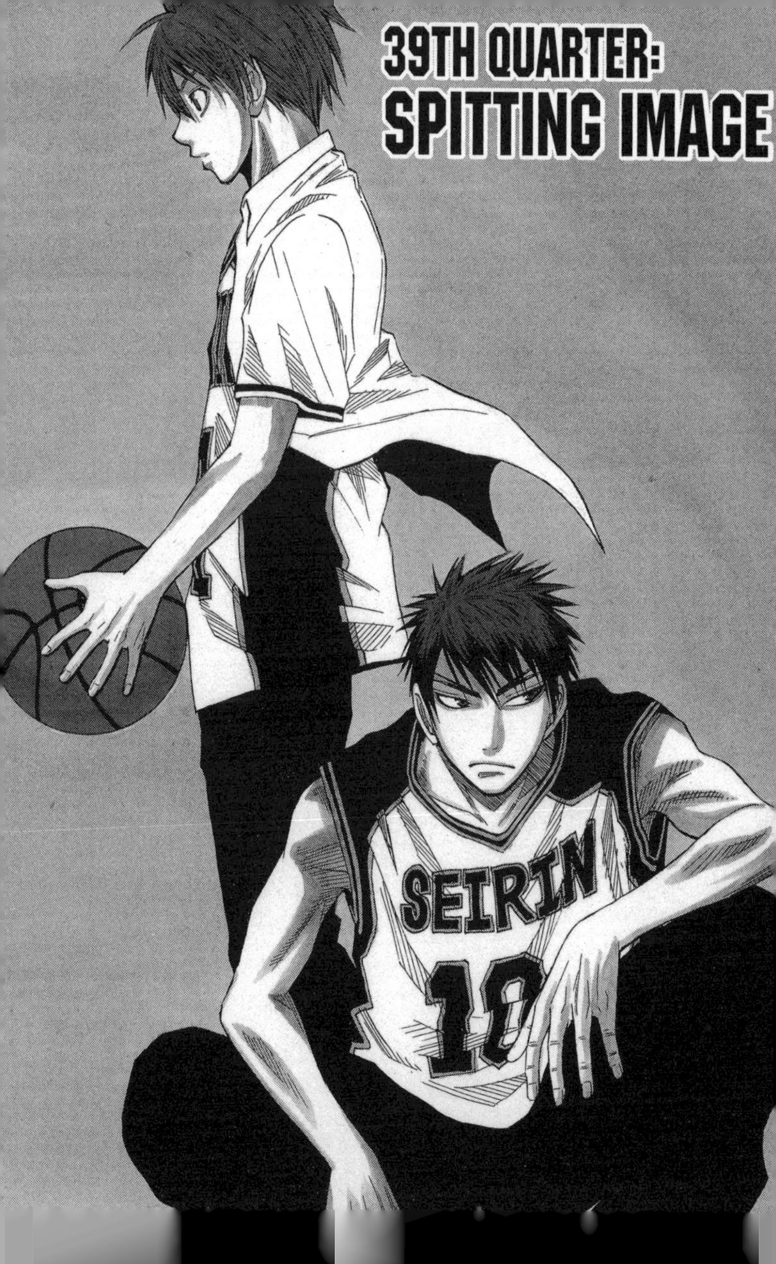
SEIRIN
10

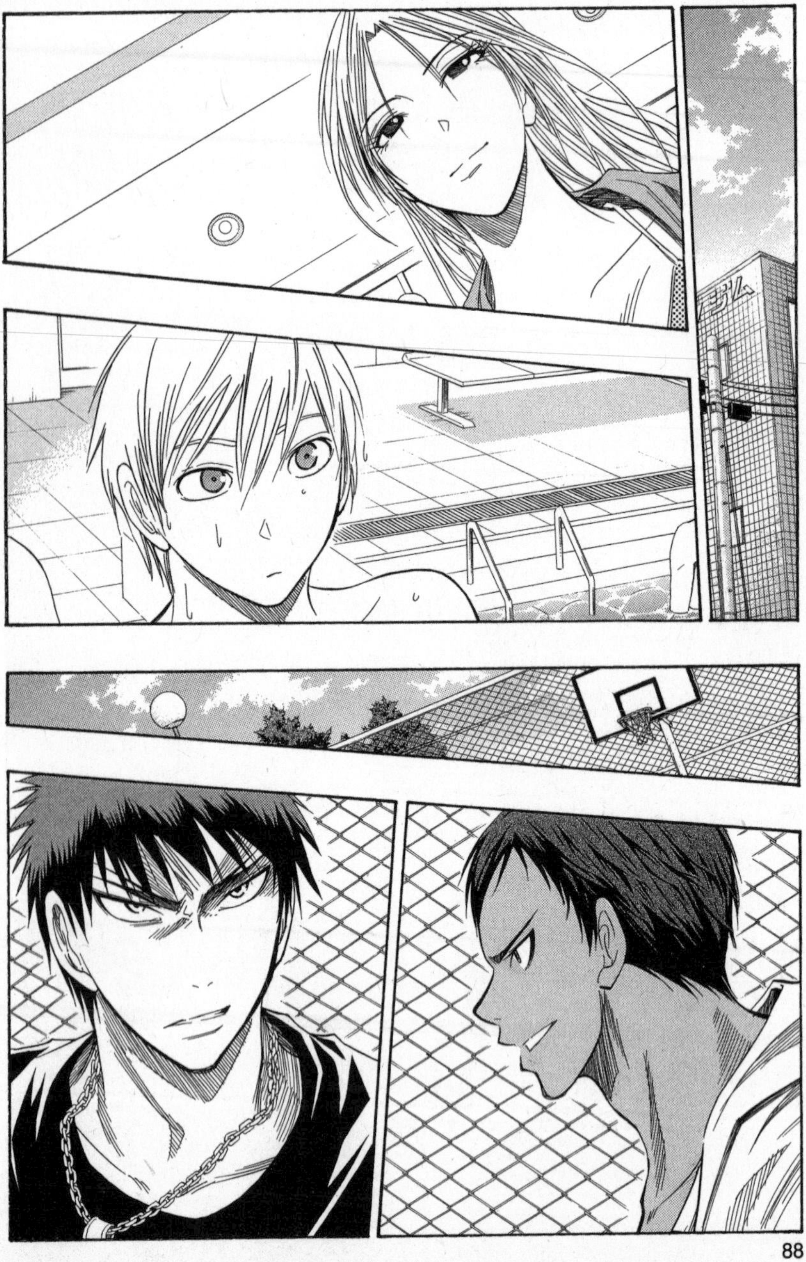

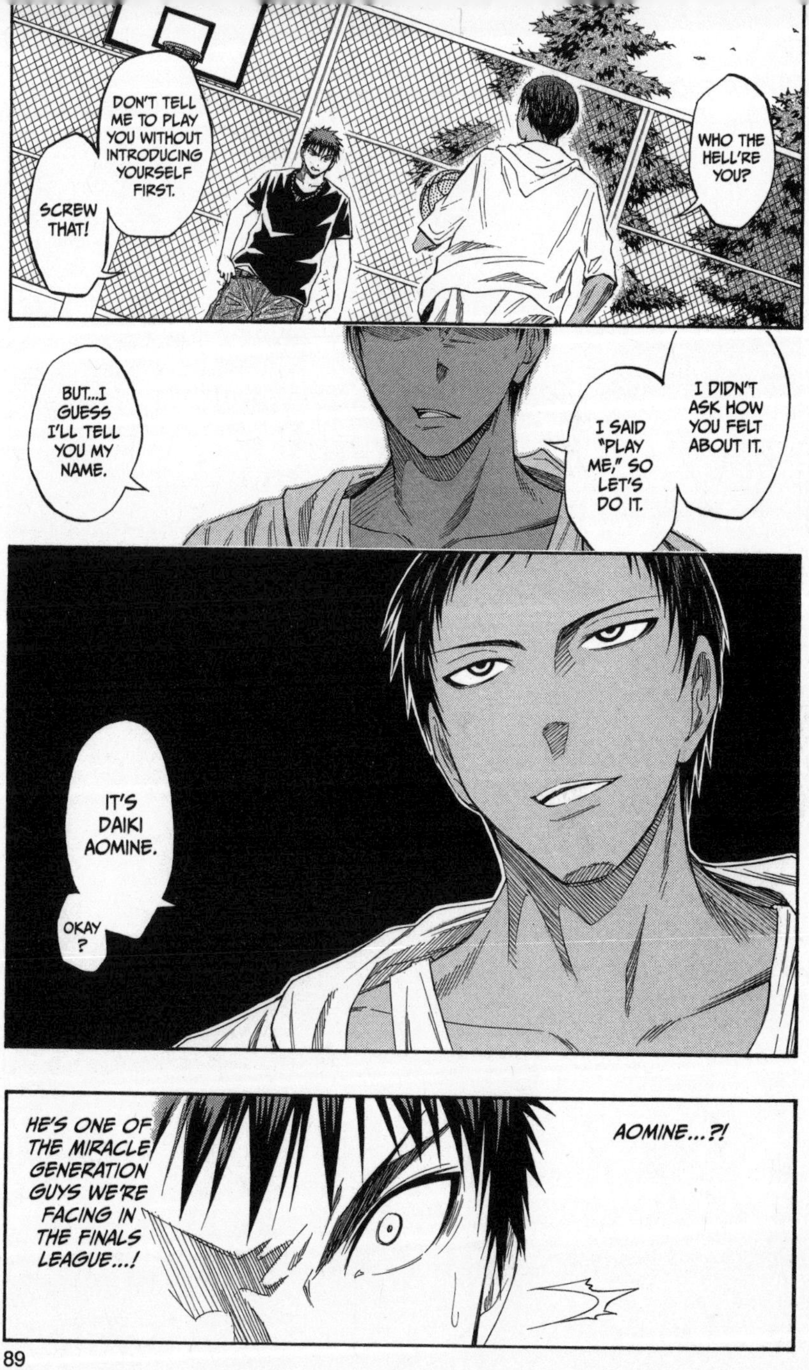
WHO THE HELL'RE YOU?
DON'T TELL ME TO PLAY YOU WITHOUT INTRODUCING YOURSELF FIRST.
SCREW THAT!
I DIDN'T ASK HOW YOU FELT ABOUT IT.
I SAID "PLAY ME," SO LET'S DO IT.
BUT...I GUESS I'LL TELL YOU MY NAME.
IT'S DAIKI AOMINE.
OKAY?
AOMINE...?!
HE'S ONE OF THE MIRACLE GENERATION GUYS WE'RE FACING IN THE FINALS LEAGUE...!

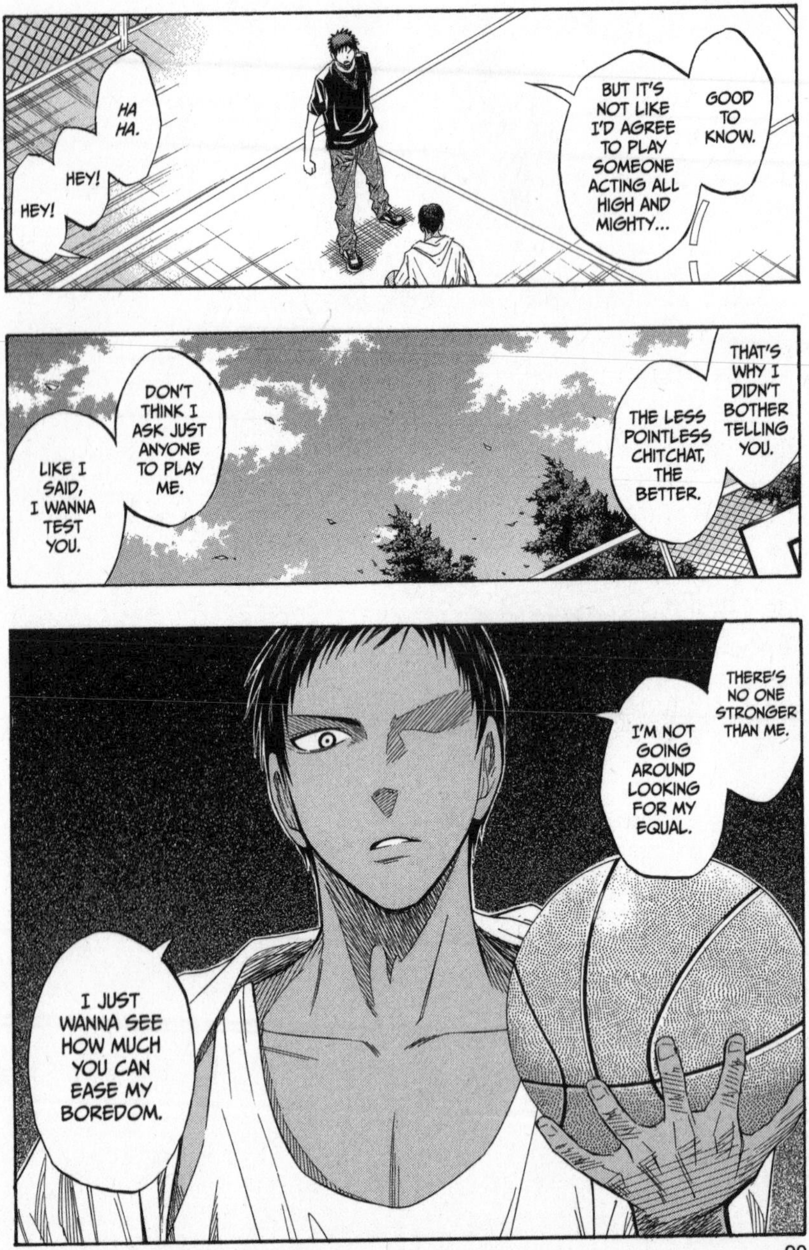
GOOD TO KNOW.
BUT IT'S NOT LIKE I'D AGREE TO PLAY SOMEONE ACTING ALL HIGH AND MIGHTY...
HA HA.
HEY!
HEY!
THAT'S WHY I DIDN'T BOTHER TELLING YOU.
THE LESS POINTLESS CHITCHAT, THE BETTER.
DON'T THINK I ASK JUST ANYONE TO PLAY ME.
LIKE I SAID, I WANNA TEST YOU.
THERE'S NO ONE STRONGER THAN ME.
I'M NOT GOING AROUND LOOKING FOR MY EQUAL.
I JUST WANNA SEE HOW MUCH YOU CAN EASE MY BOREDOM.

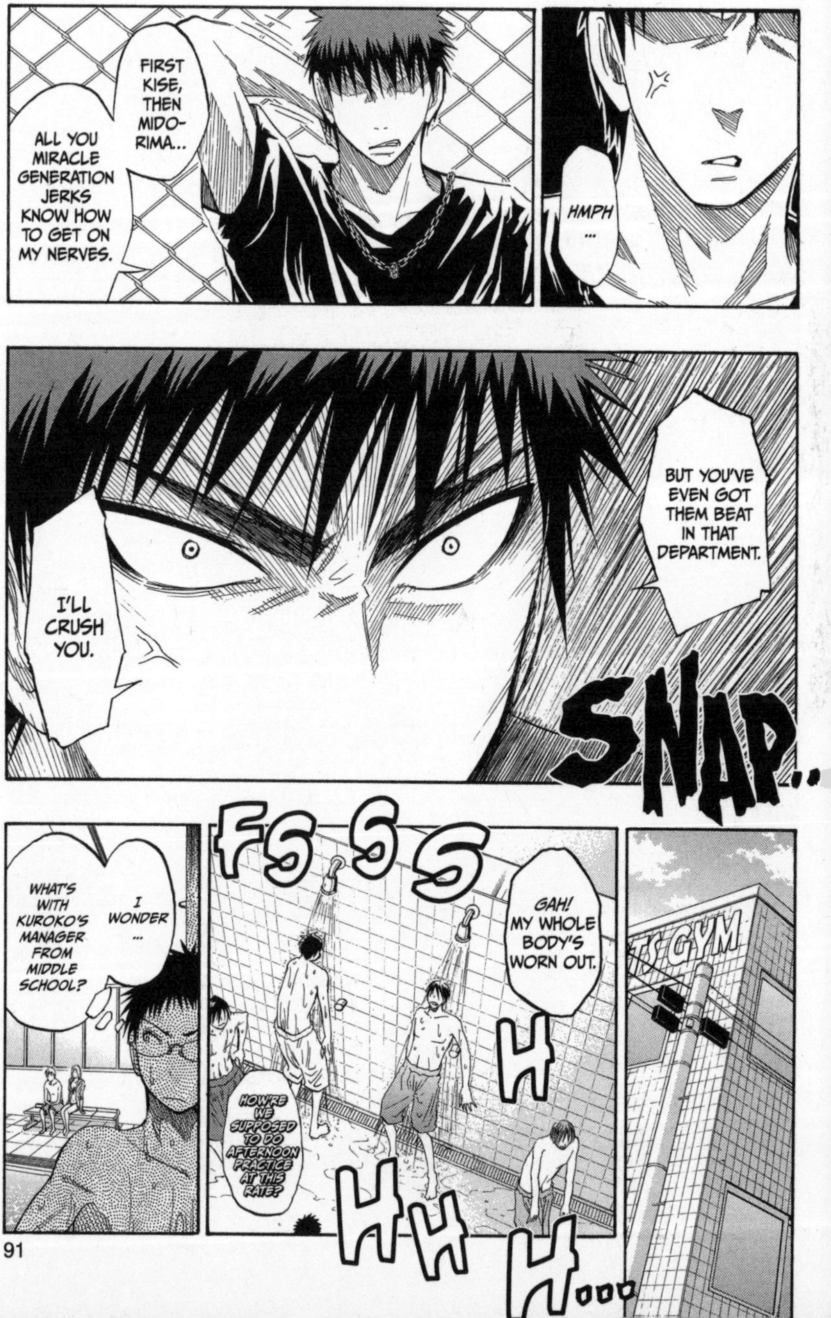
HMPH...
FIRST KISE, THEN MIDO-RIMA...
ALL YOU MIRACLE GENERATION JERKS KNOW HOW TO GET ON MY NERVES.
BUT YOU'VE EVEN GOT THEM BEAT IN THAT DEPARTMENT.
I'LL CRUSH YOU.
SNAP..
TS GYM
FSSS
GAH! MY WHOLE BODY'S WORN OUT.
HHHH...
HOW'RE WE SUPPOSED TO DO AFTERNOON PRACTICE AT THIS RATE?
WHAT'S WITH KUROKO'S MANAGER FROM MIDDLE SCHOOL?
I WONDER...

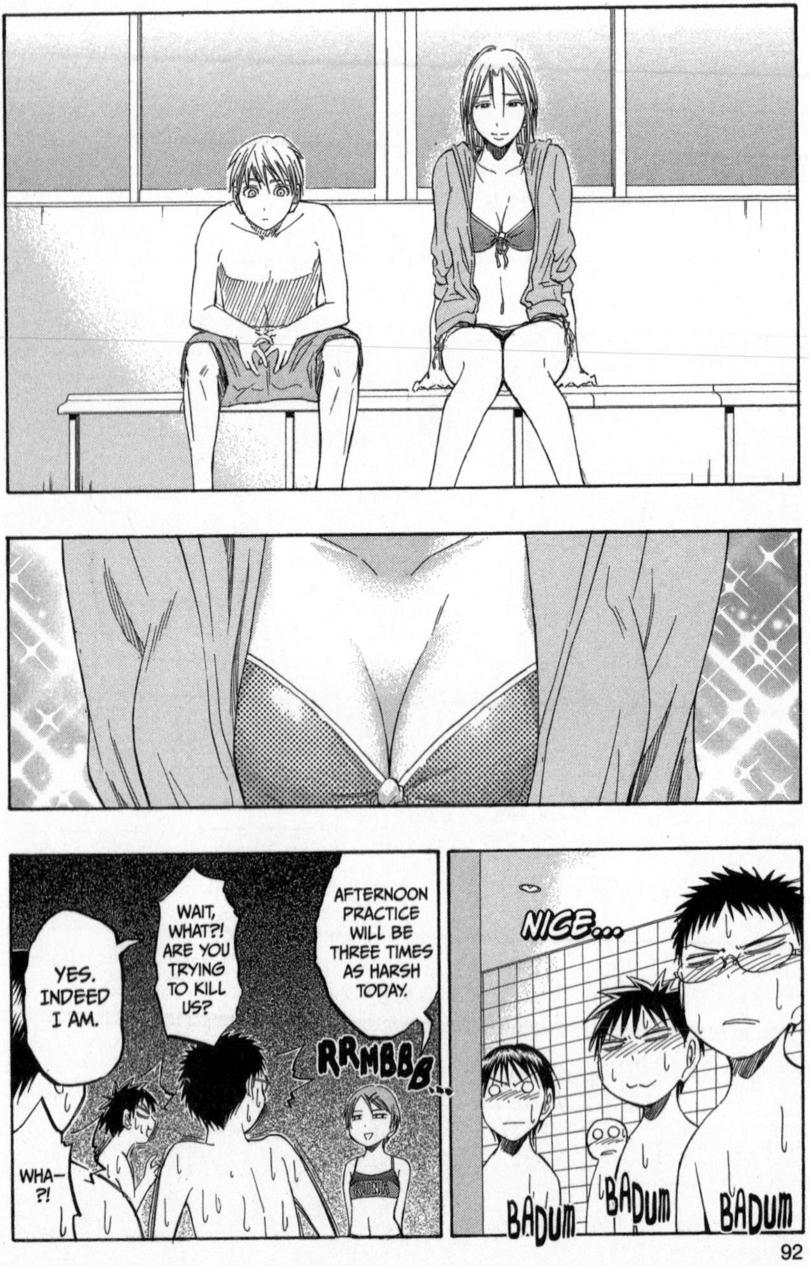
NICE...
BADUM
BADUM
BADUM
AFTERNOON PRACTICE WILL BE THREE TIMES AS HARSH TODAY.
RRMBBB...
WAIT, WHAT?! ARE YOU TRYING TO KILL US?
YES. INDEED I AM.
WHA- ?!

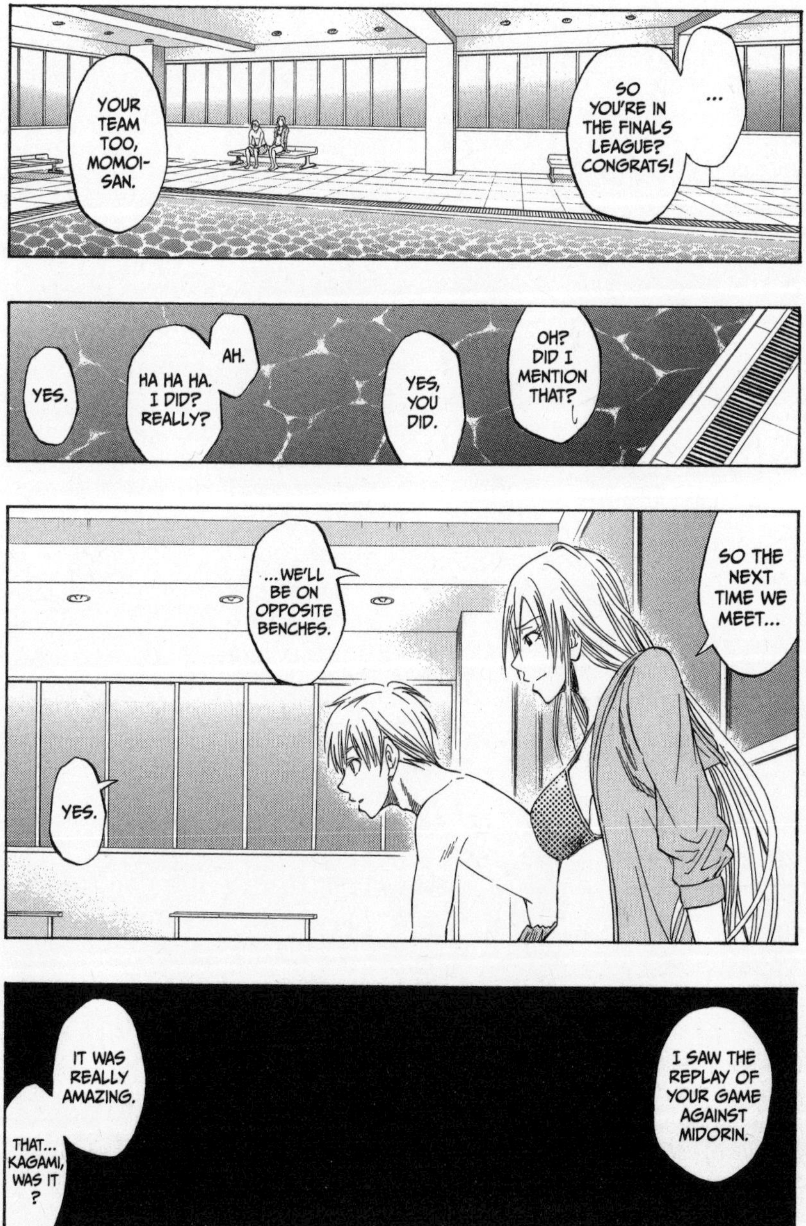
...
SO YOU'RE IN THE FINALS LEAGUE? CONGRATS!
YOUR TEAM TOO, MOMOI-SAN.
OH? DID I MENTION THAT?
YES, YOU DID.
AH.
HA HA HA. I DID? REALLY?
YES.
SO THE NEXT TIME WE MEET...
...WE'LL BE ON OPPOSITE BENCHES.
YES.
I SAW THE REPLAY OF YOUR GAME AGAINST MIDORIN.
IT WAS REALLY AMAZING.
THAT... KAGAMI, WAS IT ?

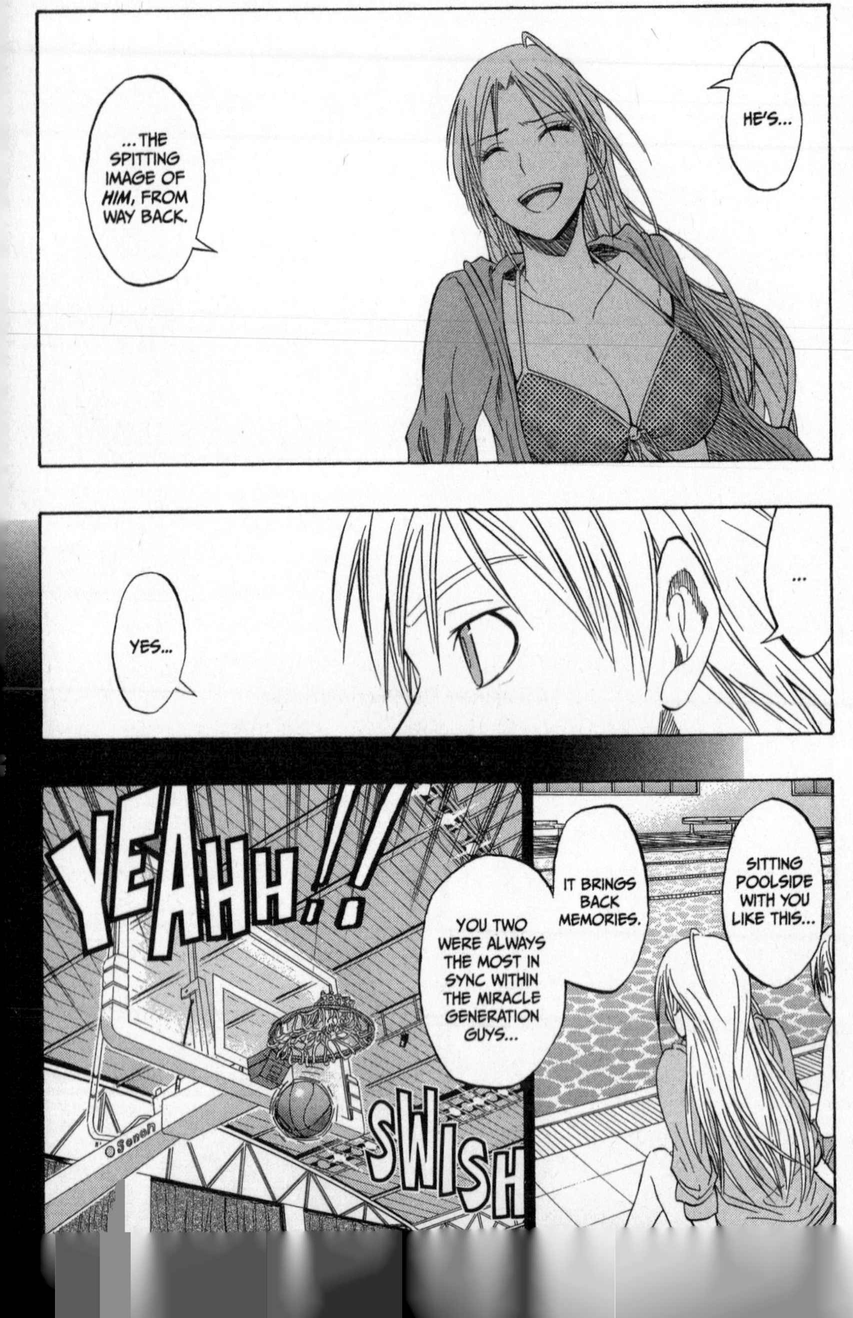
HE'S...
...THE SPITTING IMAGE OF *HIM*, FROM WAY BACK.
...
YES...
SITTING POOLSIDE WITH YOU LIKE THIS...
IT BRINGS BACK MEMORIES.
YOU TWO WERE ALWAYS THE MOST IN SYNC WITHIN THE MIRACLE GENERATION GUYS...
YEAHH!!
SWISH

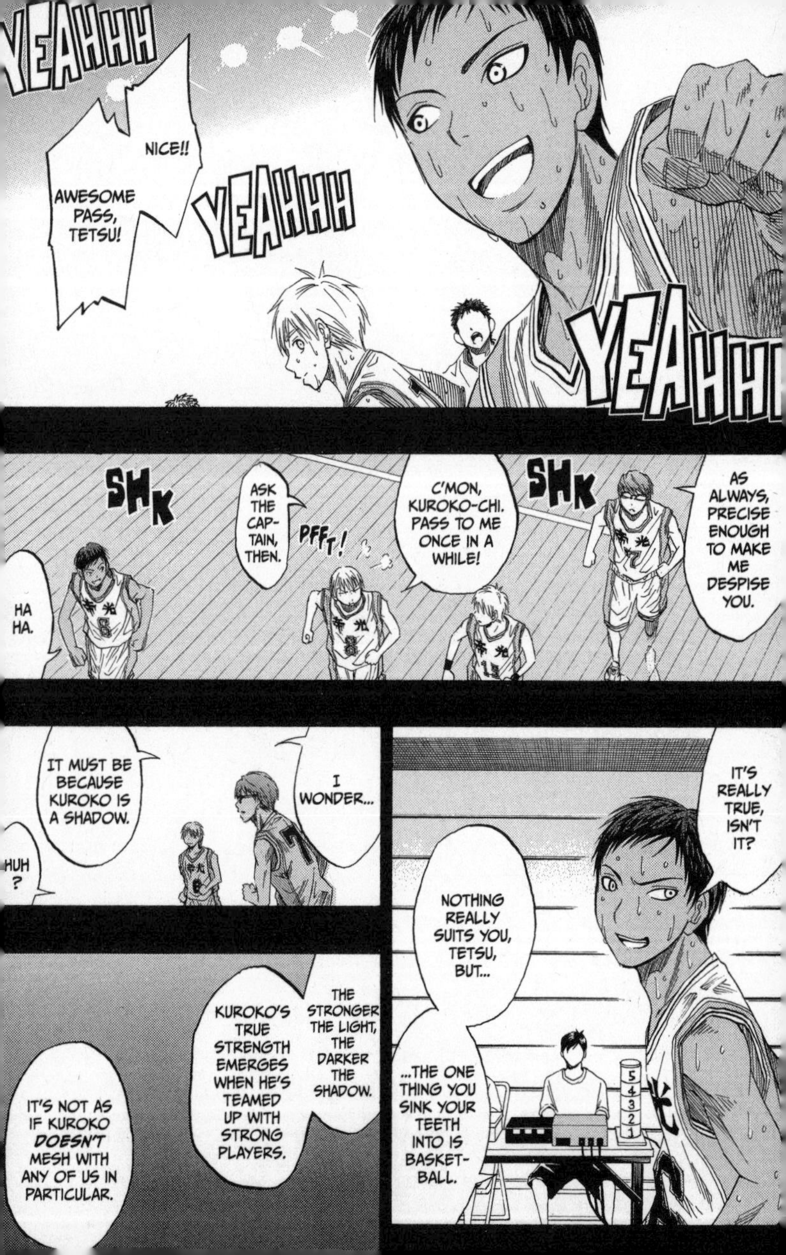
YEAHHH
YEAHHH
NICE!!
AWESOME PASS, TETSU!
YEAHHH
AS ALWAYS, PRECISE ENOUGH TO MAKE ME DESPISE YOU.
SHK
C'MON, KUROKO-CHI. PASS TO ME ONCE IN A WHILE!
PFFT!
ASK THE CAP-TAIN, THEN.
SHK
HA HA.
IT'S REALLY TRUE, ISN'T IT?
NOTHING REALLY SUITS YOU, TETSU, BUT...
...THE ONE THING YOU SINK YOUR TEETH INTO IS BASKET-BALL.
I WONDER...
IT MUST BE BECAUSE KUROKO IS A SHADOW.
HUH?
THE STRONGER THE LIGHT, THE DARKER THE SHADOW.
KUROKO'S TRUE STRENGTH EMERGES WHEN HE'S TEAMED UP WITH STRONG PLAYERS.
IT'S NOT AS IF KUROKO *DOESN'T* MESH WITH ANY OF US IN PARTICULAR.

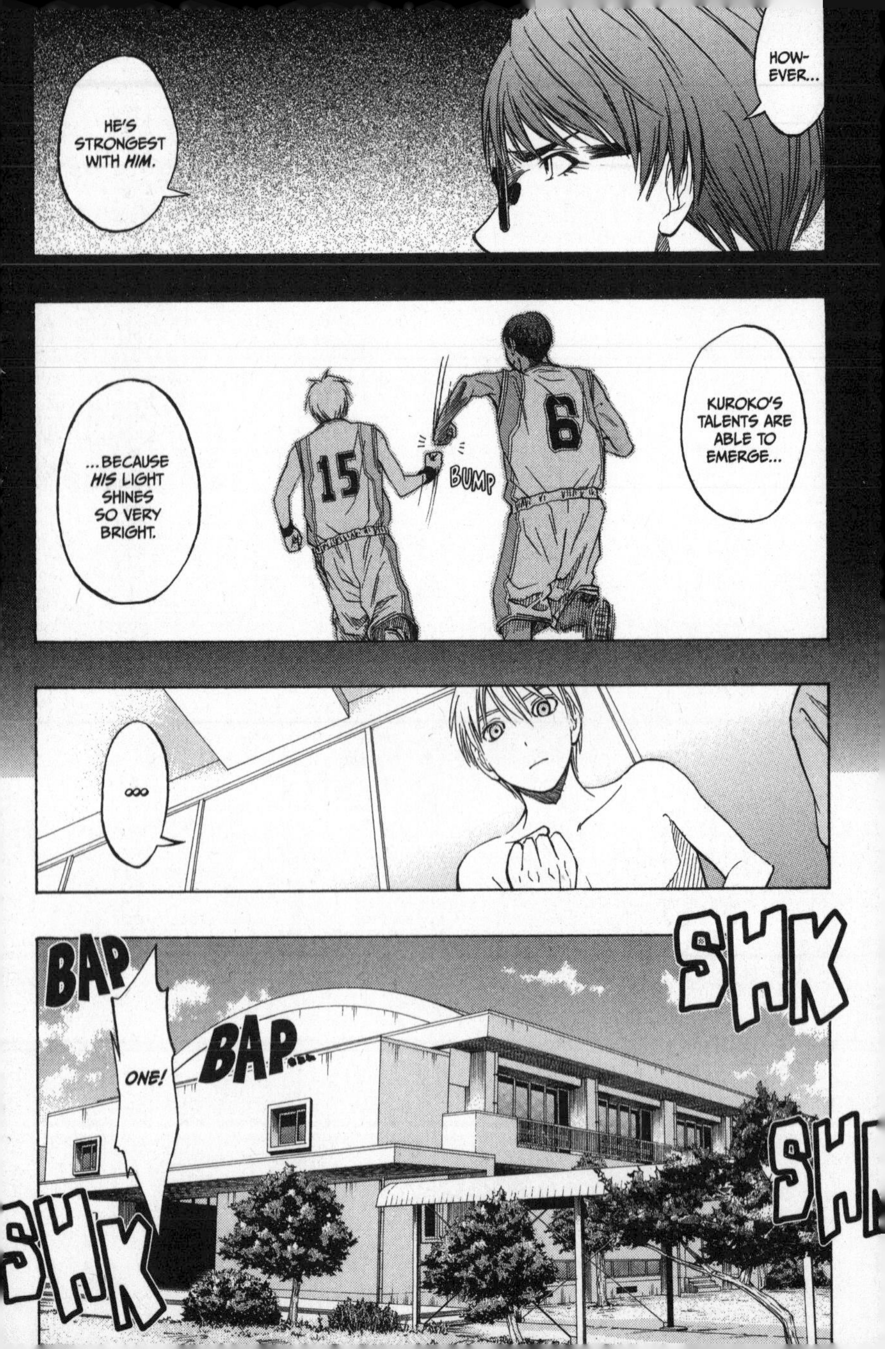
HOW-EVER...
HE'S STRONGEST WITH *HIM*.
KUROKO'S TALENTS ARE ABLE TO EMERGE...
BUMP
...BECAUSE *HIS* LIGHT SHINES SO VERY BRIGHT.
...
SHK
BAP
BAP...
ONE!
SHK
SHK

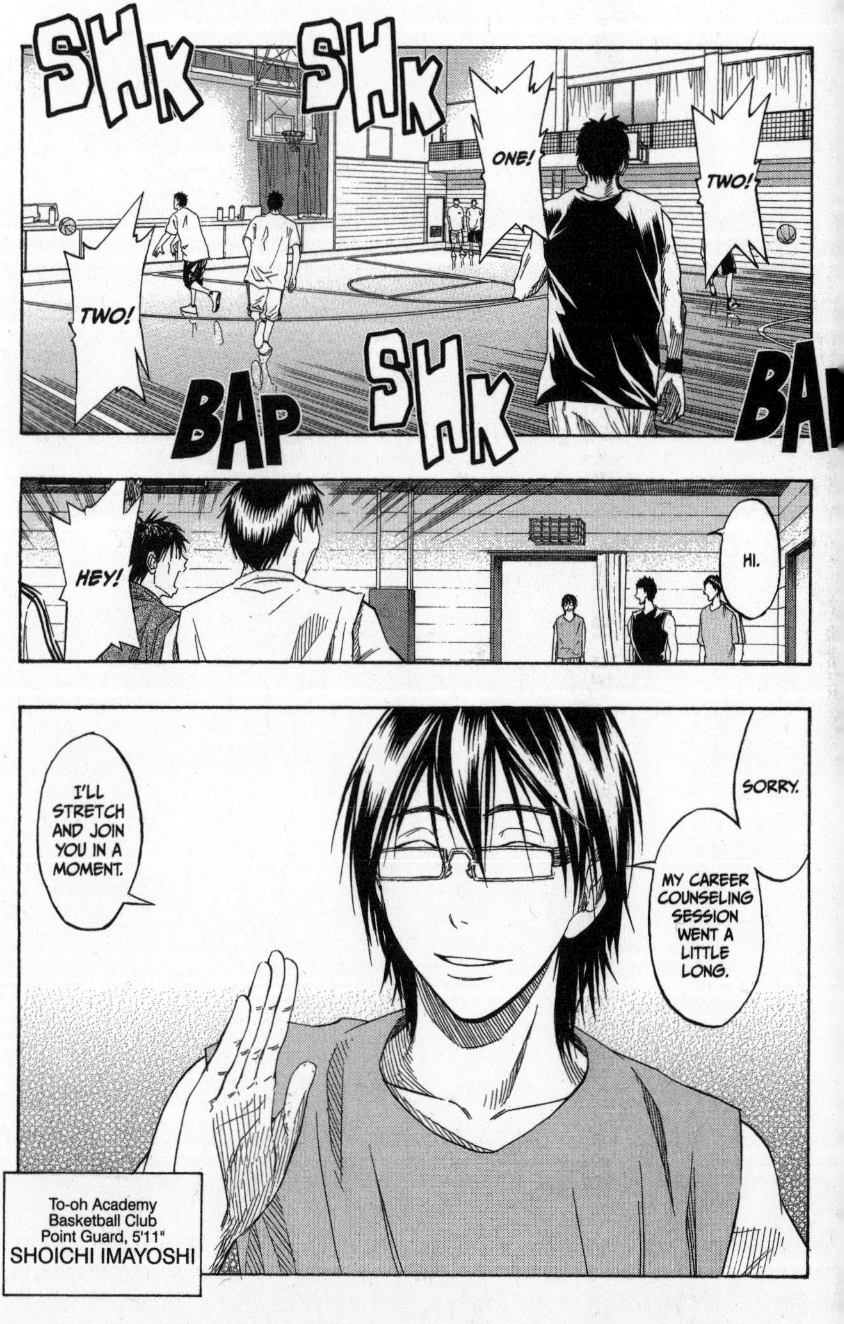
BA
TWO!
ONE!
SHK
SHK
SHK
BAP
TWO!
HI.
HEY!
SORRY.
MY CAREER COUNSELING SESSION WENT A LITTLE LONG.
I'LL STRETCH AND JOIN YOU IN A MOMENT.
To-oh Academy Basketball Club Point Guard, 5'11"
SHOICHI IMAYOSHI

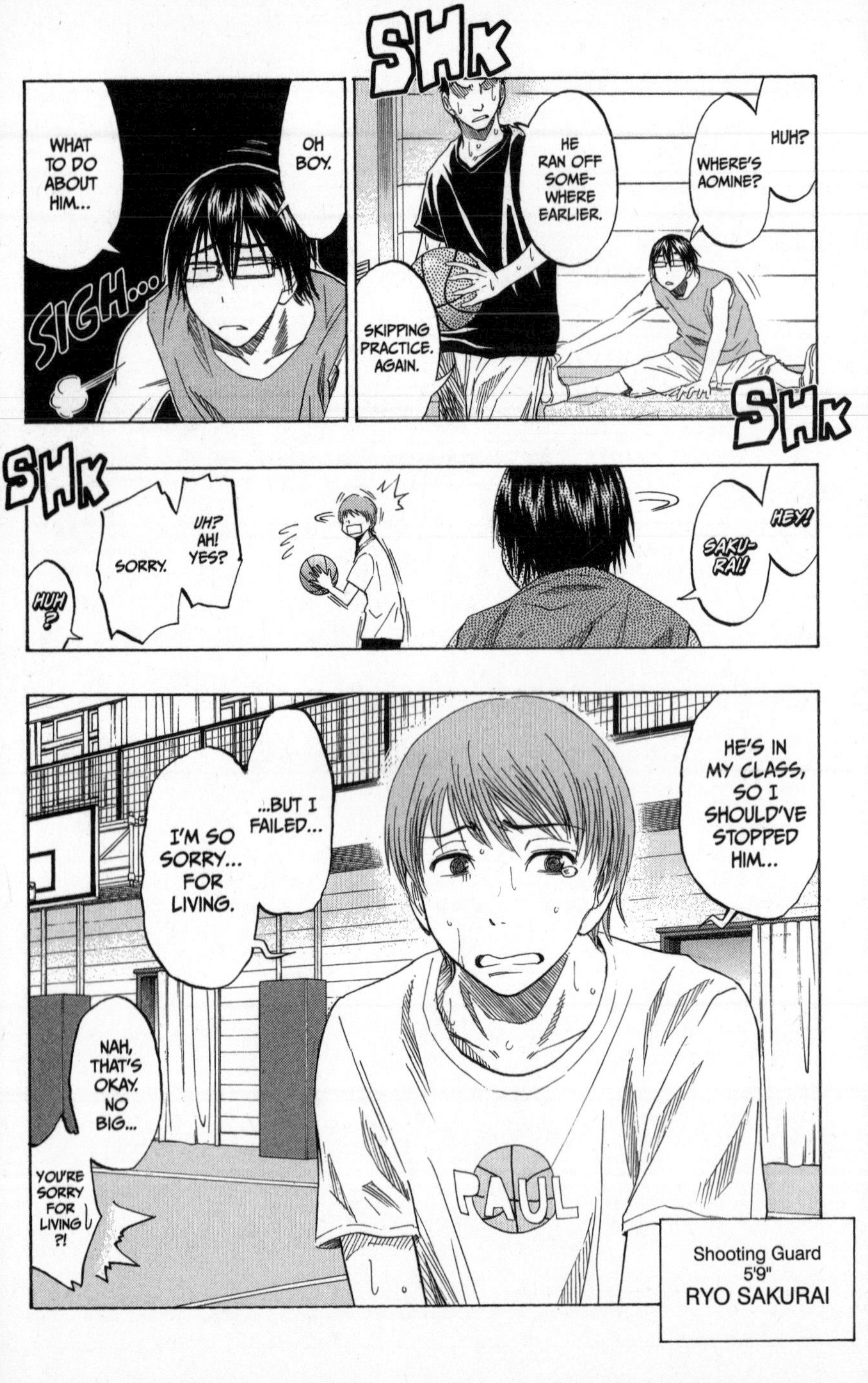
SHK
HUH?
WHERE'S AOMINE?
HE RAN OFF SOMEWHERE EARLIER.
SKIPPING PRACTICE. AGAIN.
SHK
OH BOY.
WHAT TO DO ABOUT HIM...
SIGH...
HEY!
SAKURAI!
UH? AH! YES?
SORRY.
HUH?
SHK
HE'S IN MY CLASS, SO I SHOULD'VE STOPPED HIM...
...BUT I FAILED...
I'M SO SORRY... FOR LIVING.
NAH, THAT'S OKAY. NO BIG...
YOU'RE SORRY FOR LIVING?!
Shooting Guard
5'9"
RYO SAKURAI

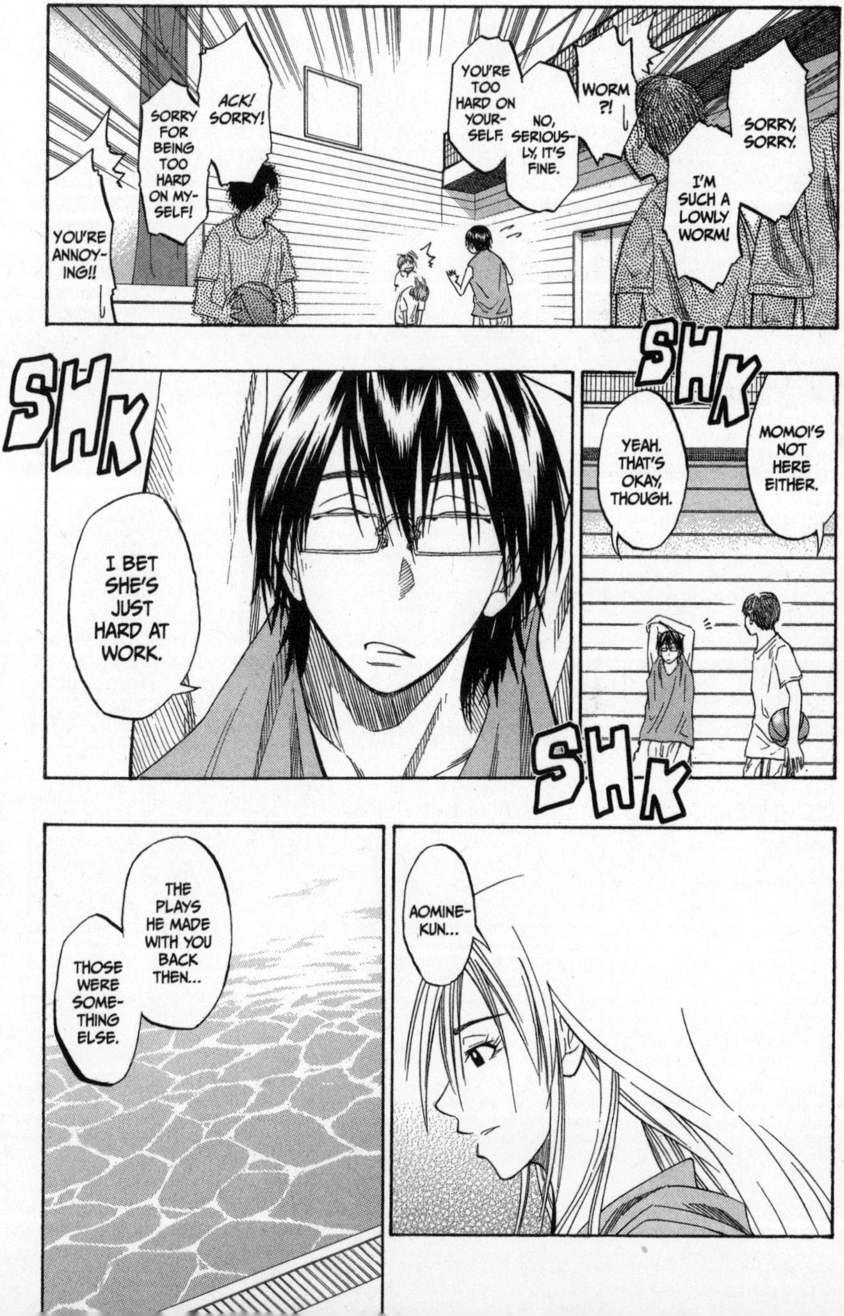
SORRY, SORRY.
I'M SUCH A LOWLY WORM!
WORM ?!
NO, SERIOUSLY, IT'S FINE.
YOU'RE TOO HARD ON YOURSELF.
ACK! SORRY!
SORRY FOR BEING TOO HARD ON MYSELF!
YOU'RE ANNOYING!!
SHK
MOMOI'S NOT HERE EITHER.
YEAH. THAT'S OKAY, THOUGH.
SHK
SHK
I BET SHE'S JUST HARD AT WORK.
AOMINE-KUN...
THE PLAYS HE MADE WITH YOU BACK THEN...
THOSE WERE SOMETHING ELSE.

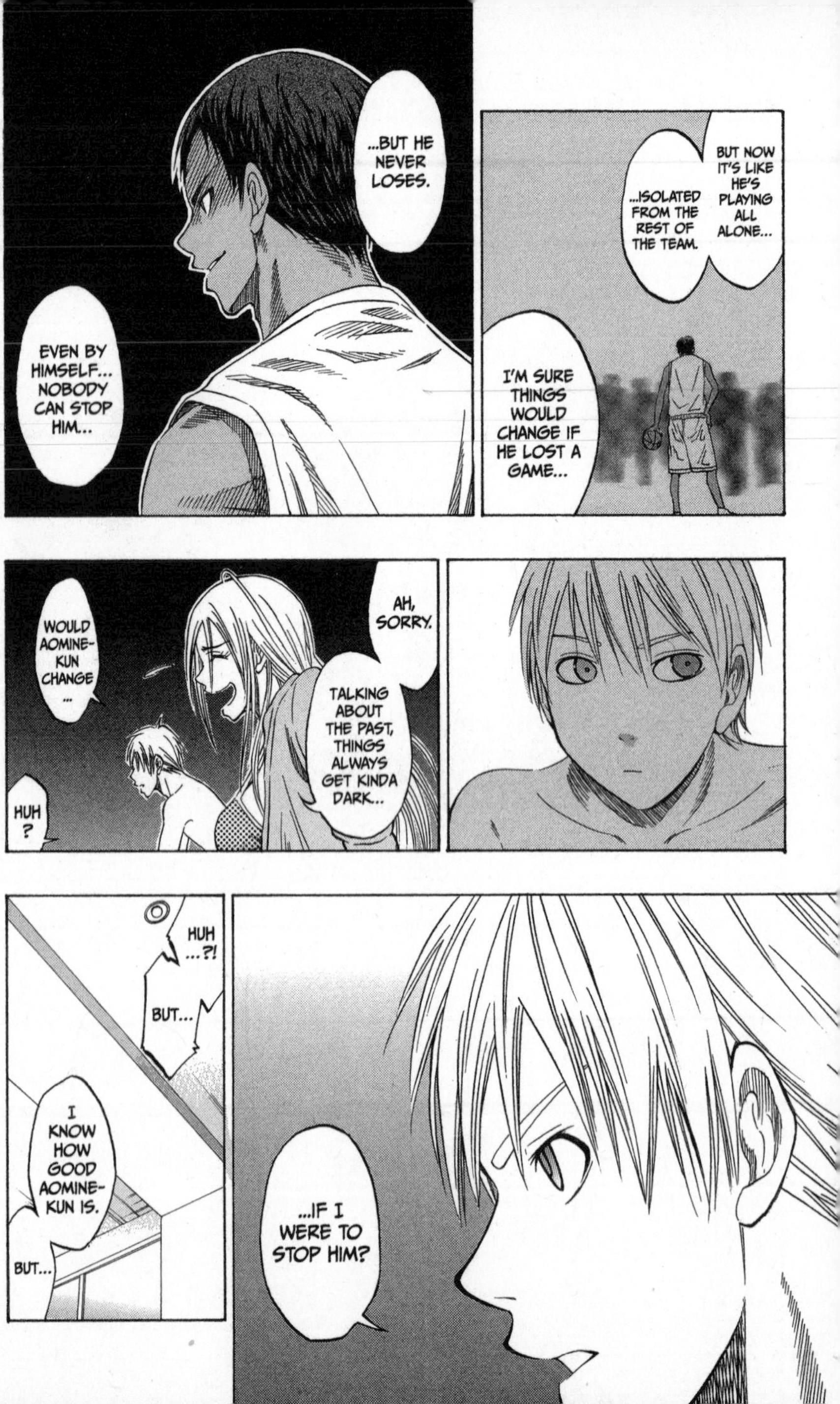
BUT NOW IT'S LIKE HE'S PLAYING ALL ALONE...
...ISOLATED FROM THE REST OF THE TEAM.
I'M SURE THINGS WOULD CHANGE IF HE LOST A GAME...
...BUT HE NEVER LOSES.
EVEN BY HIMSELF... NOBODY CAN STOP HIM...
AH, SORRY.
TALKING ABOUT THE PAST, THINGS ALWAYS GET KINDA DARK...
WOULD AOMINE-KUN CHANGE...
HUH?
...IF I WERE TO STOP HIM?
HUH...?!
BUT...
I KNOW HOW GOOD AOMINE-KUN IS.
BUT...

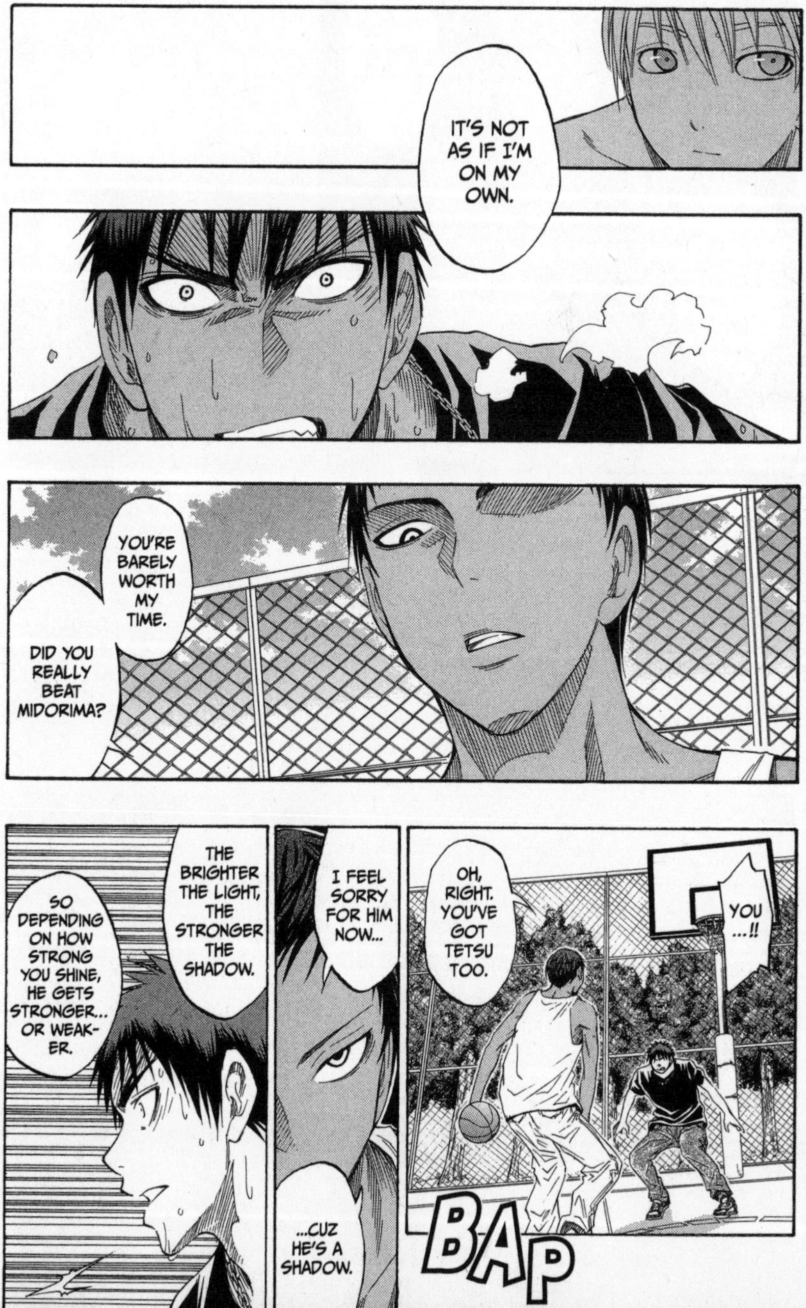
IT'S NOT AS IF I'M ON MY OWN.
YOU'RE BARELY WORTH MY TIME.
DID YOU REALLY BEAT MIDORIMA?
YOU ...!!
OH, RIGHT. YOU'VE GOT TETSU TOO.
BAP
I FEEL SORRY FOR HIM NOW...
...CUZ HE'S A SHADOW.
THE BRIGHTER THE LIGHT, THE STRONGER THE SHADOW.
SO DEPENDING ON HOW STRONG YOU SHINE, HE GETS STRONGER... OR WEAKER.

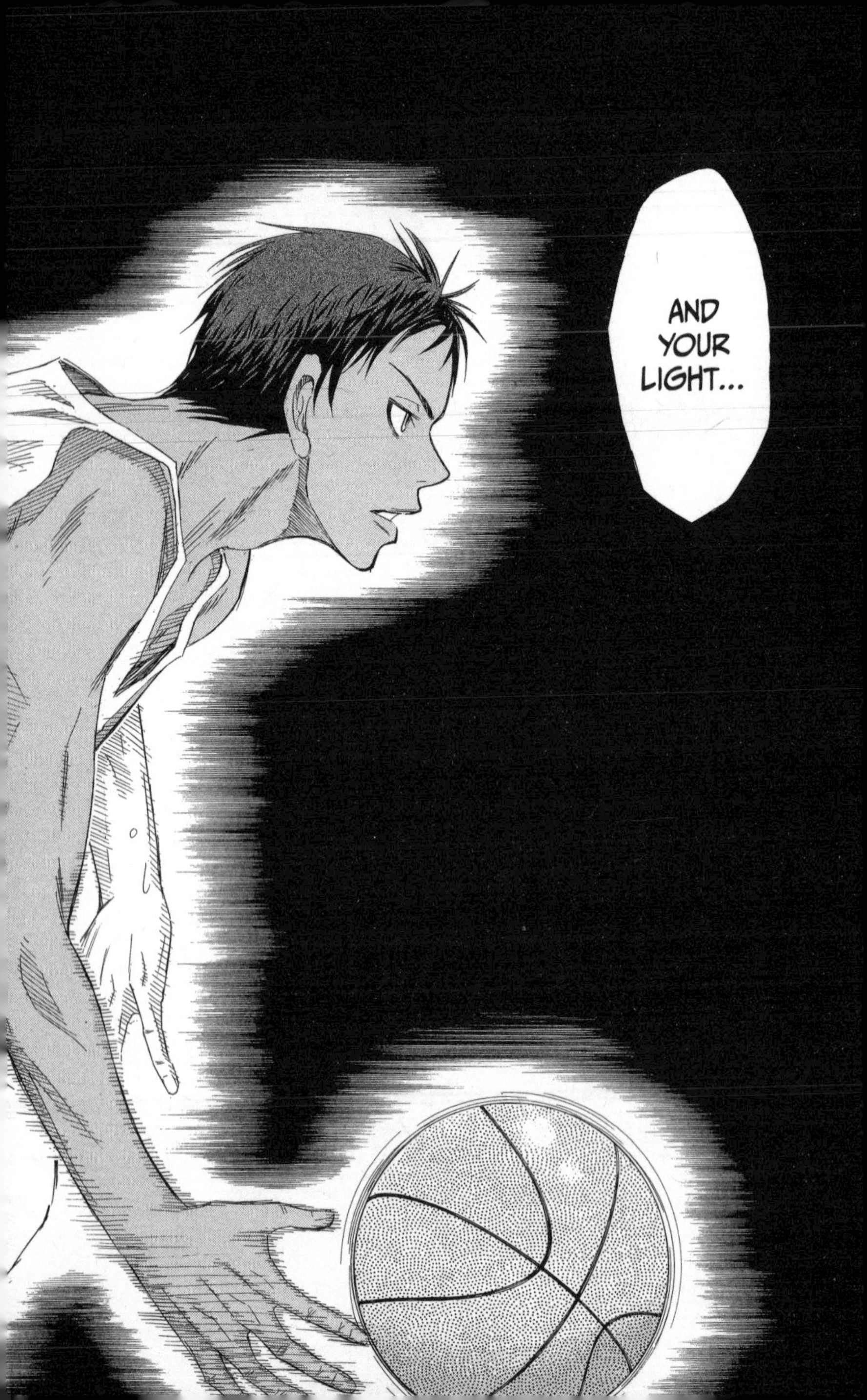
AND YOUR LIGHT...

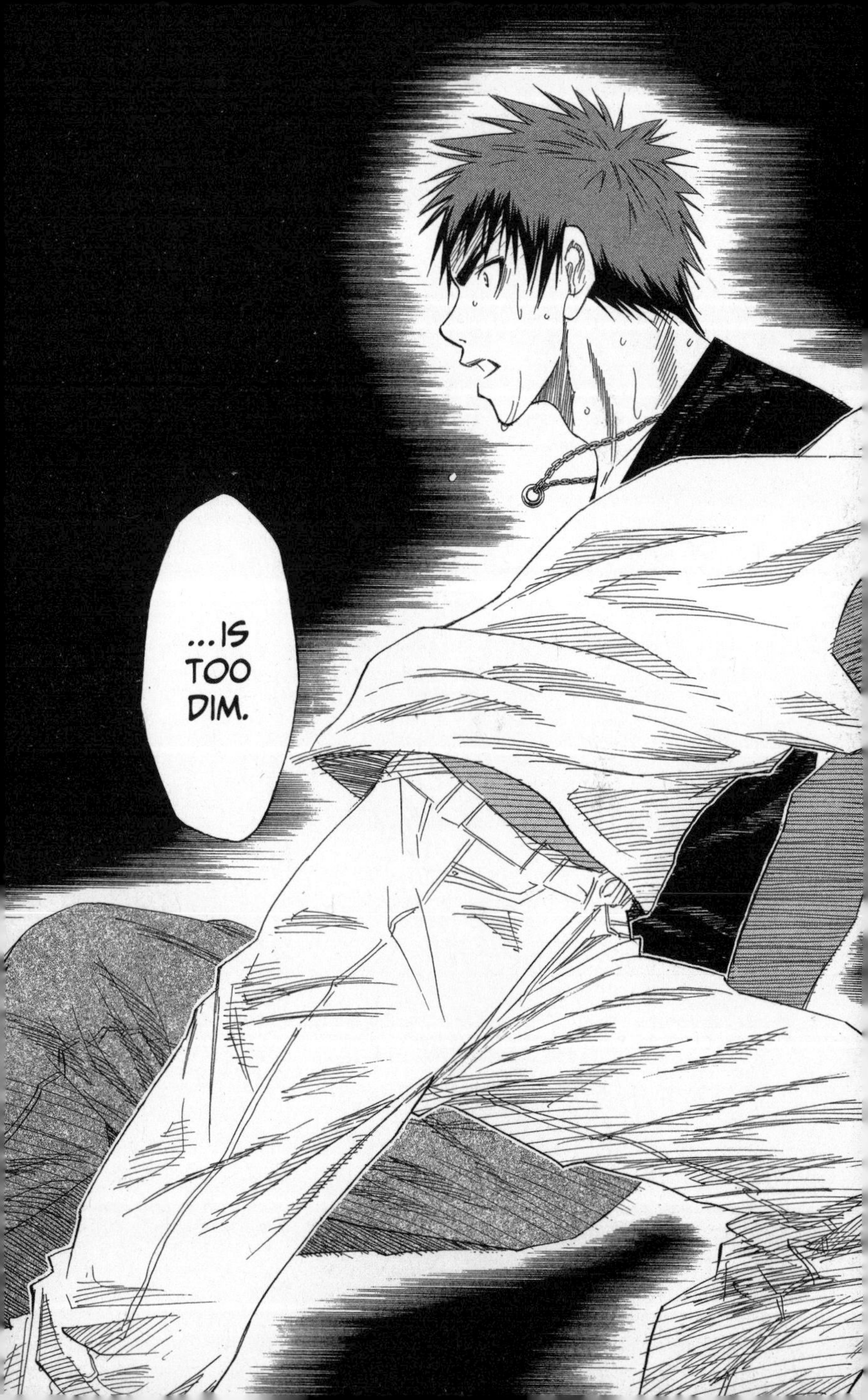
...IS TOO DIM.

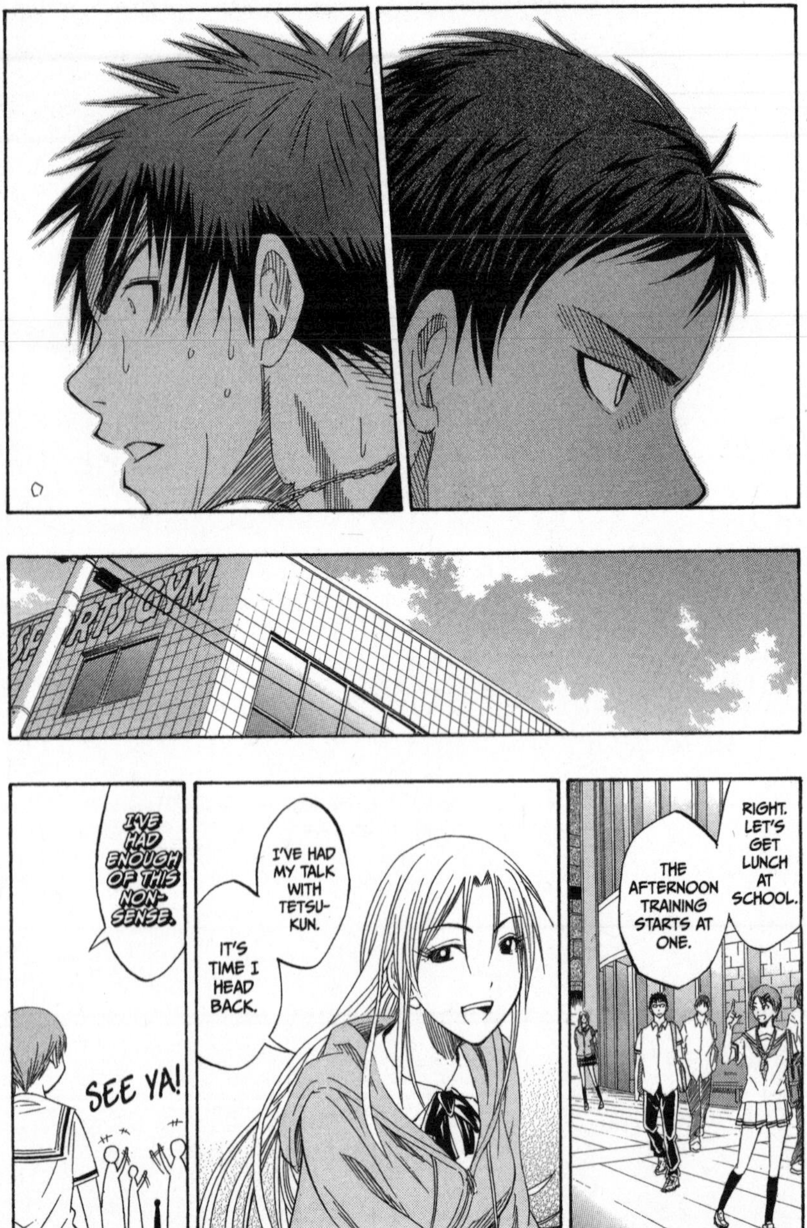
RIGHT. LET'S GET LUNCH AT SCHOOL.
THE AFTERNOON TRAINING STARTS AT ONE.
I'VE HAD MY TALK WITH TETSU-KUN.
IT'S TIME I HEAD BACK.
I'VE HAD ENOUGH OF THIS NON-SENSE.
SEE YA!

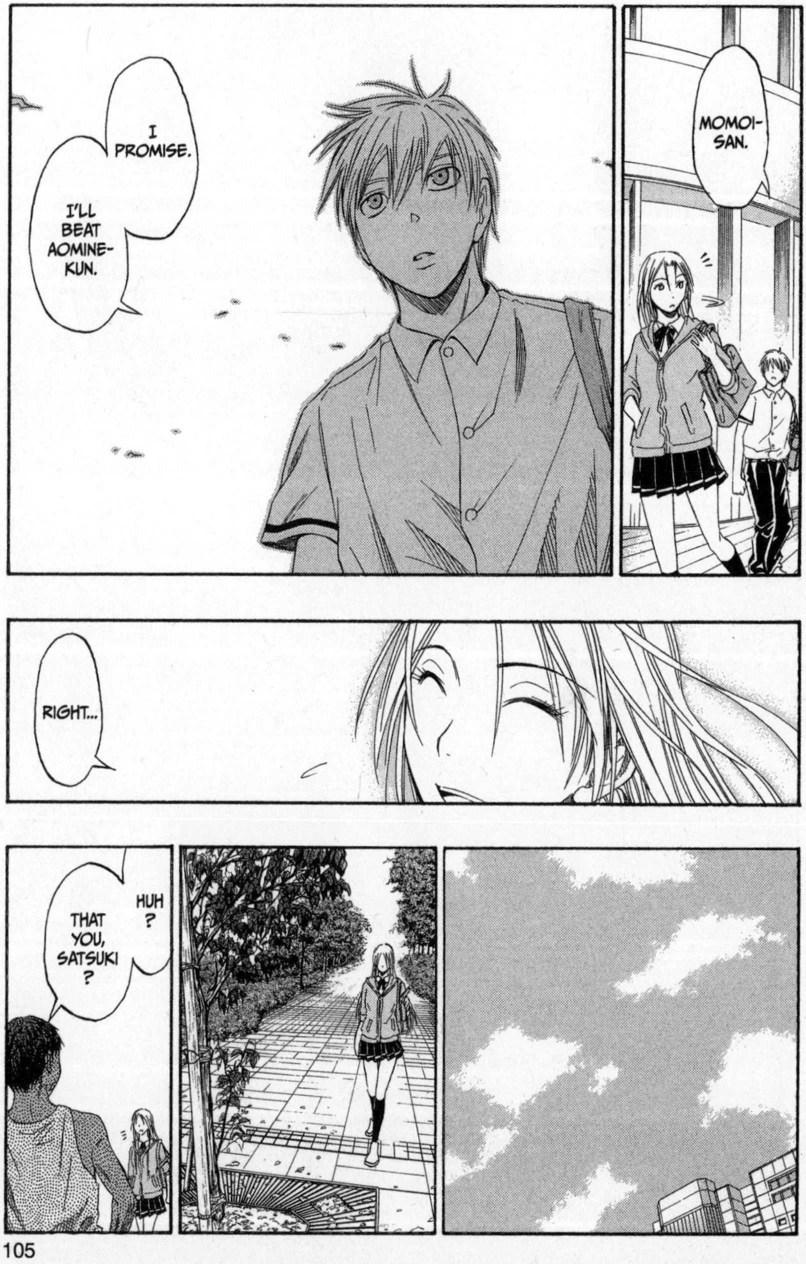
MOMOI-SAN.
I PROMISE.
I'LL BEAT AOMINE-KUN.
RIGHT...
HUH?
THAT YOU, SATSUKI?

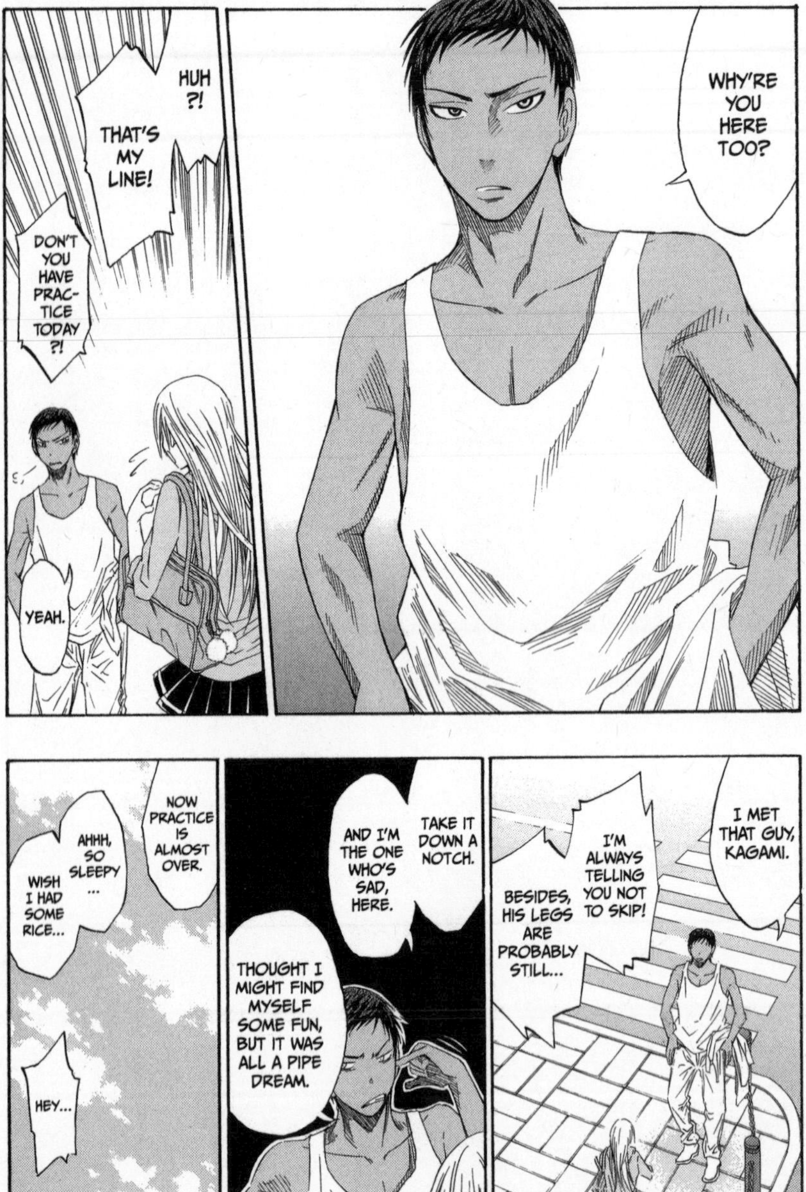
WHY'RE YOU HERE TOO?
HUH ?!
THAT'S MY LINE!
DON'T YOU HAVE PRAC- TICE TODAY ?!
YEAH.
I MET THAT GUY, KAGAMI.
I'M ALWAYS TELLING YOU NOT TO SKIP!
BESIDES, HIS LEGS ARE PROBABLY STILL...
TAKE IT DOWN A NOTCH.
AND I'M THE ONE WHO'S SAD, HERE.
THOUGHT I MIGHT FIND MYSELF SOME FUN, BUT IT WAS ALL A PIPE DREAM.
NOW PRACTICE IS ALMOST OVER.
AHHH, SO SLEEPY ...
WISH I HAD SOME RICE...
HEY...

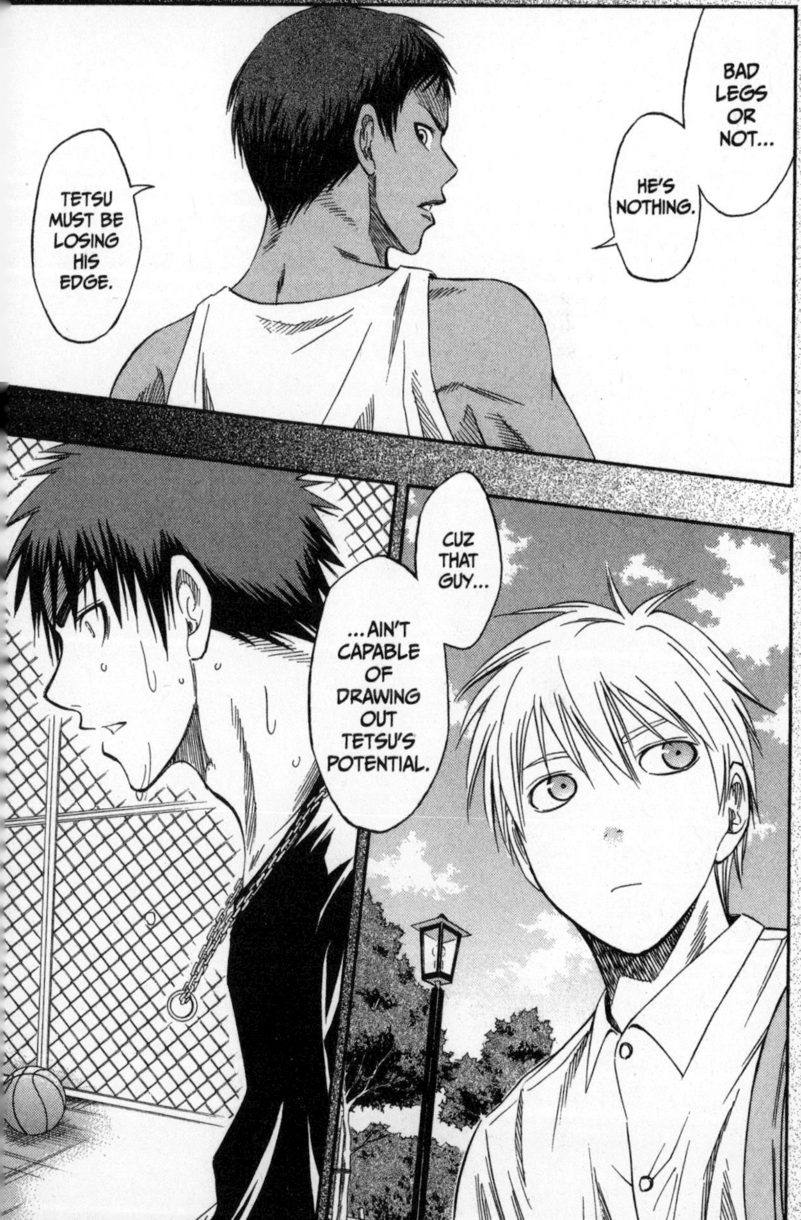
BAD LEGS OR NOT...
HE'S NOTHING.
TETSU MUST BE LOSING HIS EDGE.
CUZ THAT GUY...
...AIN'T CAPABLE OF DRAWING OUT TETSU'S POTENTIAL.

KUROKO'S BASKETBALL BLOOPERS TAKE 2

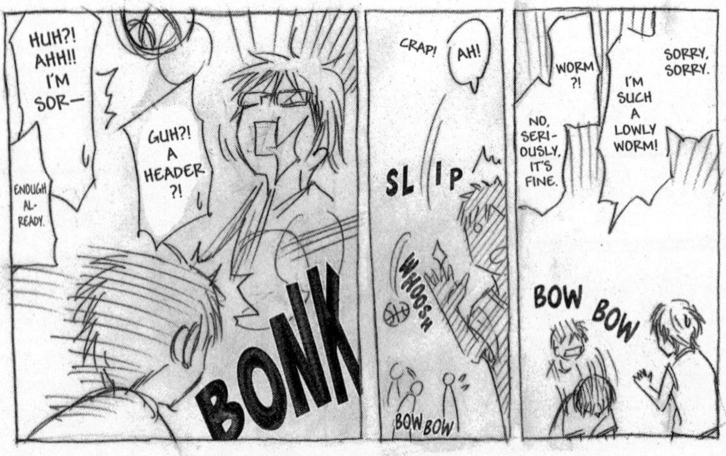
SORRY, SORRY.
I'M SUCH A LOWLY WORM!
WORM ?!
NO, SERIOUSLY, IT'S FINE.
BOW
BOW
AH!
CRAP!
SLIP
WHOOSH
BOW BOW
GUH?! A HEADER ?!
HUH?! AHH!! I'M SOR—
ENOUGH AL-READY.
BONK

40TH QUARTER: DON'T MAKE ME LAUGH

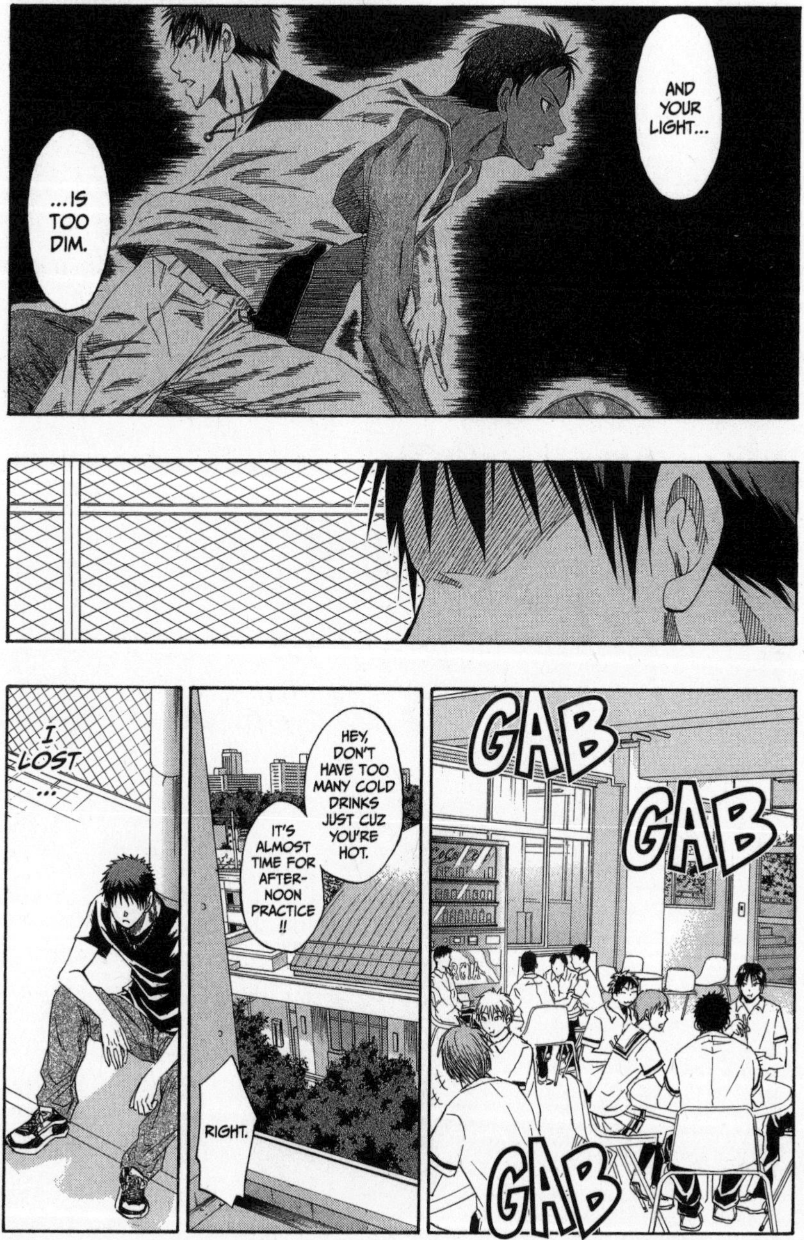
AND YOUR LIGHT...
...IS TOO DIM.
GAB
GAB
GAB
HEY, DON'T HAVE TOO MANY COLD DRINKS JUST CUZ YOU'RE HOT.
IT'S ALMOST TIME FOR AFTER-NOON PRACTICE!!
RIGHT.
I LOST...

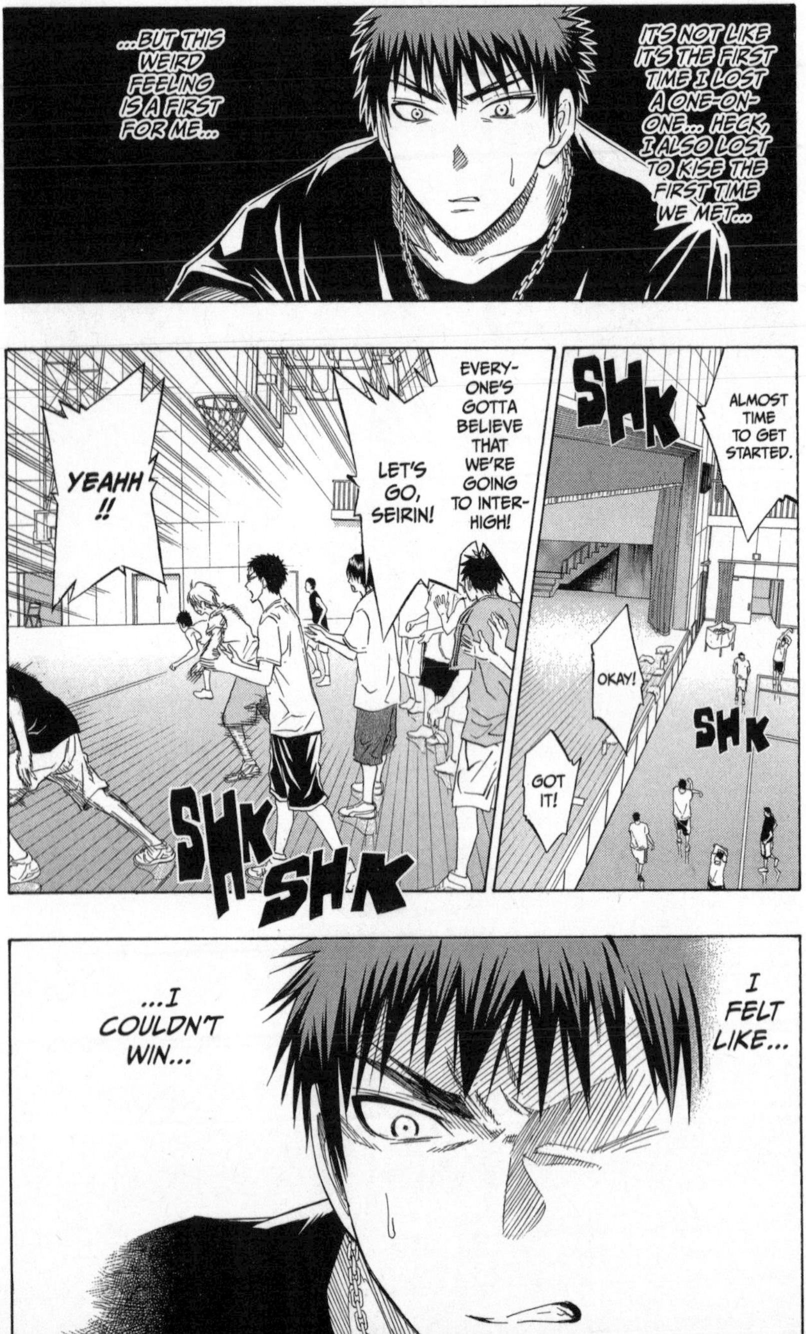
IT'S NOT LIKE IT'S THE FIRST TIME I LOST A ONE-ON-ONE... HECK, I ALSO LOST TO KISE THE FIRST TIME WE MET...
...BUT THIS WEIRD FEELING IS A FIRST FOR ME...
SHK
ALMOST TIME TO GET STARTED.
OKAY!
SHK
GOT IT!
EVERY-ONE'S GOTTA BELIEVE THAT WE'RE GOING TO INTER-HIGH!
LET'S GO, SEIRIN!
YEAHH!!
SHK
SHK
I FELT LIKE...
...I COULDN'T WIN...

40TH QUARTER: DON'T MAKE ME LAUGH

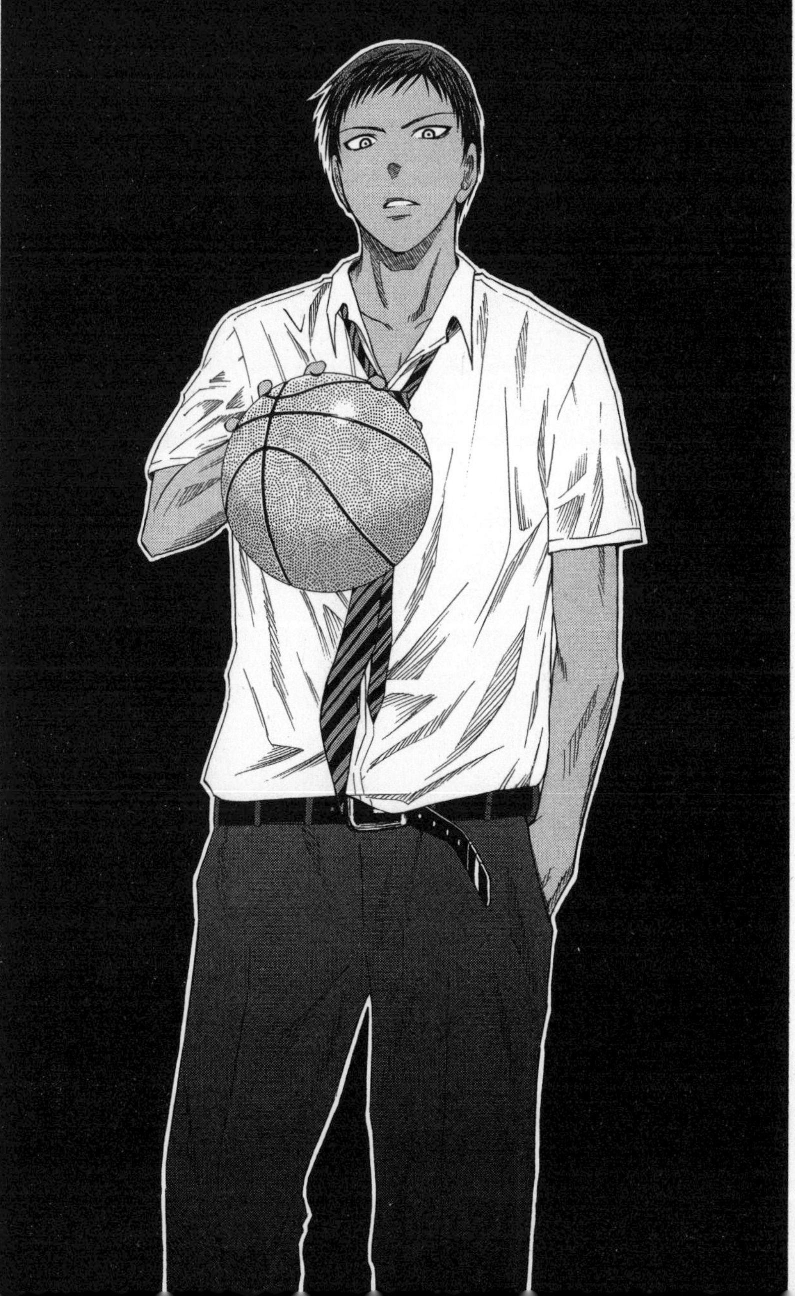

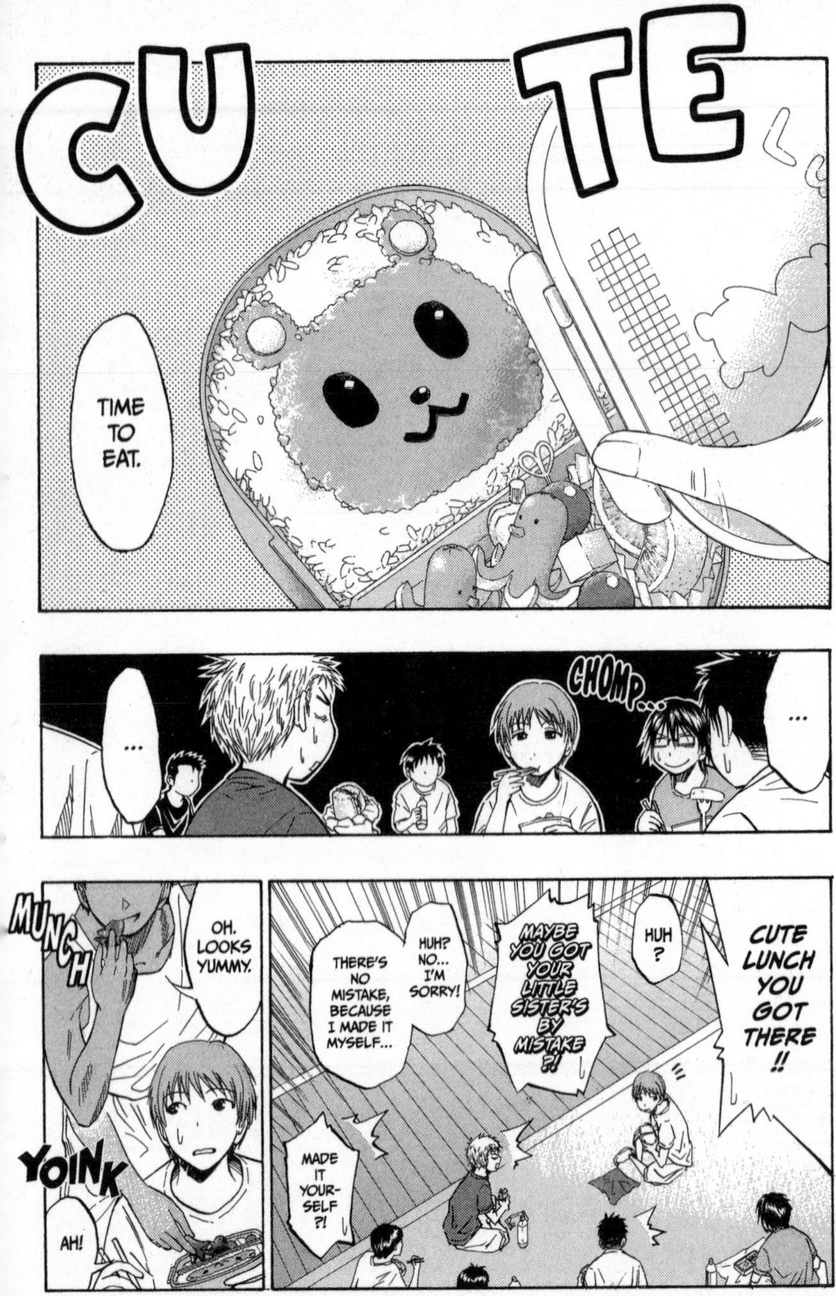
CUTE
TIME TO EAT.
...
CHOMP...
...
CUTE LUNCH YOU GOT THERE!!
HUH?
MAYBE YOU GOT YOUR LITTLE SISTER'S BY MISTAKE?!
HUH? NO... I'M SORRY!
THERE'S NO MISTAKE, BECAUSE I MADE IT MYSELF...
MADE IT YOURSELF?!
OH. LOOKS YUMMY.
MUNCH
YOINK
AH!

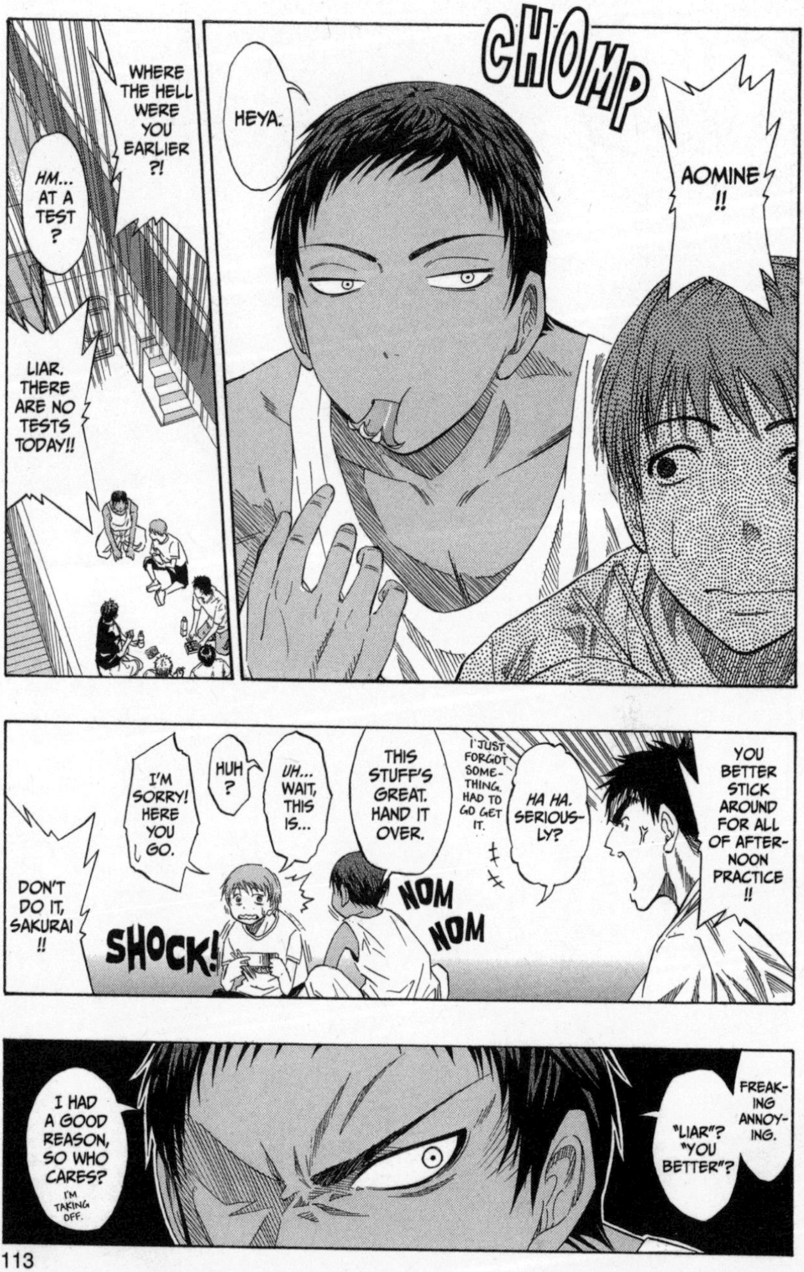
CHOMP
AOMINE!!
HEYA.
WHERE THE HELL WERE YOU EARLIER?!
HM... AT A TEST?
LIAR. THERE ARE NO TESTS TODAY!!
YOU BETTER STICK AROUND FOR ALL OF AFTERNOON PRACTICE!!
HA HA. SERIOUSLY?
I JUST FORGOT SOMETHING. HAD TO GO GET IT.
THIS STUFF'S GREAT. HAND IT OVER.
NOM NOM
UH... WAIT, THIS IS...
HUH?
I'M SORRY! HERE YOU GO.
SHOCK!
DON'T DO IT, SAKURAI!!
FREAKING ANNOYING.
"LIAR"? "YOU BETTER"?
I HAD A GOOD REASON, SO WHO CARES?
I'M TAKING OFF.

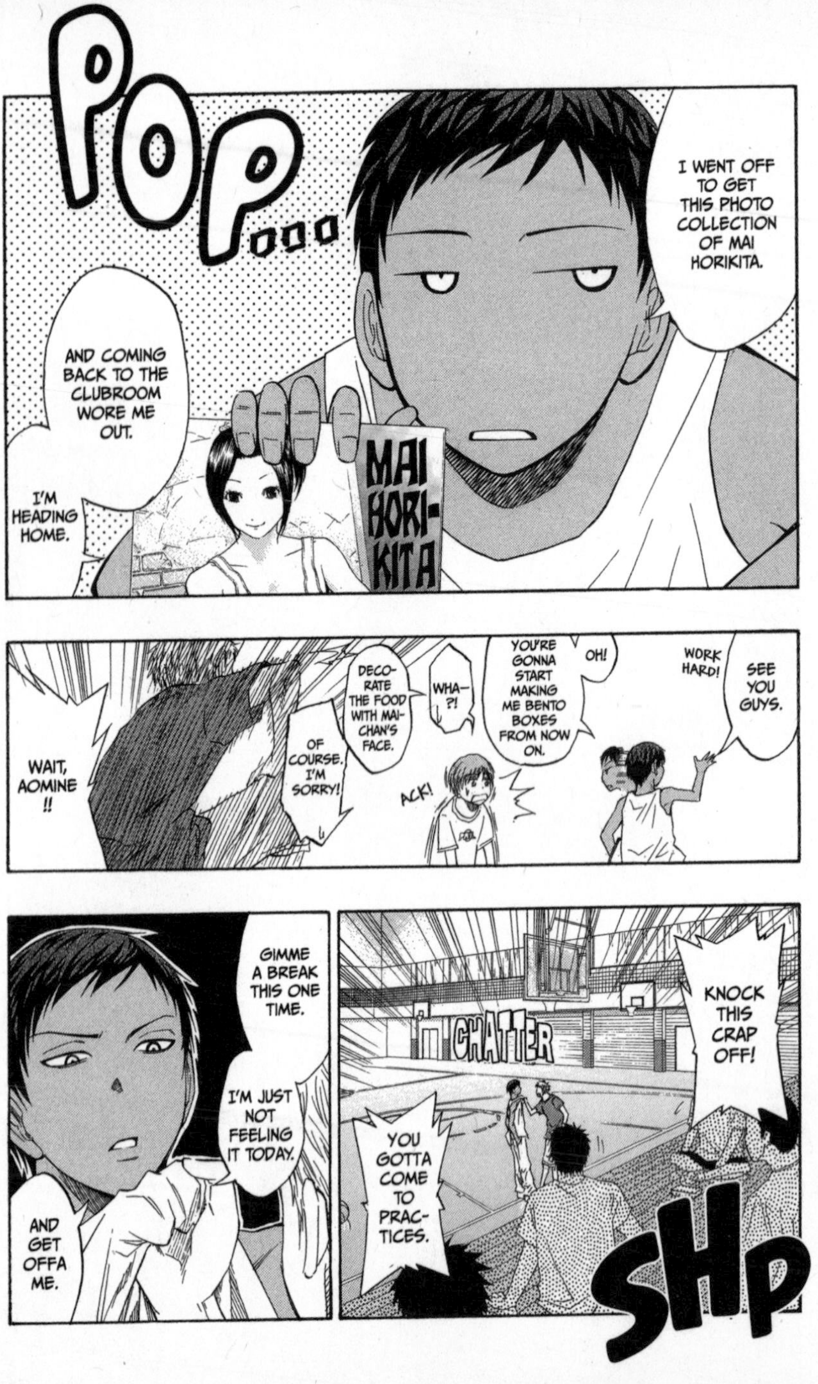
POP...
I WENT OFF TO GET THIS PHOTO COLLECTION OF MAI HORIKITA.
AND COMING BACK TO THE CLUBROOM WORE ME OUT.
MAI HORI-KITA
I'M HEADING HOME.
SEE YOU GUYS.
WORK HARD!
OH!
YOU'RE GONNA START MAKING ME BENTO BOXES FROM NOW ON.
ACK!
WHA-?!
DECO-RATE THE FOOD WITH MAI-CHAN'S FACE.
OF COURSE. I'M SORRY!
WAIT, AOMINE!!
KNOCK THIS CRAP OFF!
CHATTER
YOU GOTTA COME TO PRAC-TICES.
SHP
GIMME A BREAK THIS ONE TIME.
I'M JUST NOT FEELING IT TODAY.
AND GET OFFA ME.

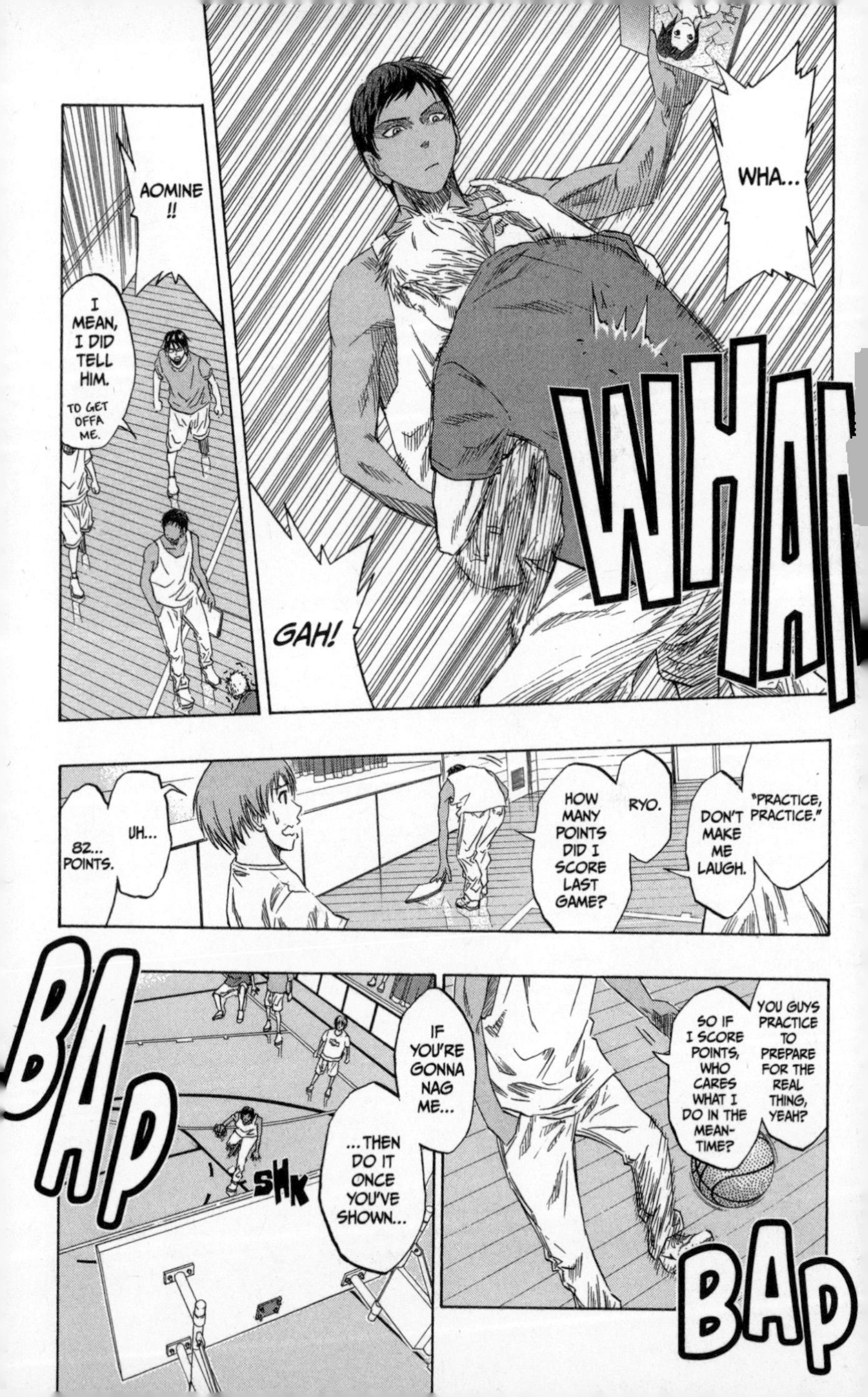
WHA...
WHA
GAH!
AOMINE !!
I MEAN, I DID TELL HIM.
TO GET OFFA ME.
"PRACTICE, PRACTICE."
DON'T MAKE ME LAUGH.
RYO.
HOW MANY POINTS DID I SCORE LAST GAME?
UH...
82... POINTS.
YOU GUYS PRACTICE TO PREPARE FOR THE REAL THING, YEAH?
SO IF I SCORE POINTS, WHO CARES WHAT I DO IN THE MEAN-TIME?
BAP
BAP
IF YOU'RE GONNA NAG ME...
...THEN DO IT ONCE YOU'VE SHOWN...
SHK

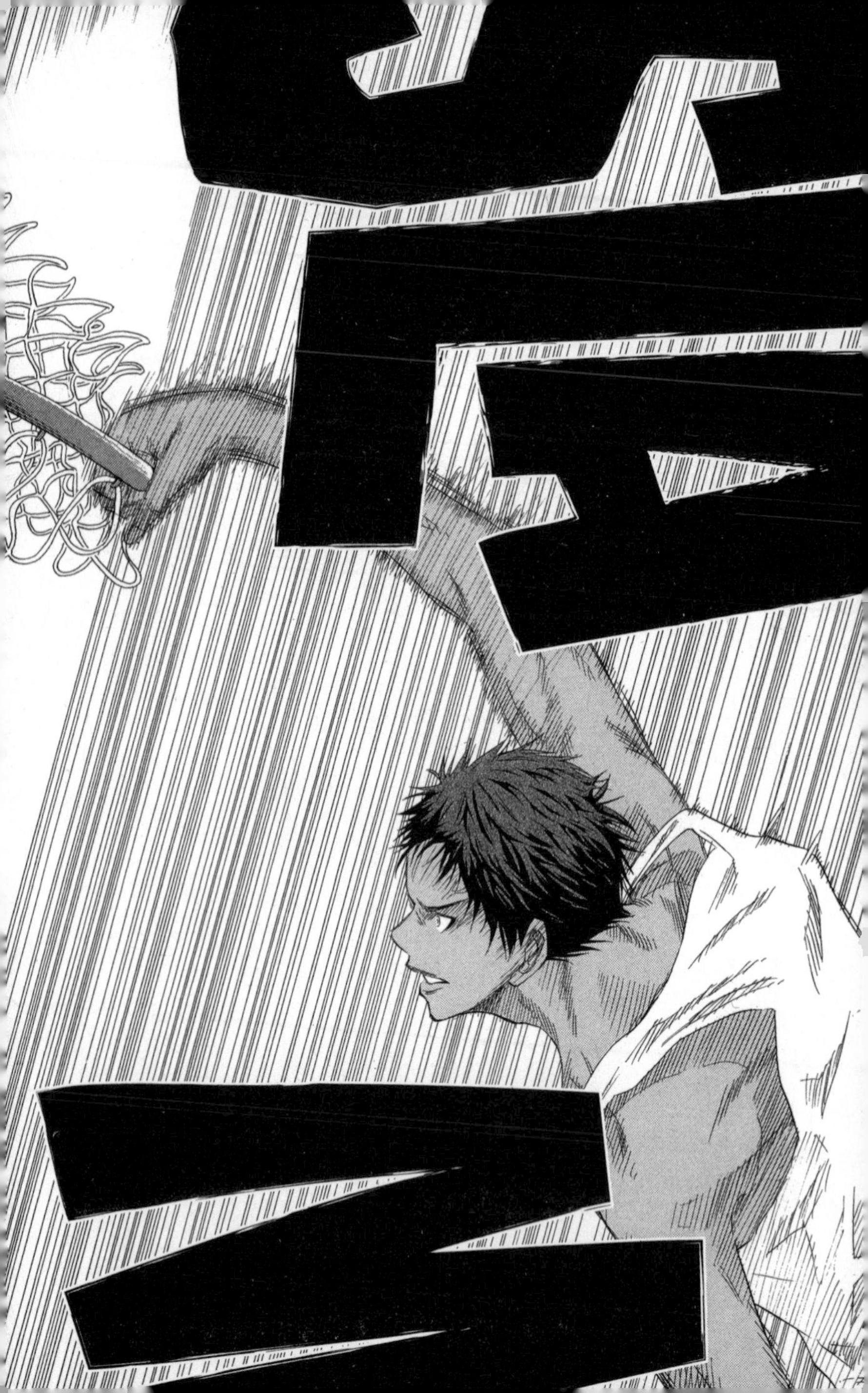

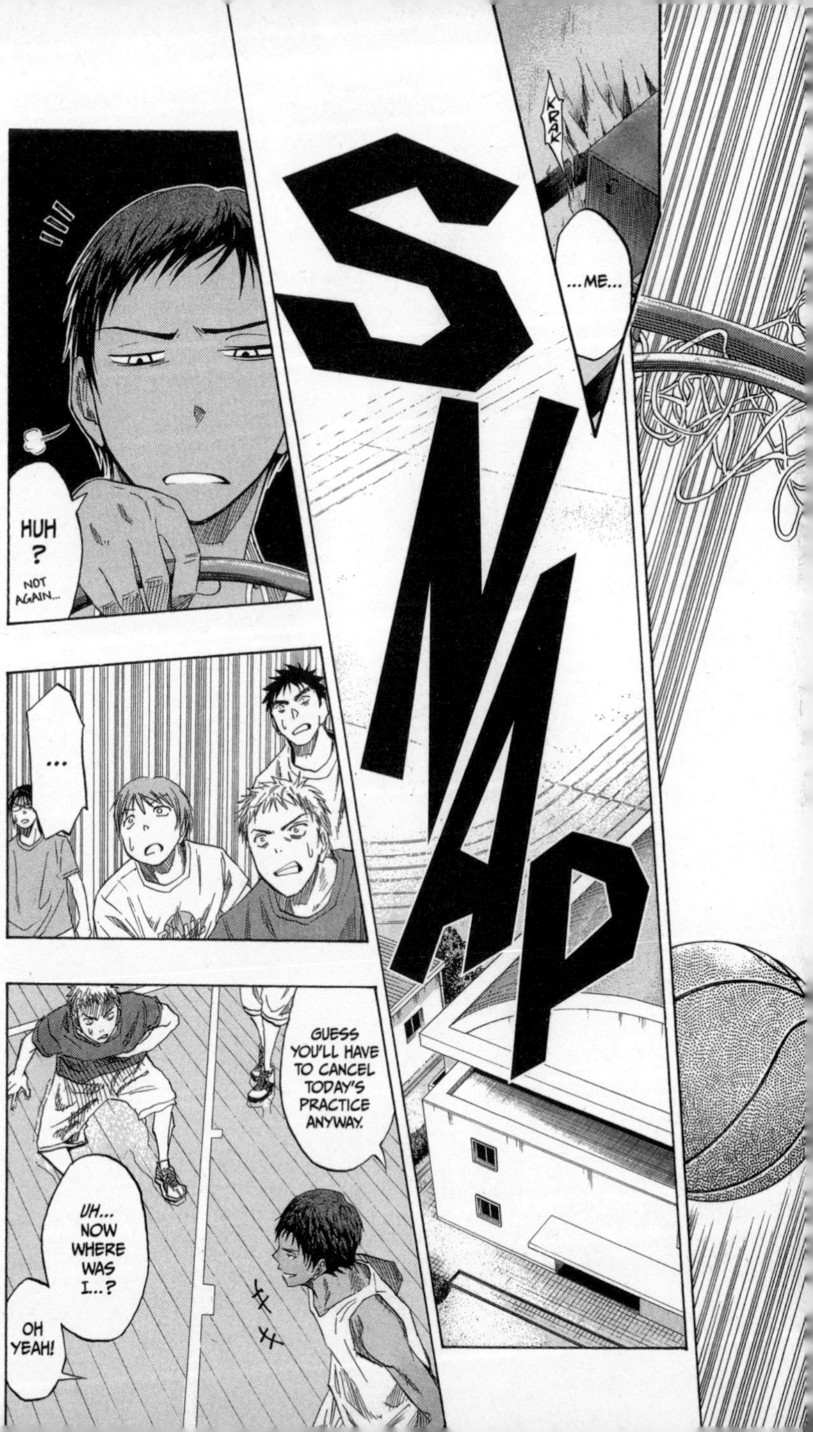
KRAK
...ME...
SNAP
HUH? NOT AGAIN...
...
GUESS YOU'LL HAVE TO CANCEL TODAY'S PRACTICE ANYWAY.
UH... NOW WHERE WAS I...?
OH YEAH!

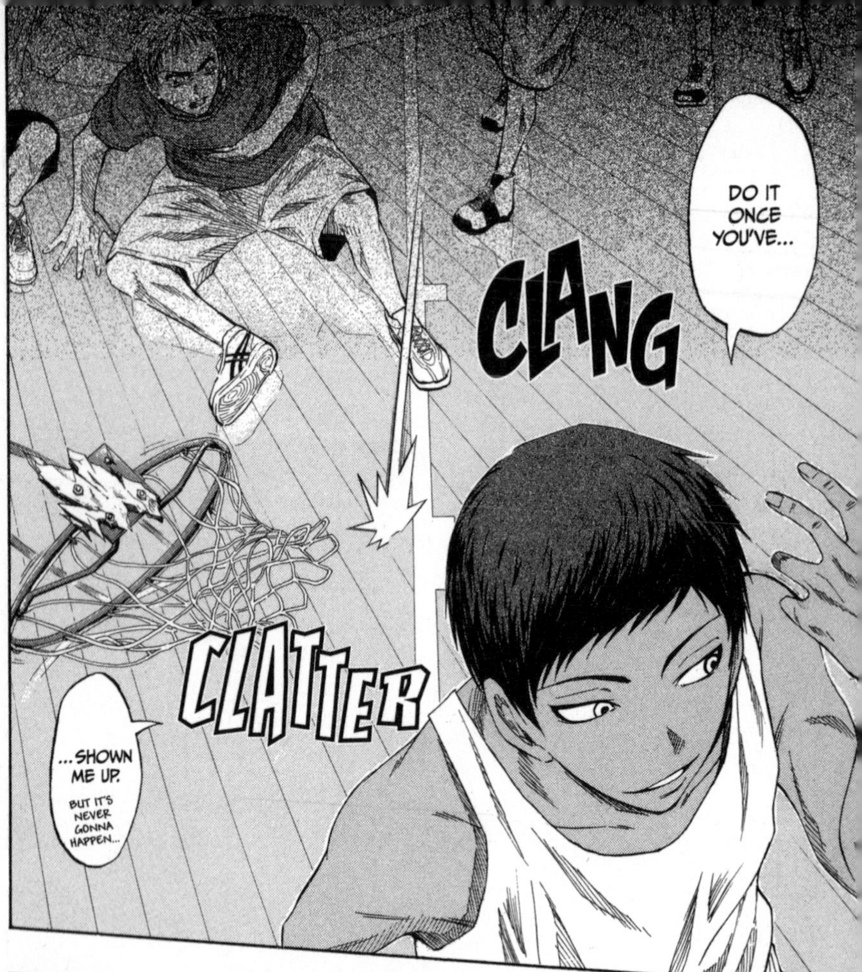
DO IT ONCE YOU'VE...
CLANG
CLATTER
...SHOWN ME UP.
BUT IT'S NEVER GONNA HAPPEN...
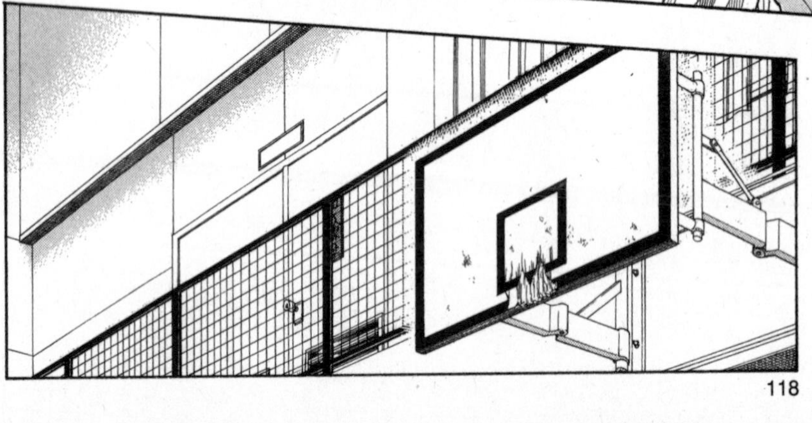

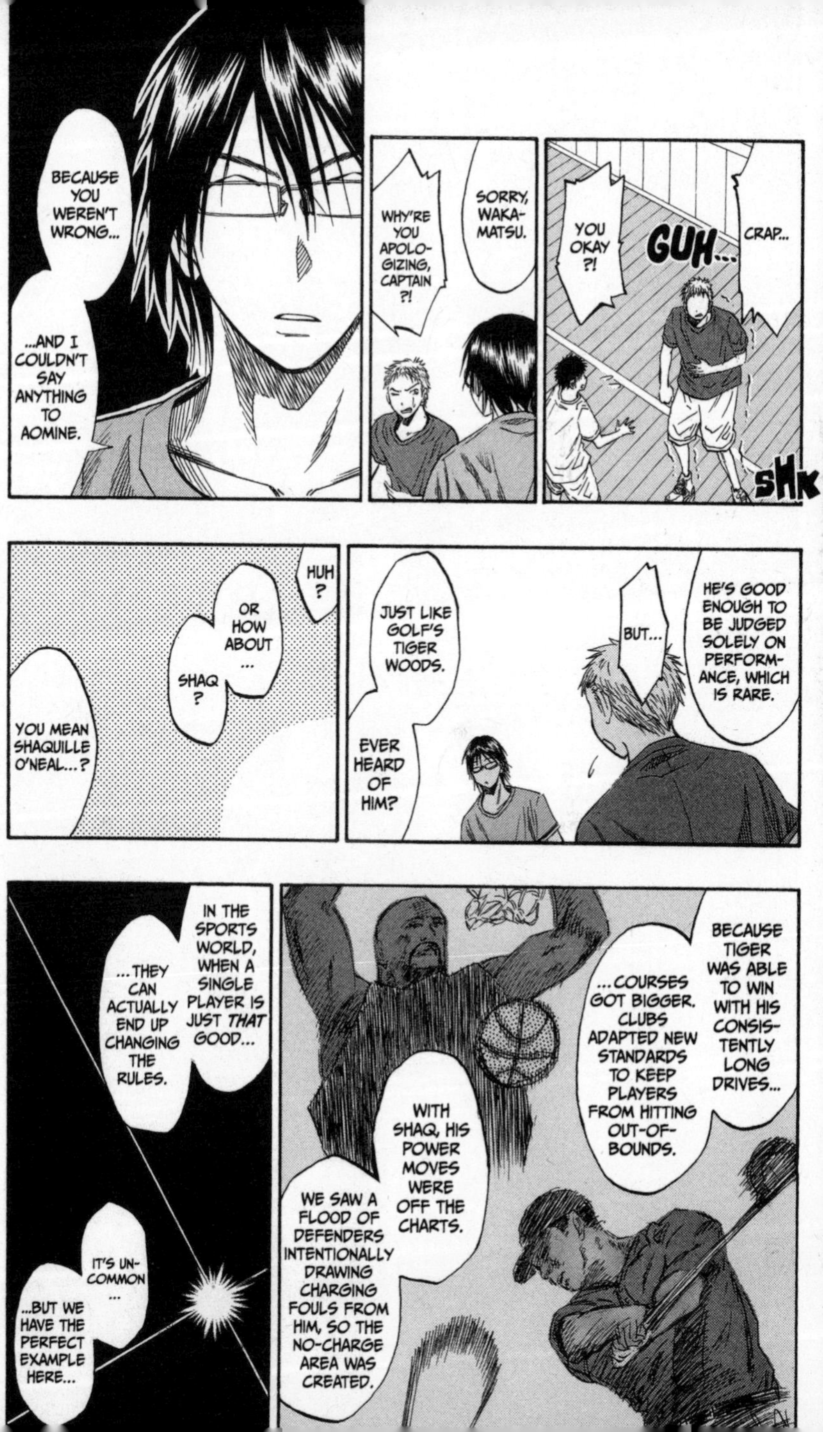
CRAP...
GUH...
YOU OKAY?!
SHK
SORRY, WAKAMATSU.
WHY'RE YOU APOLOGIZING, CAPTAIN?!
BECAUSE YOU WEREN'T WRONG...
...AND I COULDN'T SAY ANYTHING TO AOMINE.
HE'S GOOD ENOUGH TO BE JUDGED SOLELY ON PERFORMANCE, WHICH IS RARE.
BUT...
JUST LIKE GOLF'S TIGER WOODS.
EVER HEARD OF HIM?
HUH?
OR HOW ABOUT...
SHAQ?
YOU MEAN SHAQUILLE O'NEAL...?
BECAUSE TIGER WAS ABLE TO WIN WITH HIS CONSISTENTLY LONG DRIVES...
...COURSES GOT BIGGER. CLUBS ADAPTED NEW STANDARDS TO KEEP PLAYERS FROM HITTING OUT-OF-BOUNDS.
WITH SHAQ, HIS POWER MOVES WERE OFF THE CHARTS.
WE SAW A FLOOD OF DEFENDERS INTENTIONALLY DRAWING CHARGING FOULS FROM HIM, SO THE NO-CHARGE AREA WAS CREATED.
IN THE SPORTS WORLD, WHEN A SINGLE PLAYER IS JUST *THAT* GOOD...
...THEY CAN ACTUALLY END UP CHANGING THE RULES.
IT'S UNCOMMON...
...BUT WE HAVE THE PERFECT EXAMPLE HERE...

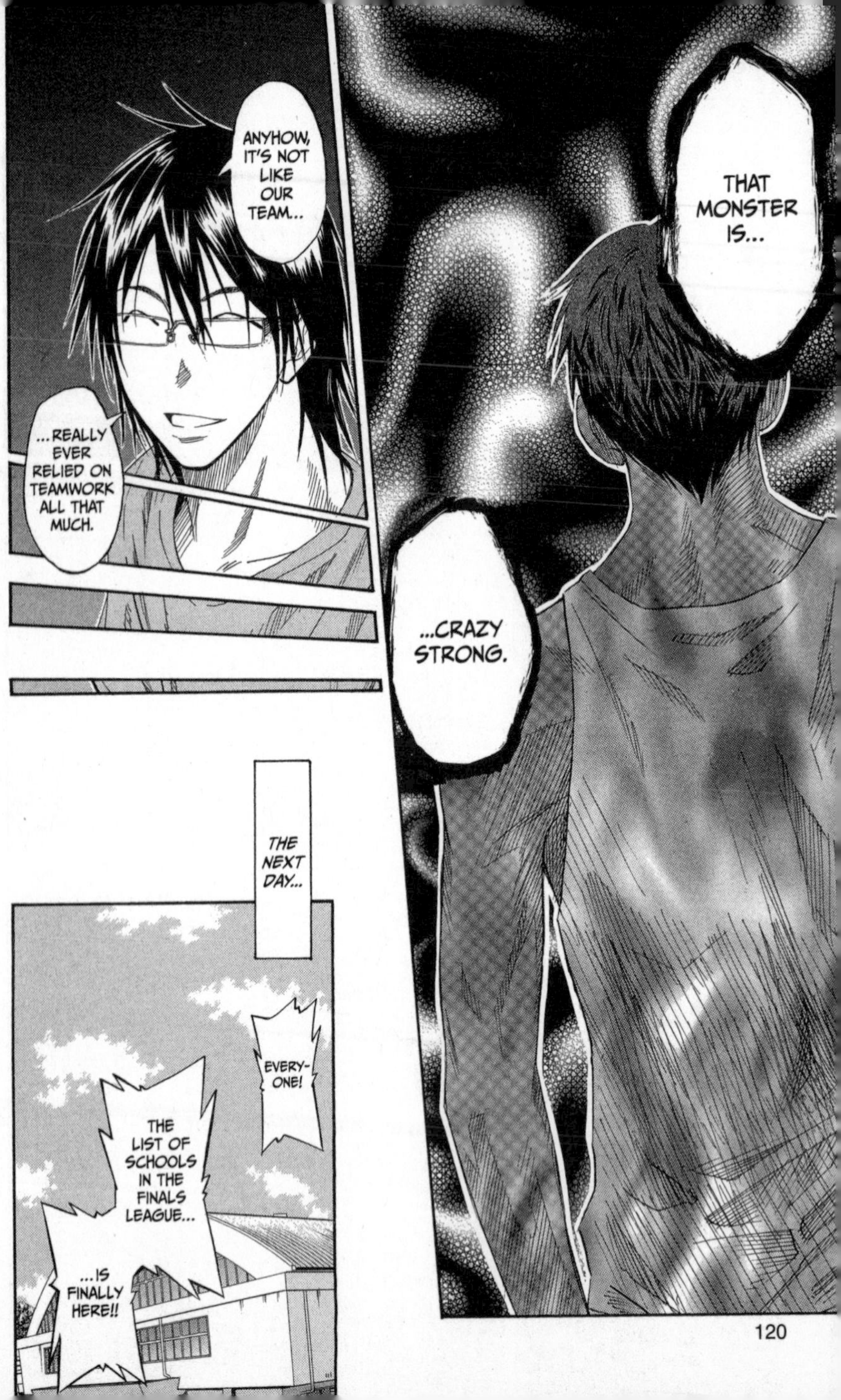
THAT MONSTER IS...
...CRAZY STRONG.
ANYHOW, IT'S NOT LIKE OUR TEAM...
...REALLY EVER RELIED ON TEAMWORK ALL THAT MUCH.
THE NEXT DAY...
EVERY-ONE!
THE LIST OF SCHOOLS IN THE FINALS LEAGUE...
...IS FINALLY HERE!!

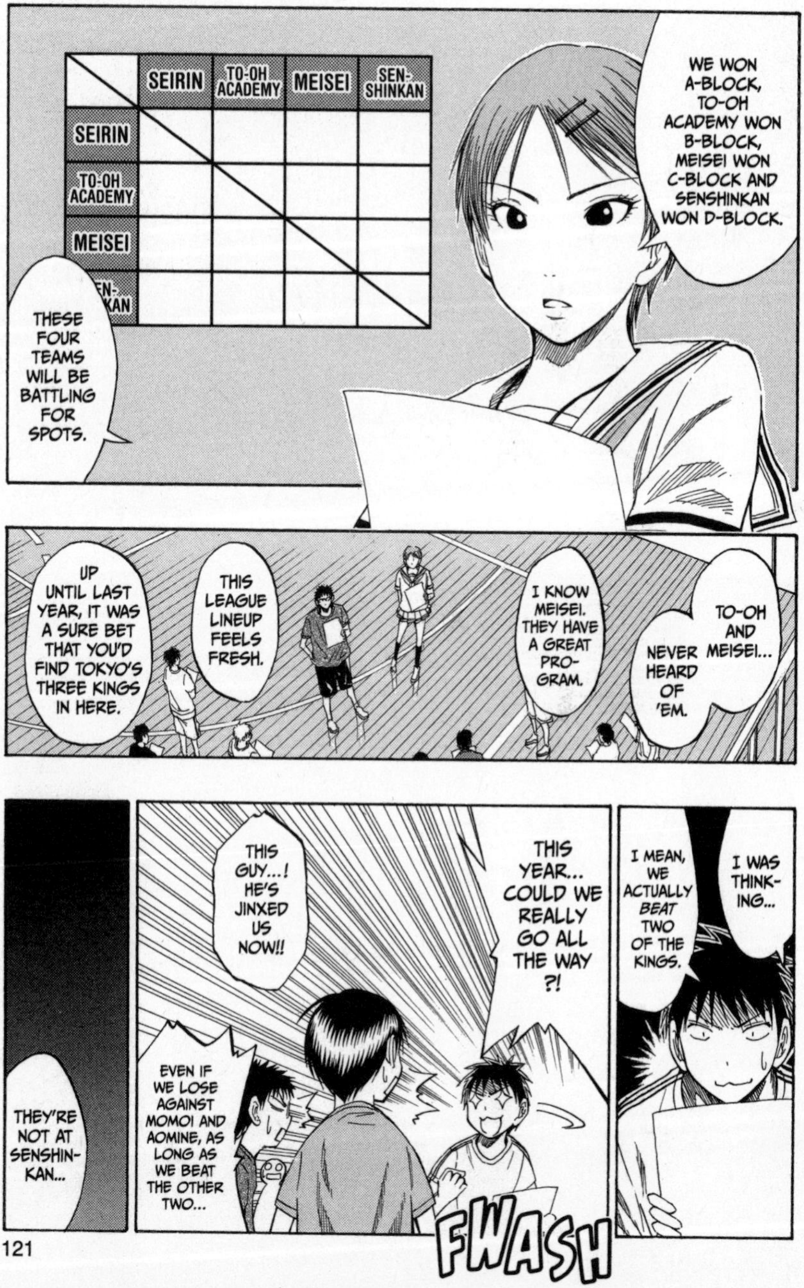
WE WON A-BLOCK, TO-OH ACADEMY WON B-BLOCK, MEISEI WON C-BLOCK AND SENSHINKAN WON D-BLOCK.
SEIRIN
TO-OH ACADEMY
MEISEI
SEN-SHINKAN
THESE FOUR TEAMS WILL BE BATTLING FOR SPOTS.
TO-OH AND MEISEI...
NEVER HEARD OF 'EM.
I KNOW MEISEI. THEY HAVE A GREAT PRO-GRAM.
THIS LEAGUE LINEUP FEELS FRESH.
UP UNTIL LAST YEAR, IT WAS A SURE BET THAT YOU'D FIND TOKYO'S THREE KINGS IN HERE.
I WAS THINK-ING...
I MEAN, WE ACTUALLY *BEAT* TWO OF THE KINGS.
THIS YEAR... COULD WE REALLY GO ALL THE WAY ?!
THIS GUY...! HE'S JINXED US NOW!!
EVEN IF WE LOSE AGAINST MOMOI AND AOMINE, AS LONG AS WE BEAT THE OTHER TWO...
FWASH
THEY'RE NOT AT SENSHIN-KAN...

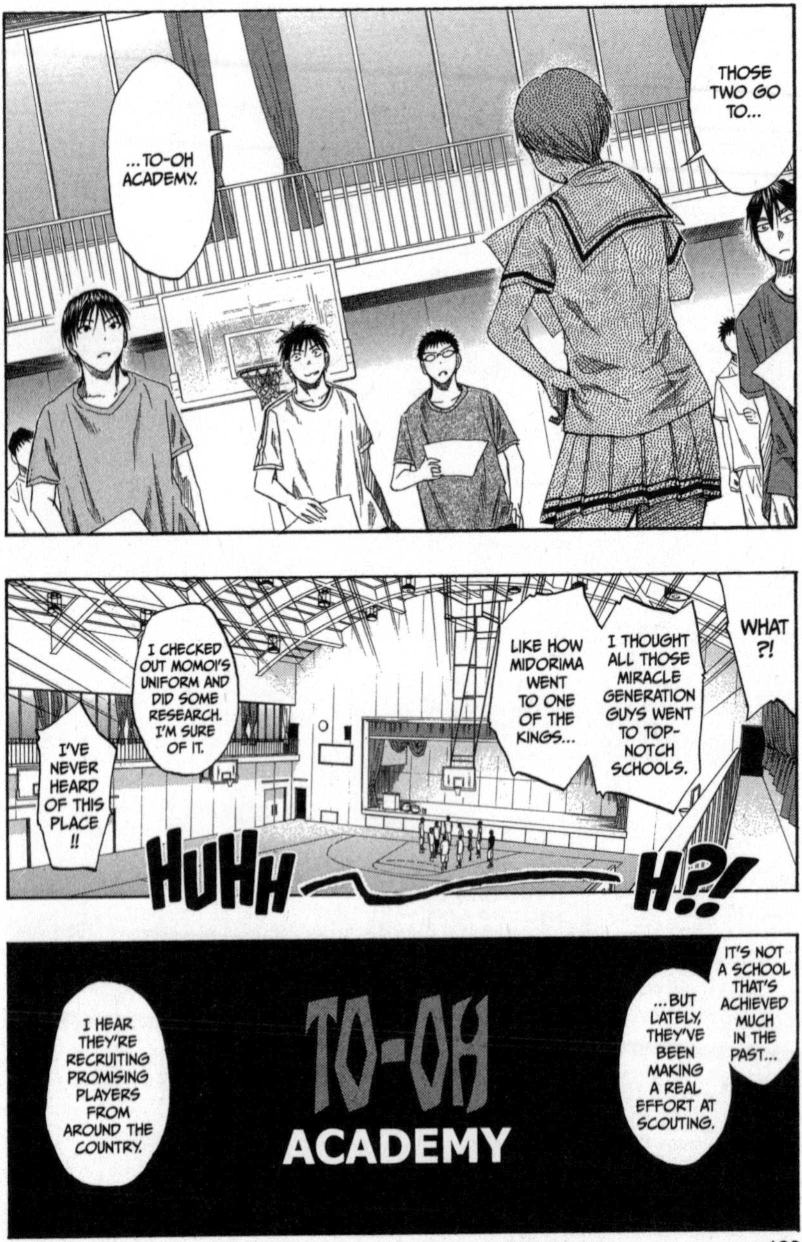
THOSE TWO GO TO...
...TO-OH ACADEMY.
WHAT ?!
I THOUGHT ALL THOSE MIRACLE GENERATION GUYS WENT TO TOP-NOTCH SCHOOLS.
LIKE HOW MIDORIMA WENT TO ONE OF THE KINGS...
I CHECKED OUT MOMOI'S UNIFORM AND DID SOME RESEARCH. I'M SURE OF IT.
I'VE NEVER HEARD OF THIS PLACE !!
HUHH—H?!
IT'S NOT A SCHOOL THAT'S ACHIEVED MUCH IN THE PAST...
...BUT LATELY, THEY'VE BEEN MAKING A REAL EFFORT AT SCOUTING.
TO-OH ACADEMY
I HEAR THEY'RE RECRUITING PROMISING PLAYERS FROM AROUND THE COUNTRY.

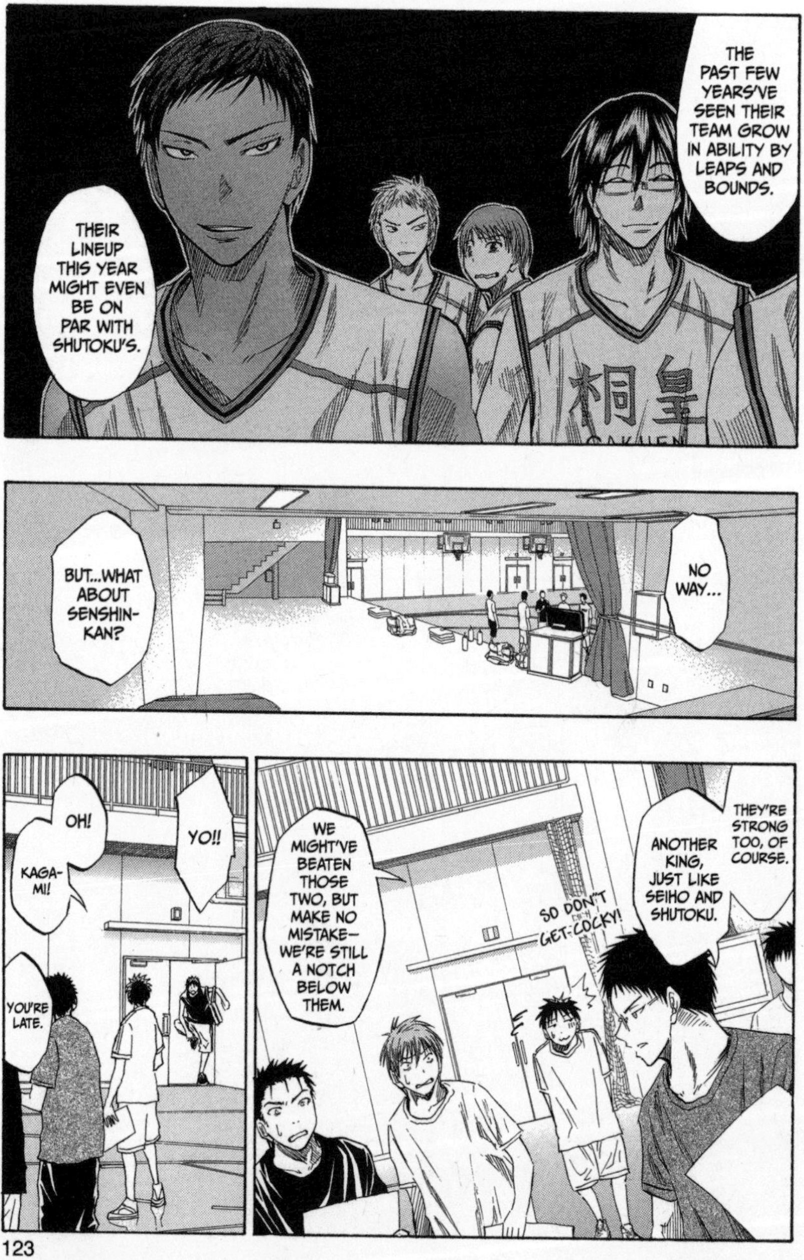
THE PAST FEW YEARS'VE SEEN THEIR TEAM GROW IN ABILITY BY LEAPS AND BOUNDS.
THEIR LINEUP THIS YEAR MIGHT EVEN BE ON PAR WITH SHUTOKU'S.
NO WAY...
BUT...WHAT ABOUT SENSHIN-KAN?
THEY'RE STRONG TOO, OF COURSE.
ANOTHER KING, JUST LIKE SEIHO AND SHUTOKU.
SO DON'T GET COCKY!
WE MIGHT'VE BEATEN THOSE TWO, BUT MAKE NO MISTAKE– WE'RE STILL A NOTCH BELOW THEM.
YO!!
OH!
KAGA-MI!
YOU'RE LATE.

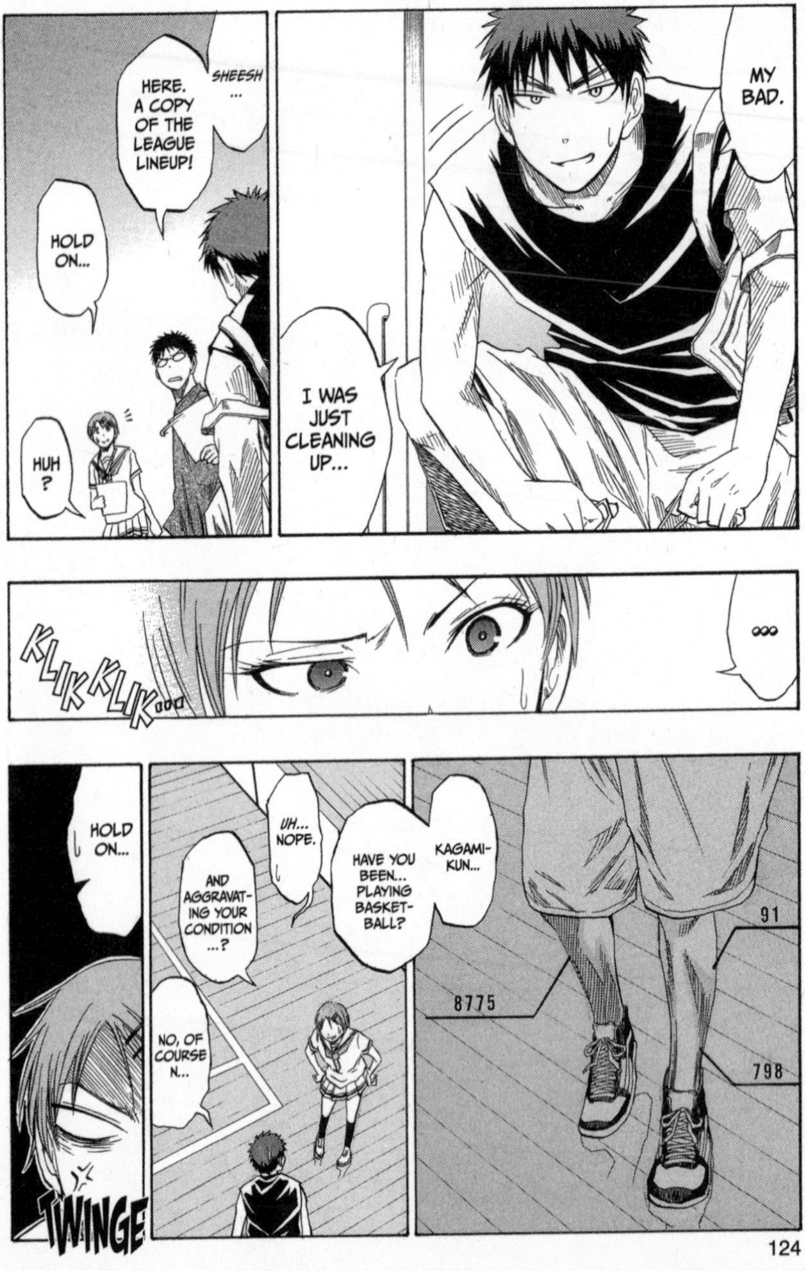
MY BAD.
I WAS JUST CLEANING UP...
SHEESH...
HERE. A COPY OF THE LEAGUE LINEUP!
HOLD ON...
HUH?
...
KLIK KLIK...
KAGAMI-KUN...
HAVE YOU BEEN... PLAYING BASKET-BALL?
91
8775
798
UH... NOPE.
AND AGGRAVAT-ING YOUR CONDITION...?
NO, OF COURSE N...
HOLD ON...
TWINGE

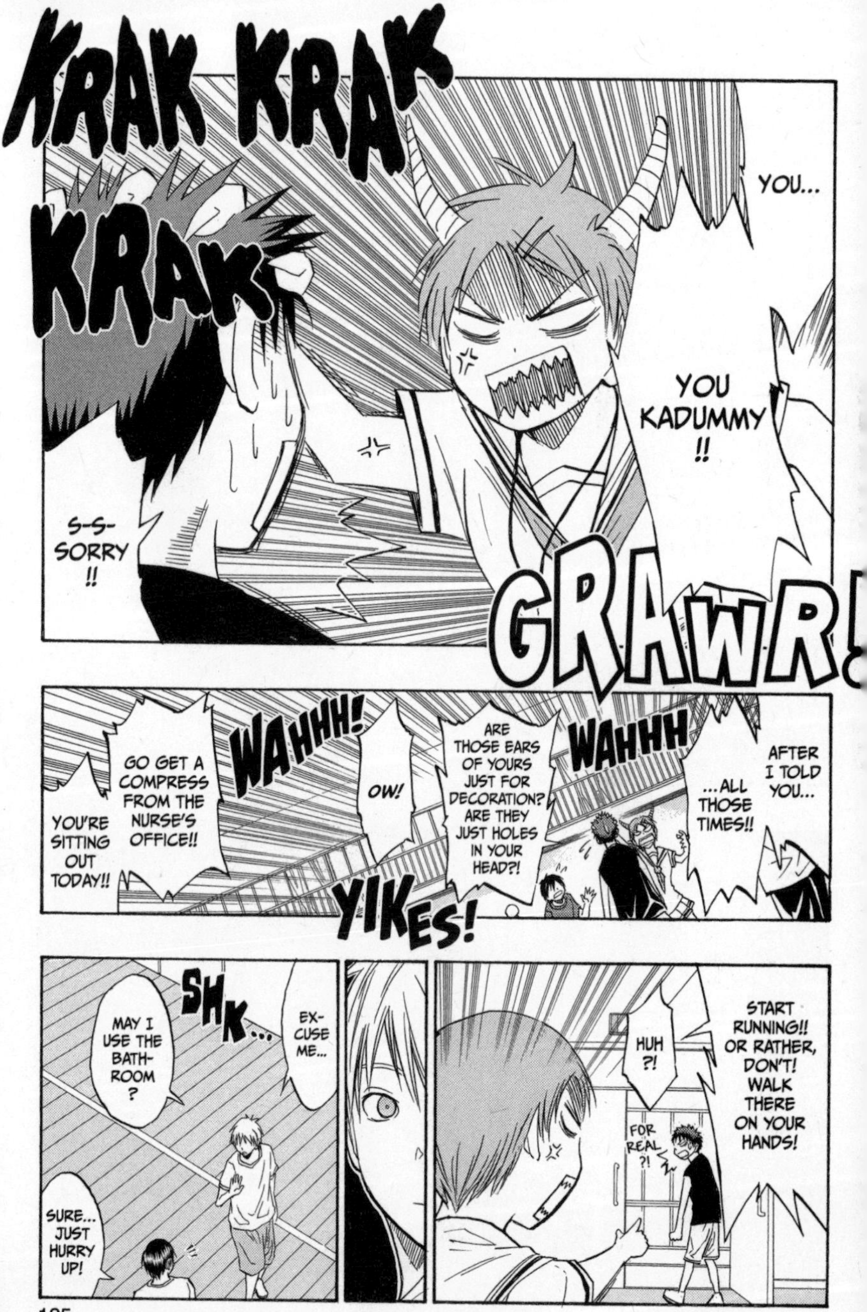
YOU...
KRAK KRAK KRAK
YOU KADUMMY !!
S-S-SORRY !!
GRAWR!
AFTER I TOLD YOU...
...ALL THOSE TIMES!!
WAHHH
ARE THOSE EARS OF YOURS JUST FOR DECORATION? ARE THEY JUST HOLES IN YOUR HEAD?!
OW!
WAHHH!
GO GET A COMPRESS FROM THE NURSE'S OFFICE!!
YOU'RE SITTING OUT TODAY!!
YIKES!
START RUNNING!! OR RATHER, DON'T! WALK THERE ON YOUR HANDS!
HUH ?!
FOR REAL ?!
EX-CUSE ME...
SHK...
MAY I USE THE BATH-ROOM ?
SURE... JUST HURRY UP!

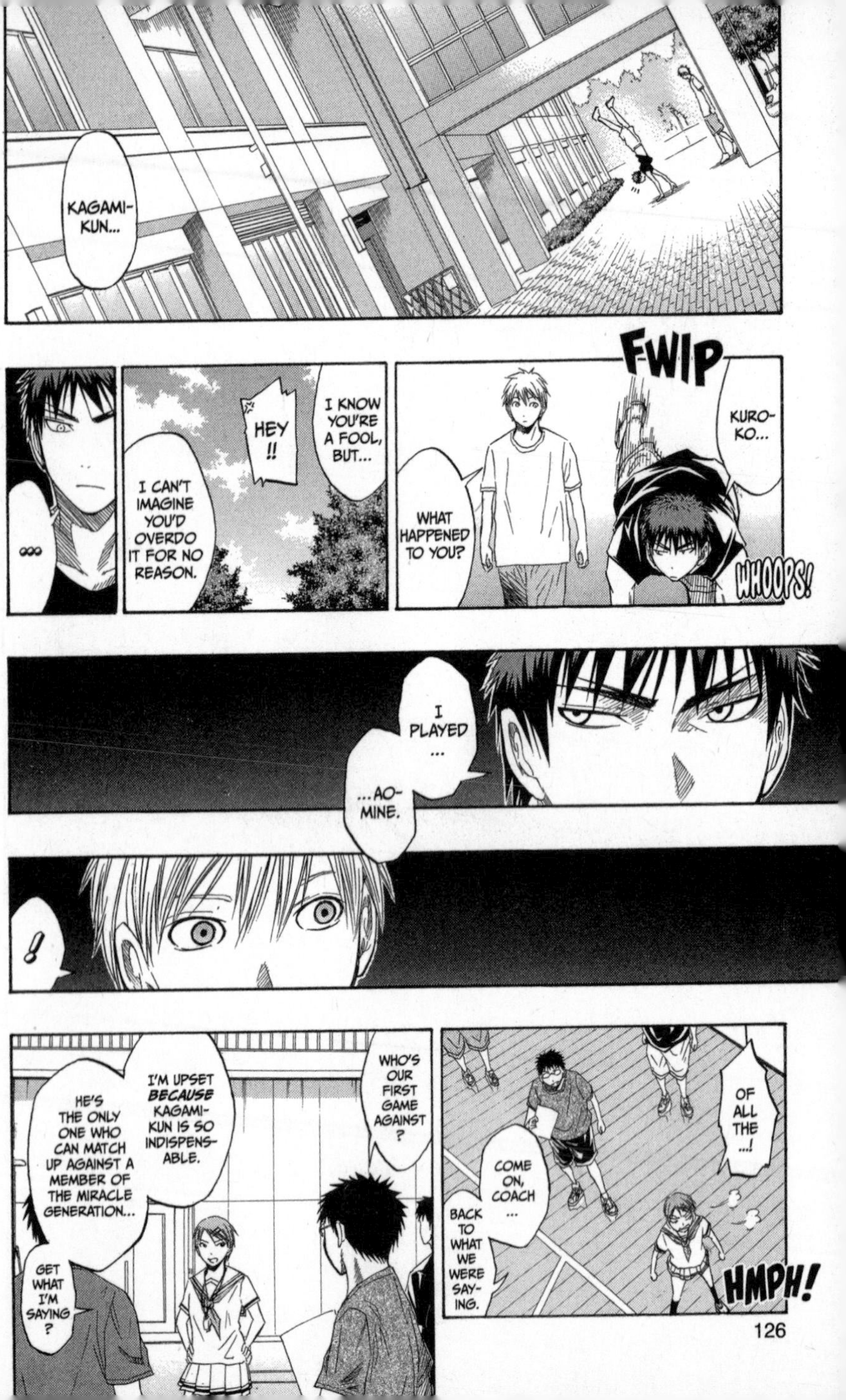
KAGAMI-KUN...
FWIP
KURO-KO...
WHOOPS!
WHAT HAPPENED TO YOU?
I KNOW YOU'RE A FOOL, BUT...
HEY !!
I CAN'T IMAGINE YOU'D OVERDO IT FOR NO REASON.
...
I PLAYED ...
...AO-MINE.
!
OF ALL THE ...!
HMPH!
COME ON, COACH ...
BACK TO WHAT WE WERE SAYING.
WHO'S OUR FIRST GAME AGAINST ?
I'M UPSET *BECAUSE* KAGAMI-KUN IS SO INDISPENSABLE.
HE'S THE ONLY ONE WHO CAN MATCH UP AGAINST A MEMBER OF THE MIRACLE GENERATION...
GET WHAT I'M SAYING ?

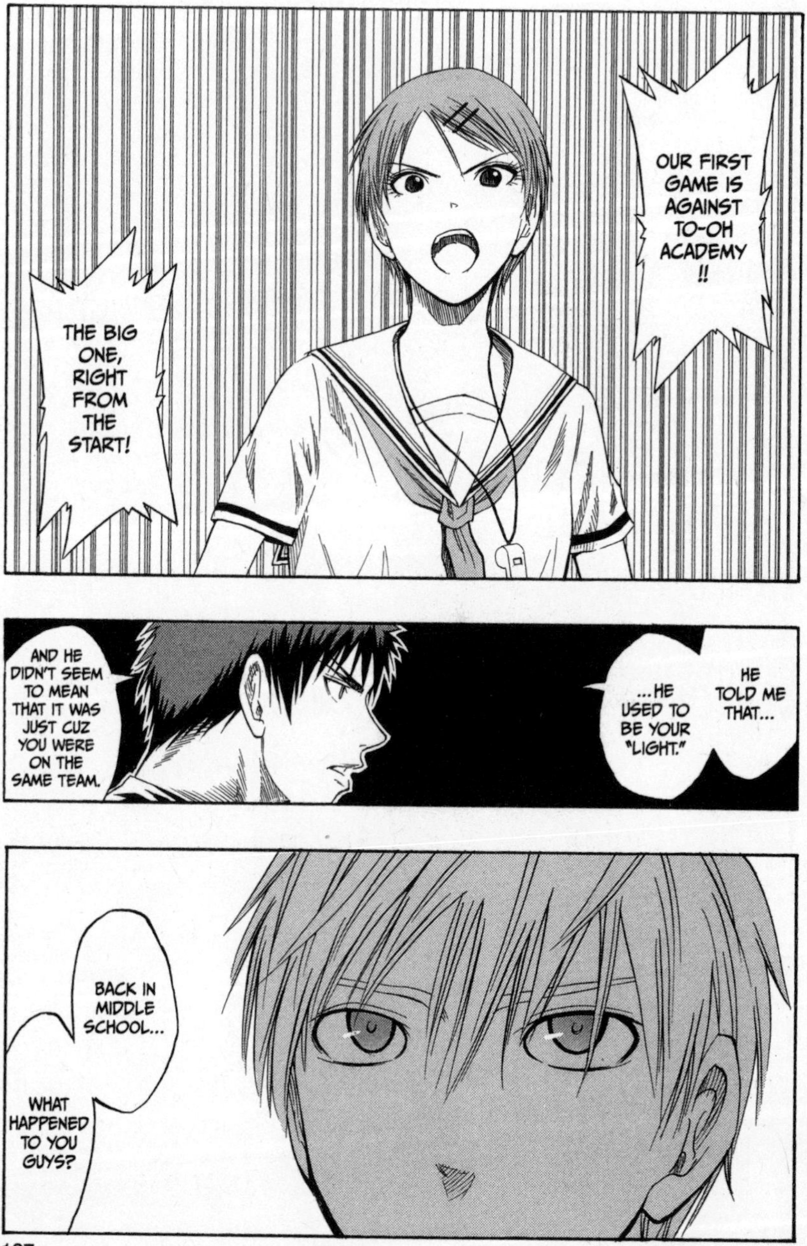
OUR FIRST GAME IS AGAINST TO-OH ACADEMY !!
THE BIG ONE, RIGHT FROM THE START!
HE TOLD ME THAT...
...HE USED TO BE YOUR "LIGHT."
AND HE DIDN'T SEEM TO MEAN THAT IT WAS JUST CUZ YOU WERE ON THE SAME TEAM.
BACK IN MIDDLE SCHOOL...
WHAT HAPPENED TO YOU GUYS?

KUROKO'S BASKETBALL BLOOPERS
TAKE 2

KAGAMI-KUN...
KURO-KO...
WHOOPS!
WHAT HAP-PENED...
BONK
...TO YOU?
SORRY, KURO... WHOA! THAT'S THE SECOND TIME I'VE KNOCKED YOU OUT!
WORMP
FWUMP

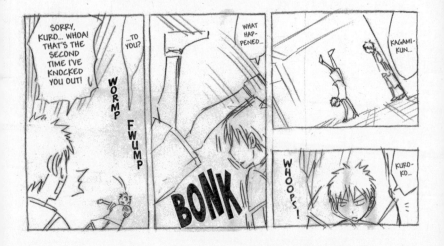

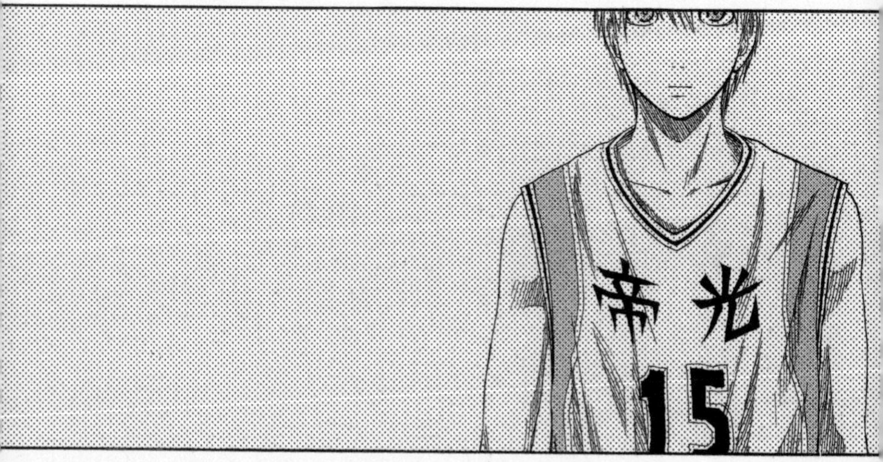

帝光
15

41ST QUARTER: IT'S "LEG," ACTUALLY

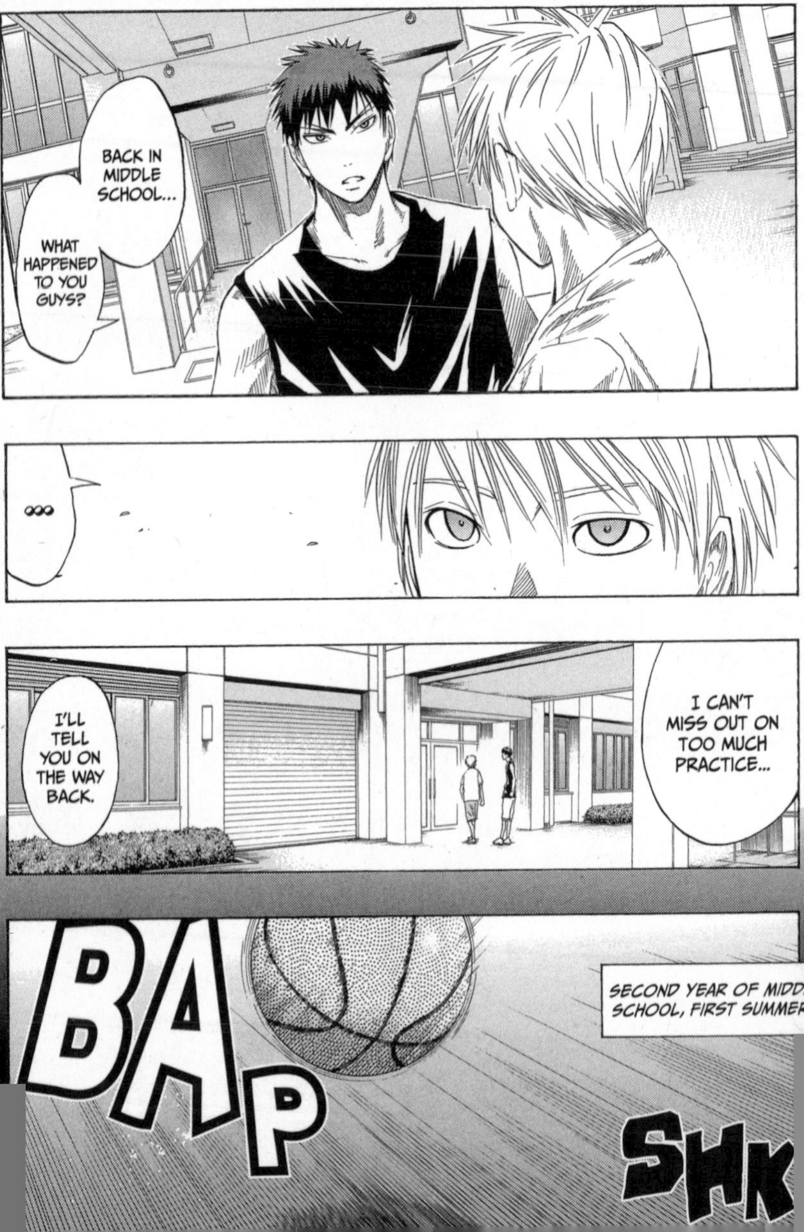
BACK IN MIDDLE SCHOOL...
WHAT HAPPENED TO YOU GUYS?
...
I CAN'T MISS OUT ON TOO MUCH PRACTICE...
I'LL TELL YOU ON THE WAY BACK.
SECOND YEAR OF MIDDLE SCHOOL, FIRST SUMMER...
SHK
BAP

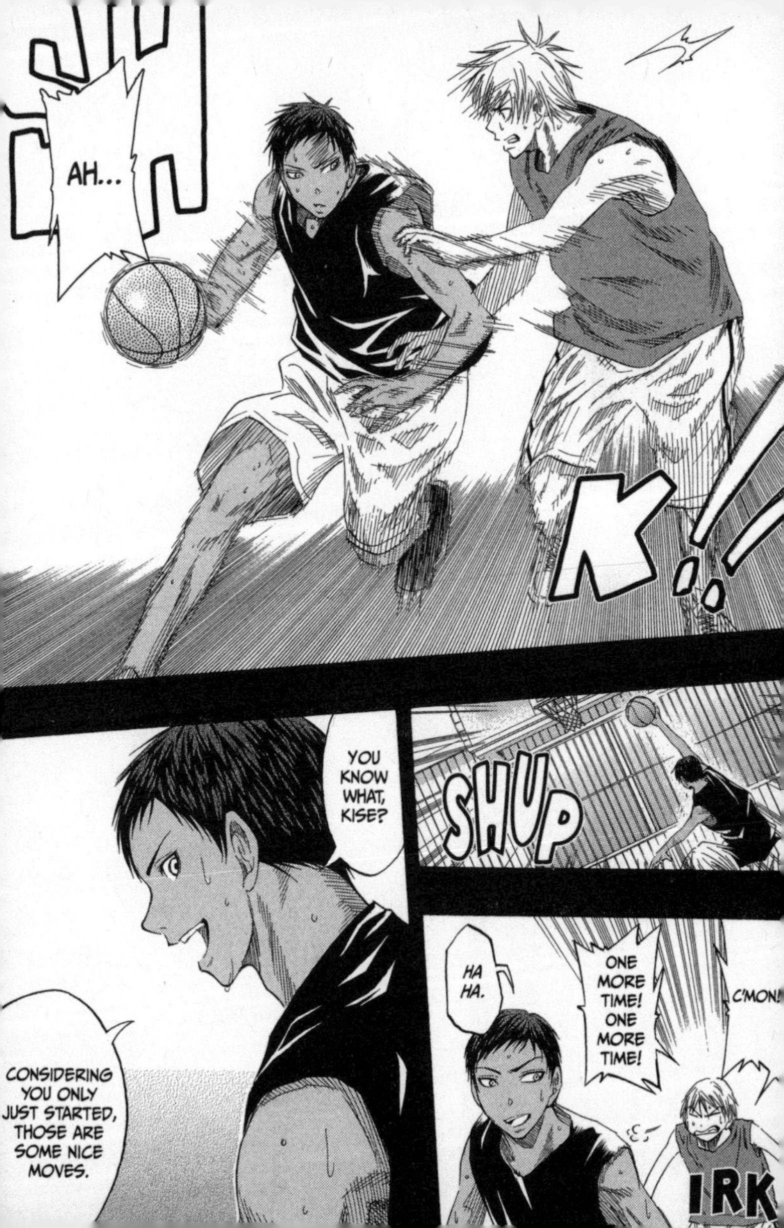
K!!
AH...
SHUP
C'MON!
ONE MORE TIME! ONE MORE TIME!
HA HA.
IRK
YOU KNOW WHAT, KISE?
CONSIDERING YOU ONLY JUST STARTED, THOSE ARE SOME NICE MOVES.

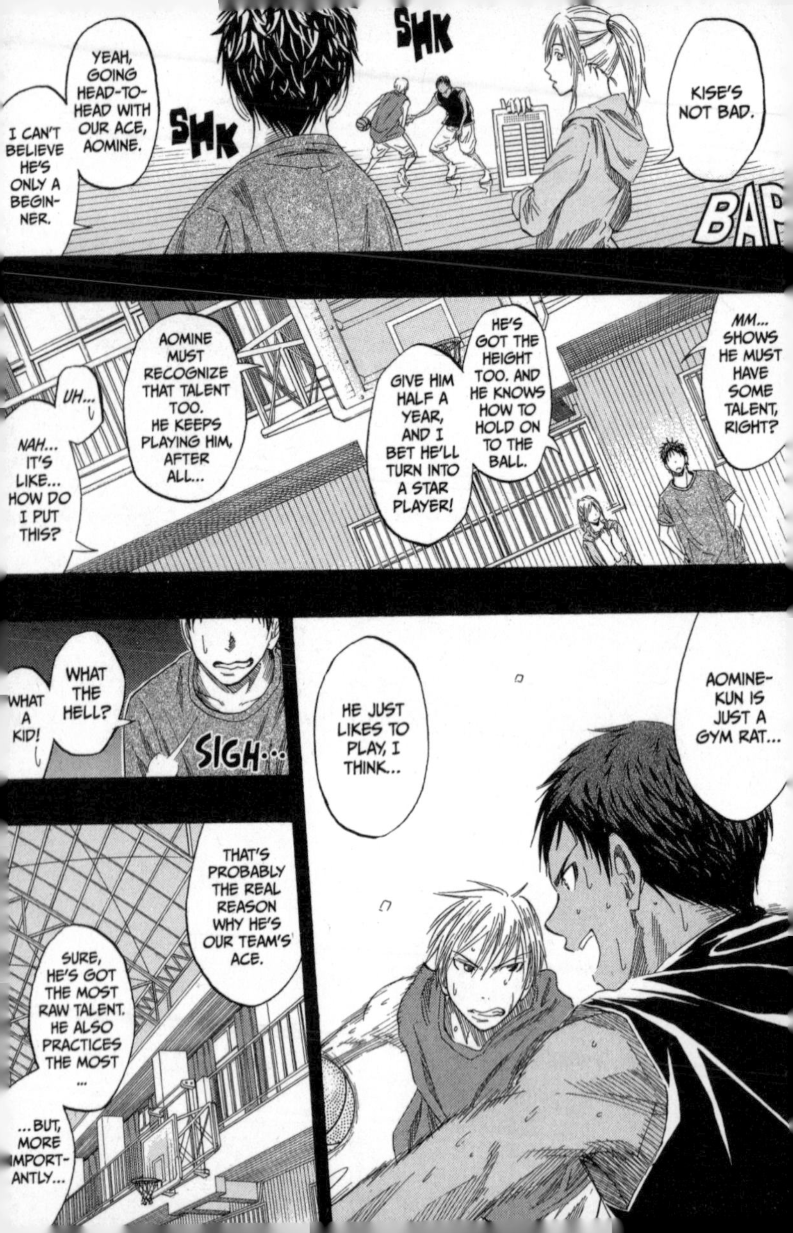
KISE'S NOT BAD.
SHK
SHK
YEAH, GOING HEAD-TO-HEAD WITH OUR ACE, AOMINE.
I CAN'T BELIEVE HE'S ONLY A BEGINNER.
BAP
MM... SHOWS HE MUST HAVE SOME TALENT, RIGHT?
HE'S GOT THE HEIGHT TOO. AND HE KNOWS HOW TO HOLD ON TO THE BALL.
GIVE HIM HALF A YEAR, AND I BET HE'LL TURN INTO A STAR PLAYER!
AOMINE MUST RECOGNIZE THAT TALENT TOO. HE KEEPS PLAYING HIM, AFTER ALL...
UH...
NAH... IT'S LIKE... HOW DO I PUT THIS?
AOMINE-KUN IS JUST A GYM RAT...
HE JUST LIKES TO PLAY, I THINK...
WHAT THE HELL?
WHAT A KID!
SIGH...
THAT'S PROBABLY THE REAL REASON WHY HE'S OUR TEAM'S ACE.
SURE, HE'S GOT THE MOST RAW TALENT. HE ALSO PRACTICES THE MOST ...
...BUT, MORE IMPORTANTLY...

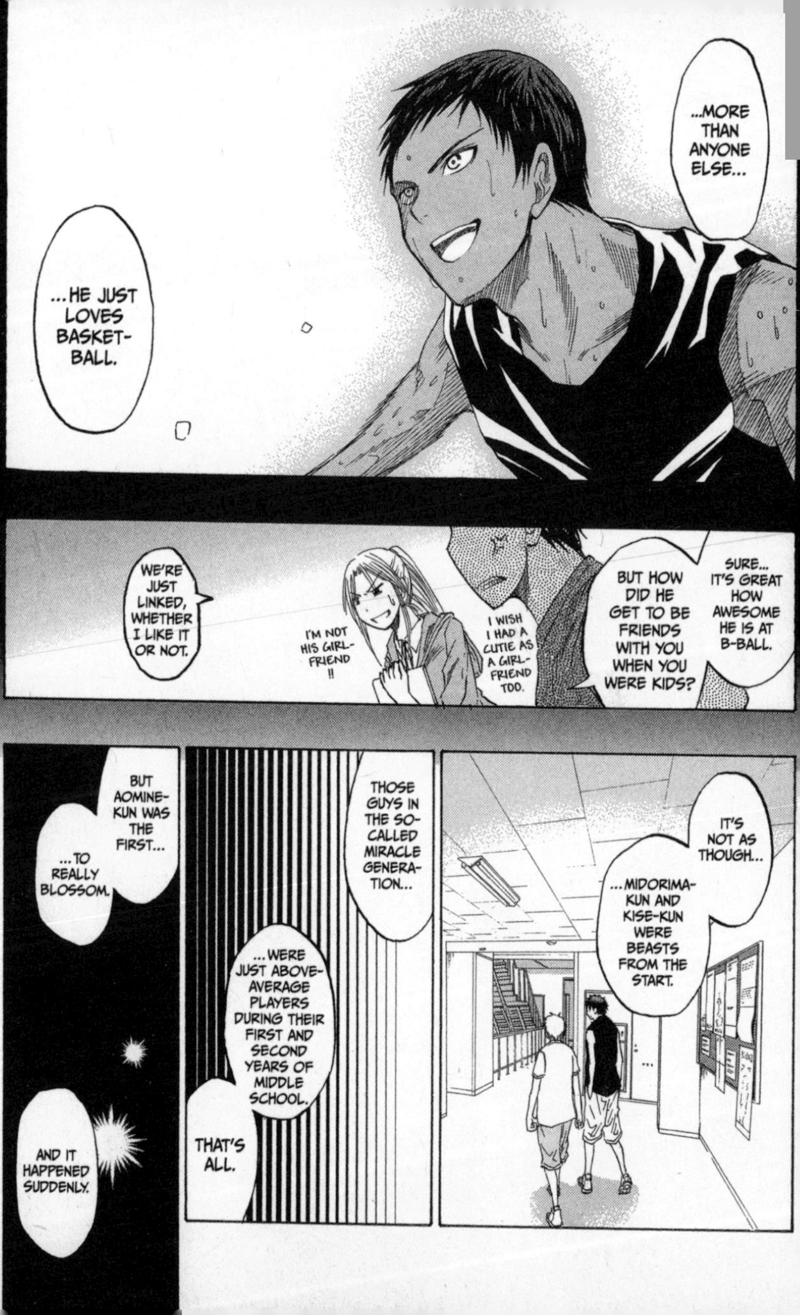
...MORE THAN ANYONE ELSE...
...HE JUST LOVES BASKET-BALL.
SURE... IT'S GREAT HOW AWESOME HE IS AT B-BALL.
BUT HOW DID HE GET TO BE FRIENDS WITH YOU WHEN YOU WERE KIDS?
I WISH I HAD A CUTIE AS A GIRL-FRIEND TOO.
I'M NOT HIS GIRL-FRIEND !!
WE'RE JUST LINKED, WHETHER I LIKE IT OR NOT.
IT'S NOT AS THOUGH...
...MIDORIMA-KUN AND KISE-KUN WERE BEASTS FROM THE START.
...
THOSE GUYS IN THE SO-CALLED MIRACLE GENERA-TION...
...WERE JUST ABOVE-AVERAGE PLAYERS DURING THEIR FIRST AND SECOND YEARS OF MIDDLE SCHOOL.
THAT'S ALL.
BUT AOMINE-KUN WAS THE FIRST...
...TO REALLY BLOSSOM.
AND IT HAPPENED SUDDENLY.

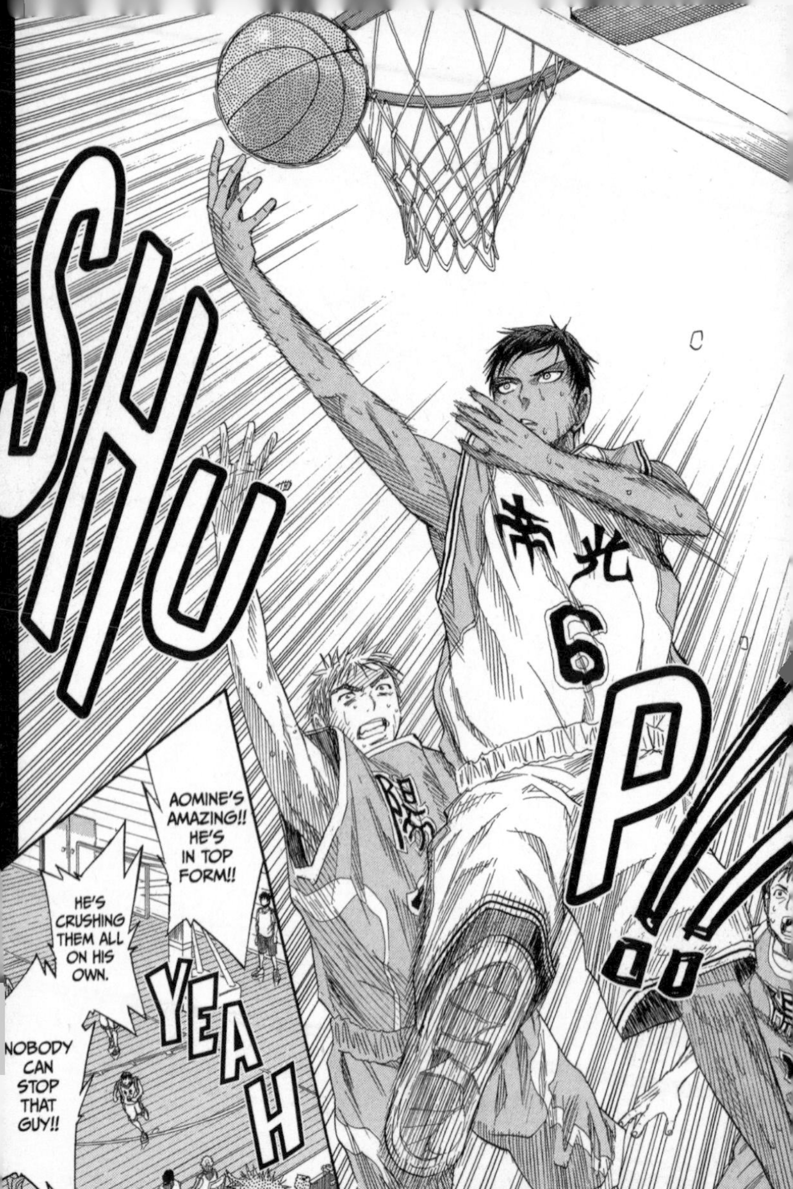
SHUP!!
AOMINE'S AMAZING!! HE'S IN TOP FORM!!
HE'S CRUSHING THEM ALL ON HIS OWN.
YEAH
NOBODY CAN STOP THAT GUY!!

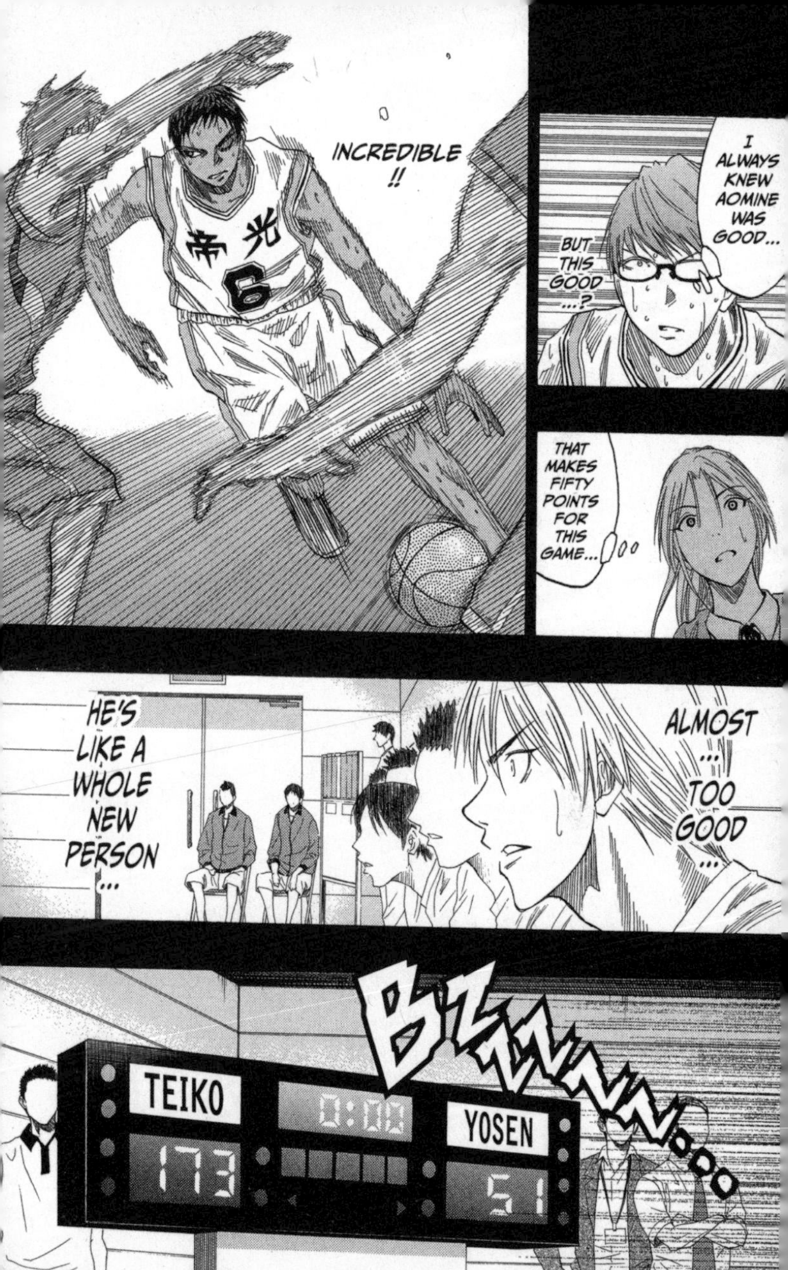
I ALWAYS KNEW AOMINE WAS GOOD...
BUT THIS GOOD ...?
THAT MAKES FIFTY POINTS FOR THIS GAME...
INCREDIBLE !!
ALMOST ... TOO GOOD ...
HE'S LIKE A WHOLE NEW PERSON ...
BZZNNN...
TEIKO
0:00
YOSEN
173
51

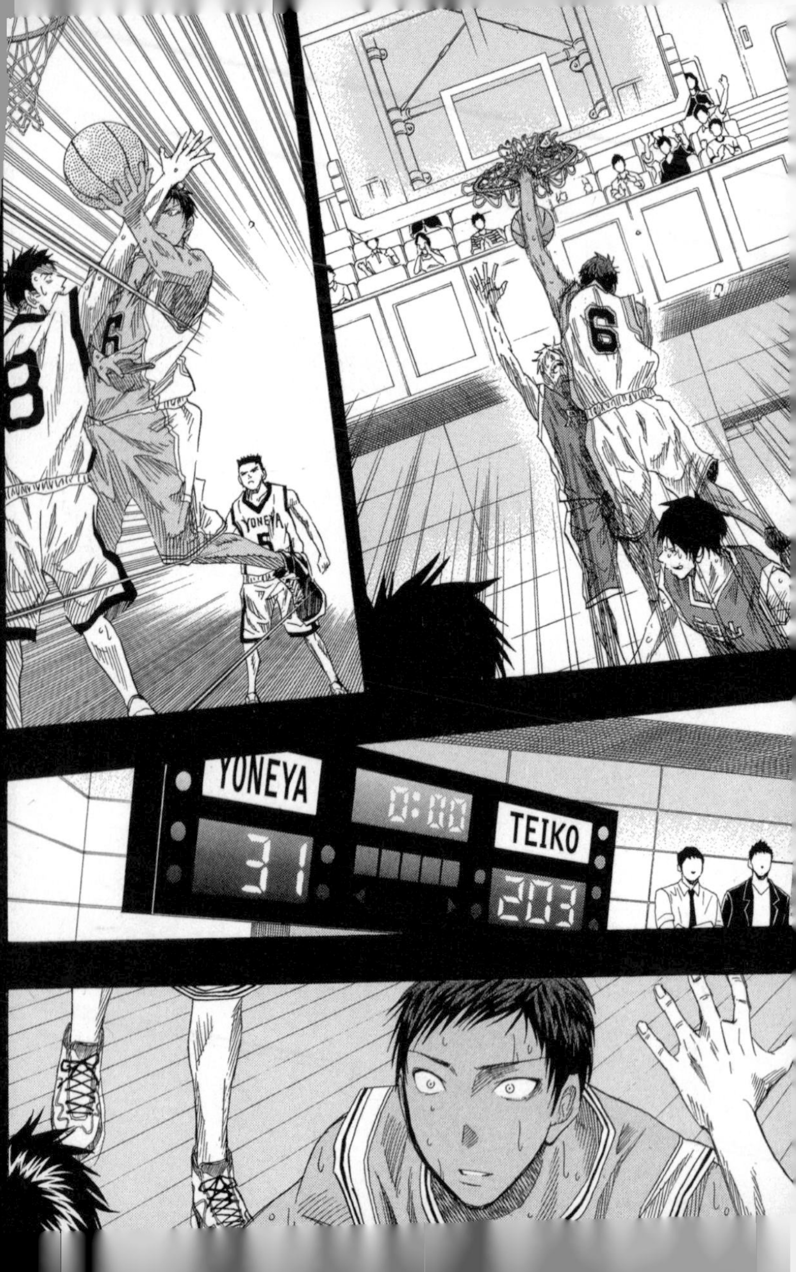
YONEYA
YONEYA
0:00
TEIKO
31
203

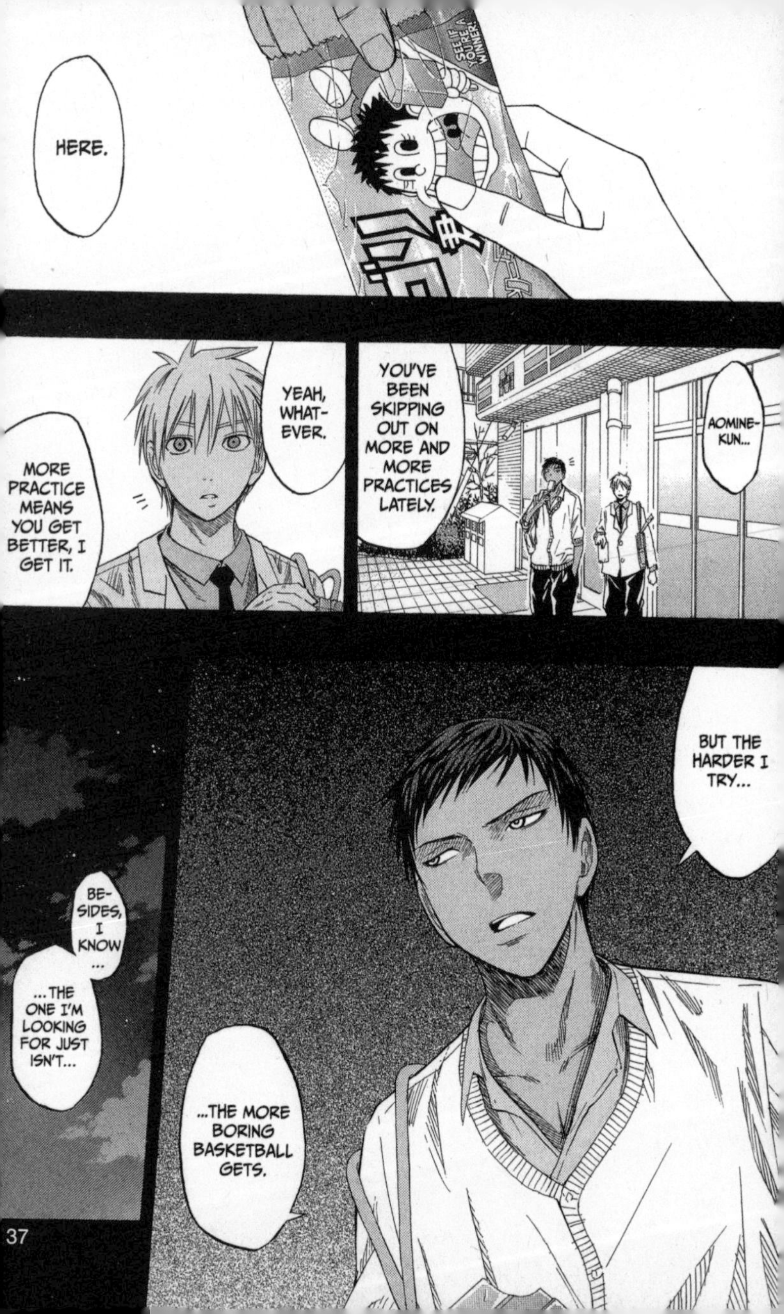
HERE.
SEE IF YOU'RE A WINNER!
AOMINE-KUN...
YOU'VE BEEN SKIPPING OUT ON MORE AND MORE PRACTICES LATELY.
YEAH, WHAT-EVER.
MORE PRACTICE MEANS YOU GET BETTER, I GET IT.
BUT THE HARDER I TRY...
...THE MORE BORING BASKETBALL GETS.
BE-SIDES, I KNOW...
...THE ONE I'M LOOKING FOR JUST ISN'T...

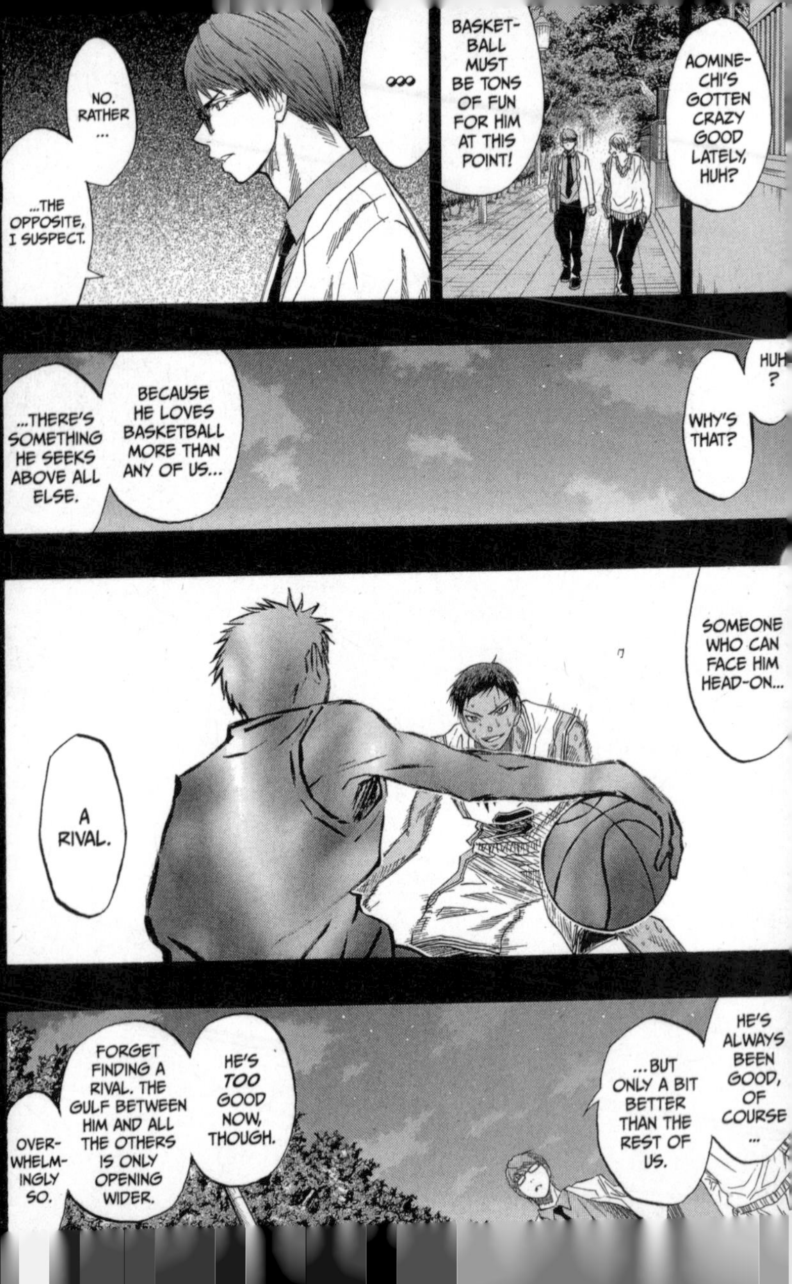
AOMINE-CHI'S GOTTEN CRAZY GOOD LATELY, HUH?
BASKETBALL MUST BE TONS OF FUN FOR HIM AT THIS POINT!
...
NO. RATHER...
...THE OPPOSITE, I SUSPECT.
HUH?
WHY'S THAT?
BECAUSE HE LOVES BASKETBALL MORE THAN ANY OF US...
...THERE'S SOMETHING HE SEEKS ABOVE ALL ELSE.
SOMEONE WHO CAN FACE HIM HEAD-ON...
A RIVAL.
HE'S ALWAYS BEEN GOOD, OF COURSE...
...BUT ONLY A BIT BETTER THAN THE REST OF US.
HE'S *TOO* GOOD NOW, THOUGH.
FORGET FINDING A RIVAL. THE GULF BETWEEN HIM AND ALL THE OTHERS IS ONLY OPENING WIDER.
OVERWHELMINGLY SO.

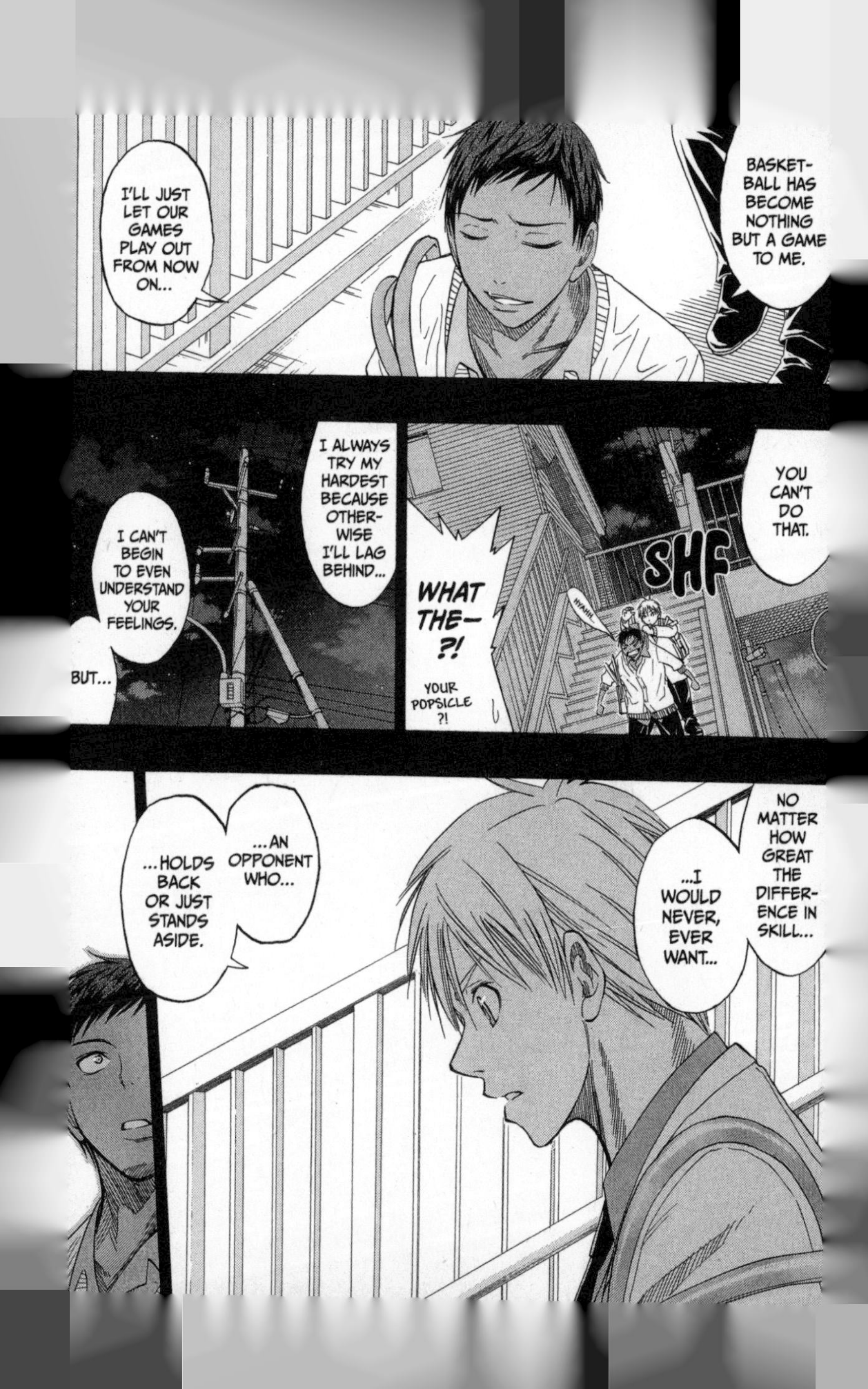
BASKET-BALL HAS BECOME NOTHING BUT A GAME TO ME.
I'LL JUST LET OUR GAMES PLAY OUT FROM NOW ON...
YOU CAN'T DO THAT.
SHF
WHAT THE—?!
YOUR POPSICLE ?!
I ALWAYS TRY MY HARDEST BECAUSE OTHER-WISE I'LL LAG BEHIND...
I CAN'T BEGIN TO EVEN UNDERSTAND YOUR FEELINGS.
BUT...
NO MATTER HOW GREAT THE DIFFER-ENCE IN SKILL...
...I WOULD NEVER, EVER WANT...
...AN OPPONENT WHO...
...HOLDS BACK OR JUST STANDS ASIDE.

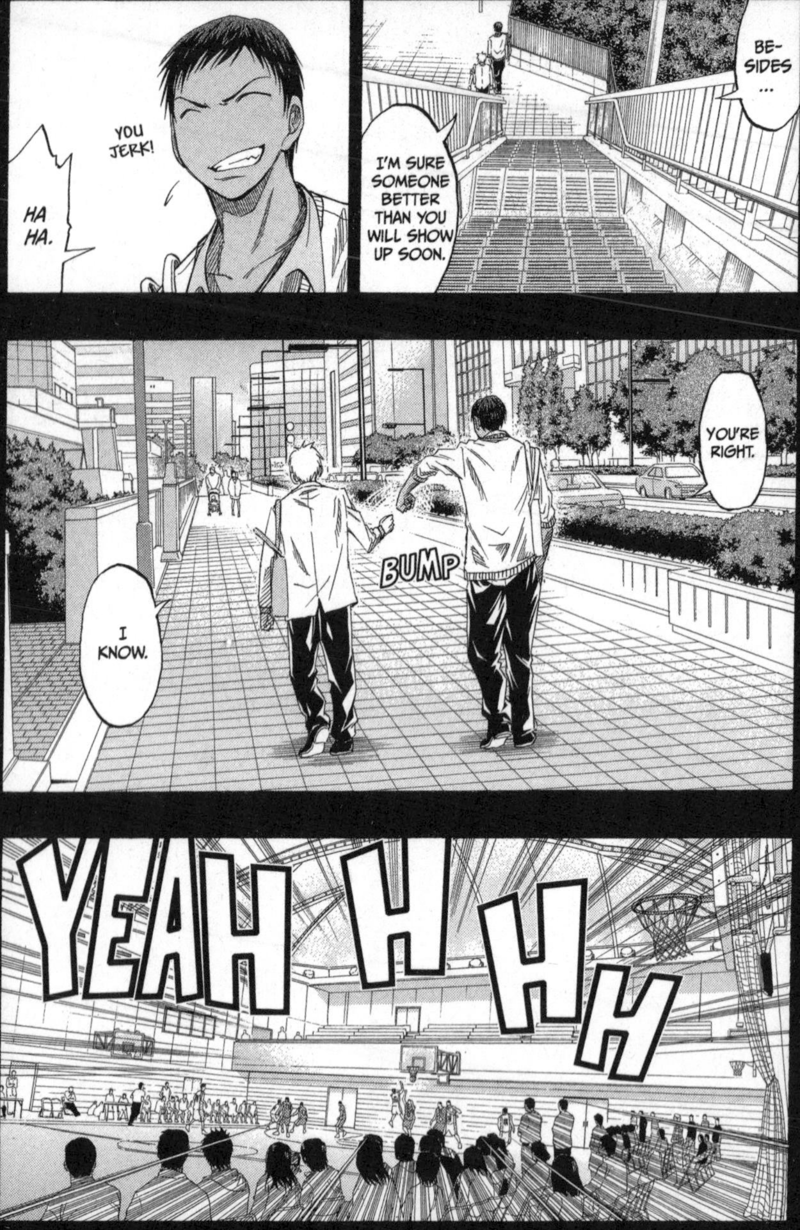
BE-SIDES ...
I'M SURE SOMEONE BETTER THAN YOU WILL SHOW UP SOON.
YOU JERK!
HA HA.
YOU'RE RIGHT.
BUMP
I KNOW.
YEAH H H H

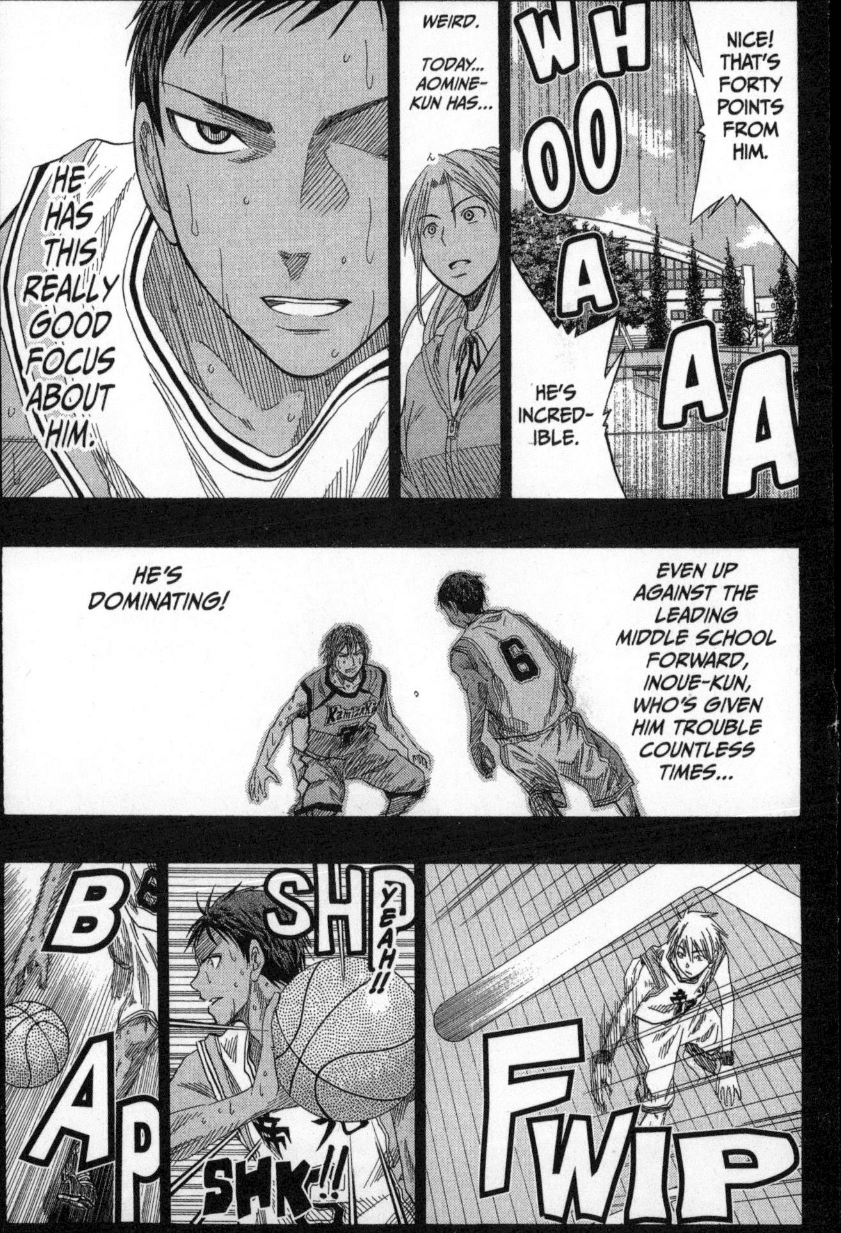
WHOOAAAA
NICE! THAT'S FORTY POINTS FROM HIM.
HE'S INCRED-IBLE.
WEIRD.
TODAY... AOMINE-KUN HAS...
HE HAS THIS REALLY GOOD FOCUS ABOUT HIM.
EVEN UP AGAINST THE LEADING MIDDLE SCHOOL FORWARD, INOUE-KUN, WHO'S GIVEN HIM TROUBLE COUNTLESS TIMES...
HE'S DOMINATING!
FWIP
SHP
YEAH!!
SHK!!
BAP

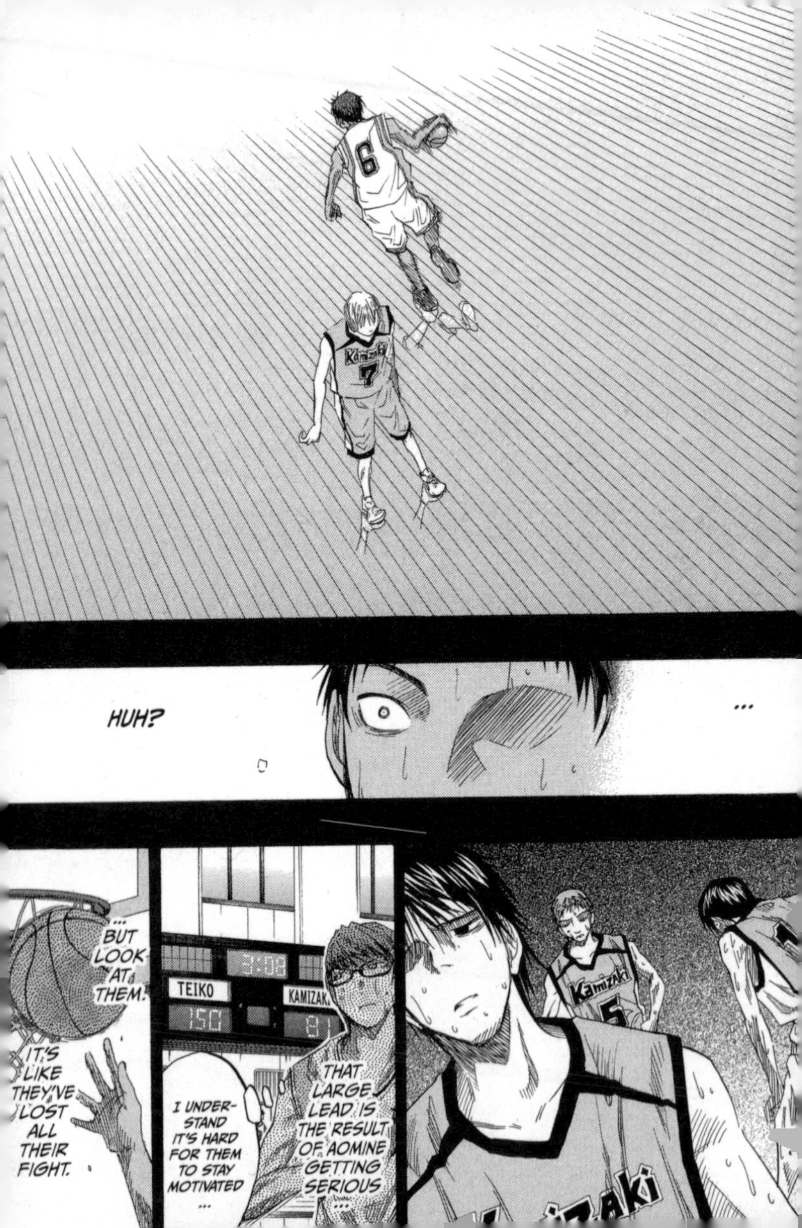
...
HUH?
THAT LARGE LEAD IS THE RESULT OF AOMINE GETTING SERIOUS...
I UNDERSTAND IT'S HARD FOR THEM TO STAY MOTIVATED...
3:08
TEIKO
KAMIZAKI
150
81
...BUT LOOK AT THEM!
IT'S LIKE THEY'VE LOST ALL THEIR FIGHT.

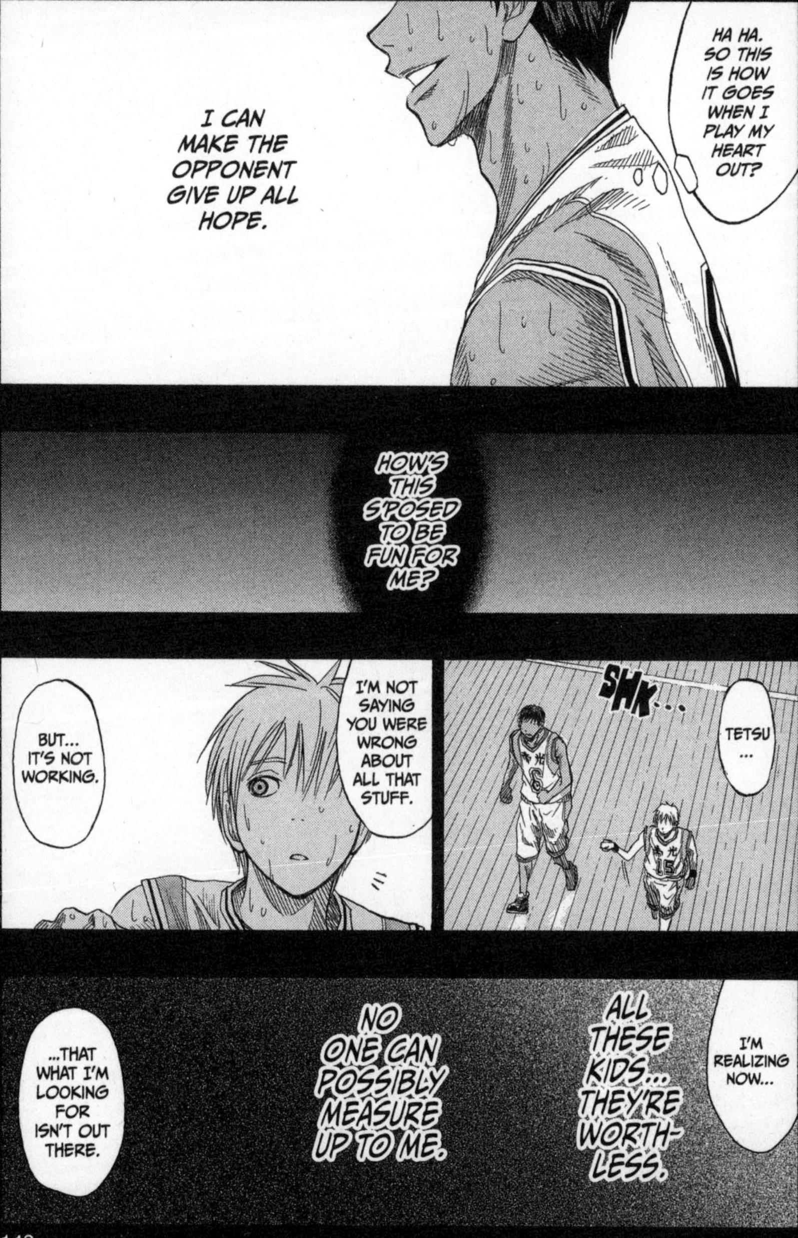
HA HA. SO THIS IS HOW IT GOES WHEN I PLAY MY HEART OUT?
I CAN MAKE THE OPPONENT GIVE UP ALL HOPE.
HOW'S THIS S'POSED TO BE FUN FOR ME?
SHK...
TETSU...
I'M NOT SAYING YOU WERE WRONG ABOUT ALL THAT STUFF.
BUT... IT'S NOT WORKING.
I'M REALIZING NOW...
ALL THESE KIDS... THEY'RE WORTH-LESS.
NO ONE CAN POSSIBLY MEASURE UP TO ME.
...THAT WHAT I'M LOOKING FOR ISN'T OUT THERE.

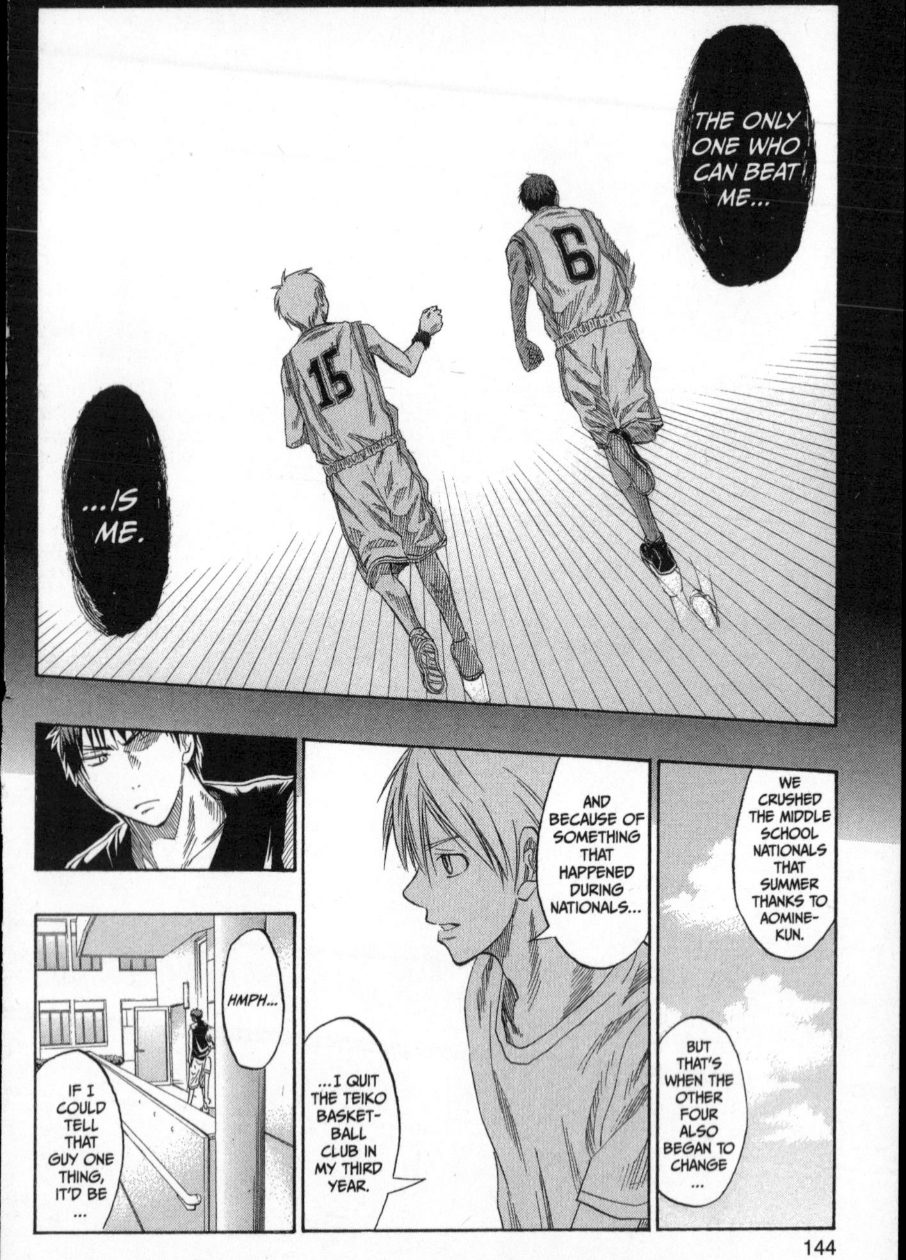
THE ONLY ONE WHO CAN BEAT ME...
...IS ME.
WE CRUSHED THE MIDDLE SCHOOL NATIONALS THAT SUMMER THANKS TO AOMINE-KUN.
BUT THAT'S WHEN THE OTHER FOUR ALSO BEGAN TO CHANGE...
AND BECAUSE OF SOMETHING THAT HAPPENED DURING NATIONALS...
...I QUIT THE TEIKO BASKET-BALL CLUB IN MY THIRD YEAR.
HMPH...
IF I COULD TELL THAT GUY ONE THING, IT'D BE...

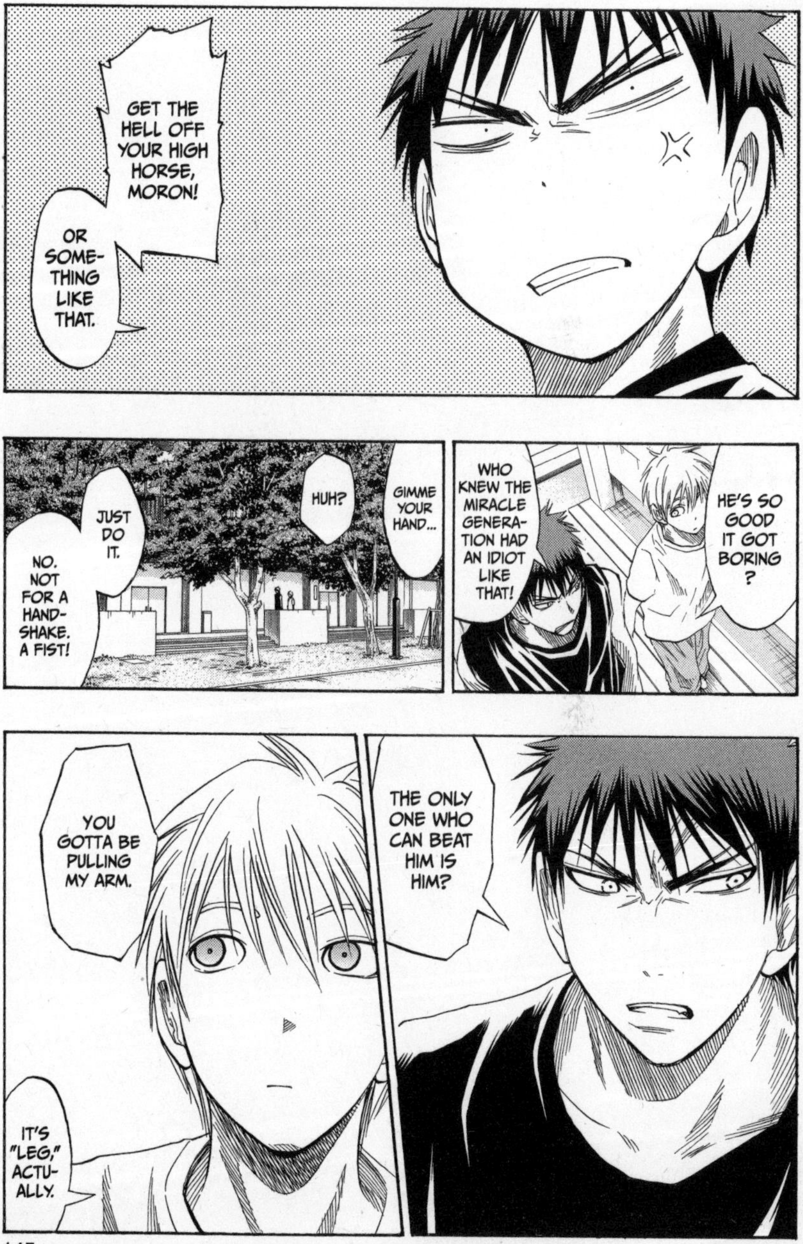
GET THE HELL OFF YOUR HIGH HORSE, MORON!
OR SOMETHING LIKE THAT.
HE'S SO GOOD IT GOT BORING?
WHO KNEW THE MIRACLE GENERATION HAD AN IDIOT LIKE THAT!
GIMME YOUR HAND...
HUH?
JUST DO IT.
NO. NOT FOR A HANDSHAKE. A FIST!
THE ONLY ONE WHO CAN BEAT HIM IS HIM?
YOU GOTTA BE PULLING MY ARM.
IT'S "LEG," ACTUALLY.

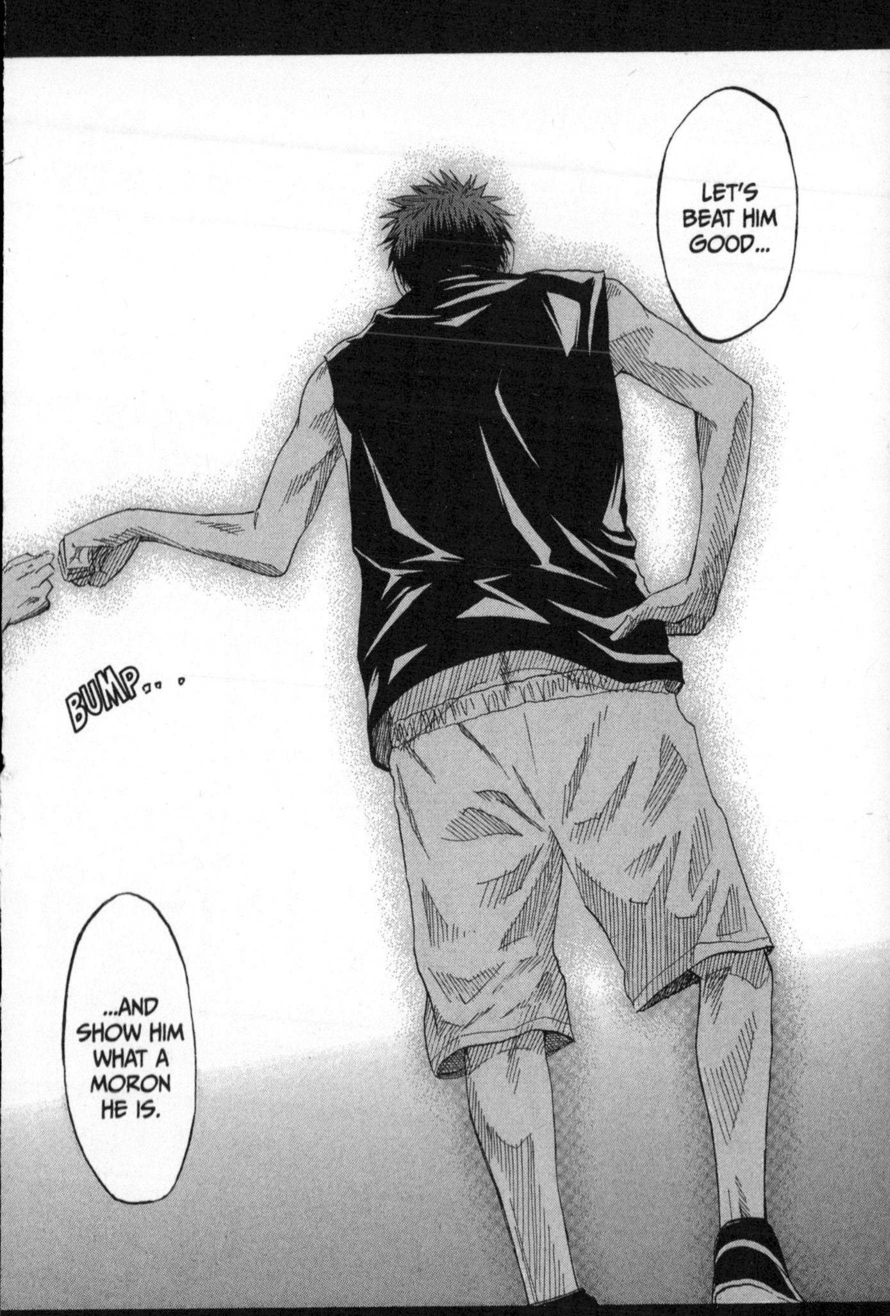
LET'S BEAT HIM GOOD...
BUMP...
...AND SHOW HIM WHAT A MORON HE IS.

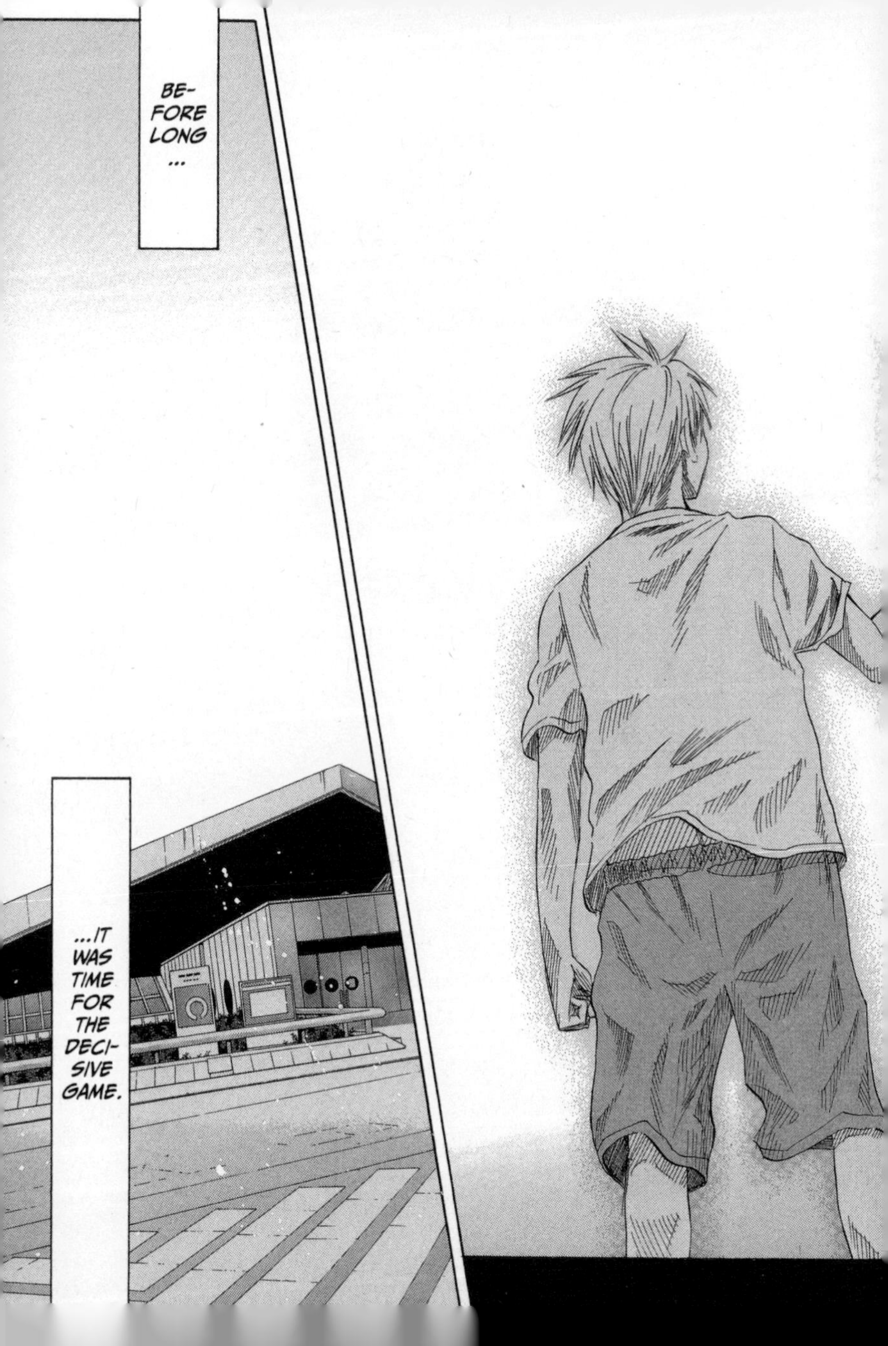
BE-FORE LONG ...
...IT WAS TIME FOR THE DECI-SIVE GAME.

KUROKO'S BASKETBALL BLOOPERS
TAKE 18

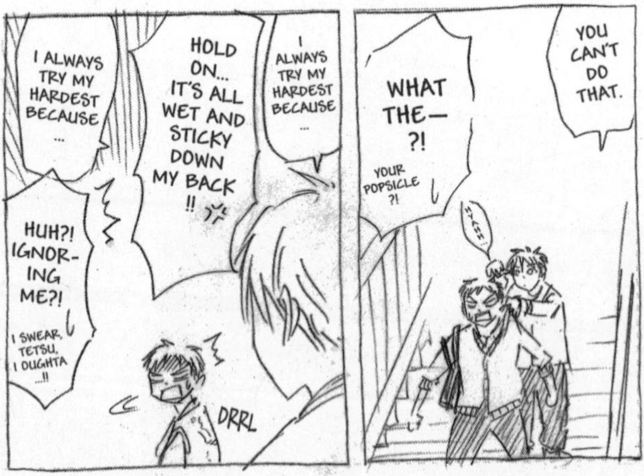
YOU CAN'T DO THAT.
WHAT THE—?!
YOUR POPSICLE ?!
I ALWAYS TRY MY HARDEST BECAUSE ...
HOLD ON... IT'S ALL WET AND STICKY DOWN MY BACK!!
I ALWAYS TRY MY HARDEST BECAUSE ...
HUH?! IGNOR-ING ME?!
I SWEAR, TETSU, I OUGHTA ...!!
DRRL

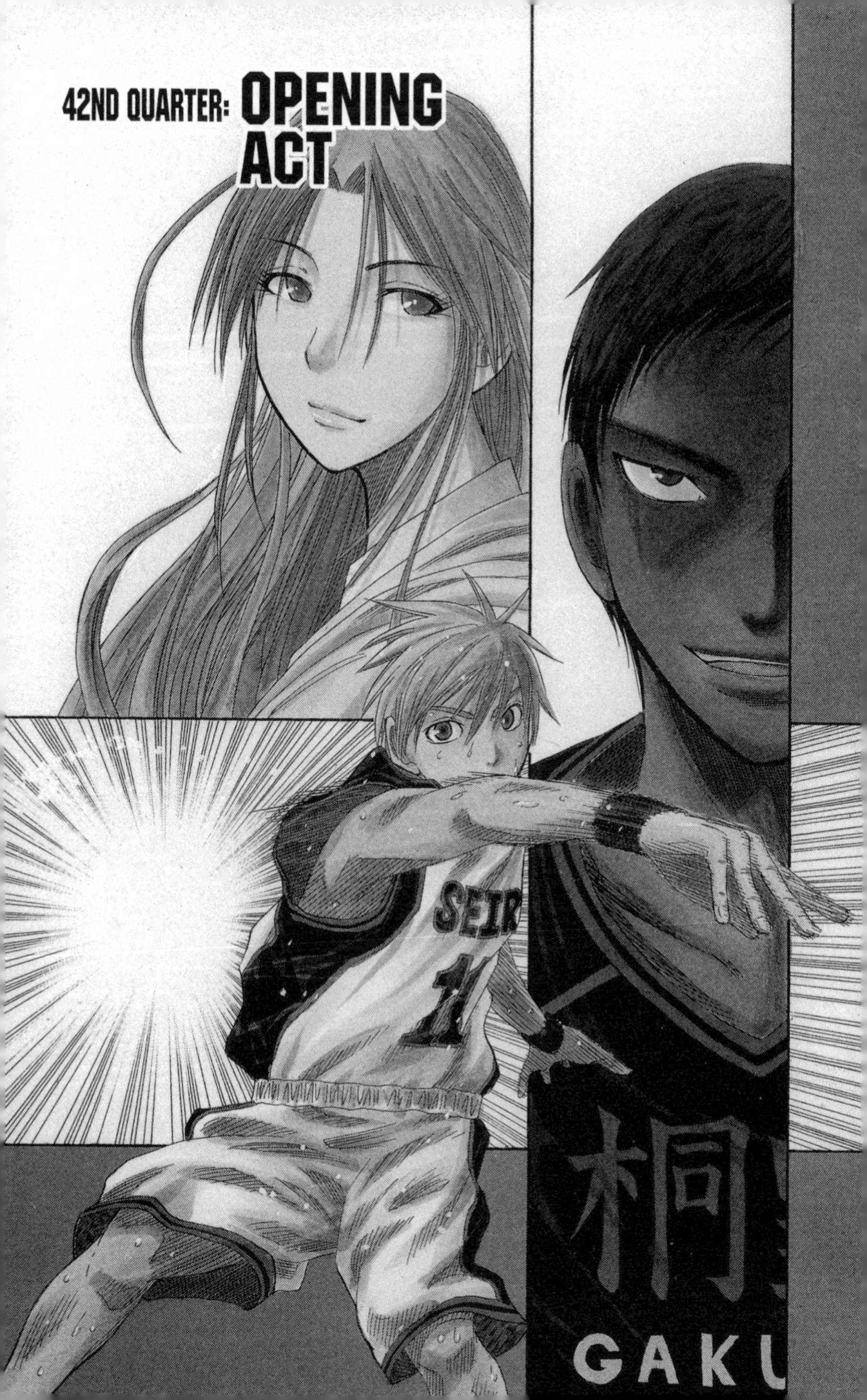
42ND QUARTER: OPENING ACT
SEIR
11
桐
GAKU

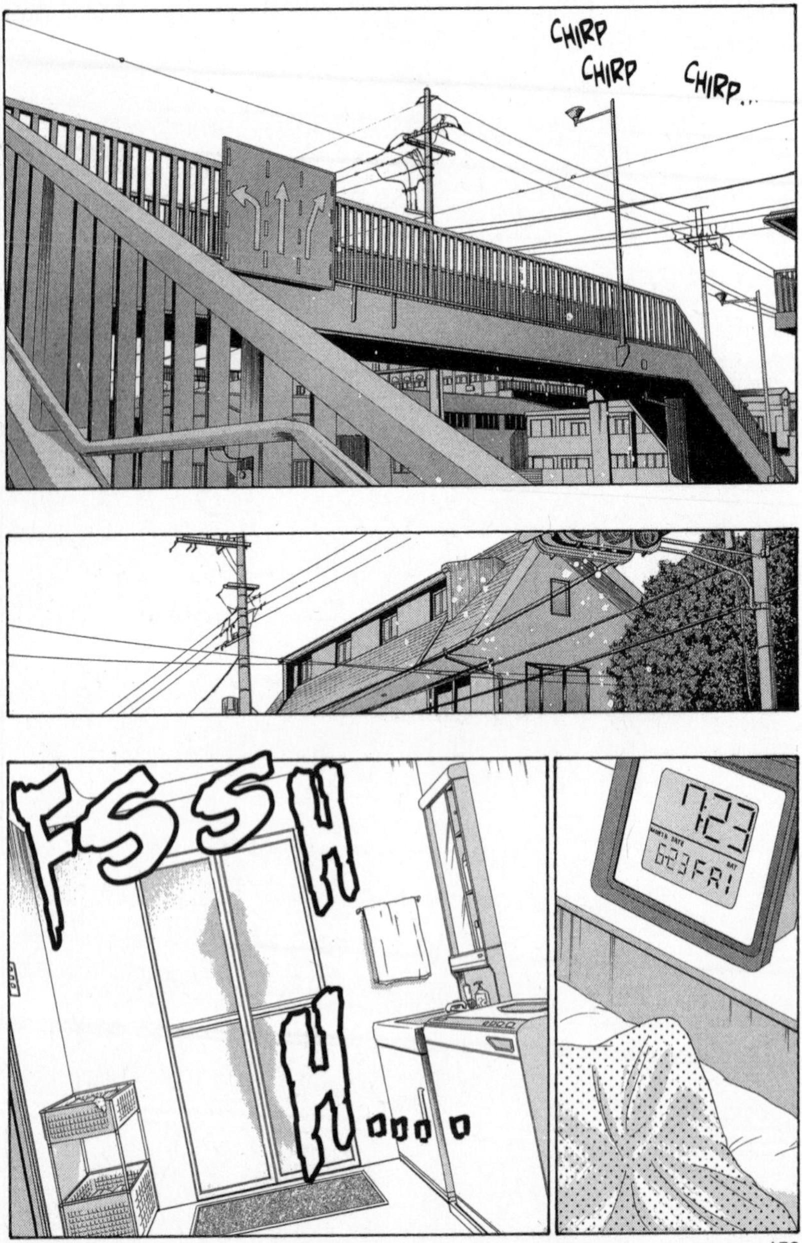
CHIRP
CHIRP
CHIRP...
7:23
6 23 FRI
FSSH
H

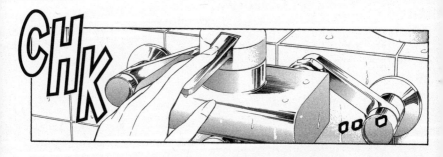

CHK

I'LL BEAT AOMINE-KUN.

I PROMISE.

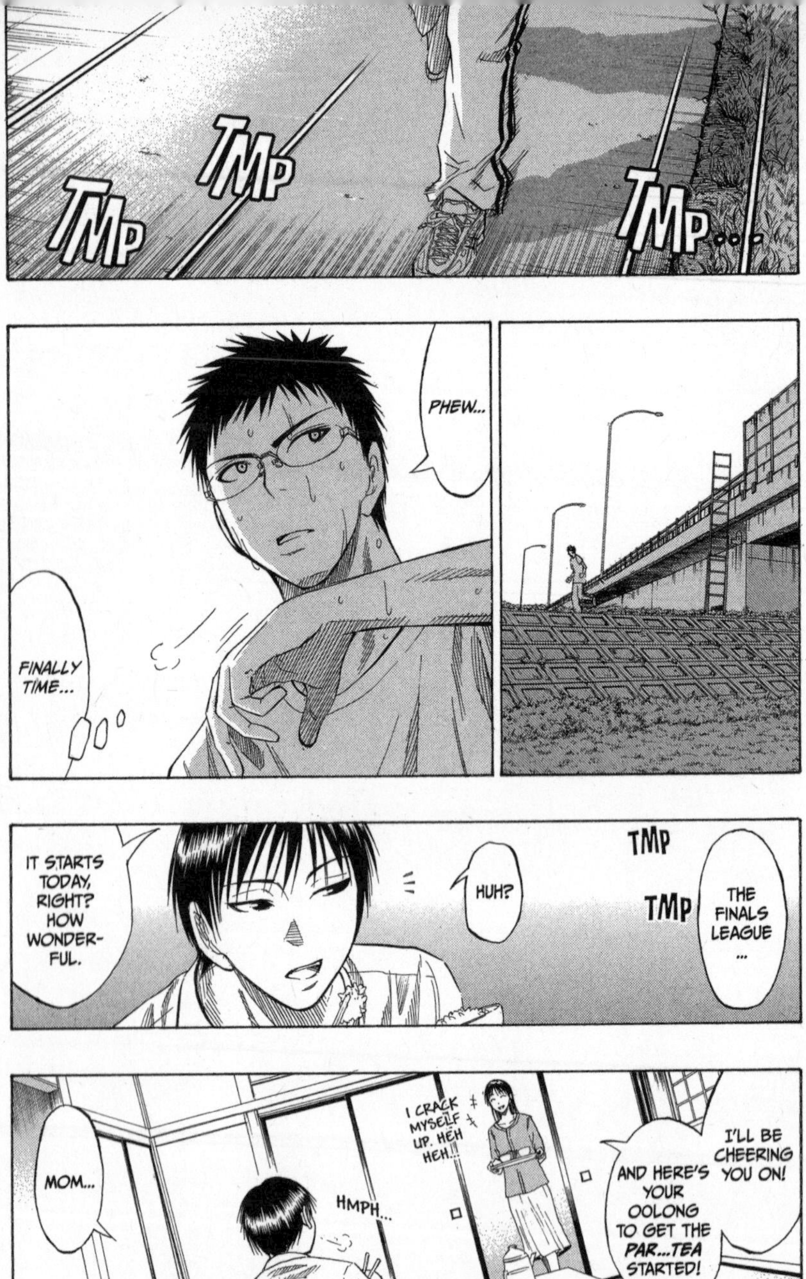
TMP...
TMP
TMP
PHEW...
FINALLY TIME...
THE FINALS LEAGUE...
TMP
TMP
HUH?
IT STARTS TODAY, RIGHT? HOW WONDERFUL.
I'LL BE CHEERING YOU ON!
AND HERE'S YOUR OOLONG TO GET THE *PAR...TEA* STARTED!
I CRACK MYSELF UP. HEH HEH...
HMPH...
MOM...

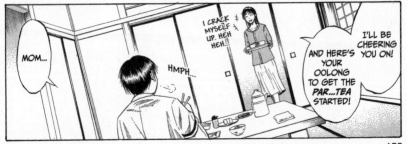

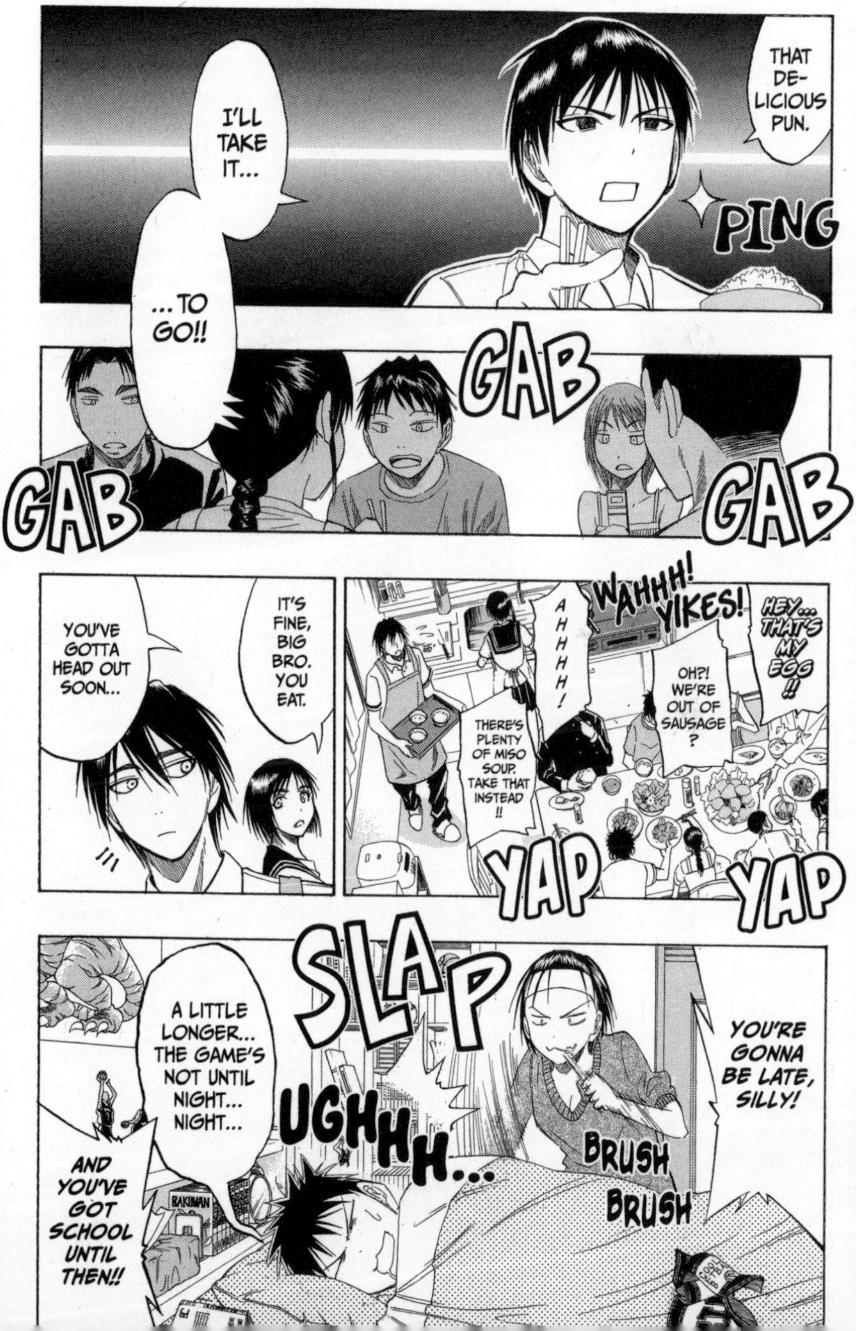
THAT DE-LICIOUS PUN.
PING
I'LL TAKE IT...
...TO GO!!
GAB
GAB
GAB
HEY... THAT'S MY EGG!!
WAHHH! YIKES!
OH?! WE'RE OUT OF SAUSAGE?
AHHHHH!
THERE'S PLENTY OF MISO SOUP. TAKE THAT INSTEAD!!
YAP
YAP
IT'S FINE, BIG BRO. YOU EAT.
YOU'VE GOTTA HEAD OUT SOON...
YOU'RE GONNA BE LATE, SILLY!
SLAP
BRUSH
BRUSH
UGHHH...
A LITTLE LONGER... THE GAME'S NOT UNTIL NIGHT... NIGHT...
AND YOU'VE GOT SCHOOL UNTIL THEN!!
BAKUMAN

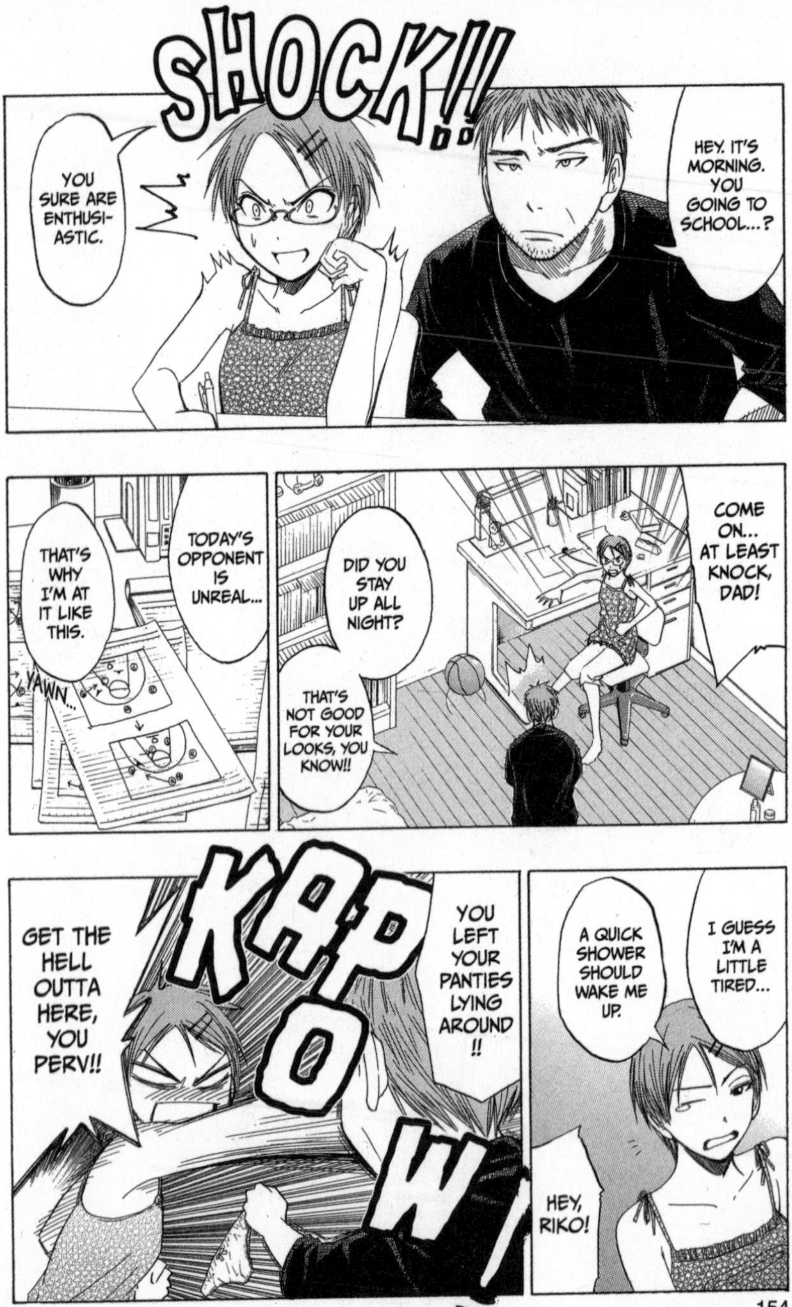
HEY. IT'S MORNING. YOU GOING TO SCHOOL...?
SHOCK!!
YOU SURE ARE ENTHUSI-ASTIC.
COME ON... AT LEAST KNOCK, DAD!
DID YOU STAY UP ALL NIGHT?
THAT'S NOT GOOD FOR YOUR LOOKS, YOU KNOW!!
TODAY'S OPPONENT IS UNREAL...
THAT'S WHY I'M AT IT LIKE THIS.
YAWN...
I GUESS I'M A LITTLE TIRED...
A QUICK SHOWER SHOULD WAKE ME UP.
HEY, RIKO!
YOU LEFT YOUR PANTIES LYING AROUND!!
KAPOW!
GET THE HELL OUTTA HERE, YOU PERV!!

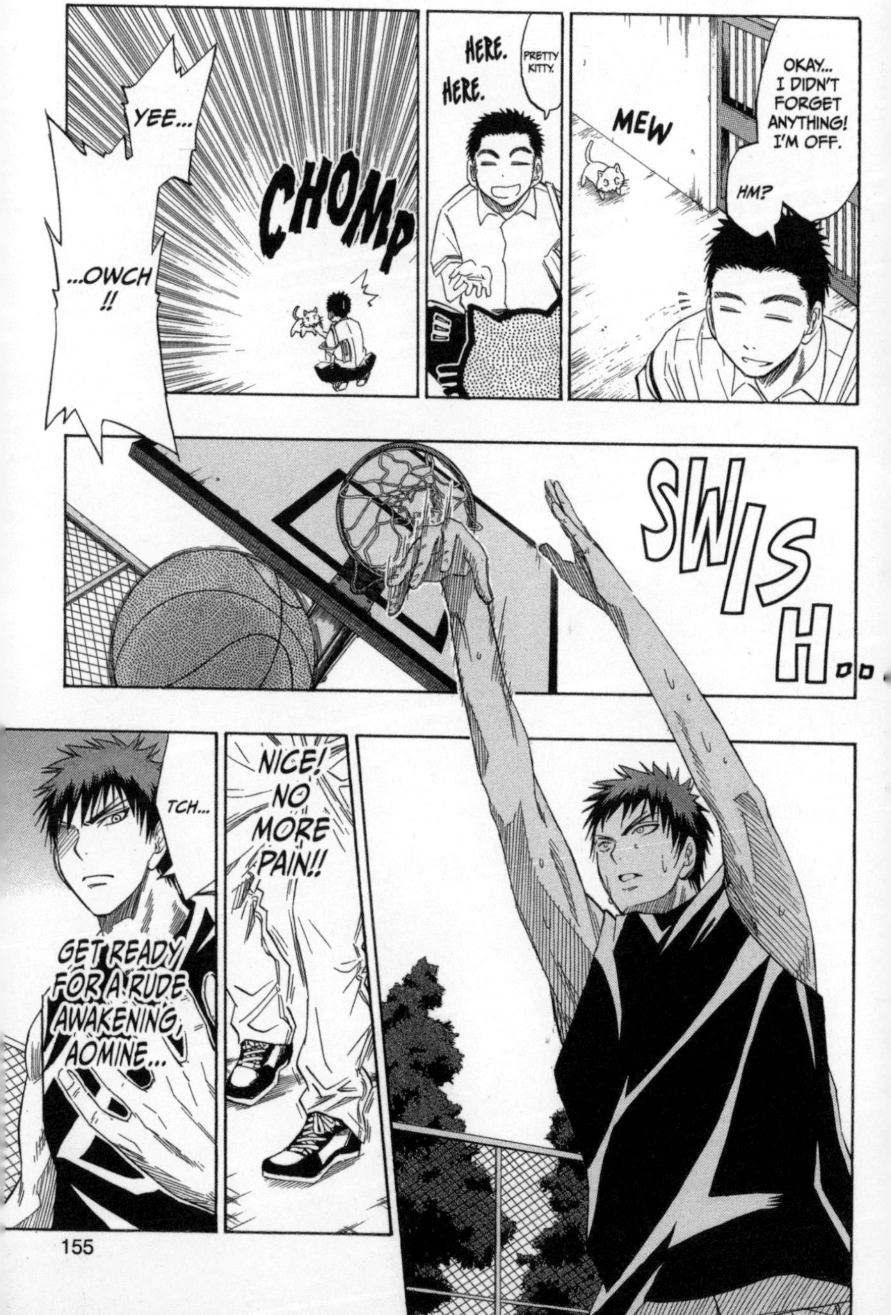
OKAY... I DIDN'T FORGET ANYTHING! I'M OFF.
MEW
HM?
PRETTY KITTY.
HERE.
HERE.
CHOMP
YEE...
...OWCH!!
SWISH..
NICE! NO MORE PAIN!!
TCH...
GET READY FOR A RUDE AWAKENING, AOMINE...

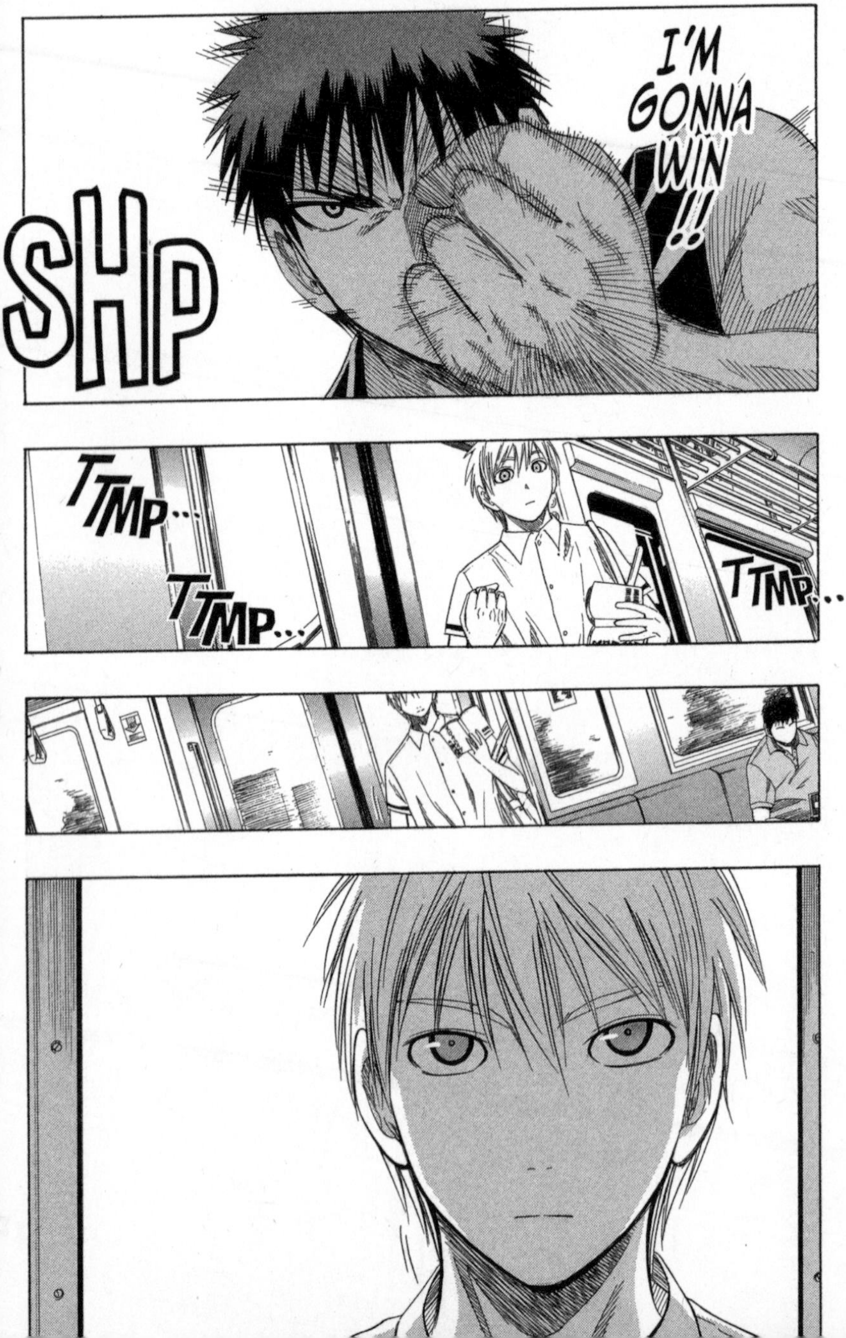
I'M GONNA WIN!!
SHP
TTMP...
TTMP...
TTMP...

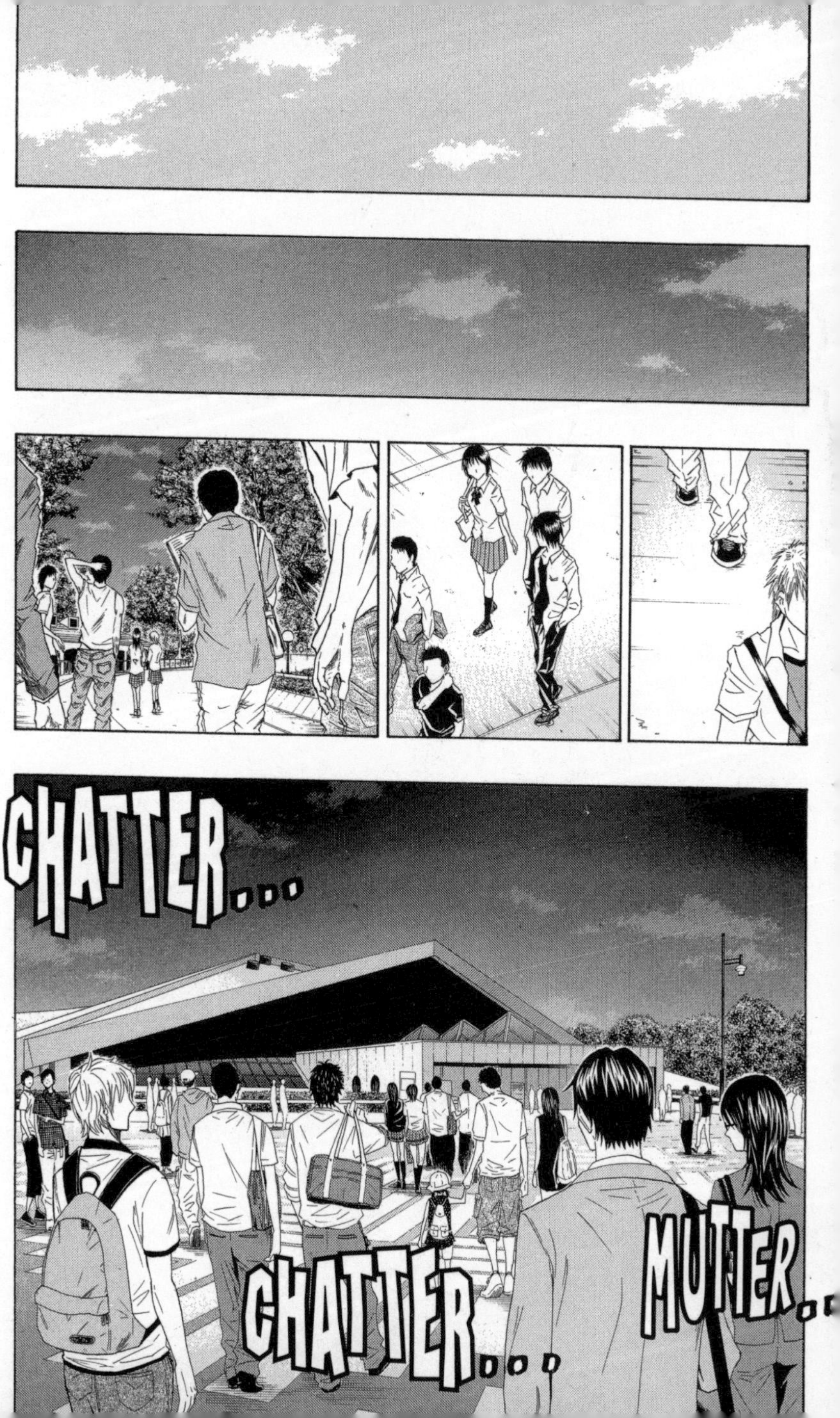
CHATTER...
MUTTER...
CHATTER...

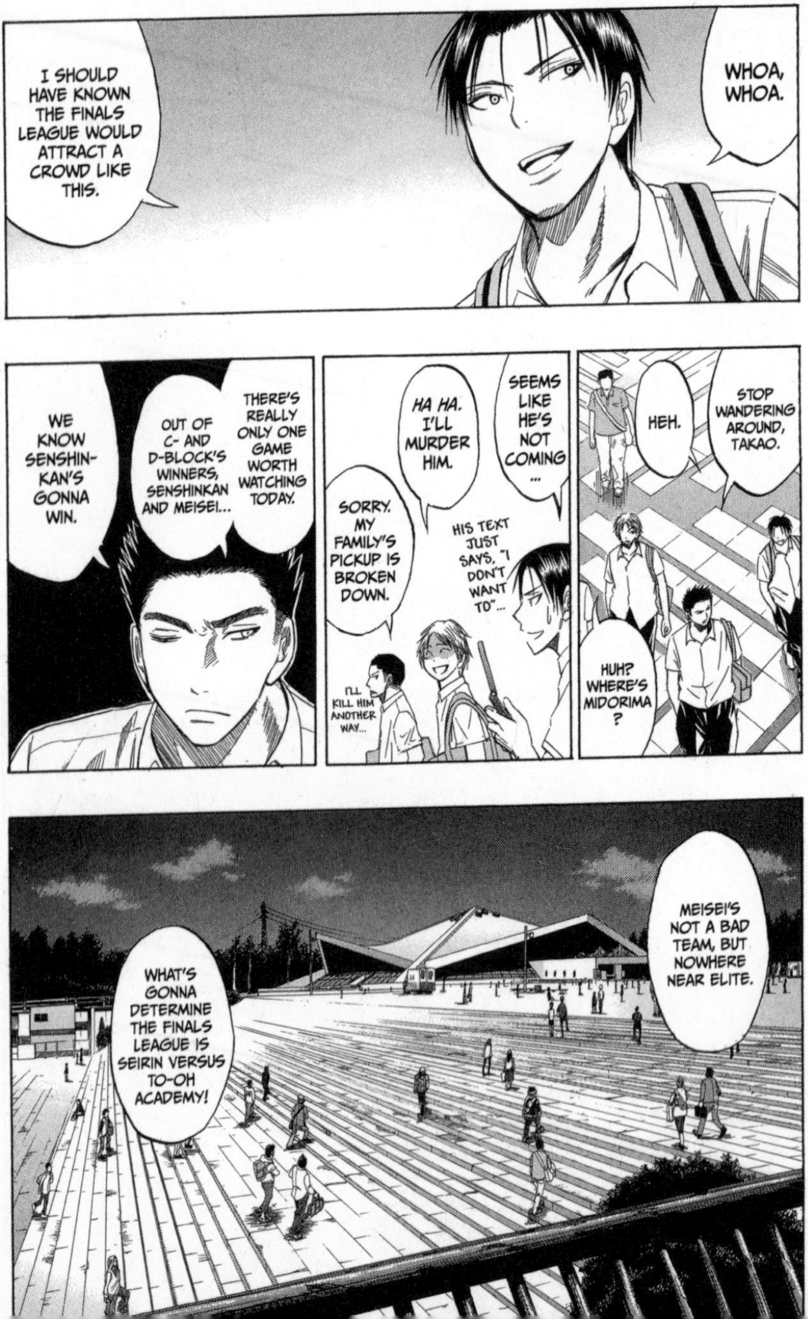
WHOA, WHOA.
I SHOULD HAVE KNOWN THE FINALS LEAGUE WOULD ATTRACT A CROWD LIKE THIS.
STOP WANDERING AROUND, TAKAO.
HEH.
HUH? WHERE'S MIDORIMA?
SEEMS LIKE HE'S NOT COMING...
HIS TEXT JUST SAYS, "I DON'T WANT TO"...
HA HA. I'LL MURDER HIM.
SORRY. MY FAMILY'S PICKUP IS BROKEN DOWN.
I'LL KILL HIM ANOTHER WAY...
THERE'S REALLY ONLY ONE GAME WORTH WATCHING TODAY.
OUT OF C- AND D-BLOCK'S WINNERS, SENSHINKAN AND MEISEI...
WE KNOW SENSHIN-KAN'S GONNA WIN.
MEISEI'S NOT A BAD TEAM, BUT NOWHERE NEAR ELITE.
WHAT'S GONNA DETERMINE THE FINALS LEAGUE IS SEIRIN VERSUS TO-OH ACADEMY!

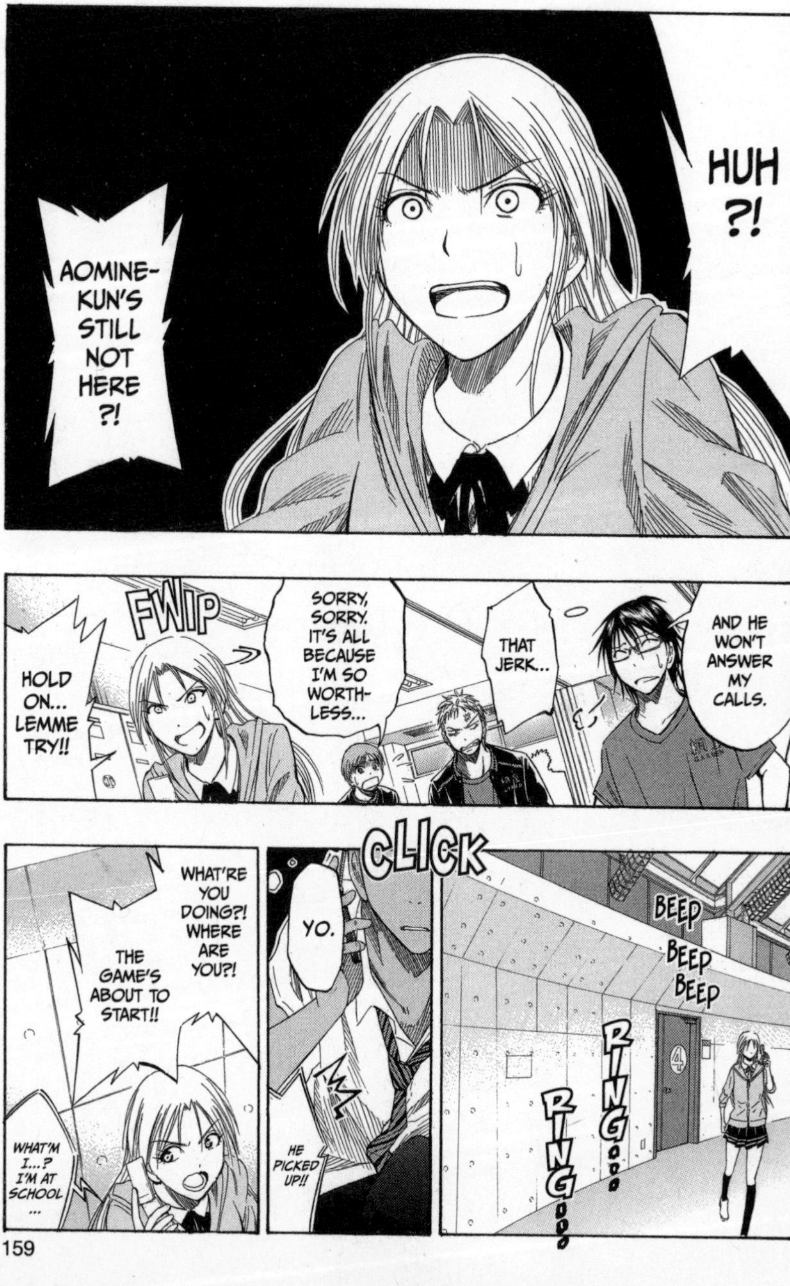
HUH ?!
AOMINE-KUN'S STILL NOT HERE ?!
AND HE WON'T ANSWER MY CALLS.
THAT JERK...
SORRY, SORRY. IT'S ALL BECAUSE I'M SO WORTHLESS...
FWIP
HOLD ON... LEMME TRY!!
BEEP
BEEP
BEEP
RING...
RING...
CLICK
YO.
HE PICKED UP!!
WHAT'RE YOU DOING?! WHERE ARE YOU?!
THE GAME'S ABOUT TO START!!
WHAT'M I...? I'M AT SCHOOL...

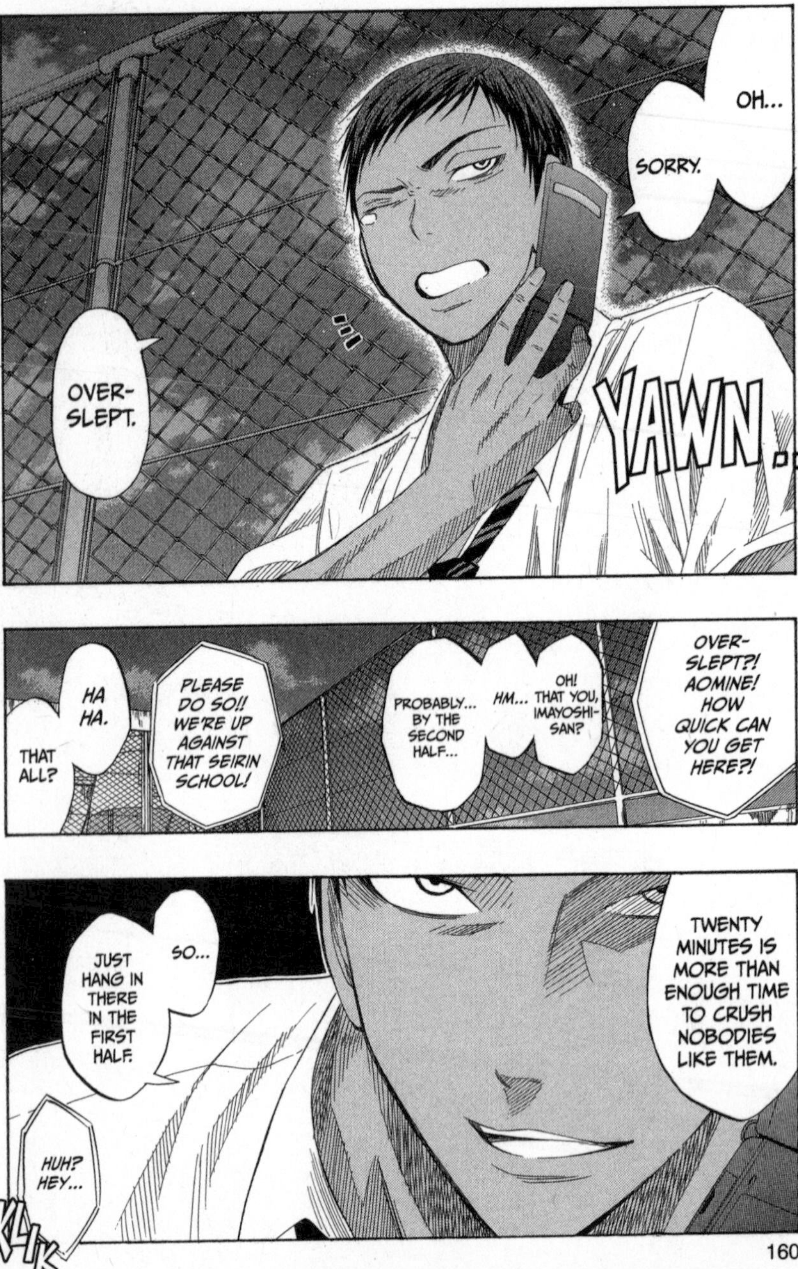
OH...
SORRY.
YAWN...
...
OVER-SLEPT.
OVER-SLEPT?! AOMINE! HOW QUICK CAN YOU GET HERE?!
OH! THAT YOU, IMAYOSHI-SAN?
HM...
PROBABLY... BY THE SECOND HALF...
PLEASE DO SO!! WE'RE UP AGAINST THAT SEIRIN SCHOOL!
HA HA.
THAT ALL?
TWENTY MINUTES IS MORE THAN ENOUGH TIME TO CRUSH NOBODIES LIKE THEM.
SO...
JUST HANG IN THERE IN THE FIRST HALF.
HUH? HEY...
KLIK

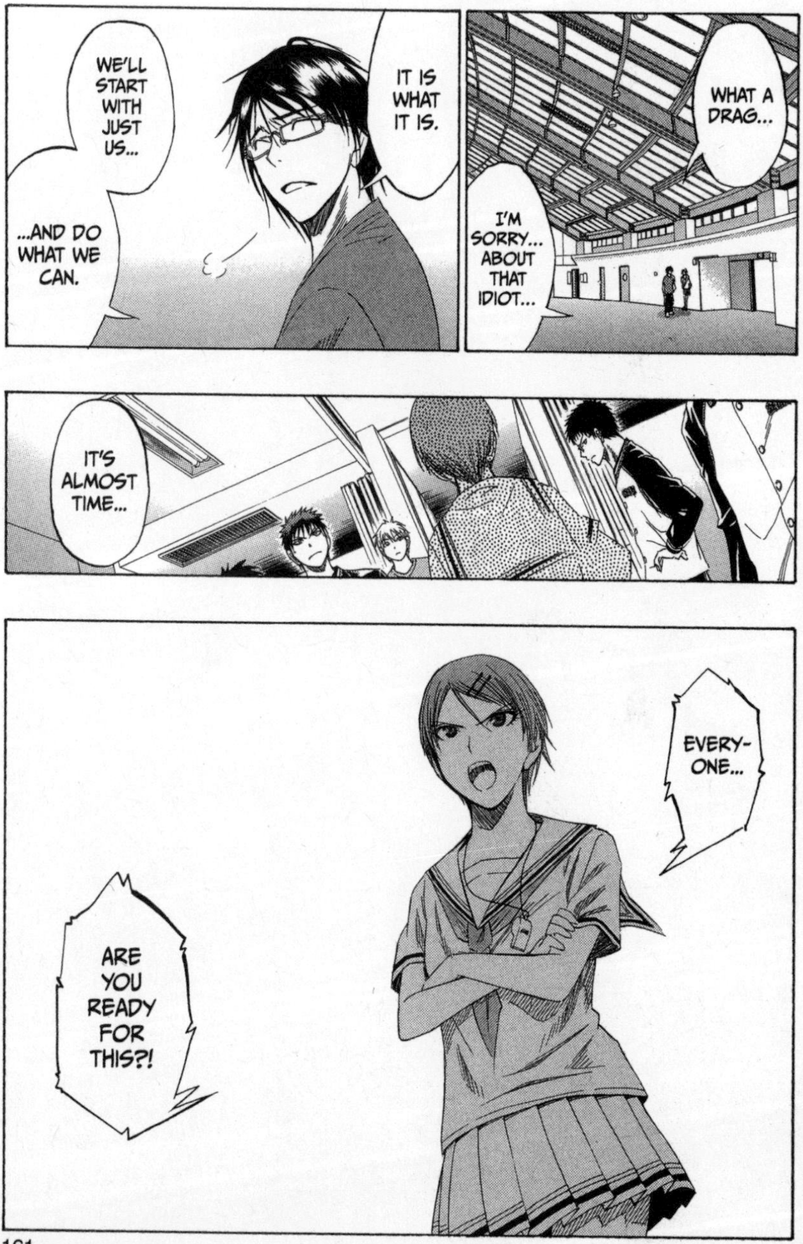
WHAT A DRAG...
I'M SORRY... ABOUT THAT IDIOT...
IT IS WHAT IT IS.
WE'LL START WITH JUST US...
...AND DO WHAT WE CAN.
IT'S ALMOST TIME...
EVERY-ONE...
ARE YOU READY FOR THIS?!

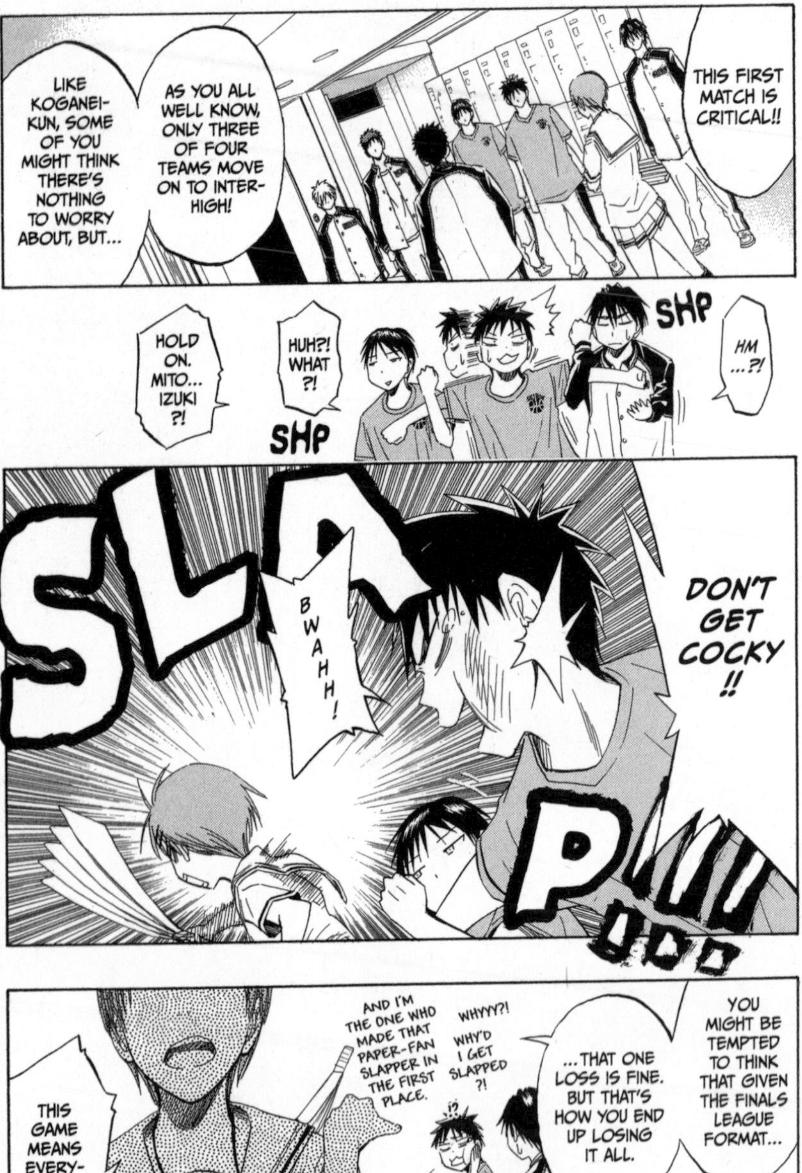
THIS FIRST MATCH IS CRITICAL!!
AS YOU ALL WELL KNOW, ONLY THREE OF FOUR TEAMS MOVE ON TO INTER-HIGH!
LIKE KOGANEI-KUN, SOME OF YOU MIGHT THINK THERE'S NOTHING TO WORRY ABOUT, BUT...
HM ...?!
SHP
HUH?! WHAT?!
HOLD ON. MITO... IZUKI?!
SHP
DON'T GET COCKY!!
SLAP
BWAHH!
YOU MIGHT BE TEMPTED TO THINK THAT GIVEN THE FINALS LEAGUE FORMAT...
...THAT ONE LOSS IS FINE. BUT THAT'S HOW YOU END UP LOSING IT ALL.
WHYYY?!
WHY'D I GET SLAPPED?!
!?
AND I'M THE ONE WHO MADE THAT PAPER-FAN SLAPPER IN THE FIRST PLACE.
THIS GAME MEANS EVERY-THING!!

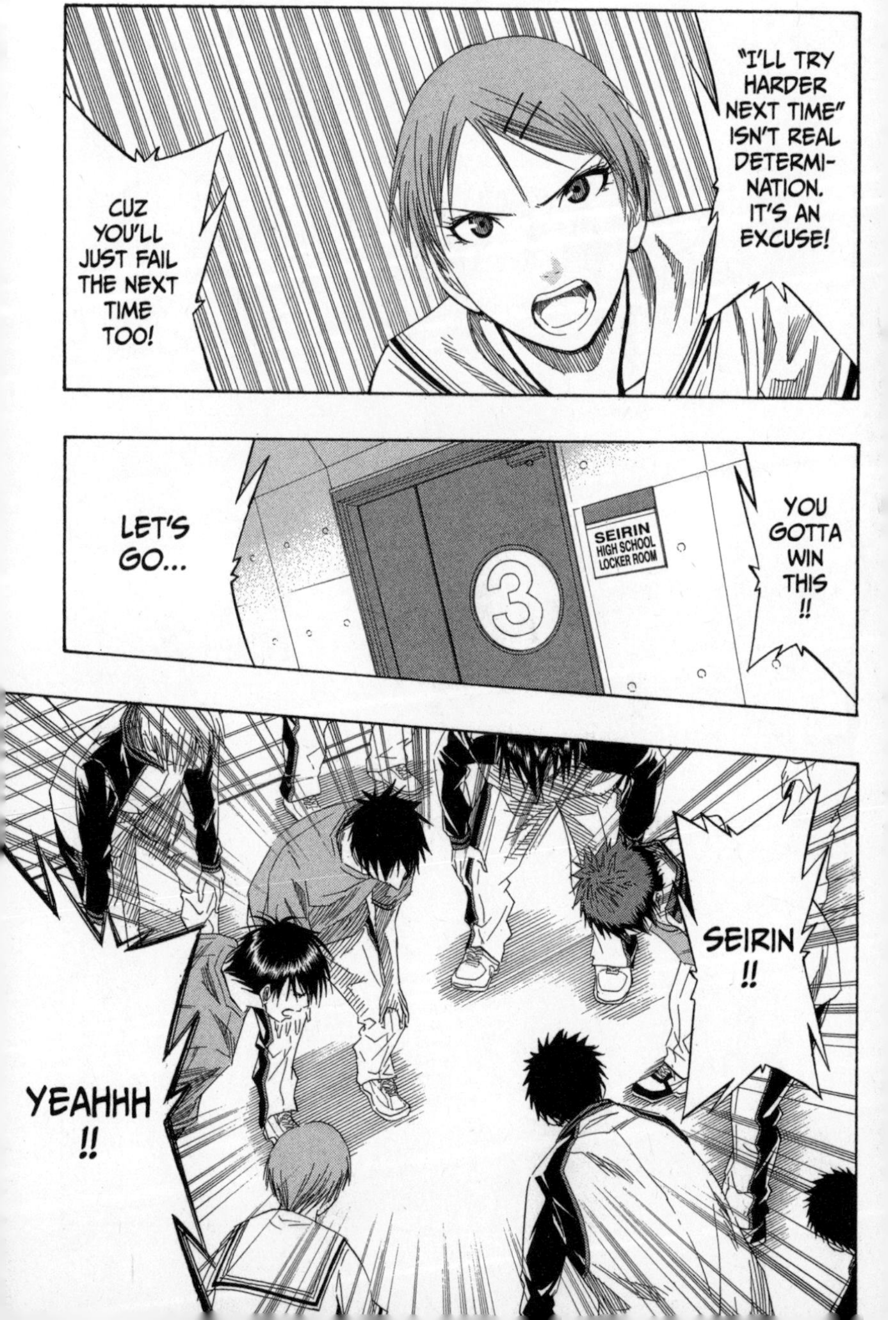
"I'LL TRY HARDER NEXT TIME" ISN'T REAL DETERMI-NATION. IT'S AN EXCUSE!
CUZ YOU'LL JUST FAIL THE NEXT TIME TOO!
YOU GOTTA WIN THIS !!
SEIRIN HIGH SCHOOL LOCKER ROOM
3
LET'S GO...
SEIRIN !!
YEAHHH !!

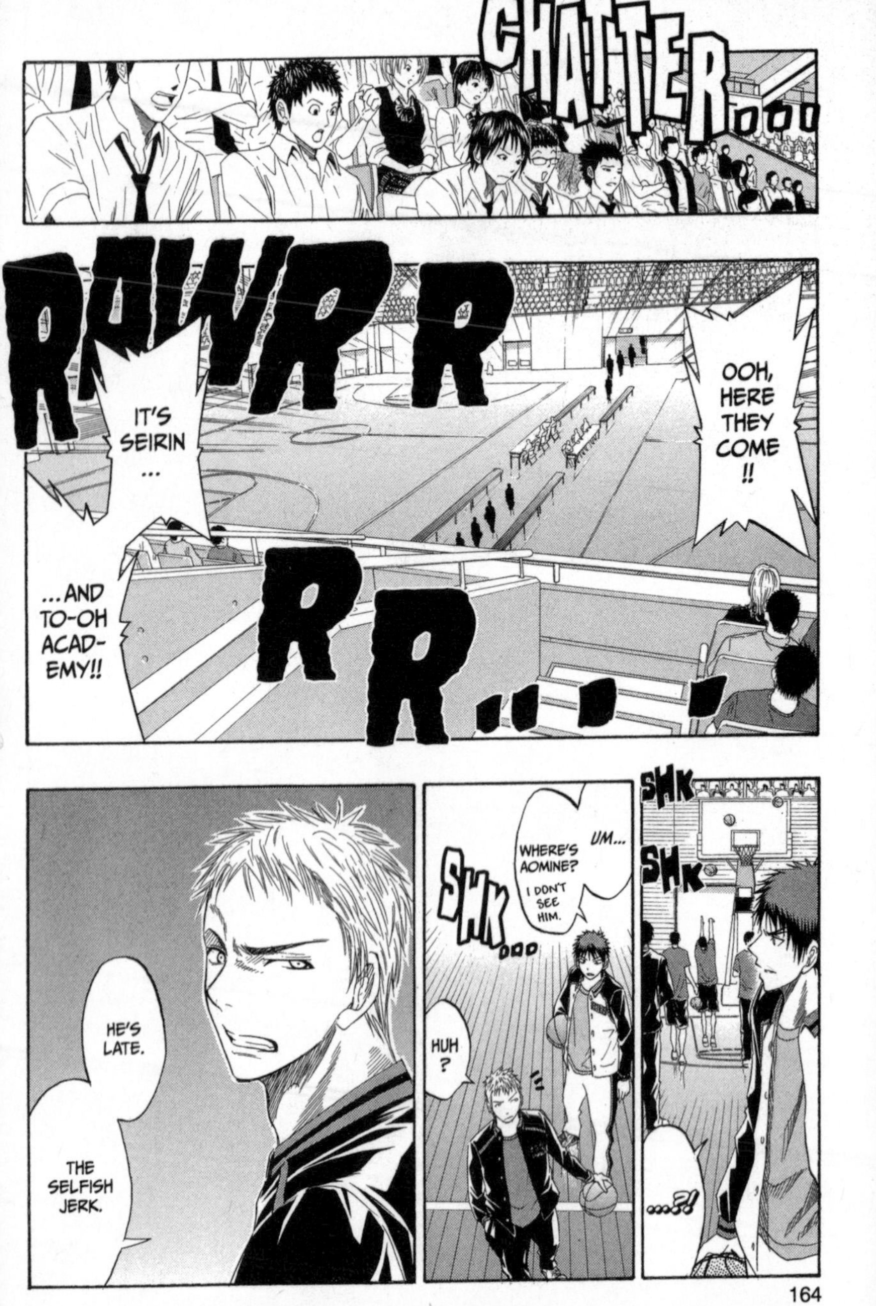
CHATTER...
OOH, HERE THEY COME!!
RAWRR
IT'S SEIRIN...
...AND TO-OH ACADEMY!!
RR...
SHK
SHK
...?!
UM...
WHERE'S AOMINE? I DON'T SEE HIM.
SHK...
HUH?
HE'S LATE.
THE SELFISH JERK.

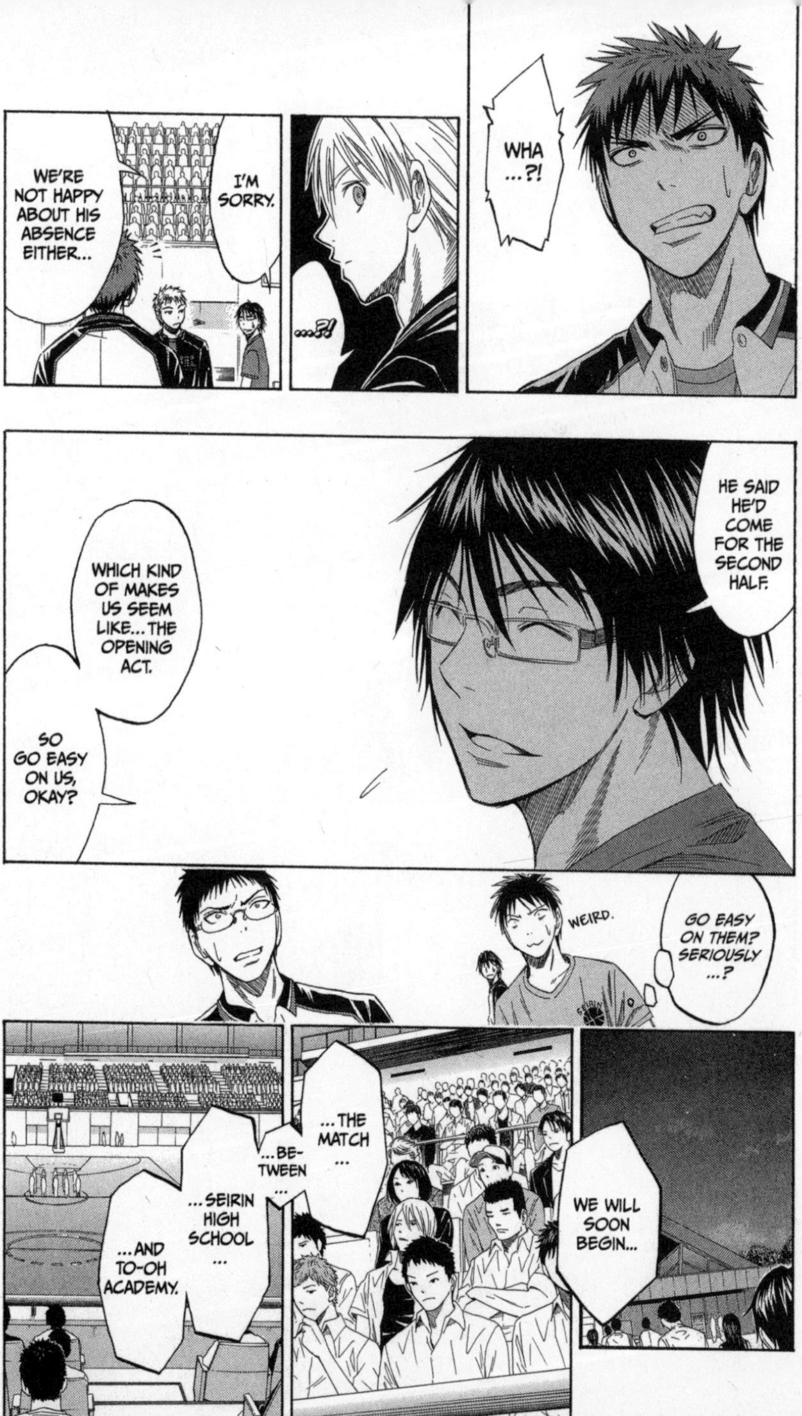
WHA ...?!
I'M SORRY.
...?!
WE'RE NOT HAPPY ABOUT HIS ABSENCE EITHER...
HE SAID HE'D COME FOR THE SECOND HALF.
WHICH KIND OF MAKES US SEEM LIKE... THE OPENING ACT.
SO GO EASY ON US, OKAY?
GO EASY ON THEM? SERIOUSLY ...?
WEIRD.
WE WILL SOON BEGIN...
...THE MATCH ...
...BE-TWEEN ...
...SEIRIN HIGH SCHOOL ...
...AND TO-OH ACADEMY.

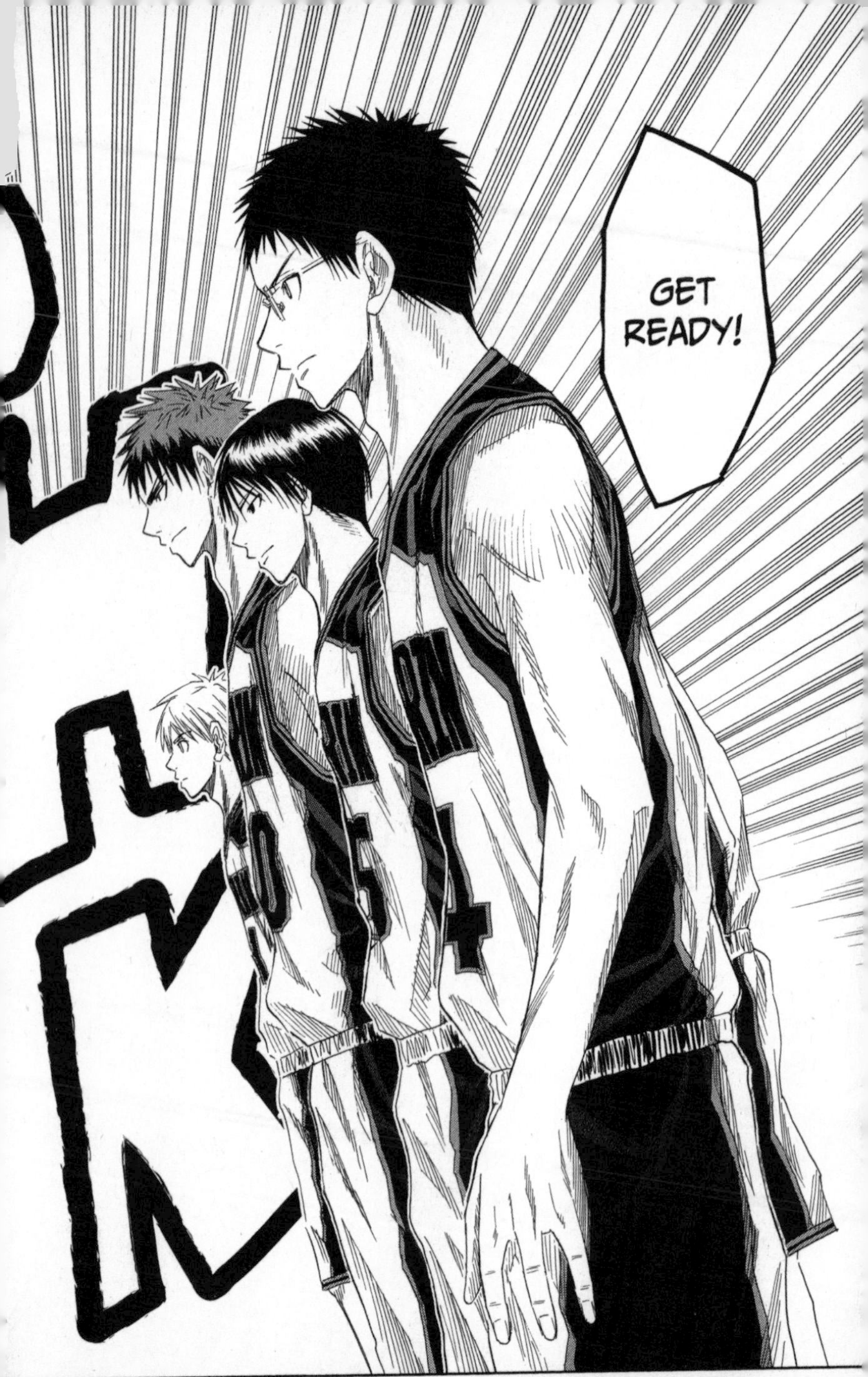
GET READY!

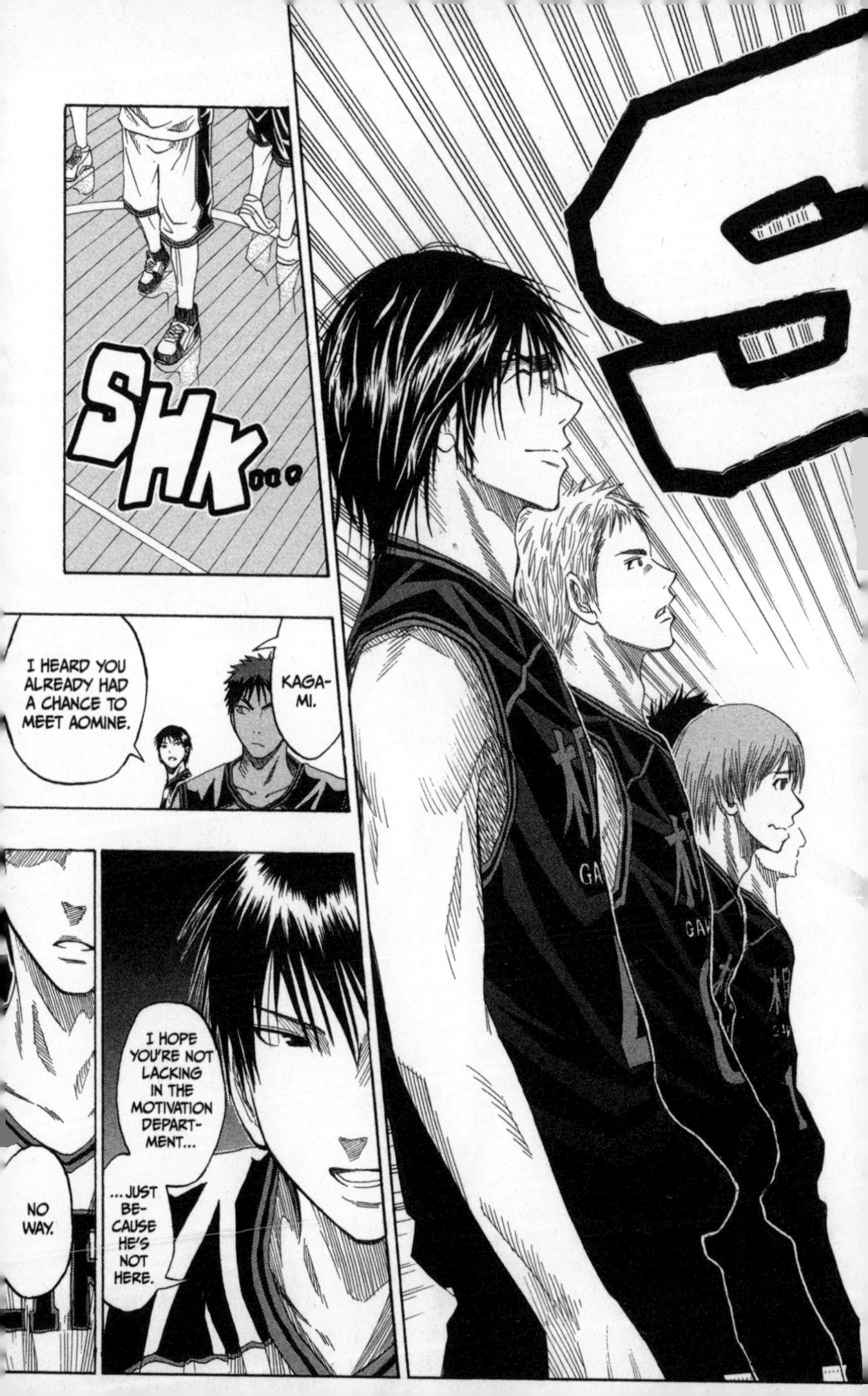
SHK...
KAGA-MI.
I HEARD YOU ALREADY HAD A CHANCE TO MEET AOMINE.
I HOPE YOU'RE NOT LACKING IN THE MOTIVATION DEPART-MENT...
...JUST BE-CAUSE HE'S NOT HERE.
NO WAY.

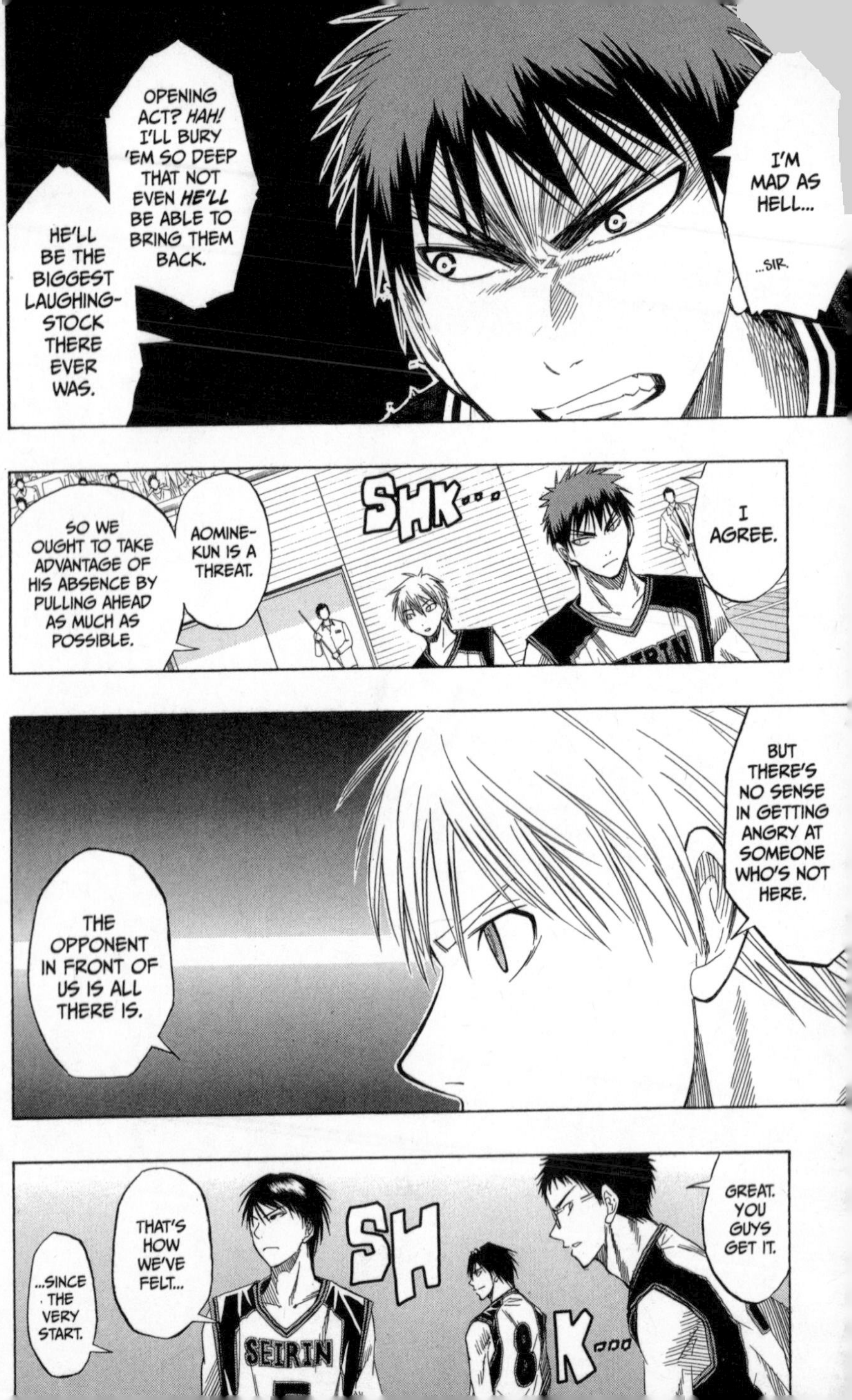
I'M MAD AS HELL...
...SIR.
OPENING ACT? *HAH!* I'LL BURY 'EM SO DEEP THAT NOT EVEN ***HE'LL*** BE ABLE TO BRING THEM BACK.
HE'LL BE THE BIGGEST LAUGHING-STOCK THERE EVER WAS.
I AGREE.
SHK...
AOMINE-KUN IS A THREAT.
SO WE OUGHT TO TAKE ADVANTAGE OF HIS ABSENCE BY PULLING AHEAD AS MUCH AS POSSIBLE.
BUT THERE'S NO SENSE IN GETTING ANGRY AT SOMEONE WHO'S NOT HERE.
THE OPPONENT IN FRONT OF US IS ALL THERE IS.
GREAT. YOU GUYS GET IT.
SHK...
THAT'S HOW WE'VE FELT...
...SINCE THE VERY START.

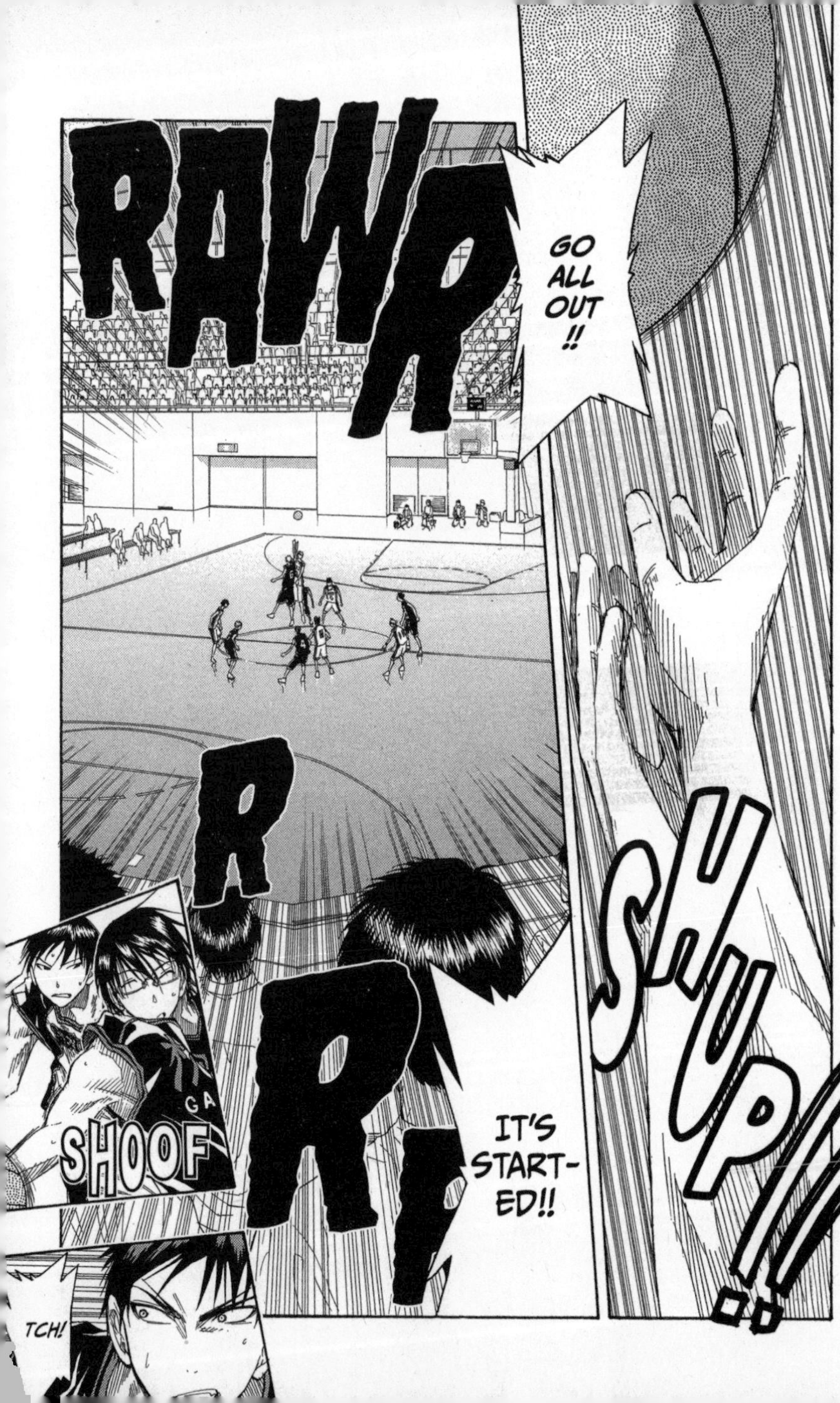
GO ALL OUT!!
SHUP!!
RAWR
RR
IT'S START-ED!!
SHOOF
TCH!

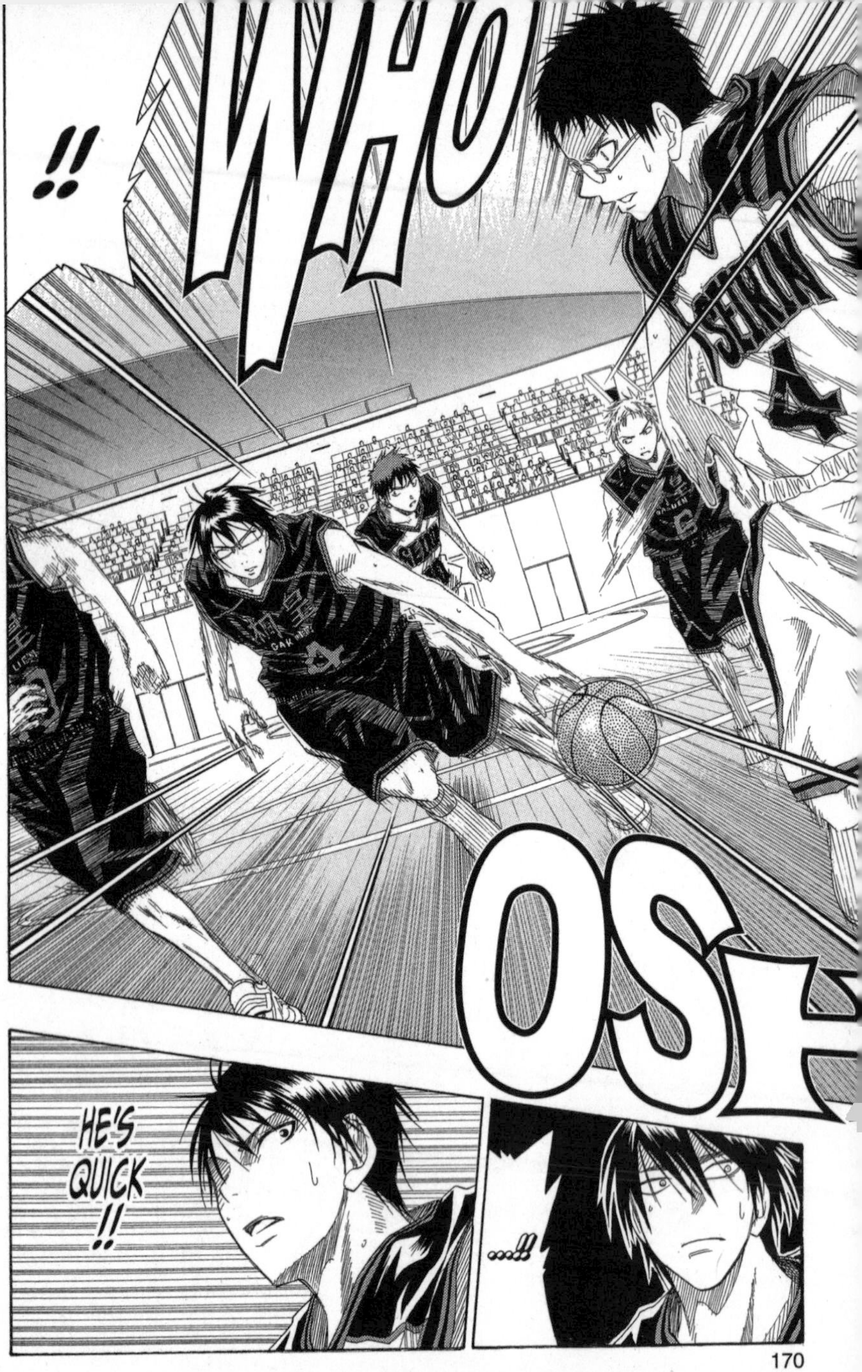

!!
WHOOSH
...!!
HE'S QUICK !!

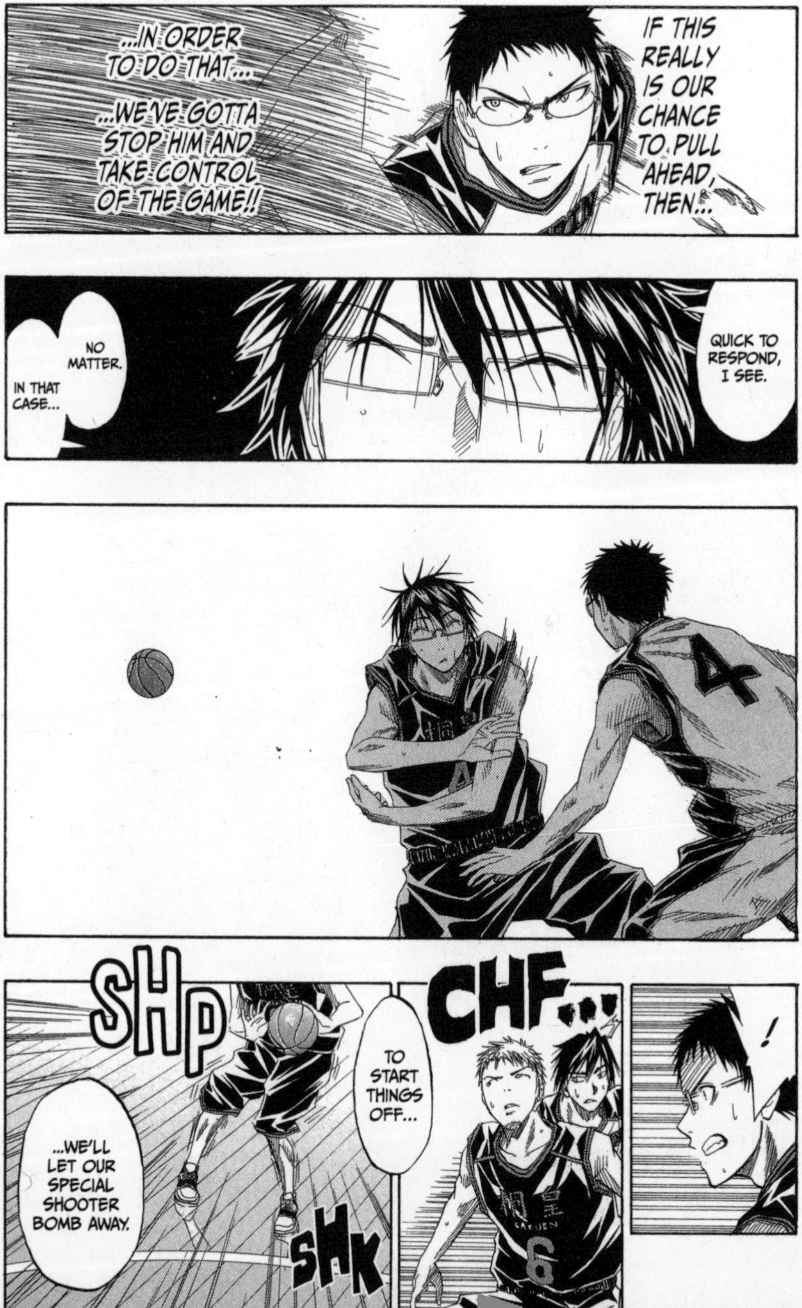
IF THIS REALLY IS OUR CHANCE TO PULL AHEAD, THEN...
...IN ORDER TO DO THAT...
...WE'VE GOTTA STOP HIM AND TAKE CONTROL OF THE GAME!!
QUICK TO RESPOND, I SEE.
NO MATTER.
IN THAT CASE...
!
CHF...
TO START THINGS OFF...
SHP
...WE'LL LET OUR SPECIAL SHOOTER BOMB AWAY.
SHK

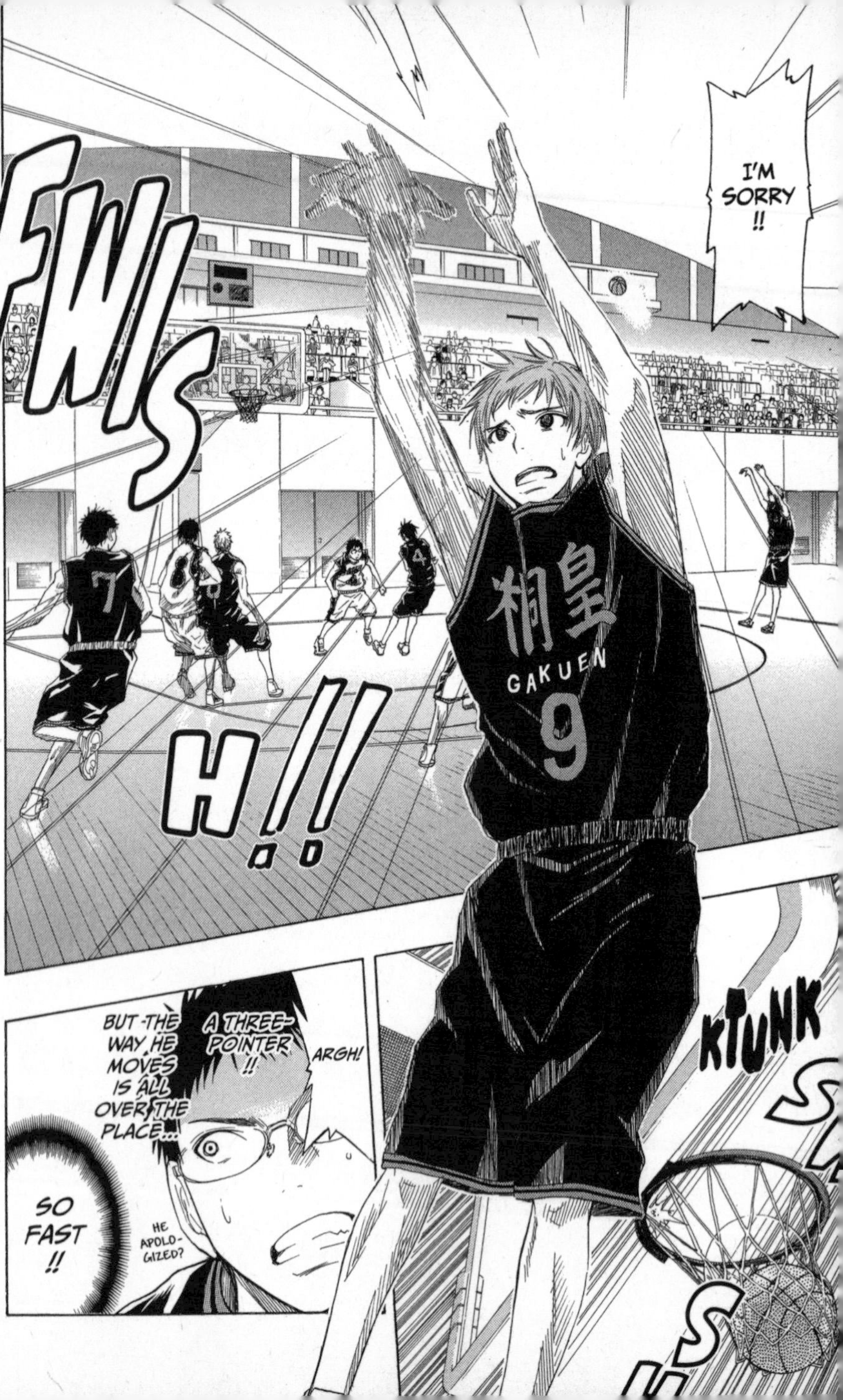
I'M SORRY !!
FWISH!!
桐皇
GAKUEN
9
KTUNK
ARGH!
A THREE-POINTER !!
BUT THE WAY HE MOVES IS ALL OVER THE PLACE...
HE APOLOGIZED?
SO FAST !!

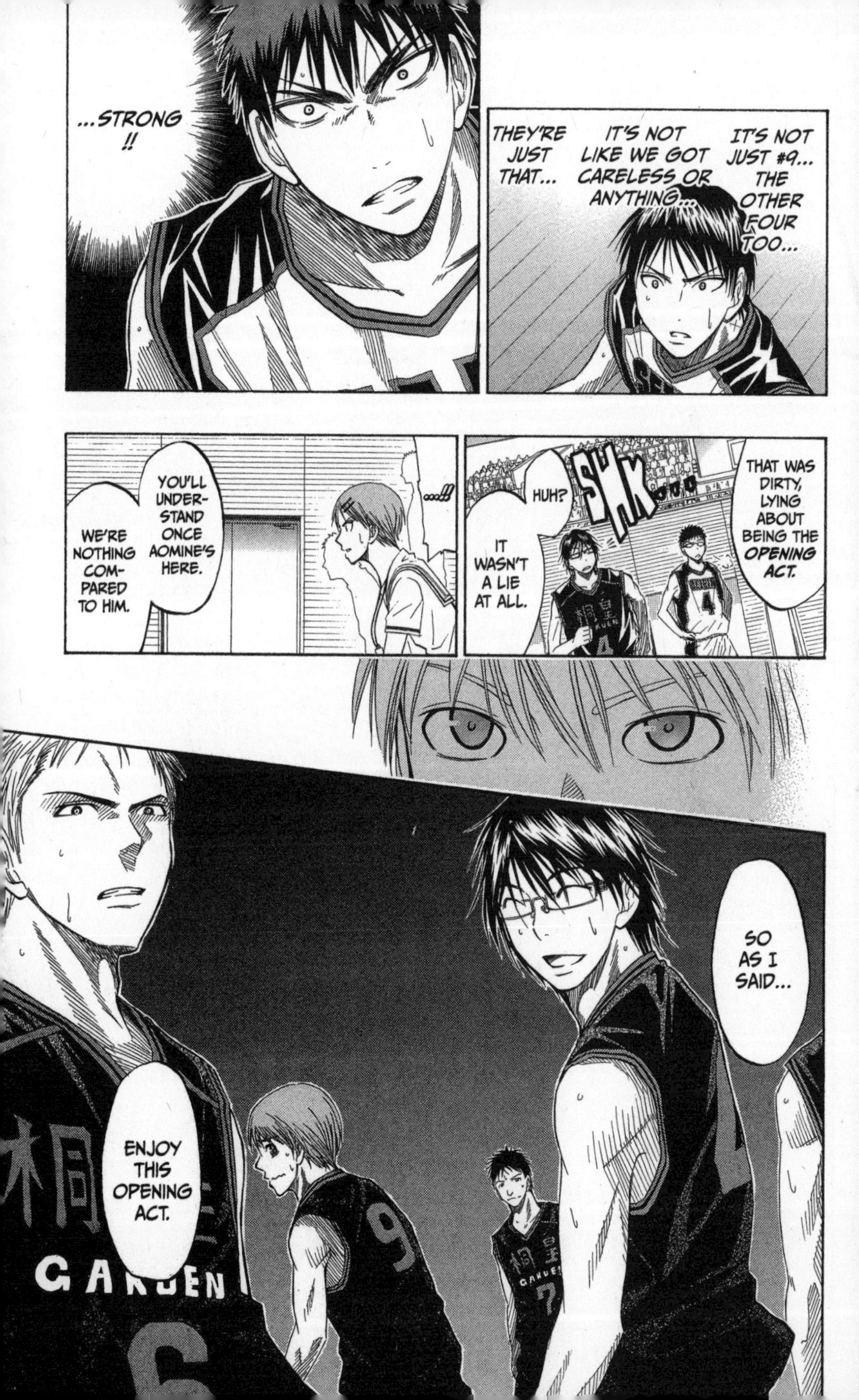
IT'S NOT JUST #9... THE OTHER FOUR TOO...
IT'S NOT LIKE WE GOT CARELESS OR ANYTHING...
THEY'RE JUST THAT...
...STRONG!!
THAT WAS DIRTY, LYING ABOUT BEING THE OPENING ACT.
SHK
HUH?
IT WASN'T A LIE AT ALL.
...!!
YOU'LL UNDER-STAND ONCE AOMINE'S HERE.
WE'RE NOTHING COM-PARED TO HIM.
SO AS I SAID...
ENJOY THIS OPENING ACT.

KUROKO'S BASKETBALL BLOOPERS TAKE 9

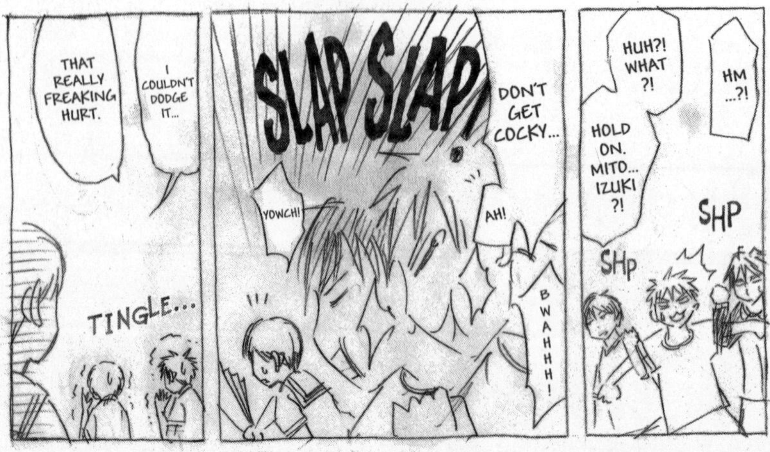
HM ...?!
HUH?! WHAT ?!
HOLD ON. MITO... IZUKI ?!
SHP
SHp
SLAP SLAP!
DON'T GET COCKY...
AH!
YOWCH!
BWAHHH!
I COULDN'T DODGE IT...
THAT REALLY FREAKING HURT.
TINGLE...

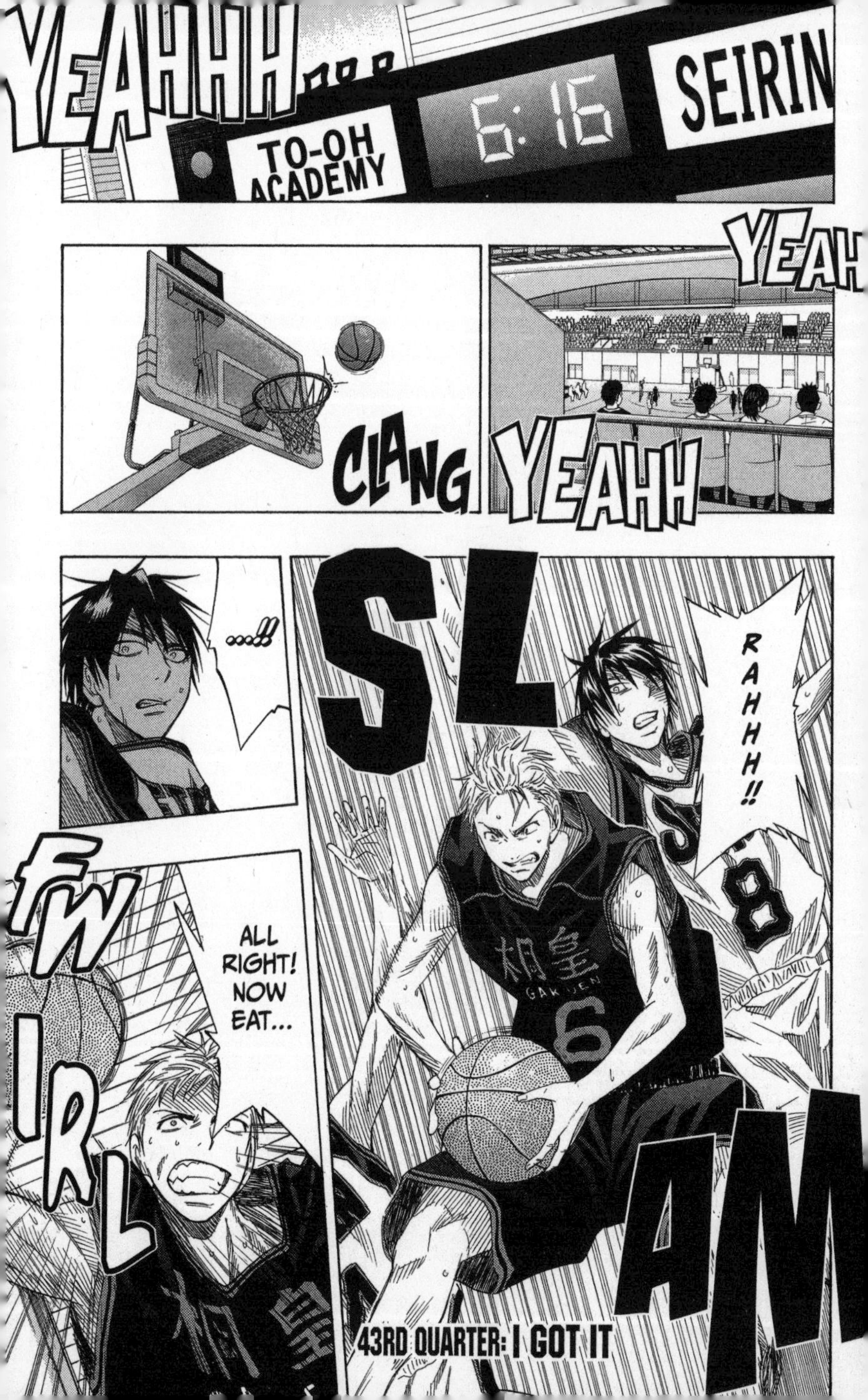
YEAHHH
SEIRIN
6:16
TO-OH ACADEMY
YEAH
YEAHH
CLANG
SLAM
RAHHHH!!
...!!
ALL RIGHT! NOW EAT...
FWIRL

43RD QUARTER: I GOT IT

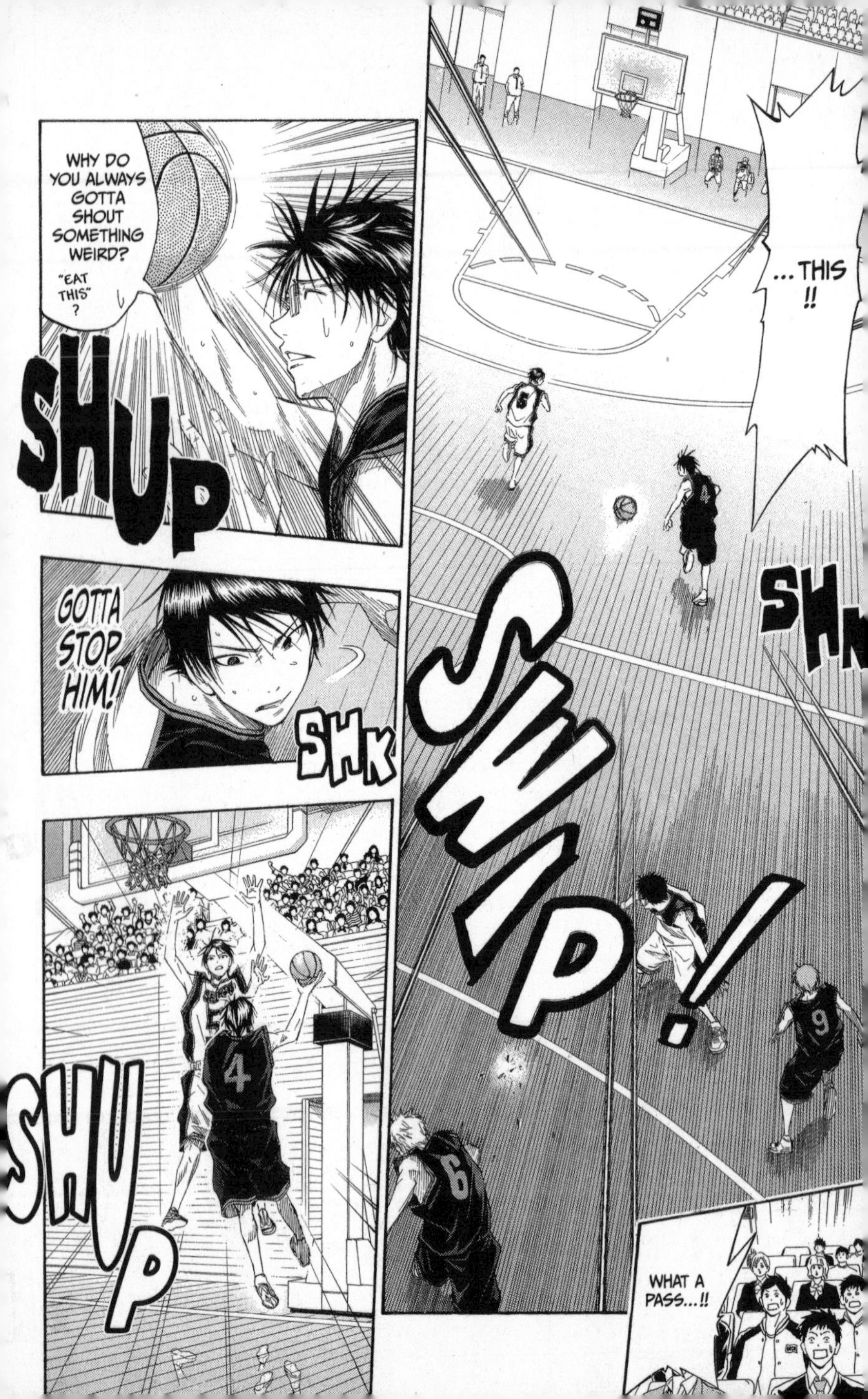
...THIS !!
SHN
SWIP!
WHAT A PASS...!!
WHY DO YOU ALWAYS GOTTA SHOUT SOMETHING WEIRD?
"EAT THIS" ?
SHUP
GOTTA STOP HIM!
SHK
SHUP

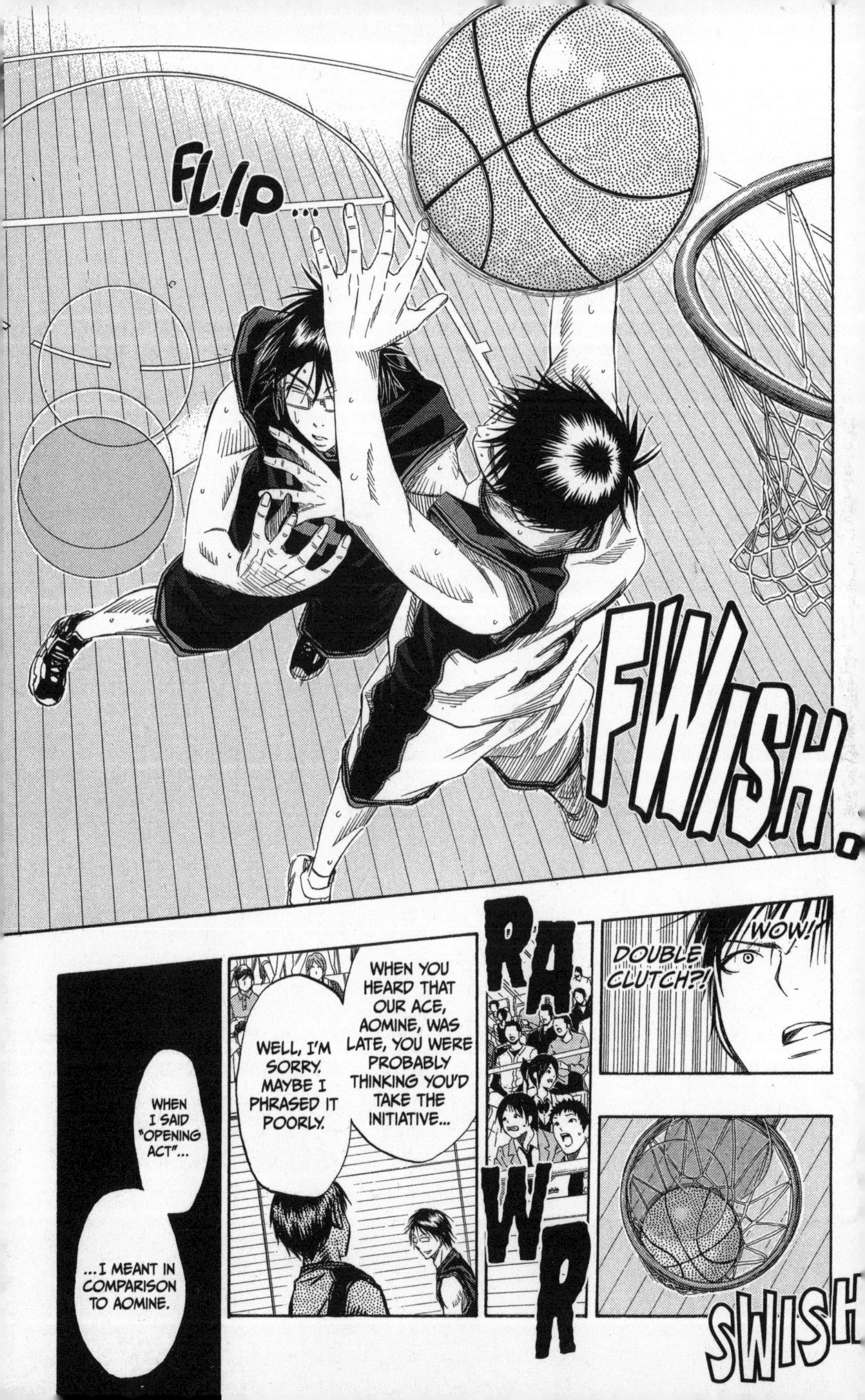
FLIP...
FWISH.
WOW!
DOUBLE CLUTCH?!
SWISH
RAWR
WHEN YOU HEARD THAT OUR ACE, AOMINE, WAS LATE, YOU WERE PROBABLY THINKING YOU'D TAKE THE INITIATIVE...
WELL, I'M SORRY. MAYBE I PHRASED IT POORLY.
WHEN I SAID "OPENING ACT"...
...I MEANT IN COMPARISON TO AOMINE.

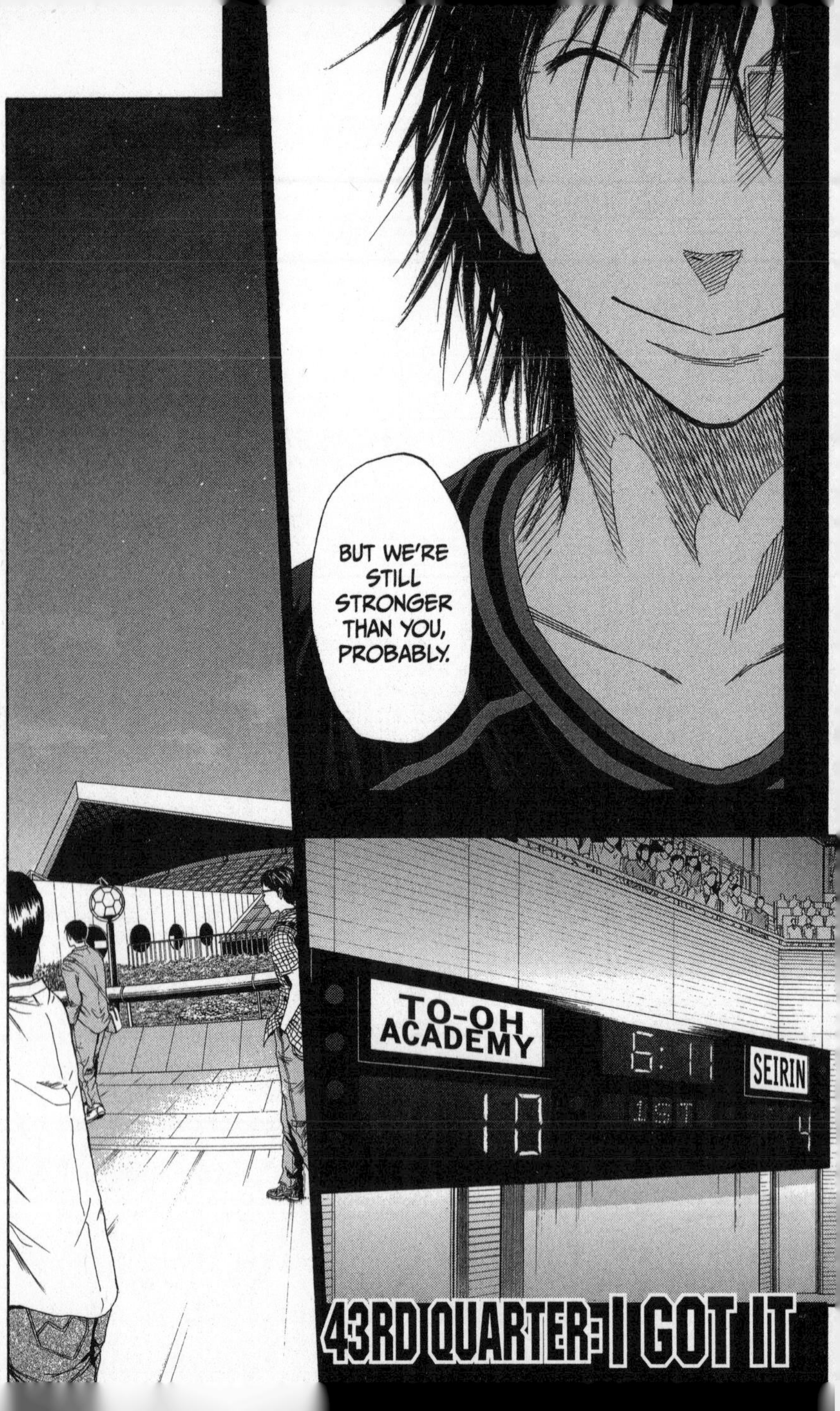
BUT WE'RE STILL STRONGER THAN YOU, PROBABLY.
TO-OH ACADEMY
6:11
SEIRIN
10
1ST
4
43RD QUARTER: I GOT IT

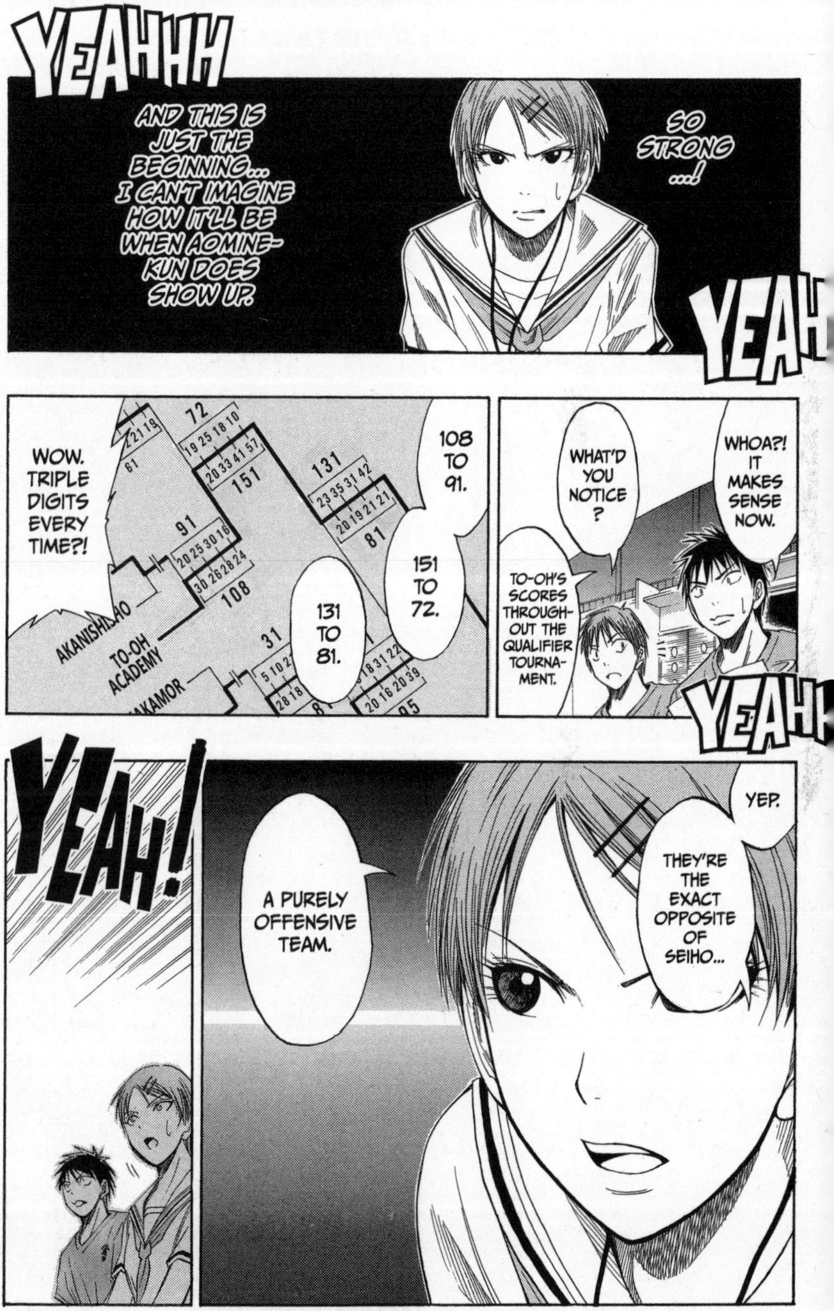
YEAHHH
SO STRONG ...!
AND THIS IS JUST THE BEGINNING... I CAN'T IMAGINE HOW IT'LL BE WHEN AOMINE-KUN DOES SHOW UP.
YEAH
WHOA?! IT MAKES SENSE NOW.
WHAT'D YOU NOTICE?
TO-OH'S SCORES THROUGHOUT THE QUALIFIER TOURNAMENT.
YEAHH
108 TO 91.
151 TO 72.
131 TO 81.
WOW. TRIPLE DIGITS EVERY TIME?!
TO-OH ACADEMY
YEP.
THEY'RE THE EXACT OPPOSITE OF SEIHO...
A PURELY OFFENSIVE TEAM.
YEAH!

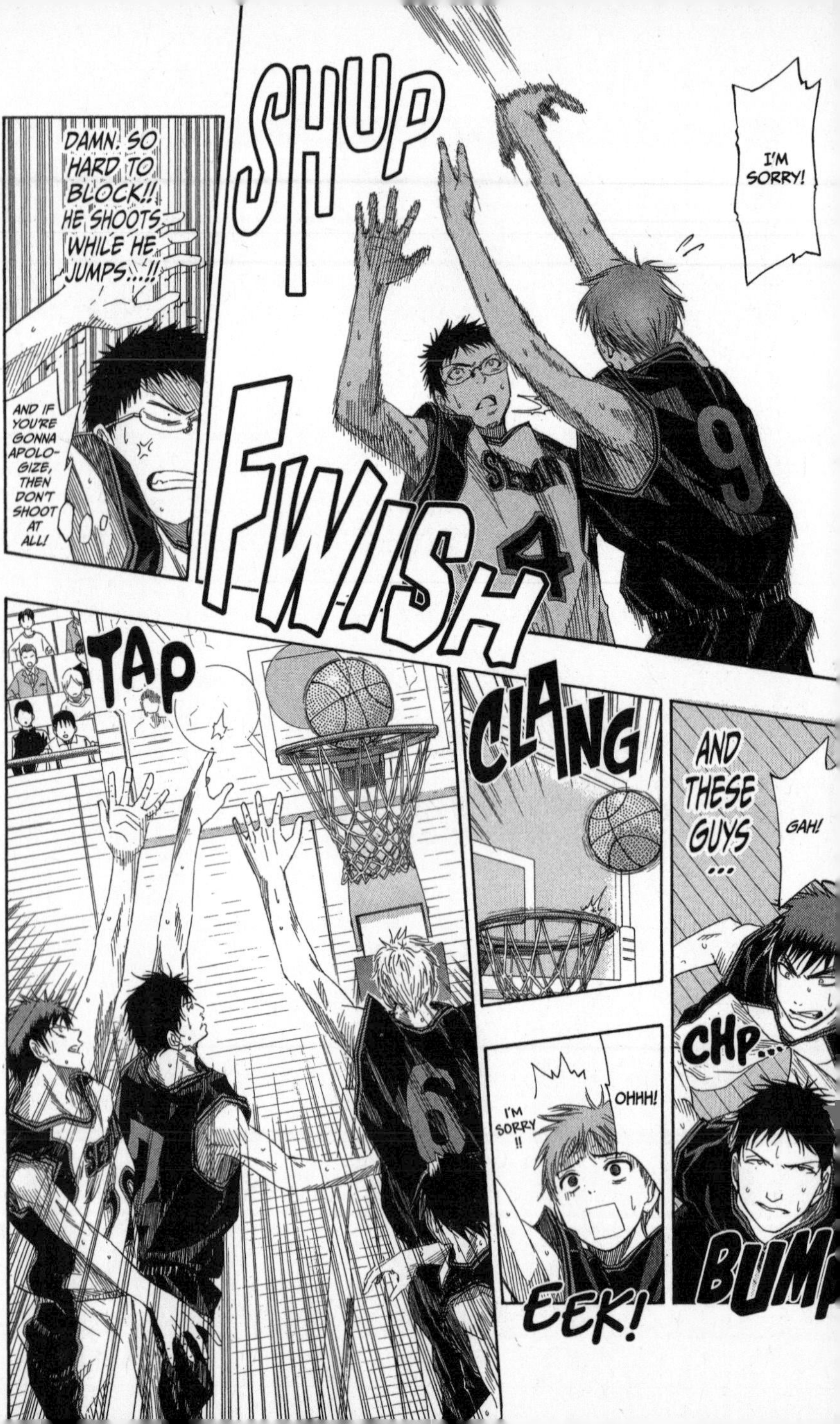
I'M SORRY!
SHUP
FWISH
DAMN. SO HARD TO BLOCK!! HE SHOOTS WHILE HE JUMPS...!!
AND IF YOU'RE GONNA APOLOGIZE, THEN DON'T SHOOT AT ALL!
AND THESE GUYS...
GAH!
CHP...
BUM
CLANG
OHHH!
I'M SORRY!!
EEK!
TAP

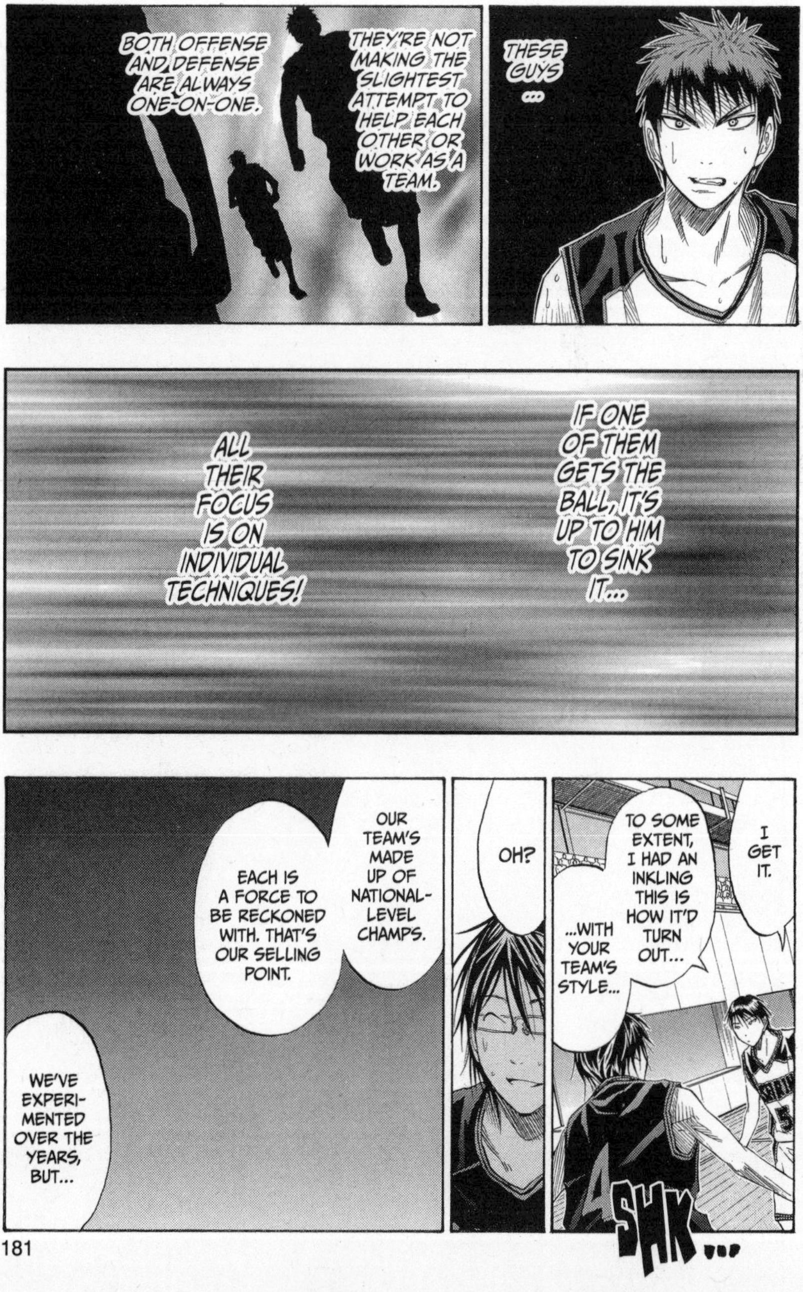
THESE GUYS...
THEY'RE NOT MAKING THE SLIGHTEST ATTEMPT TO HELP EACH OTHER OR WORK AS A TEAM.
BOTH OFFENSE AND DEFENSE ARE ALWAYS ONE-ON-ONE.
IF ONE OF THEM GETS THE BALL, IT'S UP TO HIM TO SINK IT...
ALL THEIR FOCUS IS ON INDIVIDUAL TECHNIQUES!
I GET IT.
TO SOME EXTENT, I HAD AN INKLING THIS IS HOW IT'D TURN OUT...
...WITH YOUR TEAM'S STYLE...
SHK
OH?
OUR TEAM'S MADE UP OF NATIONAL-LEVEL CHAMPS.
EACH IS A FORCE TO BE RECKONED WITH. THAT'S OUR SELLING POINT.
WE'VE EXPERIMENTED OVER THE YEARS, BUT...

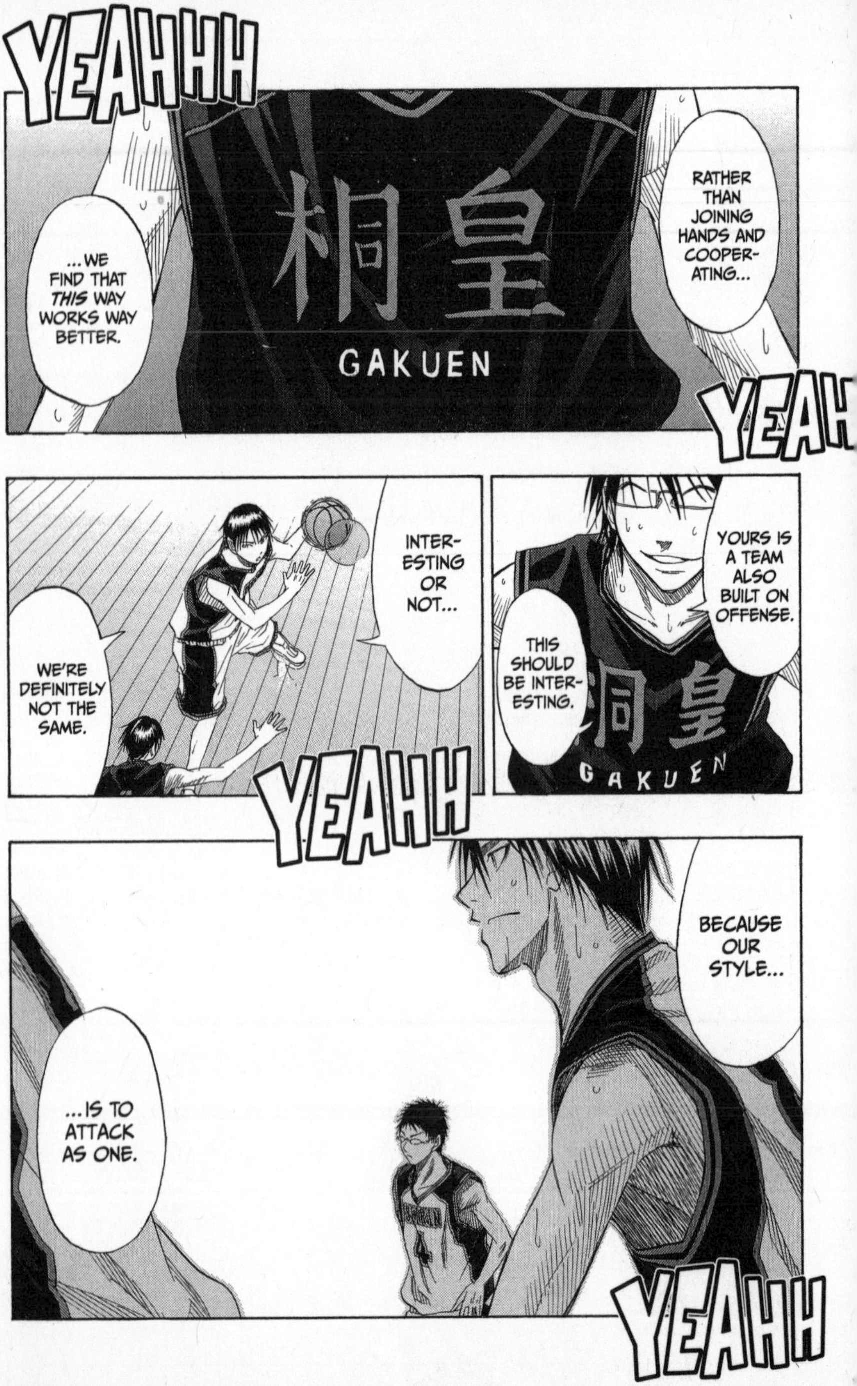
YEAHHH
RATHER THAN JOINING HANDS AND COOPER-ATING...
桐皇
GAKUEN
...WE FIND THAT *THIS* WAY WORKS WAY BETTER.
YEAH
YOURS IS A TEAM ALSO BUILT ON OFFENSE.
THIS SHOULD BE INTER-ESTING.
桐皇
GAKUEN
INTER-ESTING OR NOT...
WE'RE DEFINITELY NOT THE SAME.
YEAHH
BECAUSE OUR STYLE...
...IS TO ATTACK AS ONE.
YEAHH

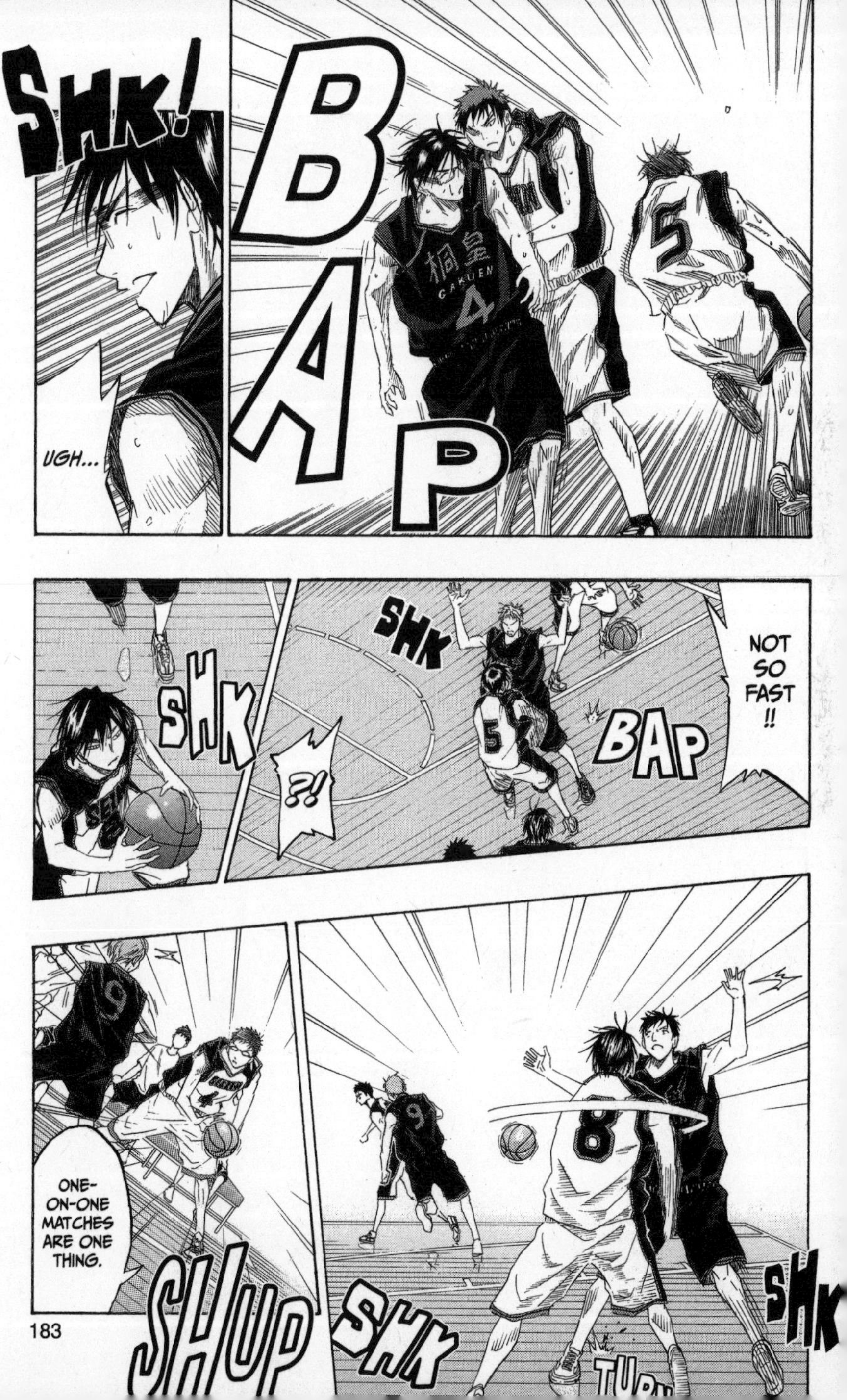
BAP
SHK!
UGH...
SHK
NOT SO FAST!!
BAP
?!
SHK
SHK
SHK
TURN
ONE-ON-ONE MATCHES ARE ONE THING.
SHUP

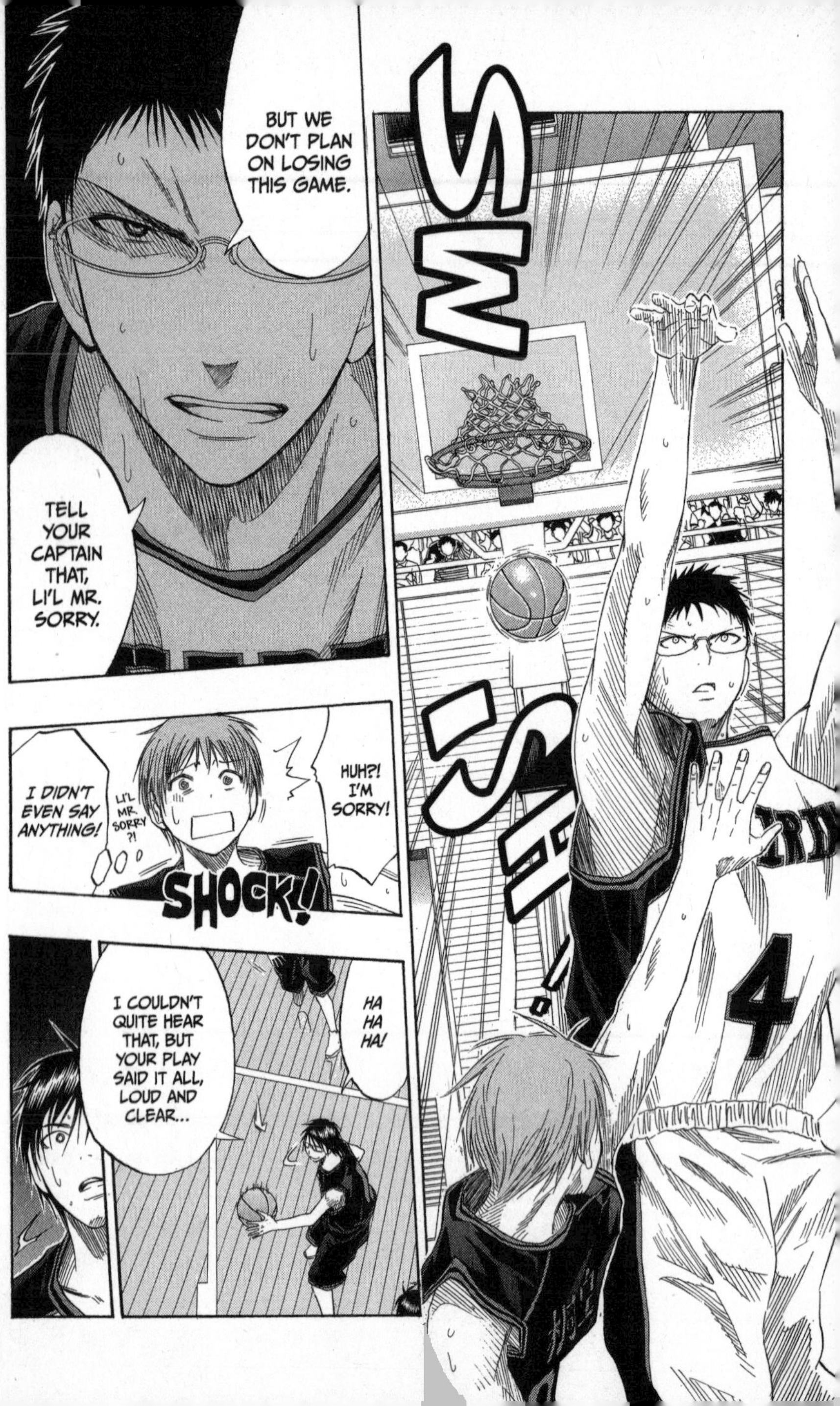
SWISH!
BUT WE DON'T PLAN ON LOSING THIS GAME.
TELL YOUR CAPTAIN THAT, LI'L MR. SORRY.
HUH?! I'M SORRY!
LI'L MR. SORRY ?!
I DIDN'T EVEN SAY ANYTHING!
SHOCK!
HA HA HA!
I COULDN'T QUITE HEAR THAT, BUT YOUR PLAY SAID IT ALL, LOUD AND CLEAR...

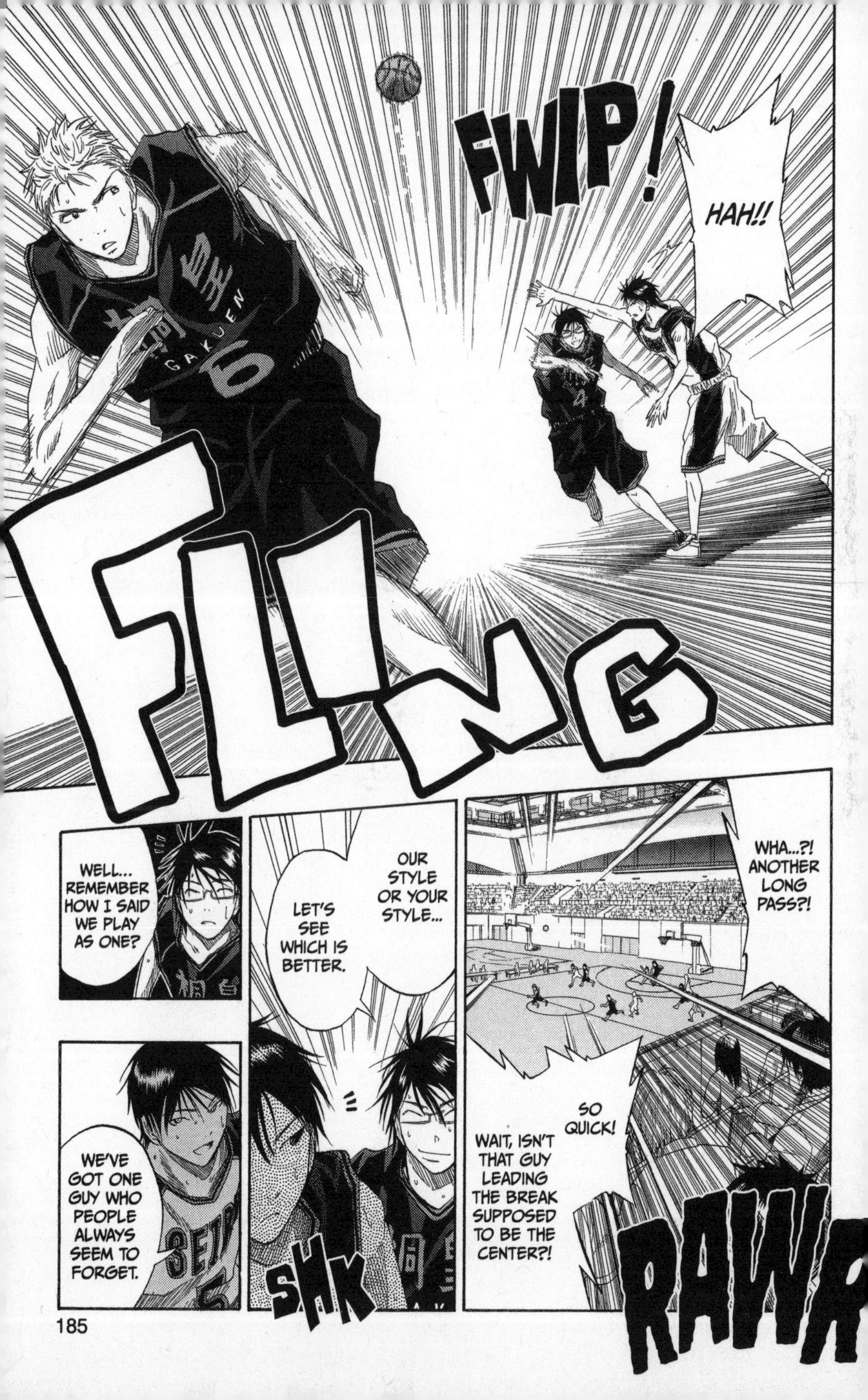
HAH!!
FWIP!
FLING
WHA...?! ANOTHER LONG PASS?!
SO QUICK!
WAIT, ISN'T THAT GUY LEADING THE BREAK SUPPOSED TO BE THE CENTER?!
RAWR
OUR STYLE OR YOUR STYLE...
LET'S SEE WHICH IS BETTER.
SHK
WELL... REMEMBER HOW I SAID WE PLAY AS ONE?
WE'VE GOT ONE GUY WHO PEOPLE ALWAYS SEEM TO FORGET.

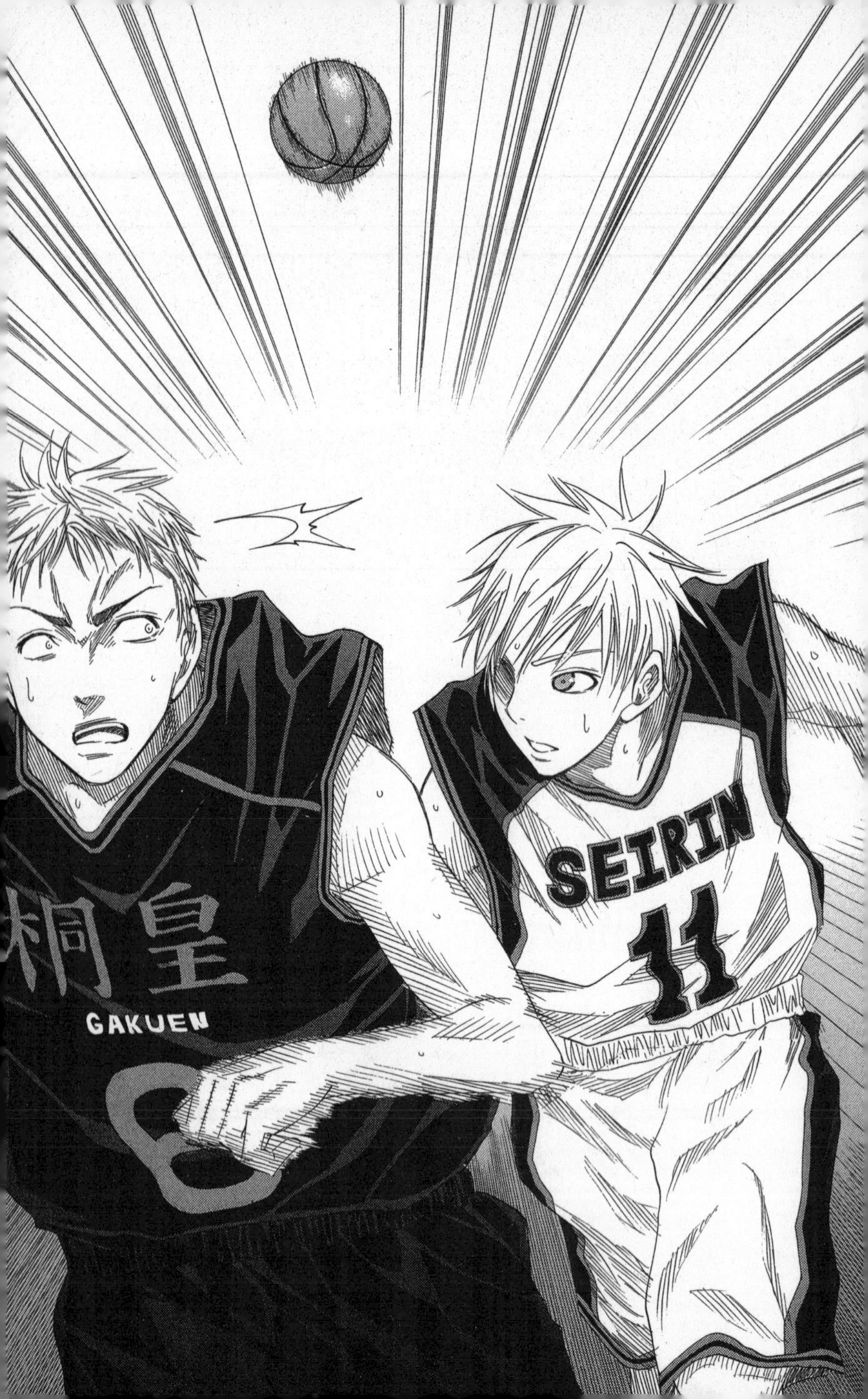
SEIRIN
11
桐皇
GAKUEN

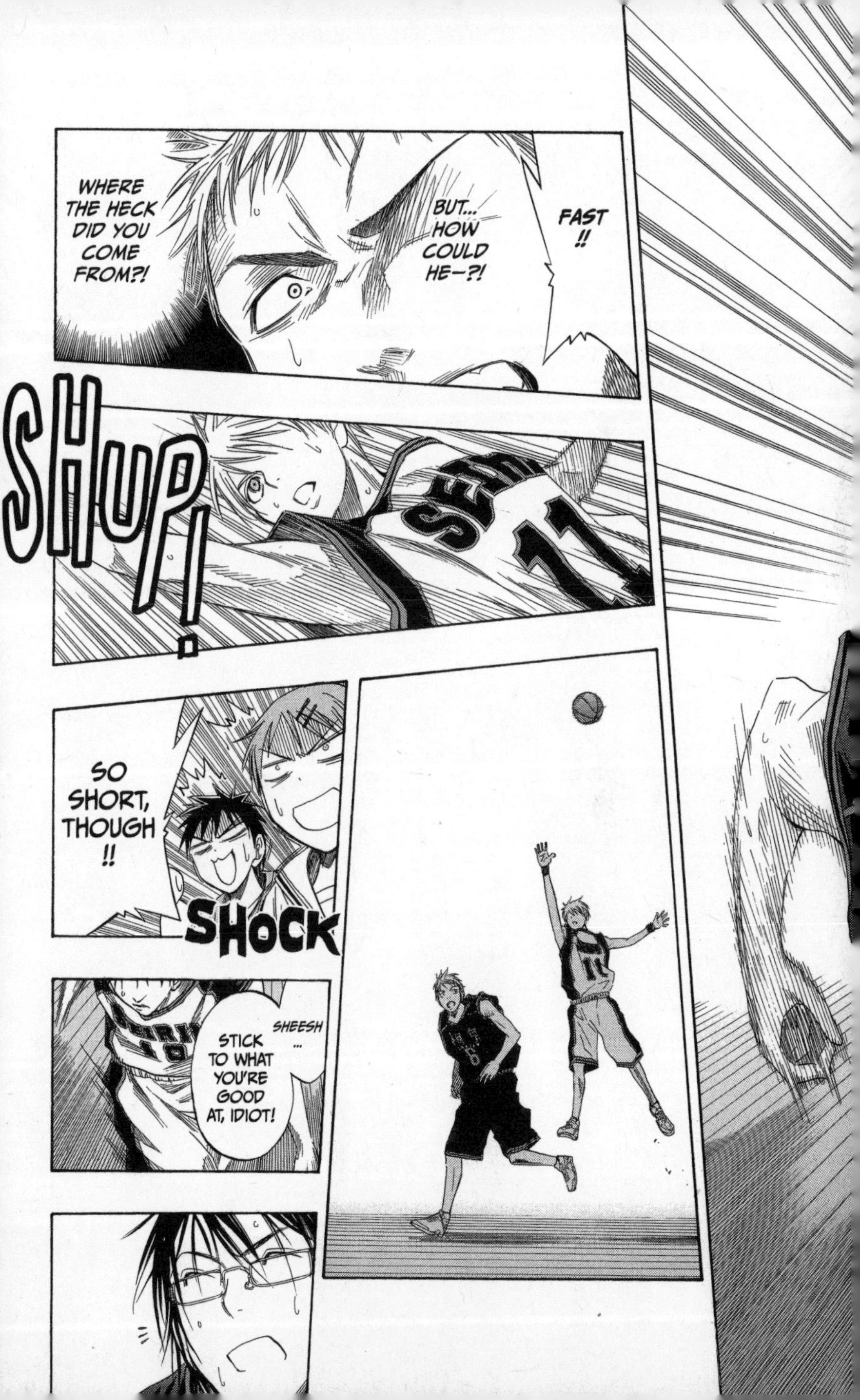
FAST !!
BUT... HOW COULD HE–?!
WHERE THE HECK DID YOU COME FROM?!
SHUP!!
SO SHORT, THOUGH !!
SHOCK
SHEESH ...
STICK TO WHAT YOU'RE GOOD AT, IDIOT!

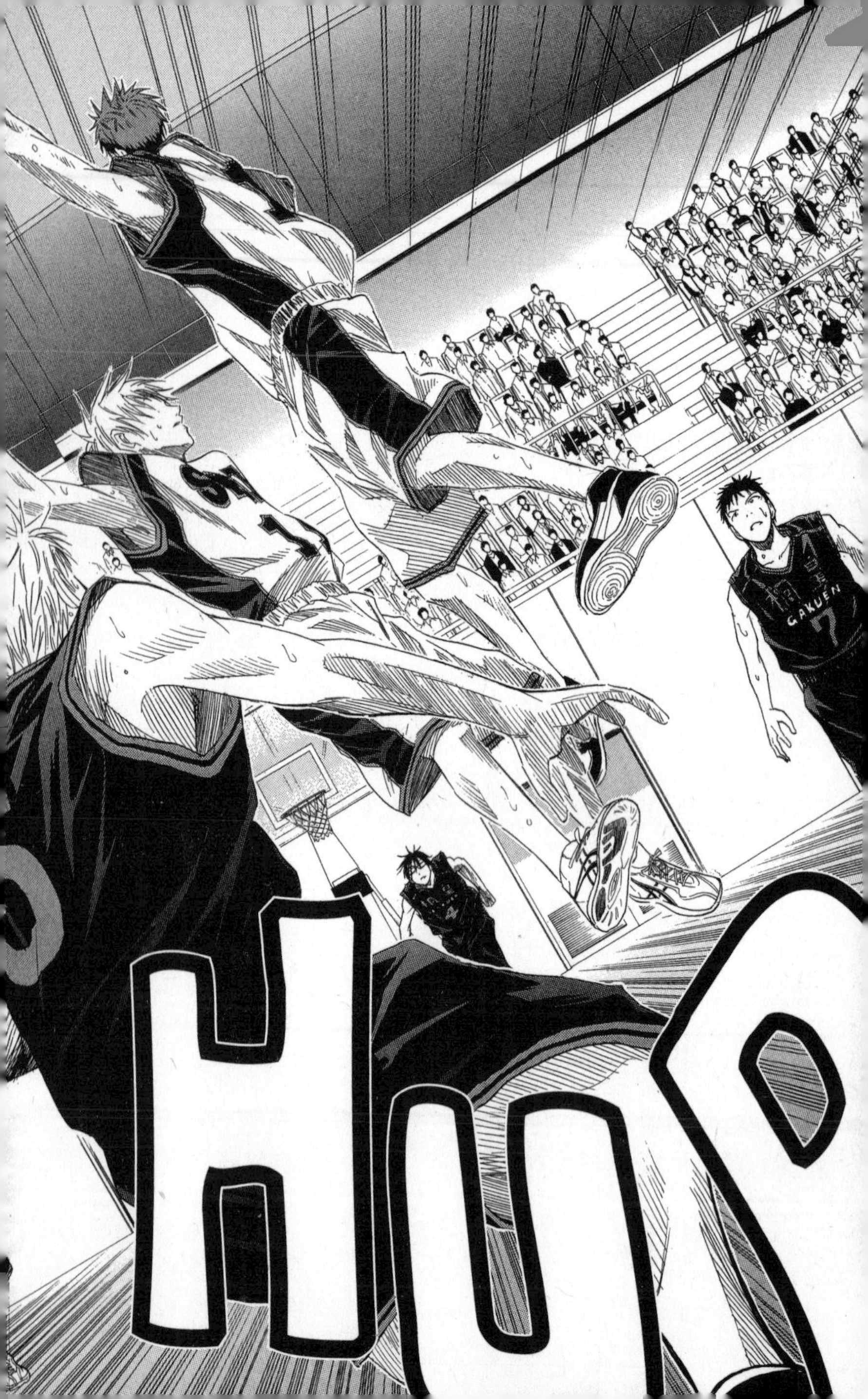
GAKUEN

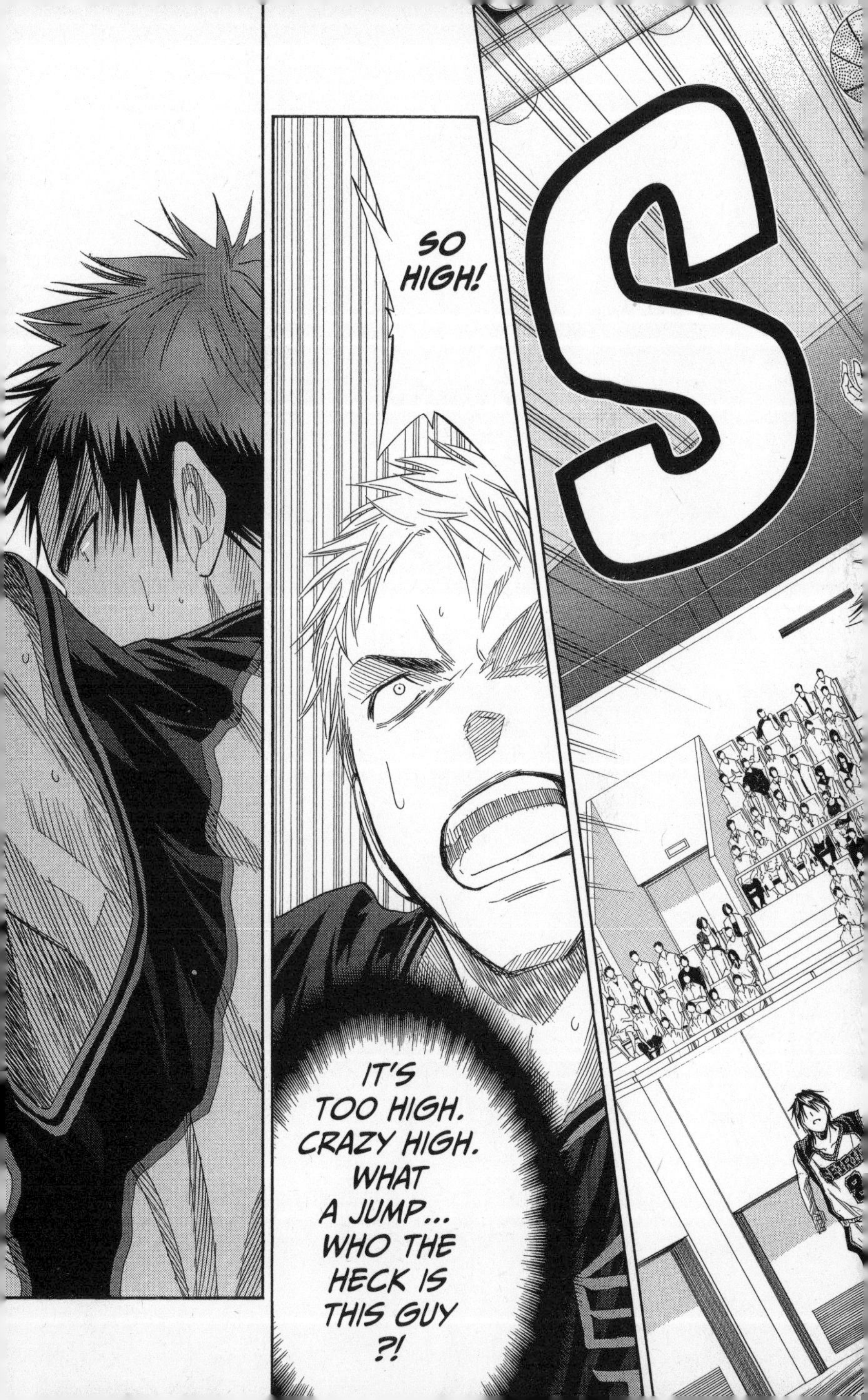
S
SO HIGH!
IT'S TOO HIGH. CRAZY HIGH. WHAT A JUMP... WHO THE HECK IS THIS GUY ?!

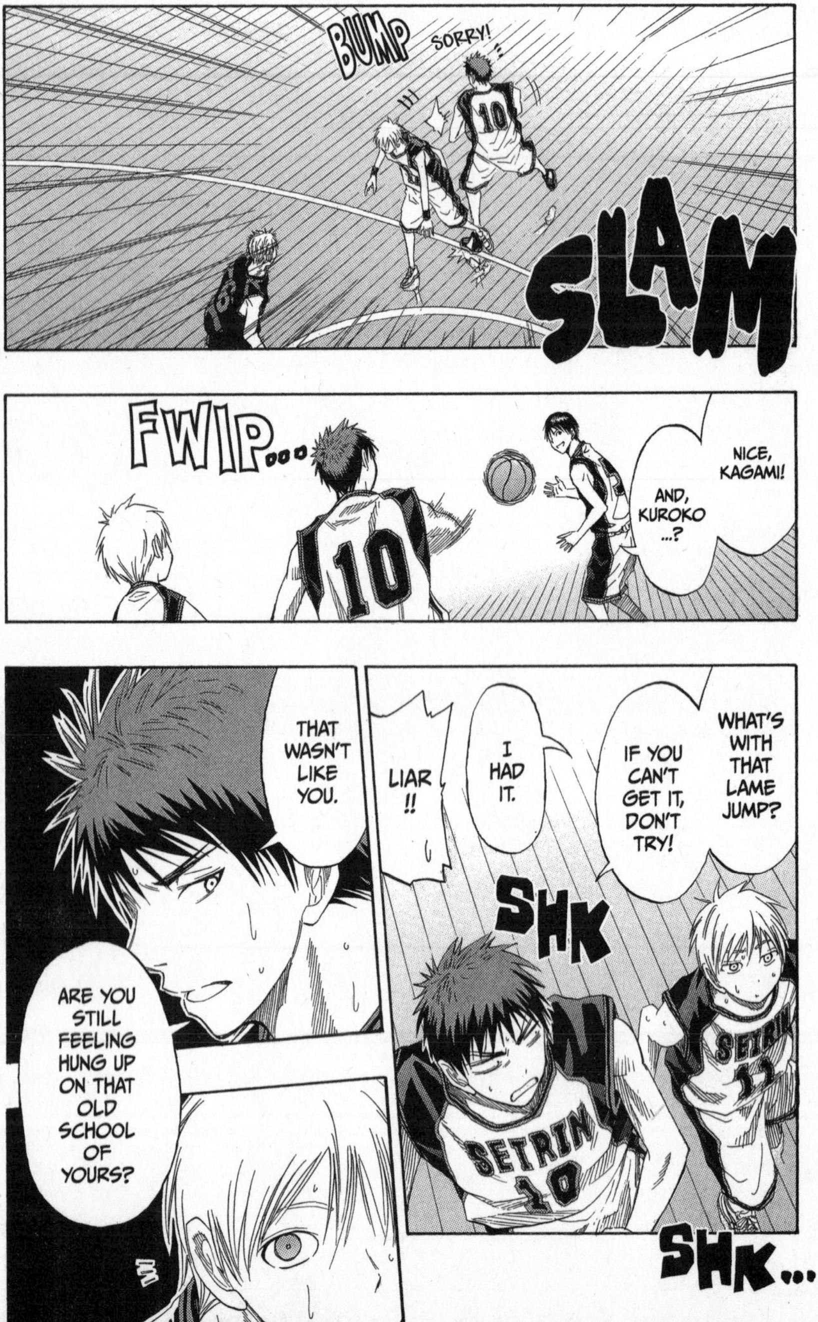
SORRY!
BUMP
SLAM
NICE, KAGAMI!
AND, KUROKO ...?
FWIP...
WHAT'S WITH THAT LAME JUMP?
IF YOU CAN'T GET IT, DON'T TRY!
I HAD IT.
LIAR !!
SHK
SHK...
THAT WASN'T LIKE YOU.
ARE YOU STILL FEELING HUNG UP ON THAT OLD SCHOOL OF YOURS?

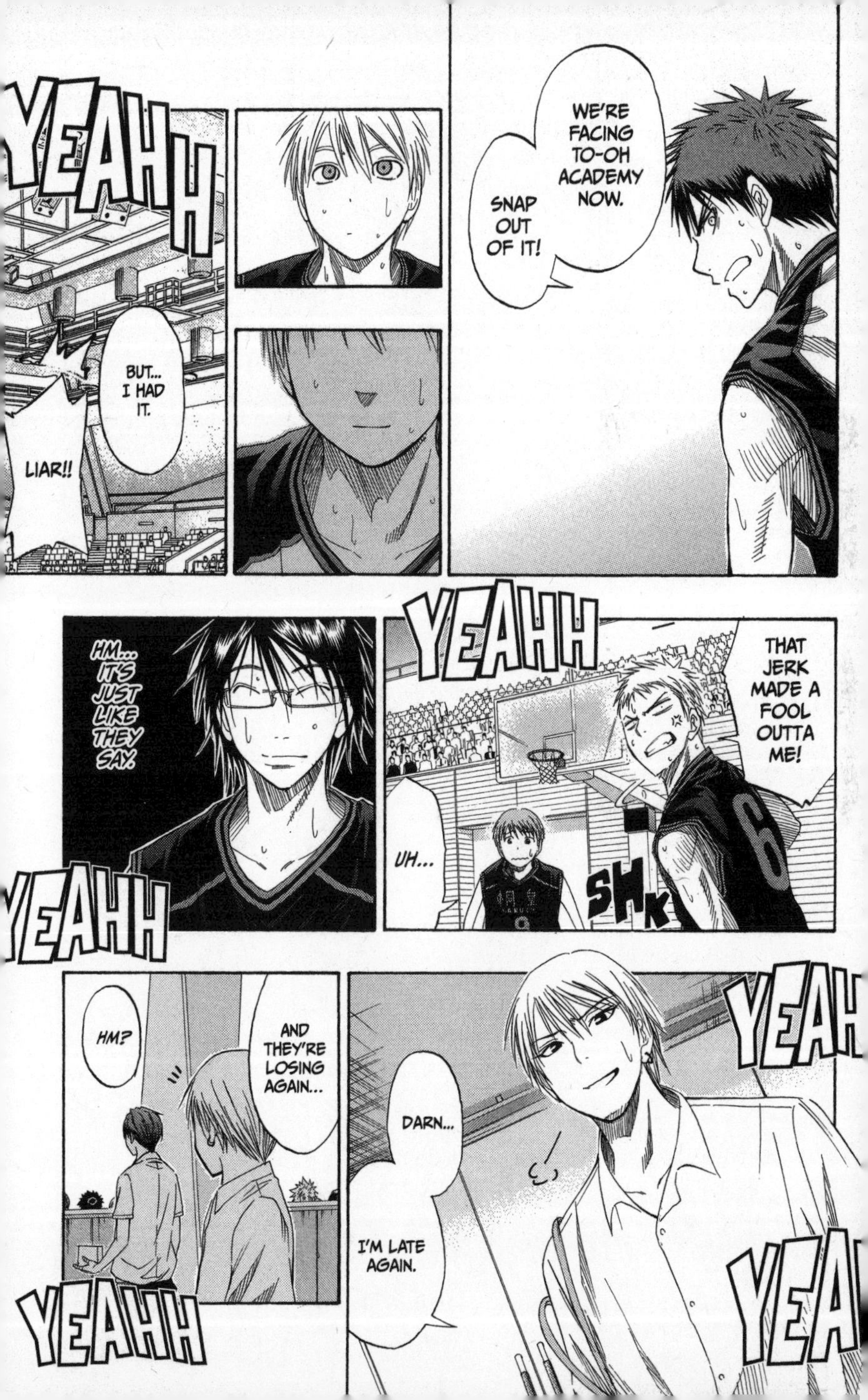
WE'RE FACING TO-OH ACADEMY NOW.
SNAP OUT OF IT!
YEAHH
BUT... I HAD IT.
LIAR!!
YEAHH
THAT JERK MADE A FOOL OUTTA ME!
UH...
SHK
HM... IT'S JUST LIKE THEY SAY.
YEAHH
YEAH
DARN...
I'M LATE AGAIN.
YEA
AND THEY'RE LOSING AGAIN...
HM?
YEAHH

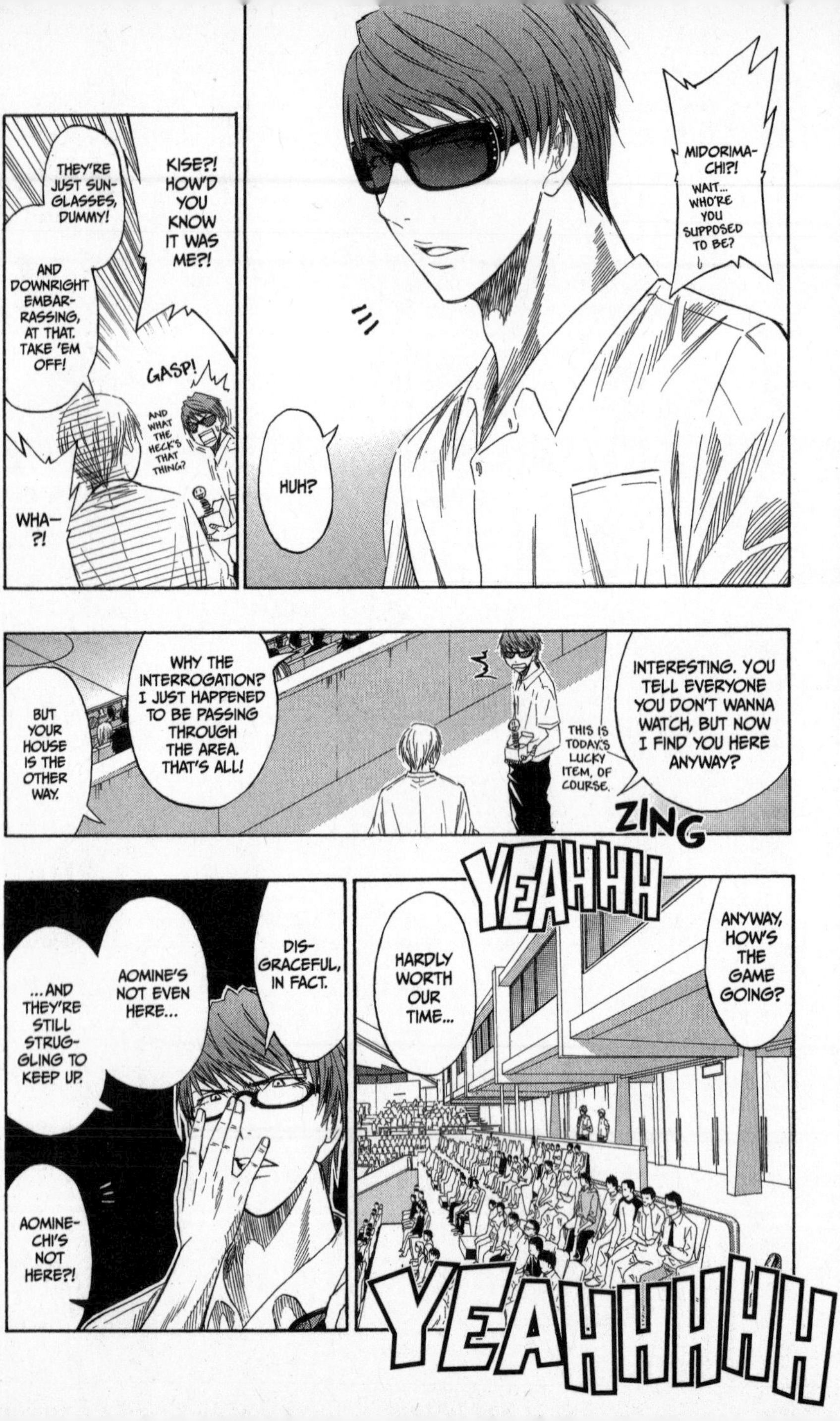
MIDORIMA-CHI?!
WAIT... WHO'RE YOU SUPPOSED TO BE?
HUH?
KISE?! HOW'D YOU KNOW IT WAS ME?!
GASP!
AND WHAT THE HECK'S THAT THING?
THEY'RE JUST SUN-GLASSES, DUMMY!
AND DOWNRIGHT EMBAR-RASSING, AT THAT. TAKE 'EM OFF!
WHA-?!
INTERESTING. YOU TELL EVERYONE YOU DON'T WANNA WATCH, BUT NOW I FIND YOU HERE ANYWAY?
THIS IS TODAY'S LUCKY ITEM, OF COURSE.
ZING
WHY THE INTERROGATION? I JUST HAPPENED TO BE PASSING THROUGH THE AREA. THAT'S ALL!
BUT YOUR HOUSE IS THE OTHER WAY.
YEAHHH
ANYWAY, HOW'S THE GAME GOING?
HARDLY WORTH OUR TIME...
YEAHHHHHH
DIS-GRACEFUL, IN FACT.
AOMINE'S NOT EVEN HERE...
...AND THEY'RE STILL STRUG-GLING TO KEEP UP.
AOMINE-CHI'S NOT HERE?!

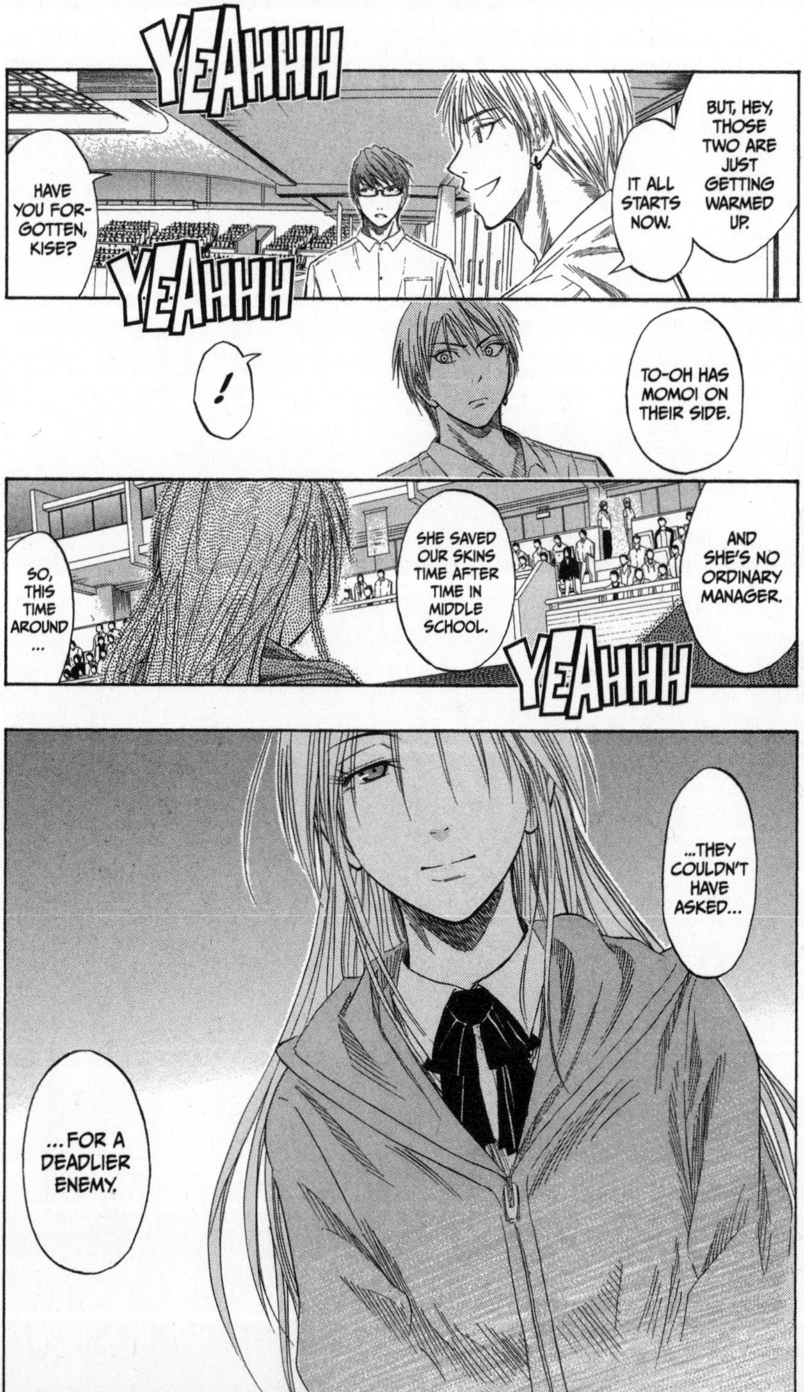
YEAHHH
BUT, HEY, THOSE TWO ARE JUST GETTING WARMED UP.
IT ALL STARTS NOW.
HAVE YOU FOR-GOTTEN, KISE?
YEAHHH
TO-OH HAS MOMOI ON THEIR SIDE.
!
AND SHE'S NO ORDINARY MANAGER.
SHE SAVED OUR SKINS TIME AFTER TIME IN MIDDLE SCHOOL.
YEAHHH
SO, THIS TIME AROUND...
...THEY COULDN'T HAVE ASKED...
...FOR A DEADLIER ENEMY.

KUROKO'S BASKETBALL BLOOPERS

TAKE 1

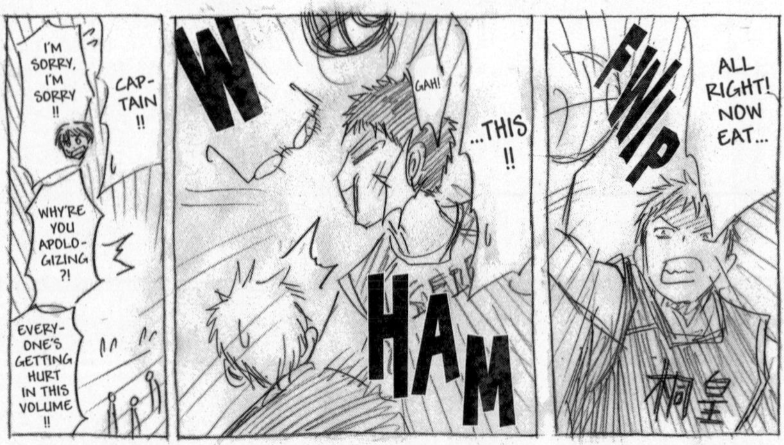
FWIP
ALL RIGHT! NOW EAT...
桐皇
GAH!
...THIS!!
W
HAM
CAPTAIN!!
I'M SORRY, I'M SORRY!!
WHY'RE YOU APOLOGIZING?!
EVERYONE'S GETTING HURT IN THIS VOLUME!!

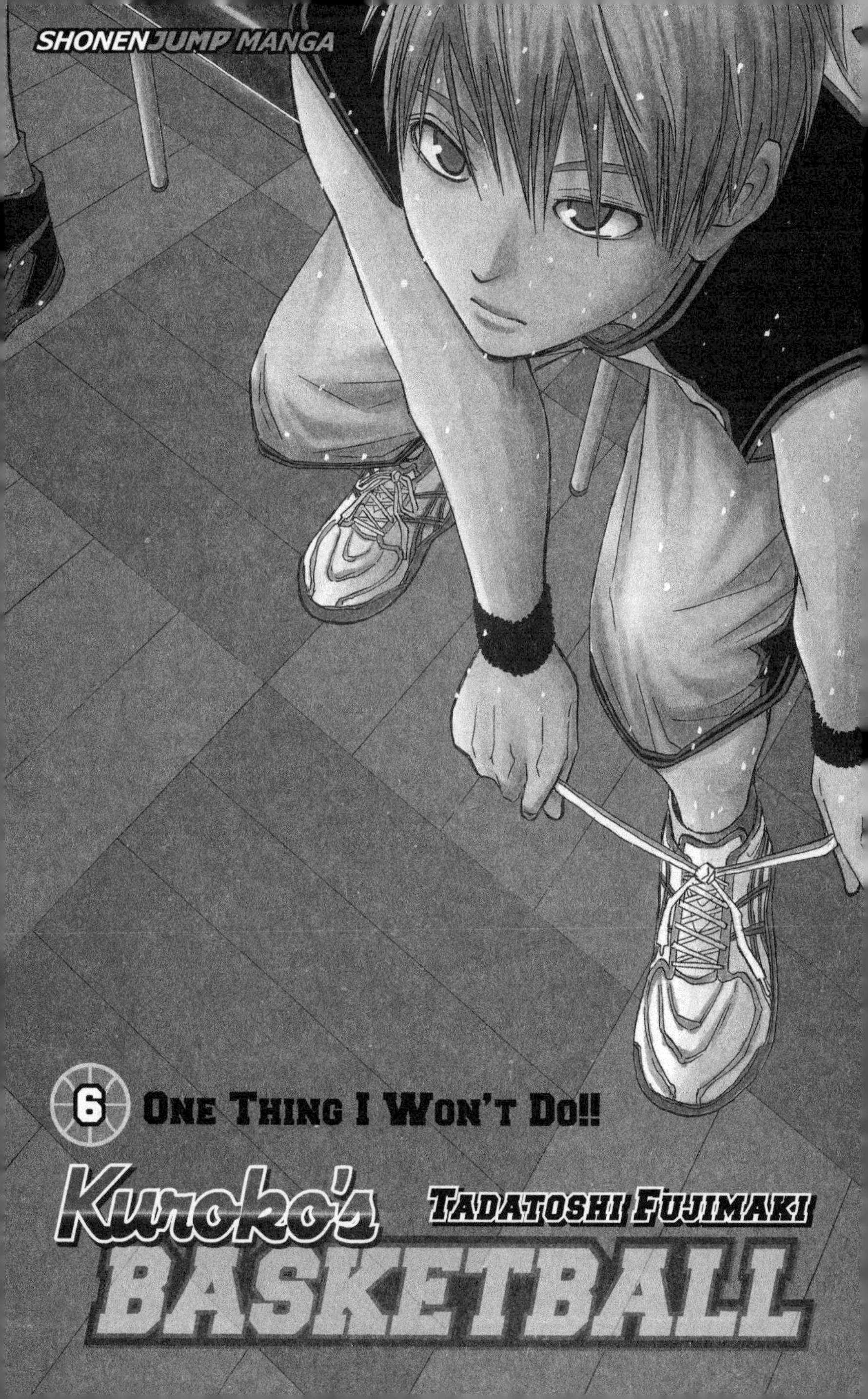
SHONEN JUMP MANGA
6 ONE THING I WON'T DO!!
Kuroko's
TADATOSHI FUJIMAKI
BASKETBALL

TADATOSHI FUJIMAKI

This isn't something I typically broadcast, but I often find myself irritated while working, thinking, "Why can't I draw better?" or "Why can't I come up with a better story?" But I believe that satisfaction means the end of passion, so I'll probably keep being irritated.

But I like drawing manga.

—2010

44TH QUARTER: NOT HER STYLE

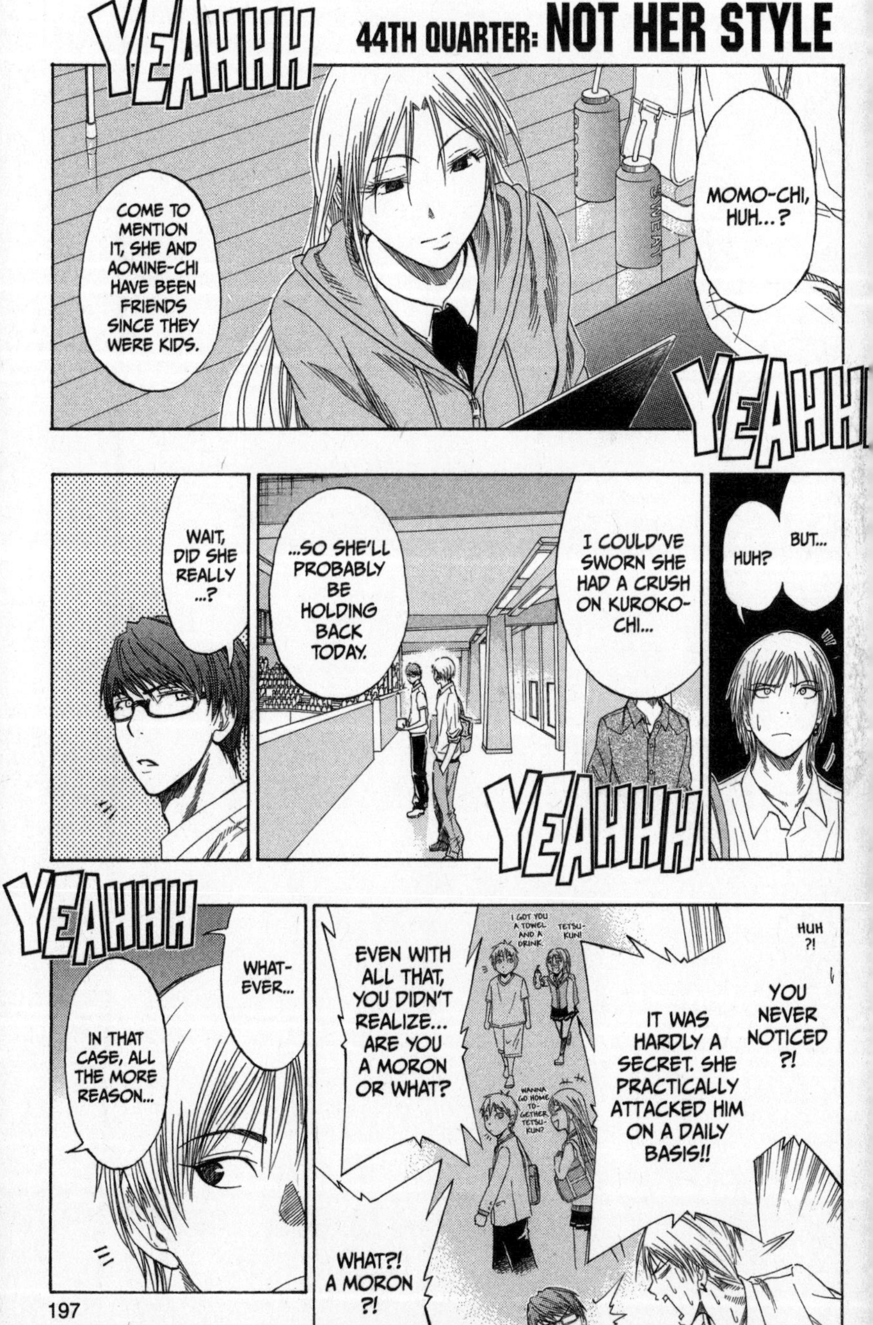

YEAHHH
MOMO-CHI, HUH...?
COME TO MENTION IT, SHE AND AOMINE-CHI HAVE BEEN FRIENDS SINCE THEY WERE KIDS.
YEAHH
BUT...
HUH?
I COULD'VE SWORN SHE HAD A CRUSH ON KUROKO-CHI...
...SO SHE'LL PROBABLY BE HOLDING BACK TODAY.
YEAHHH
WAIT, DID SHE REALLY ...?
YEAHHH
HUH ?!
YOU NEVER NOTICED ?!
IT WAS HARDLY A SECRET. SHE PRACTICALLY ATTACKED HIM ON A DAILY BASIS!!
TETSU-KUN!
I GOT YOU A TOWEL AND A DRINK.
WANNA GO HOME TO-GETHER, TETSU-KUN?
EVEN WITH ALL THAT, YOU DIDN'T REALIZE... ARE YOU A MORON OR WHAT?
WHAT?! A MORON ?!
WHAT-EVER...
IN THAT CASE, ALL THE MORE REASON...

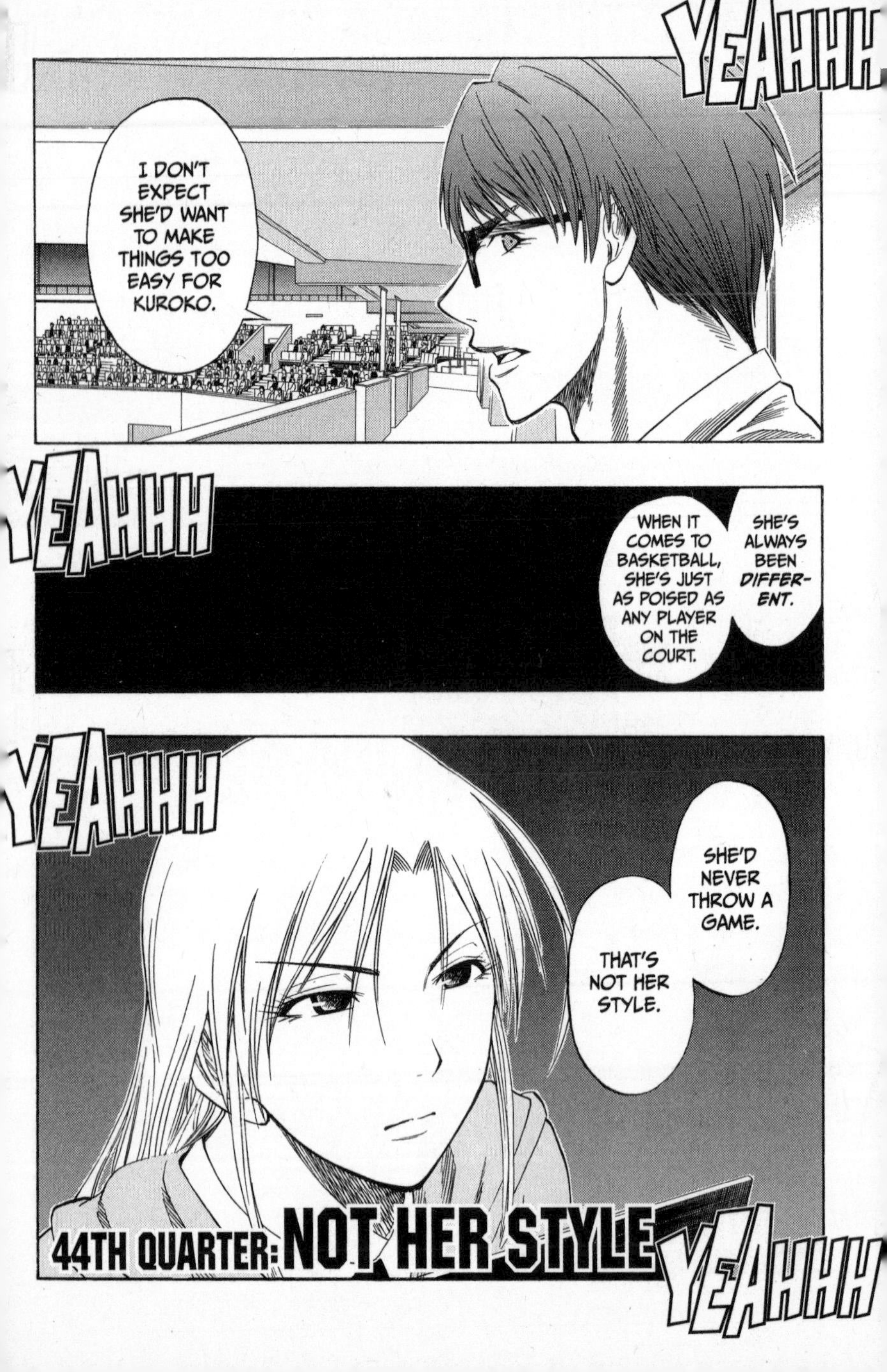
YEAHHH
I DON'T EXPECT SHE'D WANT TO MAKE THINGS TOO EASY FOR KUROKO.
YEAHHH
SHE'S ALWAYS BEEN *DIFFERENT.*
WHEN IT COMES TO BASKETBALL, SHE'S JUST AS POISED AS ANY PLAYER ON THE COURT.
YEAHHH
SHE'D NEVER THROW A GAME.
THAT'S NOT HER STYLE.
44TH QUARTER: NOT HER STYLE
YEAHHH

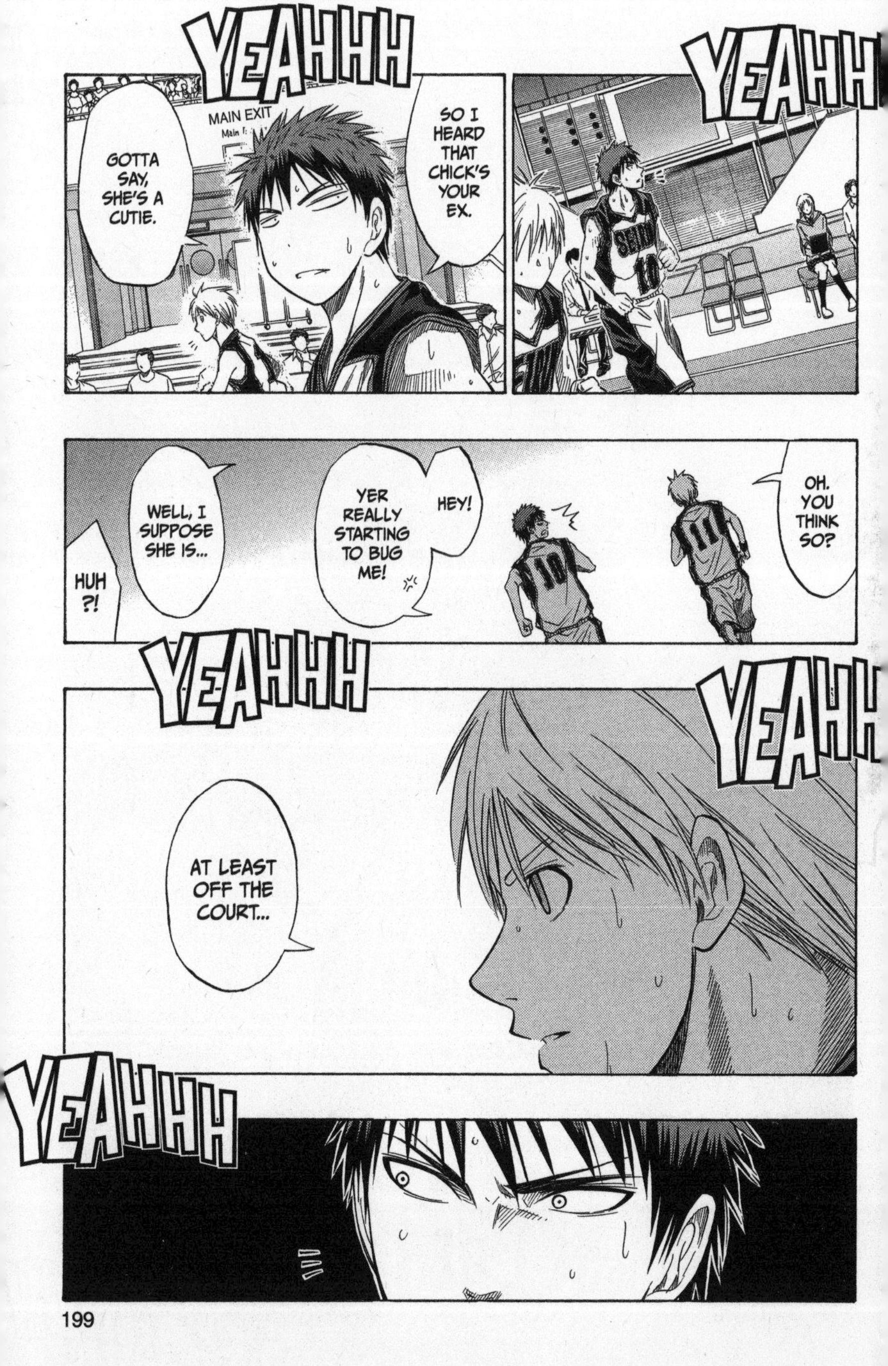
YEAHH
YEAHHH
SO I HEARD THAT CHICK'S YOUR EX.
MAIN EXIT
GOTTA SAY, SHE'S A CUTIE.
OH. YOU THINK SO?
HEY!
YER REALLY STARTING TO BUG ME!
WELL, I SUPPOSE SHE IS...
HUH ?!
YEAHH
YEAHHH
AT LEAST OFF THE COURT...
YEAHHH

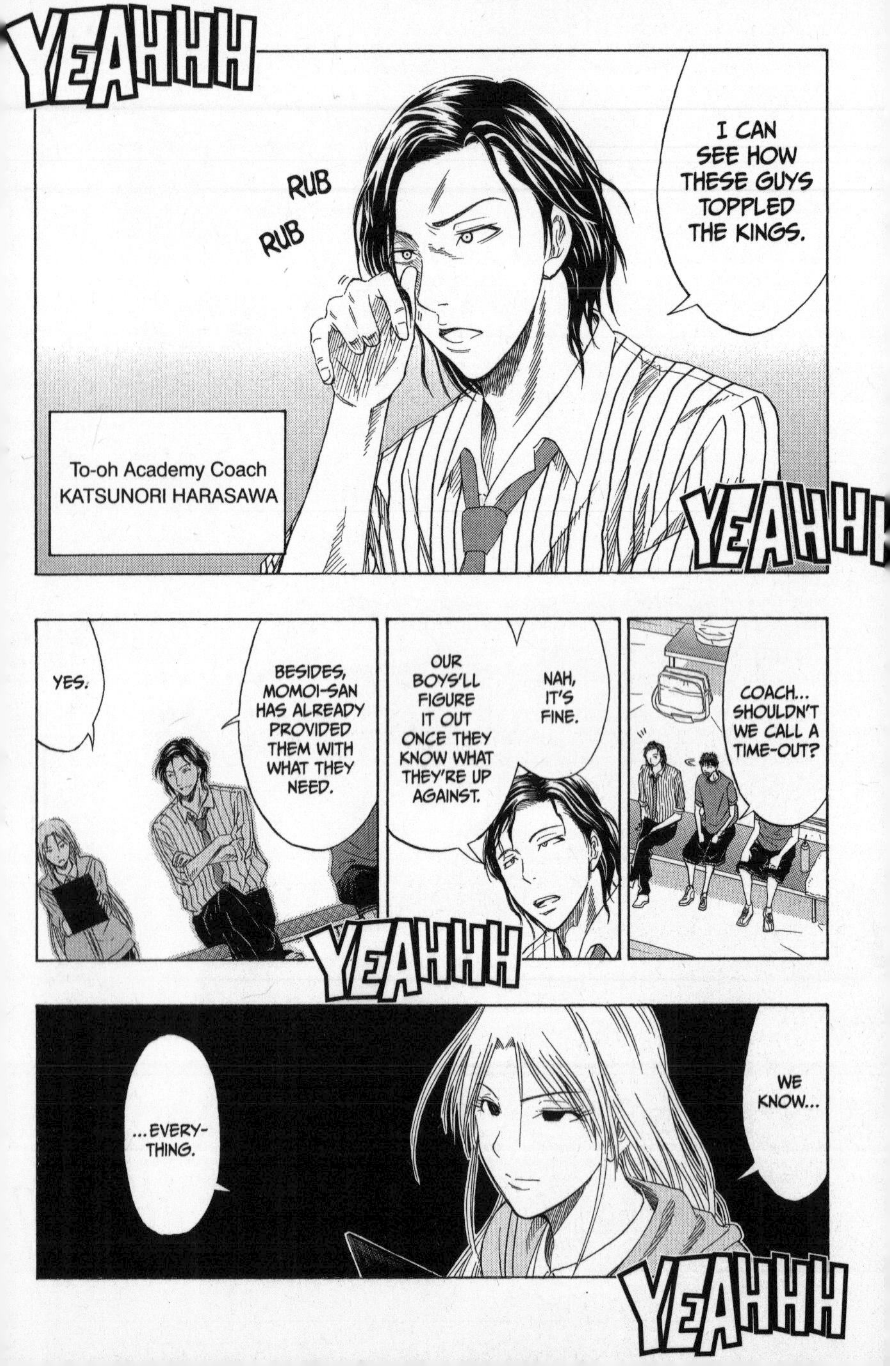

YEAHHH
I CAN SEE HOW THESE GUYS TOPPLED THE KINGS.
RUB
RUB
YEAHHH
To-oh Academy Coach
KATSUNORI HARASAWA
COACH... SHOULDN'T WE CALL A TIME-OUT?
NAH, IT'S FINE.
OUR BOYS'LL FIGURE IT OUT ONCE THEY KNOW WHAT THEY'RE UP AGAINST.
BESIDES, MOMOI-SAN HAS ALREADY PROVIDED THEM WITH WHAT THEY NEED.
YES.
YEAHHH
WE KNOW...
...EVERY-THING.
YEAHHH

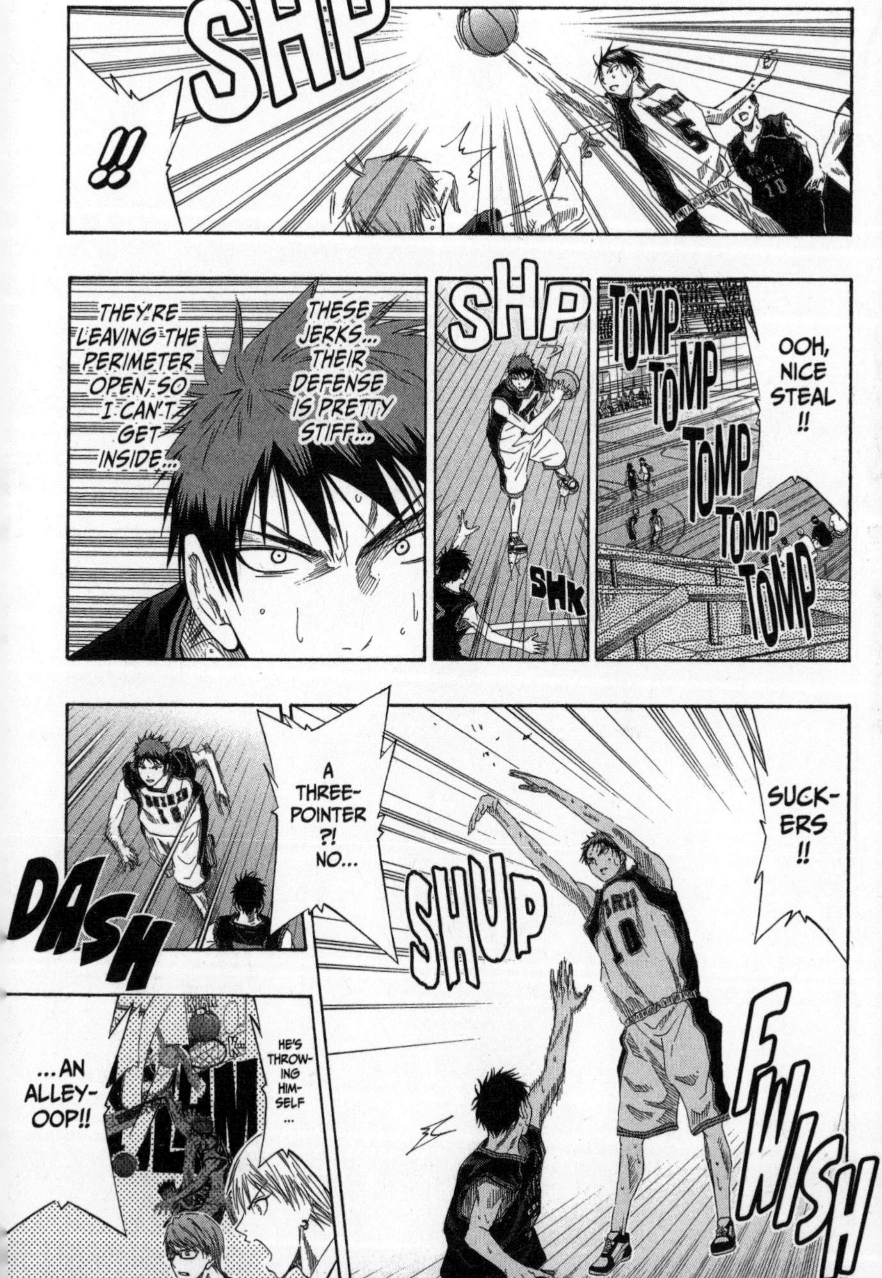
SHP
!!
TOMP
TOMP
TOMP
TOMP
TOMP
TOMP
OOH, NICE STEAL !!
SHP
SHK
THESE JERKS... THEIR DEFENSE IS PRETTY STIFF...
THEY'RE LEAVING THE PERIMETER OPEN, SO I CAN'T GET INSIDE...
SUCK-ERS !!
FWISH
SHUP
A THREE-POINTER ?! NO...
DASH
HE'S THROWING HIMSELF ...
...AN ALLEY-OOP!!

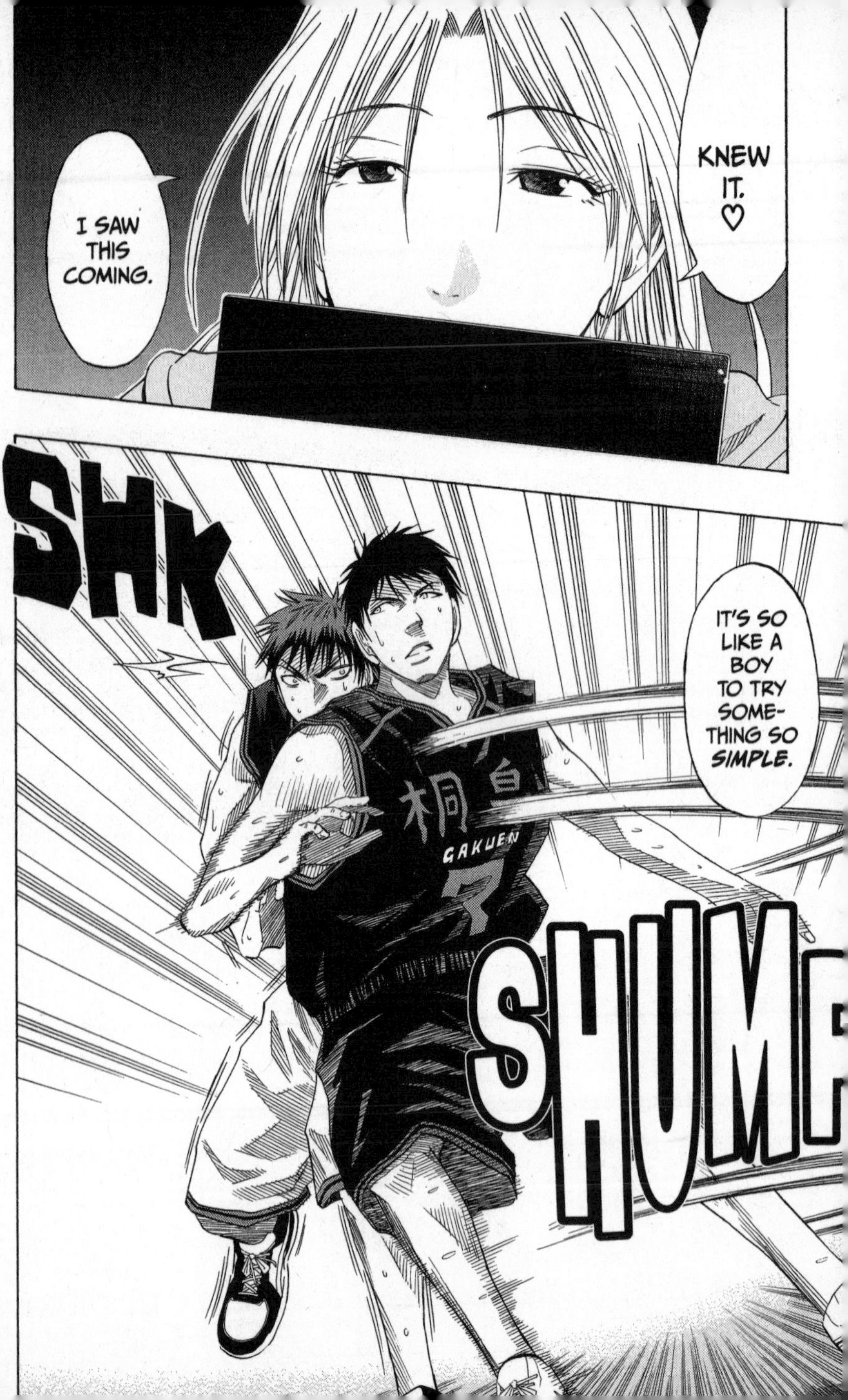
KNEW IT. ♡
I SAW THIS COMING.
IT'S SO LIKE A BOY TO TRY SOMETHING SO *SIMPLE*.
SHK
GAKUEN
SHUM

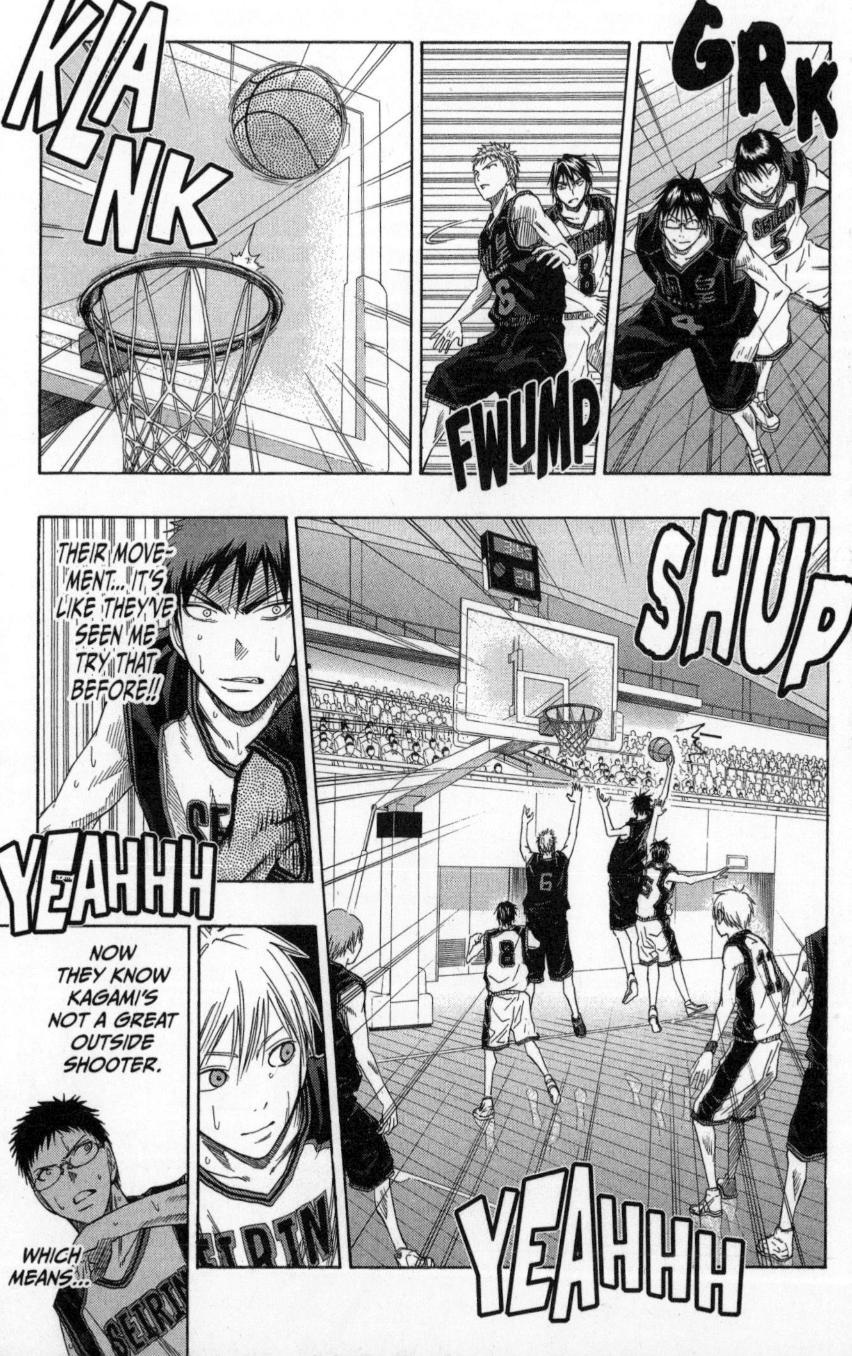
GRK
FWUMP
KLANK
SHUP
YEAHHH
THEIR MOVEMENT... IT'S LIKE THEY'VE SEEN ME TRY THAT BEFORE!!
YEAHHH
NOW THEY KNOW KAGAMI'S NOT A GREAT OUTSIDE SHOOTER.
WHICH MEANS...

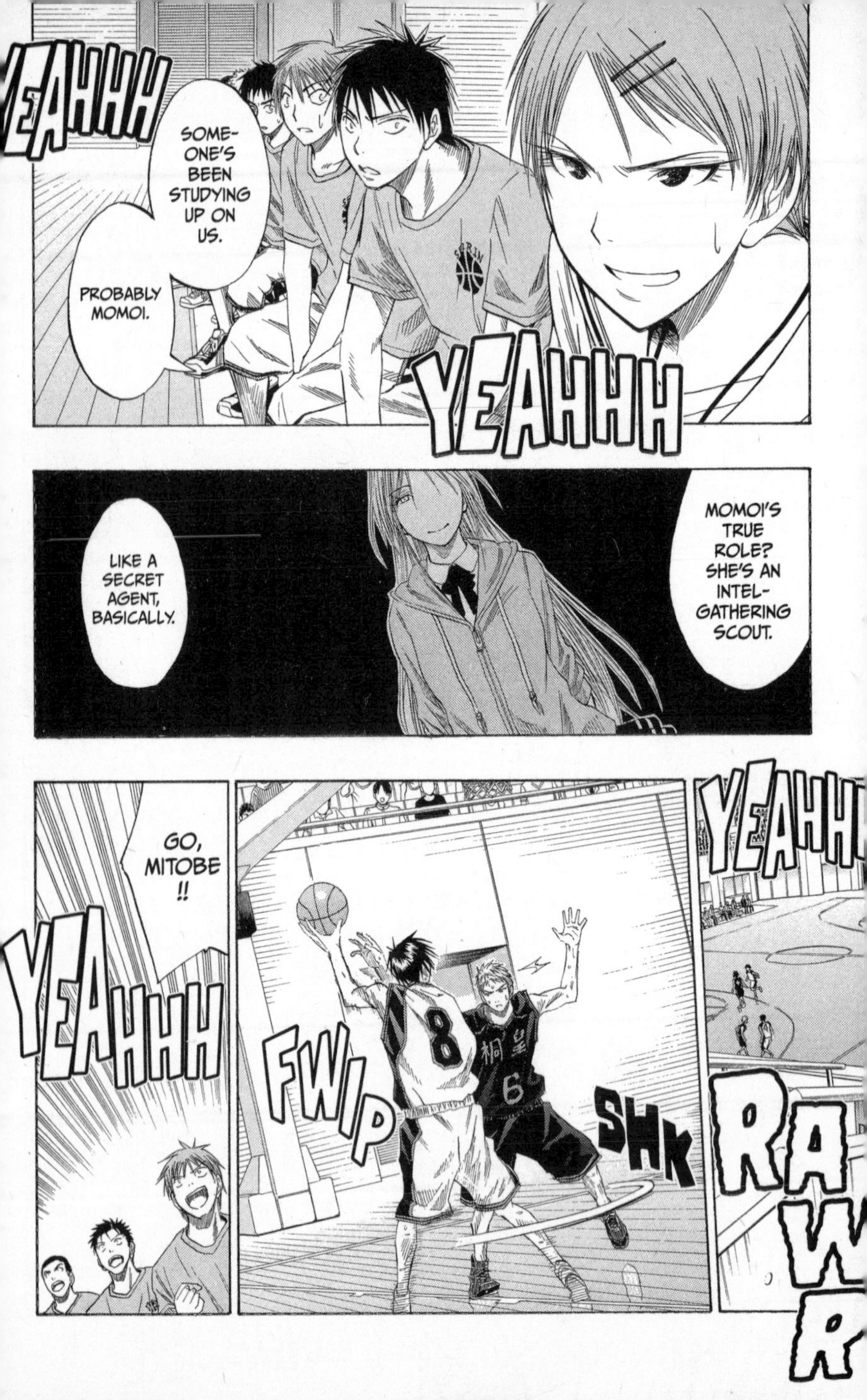

YEAHHH
SOME-ONE'S BEEN STUDYING UP ON US.
PROBABLY MOMOI.
YEAHHH
MOMOI'S TRUE ROLE? SHE'S AN INTEL-GATHERING SCOUT.
LIKE A SECRET AGENT, BASICALLY.
YEAHH
RAWR
SHK
FWIP
GO, MITOBE!!
YEAHHH

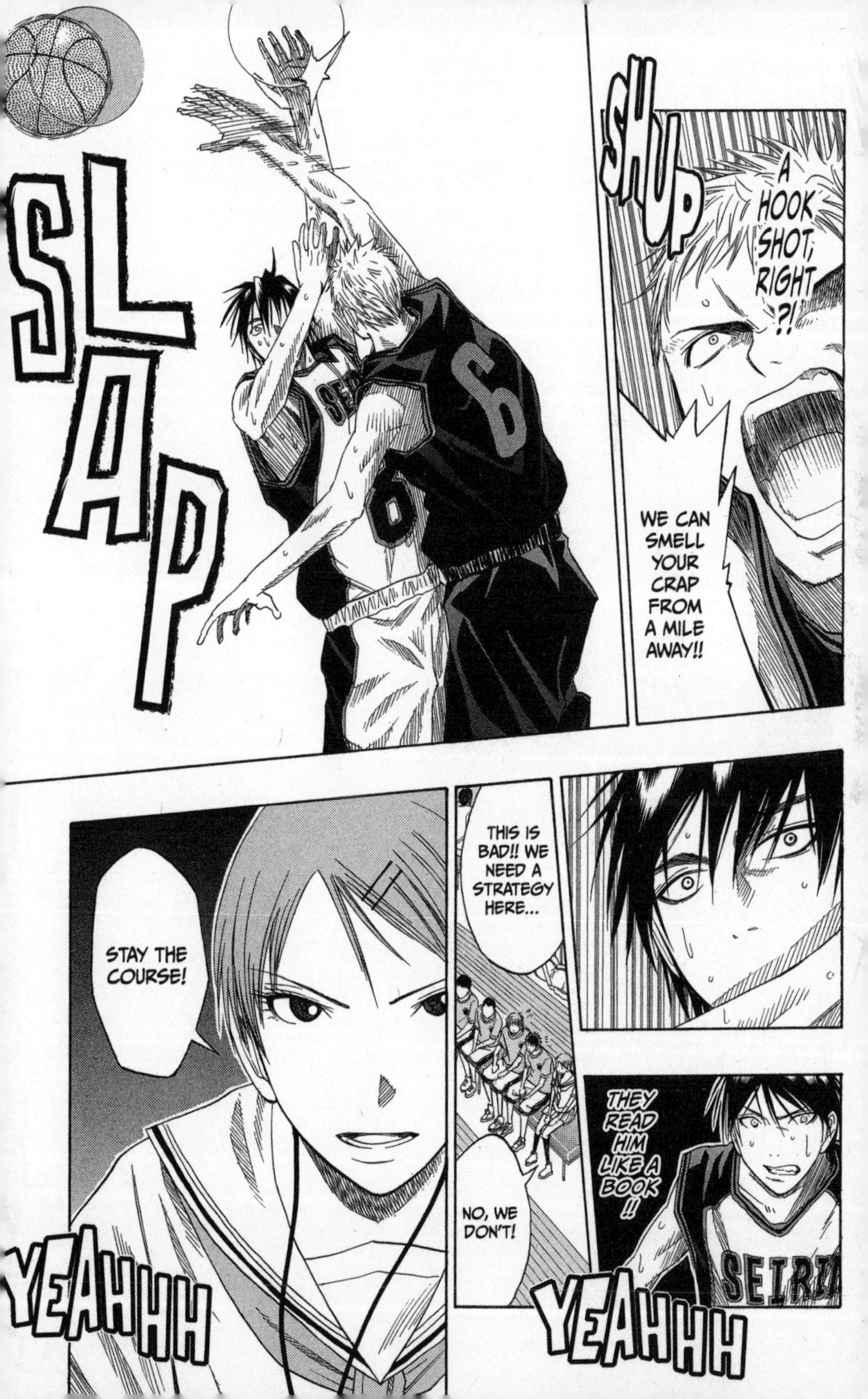
SHUP
A HOOK SHOT, RIGHT?!
WE CAN SMELL YOUR CRAP FROM A MILE AWAY!!
SLAP
THEY READ HIM LIKE A BOOK!!
YEAHHH
THIS IS BAD!! WE NEED A STRATEGY HERE...
NO, WE DON'T!
STAY THE COURSE!
YEAHHH

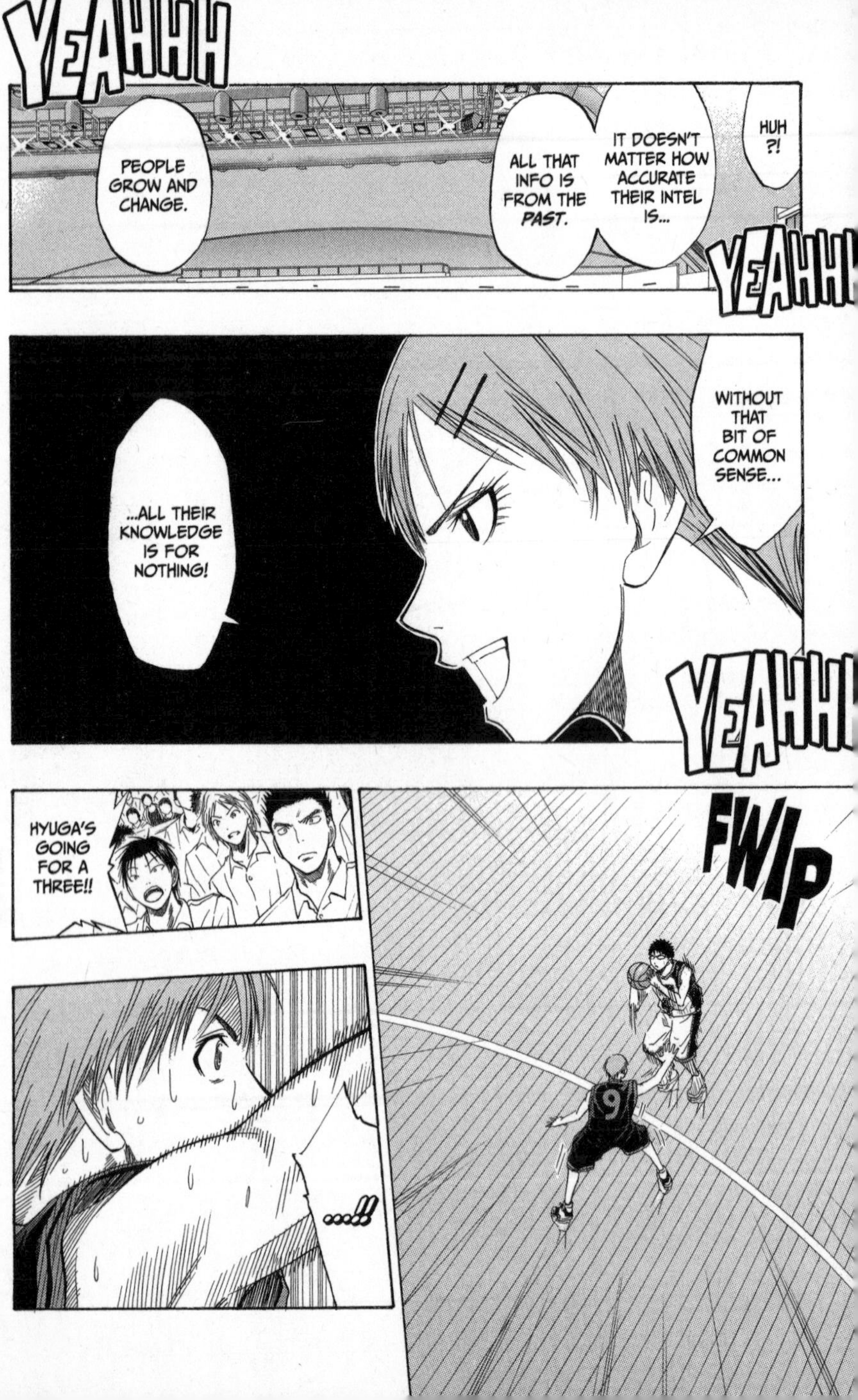
YEAHHH
HUH ?!
IT DOESN'T MATTER HOW ACCURATE THEIR INTEL IS...
ALL THAT INFO IS FROM THE PAST.
PEOPLE GROW AND CHANGE.
YEAHHH
WITHOUT THAT BIT OF COMMON SENSE...
...ALL THEIR KNOWLEDGE IS FOR NOTHING!
YEAHHH
FWIP
HYUGA'S GOING FOR A THREE!!
...!!

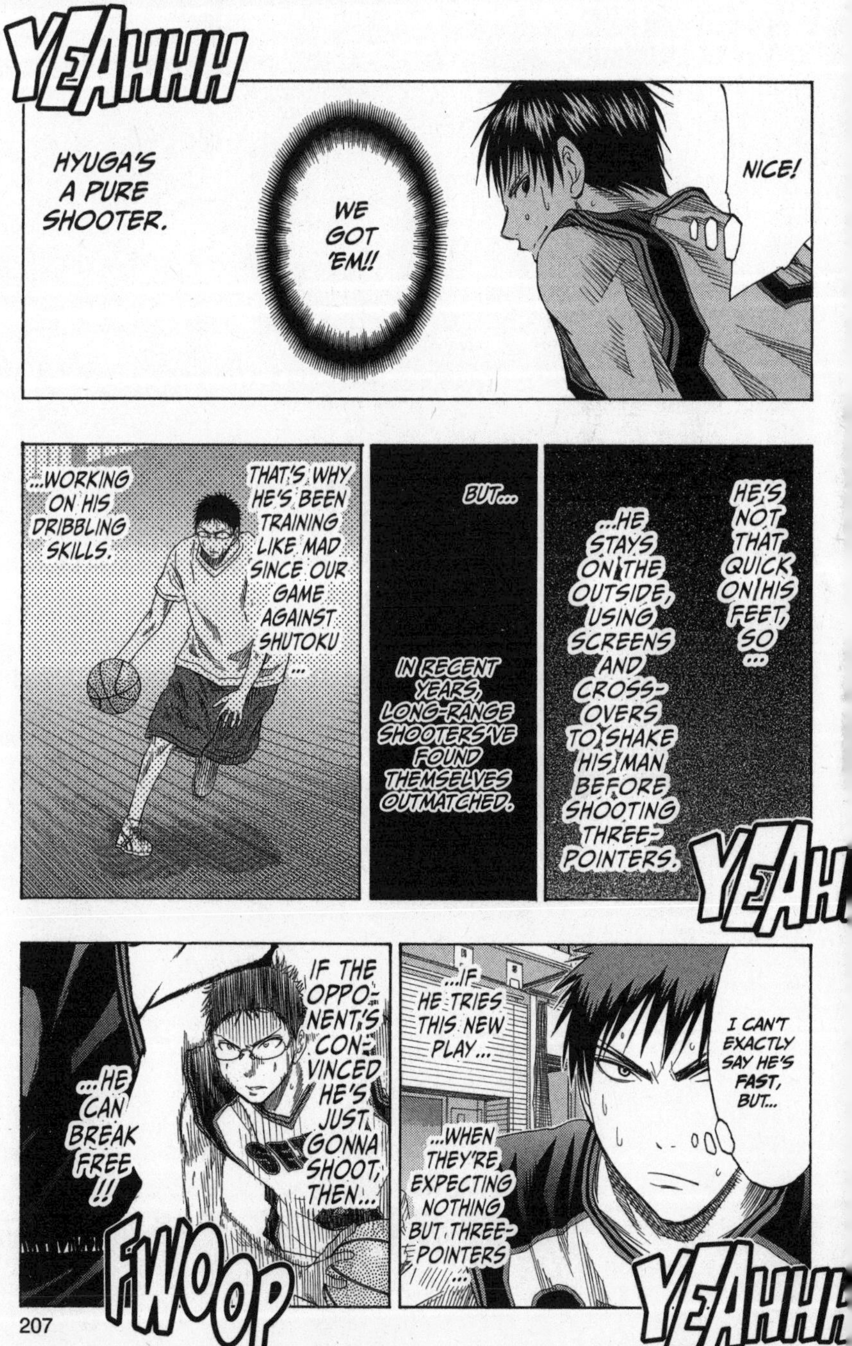
YEAHHH
NICE!
WE GOT 'EM!!
HYUGA'S A PURE SHOOTER.
HE'S NOT THAT QUICK ON HIS FEET, SO...
...HE STAYS ON THE OUTSIDE, USING SCREENS AND CROSS-OVERS TO SHAKE HIS MAN BEFORE SHOOTING THREE-POINTERS.
YEAHH
BUT...
IN RECENT YEARS, LONG-RANGE SHOOTERS'VE FOUND THEMSELVES OUTMATCHED.
THAT'S WHY HE'S BEEN TRAINING LIKE MAD SINCE OUR GAME AGAINST SHUTOKU...
...WORKING ON HIS DRIBBLING SKILLS.
I CAN'T EXACTLY SAY HE'S FAST, BUT...
...IF HE TRIES THIS NEW PLAY...
...WHEN THEY'RE EXPECTING NOTHING BUT THREE-POINTERS...
YEAHHH
IF THE OPPO-NENT'S CON-VINCED HE'S JUST GONNA SHOOT, THEN...
...HE CAN BREAK FREE!!
FWOOP

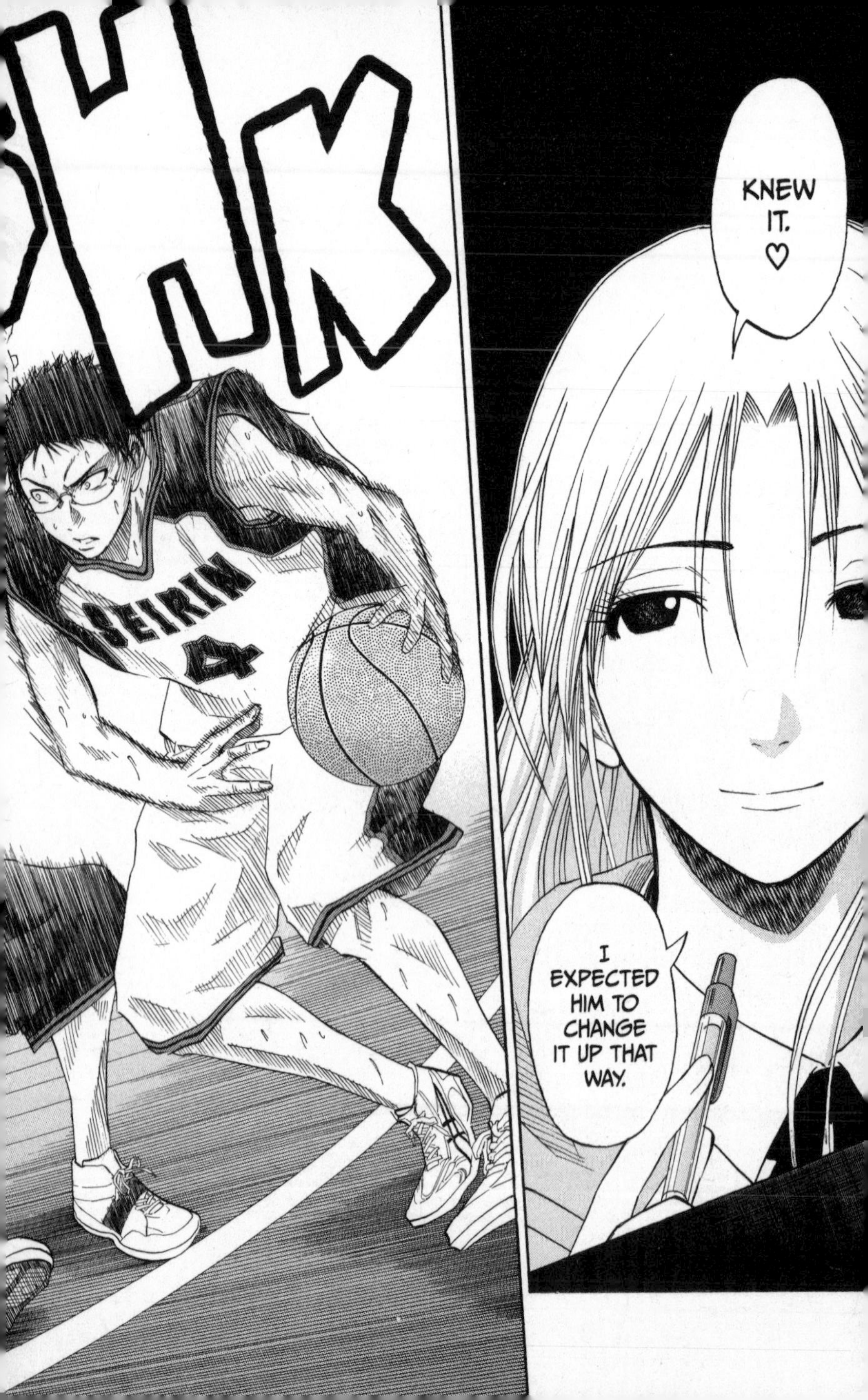
KNEW IT. ♡
I EXPECTED HIM TO CHANGE IT UP THAT WAY.
SHK

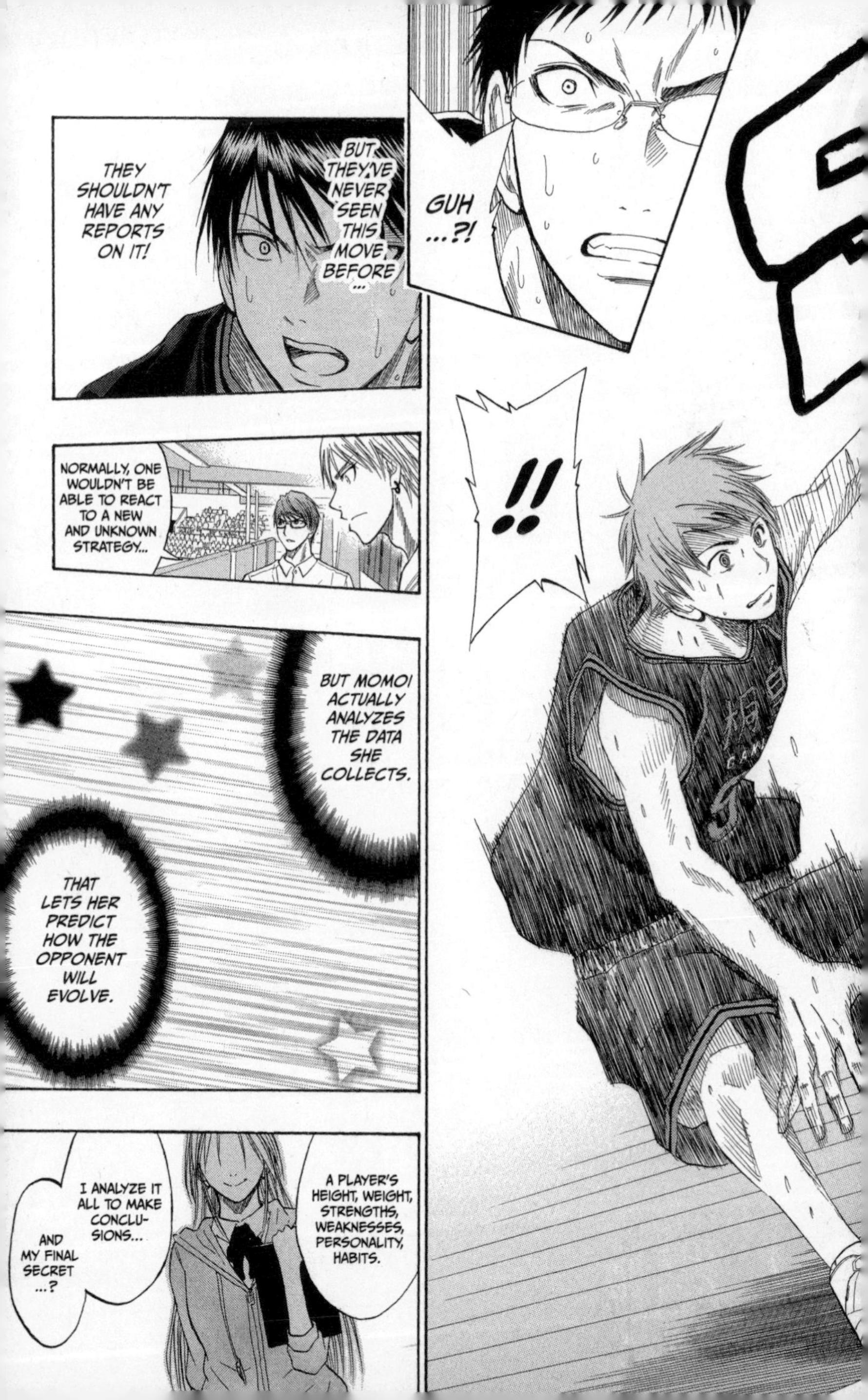
GUH ...?!
BUT THEY'VE NEVER SEEN THIS MOVE BEFORE ...
THEY SHOULDN'T HAVE ANY REPORTS ON IT!
!!
NORMALLY, ONE WOULDN'T BE ABLE TO REACT TO A NEW AND UNKNOWN STRATEGY...
BUT MOMOI ACTUALLY ANALYZES THE DATA SHE COLLECTS.
THAT LETS HER PREDICT HOW THE OPPONENT WILL EVOLVE.
A PLAYER'S HEIGHT, WEIGHT, STRENGTHS, WEAKNESSES, PERSONALITY, HABITS.
I ANALYZE IT ALL TO MAKE CONCLU- SIONS...
AND MY FINAL SECRET ...?

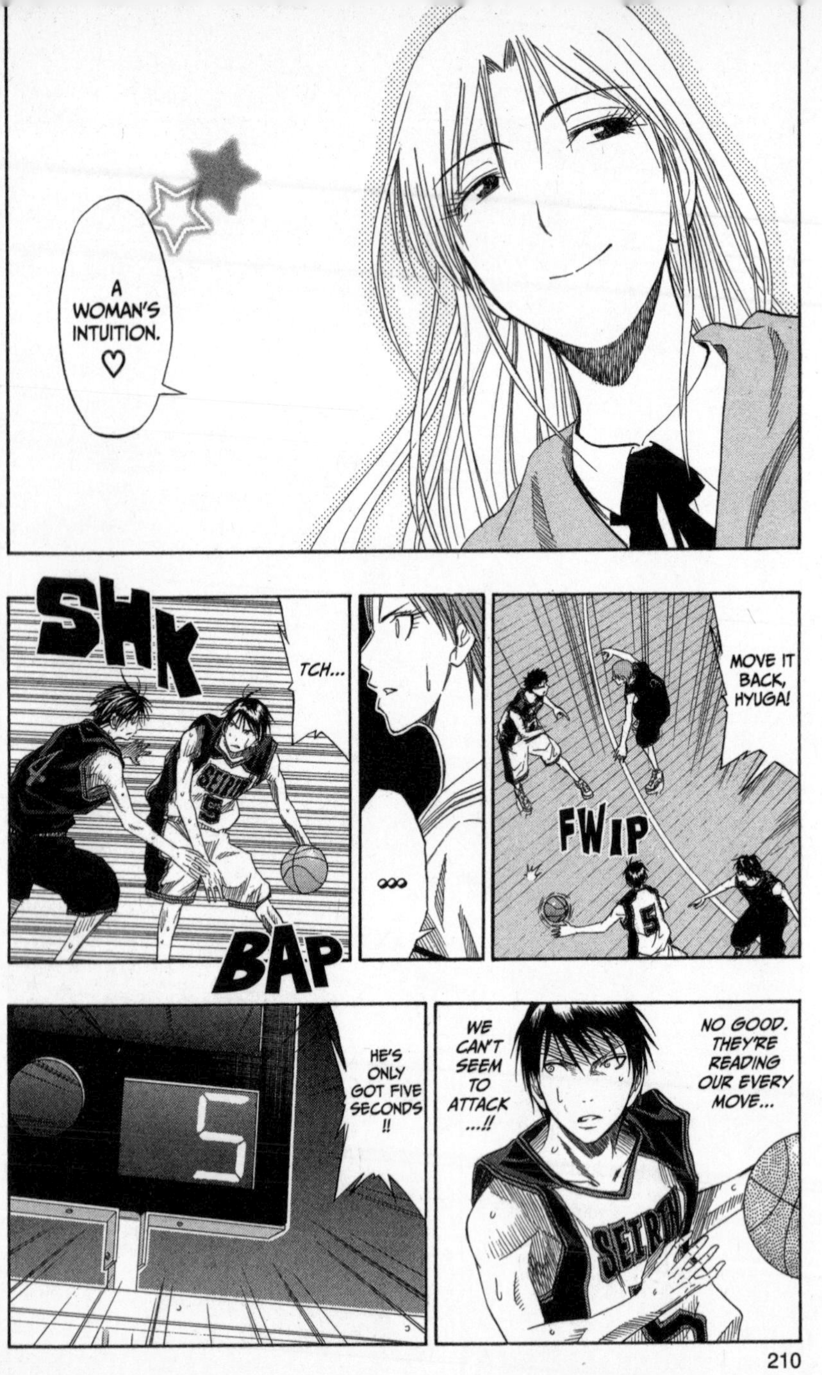
A WOMAN'S INTUITION. ♡
MOVE IT BACK, HYUGA!
FWIP
...
TCH...
SHK
BAP
NO GOOD. THEY'RE READING OUR EVERY MOVE...
WE CAN'T SEEM TO ATTACK ...!!
HE'S ONLY GOT FIVE SECONDS !!

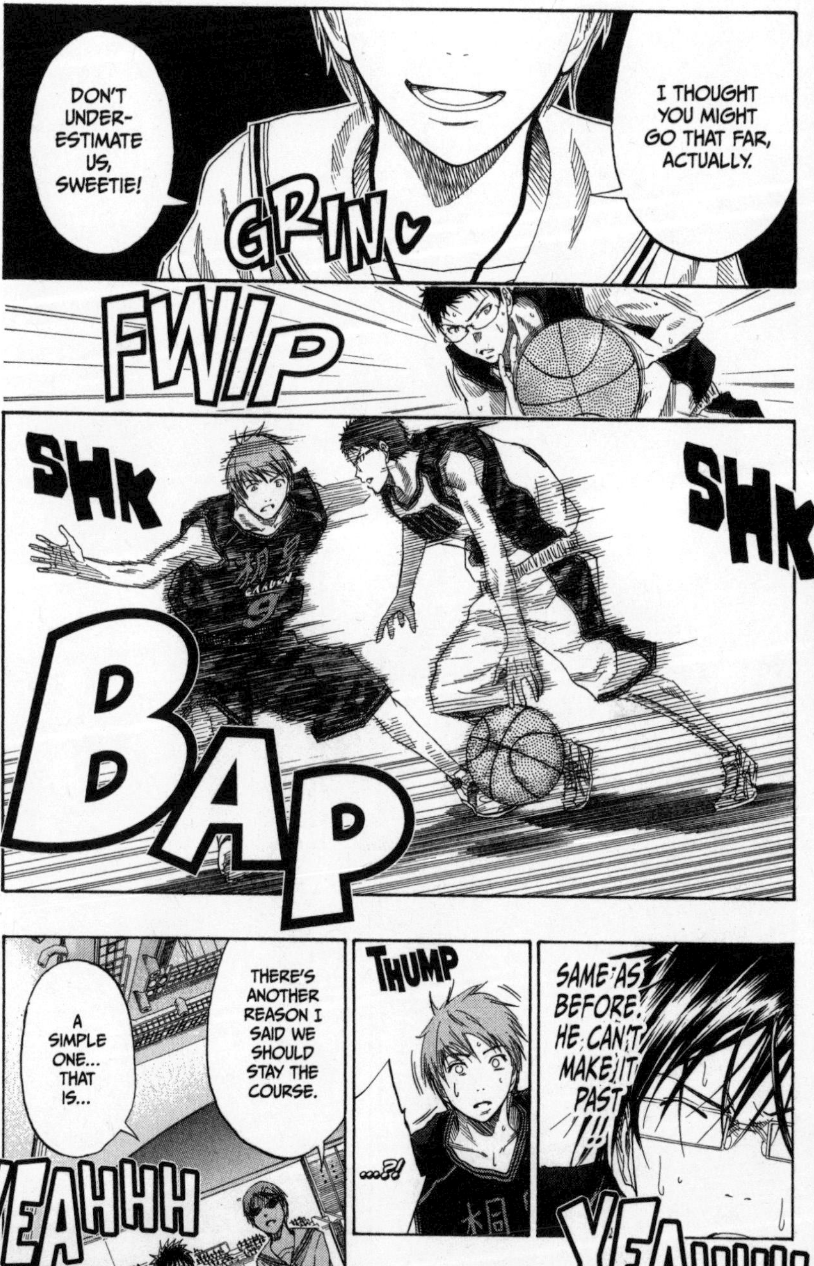
I THOUGHT YOU MIGHT GO THAT FAR, ACTUALLY.
DON'T UNDER-ESTIMATE US, SWEETIE!
GRIN
FWIP
SHK
SHK
BAP
SAME AS BEFORE. HE CAN'T MAKE IT PAST!!
YEAHHH
THUMP
...?!
THERE'S ANOTHER REASON I SAID WE SHOULD STAY THE COURSE.
A SIMPLE ONE... THAT IS...
YEAHHH

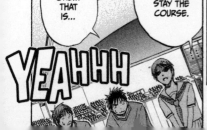

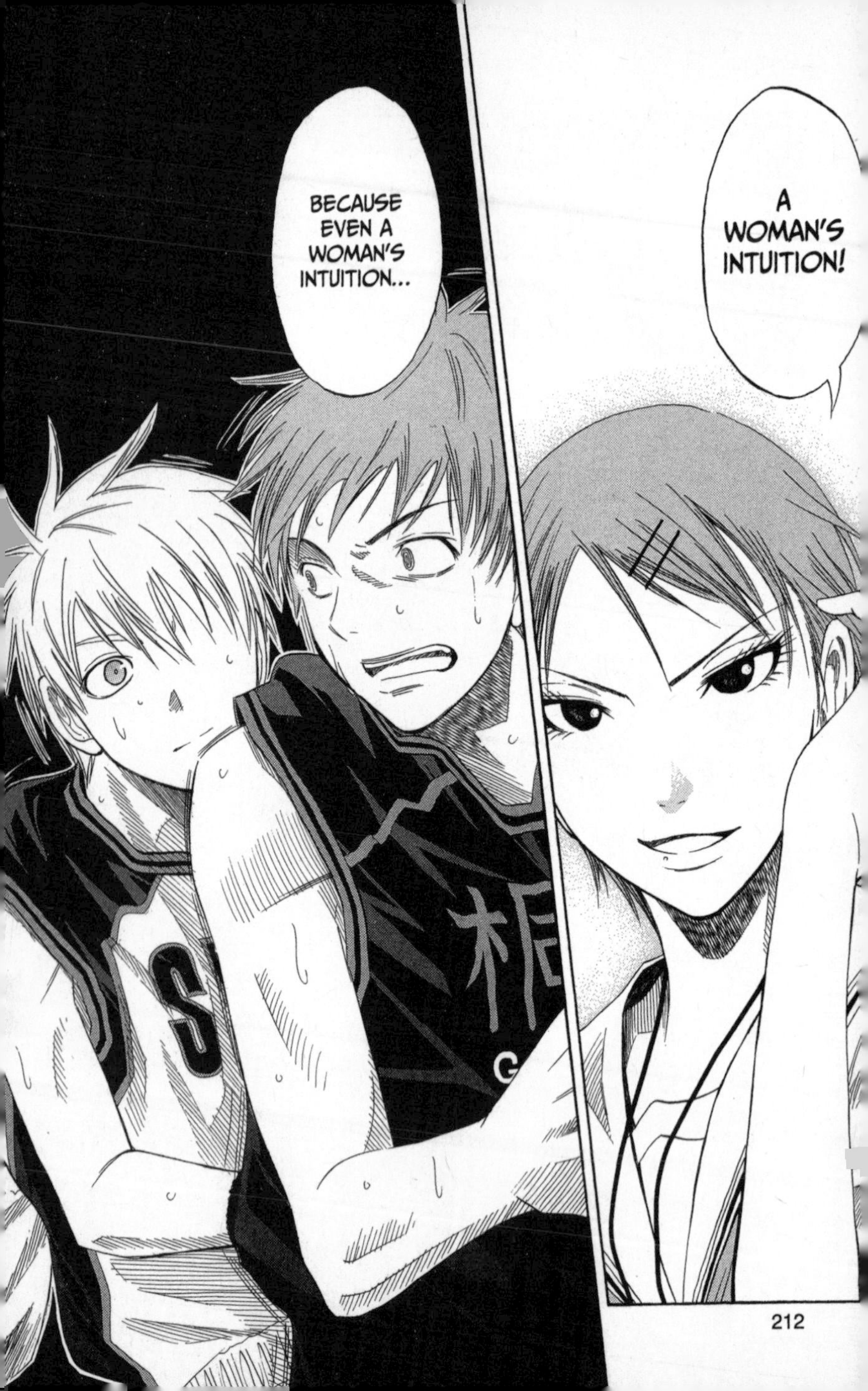
A WOMAN'S INTUITION!
BECAUSE EVEN A WOMAN'S INTUITION...

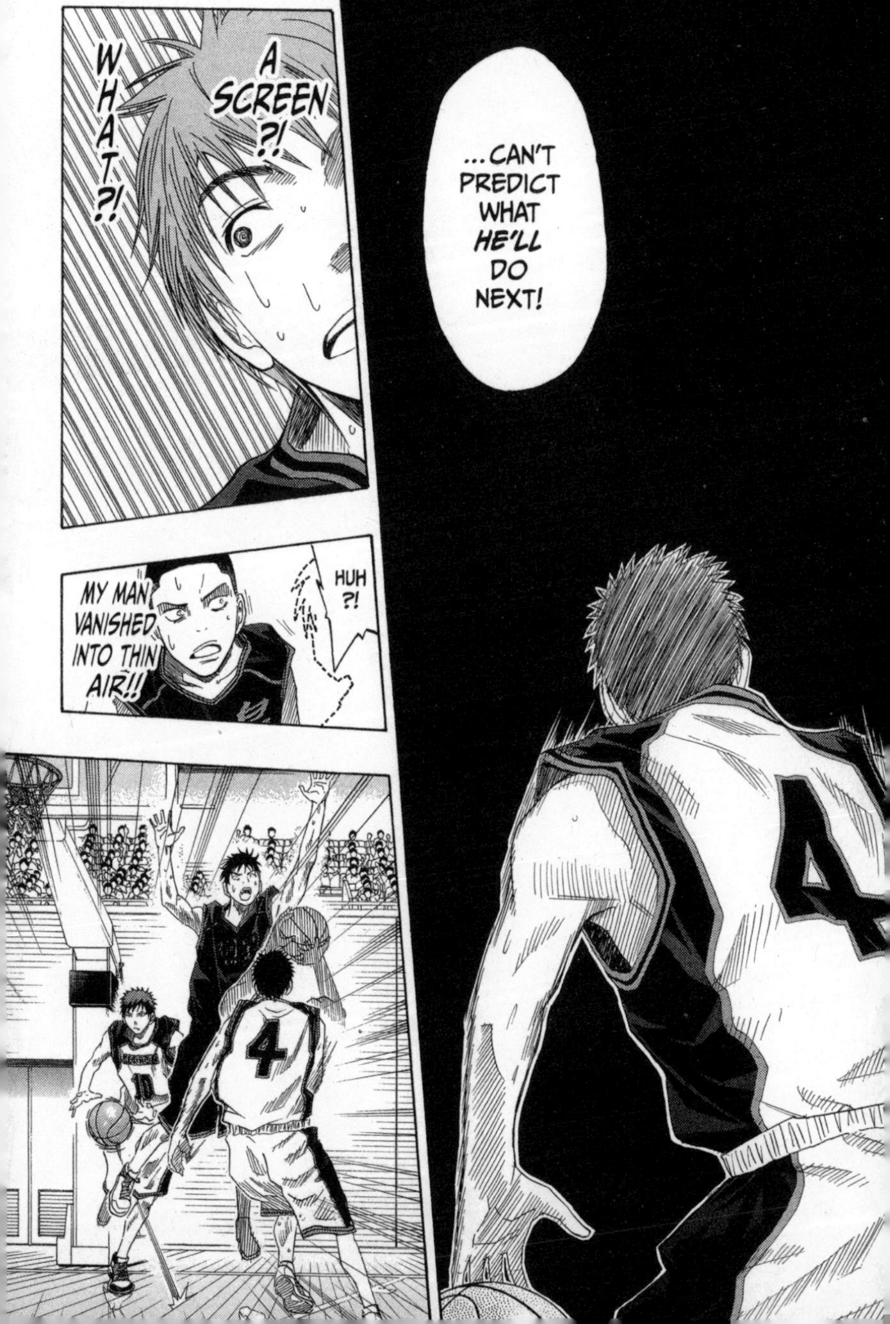

...CAN'T PREDICT WHAT *HE'LL* DO NEXT!
A SCREEN?!
WHAT?!
HUH?!
MY MAN VANISHED INTO THIN AIR!!

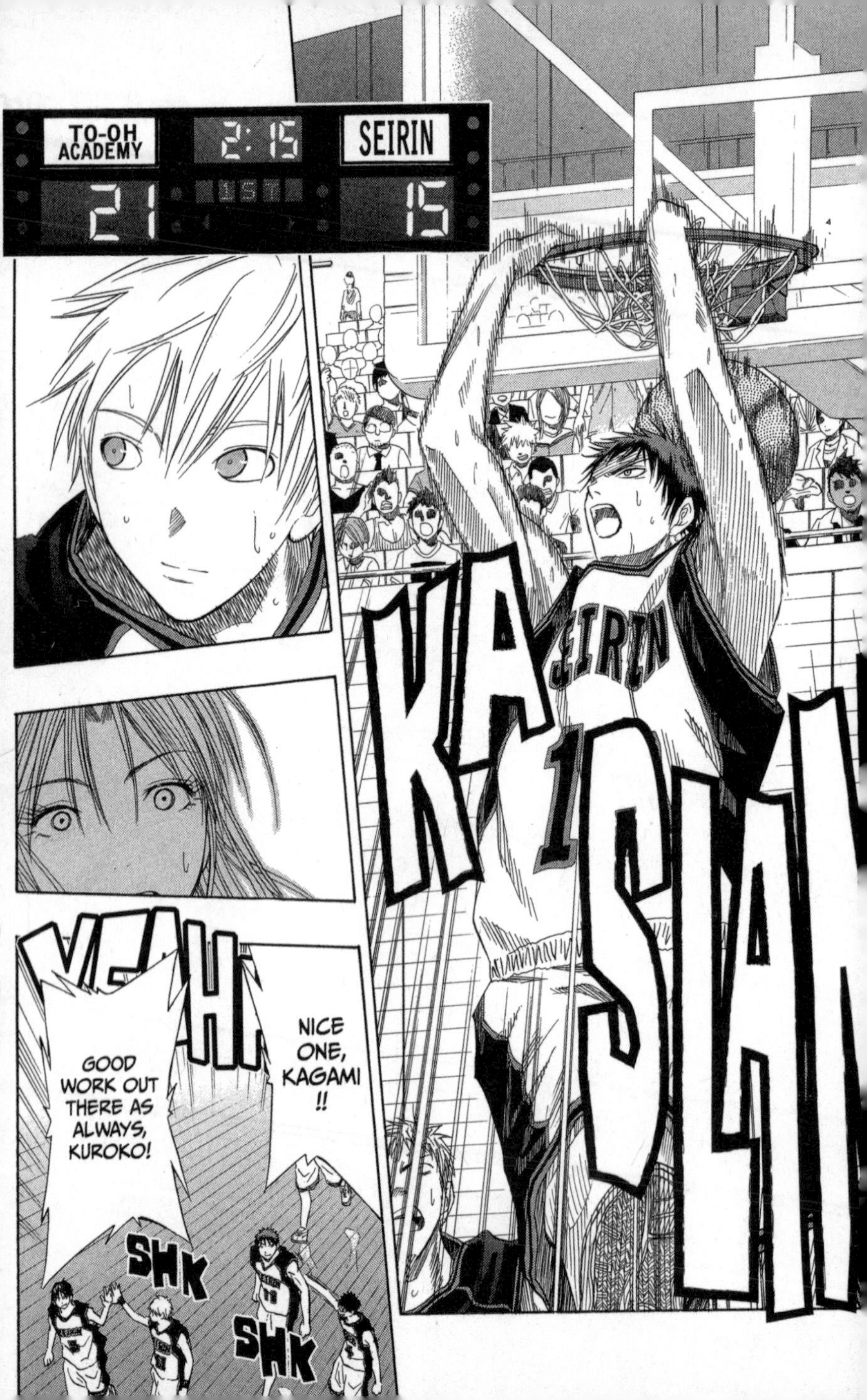
KA-SLAM
TO-OH ACADEMY
2:15
SEIRIN
21
1ST
15
NICE ONE, KAGAMI !!
GOOD WORK OUT THERE AS ALWAYS, KUROKO!
SHK
SHK

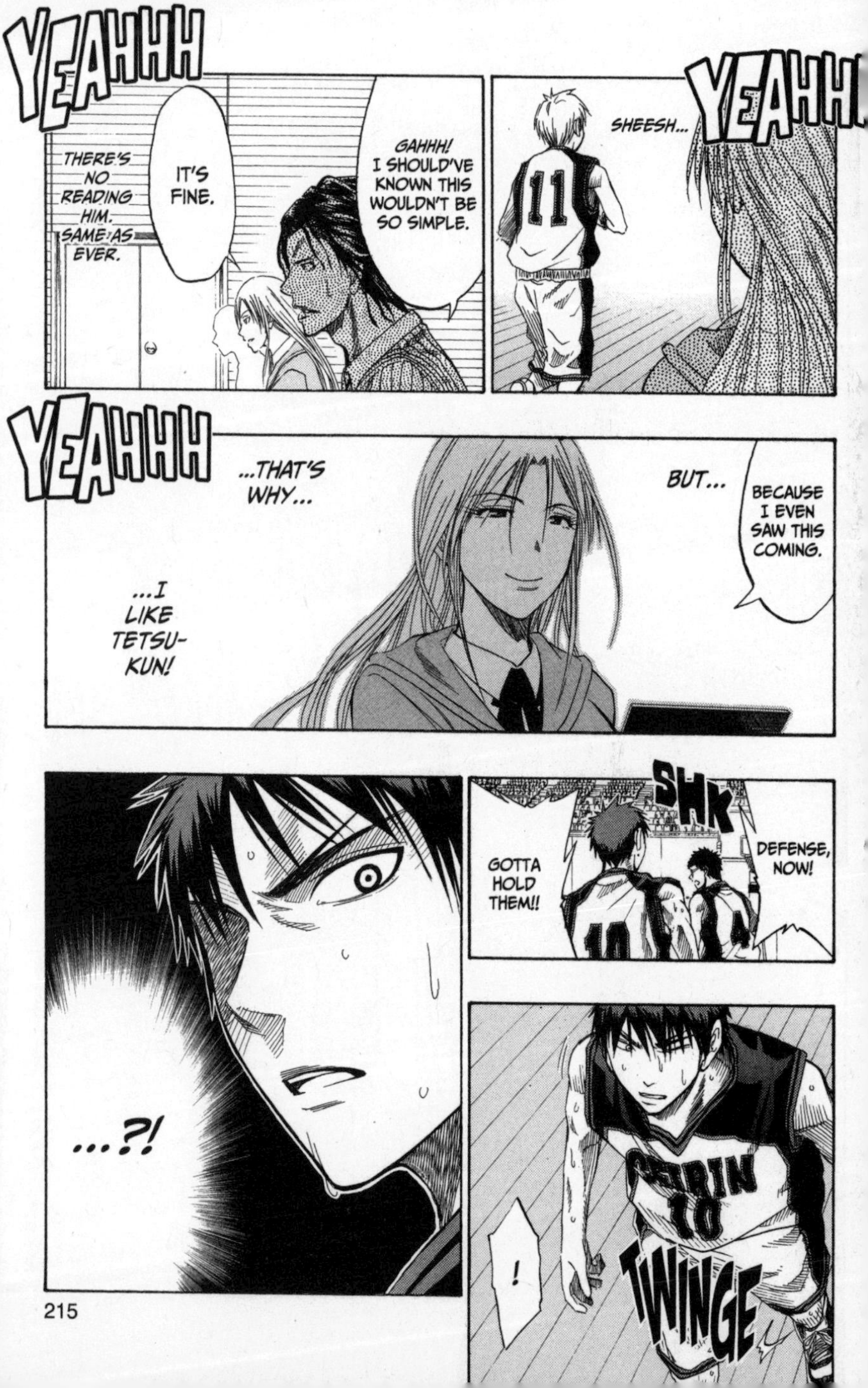
YEAHHH
SHEESH...
YEAHHH
GAHHH! I SHOULD'VE KNOWN THIS WOULDN'T BE SO SIMPLE.
IT'S FINE.
THERE'S NO READING HIM. SAME AS EVER.
BECAUSE I EVEN SAW THIS COMING.
BUT...
...THAT'S WHY...
...I LIKE TETSU-KUN!
YEAHHH
SHK
DEFENSE, NOW!
GOTTA HOLD THEM!!
TWINGE
!
...?!

KUROKO'S BASKETBALL BLOOPERS
TAKE 10

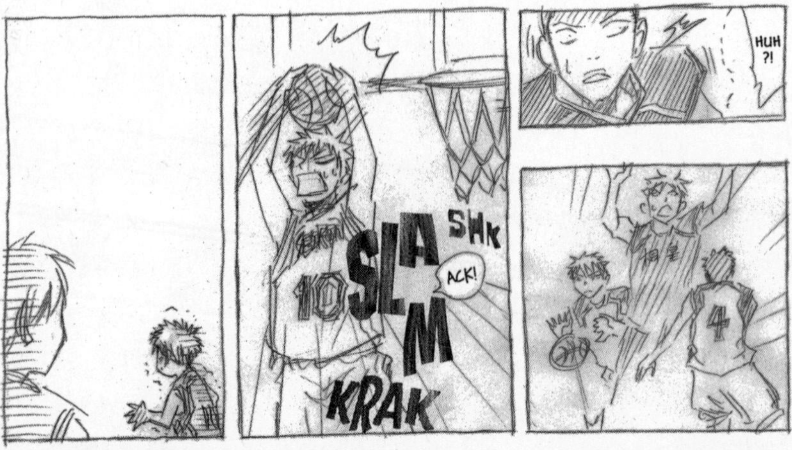
HUH ?!
SHK
SLAM
ACK!
KRAK

45TH QUARTER: LET'S DO THIS!

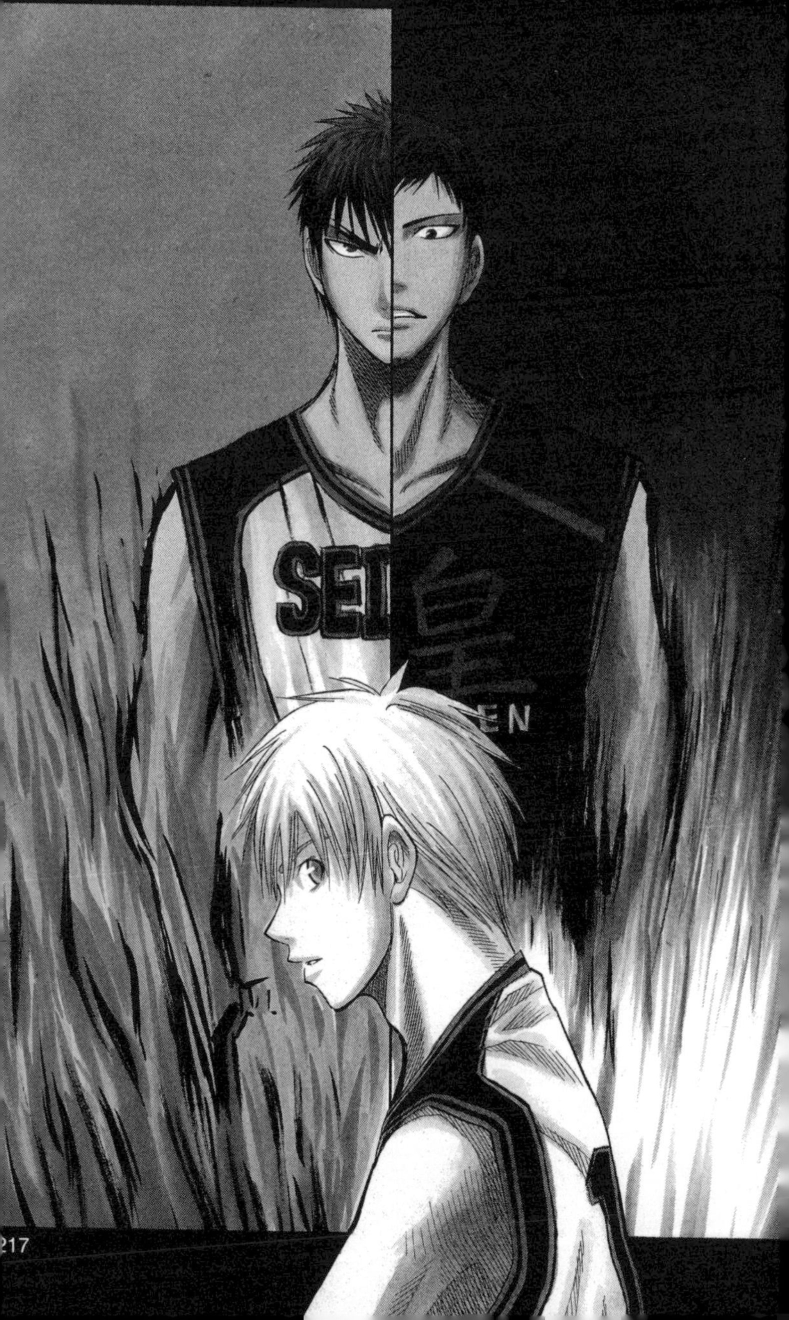

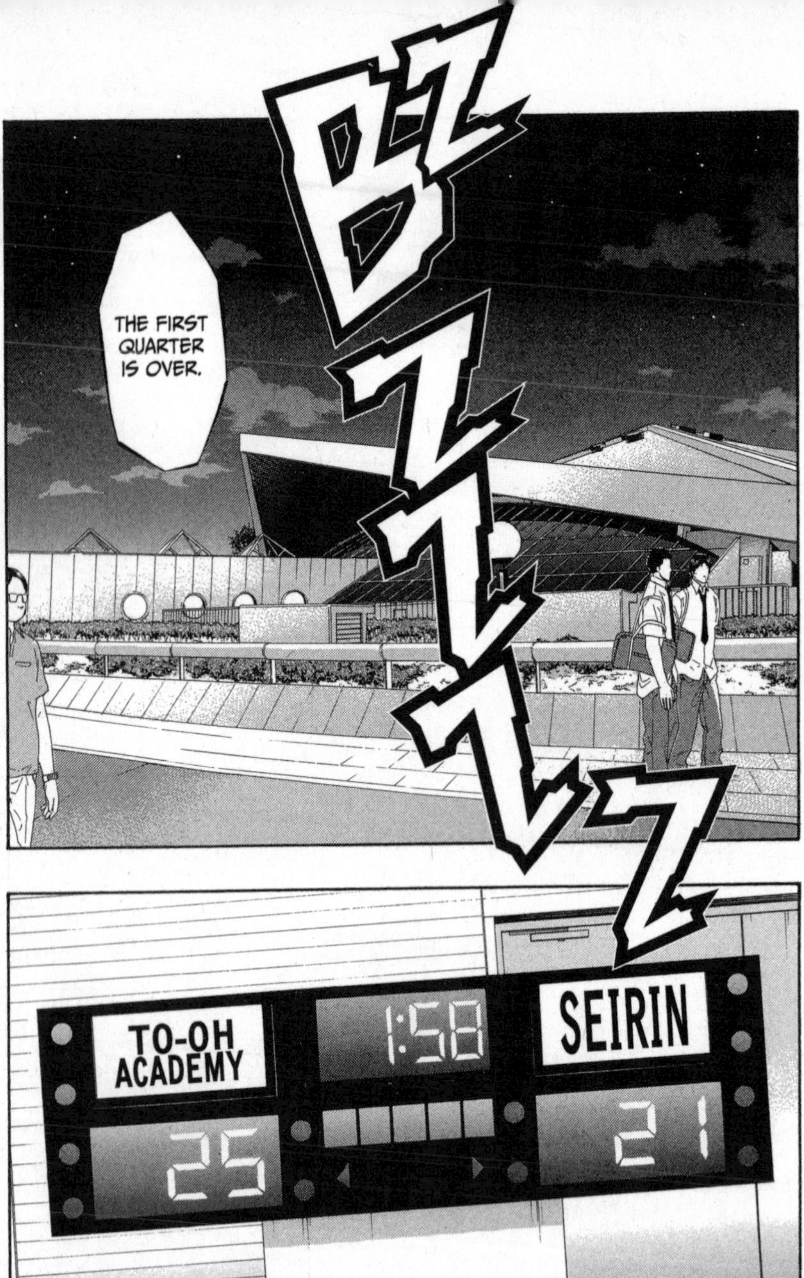
BZZZZZ
THE FIRST QUARTER IS OVER.
TO-OH ACADEMY
1:58
SEIRIN
25
21

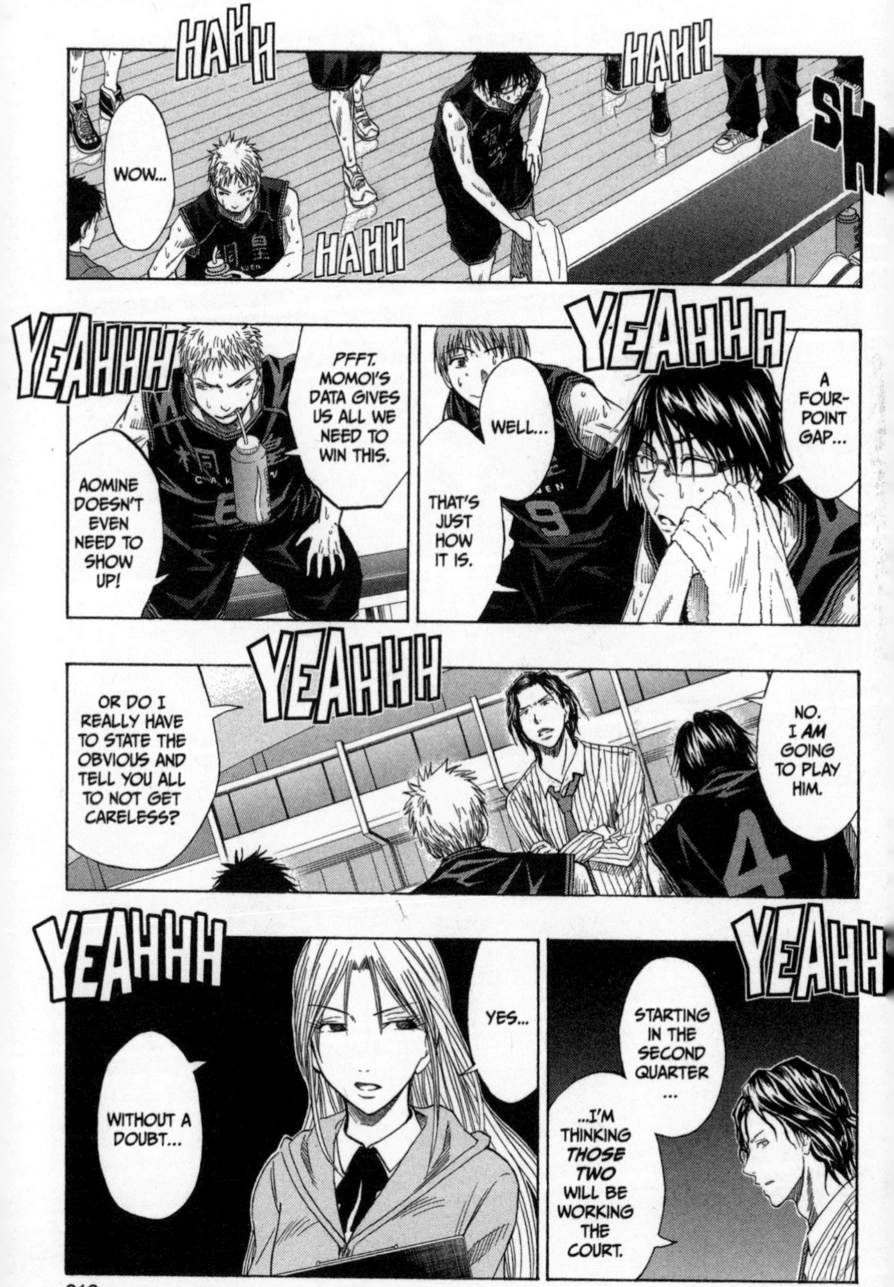
SH
HAHH
HAHH
WOW...
HAHH
YEAHHH
A FOUR-POINT GAP...
WELL...
THAT'S JUST HOW IT IS.
YEAHHH
PFFT. MOMOI'S DATA GIVES US ALL WE NEED TO WIN THIS.
AOMINE DOESN'T EVEN NEED TO SHOW UP!
NO. I *AM* GOING TO PLAY HIM.
YEAHHH
OR DO I REALLY HAVE TO STATE THE OBVIOUS AND TELL YOU ALL TO NOT GET CARELESS?
YEAHH
STARTING IN THE SECOND QUARTER ...
...I'M THINKING *THOSE TWO* WILL BE WORKING THE COURT.
YEAHHH
YES...
WITHOUT A DOUBT...

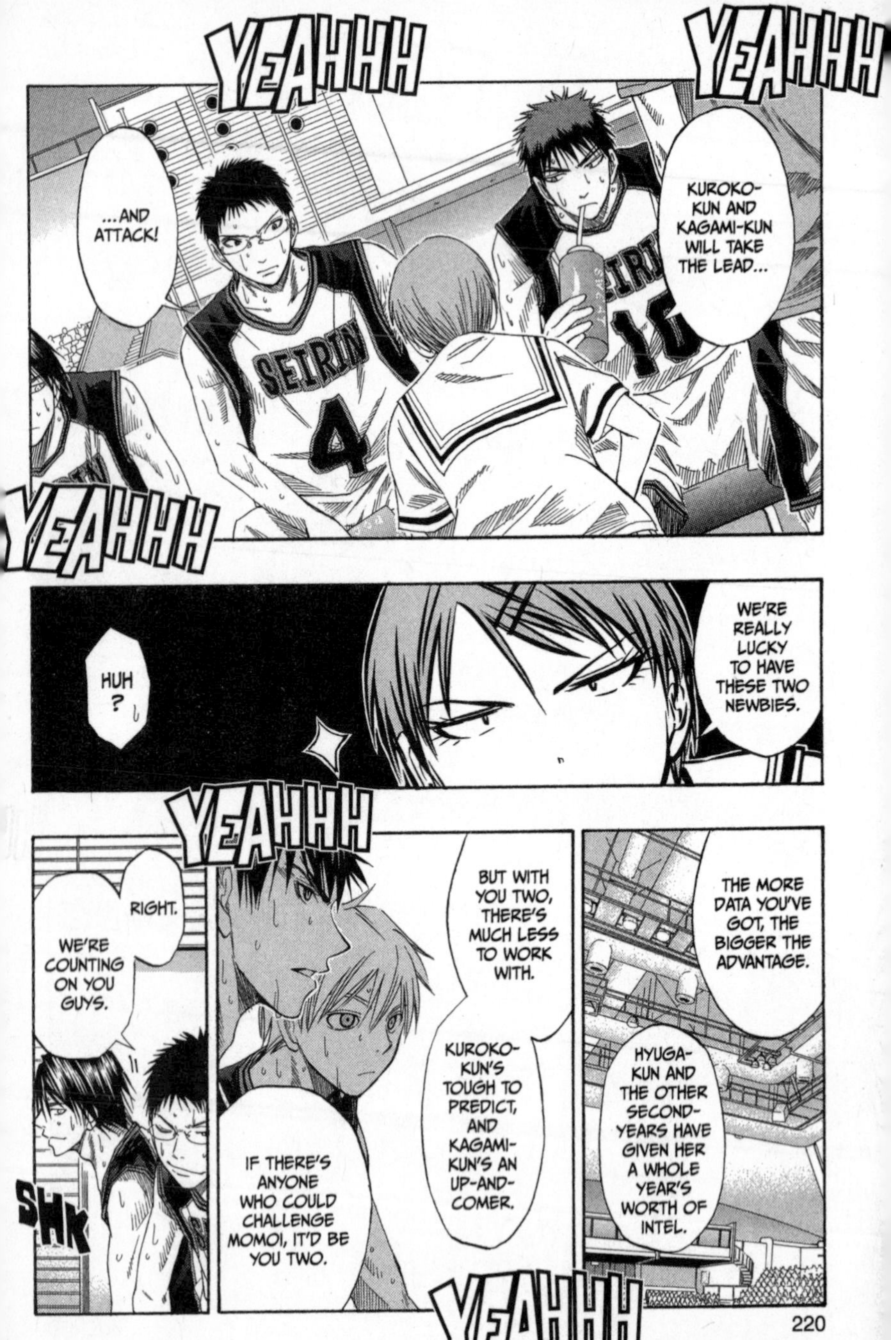
YEAHHH
YEAHHH
KUROKO-KUN AND KAGAMI-KUN WILL TAKE THE LEAD...
...AND ATTACK!
YEAHHH
WE'RE REALLY LUCKY TO HAVE THESE TWO NEWBIES.
HUH ?
YEAHHH
THE MORE DATA YOU'VE GOT, THE BIGGER THE ADVANTAGE.
HYUGA-KUN AND THE OTHER SECOND-YEARS HAVE GIVEN HER A WHOLE YEAR'S WORTH OF INTEL.
BUT WITH YOU TWO, THERE'S MUCH LESS TO WORK WITH.
KUROKO-KUN'S TOUGH TO PREDICT, AND KAGAMI-KUN'S AN UP-AND-COMER.
IF THERE'S ANYONE WHO COULD CHALLENGE MOMOI, IT'D BE YOU TWO.
RIGHT.
WE'RE COUNTING ON YOU GUYS.
SHK
YEAHHH

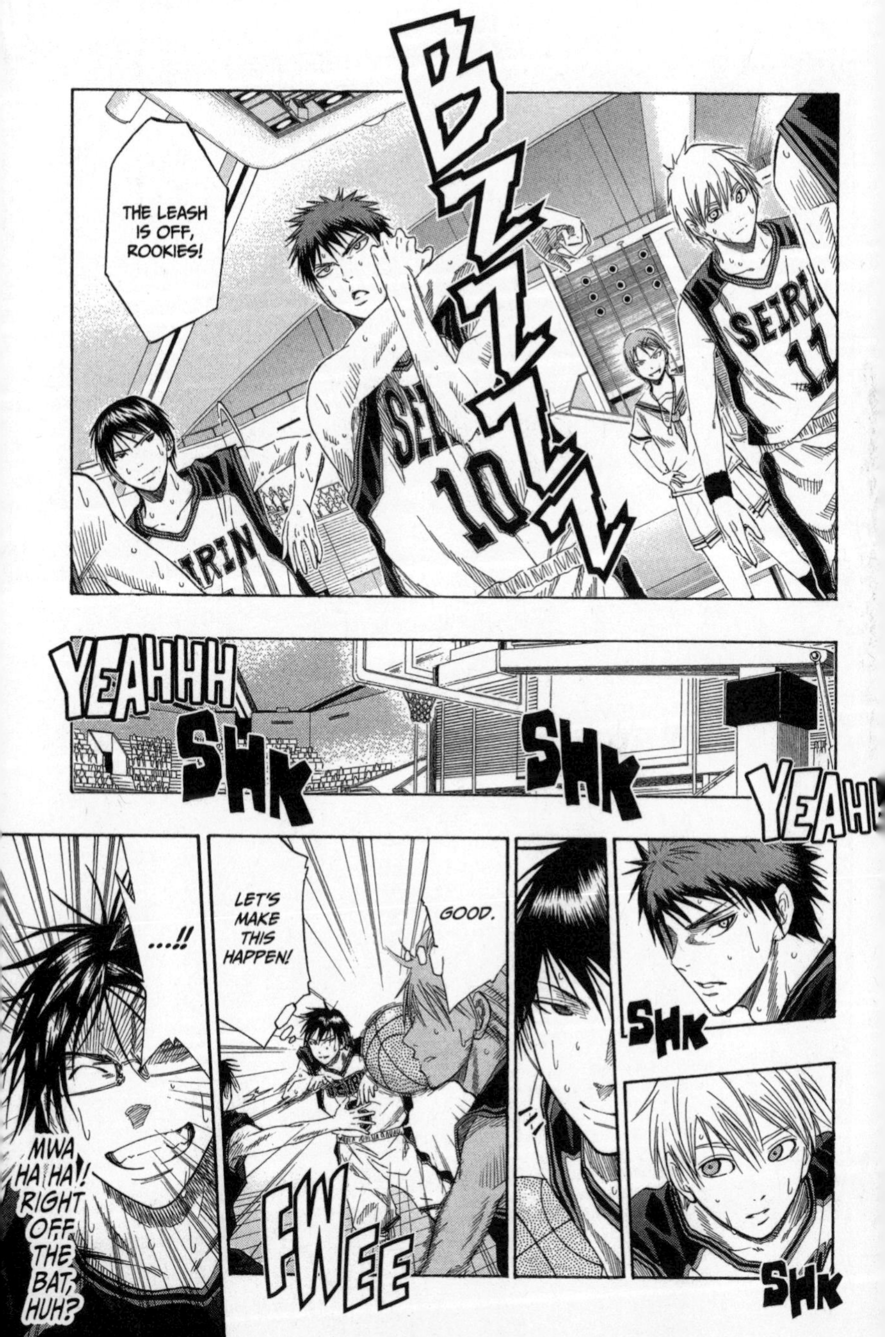
BZZZZ
THE LEASH IS OFF, ROOKIES!
YEAH!
SHK
SHK
YEAHHH
SHK
SHK
GOOD.
LET'S MAKE THIS HAPPEN!
FWEE
...!!
MWA HA HA! RIGHT OFF THE BAT, HUH?

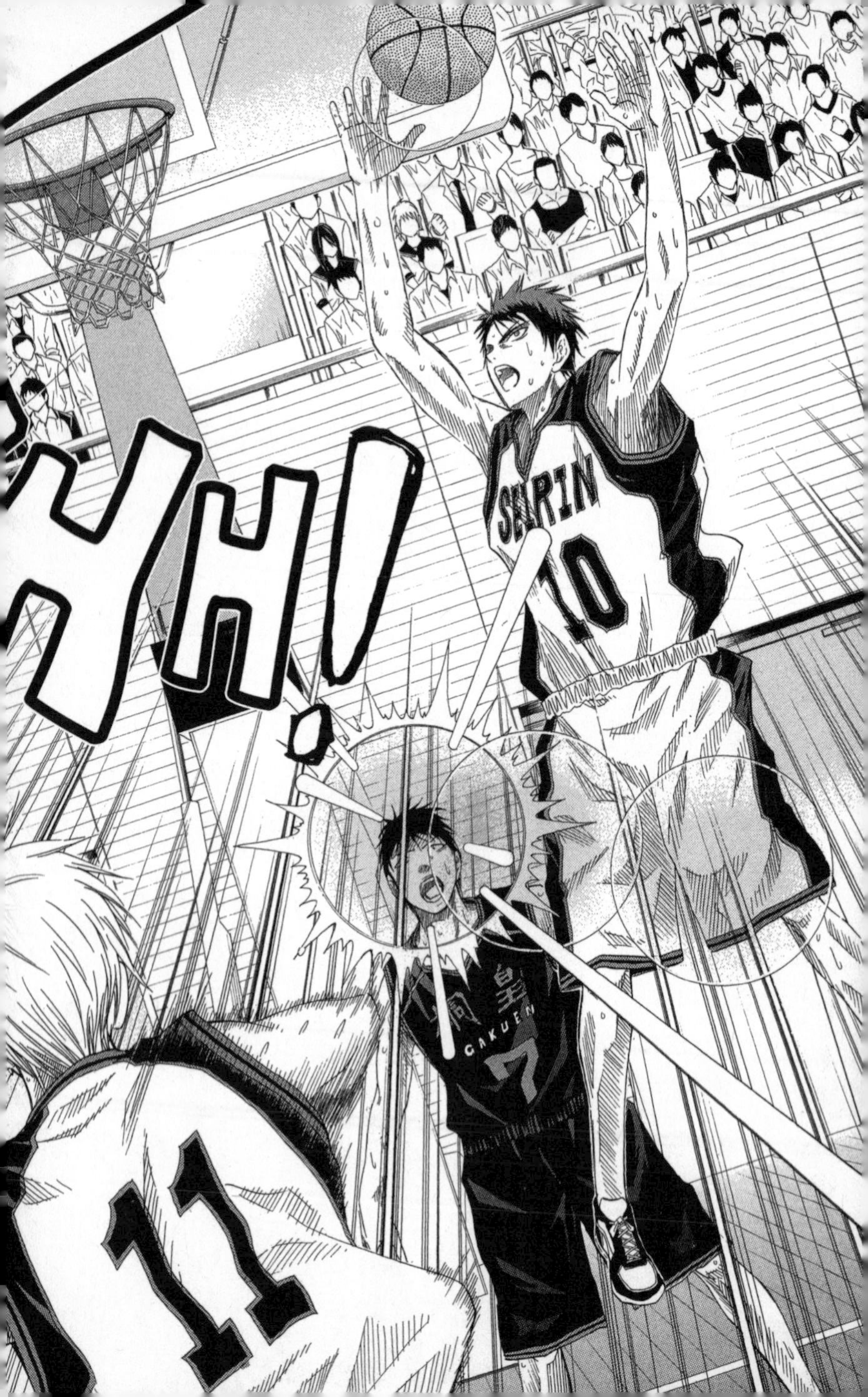
YH!

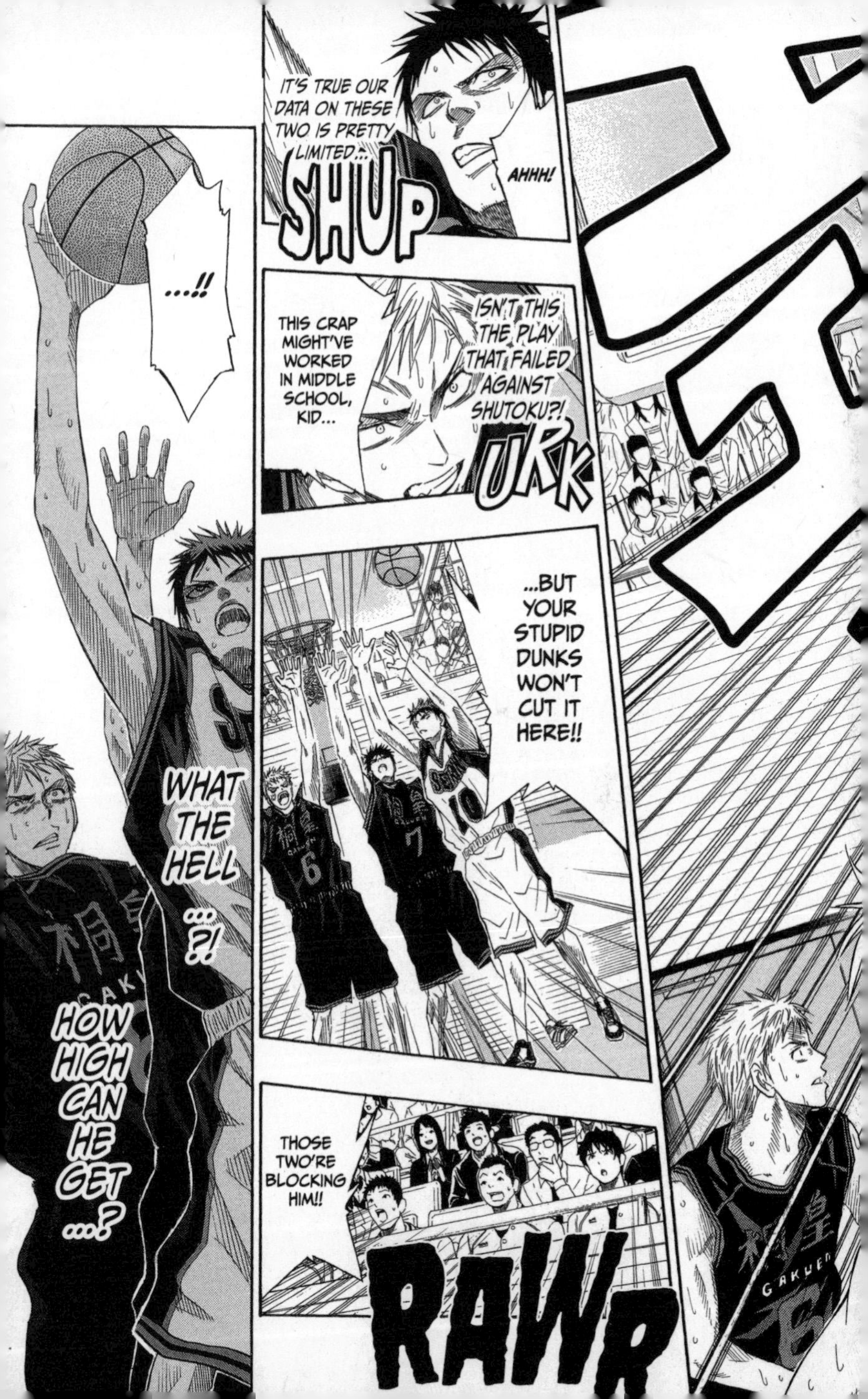

IT'S TRUE OUR DATA ON THESE TWO IS PRETTY LIMITED...
AHHH!
SHUP
ISN'T THIS THE PLAY THAT FAILED AGAINST SHUTOKU?!
URK
THIS CRAP MIGHT'VE WORKED IN MIDDLE SCHOOL, KID...
...BUT YOUR STUPID DUNKS WON'T CUT IT HERE!!
THOSE TWO'RE BLOCKING HIM!!
RAWR
...!!
WHAT THE HELL ...?!
HOW HIGH CAN HE GET ...?

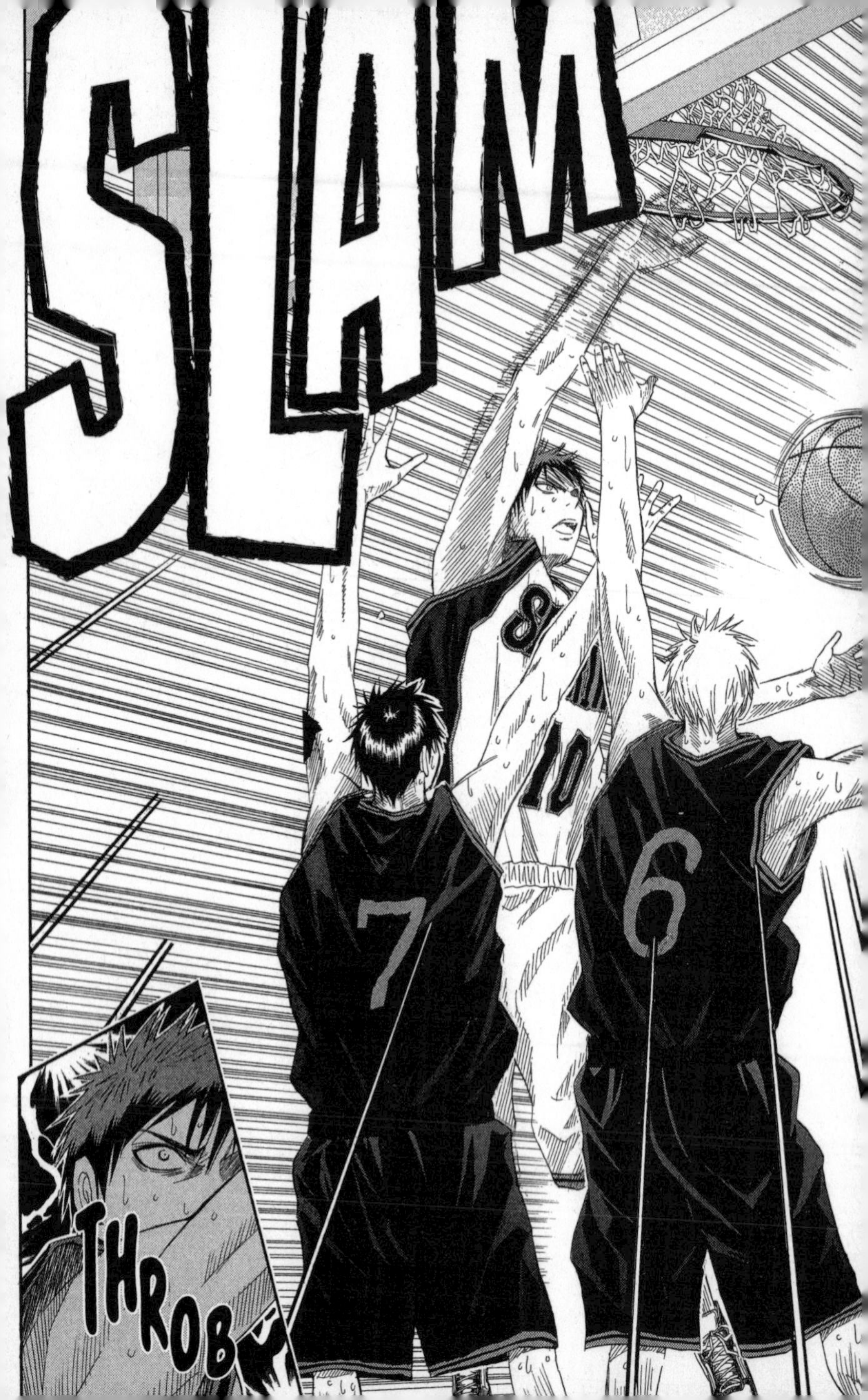
SLAM
THROB

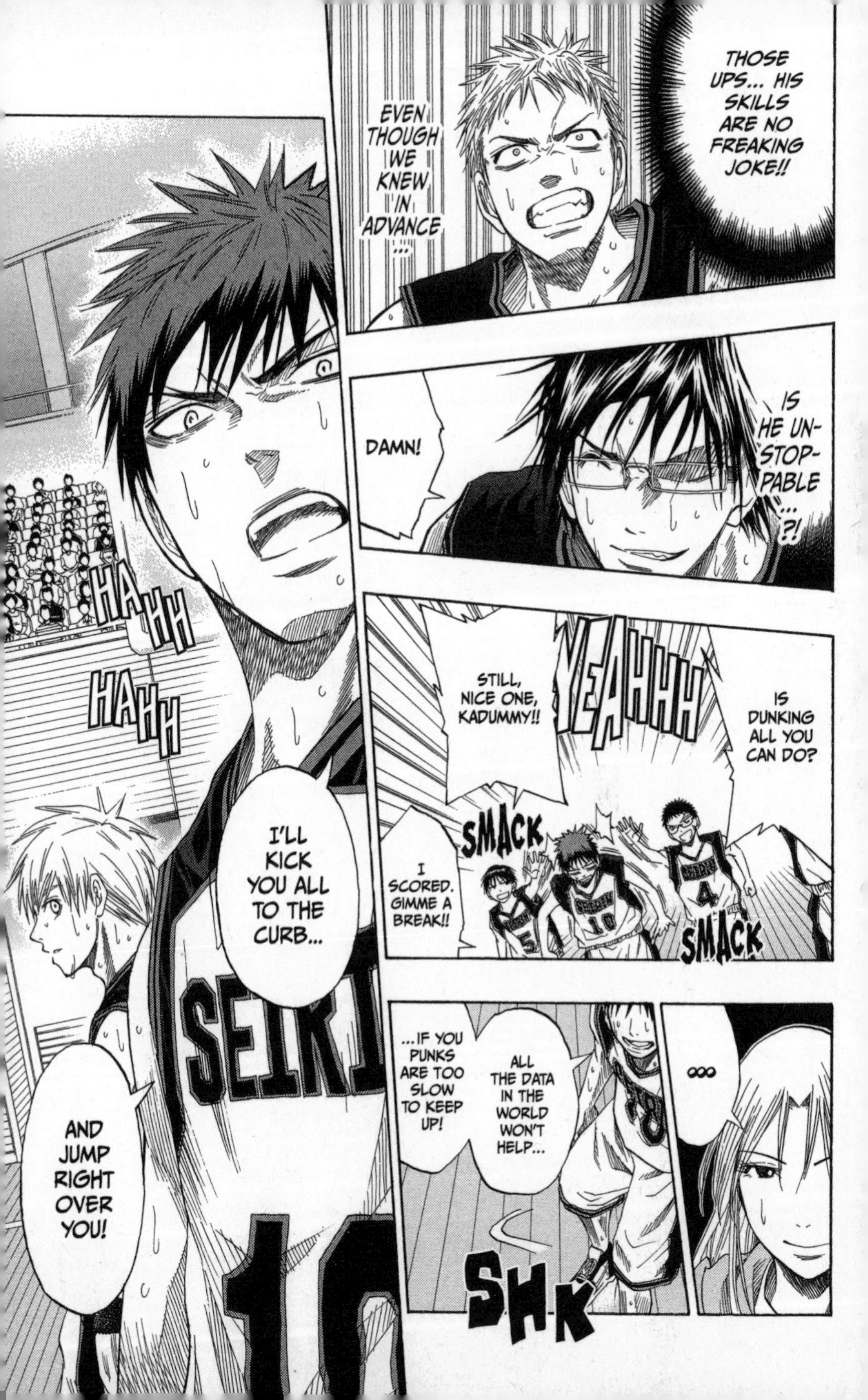
THOSE UPS... HIS SKILLS ARE NO FREAKING JOKE!!
EVEN THOUGH WE KNEW IN ADVANCE...
IS HE UN-STOPPABLE...?!
DAMN!
IS DUNKING ALL YOU CAN DO?
YEAHHHH
STILL, NICE ONE, KADUMMY!!
SMACK
I SCORED. GIMME A BREAK!!
SMACK
ooo
ALL THE DATA IN THE WORLD WON'T HELP...
...IF YOU PUNKS ARE TOO SLOW TO KEEP UP!
SHK
HAHH
HAHH
I'LL KICK YOU ALL TO THE CURB...
AND JUMP RIGHT OVER YOU!
SEIRIN

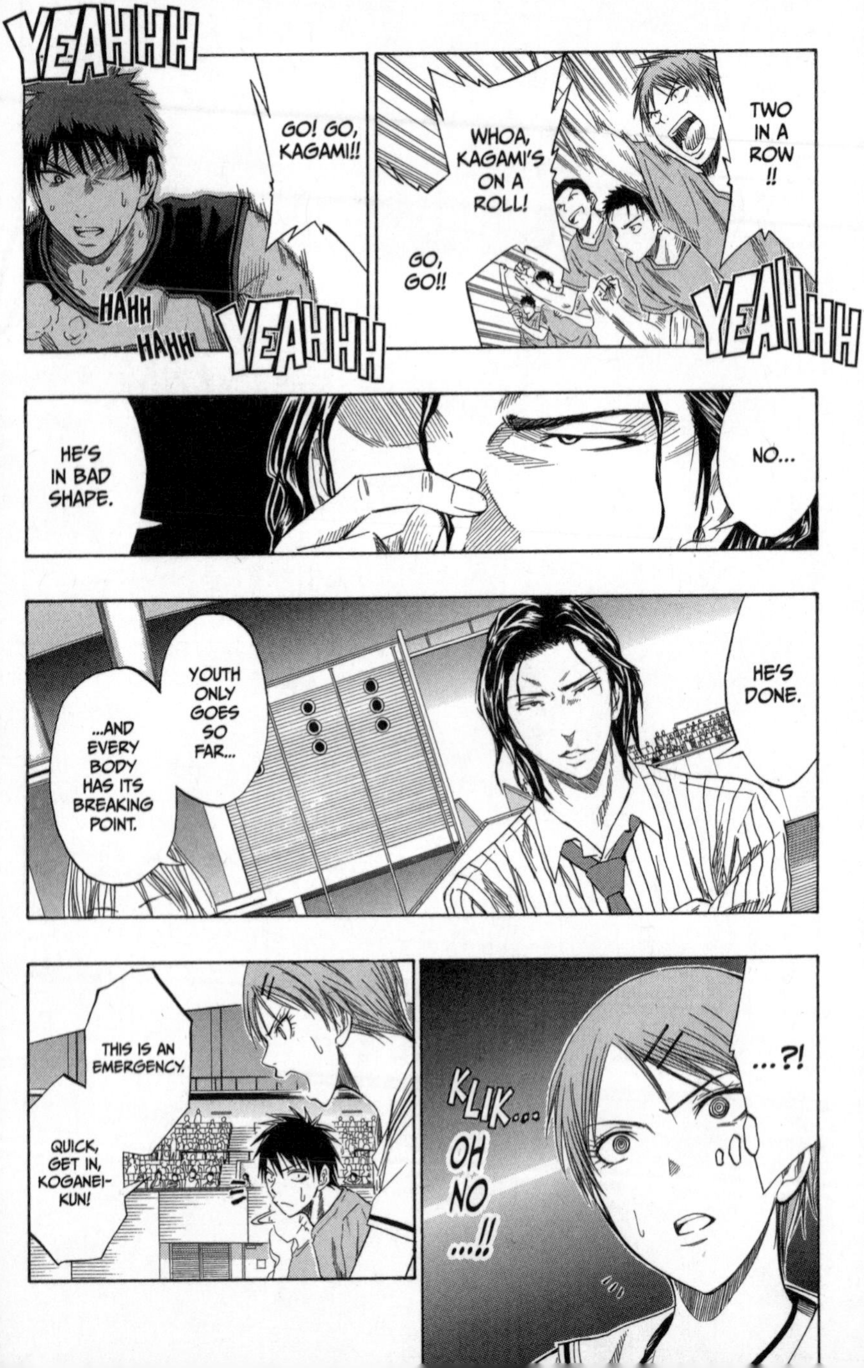

TWO IN A ROW !!
WHOA, KAGAMI'S ON A ROLL!
GO, GO!!
YEAHHH
YEAHHH
GO! GO, KAGAMI!!
HAHH HAHH
YEAHHH
NO...
HE'S IN BAD SHAPE.
HE'S DONE.
YOUTH ONLY GOES SO FAR...
...AND EVERY BODY HAS ITS BREAKING POINT.
...?!
KLIK...
OH NO ...!!
THIS IS AN EMERGENCY.
QUICK, GET IN, KOGANEI-KUN!

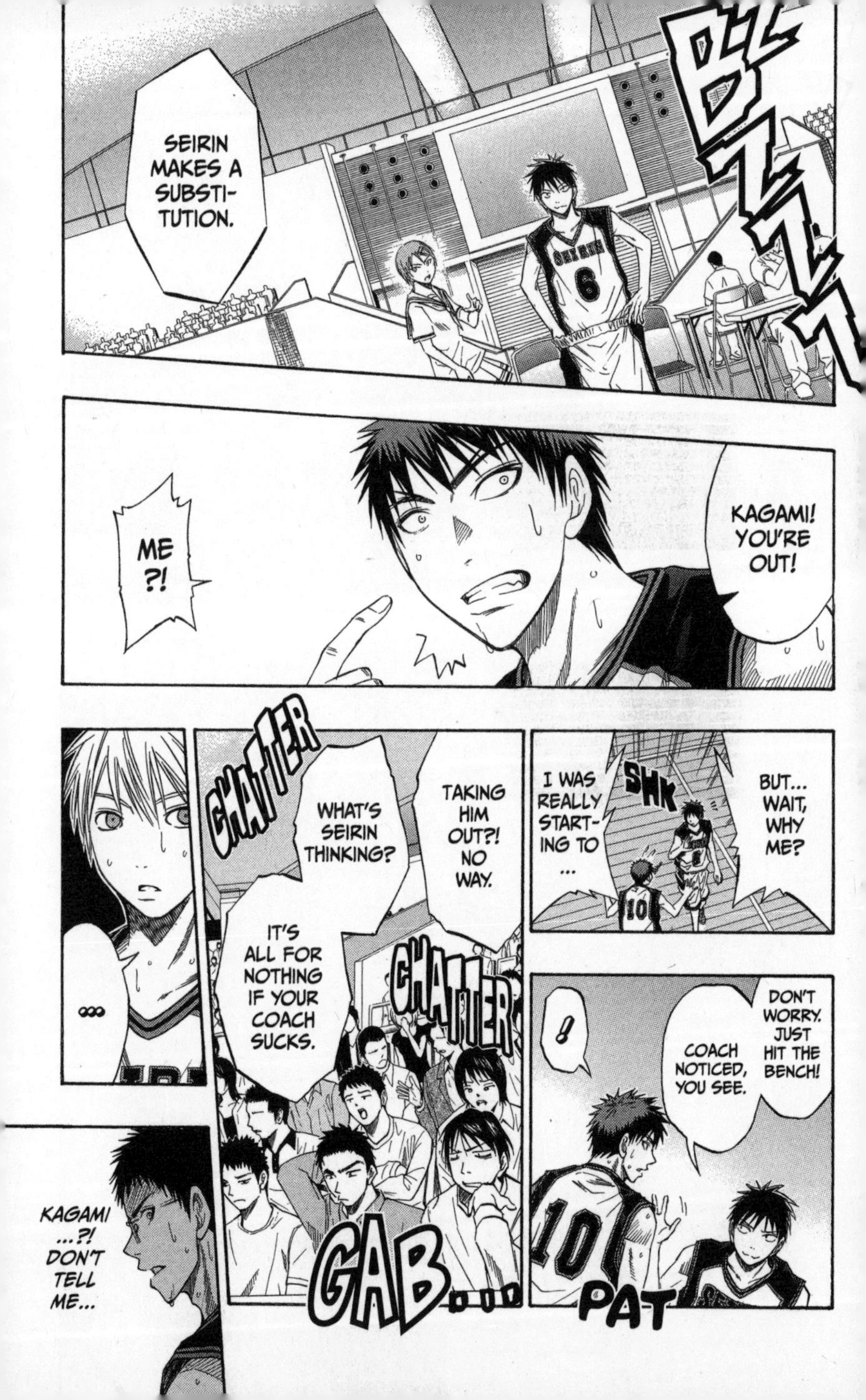

BZZZT
SEIRIN MAKES A SUBSTITUTION.
KAGAMI! YOU'RE OUT!
ME ?!
BUT... WAIT, WHY ME?
SHK
I WAS REALLY STARTING TO ...
DON'T WORRY. JUST HIT THE BENCH!
COACH NOTICED, YOU SEE.
!
PAT
CHATTER
TAKING HIM OUT?! NO WAY.
WHAT'S SEIRIN THINKING?
IT'S ALL FOR NOTHING IF YOUR COACH SUCKS.
CHATTER
GAB...
...
KAGAMI ...?! DON'T TELL ME...

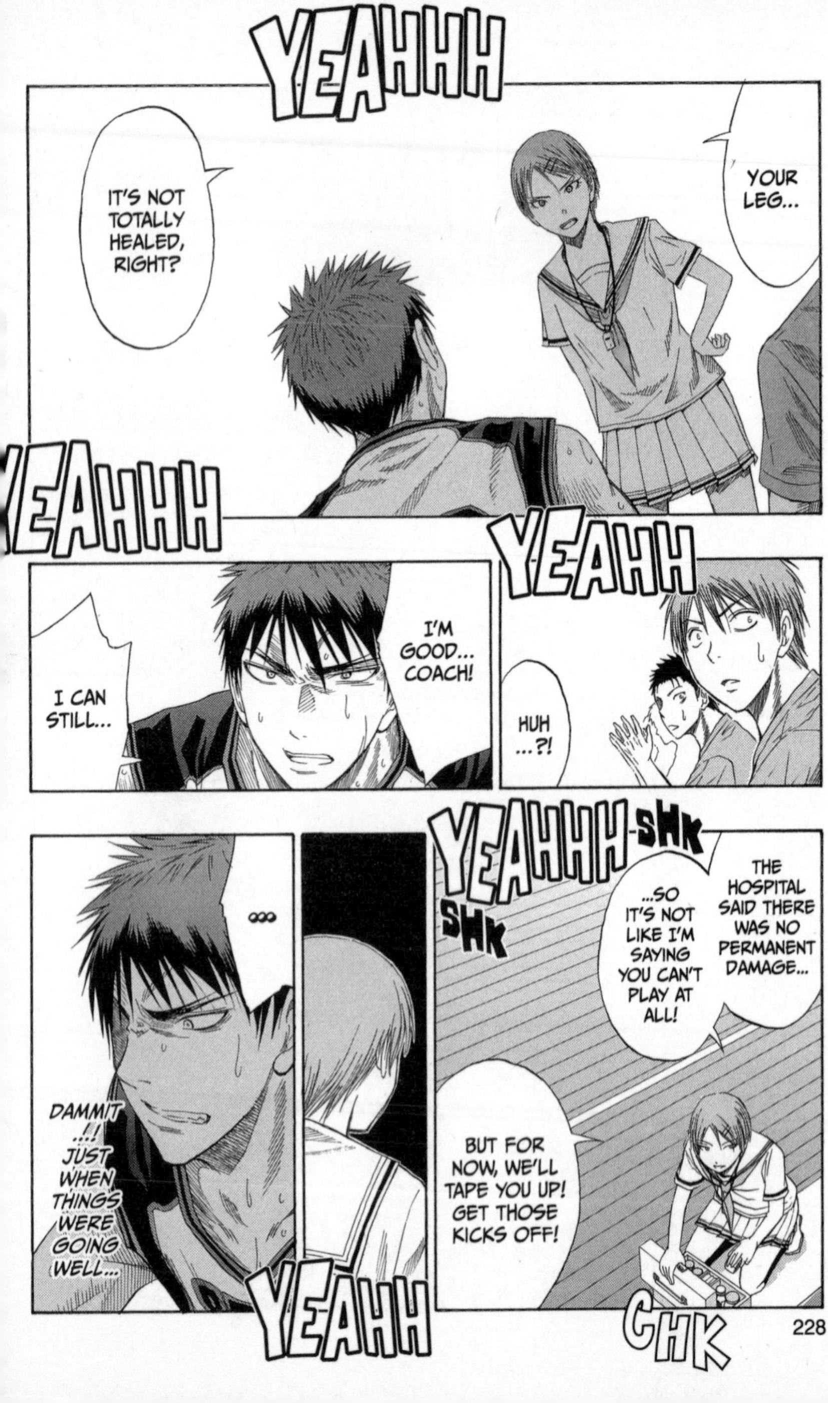
YEAHHH
YOUR LEG...
IT'S NOT TOTALLY HEALED, RIGHT?
YEAHHH
YEAHH
HUH ...?!
I'M GOOD... COACH!
I CAN STILL...
YEAHHH
SHK
SHK
THE HOSPITAL SAID THERE WAS NO PERMANENT DAMAGE...
...SO IT'S NOT LIKE I'M SAYING YOU CAN'T PLAY AT ALL!
BUT FOR NOW, WE'LL TAPE YOU UP! GET THOSE KICKS OFF!
CHK
...
DAMMIT...! JUST WHEN THINGS WERE GOING WELL...
YEAHH

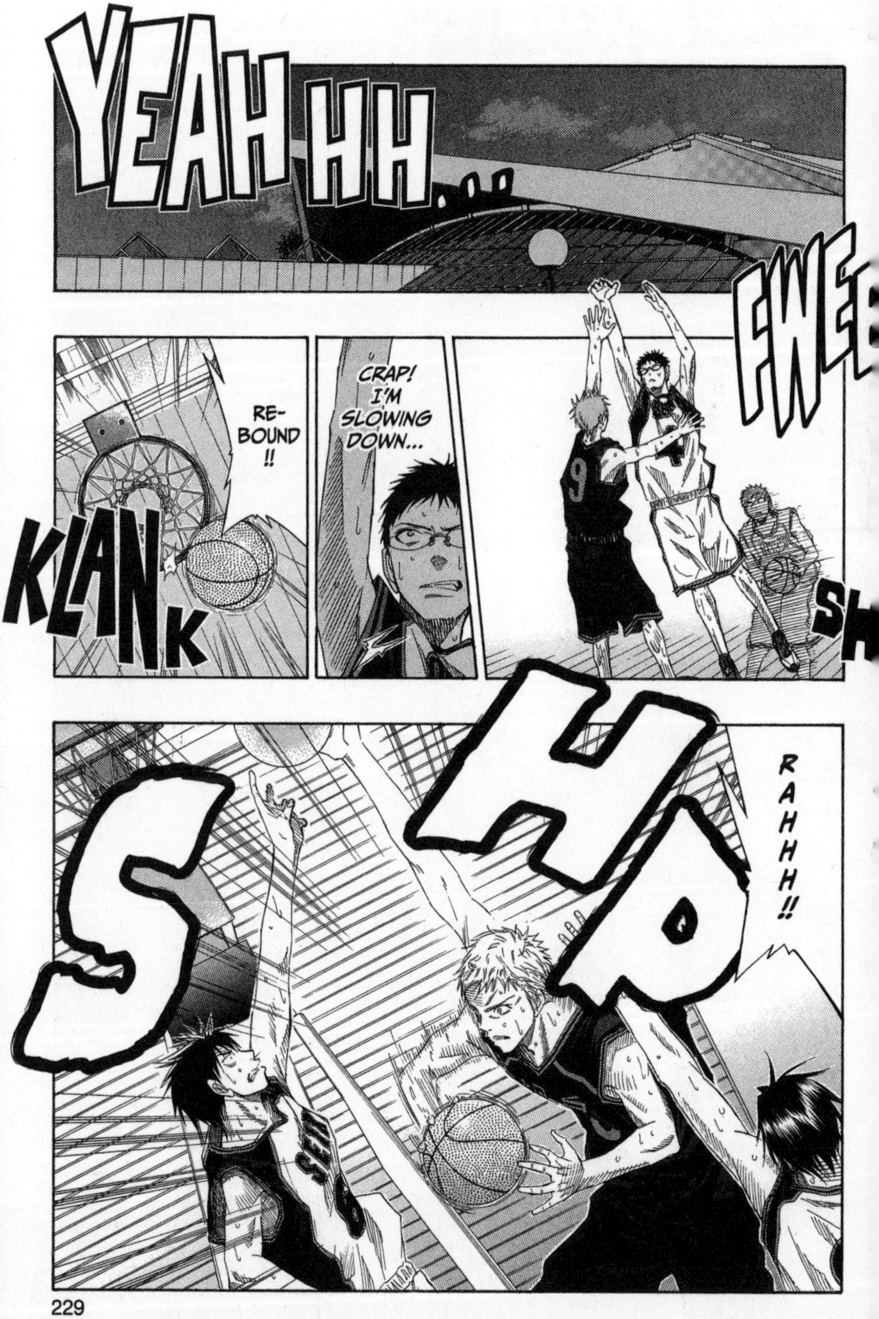
YEAHHH...
FWEE
SH
CRAP! I'M SLOWING DOWN...
RE-BOUND!!
KLANK
RAHHHH!!
SHP

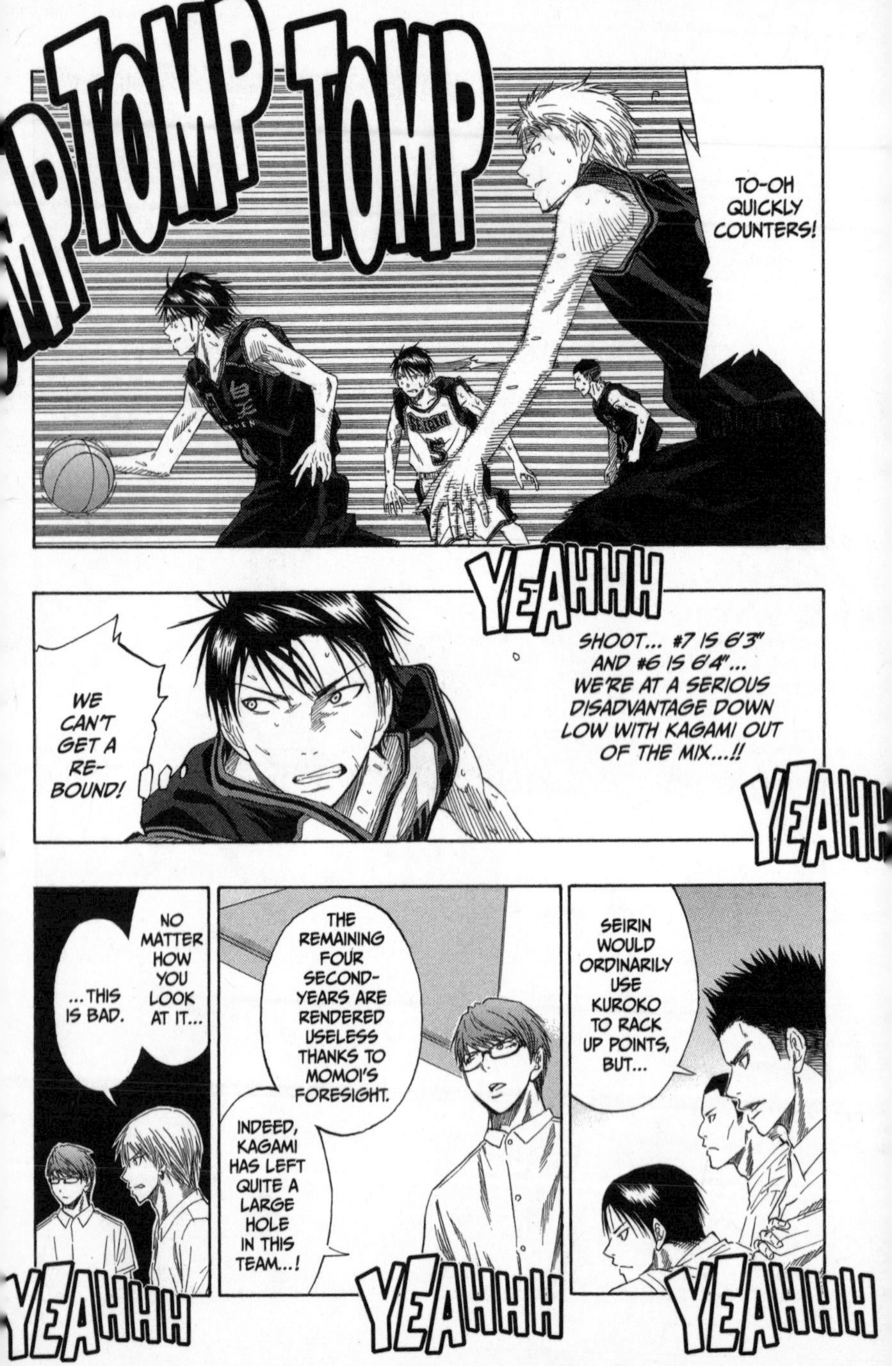
TOMP TOMP TOMP
TO-OH QUICKLY COUNTERS!
YEAHHH
SHOOT... #7 IS 6'3" AND #6 IS 6'4"... WE'RE AT A SERIOUS DISADVANTAGE DOWN LOW WITH KAGAMI OUT OF THE MIX...!!
WE CAN'T GET A RE-BOUND!
YEAHH
SEIRIN WOULD ORDINARILY USE KUROKO TO RACK UP POINTS, BUT...
YEAHHH
THE REMAINING FOUR SECOND-YEARS ARE RENDERED USELESS THANKS TO MOMOI'S FORESIGHT.
INDEED, KAGAMI HAS LEFT QUITE A LARGE HOLE IN THIS TEAM...!
YEAHHH
NO MATTER HOW YOU LOOK AT IT...
...THIS IS BAD.
YEAHHH

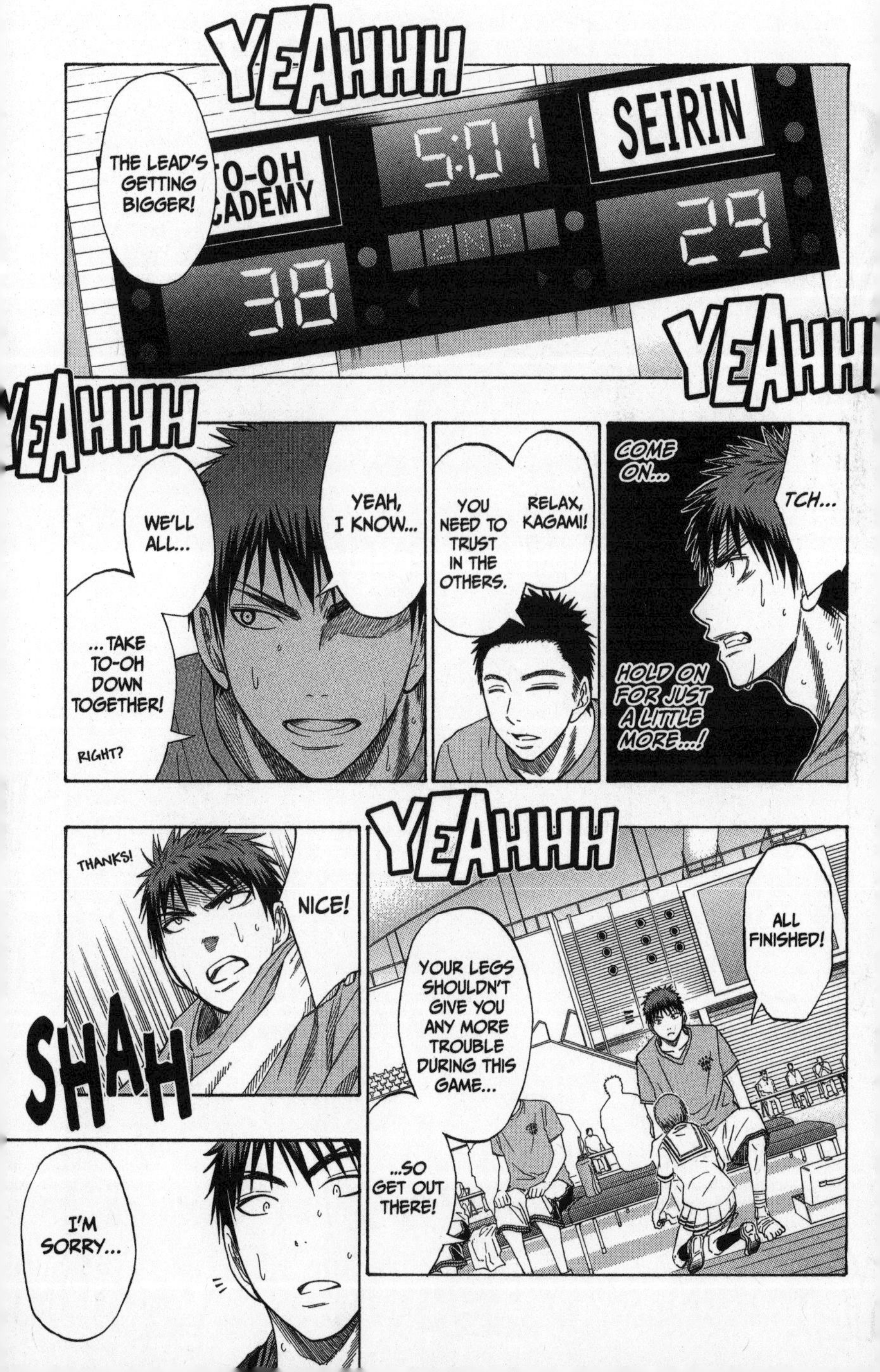
YEAHHH
THE LEAD'S GETTING BIGGER!
SEIRIN
5:01
TO-OH
CADEMY
2ND
29
38
YEAHH
YEAHHH
COME ON...
TCH...
HOLD ON FOR JUST A LITTLE MORE...!
RELAX, KAGAMI!
YOU NEED TO TRUST IN THE OTHERS.
YEAH, I KNOW...
WE'LL ALL...
...TAKE TO-OH DOWN TOGETHER!
RIGHT?
YEAHHH
ALL FINISHED!
YOUR LEGS SHOULDN'T GIVE YOU ANY MORE TROUBLE DURING THIS GAME...
...SO GET OUT THERE!
NICE!
THANKS!
SHAH
I'M SORRY...

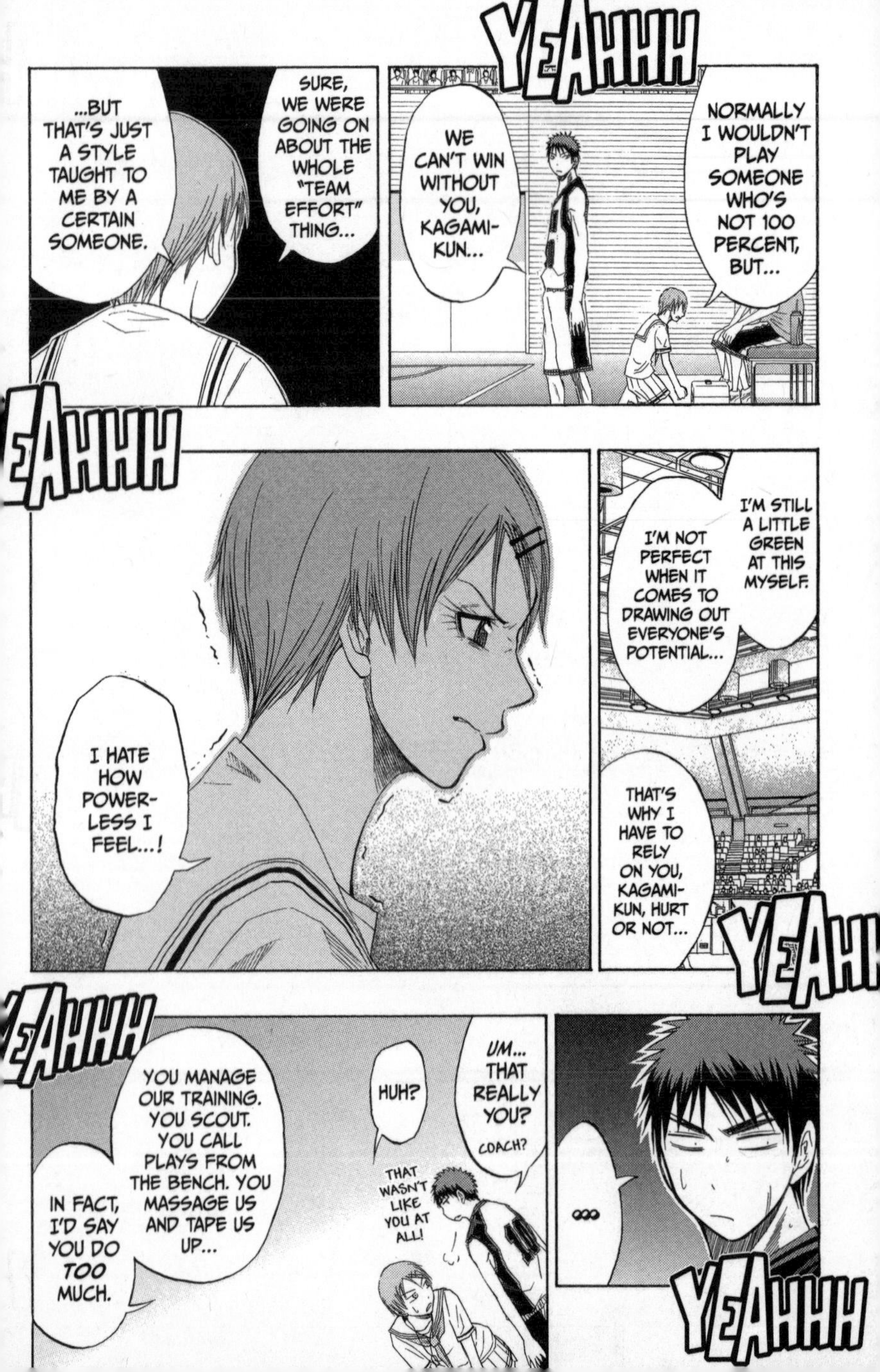
YEAHHH
NORMALLY I WOULDN'T PLAY SOMEONE WHO'S NOT 100 PERCENT, BUT...
WE CAN'T WIN WITHOUT YOU, KAGAMI-KUN...
SURE, WE WERE GOING ON ABOUT THE WHOLE "TEAM EFFORT" THING...
...BUT THAT'S JUST A STYLE TAUGHT TO ME BY A CERTAIN SOMEONE.
I'M STILL A LITTLE GREEN AT THIS MYSELF.
I'M NOT PERFECT WHEN IT COMES TO DRAWING OUT EVERYONE'S POTENTIAL...
THAT'S WHY I HAVE TO RELY ON YOU, KAGAMI-KUN, HURT OR NOT...
I HATE HOW POWERLESS I FEEL...!
...
UM... THAT REALLY YOU?
COACH?
HUH?
THAT WASN'T LIKE YOU AT ALL!
YOU MANAGE OUR TRAINING. YOU SCOUT. YOU CALL PLAYS FROM THE BENCH. YOU MASSAGE US AND TAPE US UP...
IN FACT, I'D SAY YOU DO *TOO* MUCH.
YEAHHH

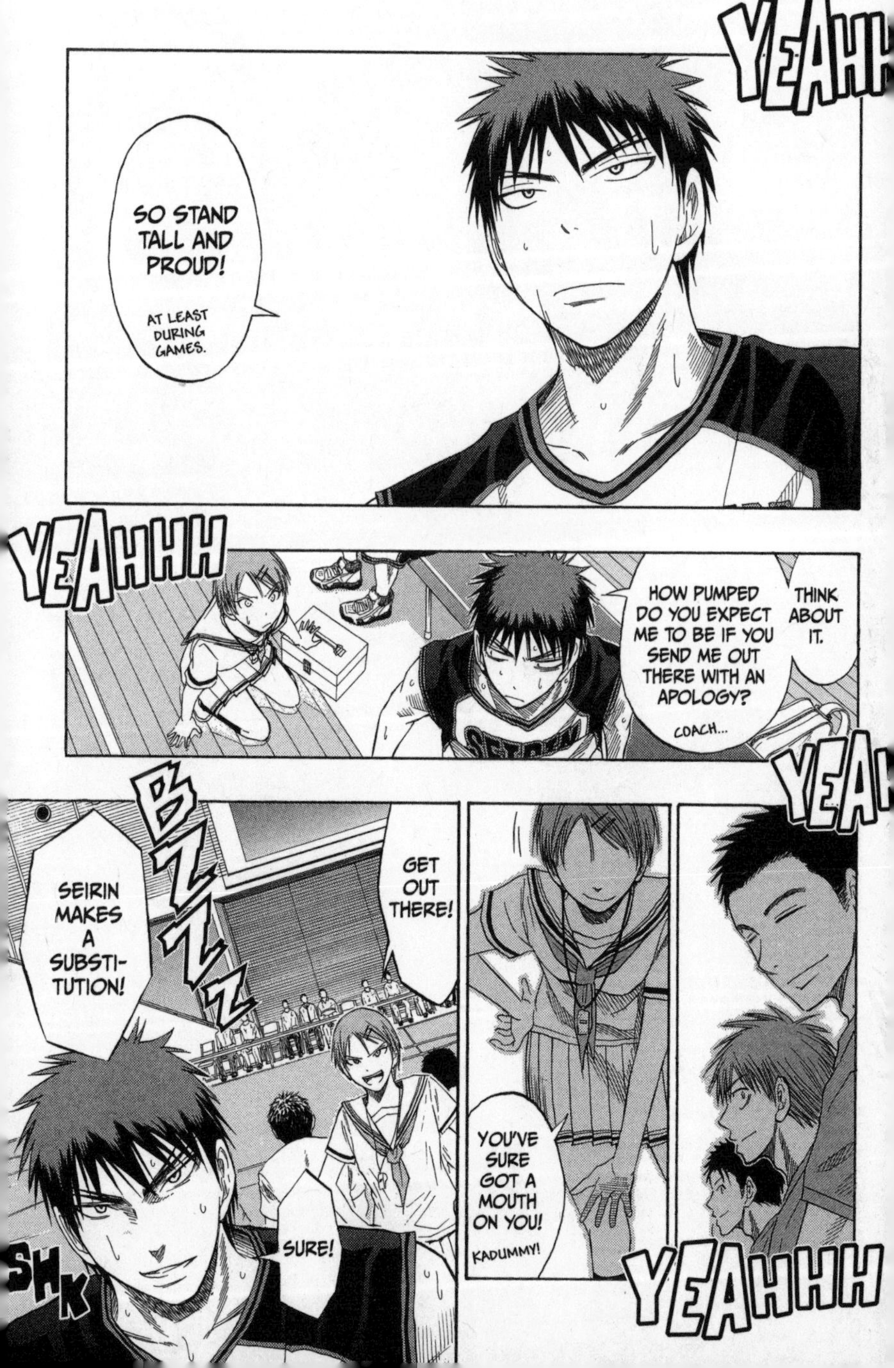
YEAHH
SO STAND TALL AND PROUD!
AT LEAST DURING GAMES.
THINK ABOUT IT.
HOW PUMPED DO YOU EXPECT ME TO BE IF YOU SEND ME OUT THERE WITH AN APOLOGY?
COACH...
YEAHHH
YEA
YEAHHH
YOU'VE SURE GOT A MOUTH ON YOU!
KADUMMY!
BZZZZ
GET OUT THERE!
SEIRIN MAKES A SUBSTITUTION!
SURE!
SHK

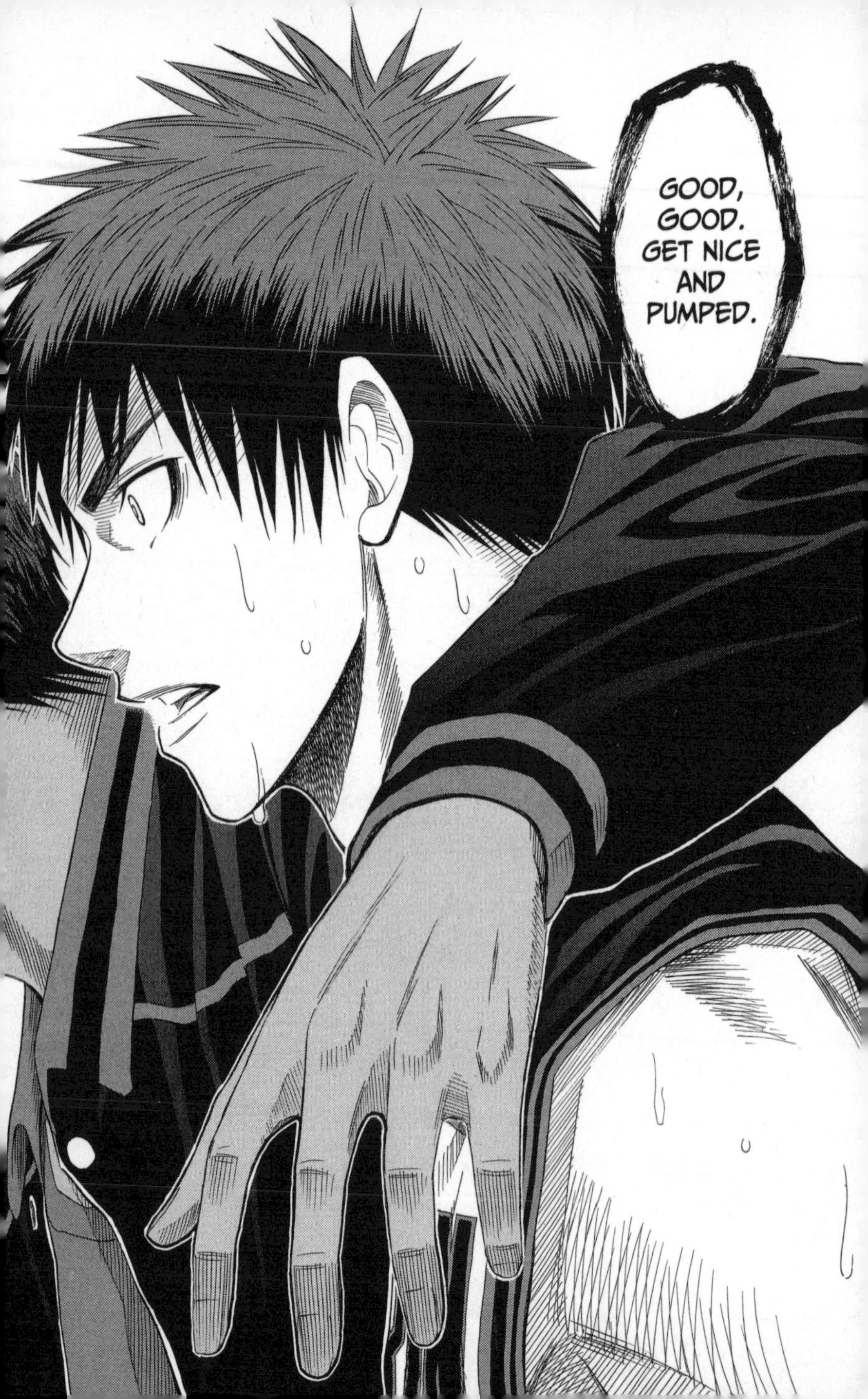
GOOD, GOOD. GET NICE AND PUMPED.

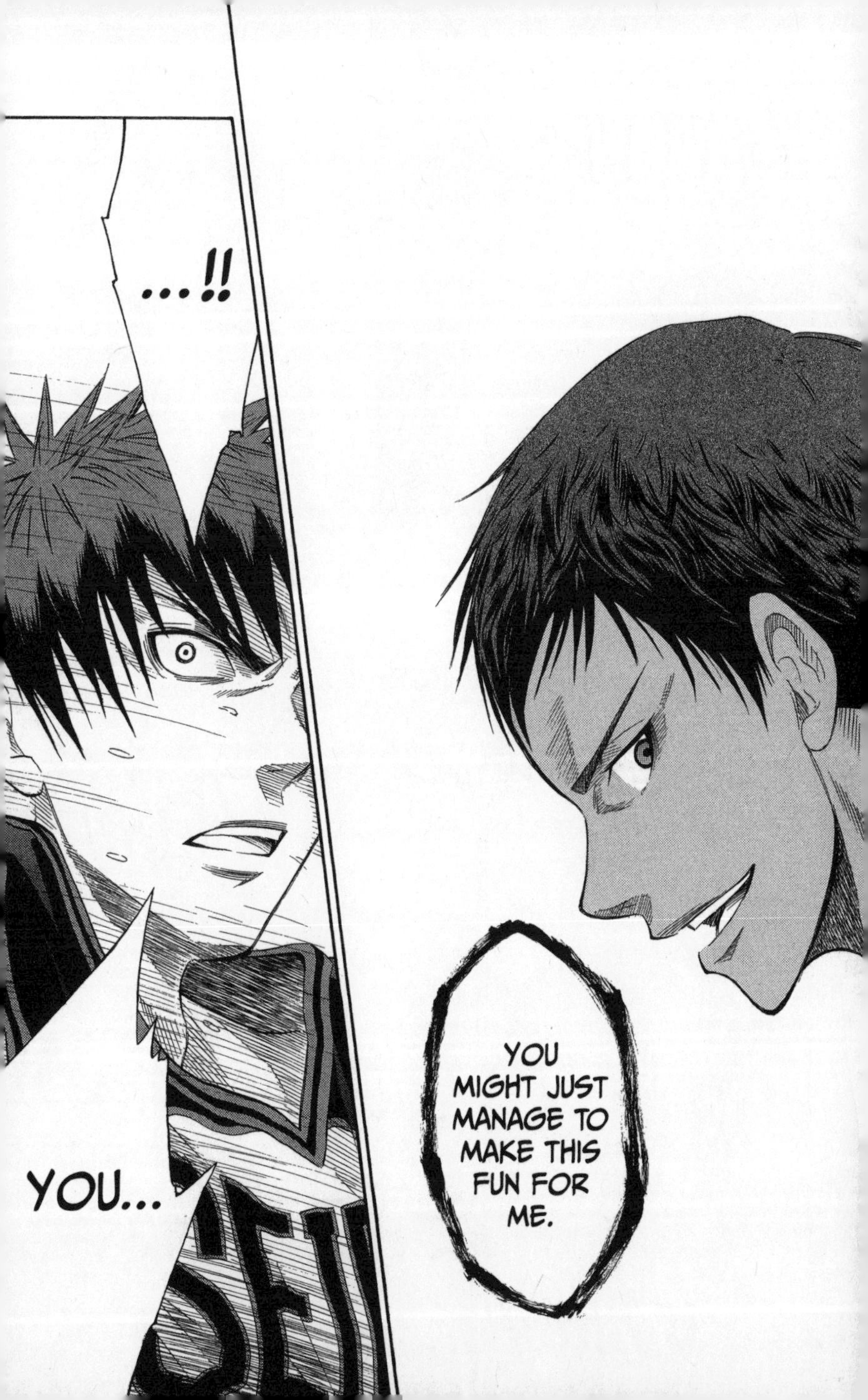
YOU MIGHT JUST MANAGE TO MAKE THIS FUN FOR ME.
...!!
YOU...

YEAHHH

AOMINE!!

SMAK!

YEAHHH

YEAHHH

NO.

HUH?

BUT WE'RE ALREADY WINNING?

GET YOUR GEAR ON AND GET OUT HERE!!

YOU'RE FINALLY HERE! SHEESH...

HIT THE COURT!

YEAHHH

YEAHHH

AND THERE'S STILL A WHOLE MINUTE LEFT IN THE SECOND QUARTER?

TO-OH ACADEMY	0:51	SEIRIN
49		39

GAH! I SHOULD'VE TAKEN MY SWEET TIME GETTING HERE.

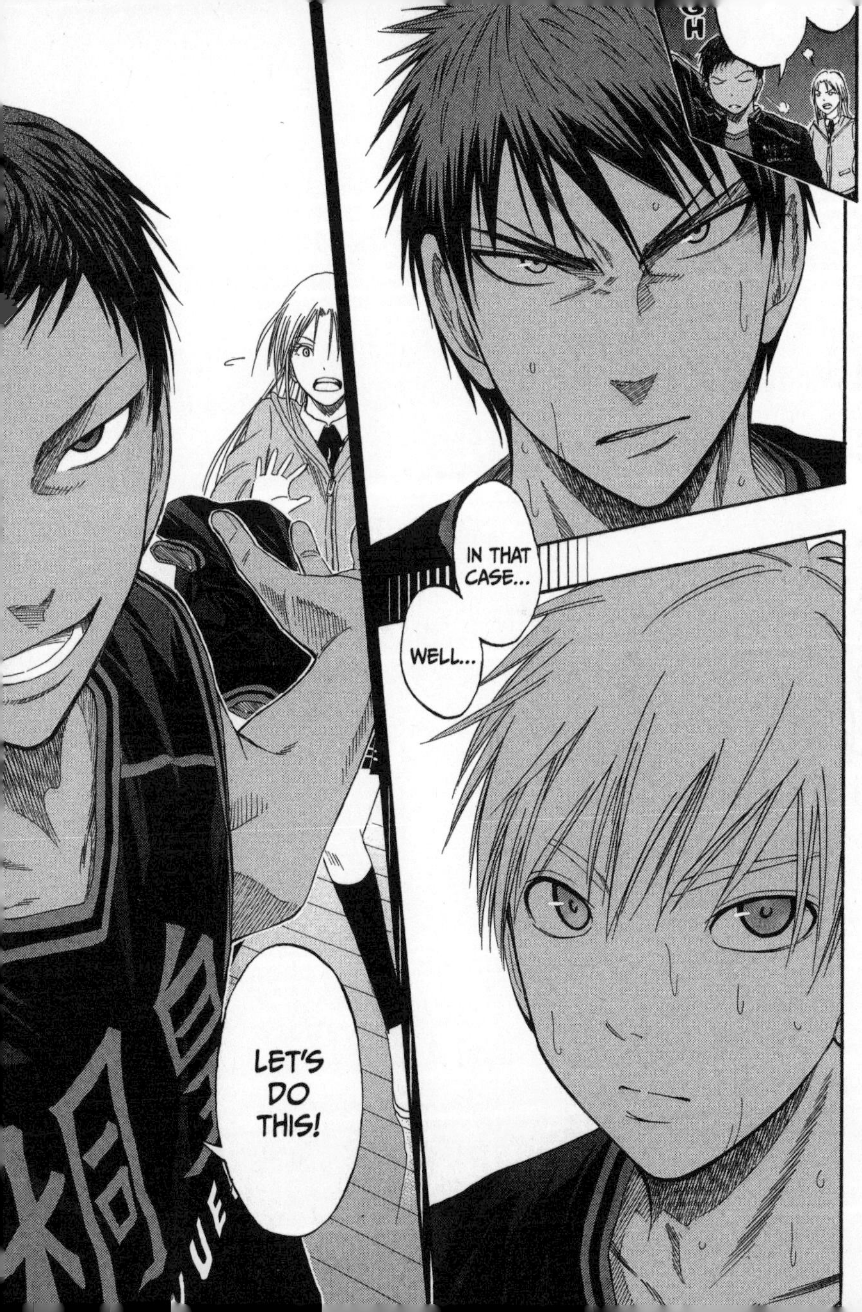
IN THAT CASE...
WELL...
LET'S DO THIS!

KUROKO'S BASKETBALL BLOOPERS TAKE 8

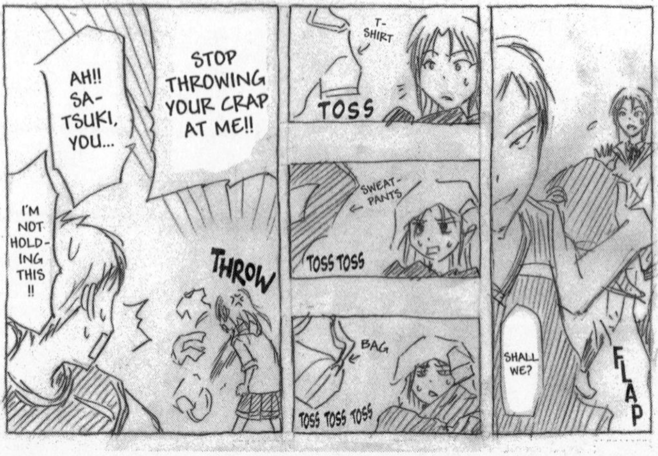

SHALL WE?
FLAP
T-SHIRT
TOSS
SWEAT-PANTS
TOSS TOSS
BAG
TOSS TOSS TOSS
STOP THROWING YOUR CRAP AT ME!!
AH!! SA-TSUKI, YOU...
THROW
I'M NOT HOLDING THIS !!

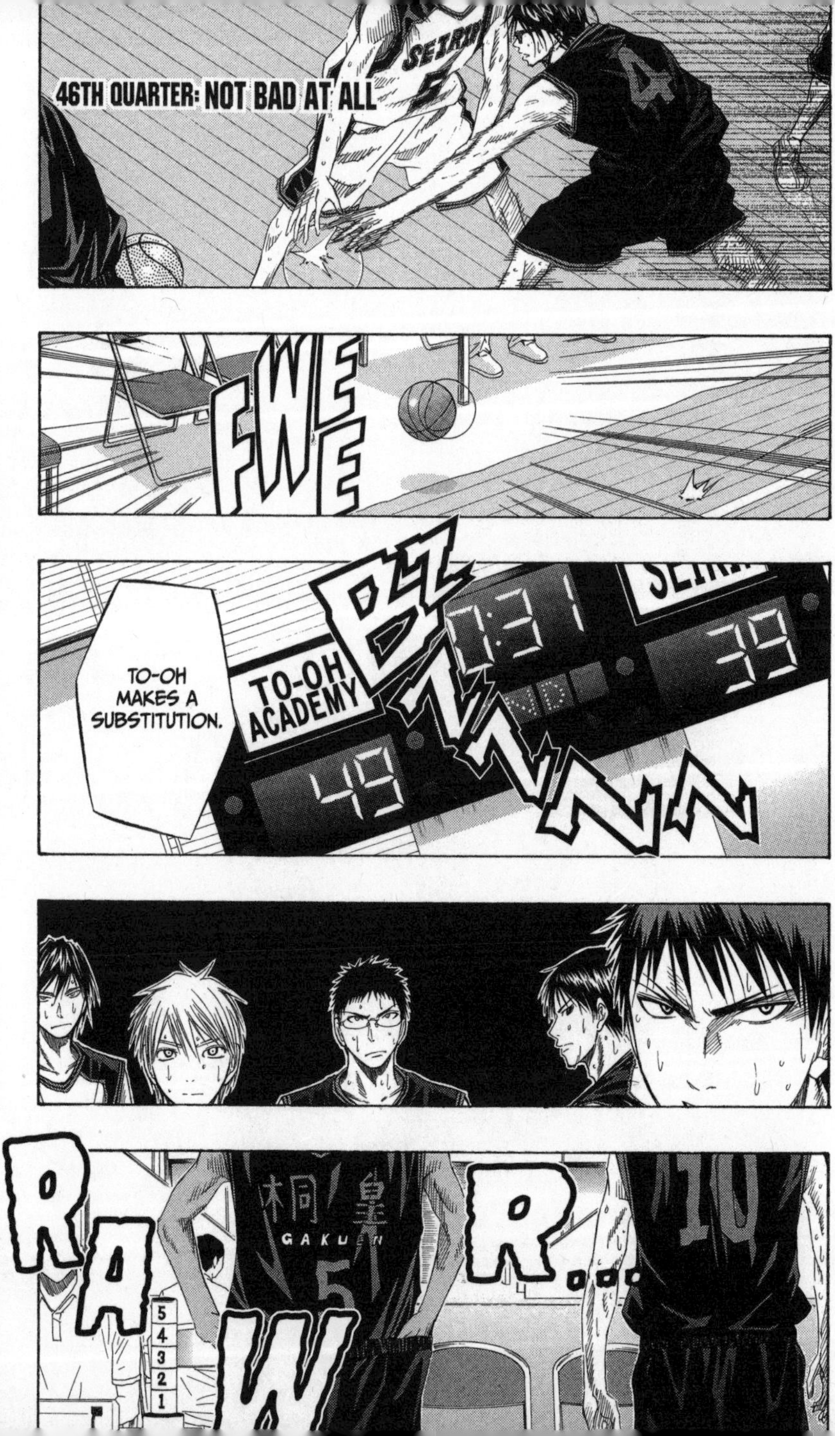
46TH QUARTER: NOT BAD AT ALL
FWE
FWE
BZZNNN
1:31
39
TO-OH ACADEMY
49
TO-OH MAKES A SUBSTITUTION.
GAKUEN
RAWR...

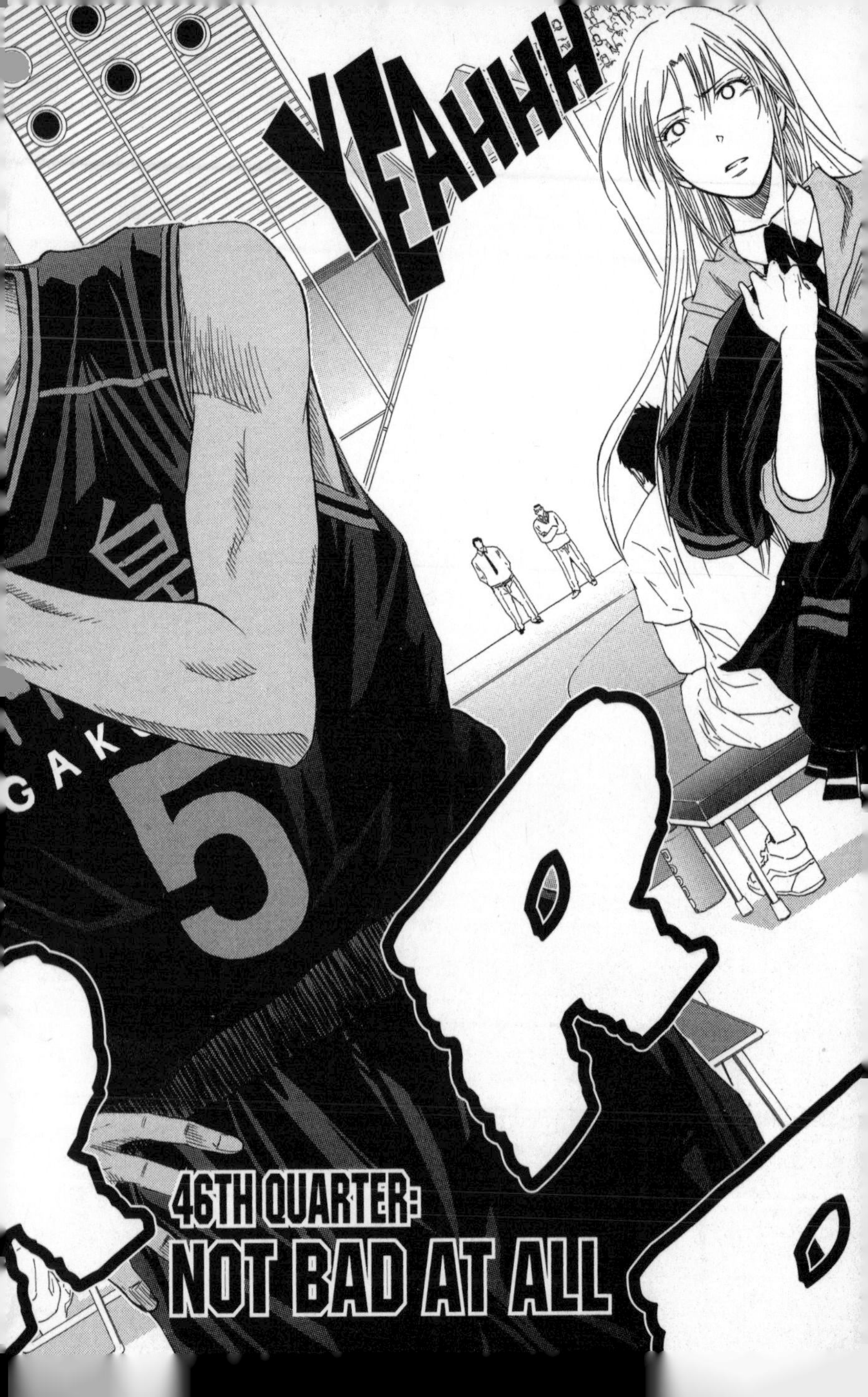
YEAHHH
GAK
5
46TH QUARTER:
NOT BAD AT ALL

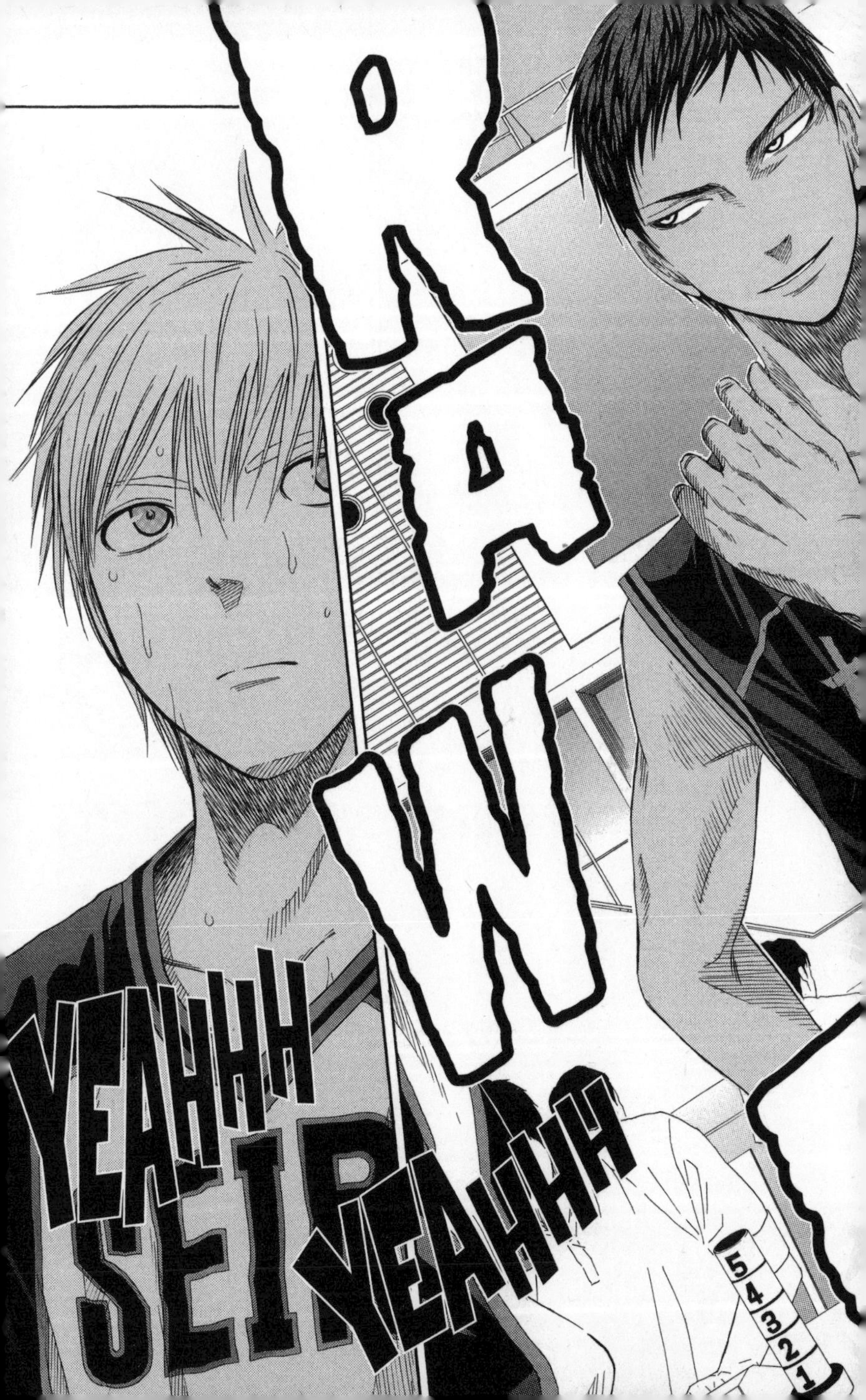
RAW
YEAHHH
YEAHHH
SEIR
54321

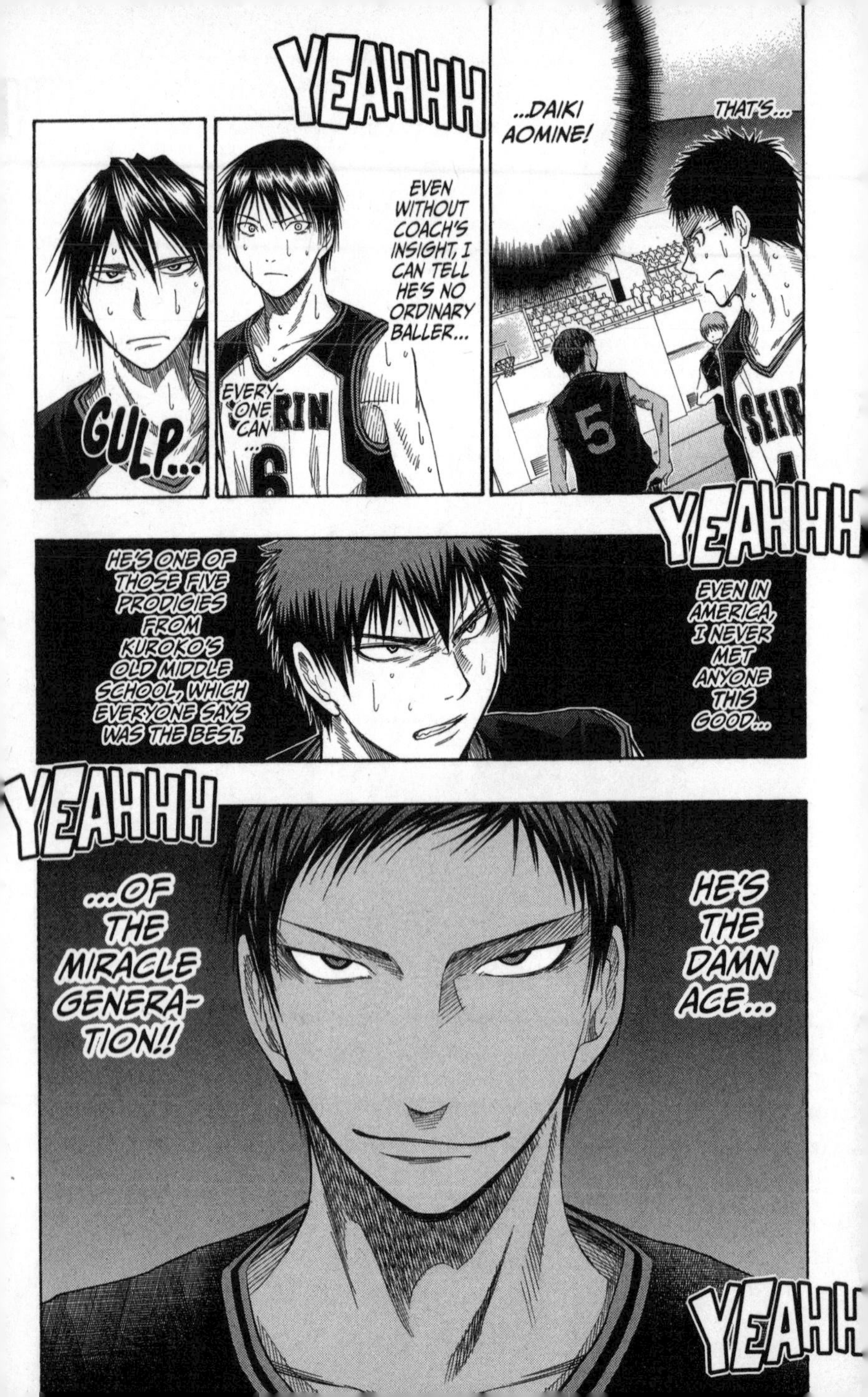
THAT'S...
...DAIKI AOMINE!
YEAHHH
EVEN WITHOUT COACH'S INSIGHT, I CAN TELL HE'S NO ORDINARY BALLER...
EVERY-ONE CAN ...
GULP...
YEAHHH
EVEN IN AMERICA, I NEVER MET ANYONE THIS GOOD...
HE'S ONE OF THOSE FIVE PRODIGIES FROM KUROKO'S OLD MIDDLE SCHOOL, WHICH EVERYONE SAYS WAS THE BEST.
YEAHHH
HE'S THE DAMN ACE...
...OF THE MIRACLE GENERA-TION!!
YEAHH

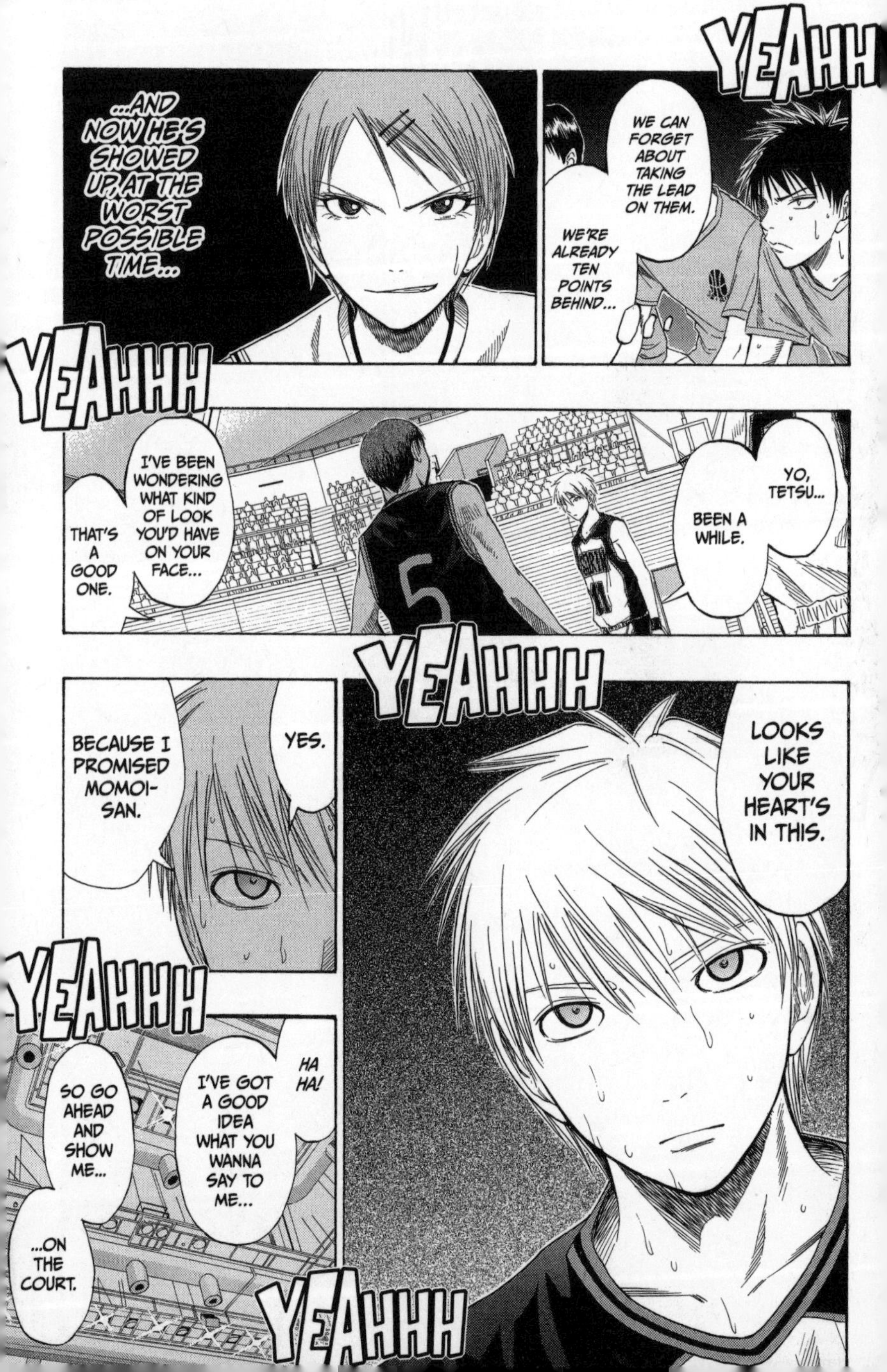
YEAHH
WE CAN FORGET ABOUT TAKING THE LEAD ON THEM.
WE'RE ALREADY TEN POINTS BEHIND...
...AND NOW HE'S SHOWED UP, AT THE WORST POSSIBLE TIME...
YEAHHH
YO, TETSU... BEEN A WHILE.
I'VE BEEN WONDERING WHAT KIND OF LOOK YOU'D HAVE ON YOUR FACE...
THAT'S A GOOD ONE.
YEAHHH
LOOKS LIKE YOUR HEART'S IN THIS.
YES.
BECAUSE I PROMISED MOMOI-SAN.
YEAHHH
HA HA!
I'VE GOT A GOOD IDEA WHAT YOU WANNA SAY TO ME...
SO GO AHEAD AND SHOW ME...
...ON THE COURT.
YEAHHH

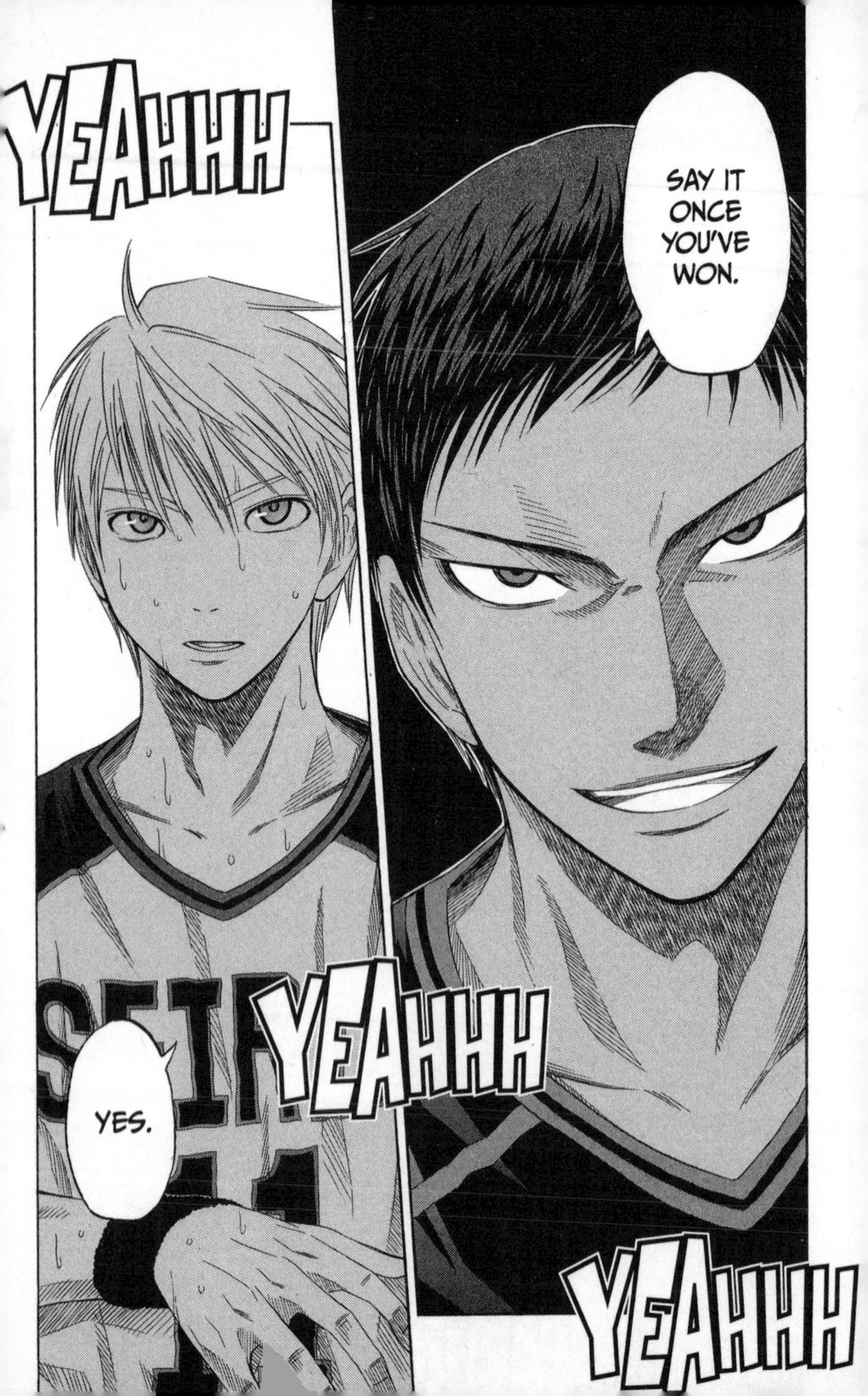
SAY IT ONCE YOU'VE WON.
YEAHHH
YEAHHH
YEAHHH
YES.

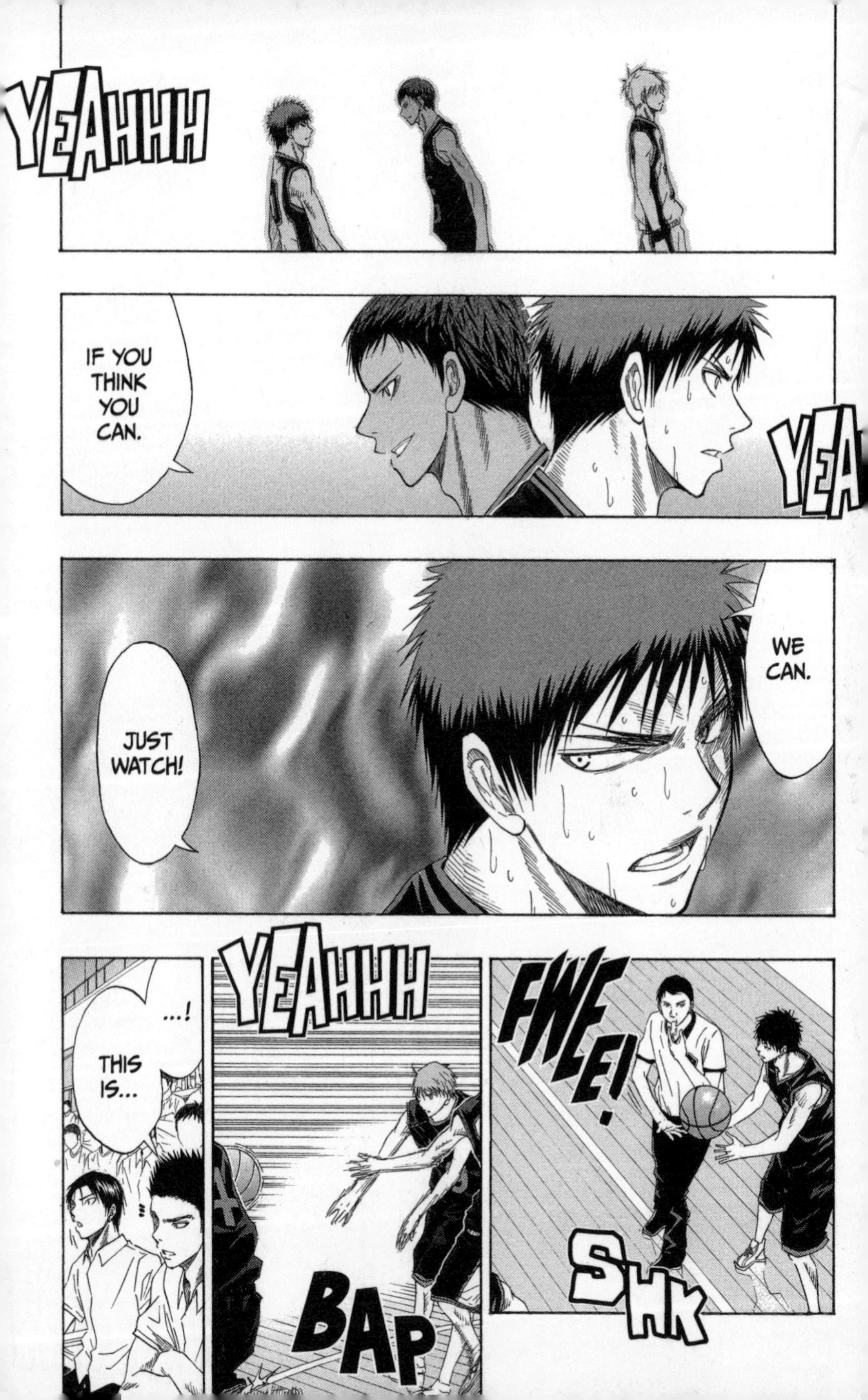
YEAHHH
YEA
IF YOU THINK YOU CAN.
WE CAN.
JUST WATCH!
FWEE!
SHK
YEAHHH
BAP
...!
THIS IS...

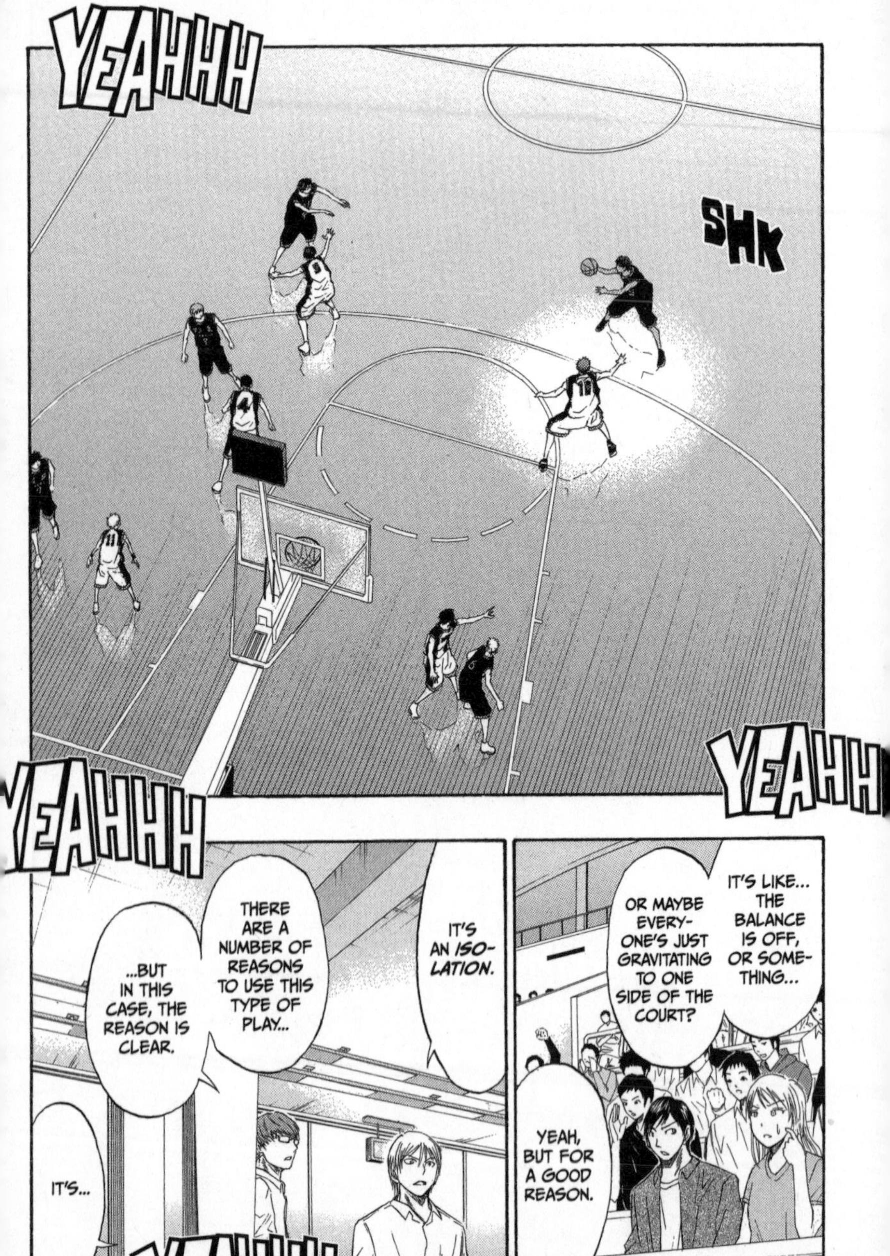
YEAHHH
SHK
YEAHH
YEAHHH
IT'S LIKE... THE BALANCE IS OFF, OR SOMETHING...
OR MAYBE EVERYONE'S JUST GRAVITATING TO ONE SIDE OF THE COURT?
YEAH, BUT FOR A GOOD REASON.
IT'S AN *ISOLATION.*
THERE ARE A NUMBER OF REASONS TO USE THIS TYPE OF PLAY...
...BUT IN THIS CASE, THE REASON IS CLEAR.
IT'S...
YEAHHH

* AN ISOLATION PLAY IS AN OFFENSIVE STRATEGY THAT GIVES ONE PLAYER SPACE TO WORK WHILE THE REMAINING PLAYERS MOVE AWAY FROM THE BALL.

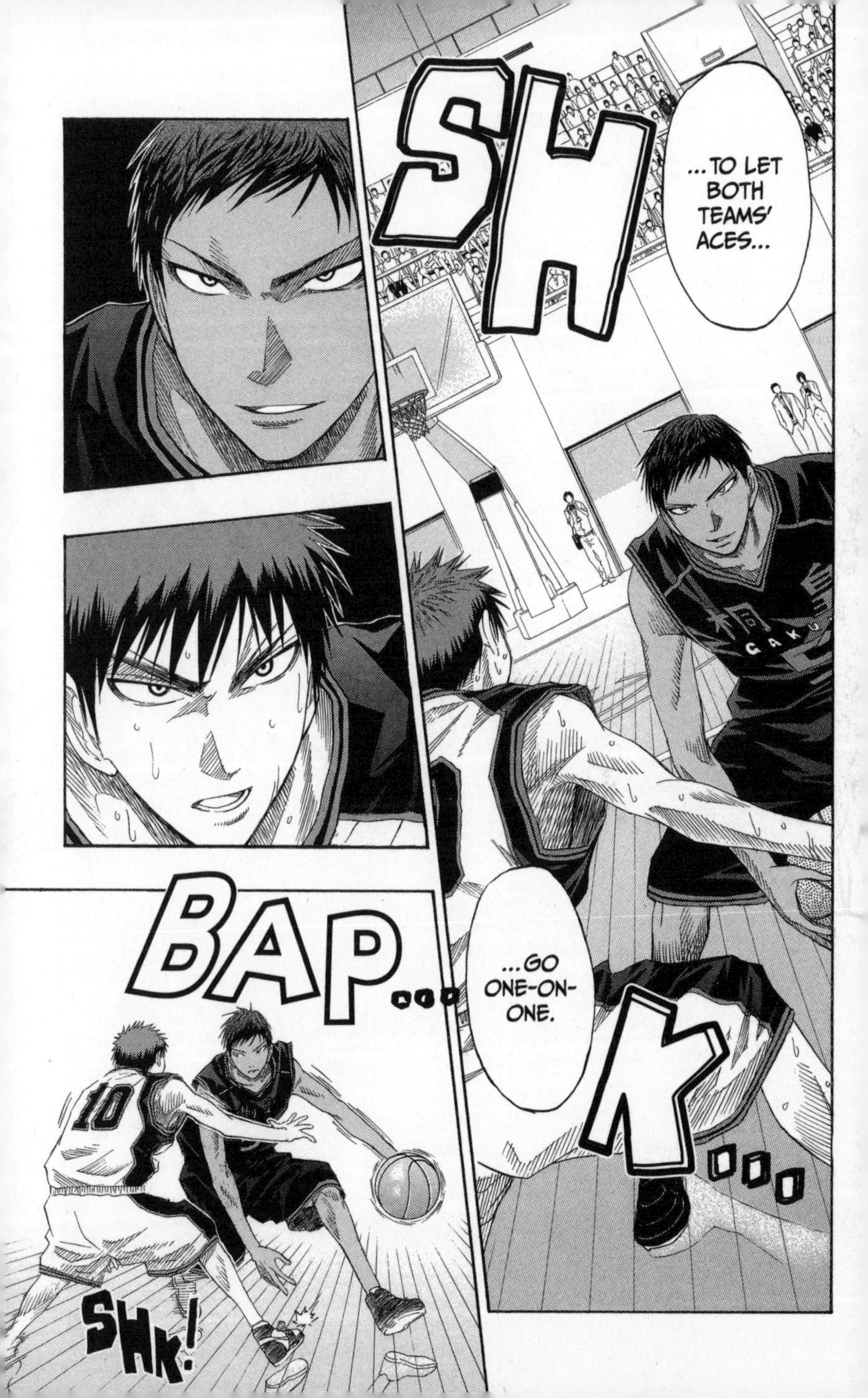
SH
...TO LET BOTH TEAMS' ACES...
...GO ONE-ON-ONE.
K...
BAP...
SHK!

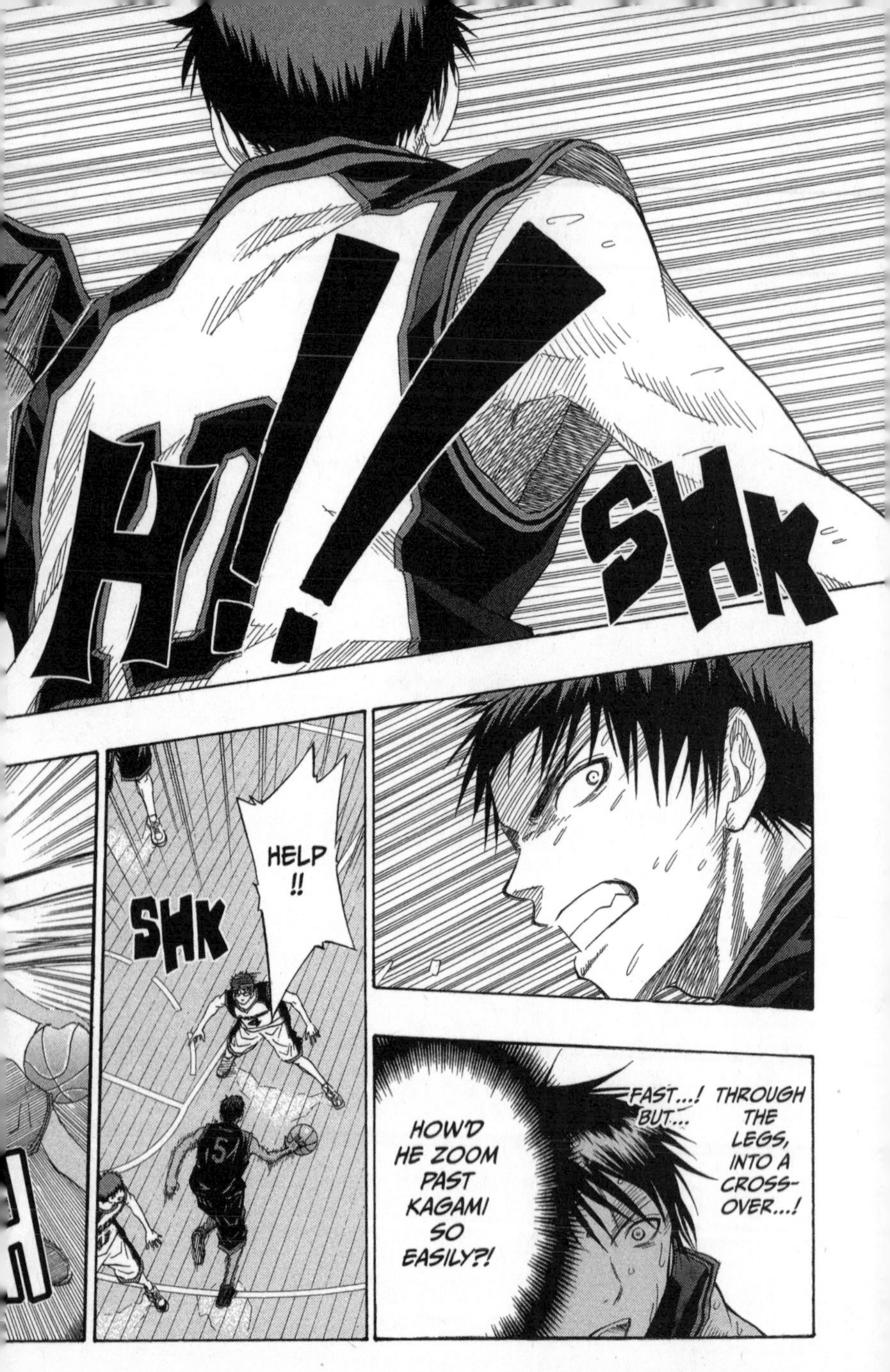
SHK
HELP!!
SHK
THROUGH THE LEGS, INTO A CROSS-OVER...!
FAST...! BUT...
HOW'D HE ZOOM PAST KAGAMI SO EASILY?!

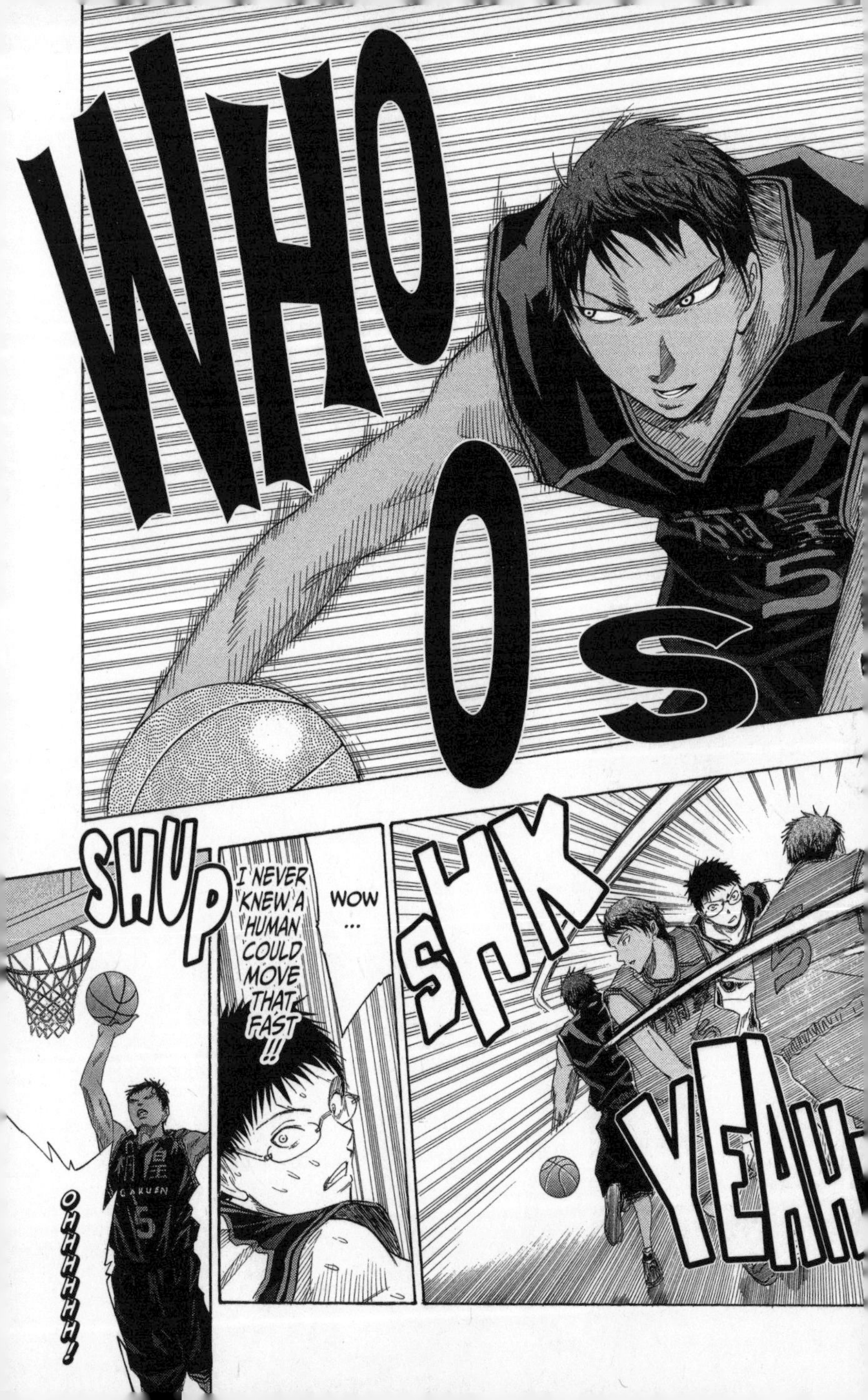
WHOOOS
SHK
YEAH
WOW...
I NEVER KNEW A HUMAN COULD MOVE THAT FAST!!
SHUP
OHHHHHHH!

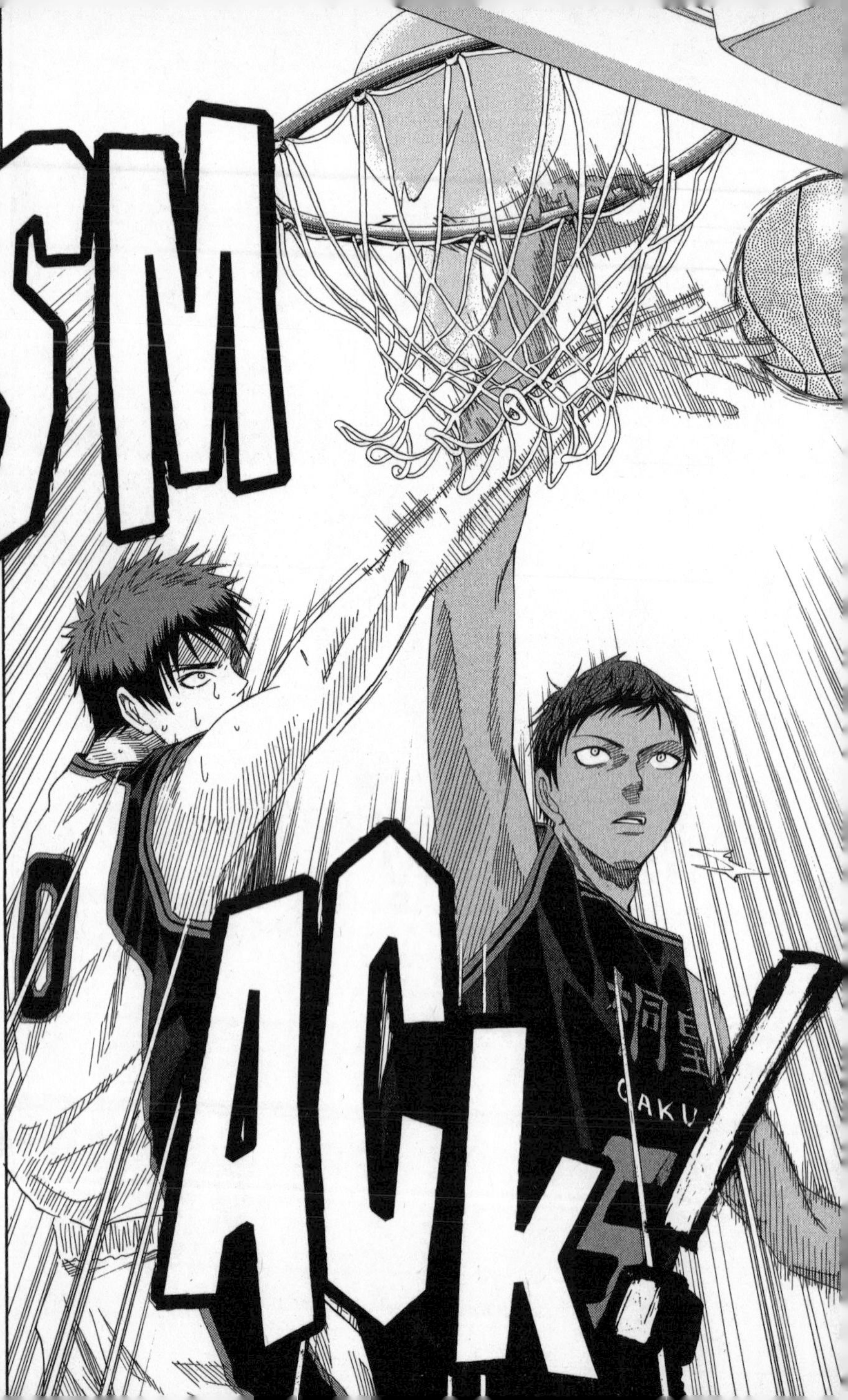
SMACK!
GAKU

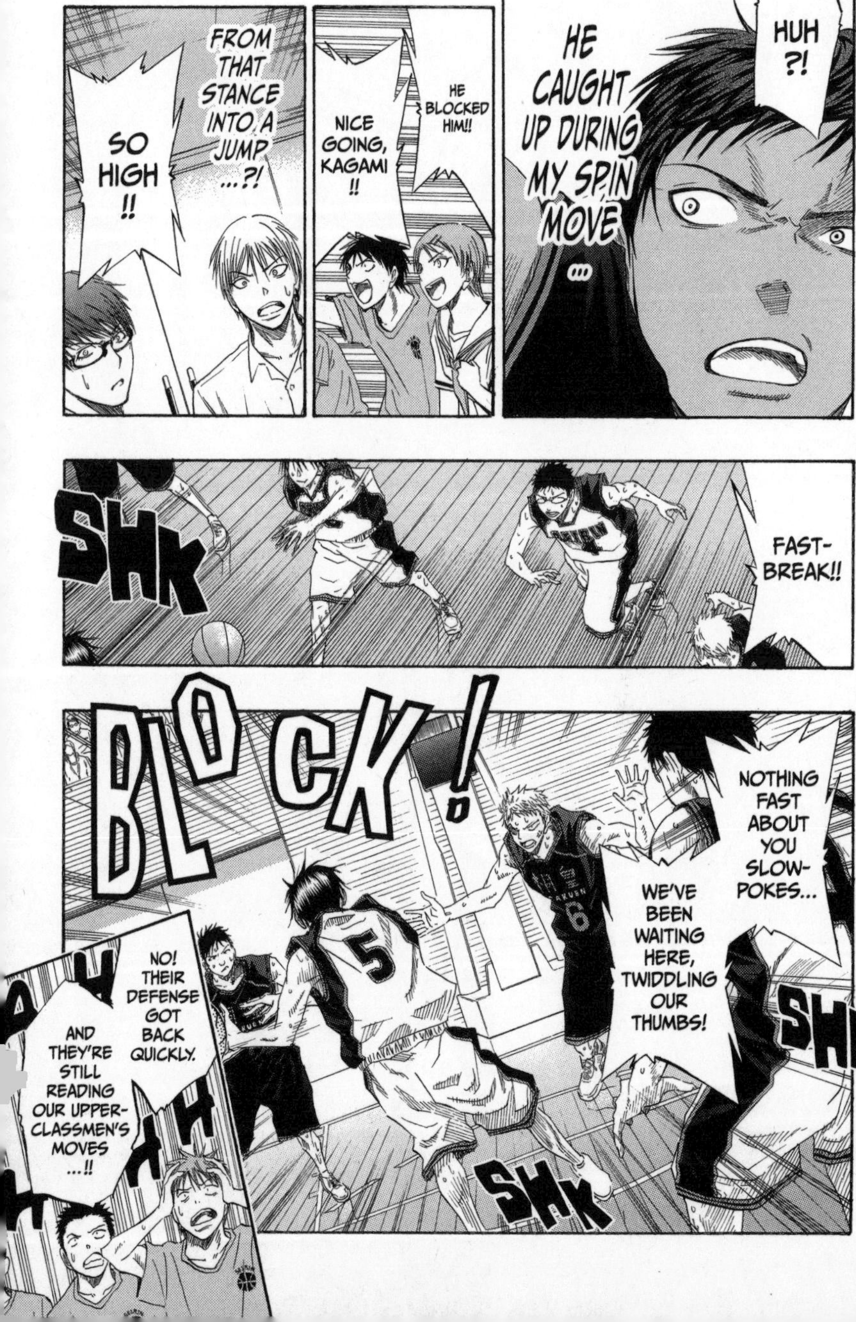
HUH ?!
HE CAUGHT UP DURING MY SPIN MOVE ...
HE BLOCKED HIM!!
NICE GOING, KAGAMI !!
FROM THAT STANCE INTO A JUMP ...?!
SO HIGH !!
FAST-BREAK!!
SHK
BLOCK!
NOTHING FAST ABOUT YOU SLOWPOKES...
WE'VE BEEN WAITING HERE, TWIDDLING OUR THUMBS!
SHK
SHK
NO! THEIR DEFENSE GOT BACK QUICKLY.
AND THEY'RE STILL READING OUR UPPERCLASSMEN'S MOVES ...!!

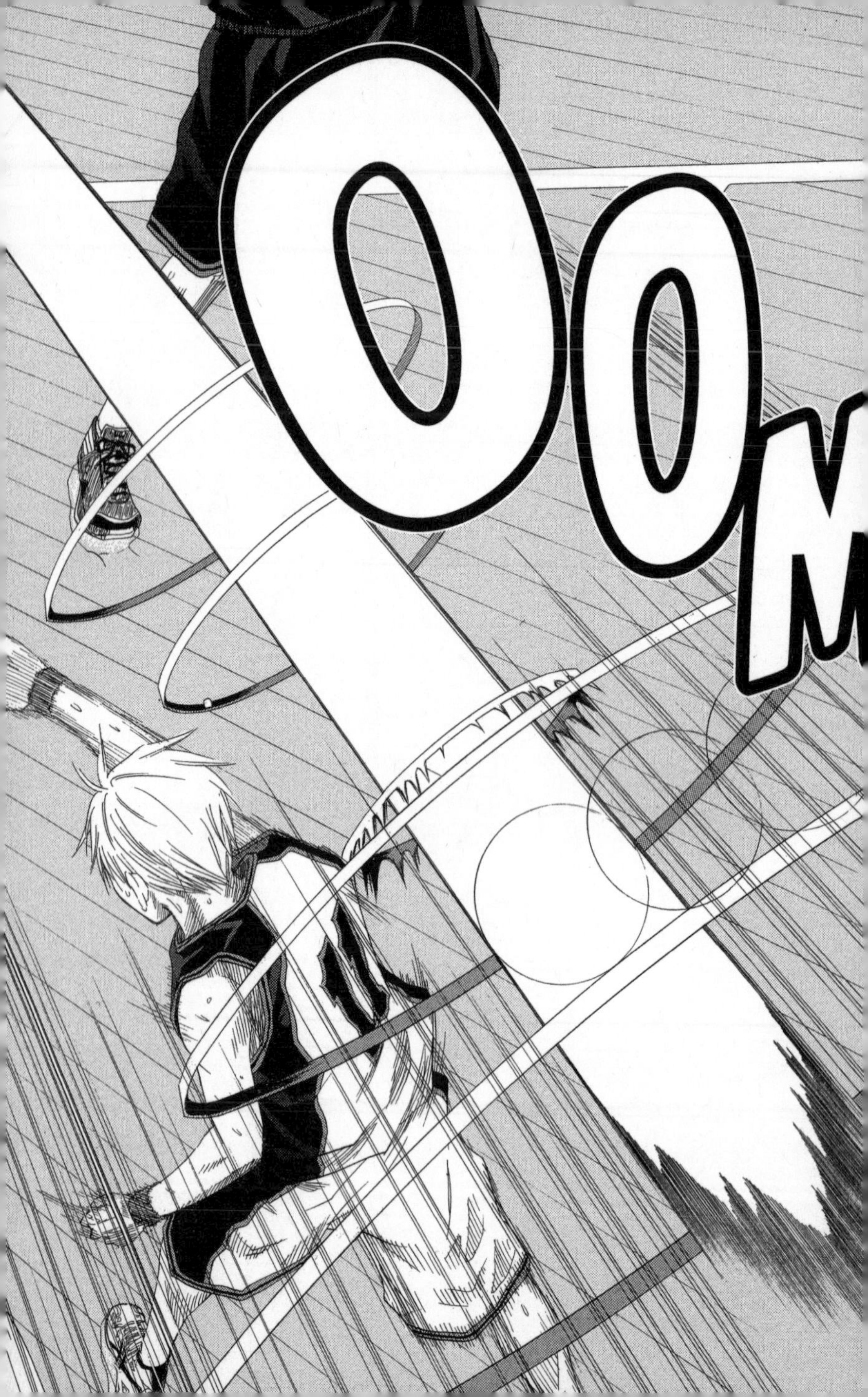
OOM

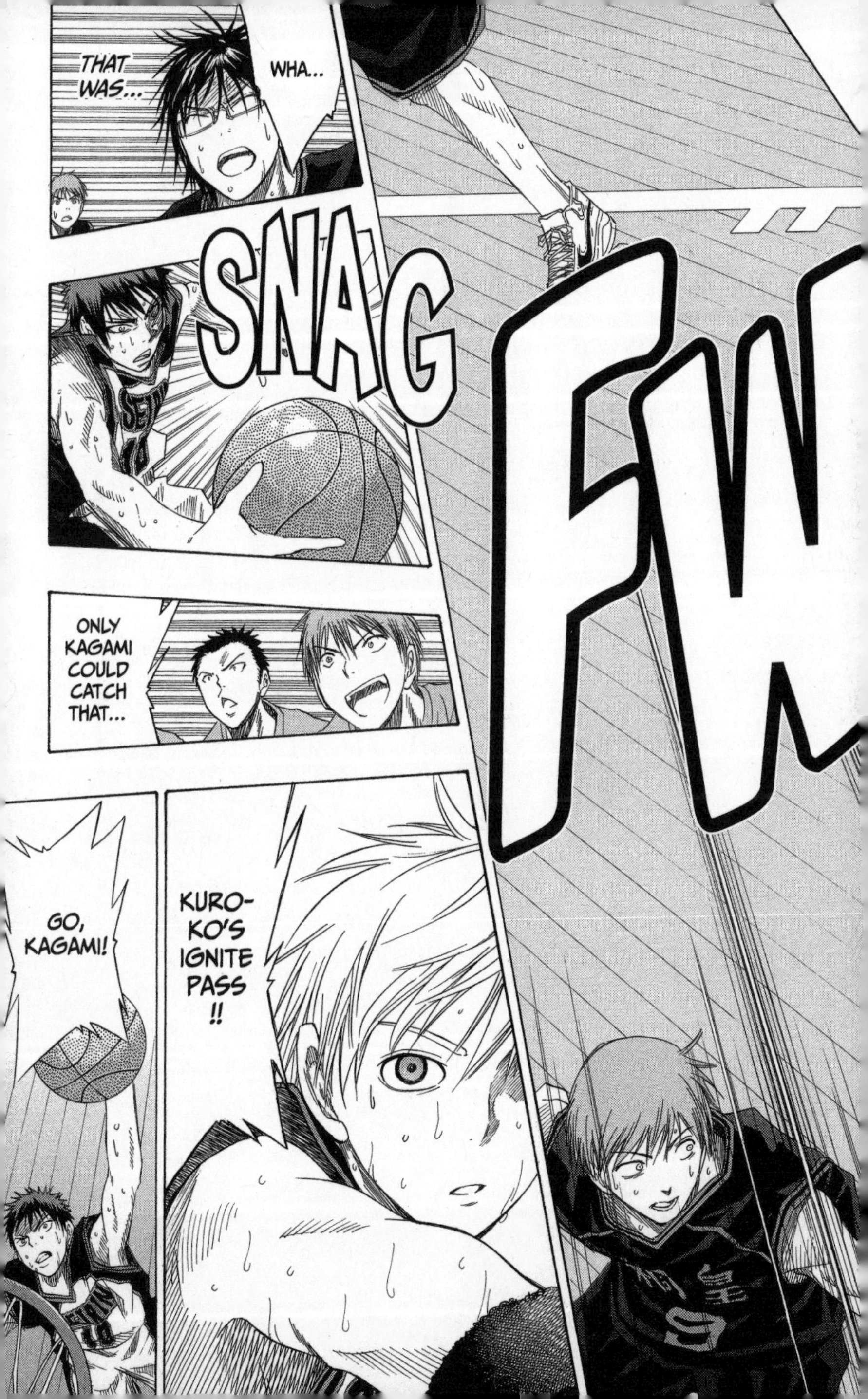
FW
WHA...
THAT WAS...
SNAG
ONLY KAGAMI COULD CATCH THAT...
KURO-KO'S IGNITE PASS!!
GO, KAGAMI!

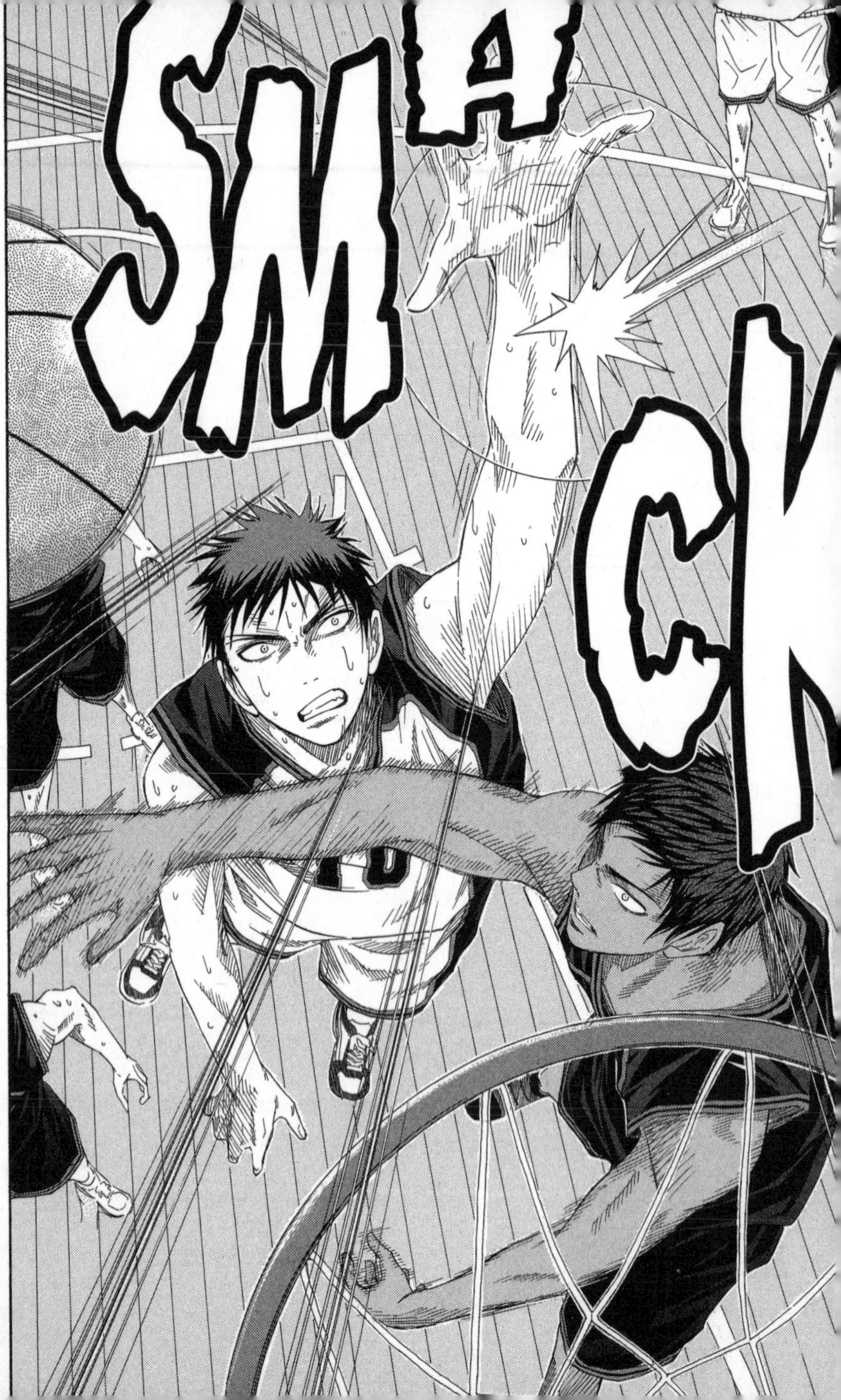
SMACK

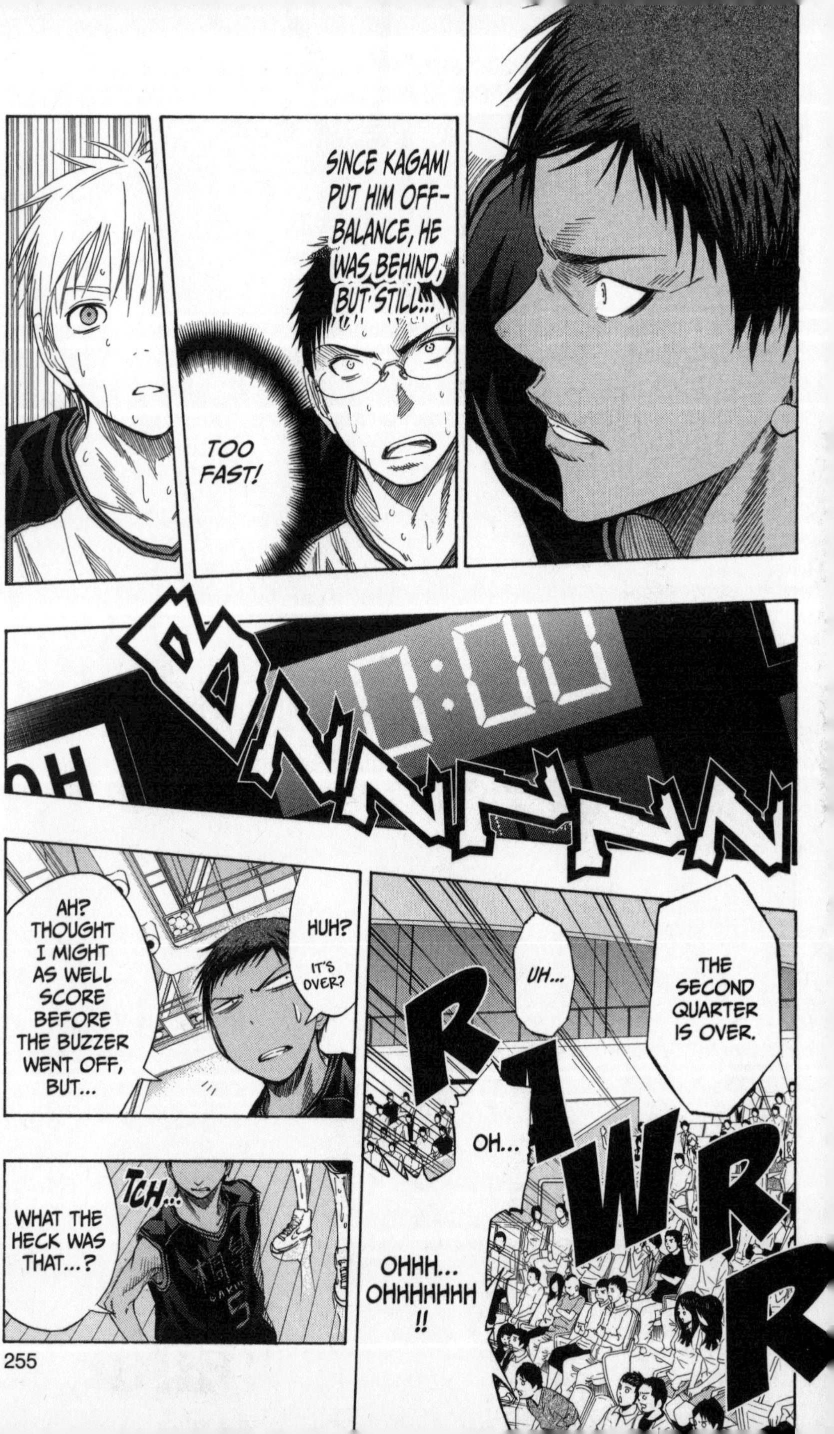

SINCE KAGAMI PUT HIM OFF-BALANCE, HE WAS BEHIND, BUT STILL...
TOO FAST!
BNNNNN
UH...
THE SECOND QUARTER IS OVER.
OH...
OHHH... OHHHHHHH!!
HUH?
IT'S OVER?
AH? THOUGHT I MIGHT AS WELL SCORE BEFORE THE BUZZER WENT OFF, BUT...
TCH...
WHAT THE HECK WAS THAT...?

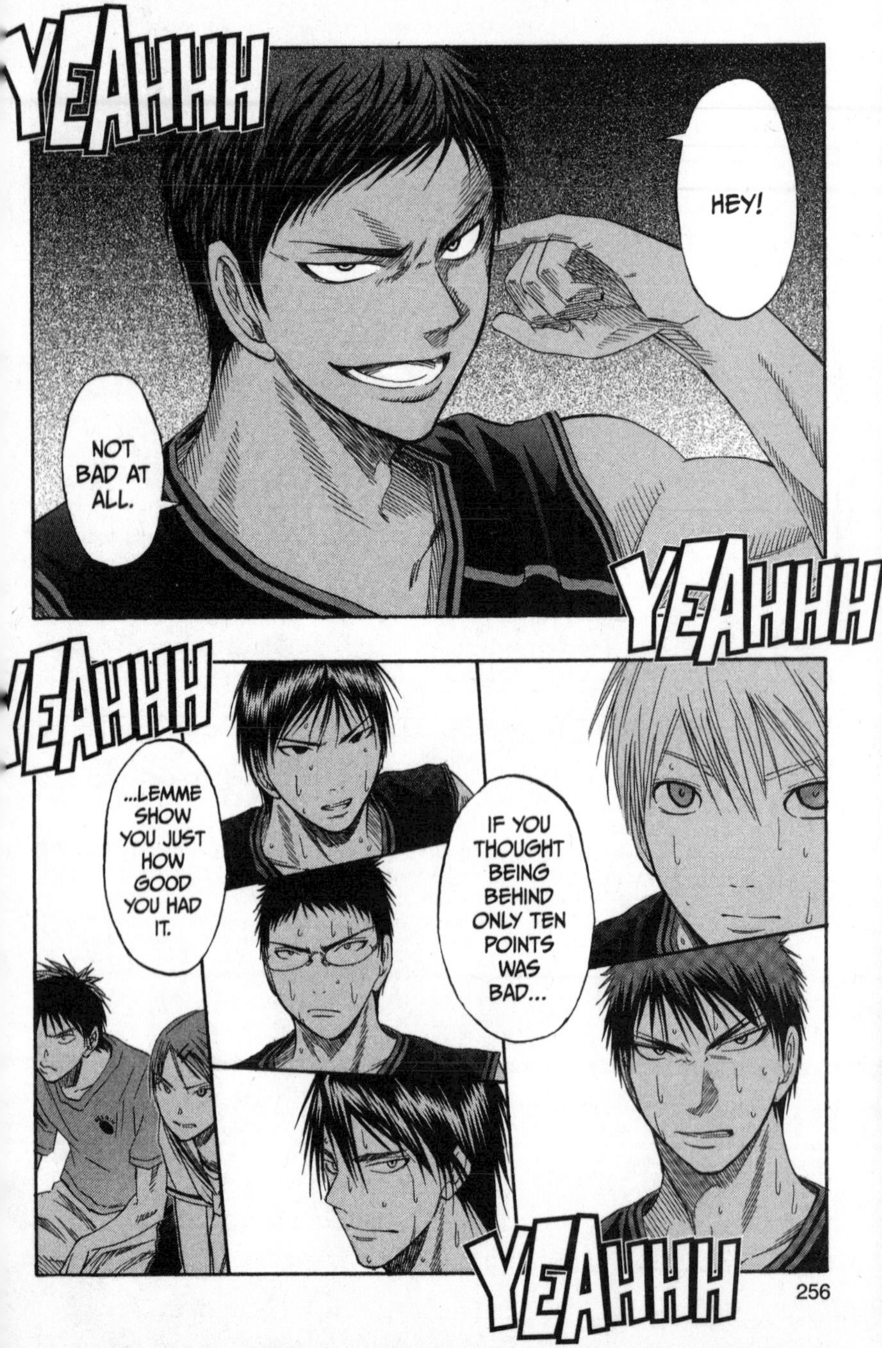
HEY!
YEAHHH
NOT BAD AT ALL.
YEAHHH
YEAHHH
IF YOU THOUGHT BEING BEHIND ONLY TEN POINTS WAS BAD...
...LEMME SHOW YOU JUST HOW GOOD YOU HAD IT.
YEAHHH

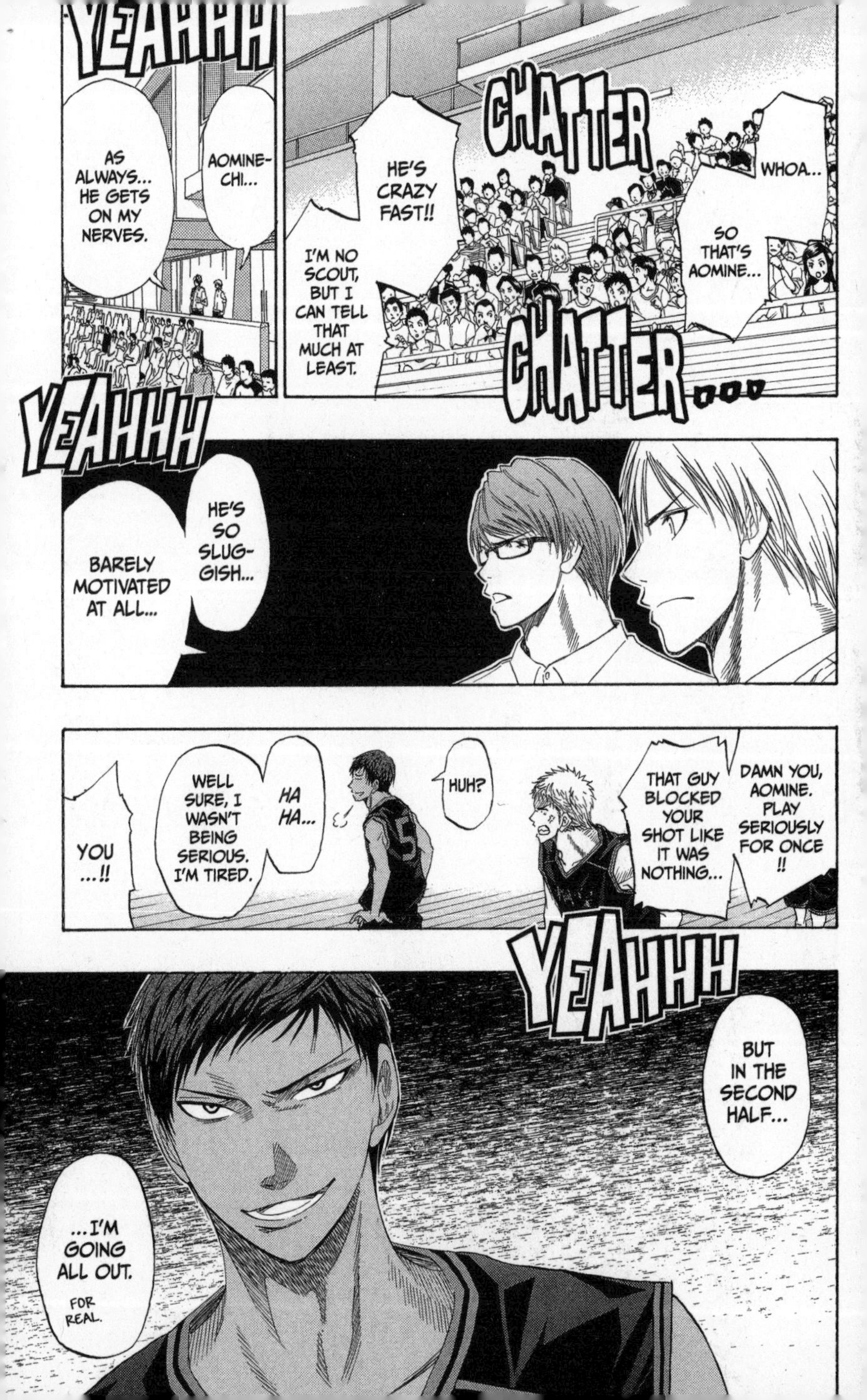
CHATTER
WHOA...
SO THAT'S AOMINE...
HE'S CRAZY FAST!!
I'M NO SCOUT, BUT I CAN TELL THAT MUCH AT LEAST.
CHATTER...
YEAHHH
AOMINE-CHI...
AS ALWAYS... HE GETS ON MY NERVES.
YEAHHH
HE'S SO SLUG-GISH...
BARELY MOTIVATED AT ALL...
DAMN YOU, AOMINE. PLAY SERIOUSLY FOR ONCE!!
THAT GUY BLOCKED YOUR SHOT LIKE IT WAS NOTHING...
HUH?
HA HA...
WELL SURE, I WASN'T BEING SERIOUS. I'M TIRED.
YOU...!!
YEAHHH
BUT IN THE SECOND HALF...
...I'M GOING ALL OUT.
FOR REAL.

KUROKO'S BASKETBALL BLOOPERS

TAKE 2

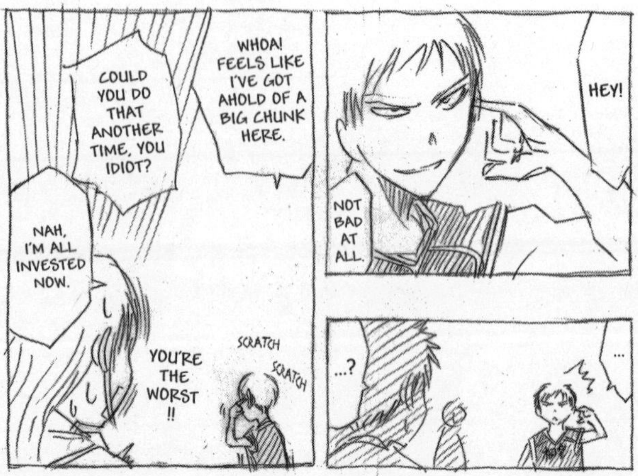
HEY!
NOT BAD AT ALL.
...
...?
WHOA! FEELS LIKE I'VE GOT AHOLD OF A BIG CHUNK HERE.
COULD YOU DO THAT ANOTHER TIME, YOU IDIOT?
NAH, I'M ALL INVESTED NOW.
SCRATCH
SCRATCH
YOU'RE THE WORST!!

47TH QUARTER:
LEAVE IT TO US

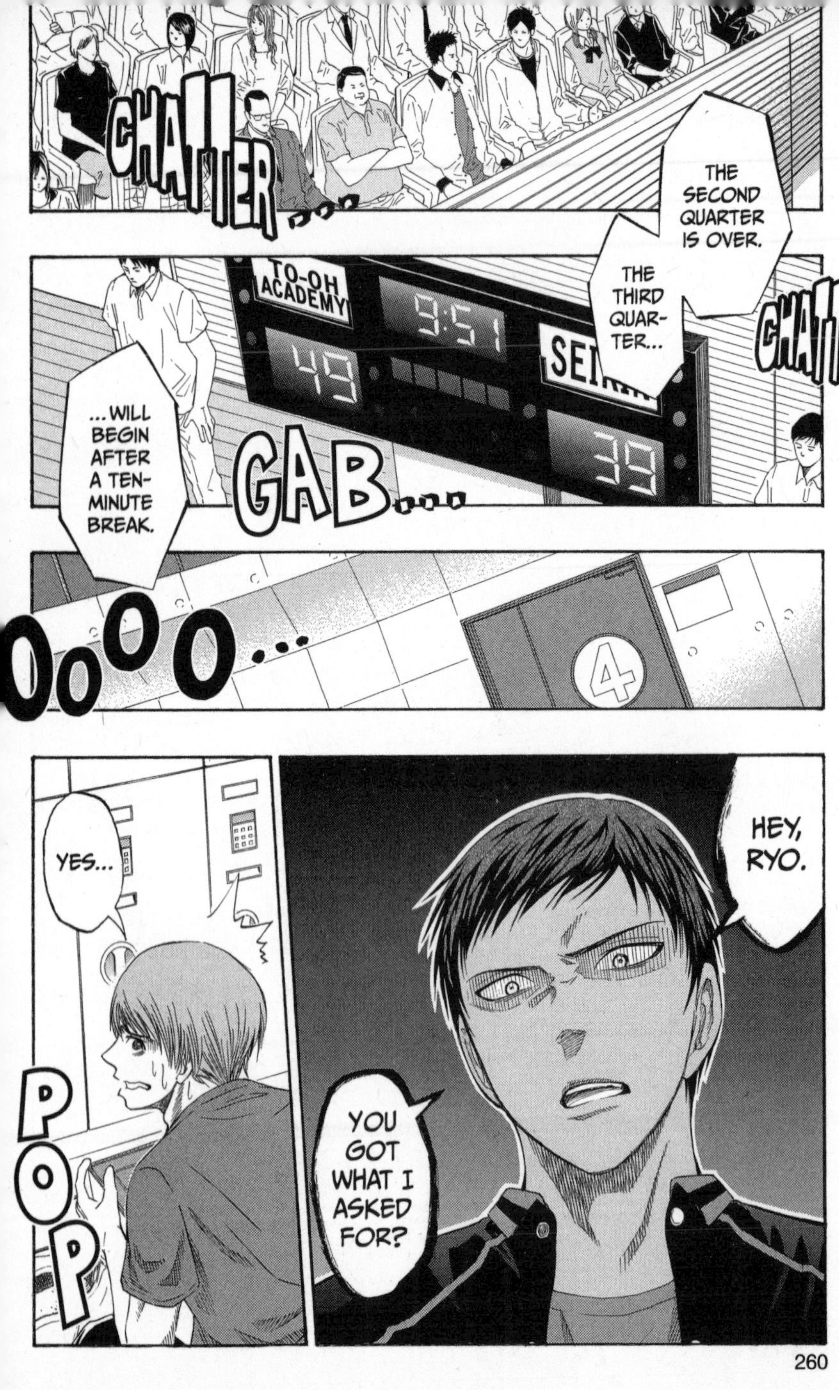
CHATTER...
THE SECOND QUARTER IS OVER.
THE THIRD QUARTER...
CHATTER
TO-OH ACADEMY
9:51
49
SEI
39
...WILL BEGIN AFTER A TEN-MINUTE BREAK.
GAB...
OoOO...
HEY, RYO.
YOU GOT WHAT I ASKED FOR?
YES...
POP

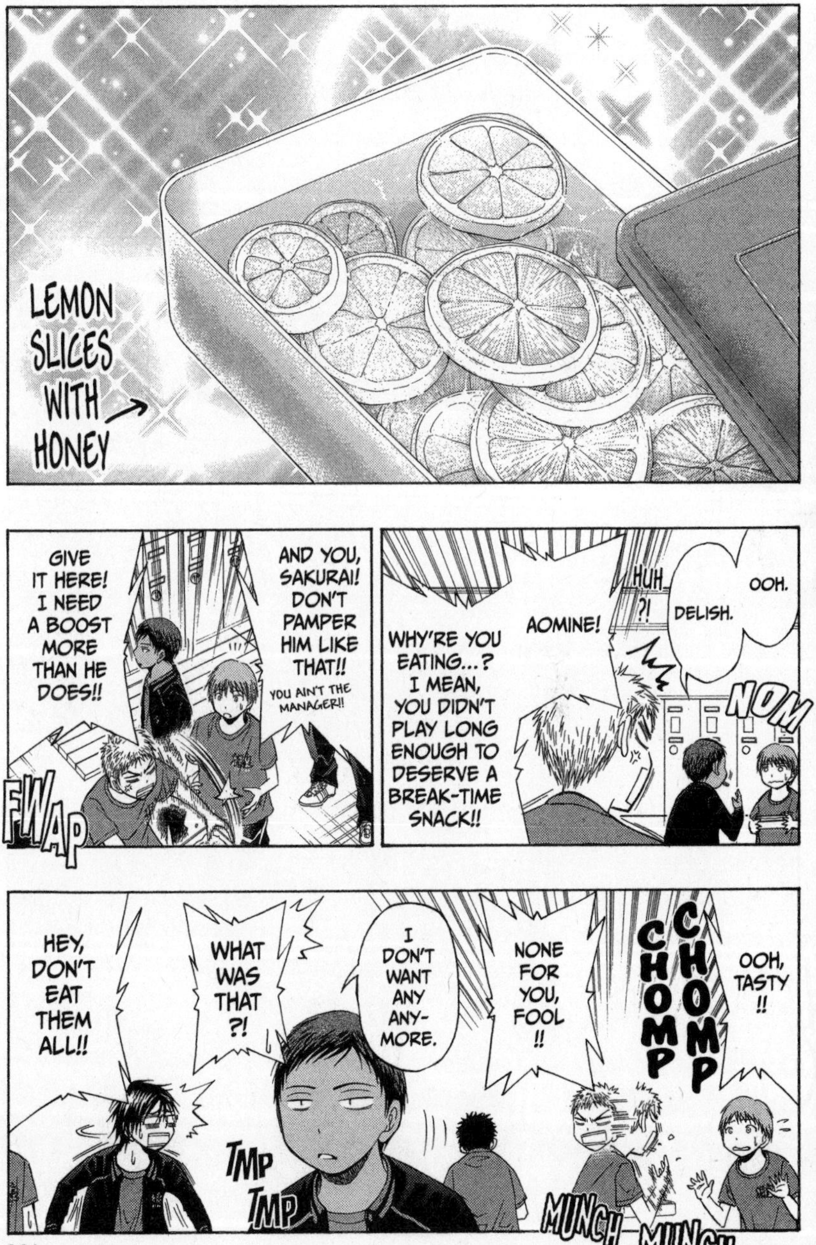
LEMON SLICES WITH HONEY
OOH. DELISH.
NOM
HUH?!
AOMINE!
WHY'RE YOU EATING...? I MEAN, YOU DIDN'T PLAY LONG ENOUGH TO DESERVE A BREAK-TIME SNACK!!
AND YOU, SAKURAI! DON'T PAMPER HIM LIKE THAT!!
YOU AIN'T THE MANAGER!!
GIVE IT HERE! I NEED A BOOST MORE THAN HE DOES!!
FWAP
OOH, TASTY!!
CHOMP CHOMP
NONE FOR YOU, FOOL!!
MUNCH MUNCH
I DON'T WANT ANY ANYMORE.
TMP TMP
WHAT WAS THAT?!
HEY, DON'T EAT THEM ALL!!

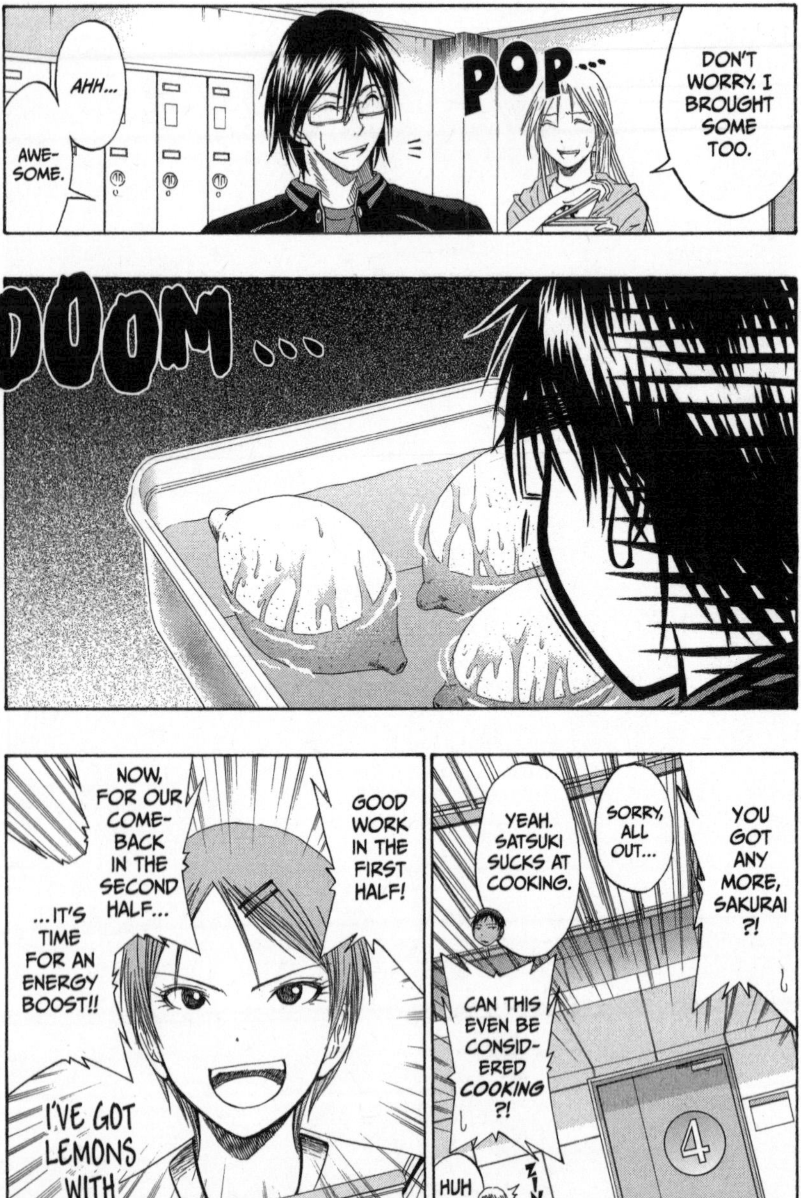
DON'T WORRY. I BROUGHT SOME TOO.
POP...
AHH... AWESOME.
DOOM...
YOU GOT ANY MORE, SAKURAI?!
SORRY, ALL OUT...
YEAH. SATSUKI SUCKS AT COOKING.
CAN THIS EVEN BE CONSIDERED COOKING?!
ZING
HUH?!
4
GOOD WORK IN THE FIRST HALF!
NOW, FOR OUR COMEBACK IN THE SECOND HALF...
...IT'S TIME FOR AN ENERGY BOOST!!
I'VE GOT LEMONS WITH HONEY!

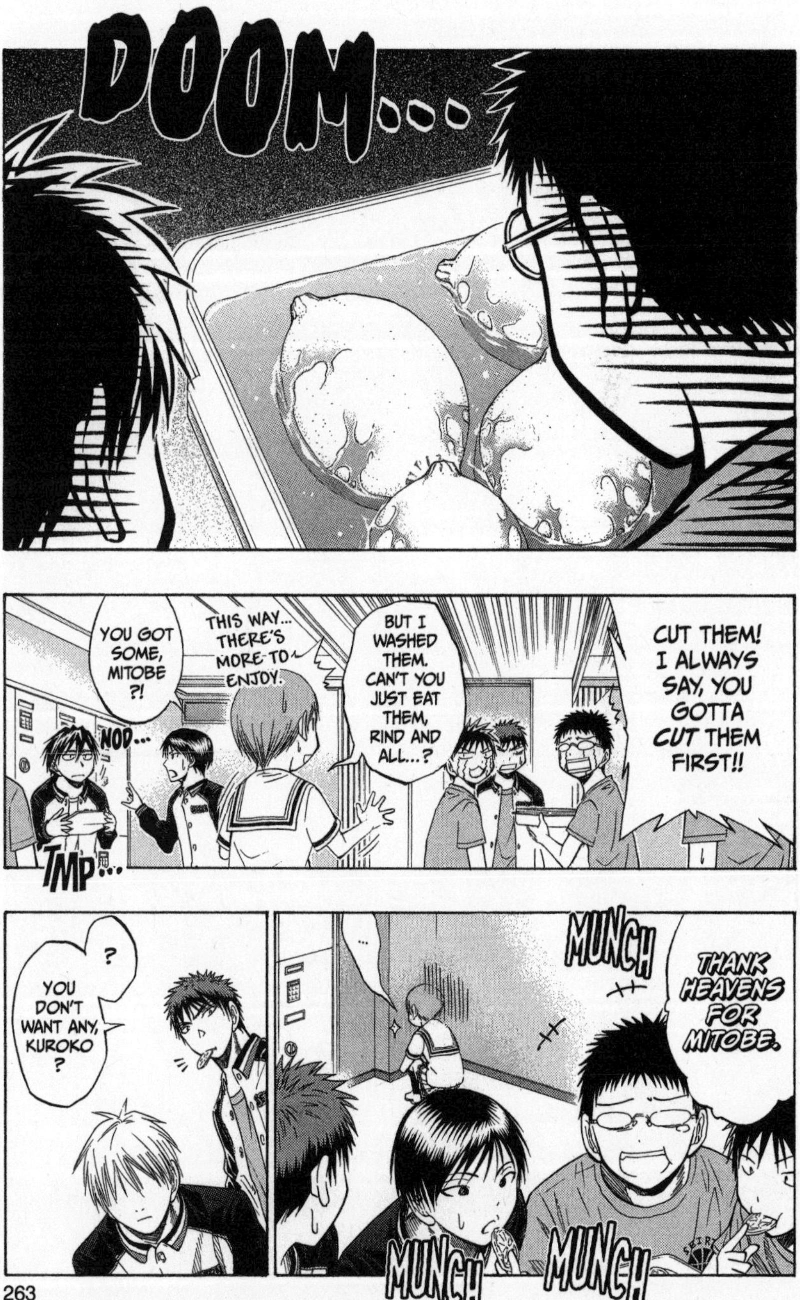
DOOM...
CUT THEM! I ALWAYS SAY, YOU GOTTA CUT THEM FIRST!!
BUT I WASHED THEM. CAN'T YOU JUST EAT THEM, RIND AND ALL...?
THIS WAY... THERE'S MORE TO ENJOY.
YOU GOT SOME, MITOBE?!
NOD...
TMP...
THANK HEAVENS FOR MITOBE.
MUNCH
...
MUNCH
MUNCH
?
YOU DON'T WANT ANY, KUROKO?

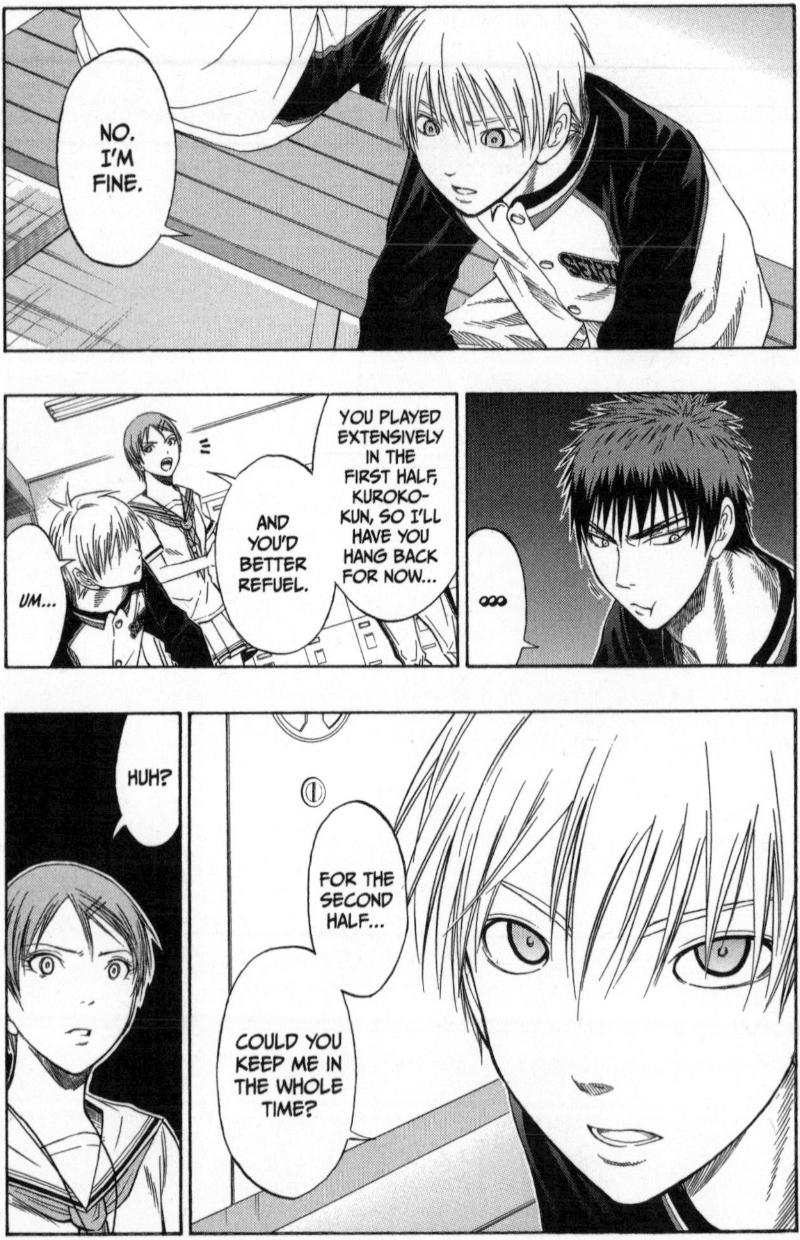
NO. I'M FINE.
...
YOU PLAYED EXTENSIVELY IN THE FIRST HALF, KUROKO-KUN, SO I'LL HAVE YOU HANG BACK FOR NOW...
AND YOU'D BETTER REFUEL.
UM...
FOR THE SECOND HALF...
COULD YOU KEEP ME IN THE WHOLE TIME?
HUH?

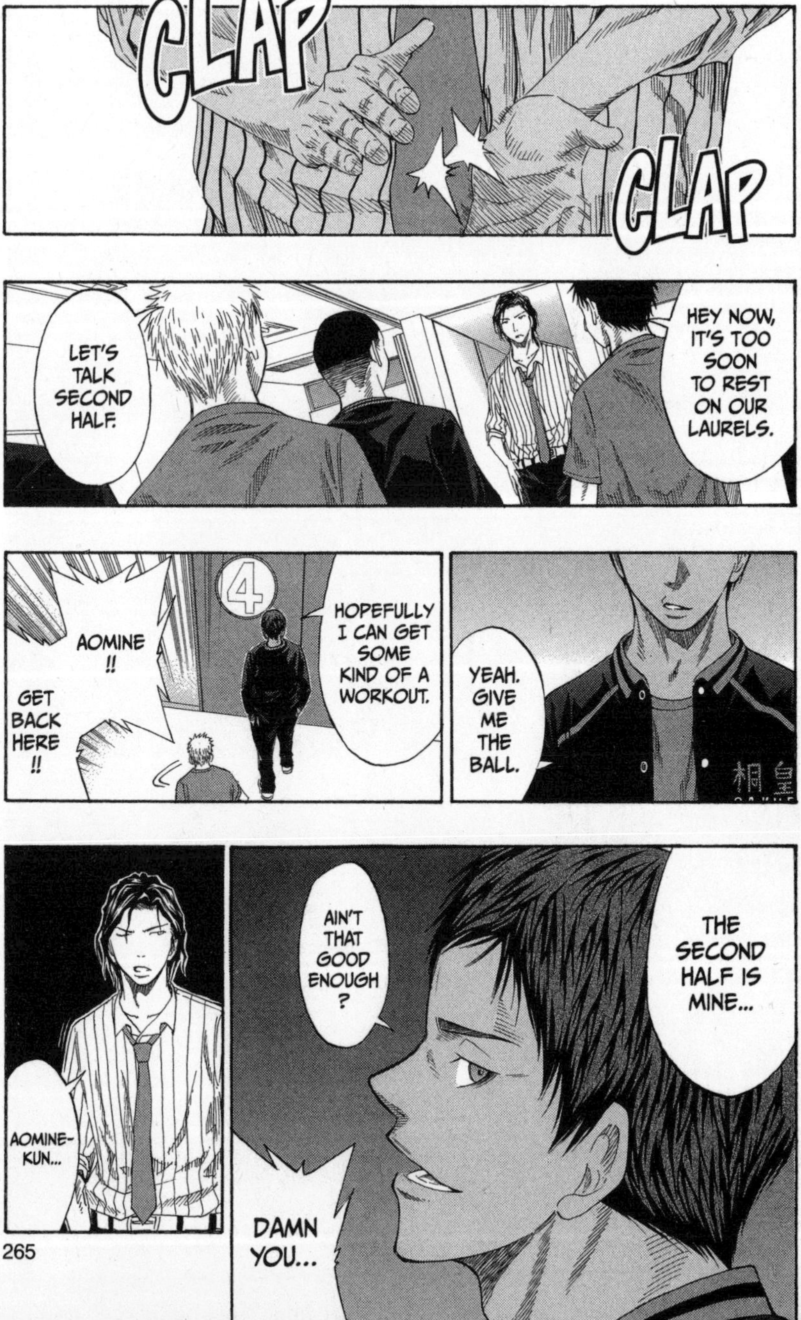
CLAP
CLAP
HEY NOW, IT'S TOO SOON TO REST ON OUR LAURELS.
LET'S TALK SECOND HALF.
YEAH. GIVE ME THE BALL.
桐皇
HOPEFULLY I CAN GET SOME KIND OF A WORKOUT.
AOMINE !!
GET BACK HERE !!
THE SECOND HALF IS MINE...
AIN'T THAT GOOD ENOUGH ?
DAMN YOU...
AOMINE-KUN...

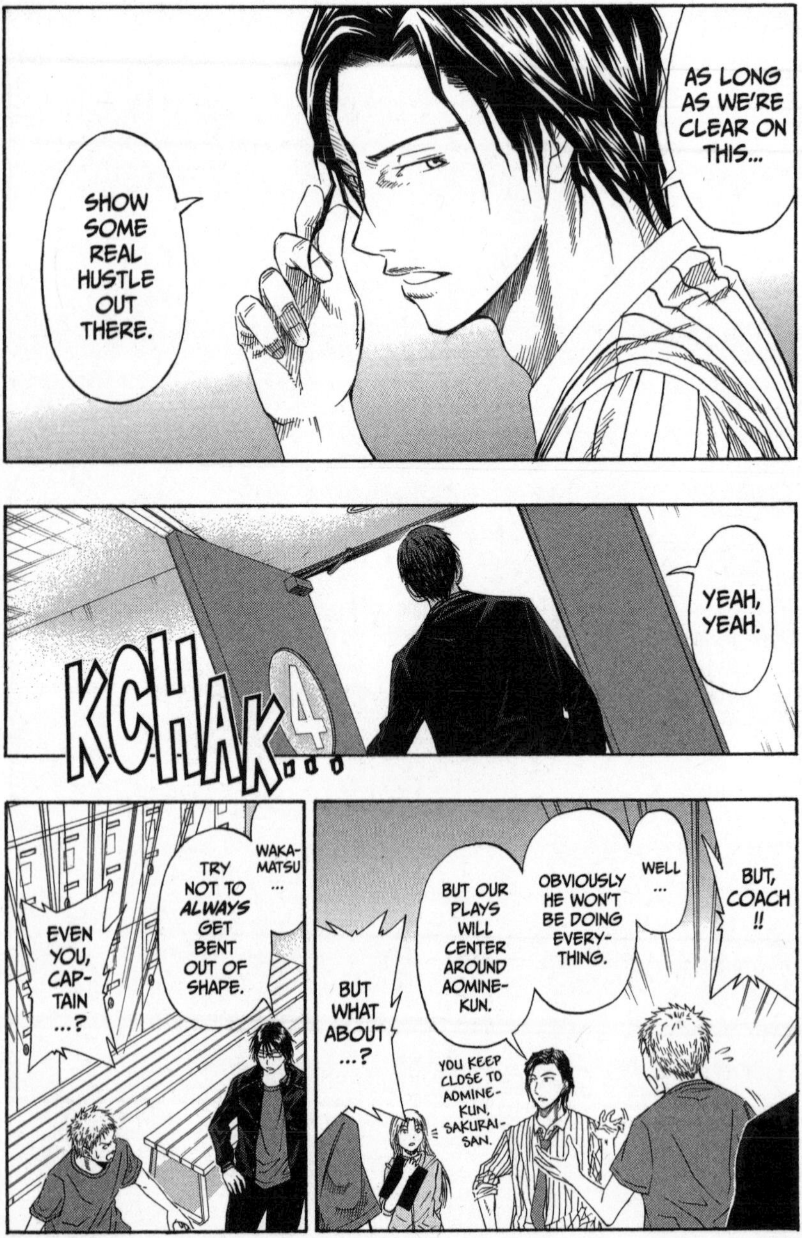
AS LONG AS WE'RE CLEAR ON THIS...
SHOW SOME REAL HUSTLE OUT THERE.
YEAH, YEAH.
KCHAK...
BUT, COACH!!
WELL...
OBVIOUSLY HE WON'T BE DOING EVERYTHING.
BUT OUR PLAYS WILL CENTER AROUND AOMINE-KUN.
BUT WHAT ABOUT...?
YOU KEEP CLOSE TO ADMINE-KUN, SAKURAI-SAN.
WAKAMATSU...
TRY NOT TO *ALWAYS* GET BENT OUT OF SHAPE.
EVEN YOU, CAPTAIN...?

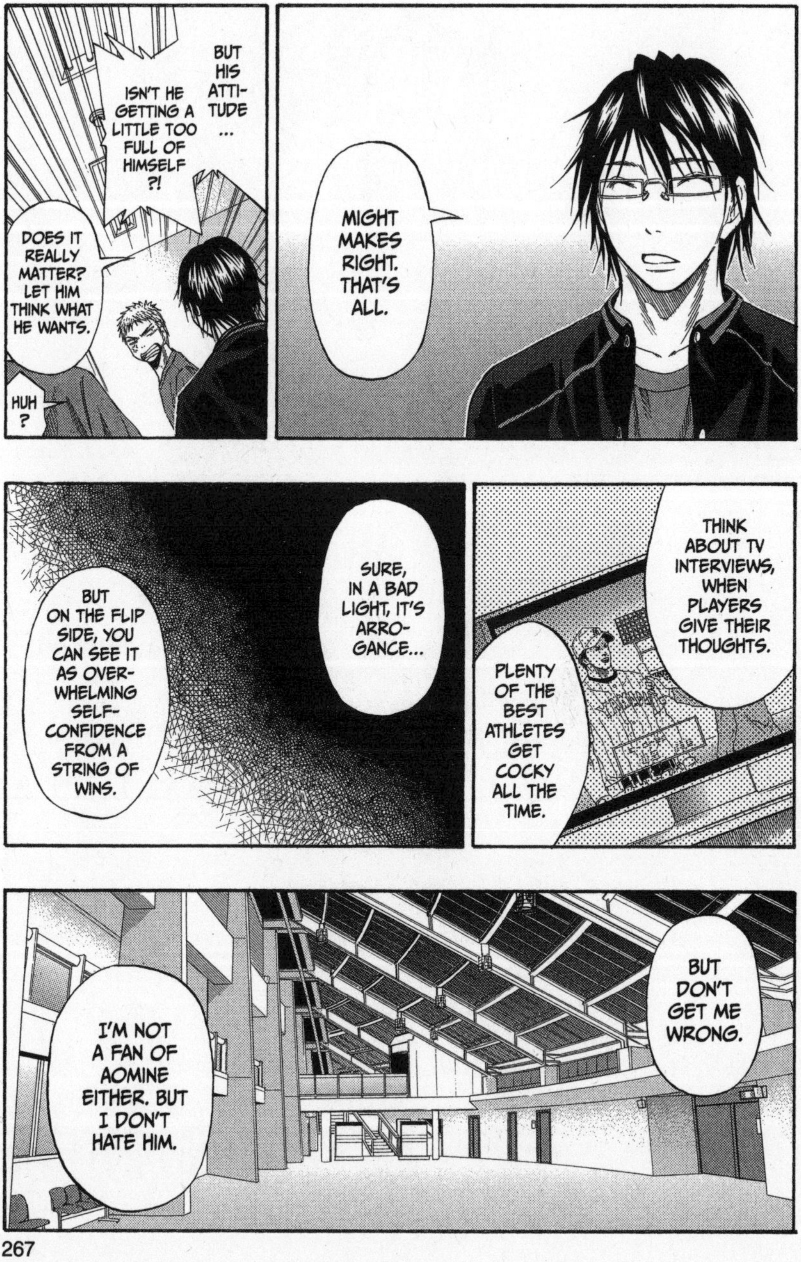
MIGHT MAKES RIGHT. THAT'S ALL.
BUT HIS ATTI-TUDE ...
ISN'T HE GETTING A LITTLE TOO FULL OF HIMSELF ?!
DOES IT REALLY MATTER? LET HIM THINK WHAT HE WANTS.
HUH ?
THINK ABOUT TV INTERVIEWS, WHEN PLAYERS GIVE THEIR THOUGHTS.
PLENTY OF THE BEST ATHLETES GET COCKY ALL THE TIME.
SURE, IN A BAD LIGHT, IT'S ARRO-GANCE...
BUT ON THE FLIP SIDE, YOU CAN SEE IT AS OVER-WHELMING SELF-CONFIDENCE FROM A STRING OF WINS.
BUT DON'T GET ME WRONG.
I'M NOT A FAN OF AOMINE EITHER. BUT I DON'T HATE HIM.

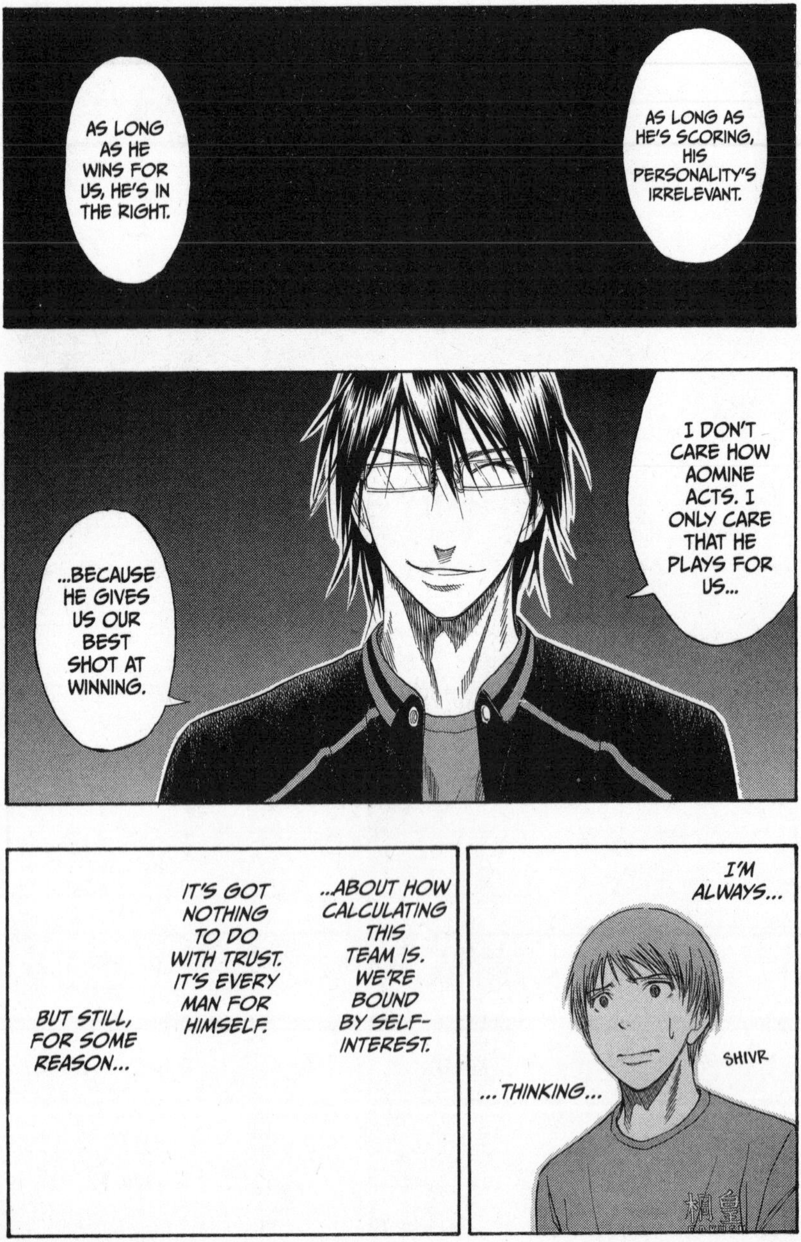
AS LONG AS HE'S SCORING, HIS PERSONALITY'S IRRELEVANT.
AS LONG AS HE WINS FOR US, HE'S IN THE RIGHT.
I DON'T CARE HOW AOMINE ACTS. I ONLY CARE THAT HE PLAYS FOR US...
...BECAUSE HE GIVES US OUR BEST SHOT AT WINNING.
I'M ALWAYS...
SHIVR
...THINKING...
...ABOUT HOW CALCULATING THIS TEAM IS. WE'RE BOUND BY SELF-INTEREST.
IT'S GOT NOTHING TO DO WITH TRUST. IT'S EVERY MAN FOR HIMSELF.
BUT STILL, FOR SOME REASON...

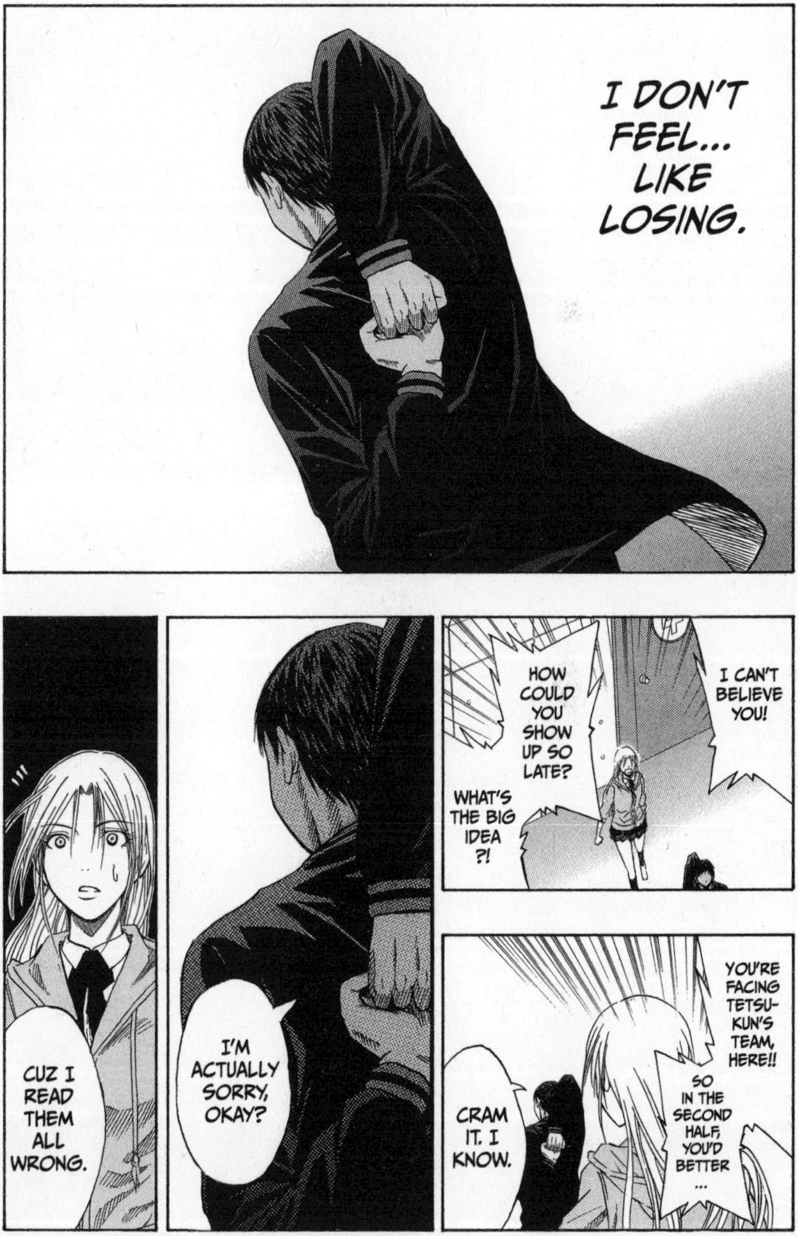
I DON'T FEEL... LIKE LOSING.
I CAN'T BELIEVE YOU!
HOW COULD YOU SHOW UP SO LATE?
WHAT'S THE BIG IDEA?!
YOU'RE FACING TETSU-KUN'S TEAM, HERE!!
SO IN THE SECOND HALF, YOU'D BETTER ...
CRAM IT. I KNOW.
I'M ACTUALLY SORRY, OKAY?
CUZ I READ THEM ALL WRONG.

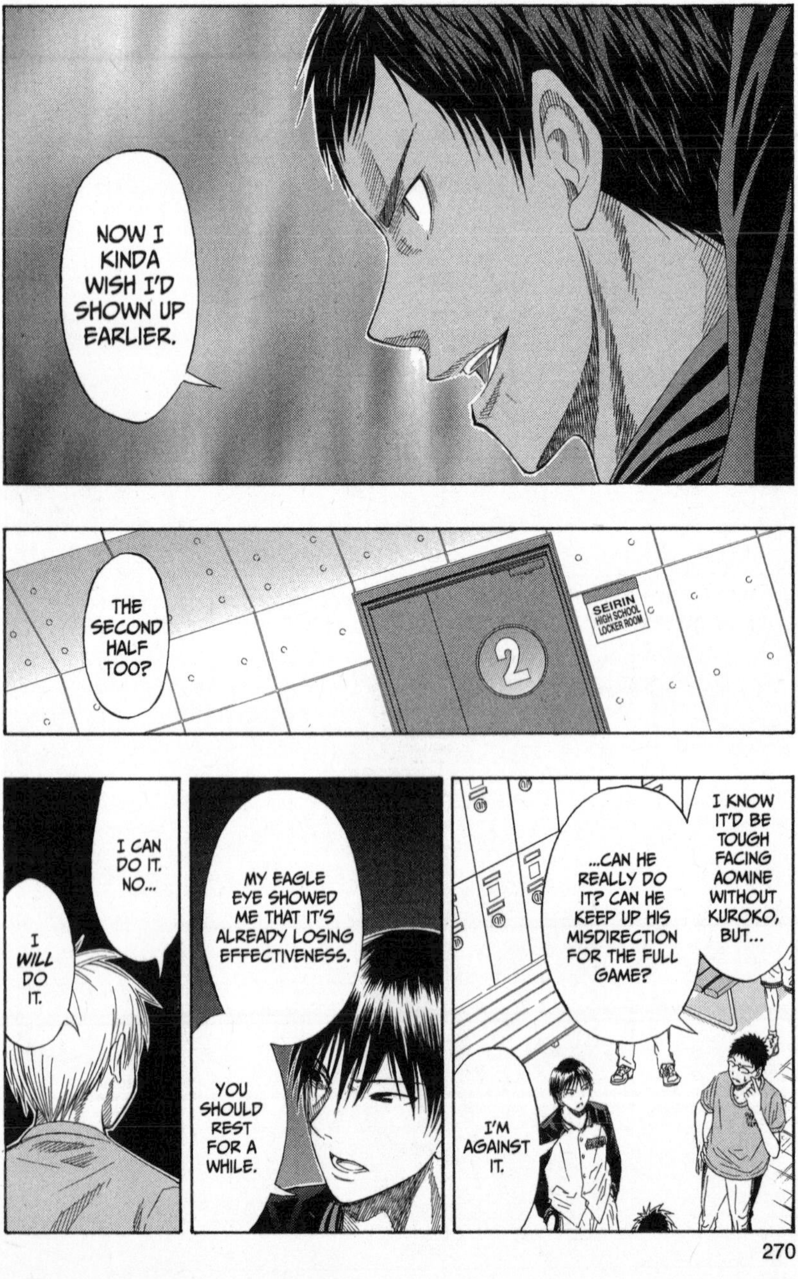
NOW I KINDA WISH I'D SHOWN UP EARLIER.
THE SECOND HALF TOO?
SEIRIN HIGH SCHOOL LOCKER ROOM
I KNOW IT'D BE TOUGH FACING AOMINE WITHOUT KUROKO, BUT...
...CAN HE REALLY DO IT? CAN HE KEEP UP HIS MISDIRECTION FOR THE FULL GAME?
I'M AGAINST IT.
MY EAGLE EYE SHOWED ME THAT IT'S ALREADY LOSING EFFECTIVENESS.
YOU SHOULD REST FOR A WHILE.
I CAN DO IT. NO...
I WILL DO IT.

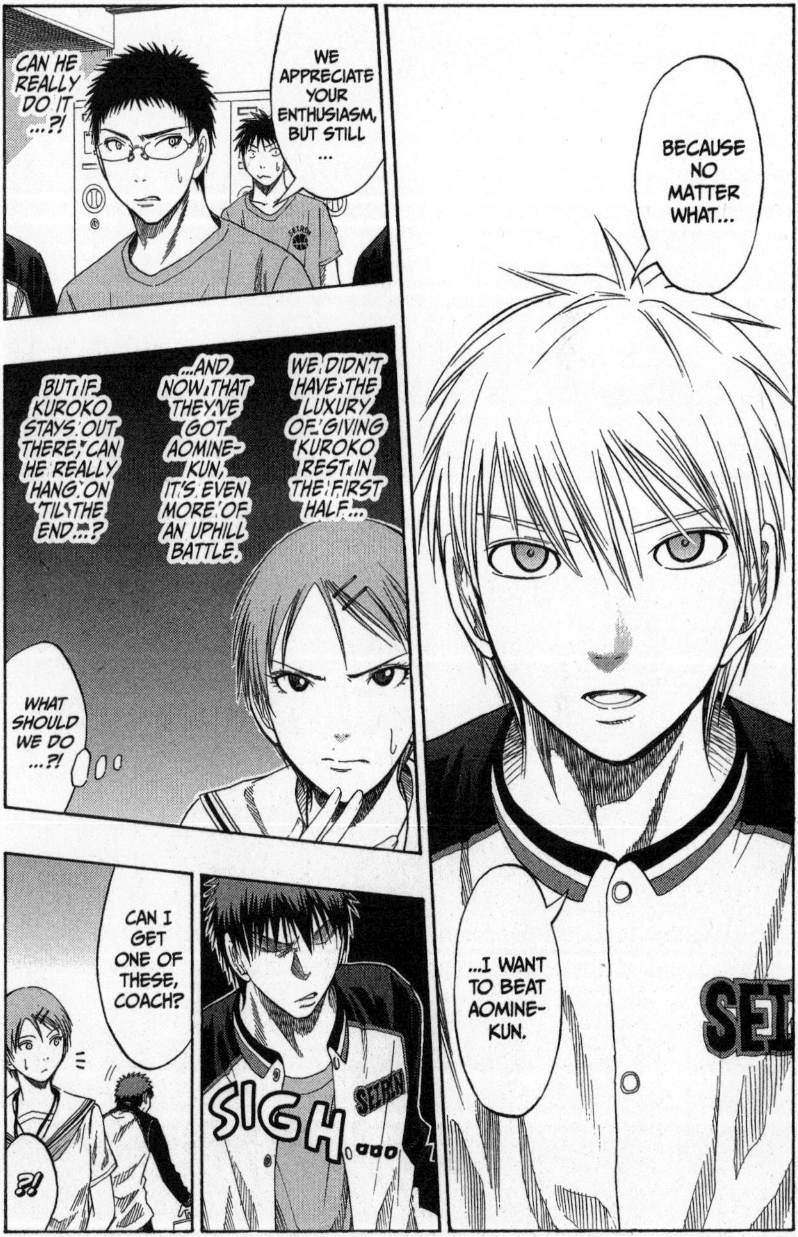
BECAUSE NO MATTER WHAT...
...I WANT TO BEAT AOMINE-KUN.
WE APPRECIATE YOUR ENTHUSIASM, BUT STILL ...
CAN HE REALLY DO IT ...?!
WE DIDN'T HAVE THE LUXURY OF GIVING KUROKO REST IN THE FIRST HALF...
...AND NOW THAT THEY'VE GOT AOMINE-KUN, IT'S EVEN MORE OF AN UPHILL BATTLE.
BUT IF KUROKO STAYS OUT THERE, CAN HE REALLY HANG ON 'TIL THE END...?
WHAT SHOULD WE DO ...?!
SIGH...
CAN I GET ONE OF THESE, COACH?
?!

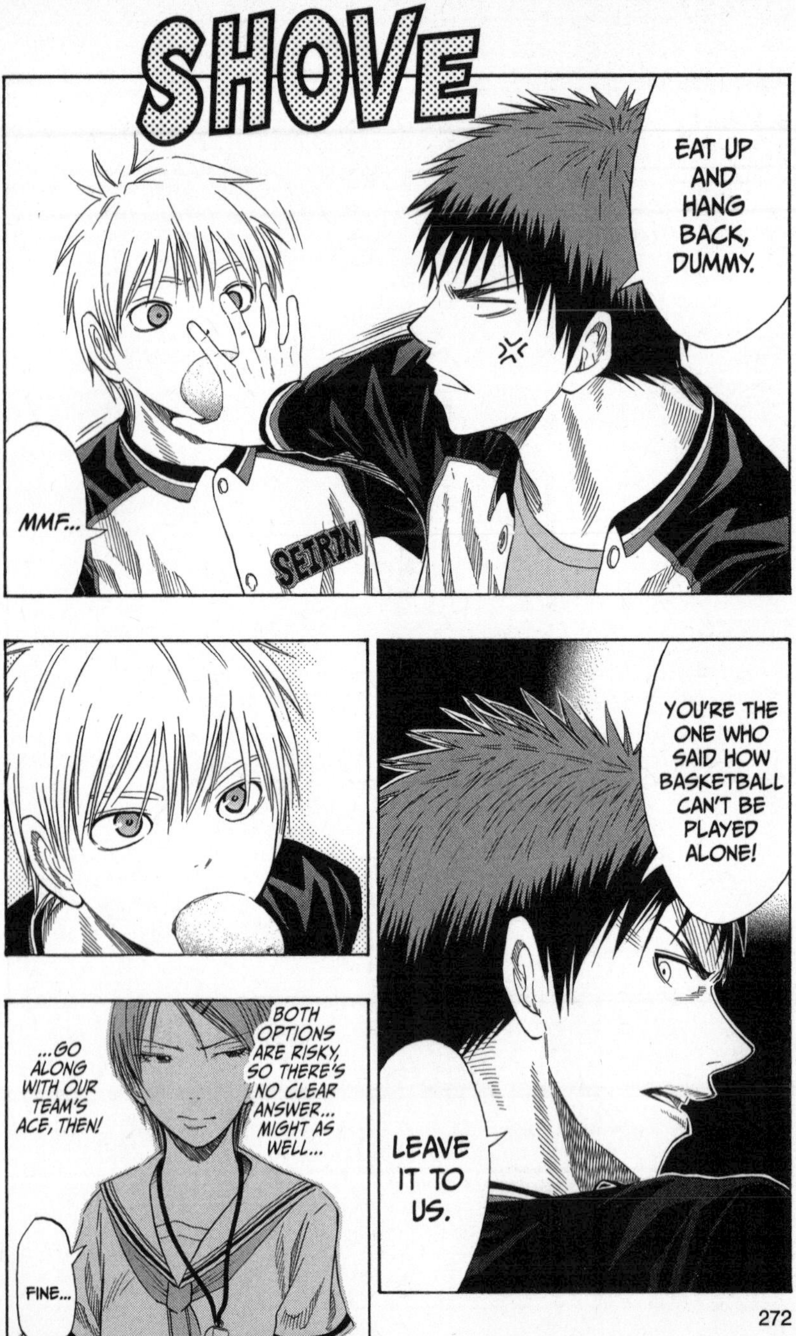
SHOVE
EAT UP AND HANG BACK, DUMMY.
MMF...
SEITRIN
YOU'RE THE ONE WHO SAID HOW BASKETBALL CAN'T BE PLAYED ALONE!
LEAVE IT TO US.
BOTH OPTIONS ARE RISKY, SO THERE'S NO CLEAR ANSWER... MIGHT AS WELL...
...GO ALONG WITH OUR TEAM'S ACE, THEN!
FINE...

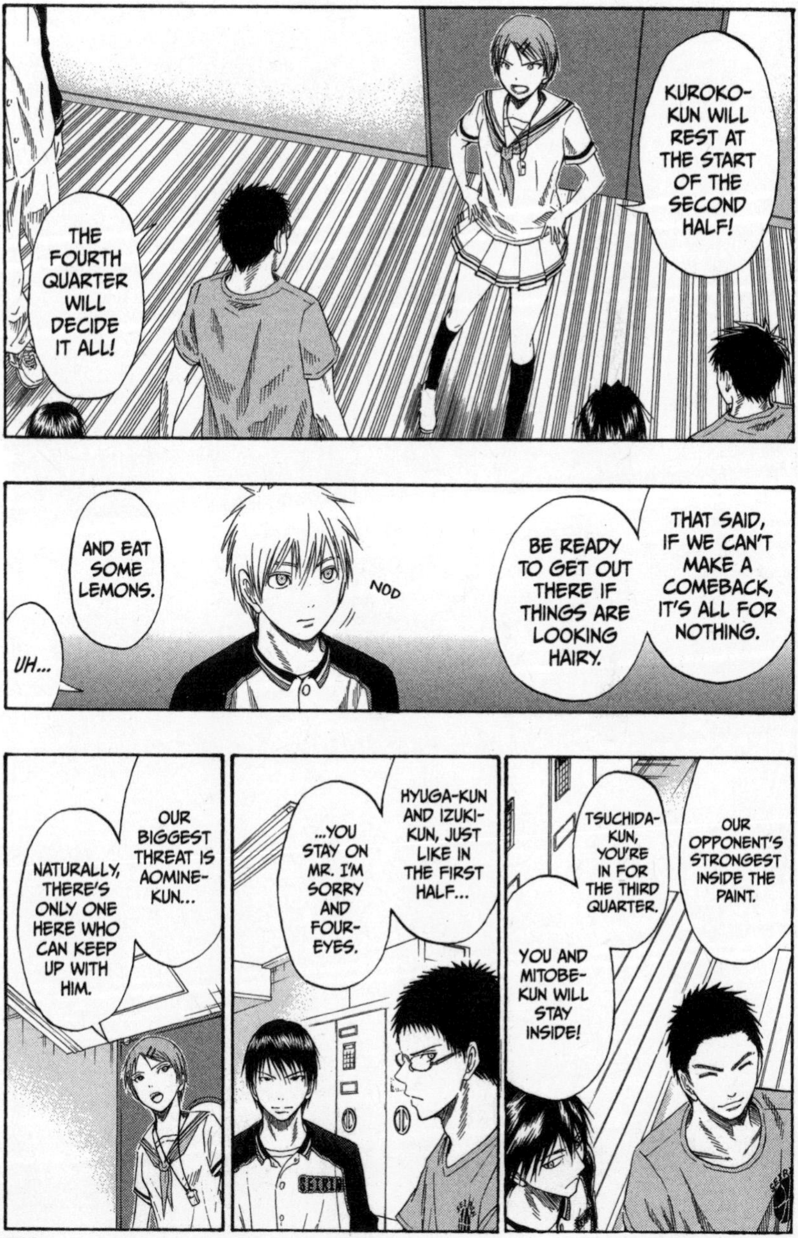
KUROKO-KUN WILL REST AT THE START OF THE SECOND HALF!
THE FOURTH QUARTER WILL DECIDE IT ALL!
THAT SAID, IF WE CAN'T MAKE A COMEBACK, IT'S ALL FOR NOTHING.
BE READY TO GET OUT THERE IF THINGS ARE LOOKING HAIRY.
NOD
AND EAT SOME LEMONS.
UH...
OUR OPPONENT'S STRONGEST INSIDE THE PAINT.
TSUCHIDA-KUN, YOU'RE IN FOR THE THIRD QUARTER.
YOU AND MITOBE-KUN WILL STAY INSIDE!
HYUGA-KUN AND IZUKI-KUN, JUST LIKE IN THE FIRST HALF...
...YOU STAY ON MR. I'M SORRY AND FOUR-EYES.
OUR BIGGEST THREAT IS AOMINE-KUN...
NATURALLY, THERE'S ONLY ONE HERE WHO CAN KEEP UP WITH HIM.
SEIRIN

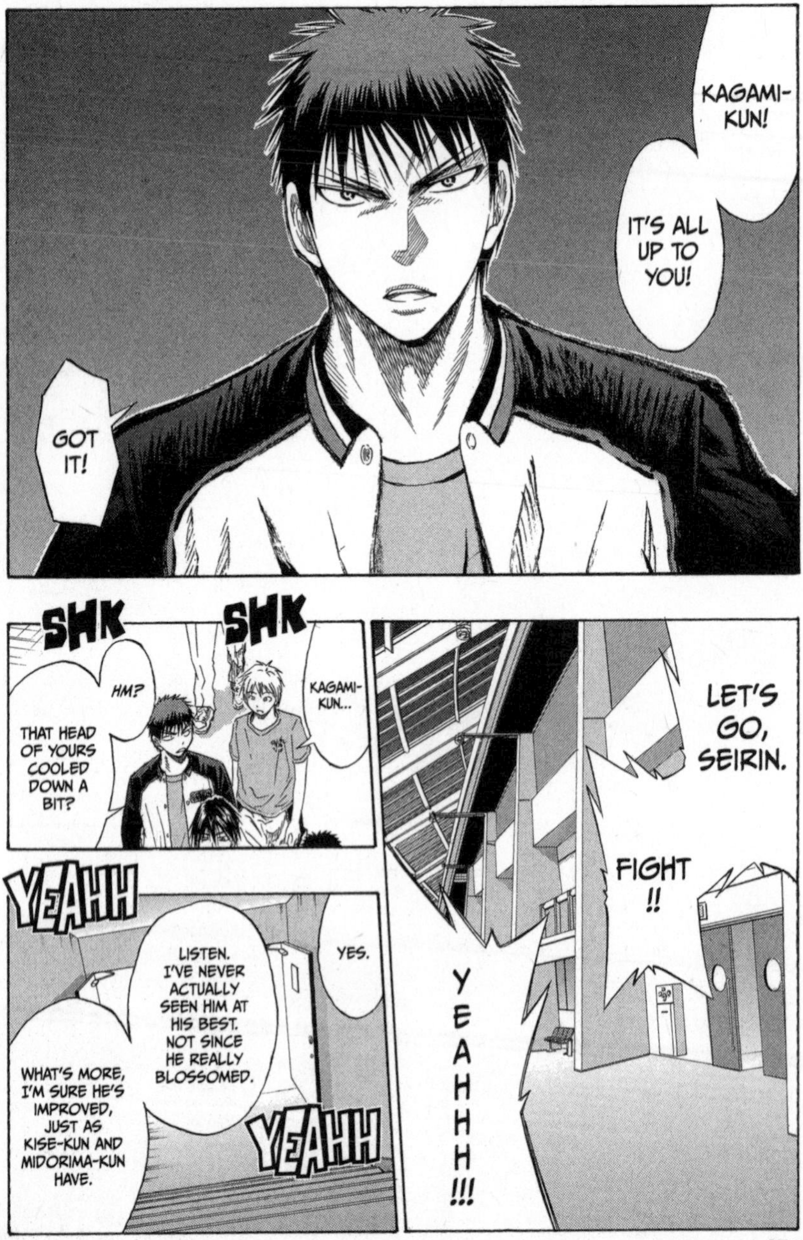
KAGAMI-KUN!
IT'S ALL UP TO YOU!
GOT IT!
LET'S GO, SEIRIN.
FIGHT!!
YEAHHH!!!
SHK
SHK
KAGAMI-KUN...
HM?
THAT HEAD OF YOURS COOLED DOWN A BIT?
YEAHH
YES.
LISTEN. I'VE NEVER ACTUALLY SEEN HIM AT HIS BEST. NOT SINCE HE REALLY BLOSSOMED.
WHAT'S MORE, I'M SURE HE'S IMPROVED, JUST AS KISE-KUN AND MIDORIMA-KUN HAVE.
YEAHH

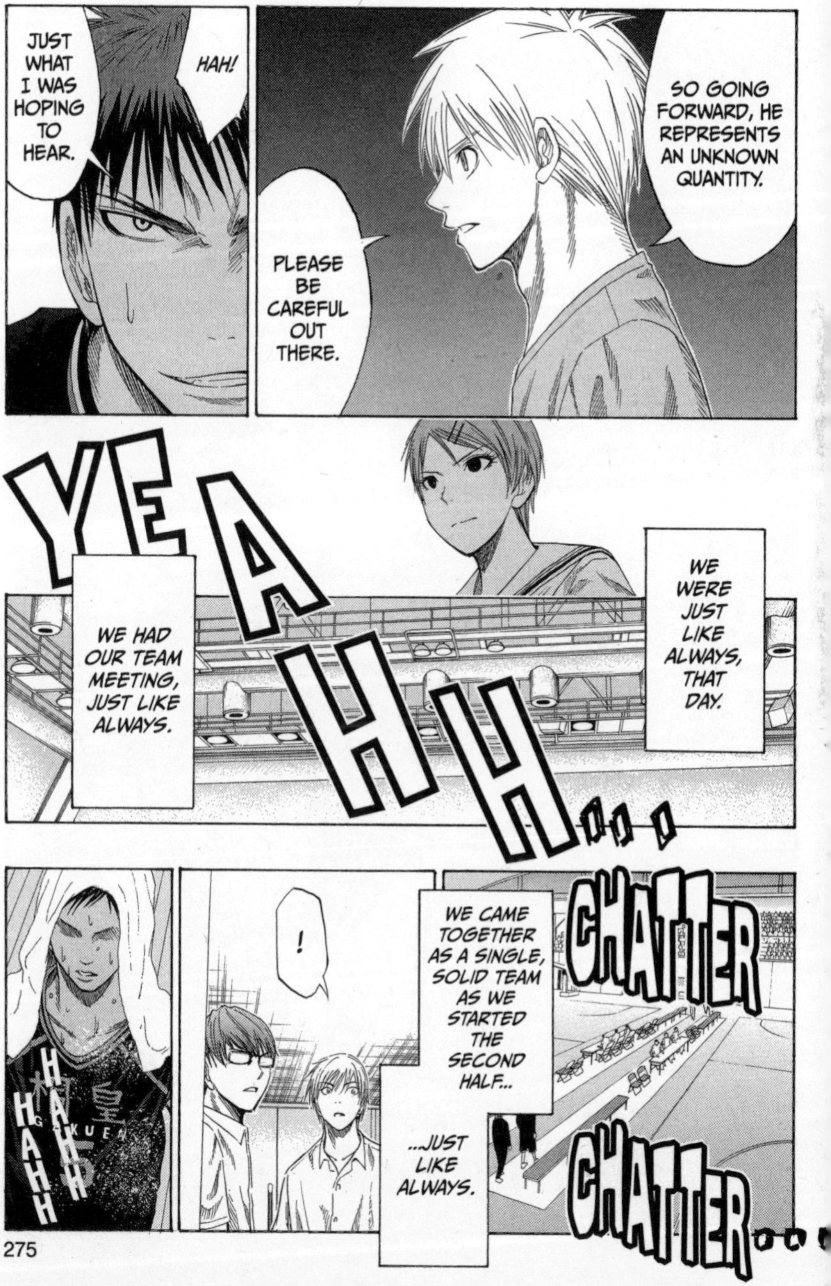
SO GOING FORWARD, HE REPRESENTS AN UNKNOWN QUANTITY.
PLEASE BE CAREFUL OUT THERE.
HAH!
JUST WHAT I WAS HOPING TO HEAR.
YEAHHH...
WE WERE JUST LIKE ALWAYS, THAT DAY.
WE HAD OUR TEAM MEETING, JUST LIKE ALWAYS.
CHATTER
WE CAME TOGETHER AS A SINGLE, SOLID TEAM AS WE STARTED THE SECOND HALF...
CHATTER...
...JUST LIKE ALWAYS.
!
HAHH
HAHH

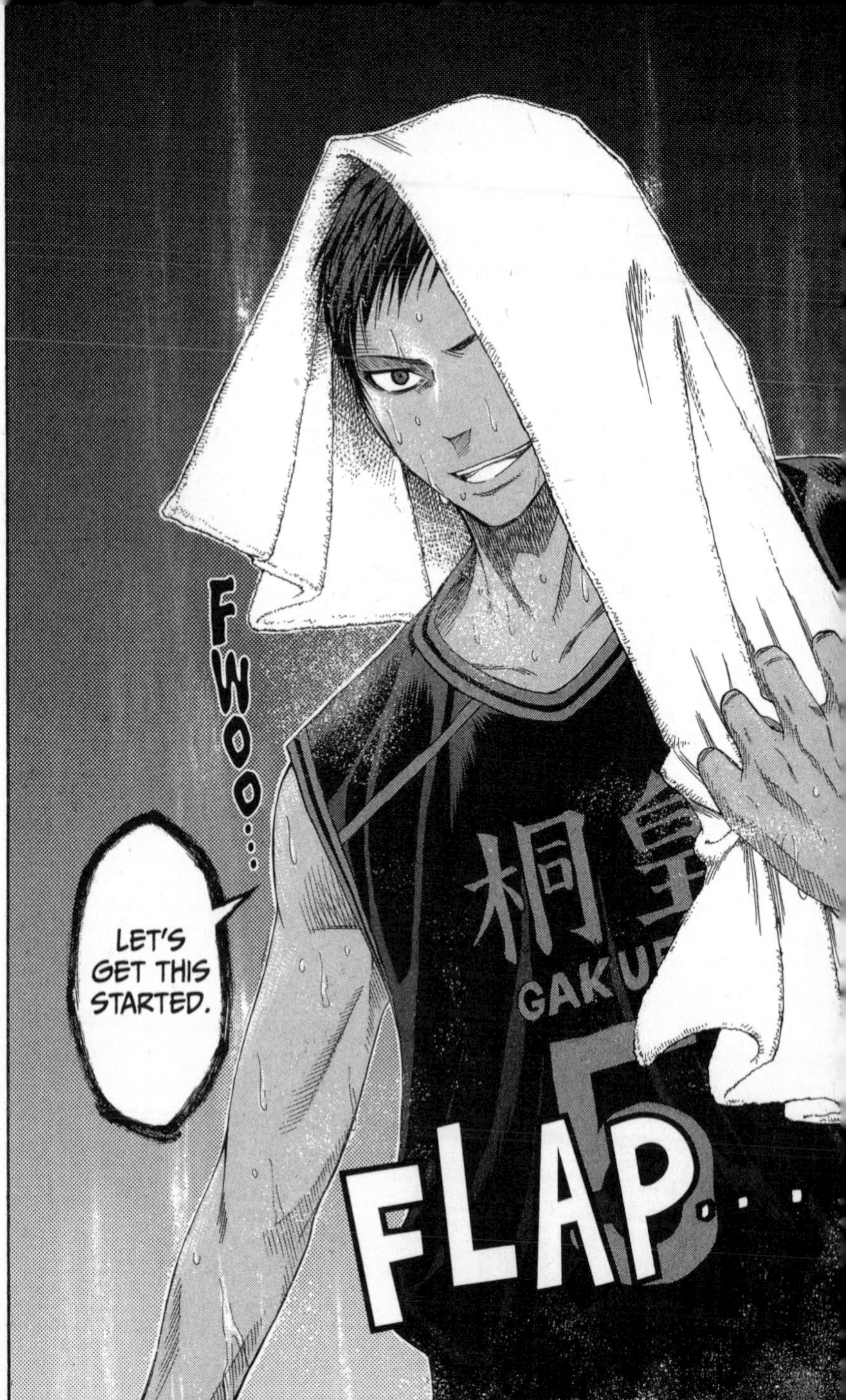
FWOO...
LET'S GET THIS STARTED.
桐皇
GAKU
FLAP...

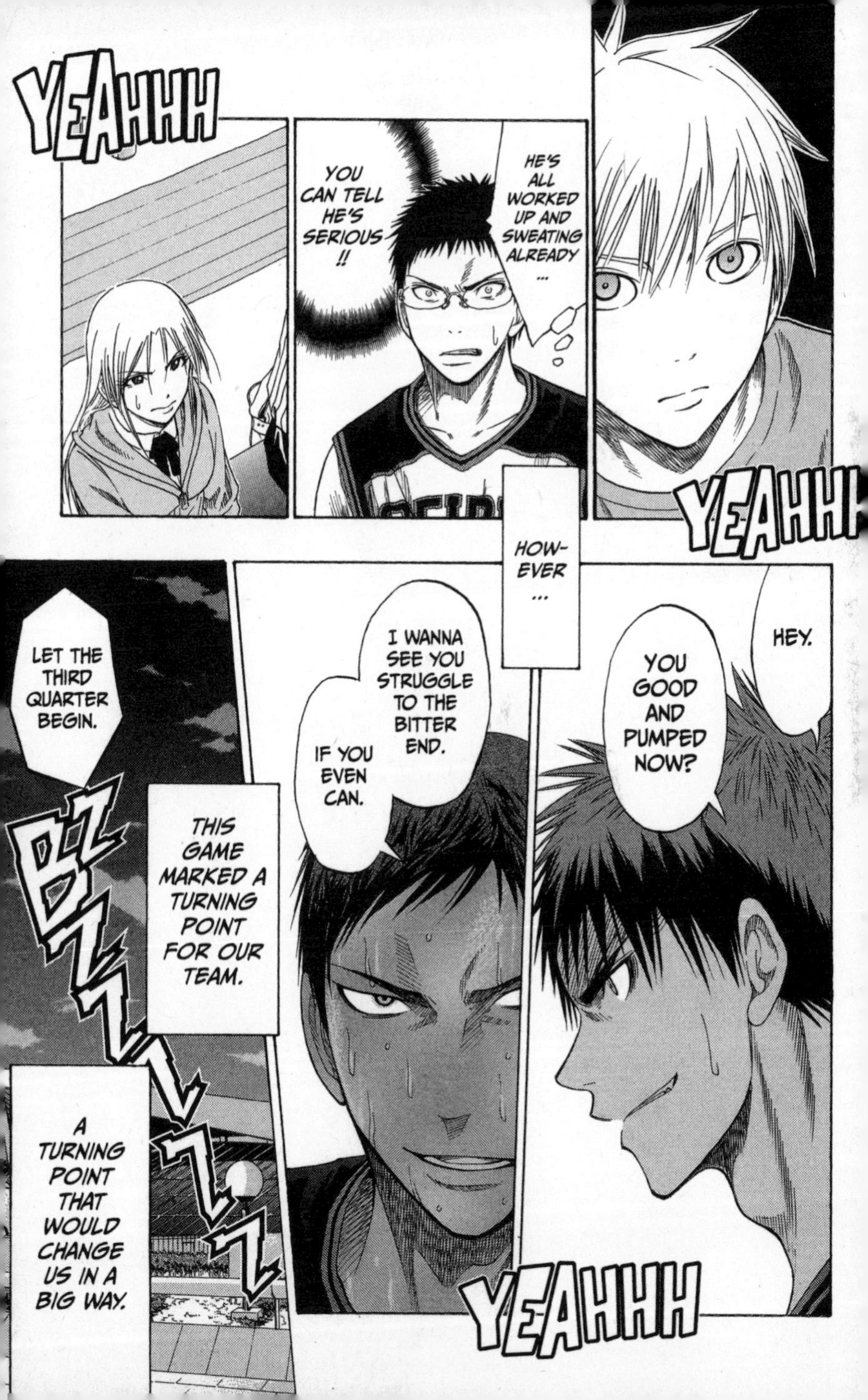
YEAHHH
HE'S ALL WORKED UP AND SWEATING ALREADY ...
YOU CAN TELL HE'S SERIOUS!!
YEAHHH
HOW-EVER ...
HEY.
YOU GOOD AND PUMPED NOW?
I WANNA SEE YOU STRUGGLE TO THE BITTER END.
IF YOU EVEN CAN.
YEAHHH
LET THE THIRD QUARTER BEGIN.
BZZZZZ
THIS GAME MARKED A TURNING POINT FOR OUR TEAM.
A TURNING POINT THAT WOULD CHANGE US IN A BIG WAY.

KUROKO'S BASKETBALL BLOOPERS

TAKE 3

EAT UP AND HANG BACK, DUMMY.
SHOVE
MMF...
YOU'RE THE ONE WHO SAID HOW BASKET-BALL...
HAGA-MEEDON... (KAGAMI-KUN...)
ISH UCK. (IT'S STUCK.)
HUH?
WHAT A FACE!!
IT'S WAY TOO GOOFY A FACE FOR THE PROTAGO-NIST TO BE MAKING!!
DON'T LET THE READERS SEE!
I SHOVED IT IN TOO FAR!!
WHOA!
EEK!

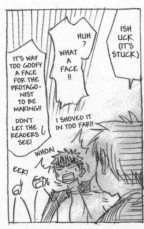

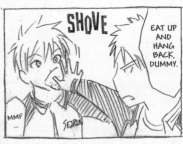

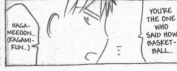

48TH QUARTER: NOTHING BUT LUNATICS

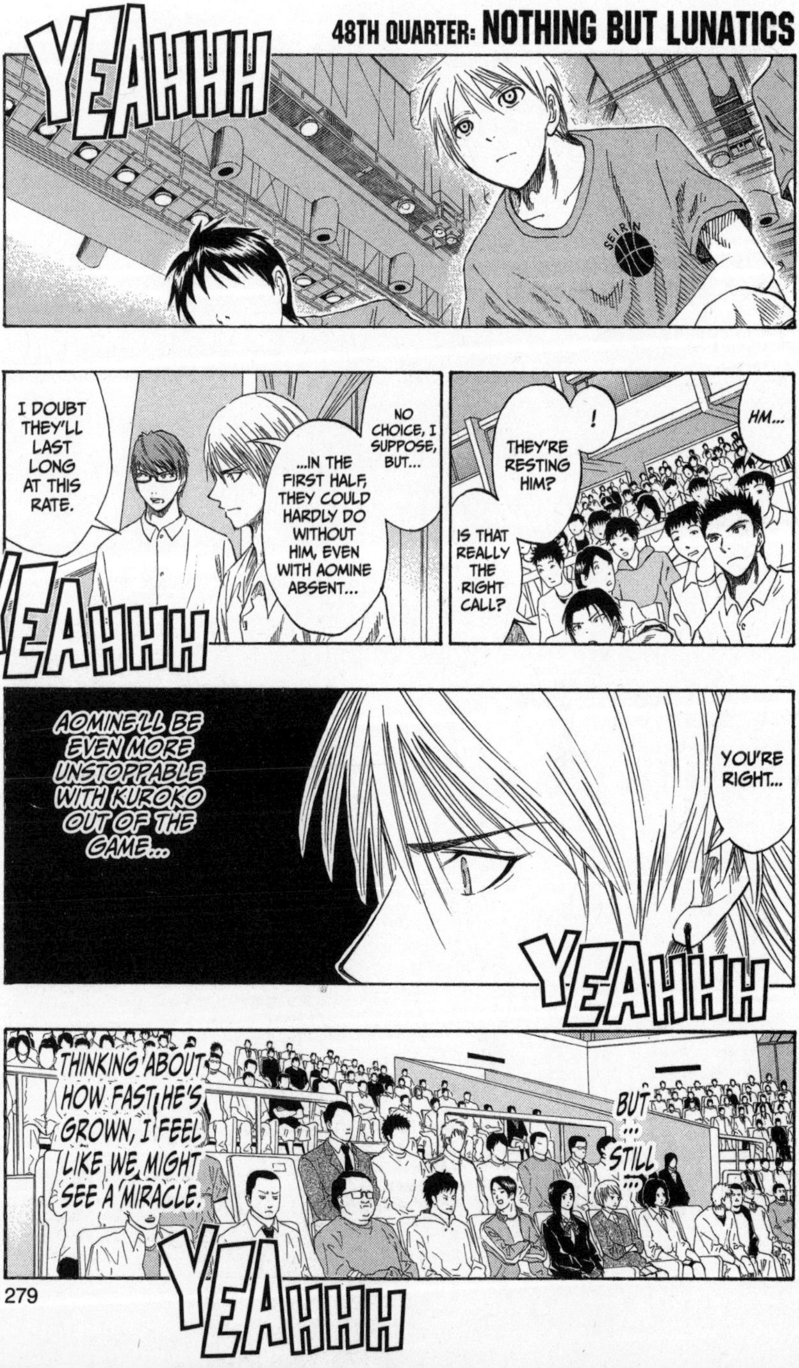
YEAHHH
HM...
!
THEY'RE RESTING HIM?
IS THAT REALLY THE RIGHT CALL?
NO CHOICE, I SUPPOSE, BUT...
...IN THE FIRST HALF, THEY COULD HARDLY DO WITHOUT HIM, EVEN WITH AOMINE ABSENT...
I DOUBT THEY'LL LAST LONG AT THIS RATE.
YEAHHH
YOU'RE RIGHT...
AOMINE'LL BE EVEN MORE UNSTOPPABLE WITH KUROKO OUT OF THE GAME...
YEAHHH
BUT... STILL...
THINKING ABOUT HOW FAST HE'S GROWN, I FEEL LIKE WE MIGHT SEE A MIRACLE.
YEAHHH

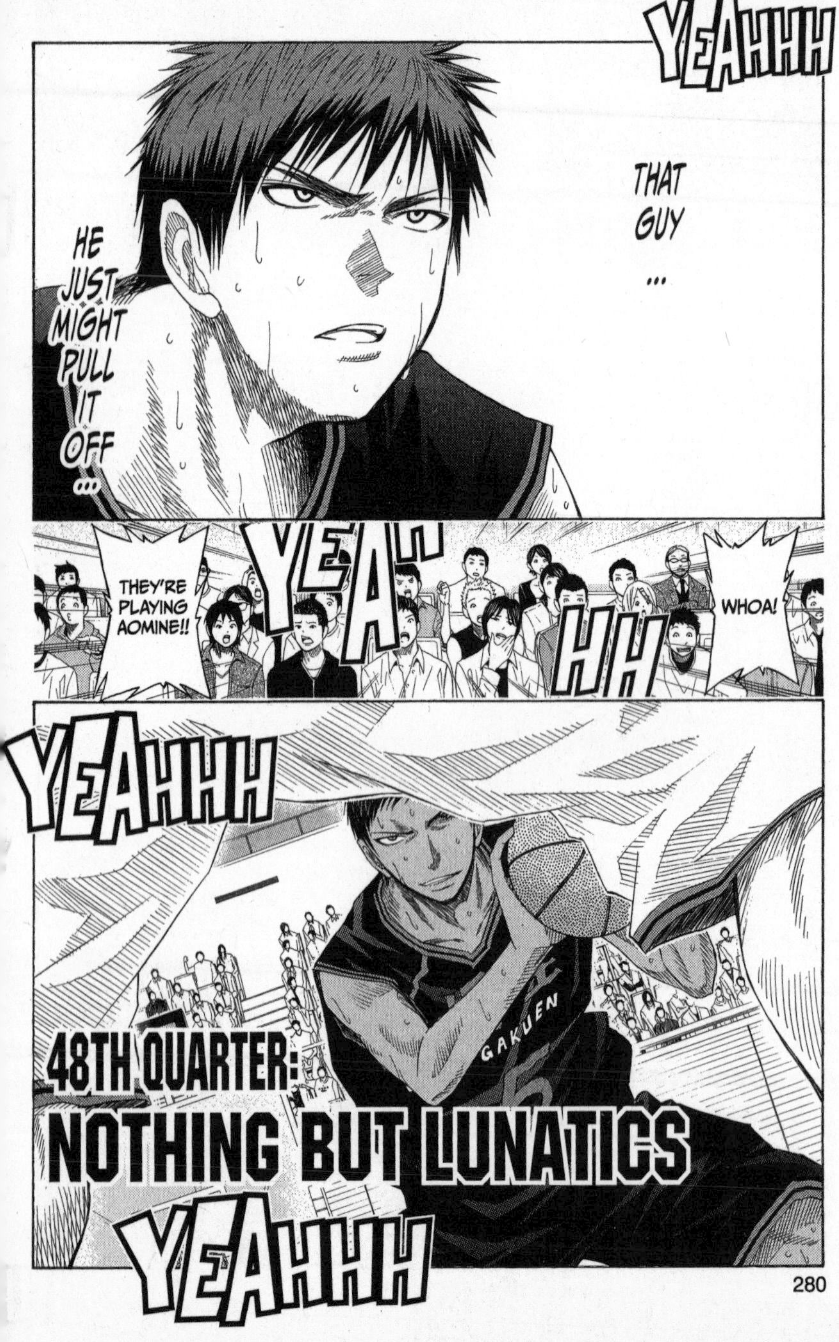
YEAHHH
THAT GUY ...
HE JUST MIGHT PULL IT OFF ...
WHOA!
YEAHHH
THEY'RE PLAYING AOMINE!!
YEAHHH
48TH QUARTER: NOTHING BUT LUNATICS
YEAHHH
GAKUEN

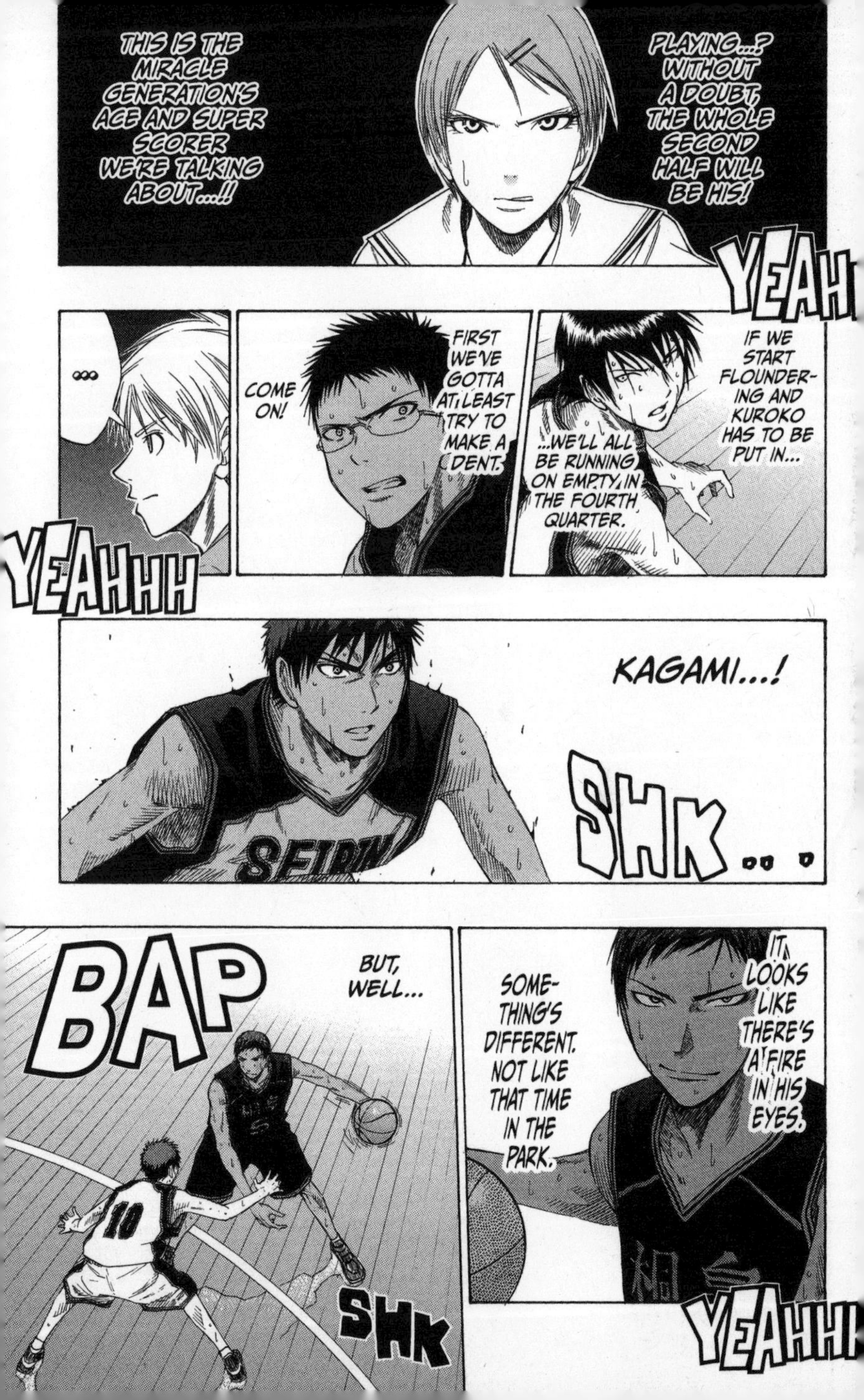
PLAYING...? WITHOUT A DOUBT, THE WHOLE SECOND HALF WILL BE HIS!
THIS IS THE MIRACLE GENERATION'S ACE AND SUPER SCORER WE'RE TALKING ABOUT...!!
YEAH
IF WE START FLOUNDERING AND KUROKO HAS TO BE PUT IN...
...WE'LL ALL BE RUNNING ON EMPTY IN THE FOURTH QUARTER.
FIRST WE'VE GOTTA AT LEAST TRY TO MAKE A DENT.
COME ON!
...
YEAHHH
KAGAMI...!
SHK...
IT LOOKS LIKE THERE'S A FIRE IN HIS EYES.
SOME-THING'S DIFFERENT. NOT LIKE THAT TIME IN THE PARK.
YEAHH
BUT, WELL...
BAP
SHK

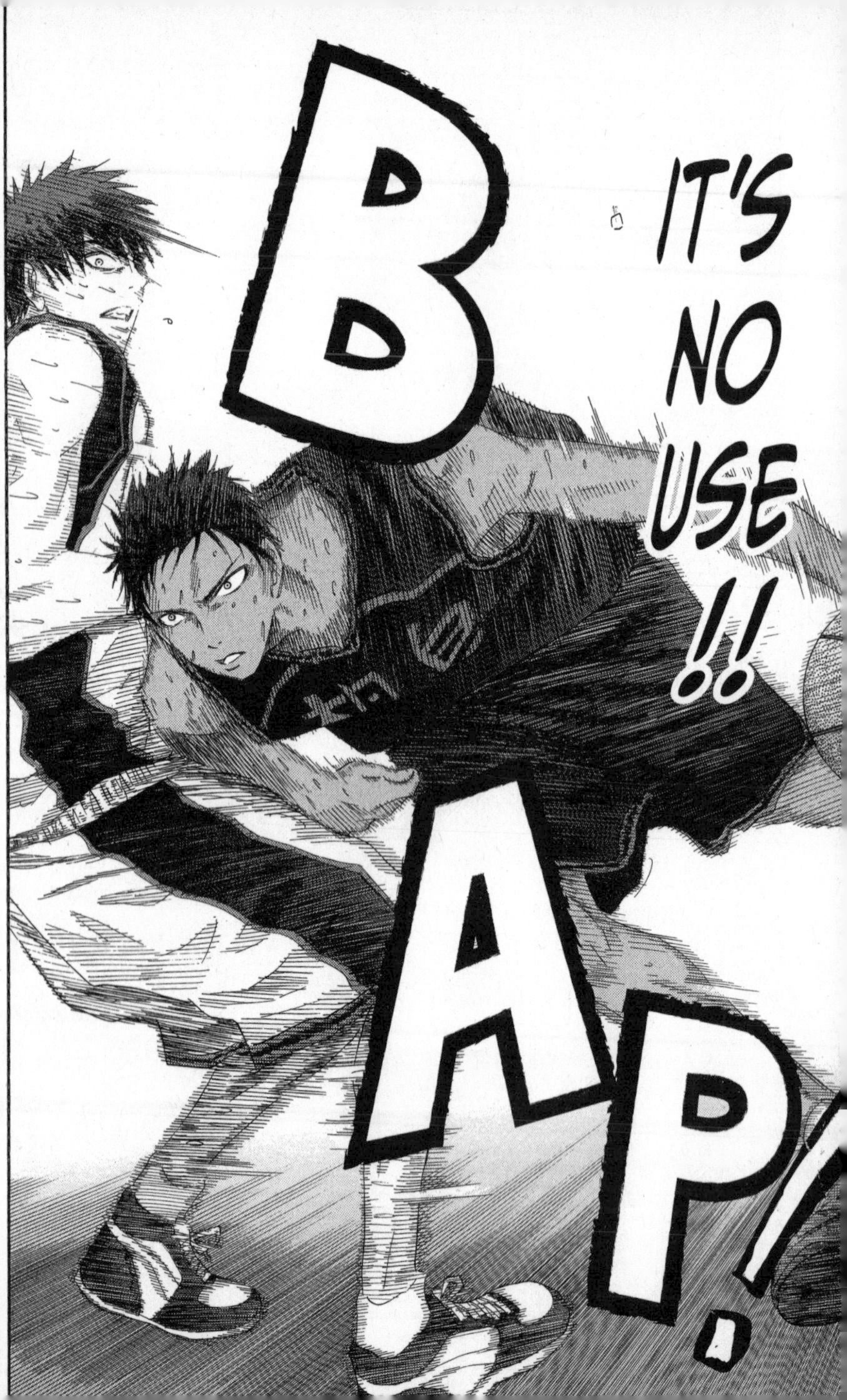
IT'S NO USE!!
BAP!

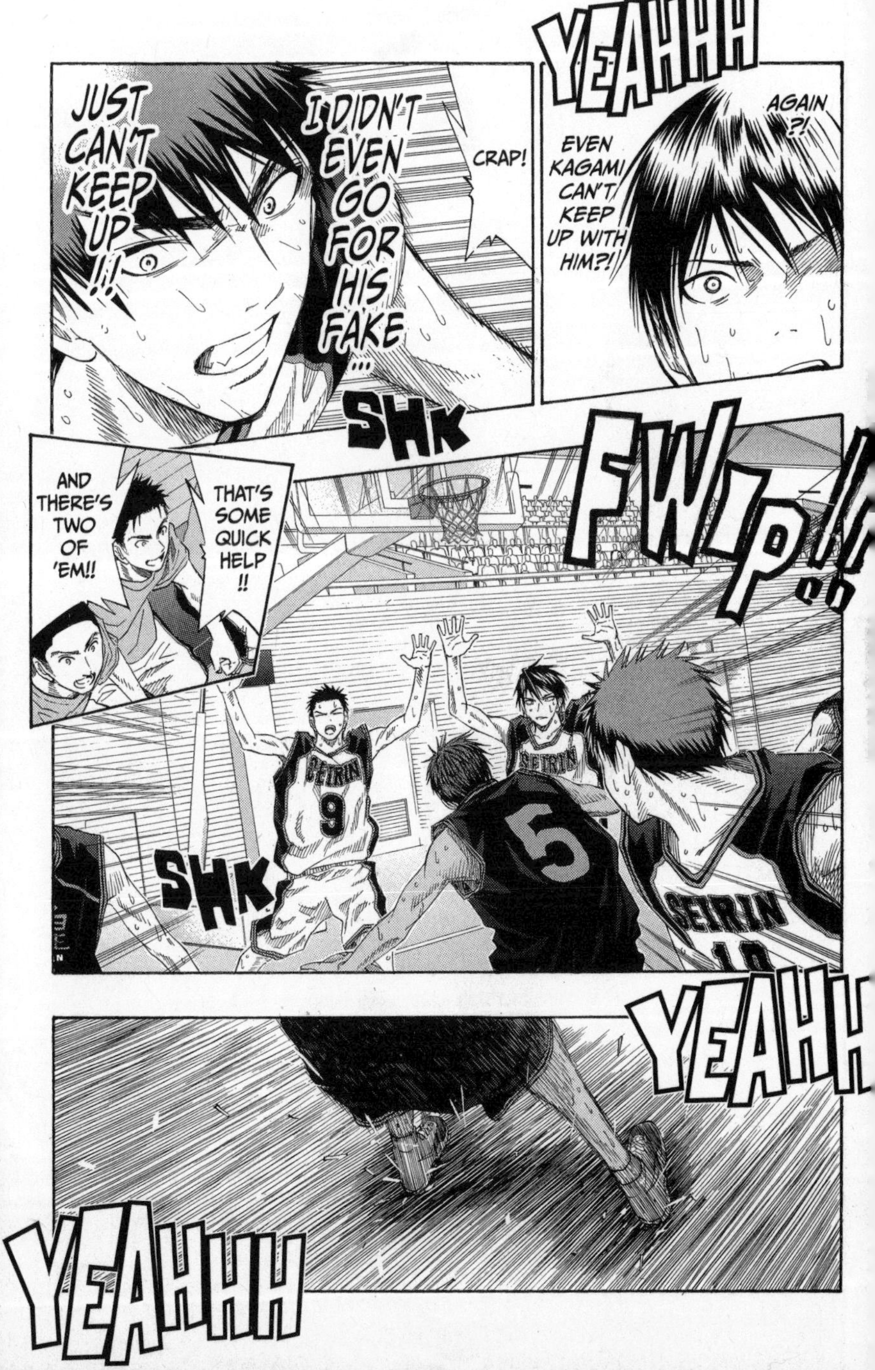
YEAHHH
AGAIN?!
EVEN KAGAMI CAN'T KEEP UP WITH HIM?!
CRAP!
I DIDN'T EVEN GO FOR HIS FAKE...
JUST CAN'T KEEP UP!!
SHK
FWIP!!
THAT'S SOME QUICK HELP!!
AND THERE'S TWO OF 'EM!!
SHK
YEAHH
YEAHHH

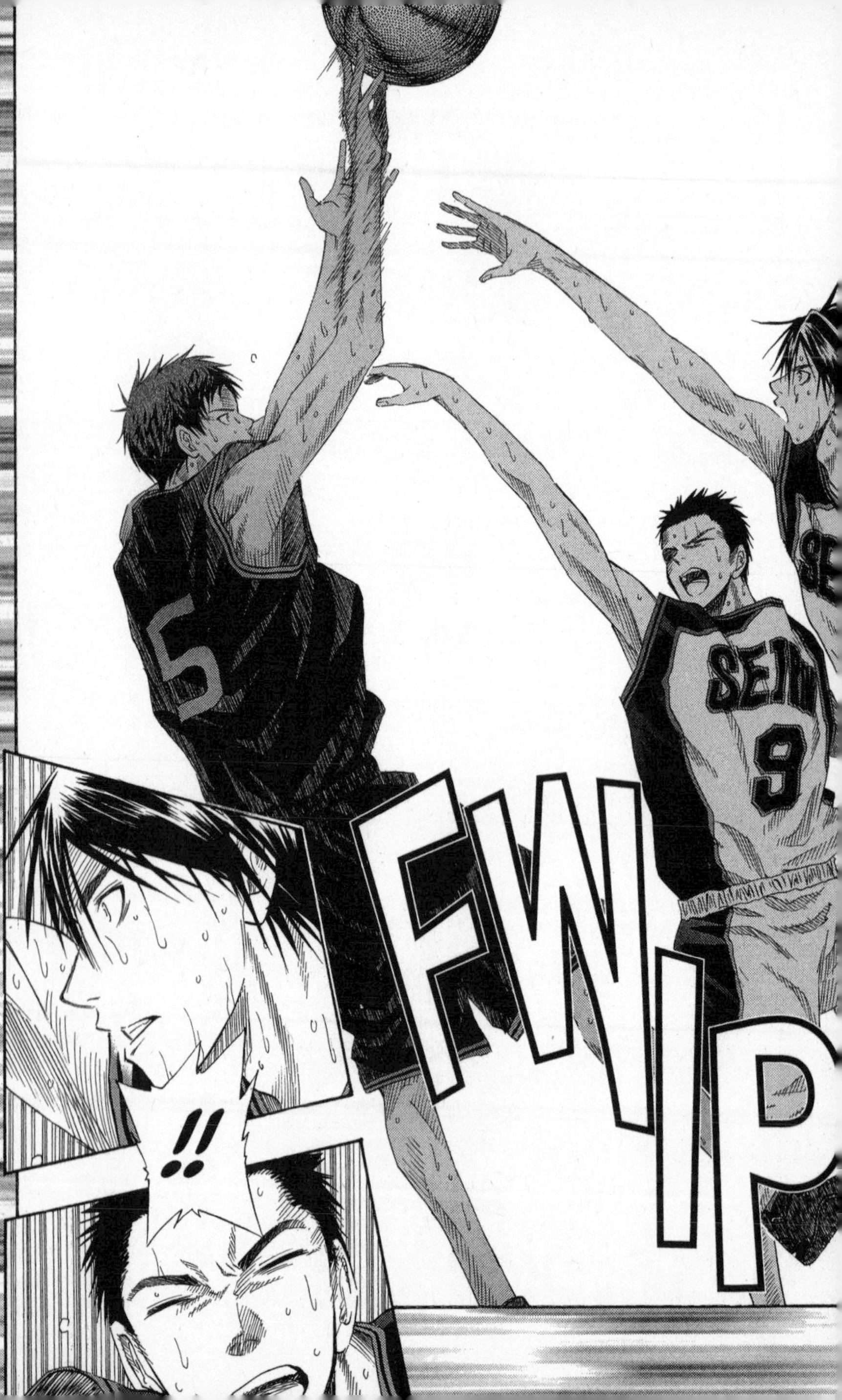
FWIP
!!

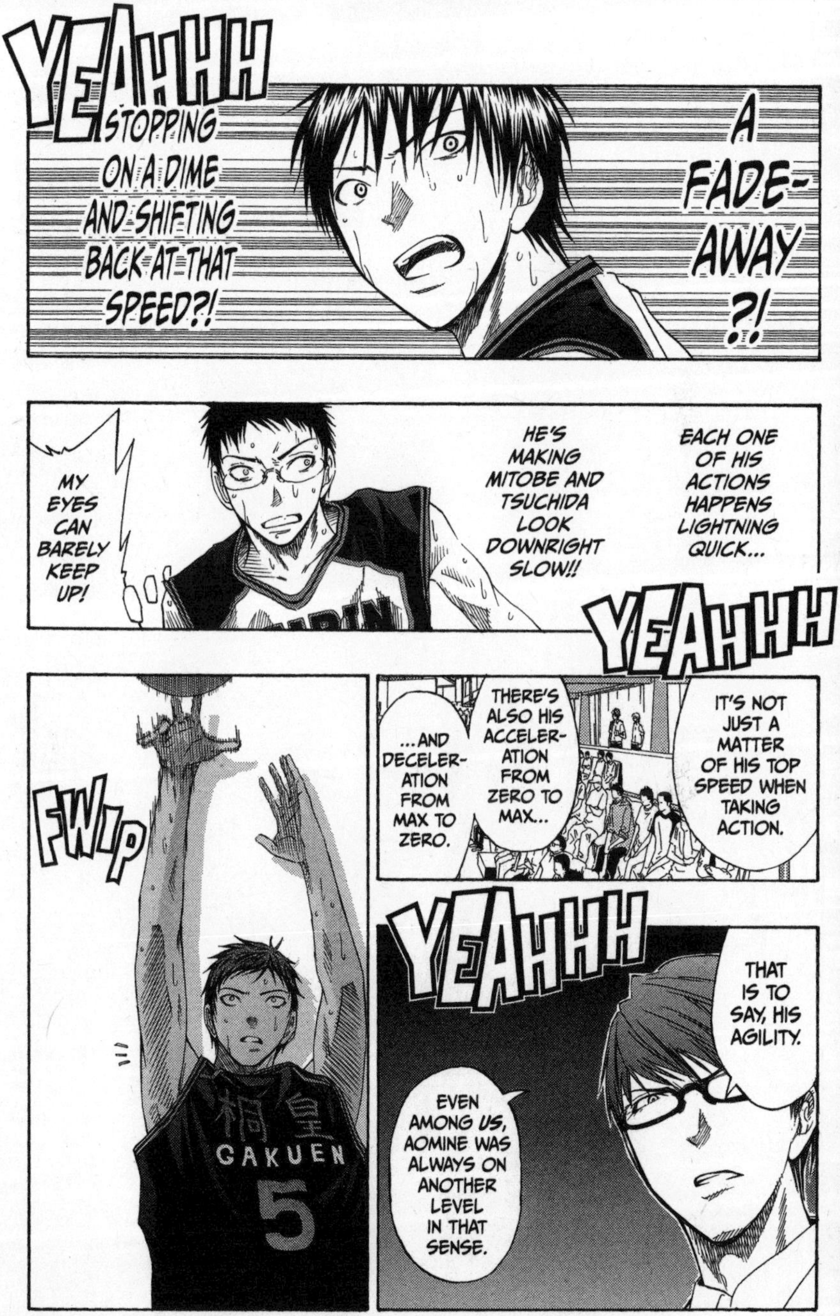
A FADE-AWAY?!
YEAHHH
STOPPING ON A DIME AND SHIFTING BACK AT THAT SPEED?!
EACH ONE OF HIS ACTIONS HAPPENS LIGHTNING QUICK...
HE'S MAKING MITOBE AND TSUCHIDA LOOK DOWNRIGHT SLOW!!
MY EYES CAN BARELY KEEP UP!
YEAHHH
IT'S NOT JUST A MATTER OF HIS TOP SPEED WHEN TAKING ACTION.
THERE'S ALSO HIS ACCELERATION FROM ZERO TO MAX...
...AND DECELERATION FROM MAX TO ZERO.
YEAHHH
THAT IS TO SAY, HIS AGILITY.
EVEN AMONG US, AOMINE WAS ALWAYS ON ANOTHER LEVEL IN THAT SENSE.
FWIP
GAKUEN
5

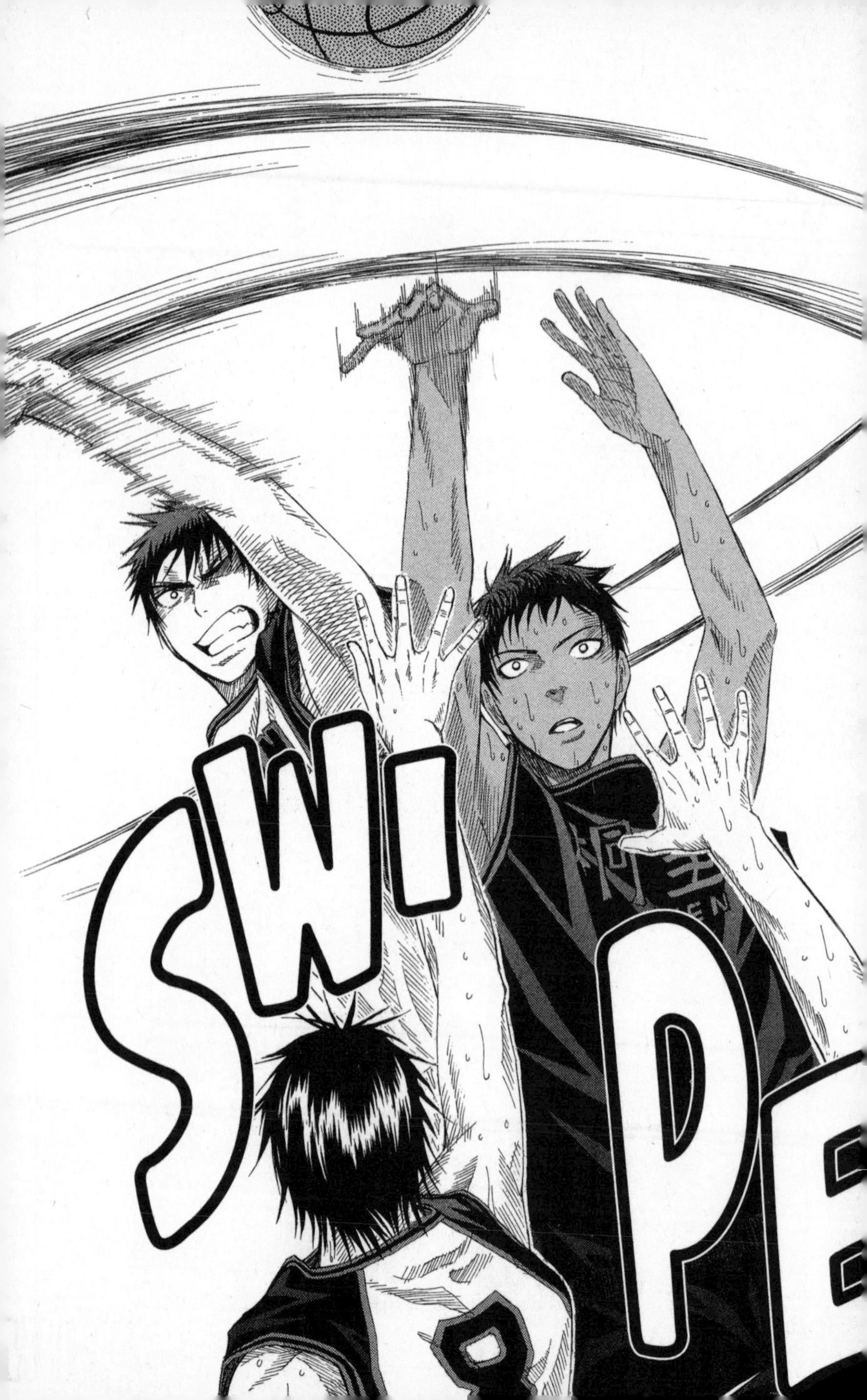
SWIPE

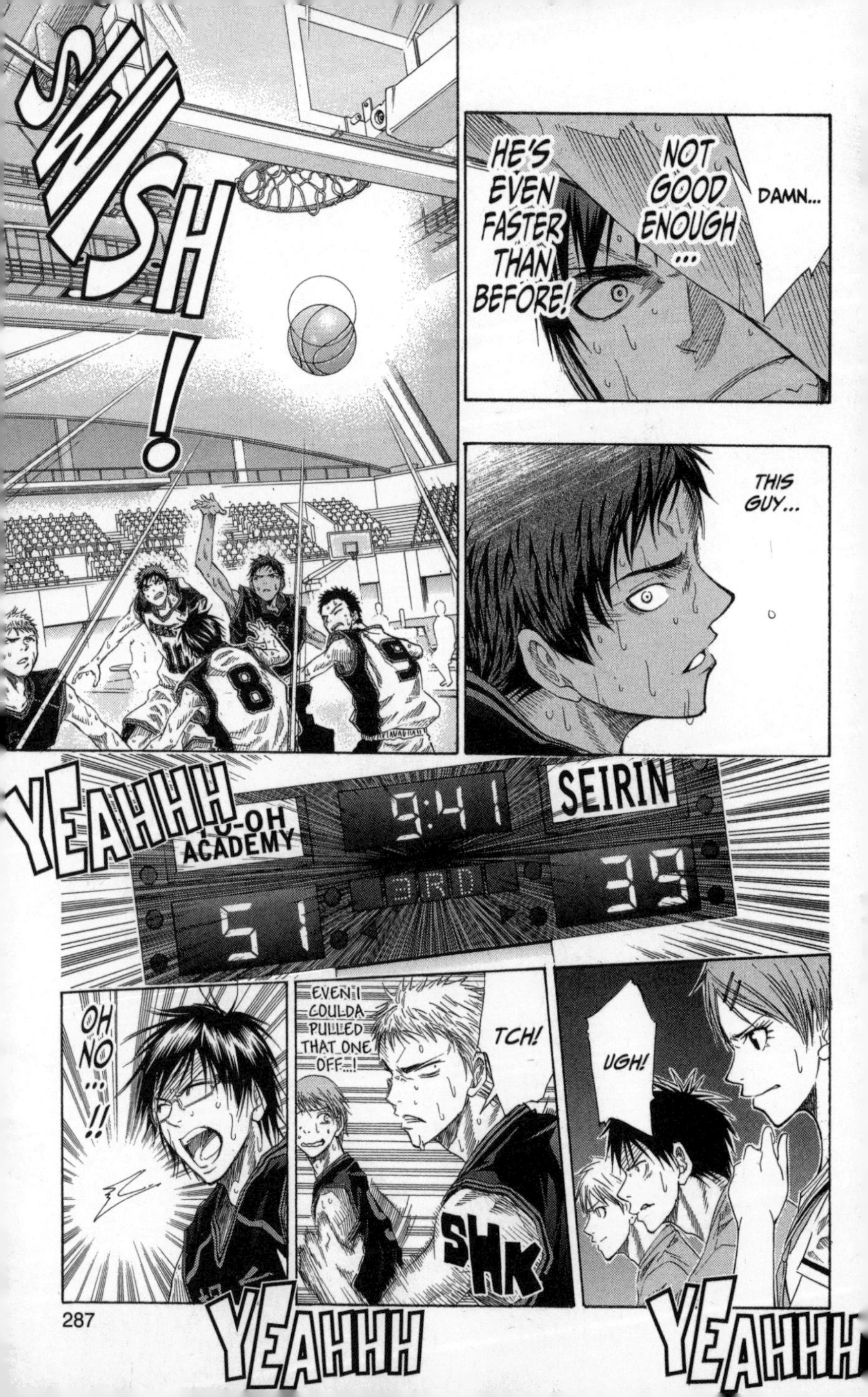
DAMN...
NOT GOOD ENOUGH...
HE'S EVEN FASTER THAN BEFORE!
THIS GUY...
SWISH!
YEAHHH
SEIRIN
9:41
O-OH ACADEMY
39
3RD
51
UGH!
TCH!
EVEN I COULDA PULLED THAT ONE OFF...!
SHK
OH NO...!!
YEAHHH
YEAHHH

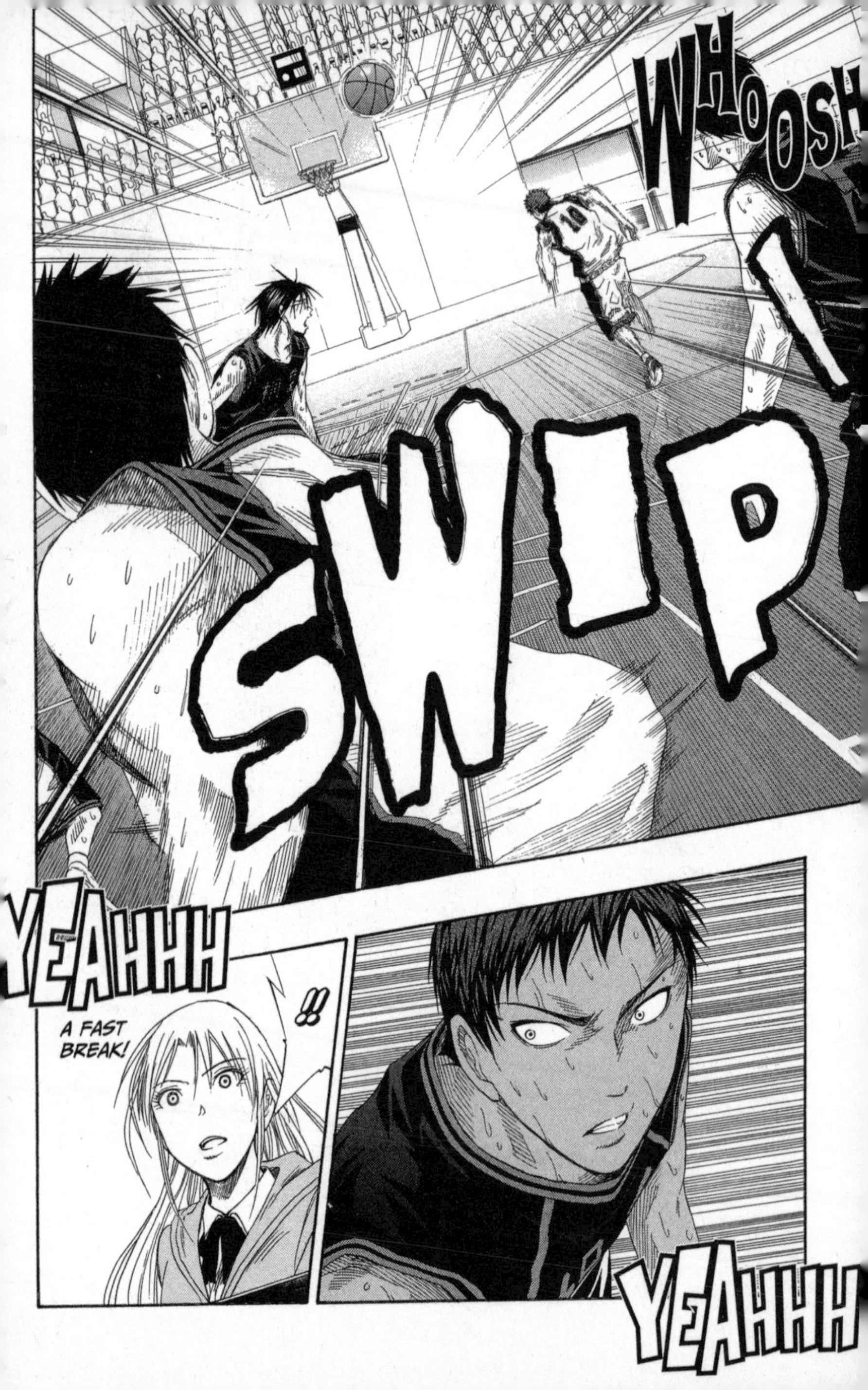
WHOOSH
SWIP
YEAHHH
!!
A FAST BREAK!
YEAHHH

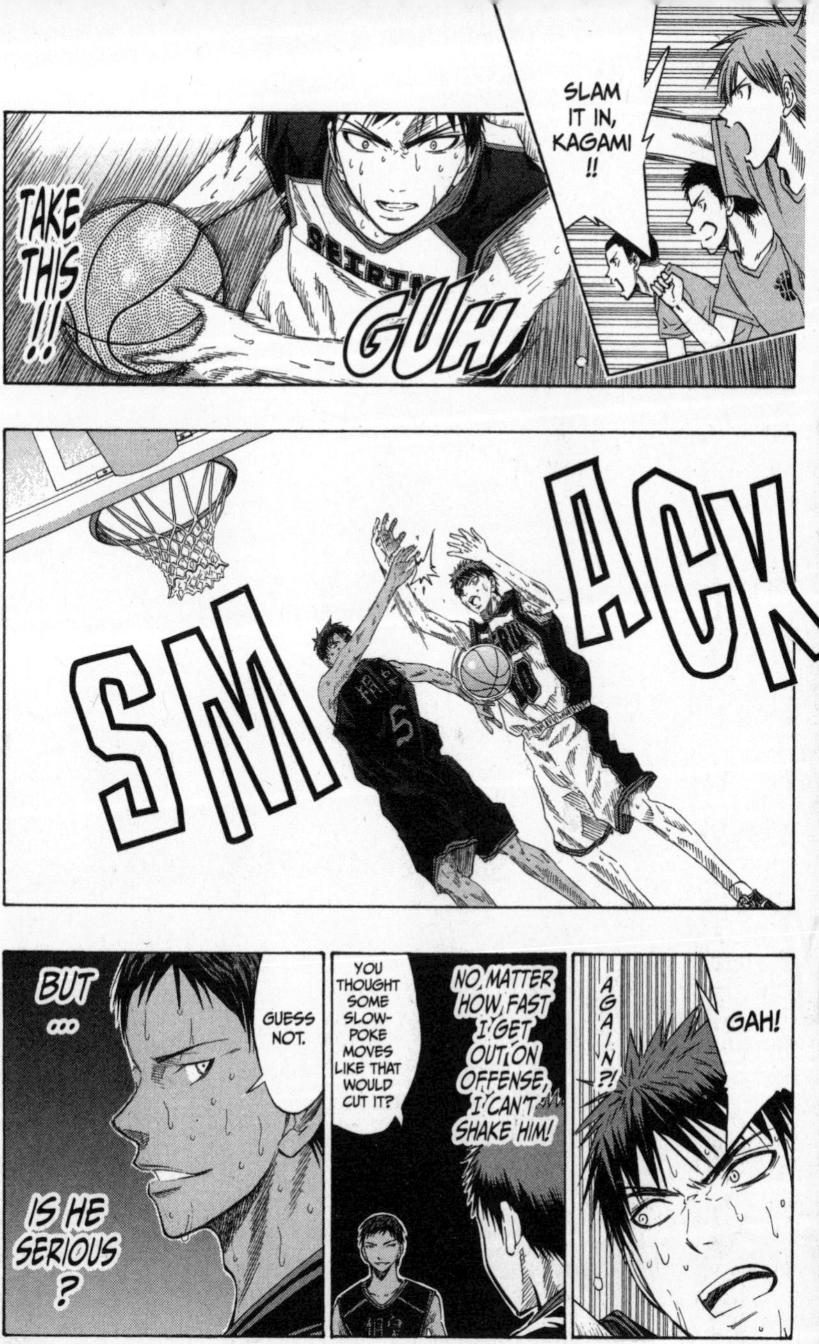
SLAM IT IN, KAGAMI!!
TAKE THIS!!
GUH
SMACK
AGAIN?!
GAH!
NO MATTER HOW FAST I GET OUT ON OFFENSE, I CAN'T SHAKE HIM!
YOU THOUGHT SOME SLOW-POKE MOVES LIKE THAT WOULD CUT IT?
GUESS NOT.
BUT...
IS HE SERIOUS?

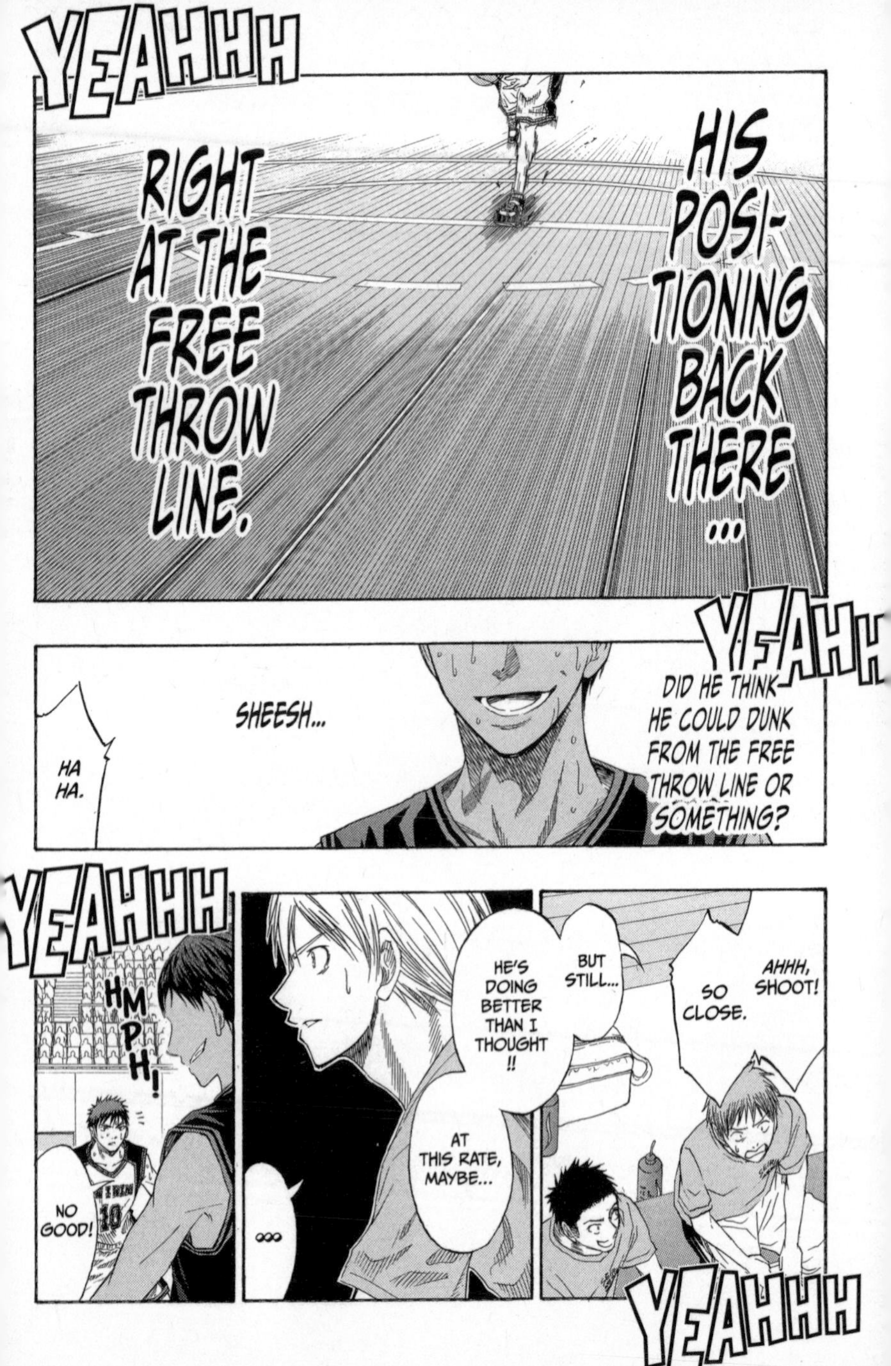
YEAHHH
HIS POSI-TIONING BACK THERE...
RIGHT AT THE FREE THROW LINE.
YEAHH
DID HE THINK HE COULD DUNK FROM THE FREE THROW LINE OR SOMETHING?
SHEESH...
HA HA.
AHHH, SHOOT!
SO CLOSE.
BUT STILL...
HE'S DOING BETTER THAN I THOUGHT!!
AT THIS RATE, MAYBE...
...
YEAHHH
HMPH!
NO GOOD!
YEAHHH

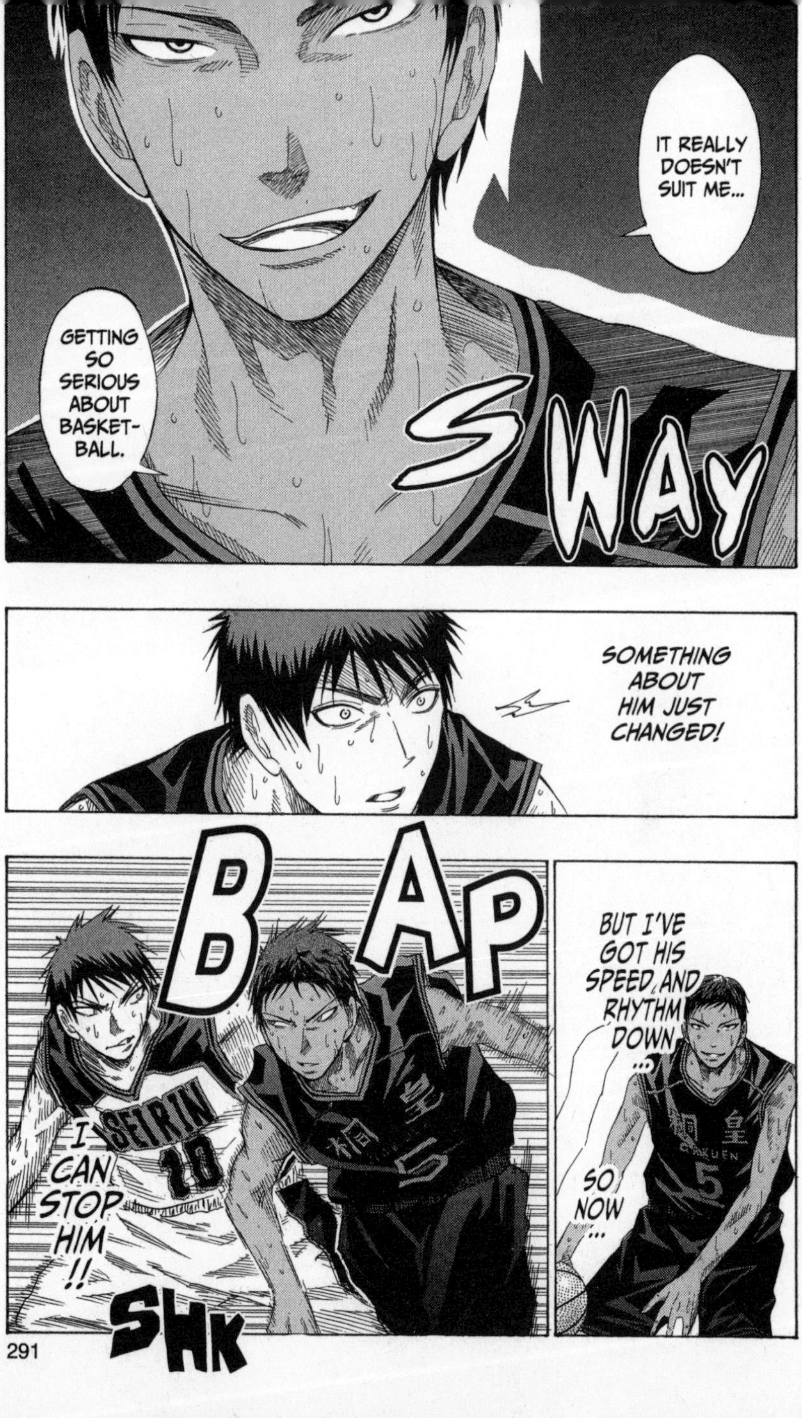
IT REALLY DOESN'T SUIT ME...
GETTING SO SERIOUS ABOUT BASKET-BALL.
SWAY
SOMETHING ABOUT HIM JUST CHANGED!
BUT I'VE GOT HIS SPEED AND RHYTHM DOWN...
SO NOW...
BAP
SEIRIN 10
I CAN STOP HIM!!
SHK

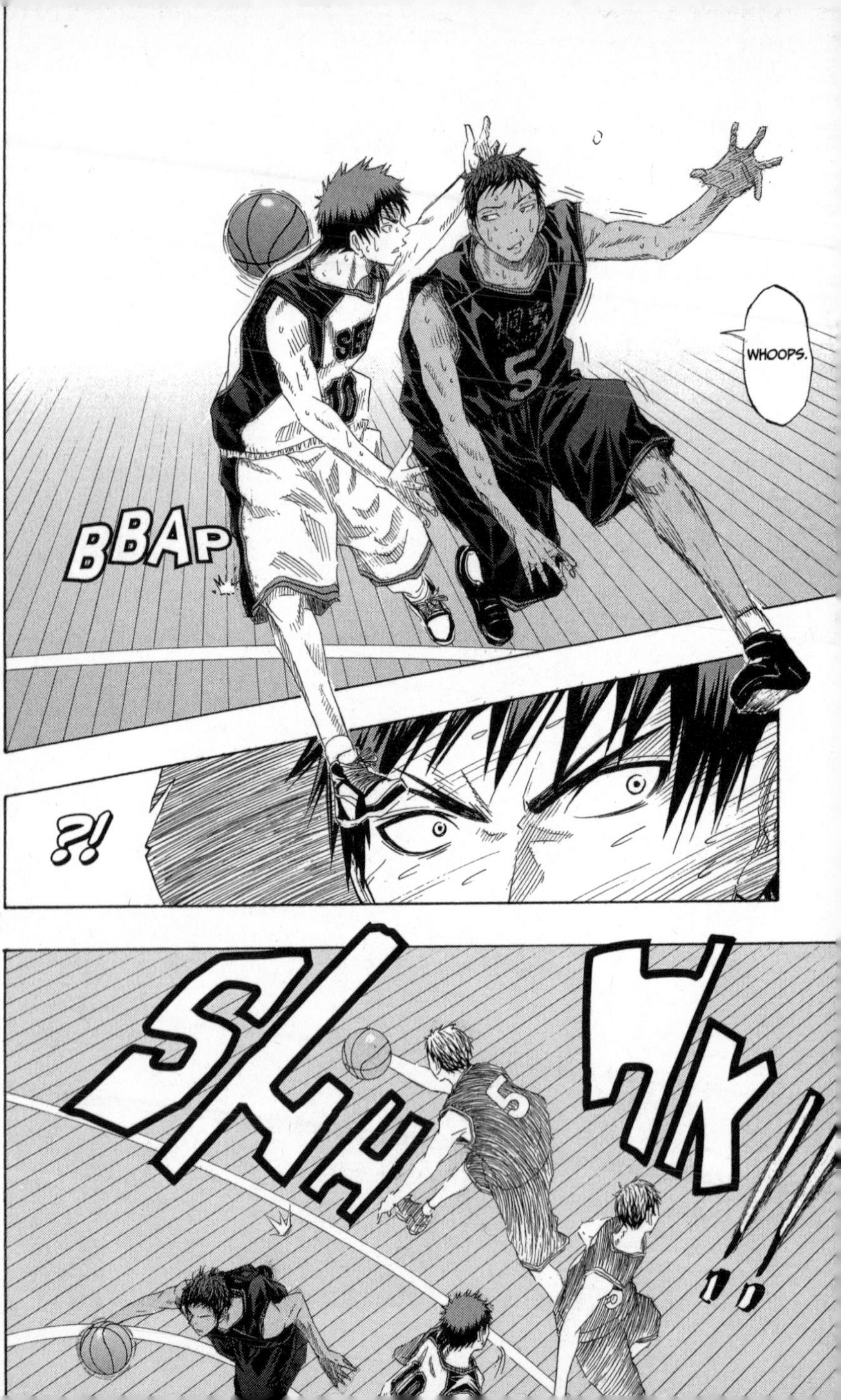
WHOOPS.
BBAP
?!
SHHNK!!

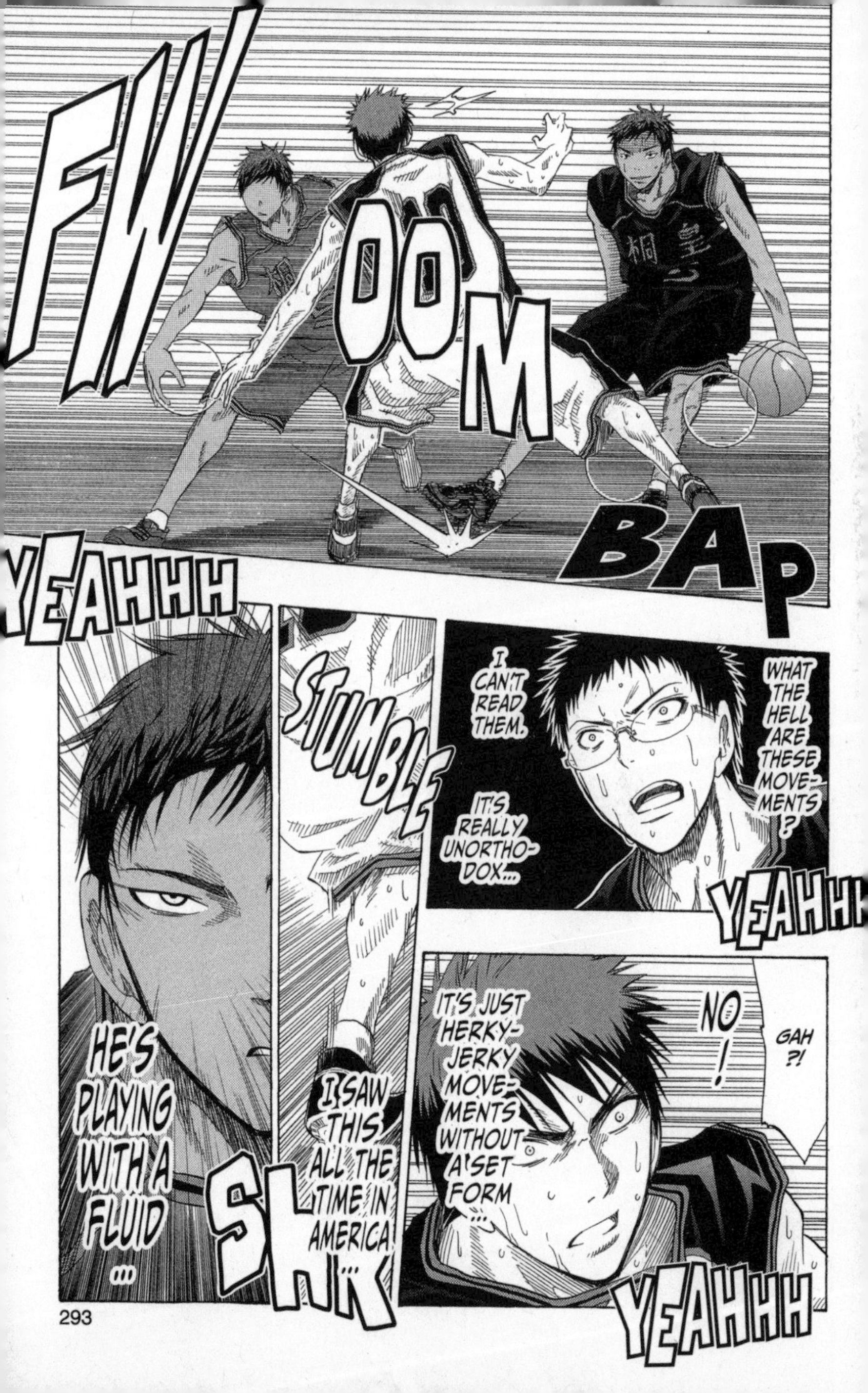
FWOOM
BAP
YEAHHH
WHAT THE HELL ARE THESE MOVE-MENTS?
I CAN'T READ THEM.
IT'S REALLY UNORTHO-DOX...
YEAHH
GAH ?!
NO!
IT'S JUST HERKY-JERKY MOVE-MENTS WITHOUT A SET FORM...
YEAHHH
STUMBLE
I SAW THIS ALL THE TIME IN AMERICA...
SHK
HE'S PLAYING WITH A FLUID...

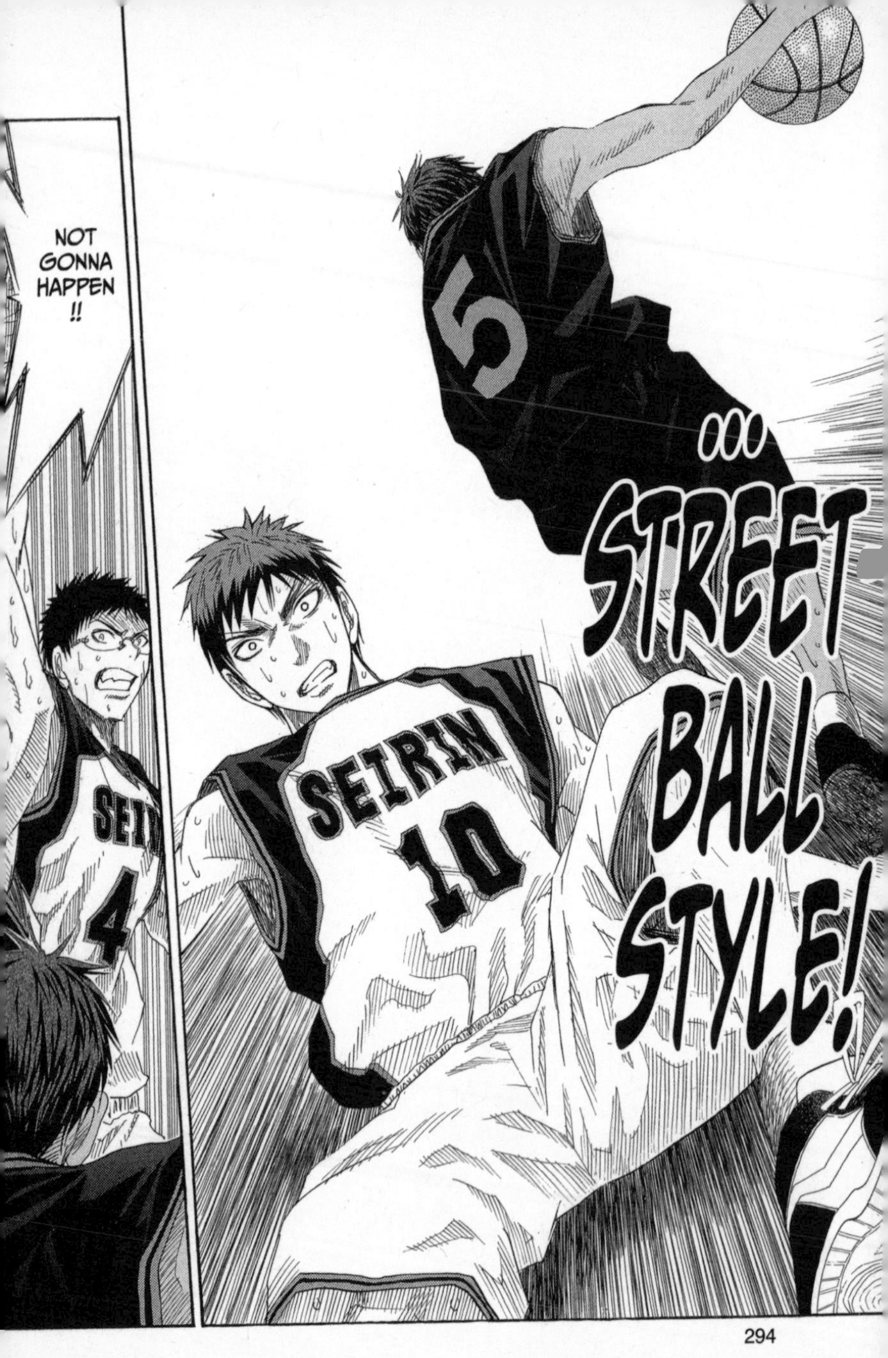
...STREET BALL STYLE!
NOT GONNA HAPPEN !!

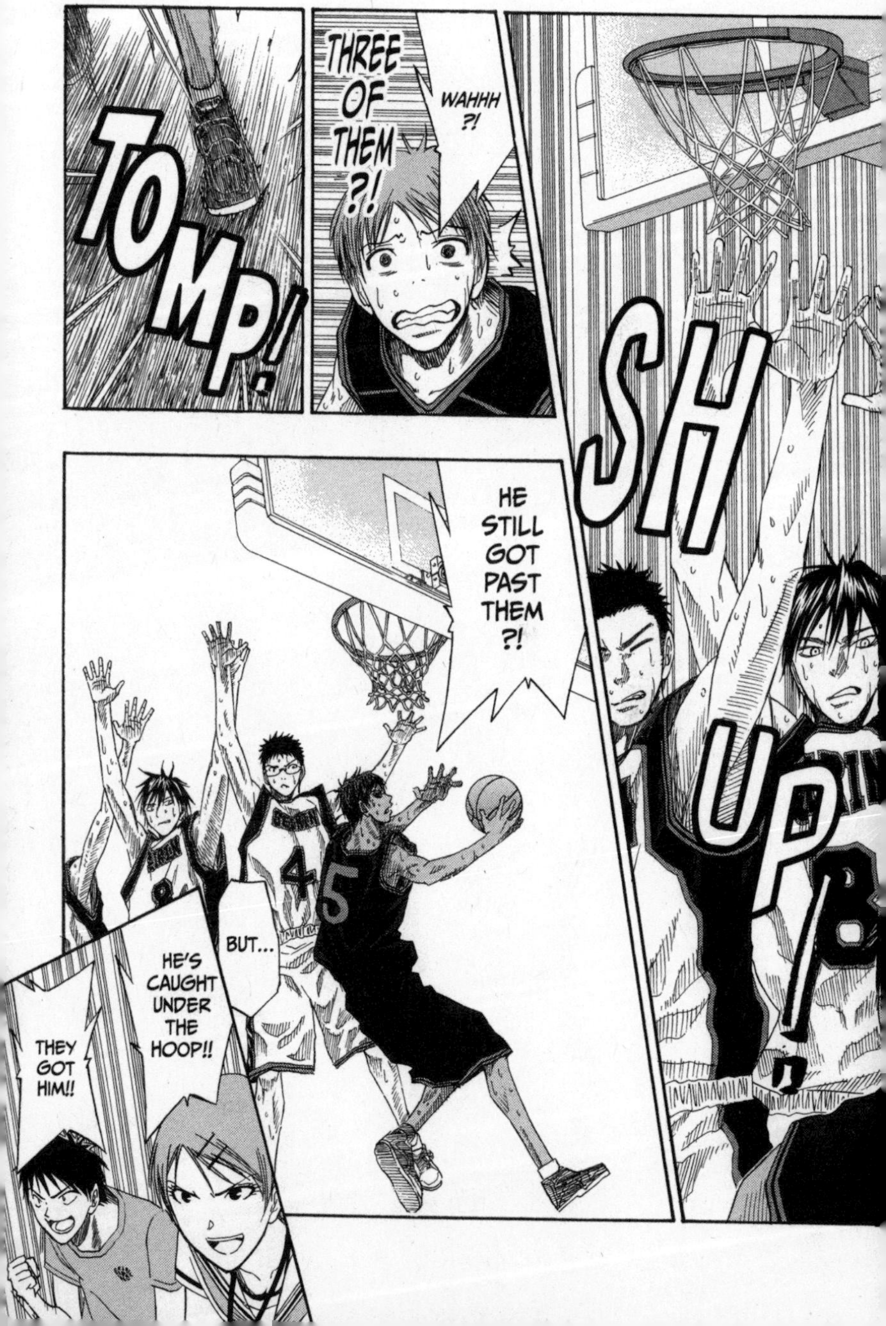
SHUP!
WAHHH ?!
THREE OF THEM ?!
TOMP!
HE STILL GOT PAST THEM ?!
BUT...
HE'S CAUGHT UNDER THE HOOP!!
THEY GOT HIM!!

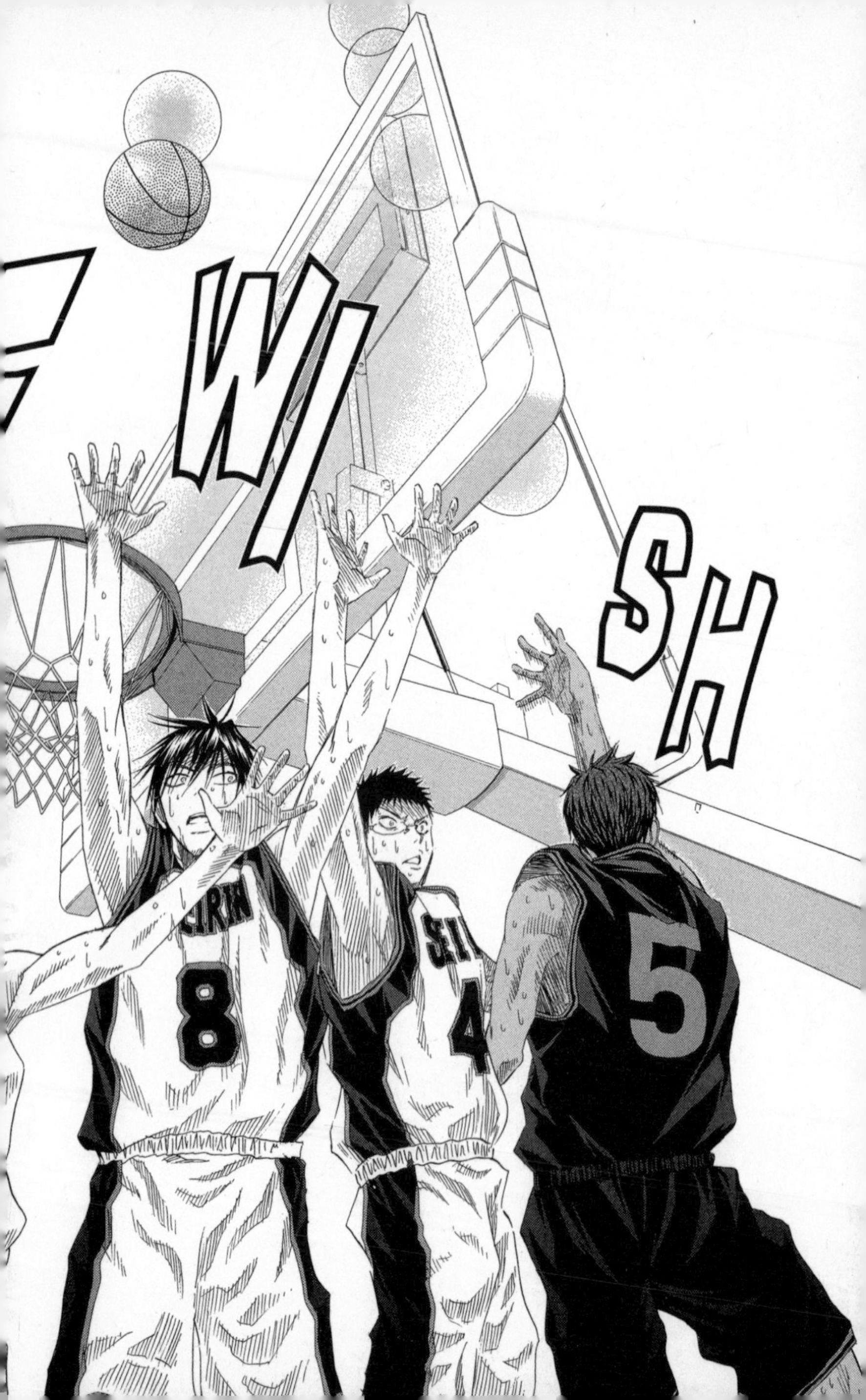
WI
SH

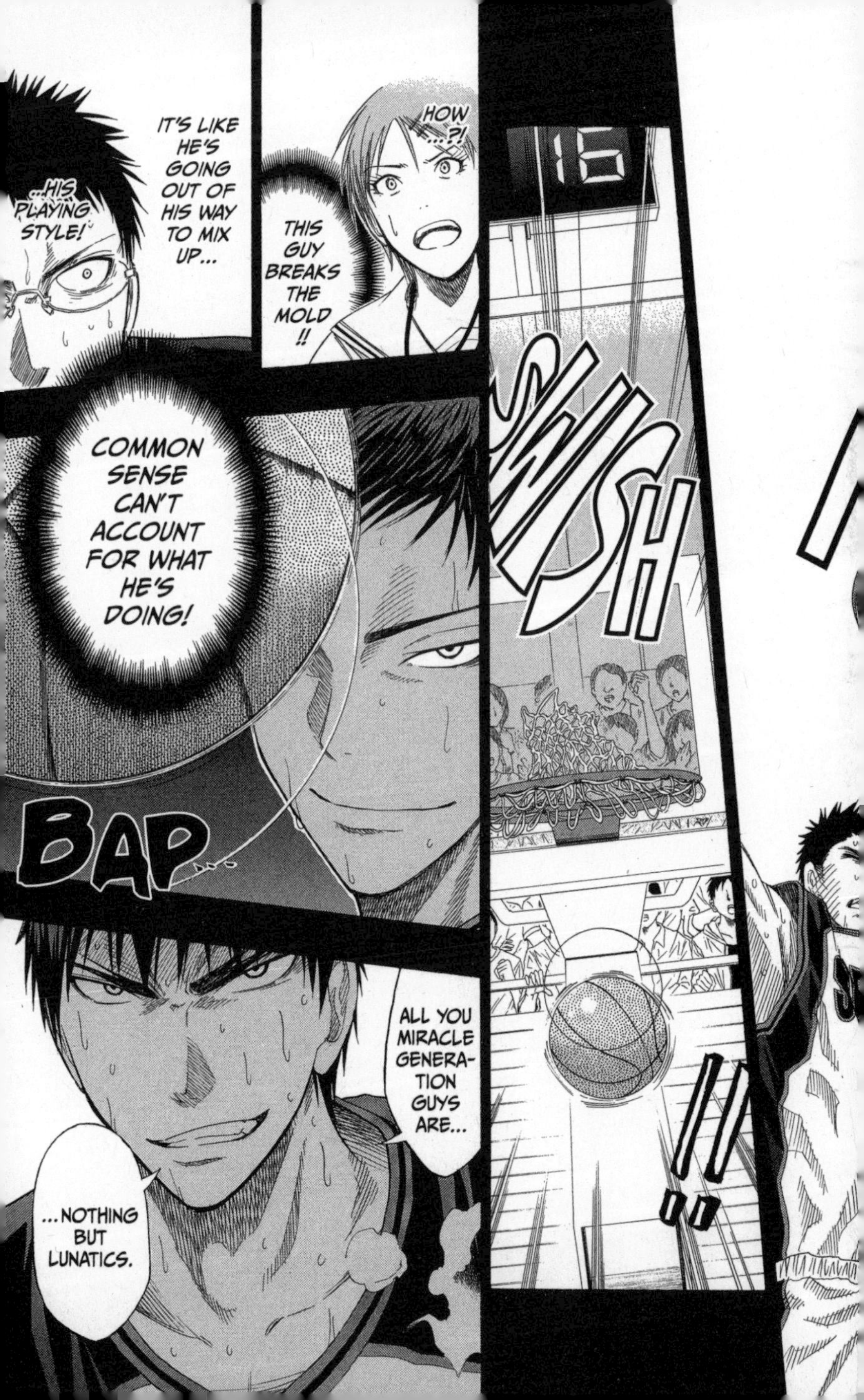

16
SWISH
!!
HOW ...?!
THIS GUY BREAKS THE MOLD!!
IT'S LIKE HE'S GOING OUT OF HIS WAY TO MIX UP...
...HIS PLAYING STYLE!
COMMON SENSE CAN'T ACCOUNT FOR WHAT HE'S DOING!
BAP
ALL YOU MIRACLE GENERA-TION GUYS ARE...
...NOTHING BUT LUNATICS.

KUROKO'S BASKETBALL BLOOPERS TAKE 1

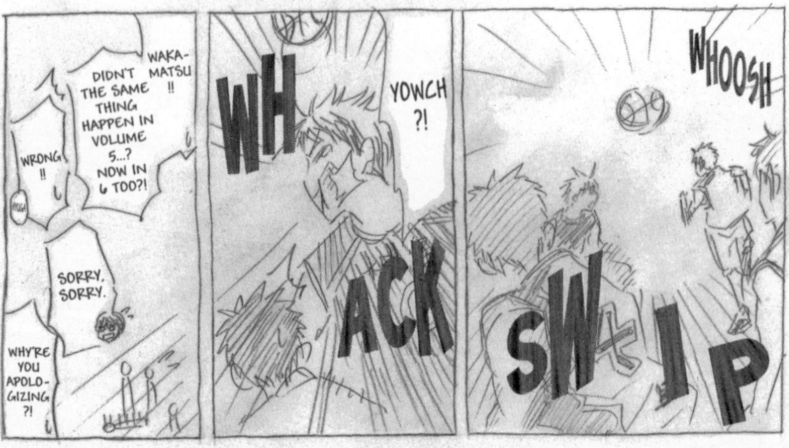
WHOOSH
SWIP
WHACK
YOWCH ?!
WAKAMATSU !!
DIDN'T THE SAME THING HAPPEN IN VOLUME 5...? NOW IN 6 TOO?!
WRONG !!
SORRY, SORRY.
WHY'RE YOU APOLOGIZING ?!

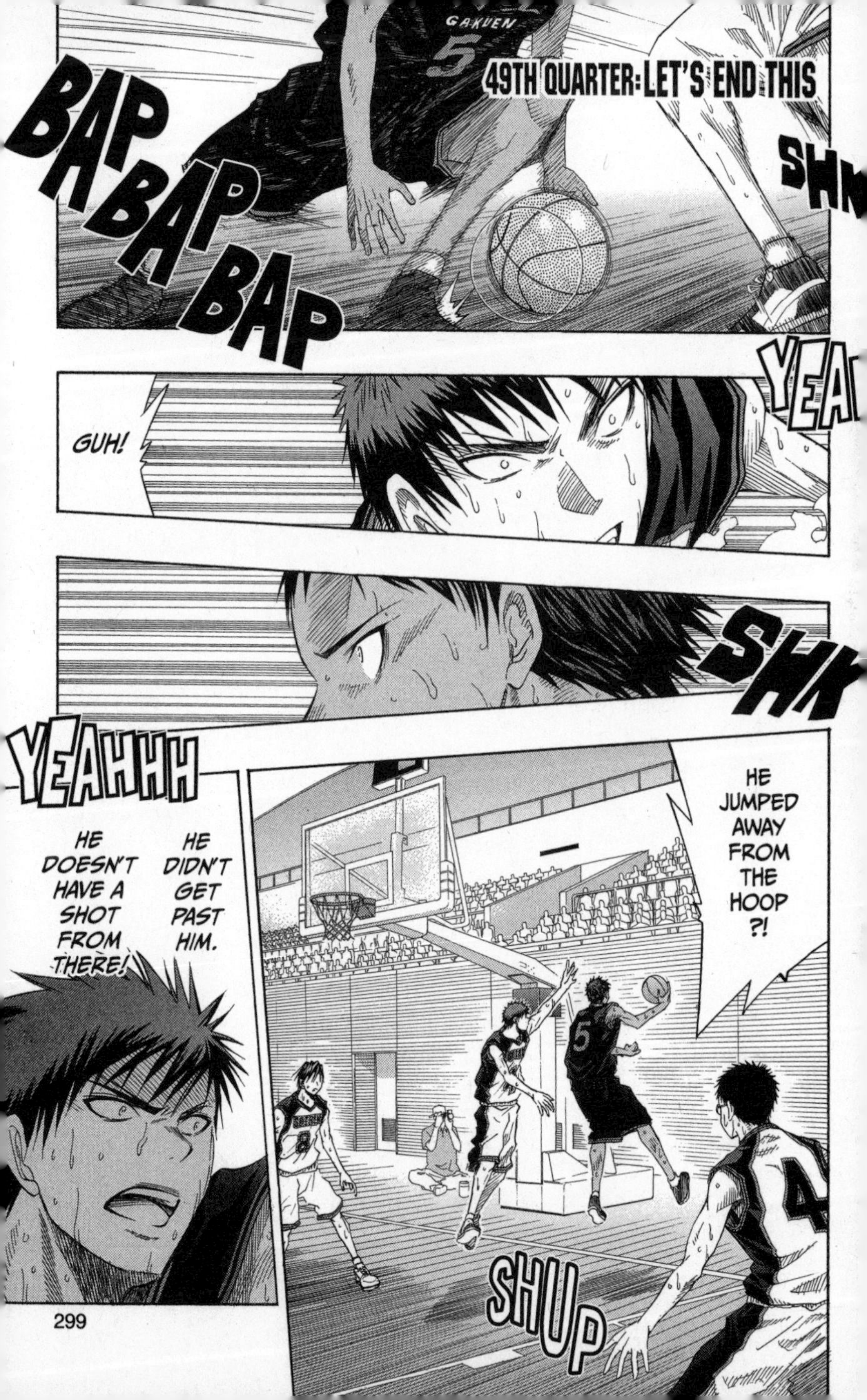
49TH QUARTER: LET'S END THIS
SHK
BAP BAP BAP BAP
YEA
GUH!
SHK
HE JUMPED AWAY FROM THE HOOP ?!
SHUP
HE DIDN'T GET PAST HIM.
HE DOESN'T HAVE A SHOT FROM THERE!
YEAHHH

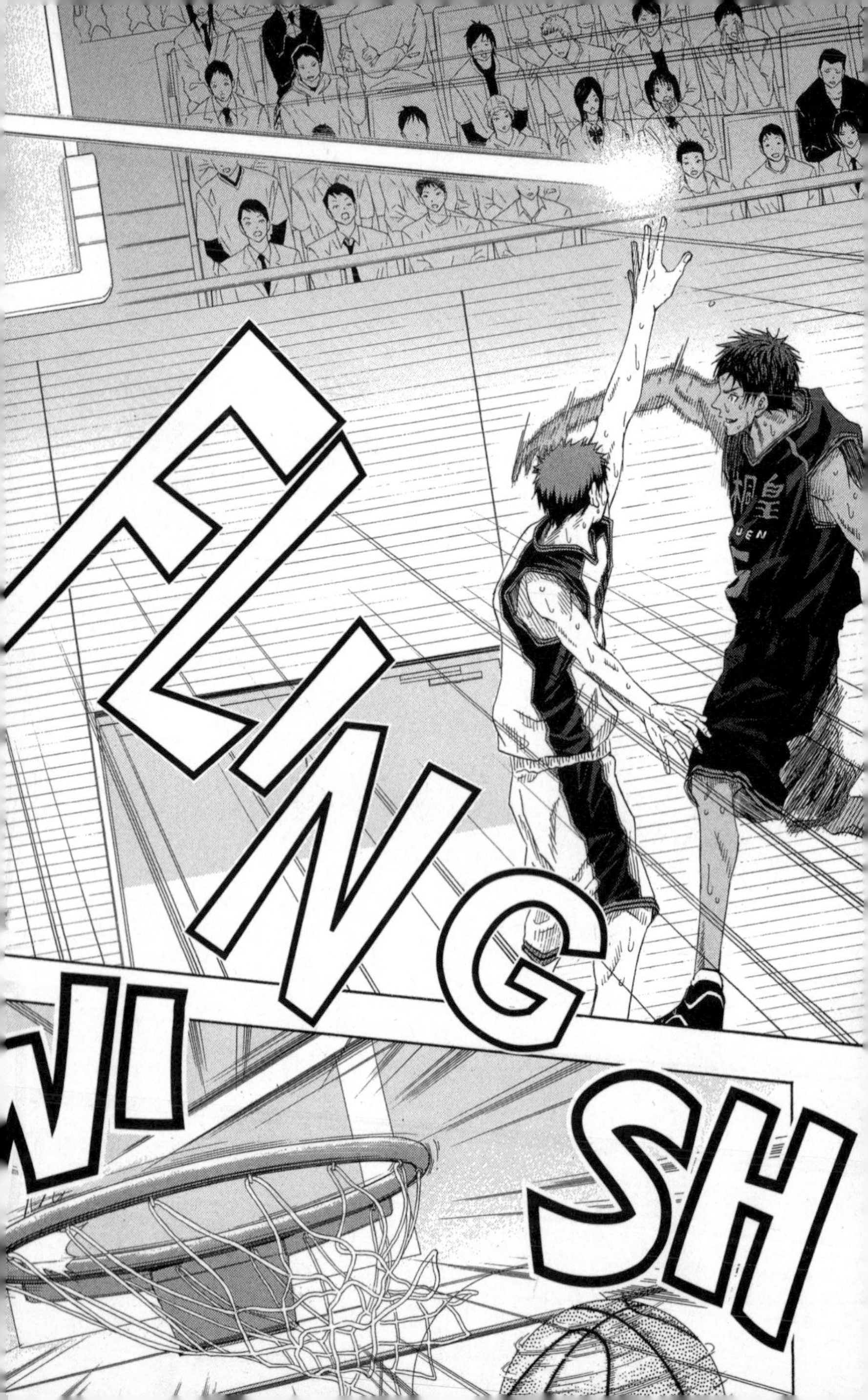
FLING
WI
SH

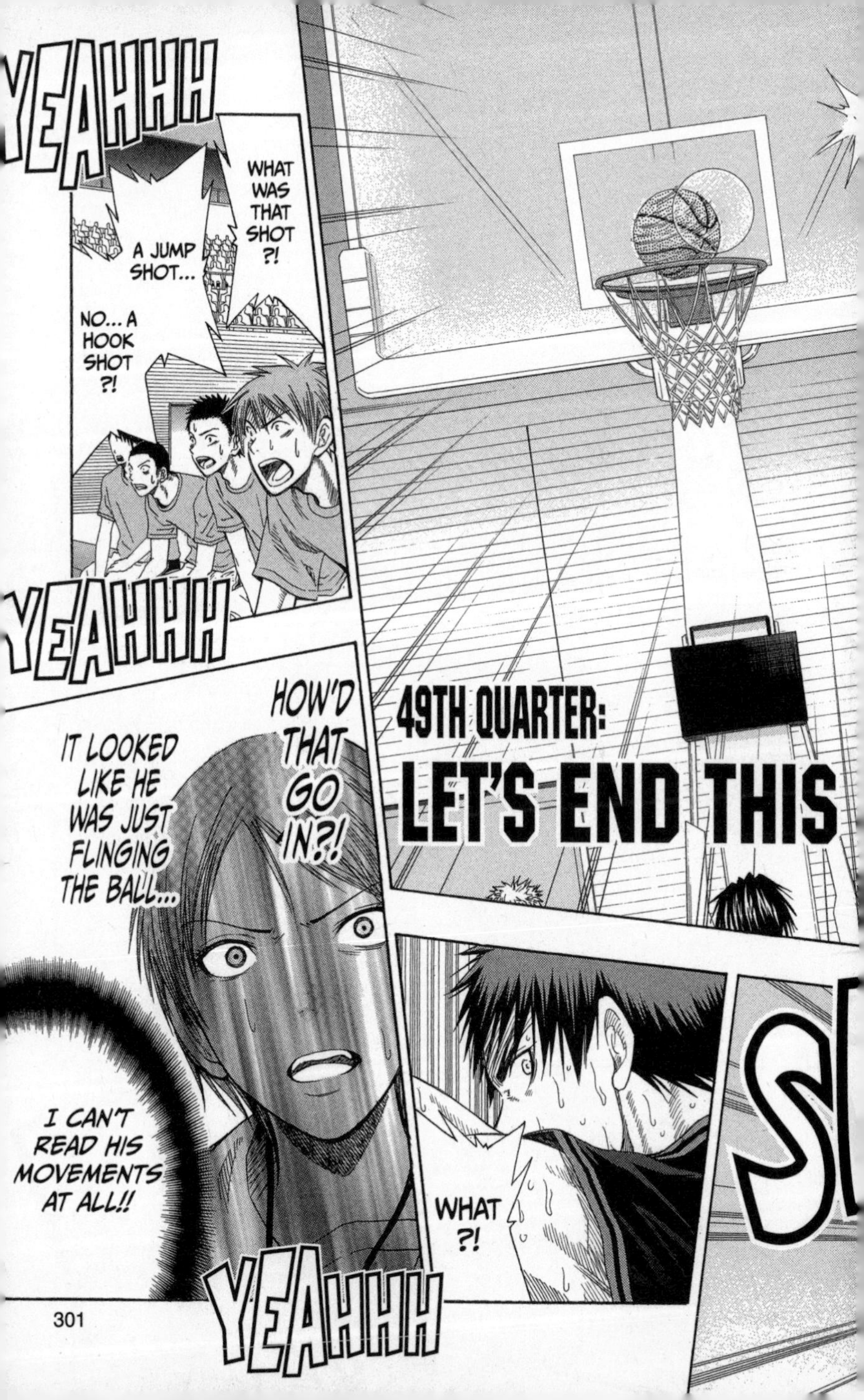
49TH QUARTER:
LET'S END THIS
YEAHHH
WHAT WAS THAT SHOT?!
A JUMP SHOT...
NO... A HOOK SHOT?!
YEAHHH
WHAT?!
HOW'D THAT GO IN?!
IT LOOKED LIKE HE WAS JUST FLINGING THE BALL...
I CAN'T READ HIS MOVEMENTS AT ALL!!
YEAHHH

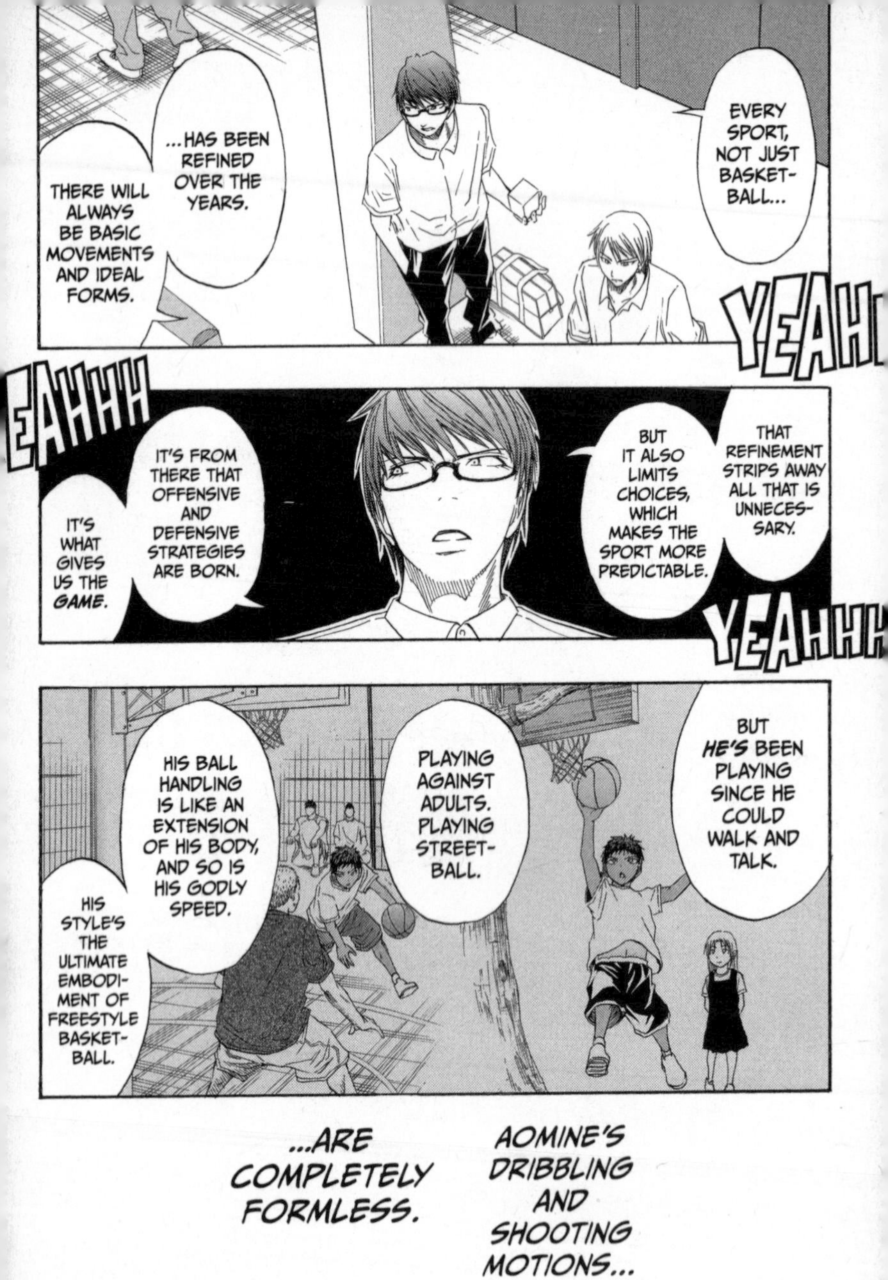
EVERY SPORT, NOT JUST BASKETBALL...
...HAS BEEN REFINED OVER THE YEARS.
THERE WILL ALWAYS BE BASIC MOVEMENTS AND IDEAL FORMS.
YEAH
EAHHH
THAT REFINEMENT STRIPS AWAY ALL THAT IS UNNECESSARY.
BUT IT ALSO LIMITS CHOICES, WHICH MAKES THE SPORT MORE PREDICTABLE.
IT'S FROM THERE THAT OFFENSIVE AND DEFENSIVE STRATEGIES ARE BORN.
IT'S WHAT GIVES US THE *GAME*.
YEAHHH
BUT *HE'S* BEEN PLAYING SINCE HE COULD WALK AND TALK.
PLAYING AGAINST ADULTS. PLAYING STREETBALL.
HIS BALL HANDLING IS LIKE AN EXTENSION OF HIS BODY, AND SO IS HIS GODLY SPEED.
HIS STYLE'S THE ULTIMATE EMBODIMENT OF FREESTYLE BASKETBALL.
AOMINE'S DRIBBLING AND SHOOTING MOTIONS...
...ARE COMPLETELY FORMLESS.

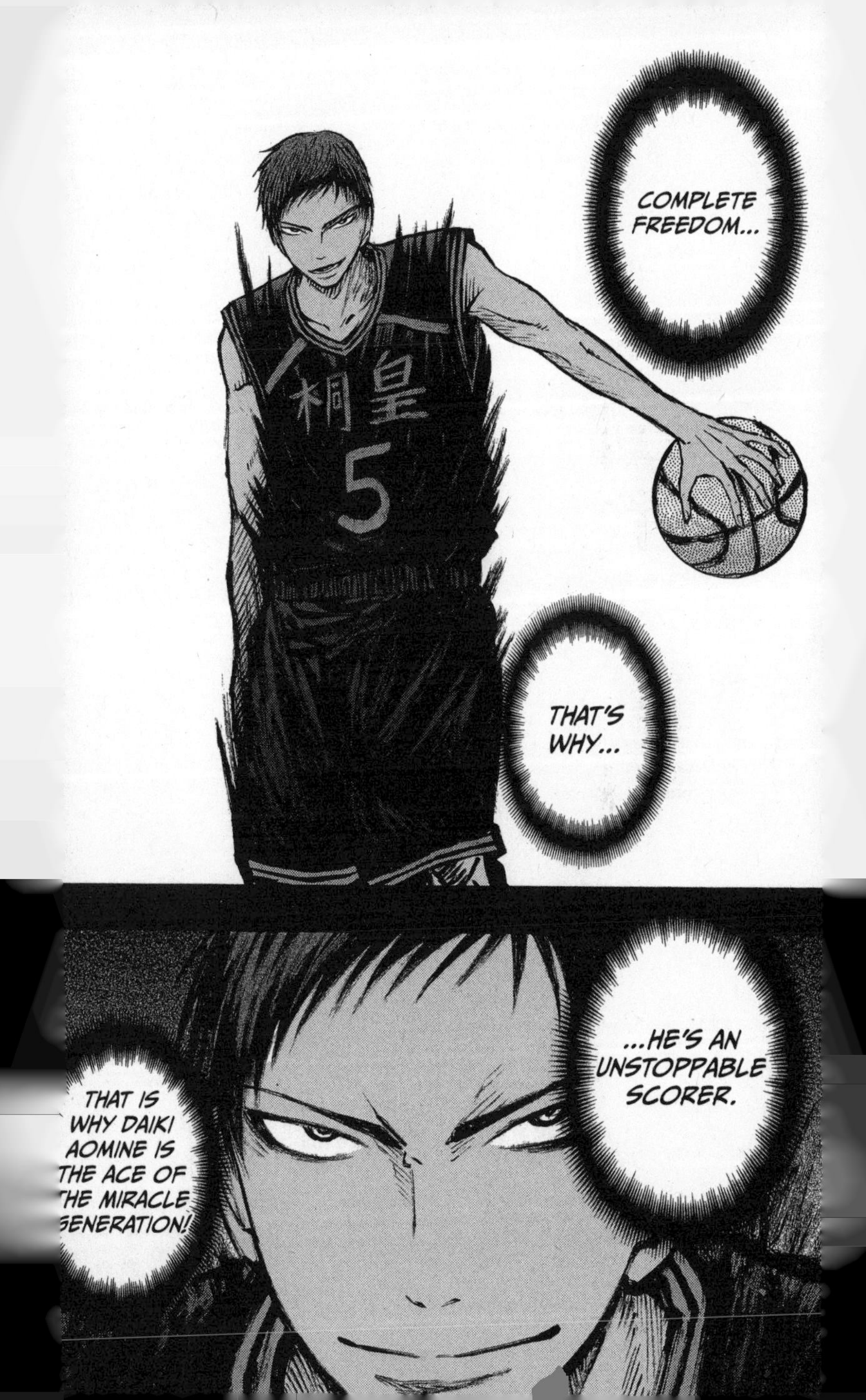
COMPLETE FREEDOM...
桐皇
5
THAT'S WHY...
...HE'S AN UNSTOPPABLE SCORER.
THAT IS WHY DAIKI AOMINE IS THE ACE OF THE MIRACLE GENERATION!

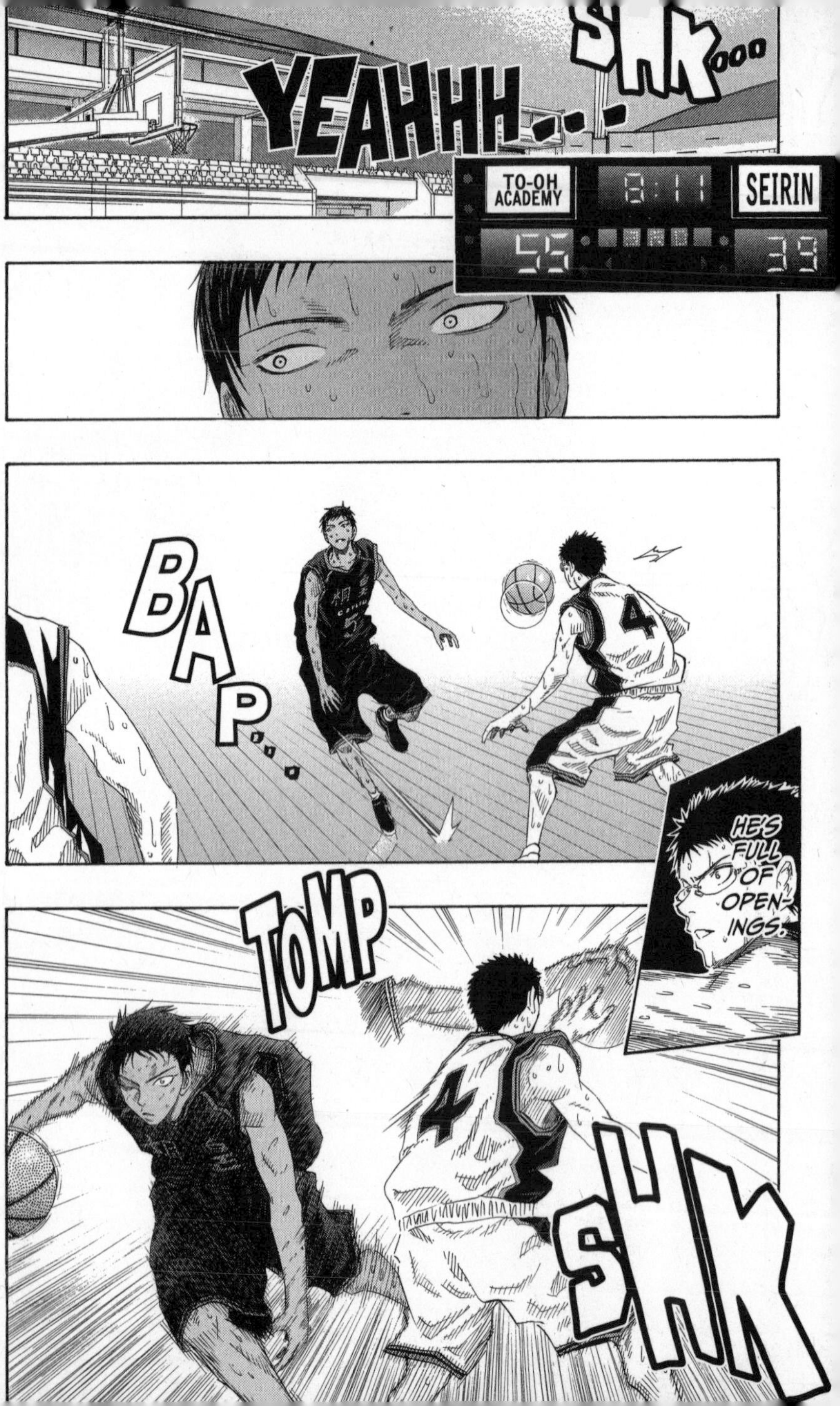
SHK...
YEAHHH...
TO-OH ACADEMY
8:11
SEIRIN
55
39
BAP...
HE'S FULL OF OPENINGS.
TOMP
SHK

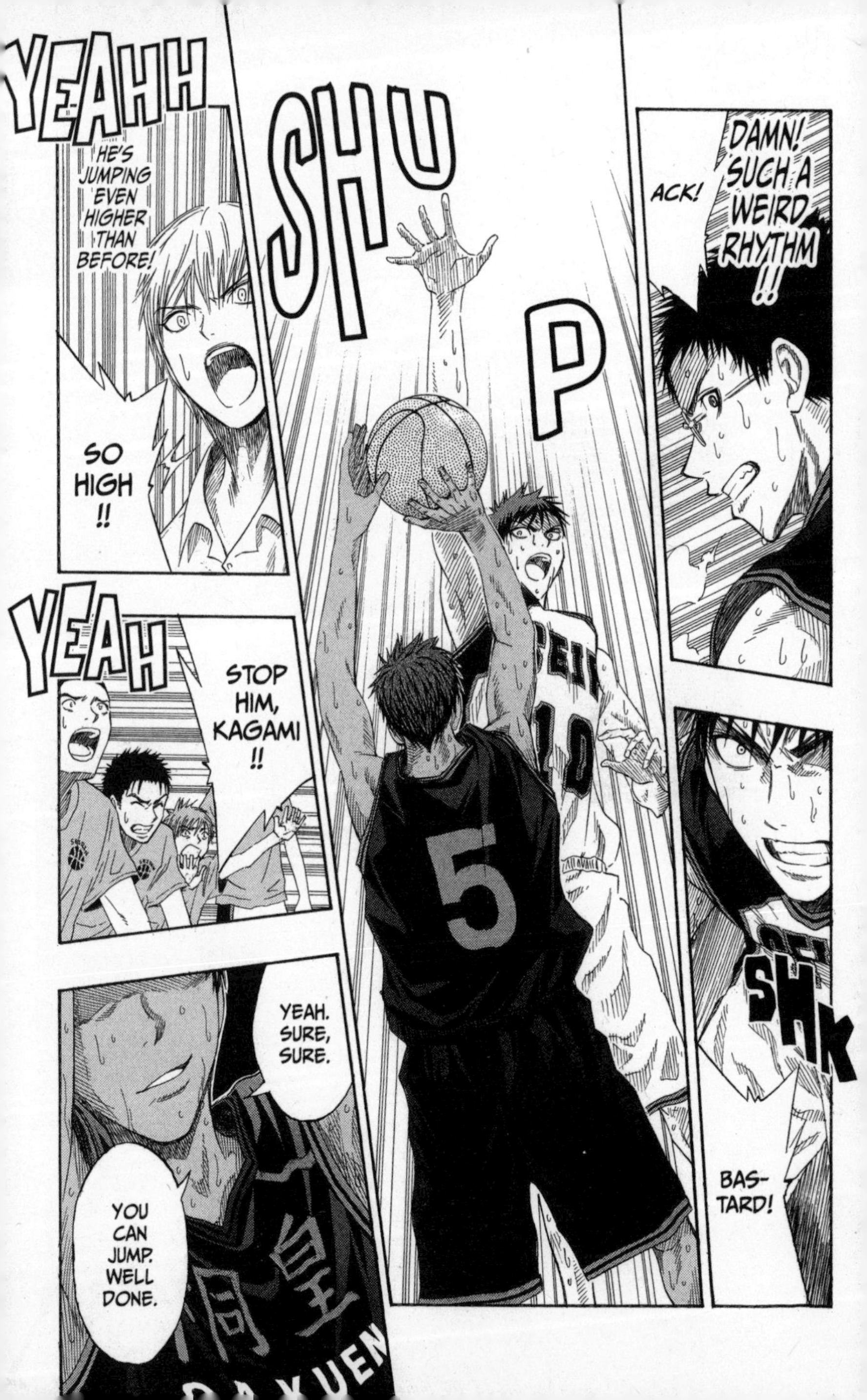
DAMN! SUCH A WEIRD RHYTHM!!
ACK!
SHK
BASTARD!
SHUP
HE'S JUMPING EVEN HIGHER THAN BEFORE!
YEAHH
SO HIGH!!
STOP HIM, KAGAMI!!
YEAH
YEAH. SURE, SURE.
YOU CAN JUMP. WELL DONE.

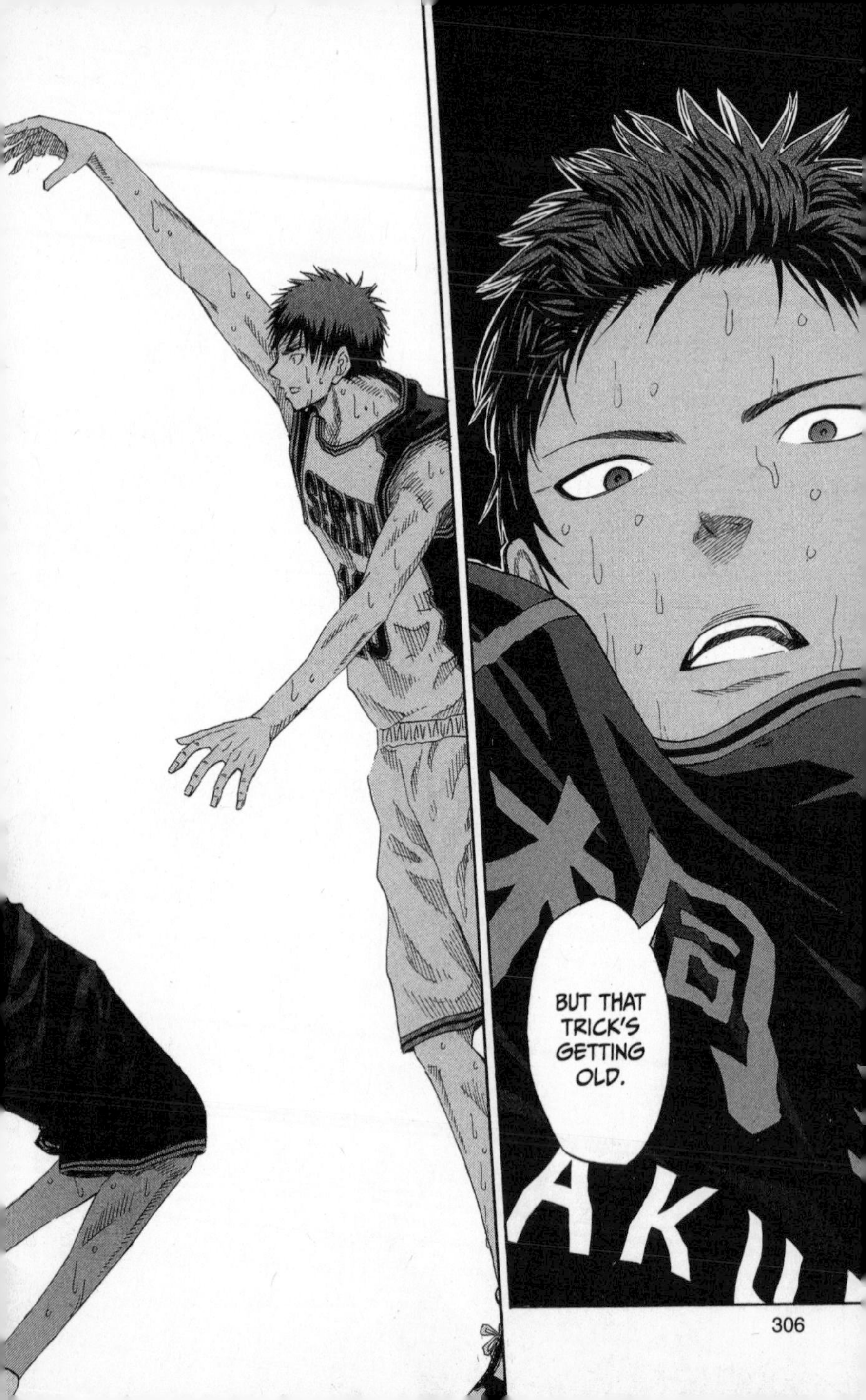
BUT THAT TRICK'S GETTING OLD.

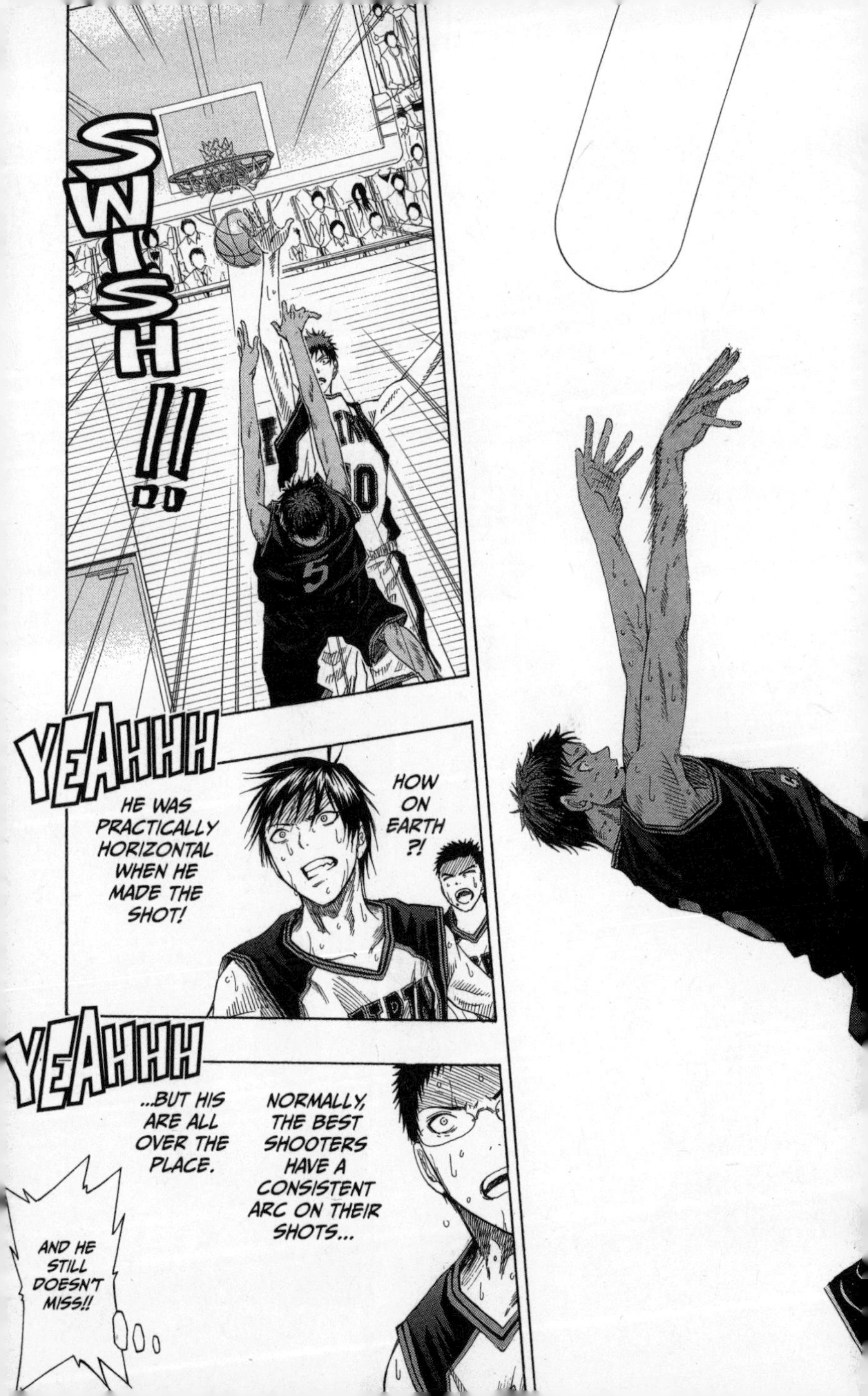
SWISH!!
YEAHHH
HOW ON EARTH ?!
HE WAS PRACTICALLY HORIZONTAL WHEN HE MADE THE SHOT!
YEAHHH
NORMALLY, THE BEST SHOOTERS HAVE A CONSISTENT ARC ON THEIR SHOTS...
...BUT HIS ARE ALL OVER THE PLACE.
AND HE STILL DOESN'T MISS!!

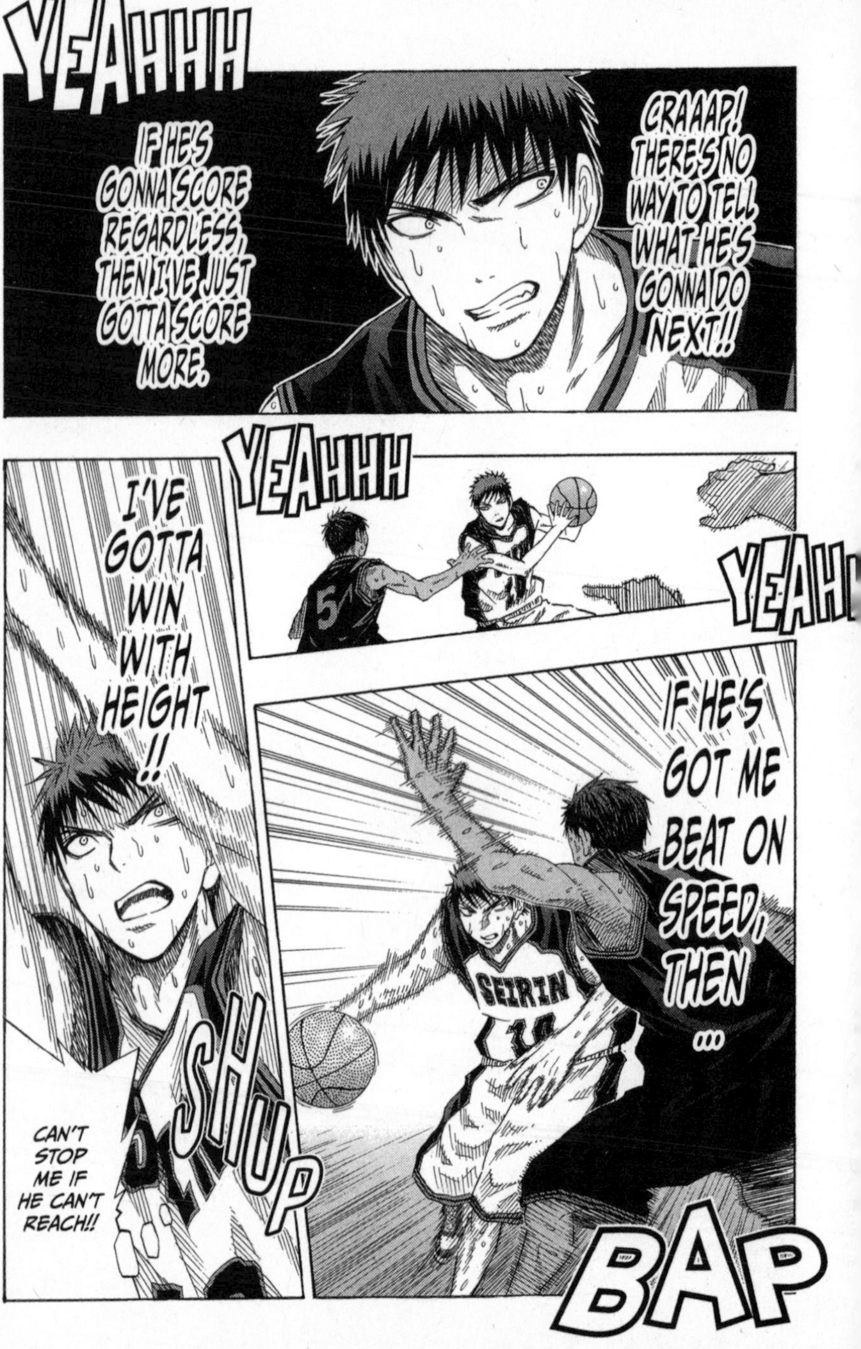
CRAAAP! THERE'S NO WAY TO TELL WHAT HE'S GONNA DO NEXT!!
YEAHHH
IF HE'S GONNA SCORE REGARDLESS, THEN I'VE JUST GOTTA SCORE MORE.
YEAHHH
YEAH
IF HE'S GOT ME BEAT ON SPEED, THEN ...
BAP
I'VE GOTTA WIN WITH HEIGHT!!
SHUP
CAN'T STOP ME IF HE CAN'T REACH!!

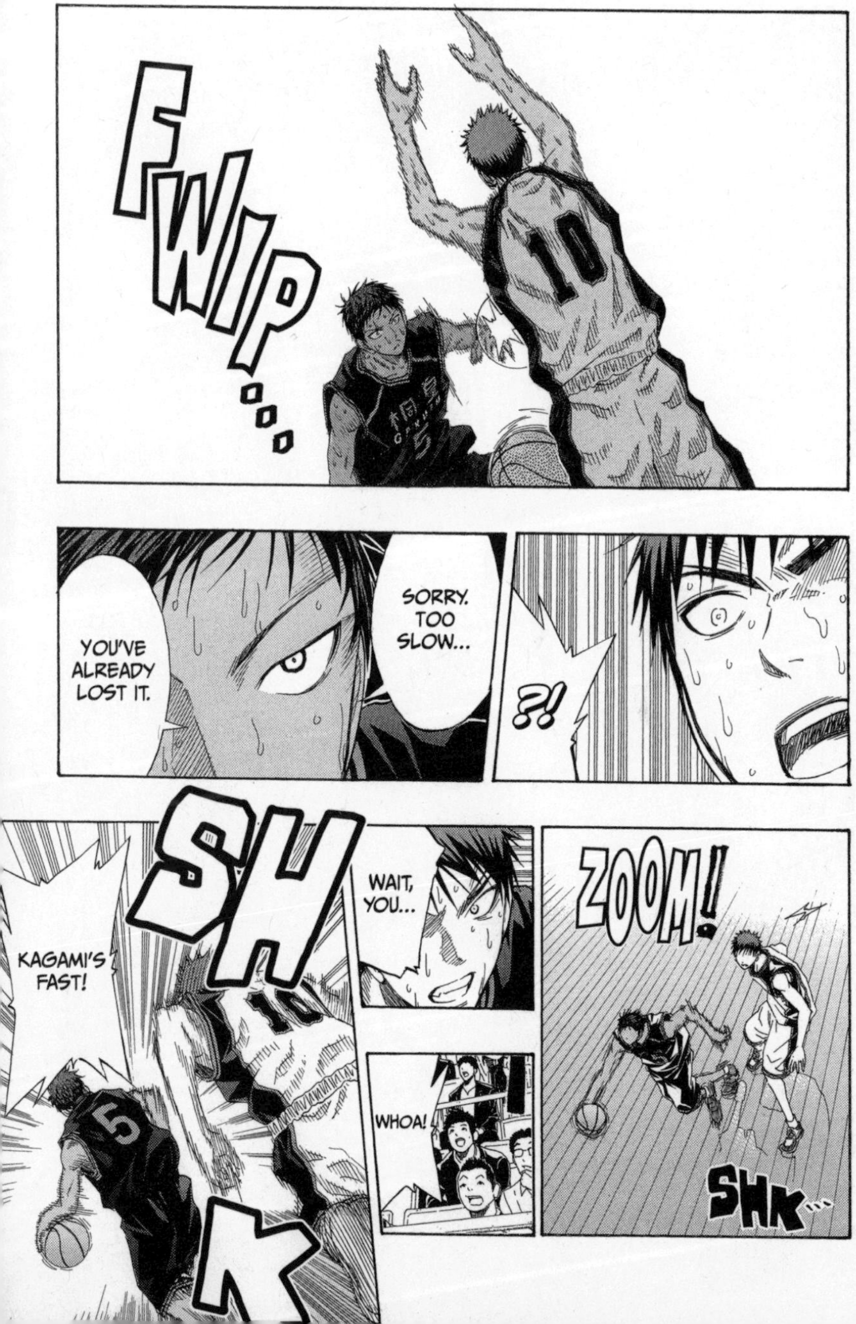
FWIP...
?!
SORRY. TOO SLOW...
YOU'VE ALREADY LOST IT.
ZOOM!!
SHK...
WAIT, YOU...
WHOA!
SH
KAGAMI'S FAST!
K

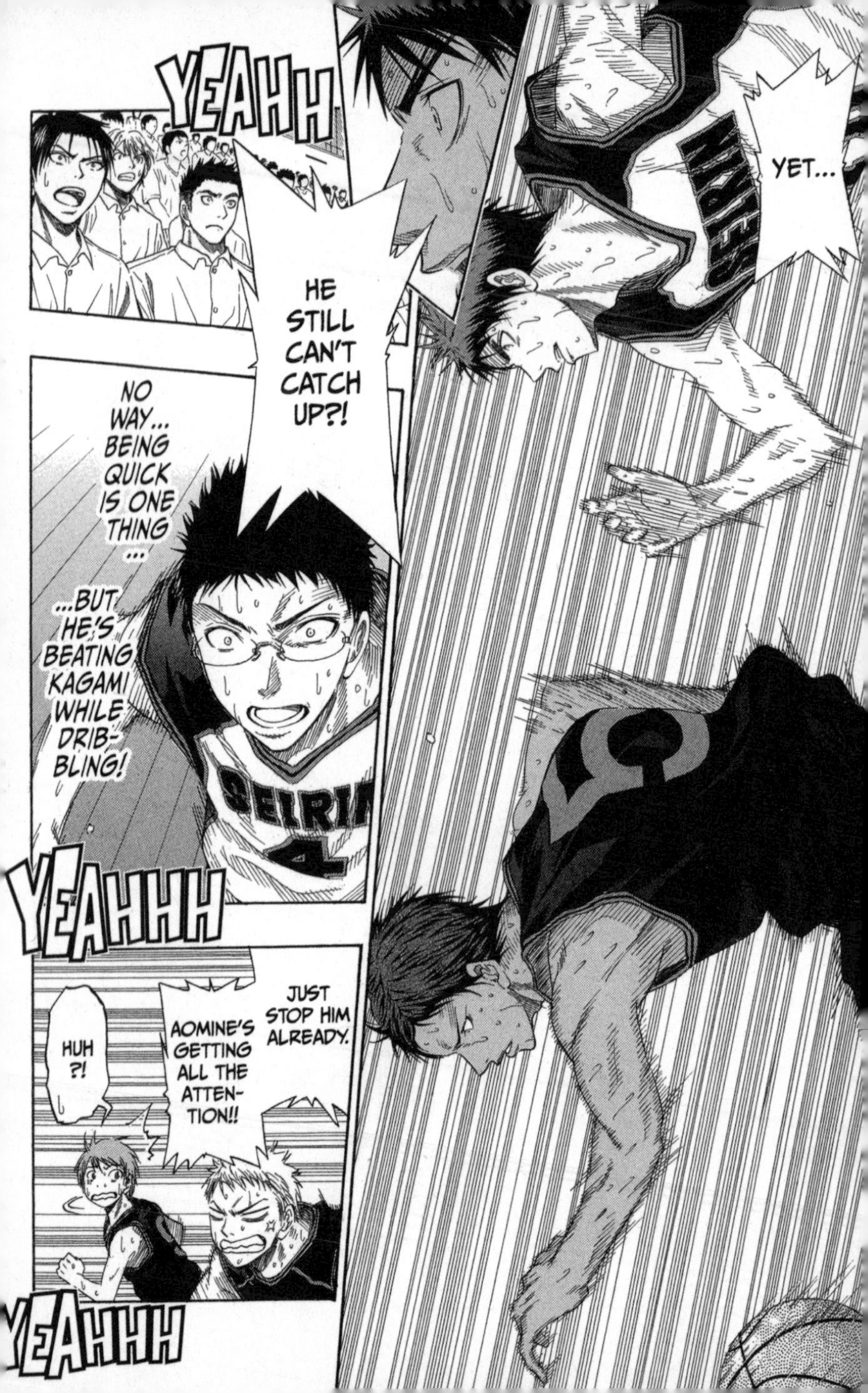
YET...
HE STILL CAN'T CATCH UP?!
YEAHH
NO WAY... BEING QUICK IS ONE THING...
...BUT HE'S BEATING KAGAMI WHILE DRIBBLING!
YEAHHH
JUST STOP HIM ALREADY.
AOMINE'S GETTING ALL THE ATTENTION!!
HUH?!
YEAHHH

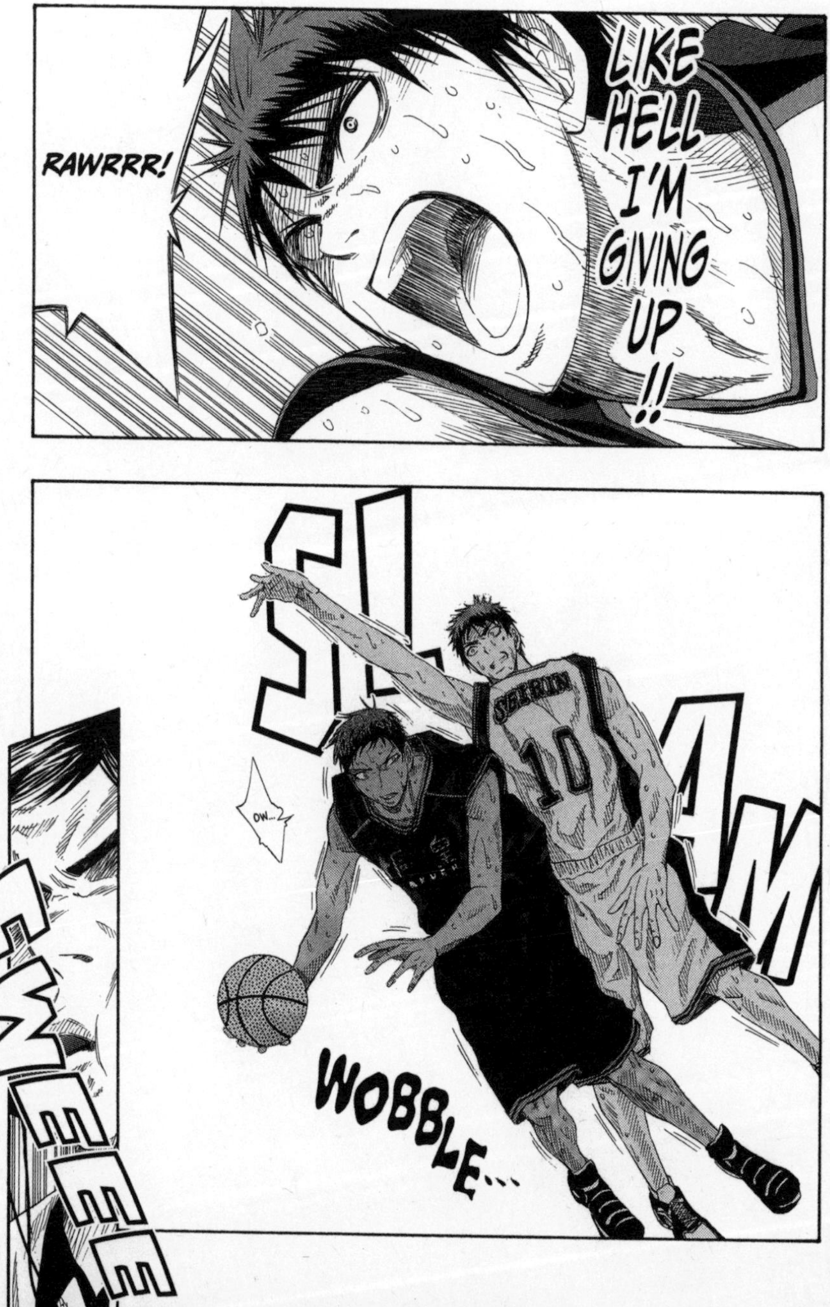
LIKE HELL I'M GIVING UP!!
RAWRRR!
SLAM
OW...
WOBBLE...
SWEEEE

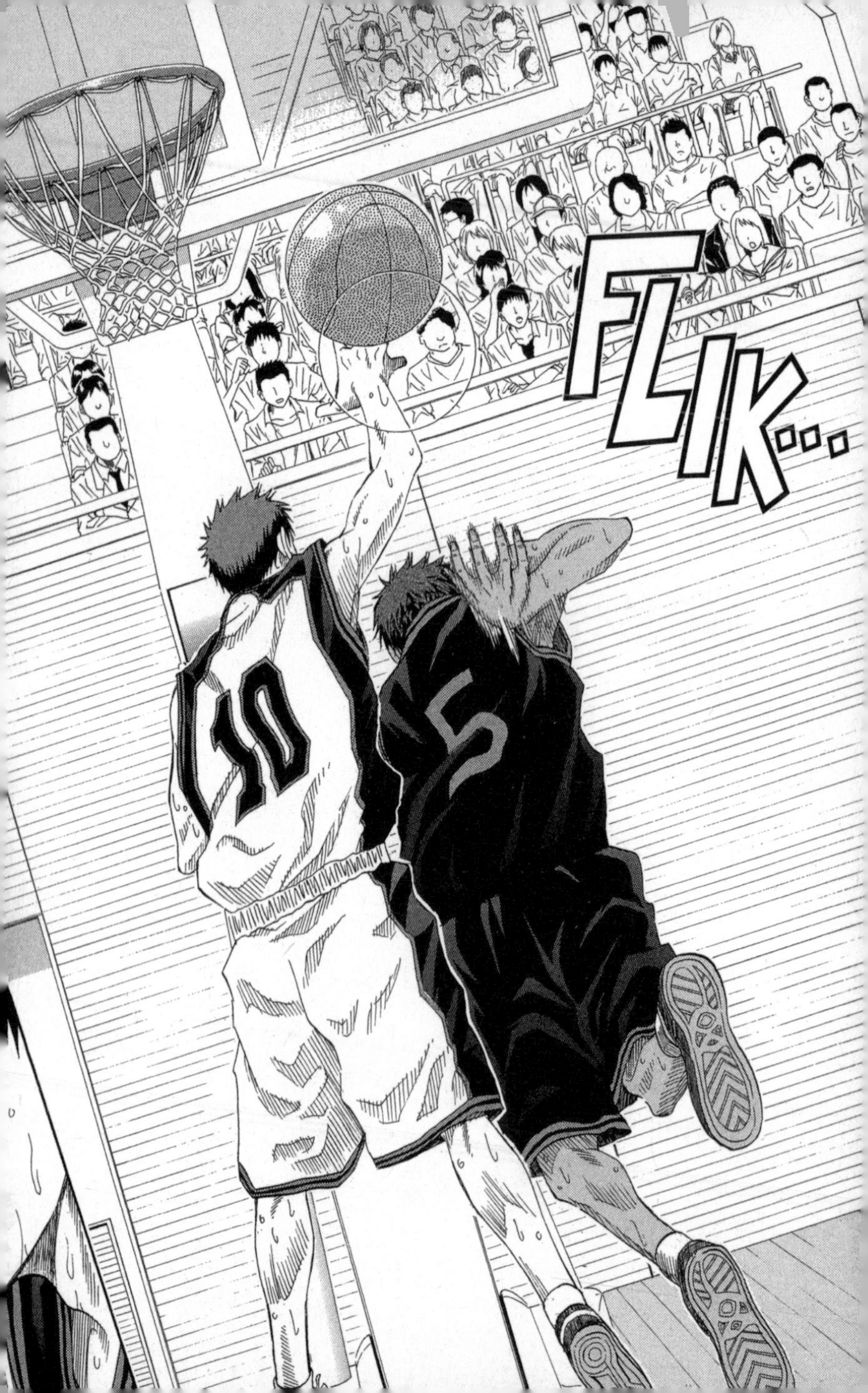
FLIK...

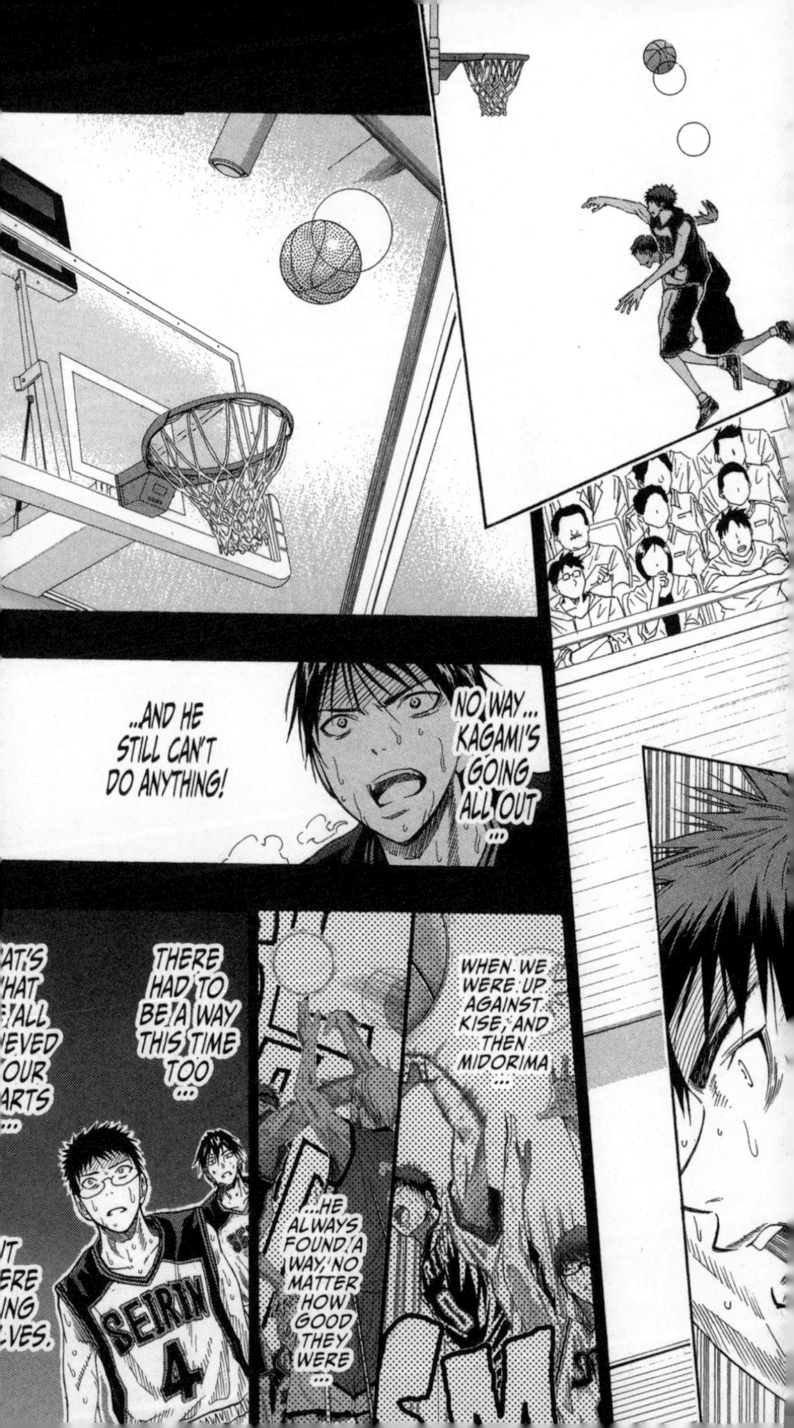
NO WAY... KAGAMI'S GOING ALL OUT ...
...AND HE STILL CAN'T DO ANYTHING!
WHEN WE WERE UP AGAINST KISE, AND THEN MIDORIMA ...
...HE ALWAYS FOUND A WAY, NO MATTER HOW GOOD THEY WERE ...
THERE HAD TO BE A WAY THIS TIME TOO ...
SEIRIN
4

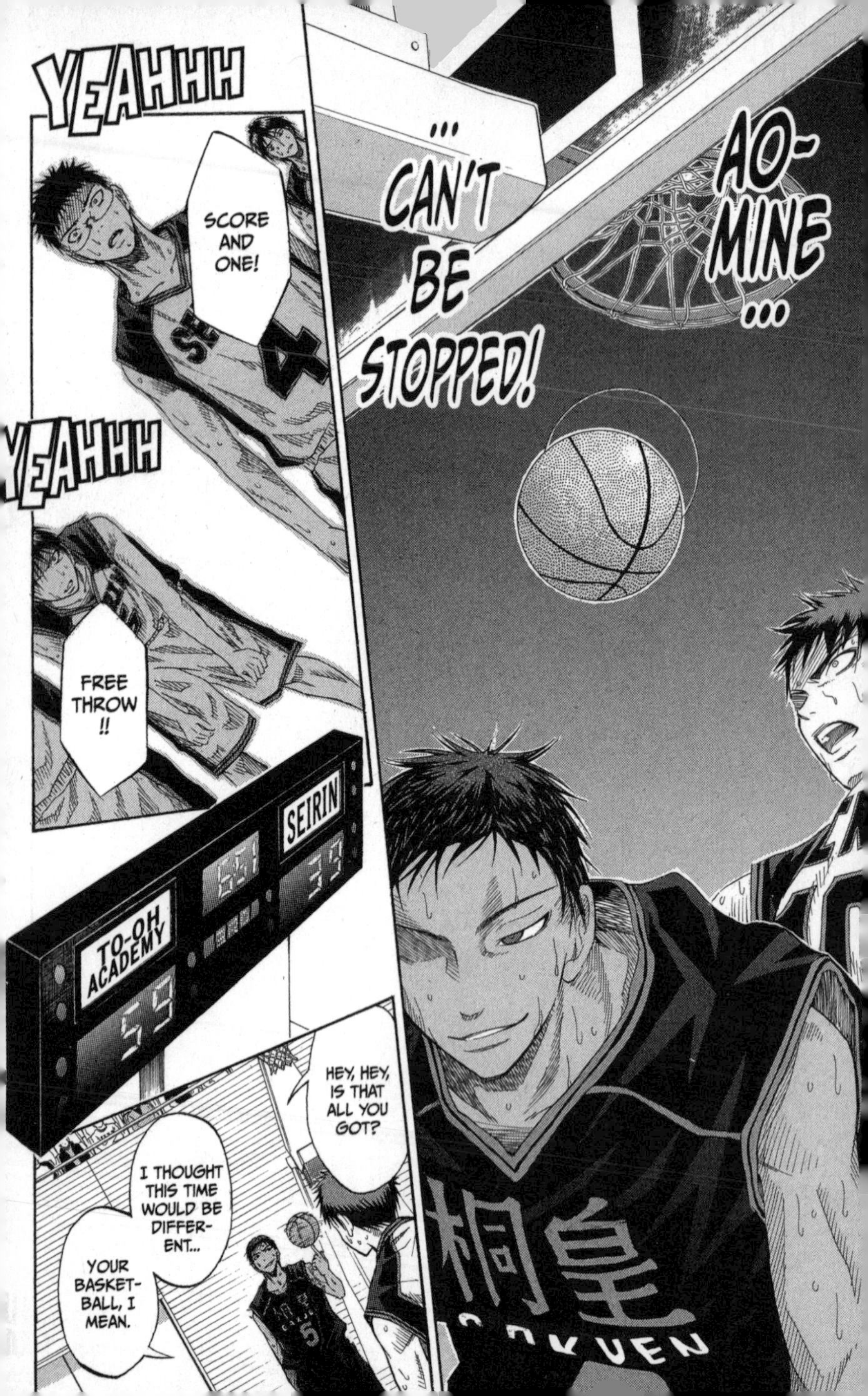
AO-MINE...
... CAN'T BE STOPPED!
YEAHHH
SCORE AND ONE!
YEAHHH
FREE THROW !!
SEIRIN
39
TO-OH ACADEMY
59
HEY, HEY, IS THAT ALL YOU GOT?
I THOUGHT THIS TIME WOULD BE DIFFER-ENT...
YOUR BASKET-BALL, I MEAN.

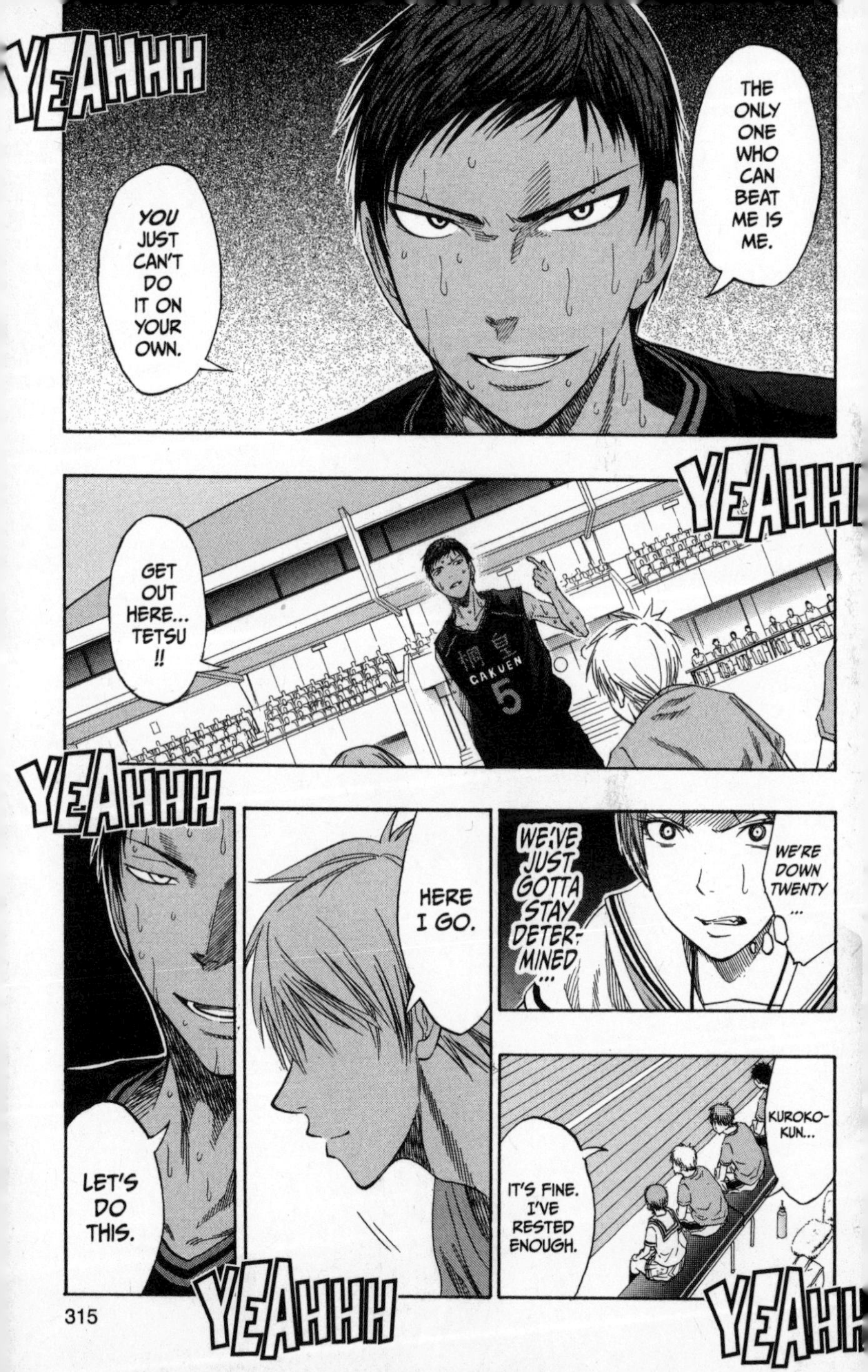
THE ONLY ONE WHO CAN BEAT ME IS ME.
YOU JUST CAN'T DO IT ON YOUR OWN.
YEAHHH
YEAHHH
GET OUT HERE... TETSU !!
WE'RE DOWN TWENTY ...
WE'VE JUST GOTTA STAY DETER-MINED ...
KUROKO-KUN...
IT'S FINE. I'VE RESTED ENOUGH.
YEAHH
HERE I GO.
YEAHHH
YEAHHH
LET'S DO THIS.

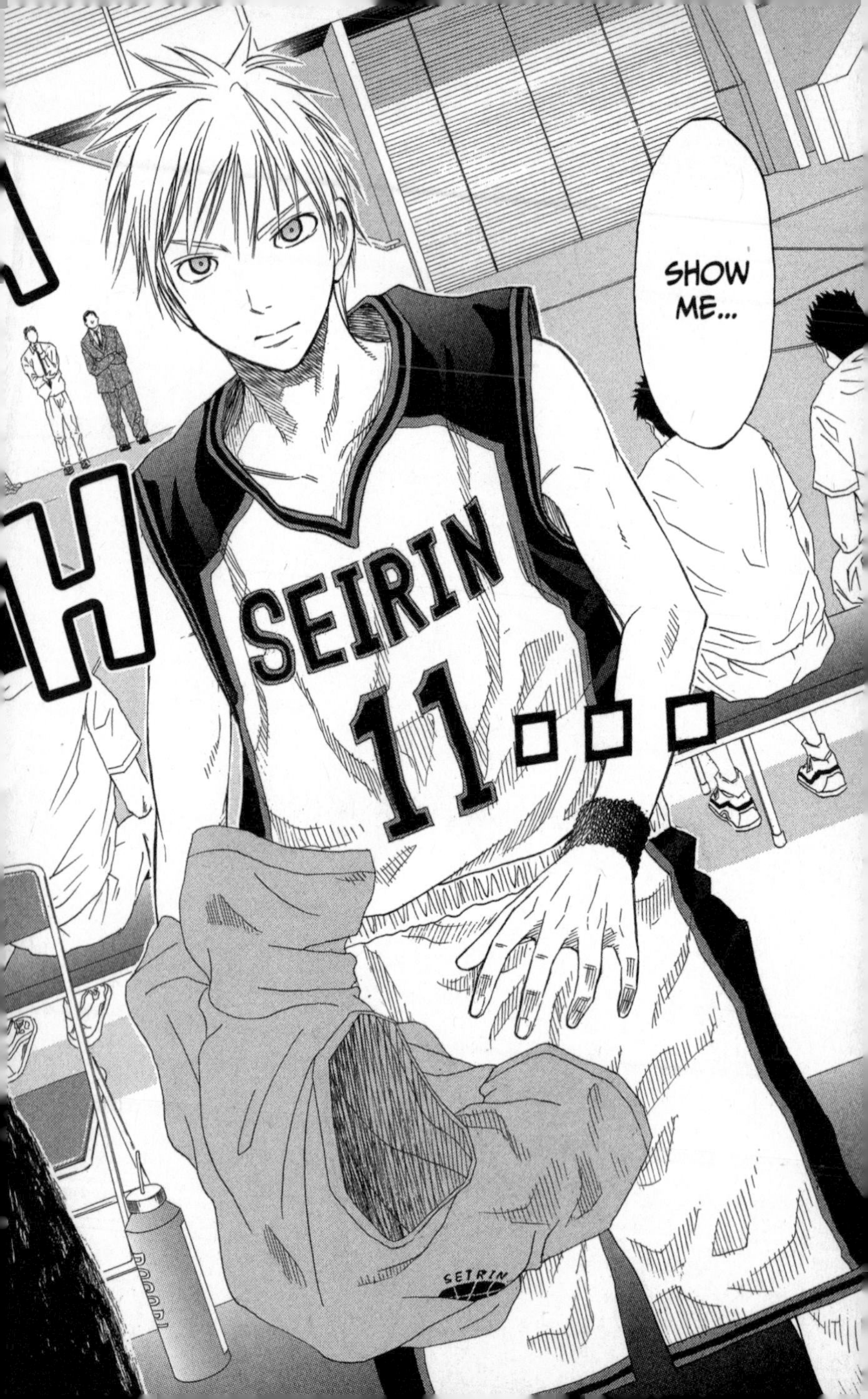
SHOW ME...
SEIRIN
11
SEIRIN

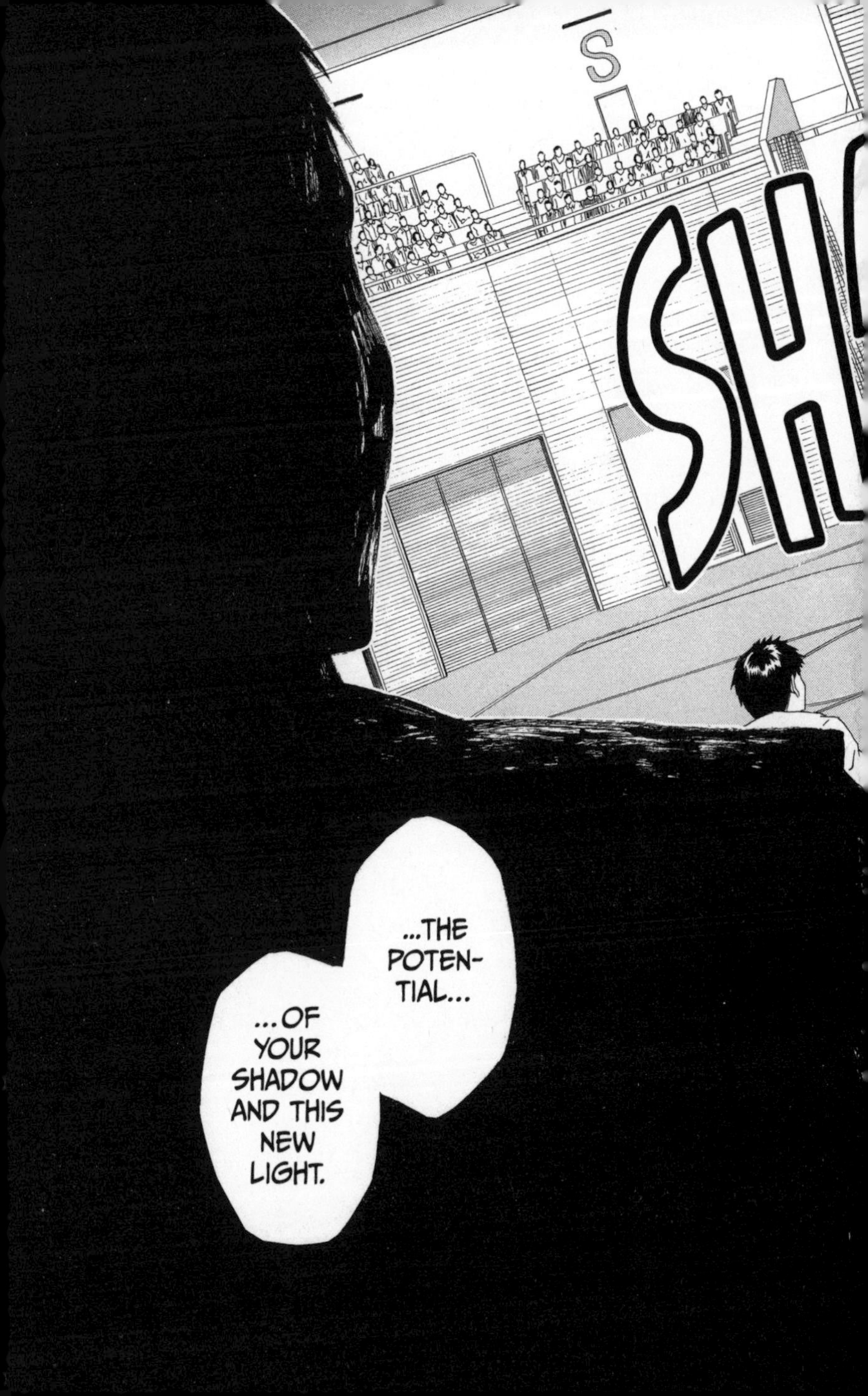
SH
...THE POTEN-TIAL...
...OF YOUR SHADOW AND THIS NEW LIGHT.

KUROKO'S BASKETBALL BLOOPERS TAKE 9

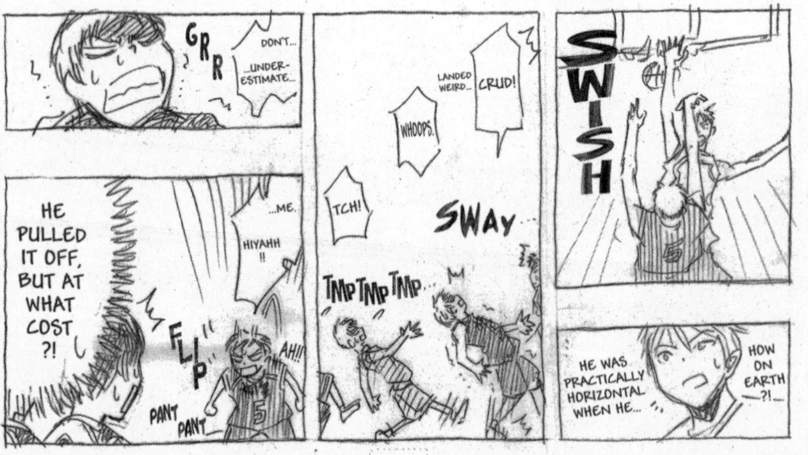
SWISH
HOW ON EARTH—?!...
HE WAS PRACTICALLY HORIZONTAL WHEN HE...
CRUD!
LANDED WEIRD...
WHOOPS.
TCH!
SWAY...
TMP TMP TMP...
DON'T...
...UNDER-ESTIMATE...
GRR
...ME.
HIYAHH!!
AH!!
FLIP
PANT PANT
HE PULLED IT OFF, BUT AT WHAT COST?!

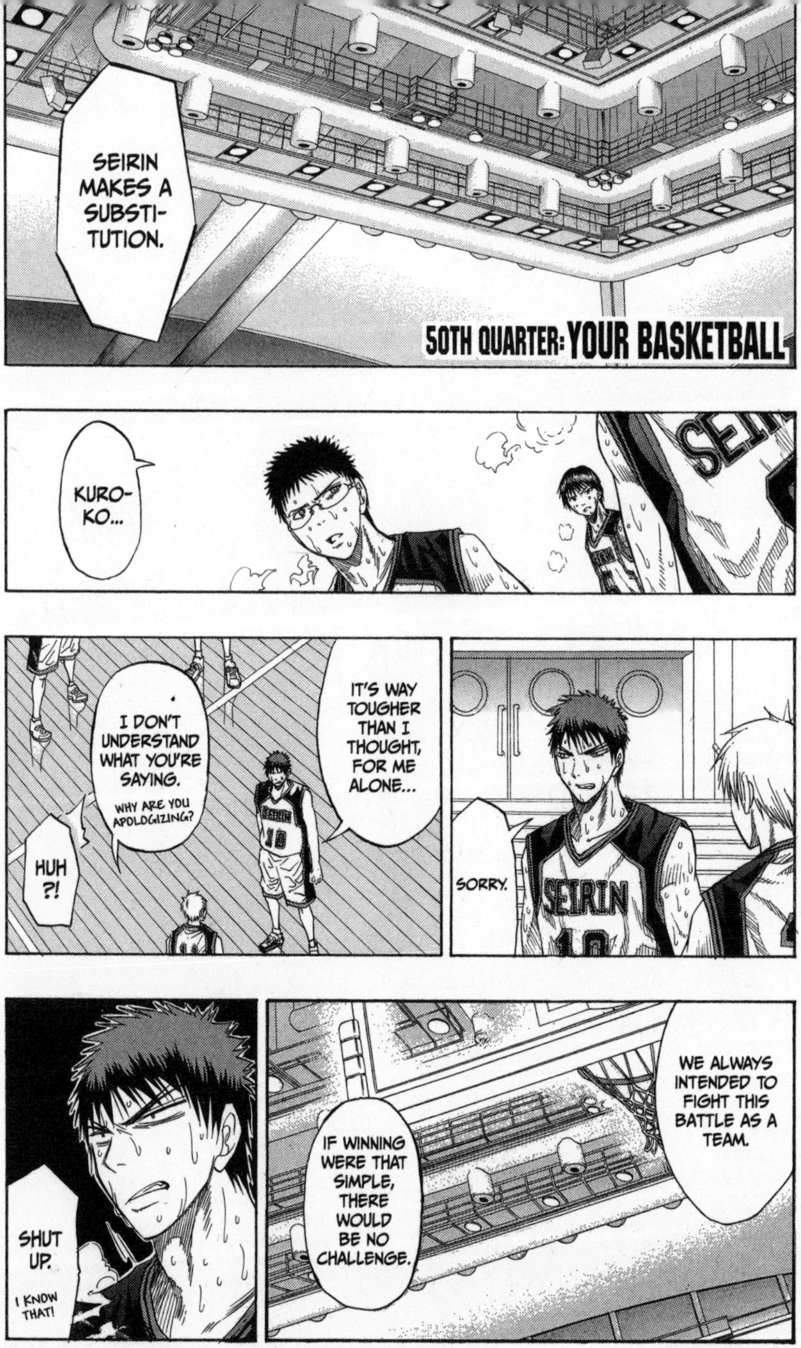
SEIRIN MAKES A SUBSTITUTION.
50TH QUARTER: YOUR BASKETBALL
KURO-KO...
SEIRIN
SORRY.
IT'S WAY TOUGHER THAN I THOUGHT, FOR ME ALONE...
I DON'T UNDERSTAND WHAT YOU'RE SAYING.
WHY ARE YOU APOLOGIZING?
HUH ?!
WE ALWAYS INTENDED TO FIGHT THIS BATTLE AS A TEAM.
IF WINNING WERE THAT SIMPLE, THERE WOULD BE NO CHALLENGE.
SHUT UP.
I KNOW THAT!

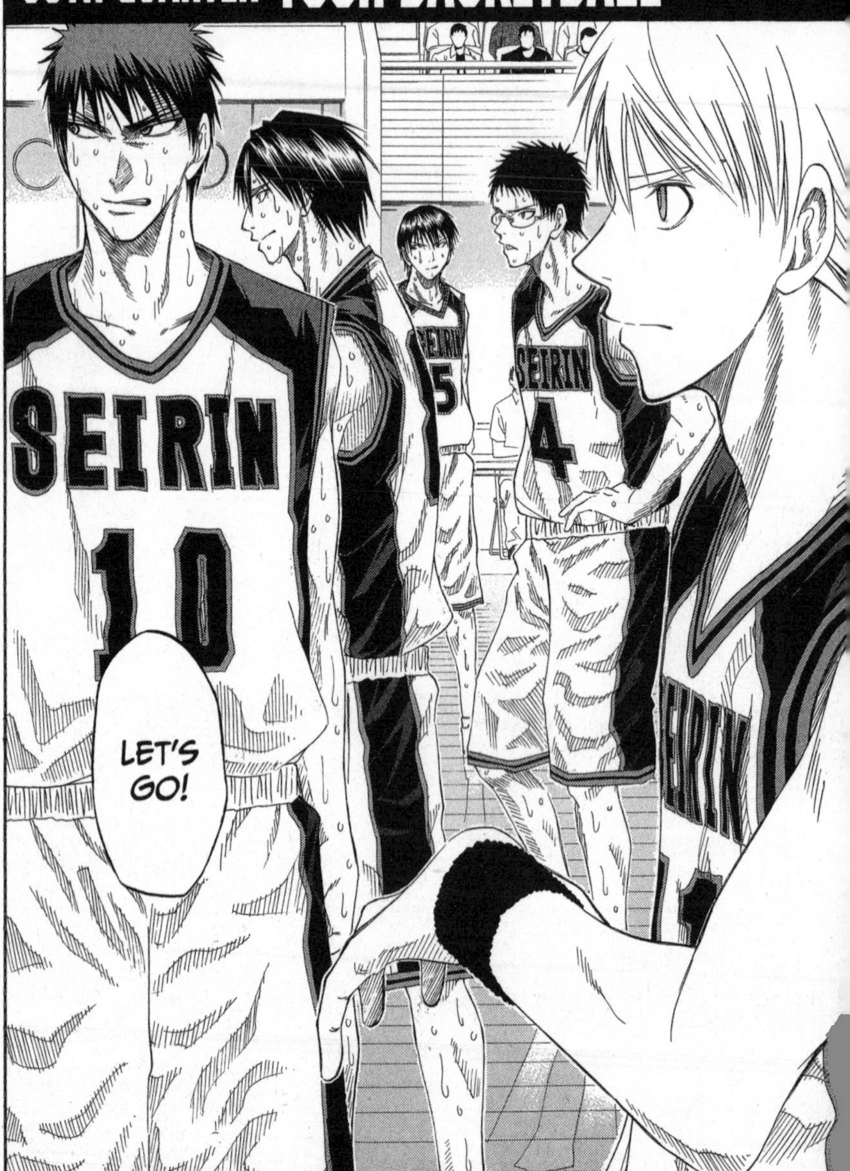
LET'S GO!

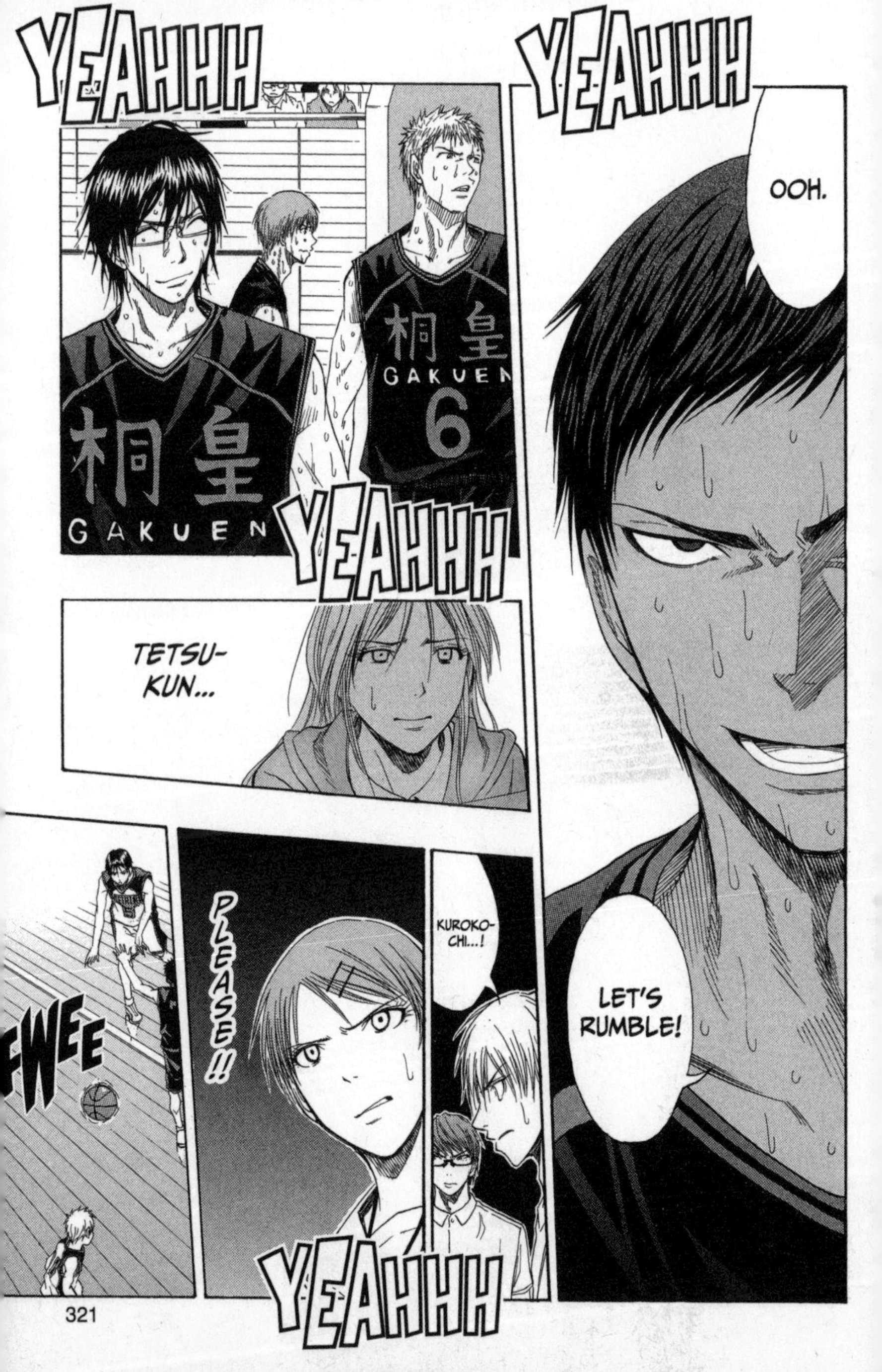
YEAHHH
OOH.
LET'S RUMBLE!
YEAHHH
YEAHHH
TETSU-KUN...
KUROKO-CHI...!
PLEASE!!
FWEE
YEAHHH

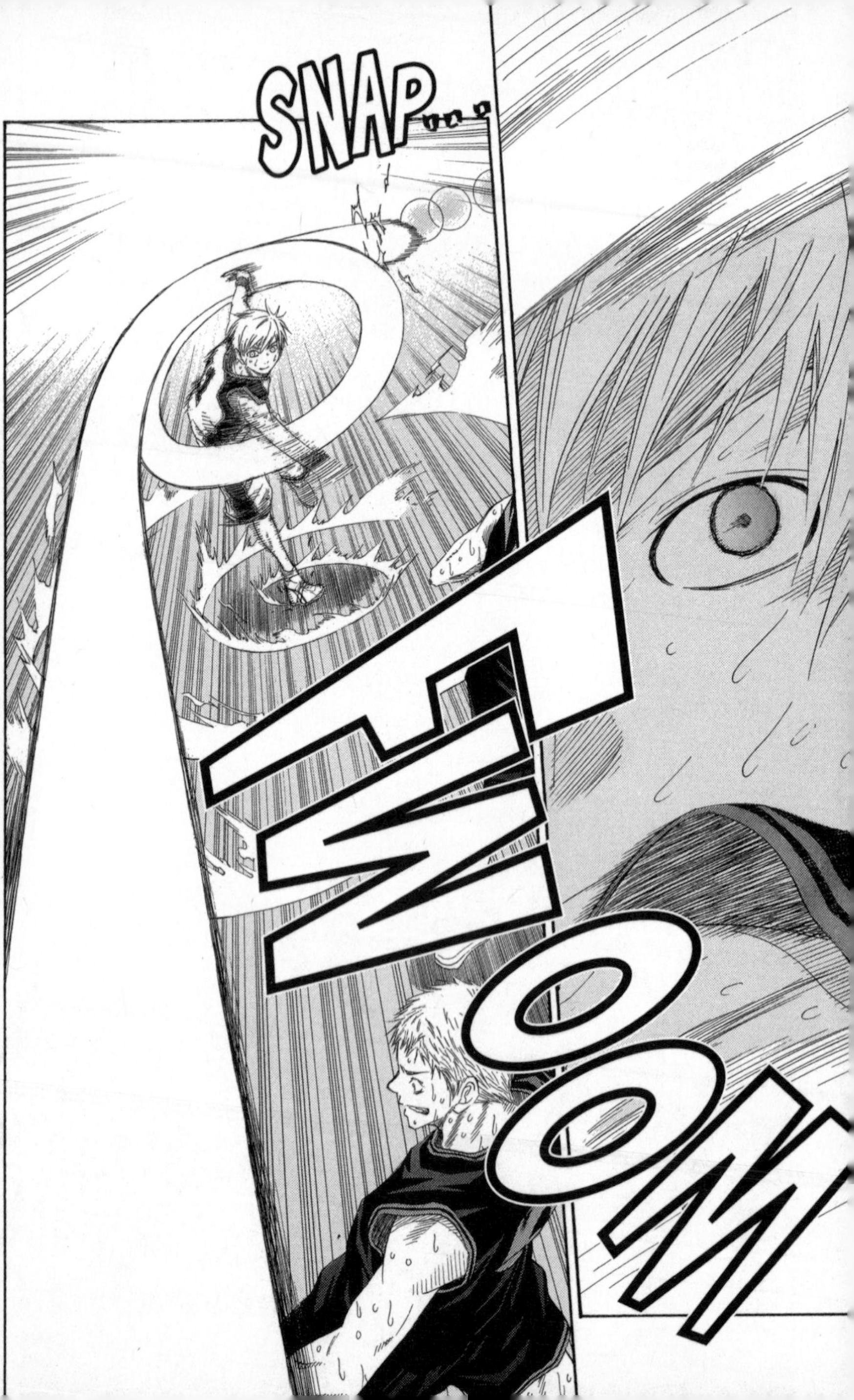
SNAP
FWOOM

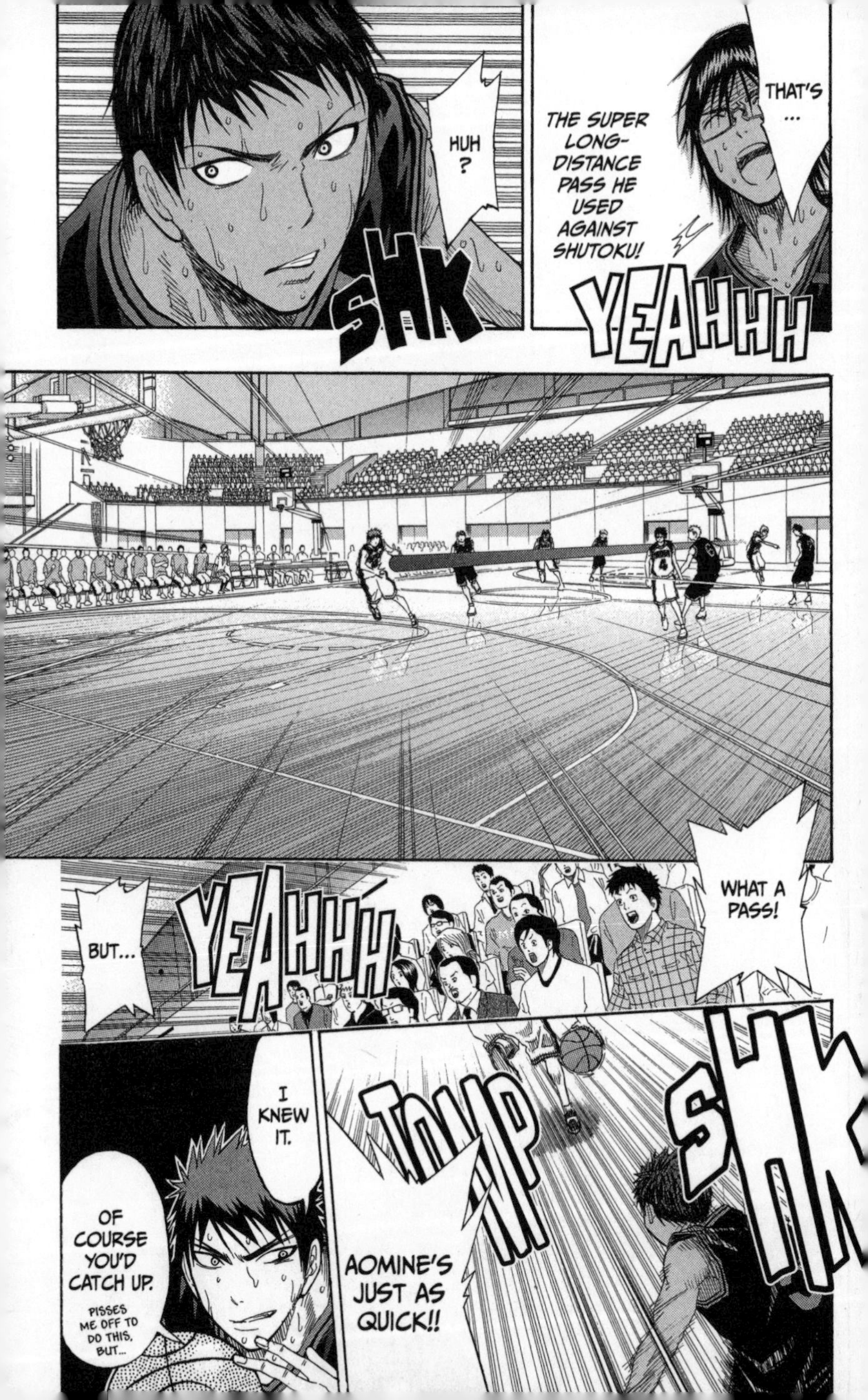
THAT'S ...
THE SUPER LONG-DISTANCE PASS HE USED AGAINST SHUTOKU!
YEAHHH
HUH?
SHK
WHAT A PASS!
YEAHHH
BUT...
SHK
TMP
AOMINE'S JUST AS QUICK!!
I KNEW IT.
OF COURSE YOU'D CATCH UP.
PISSES ME OFF TO DO THIS, BUT...

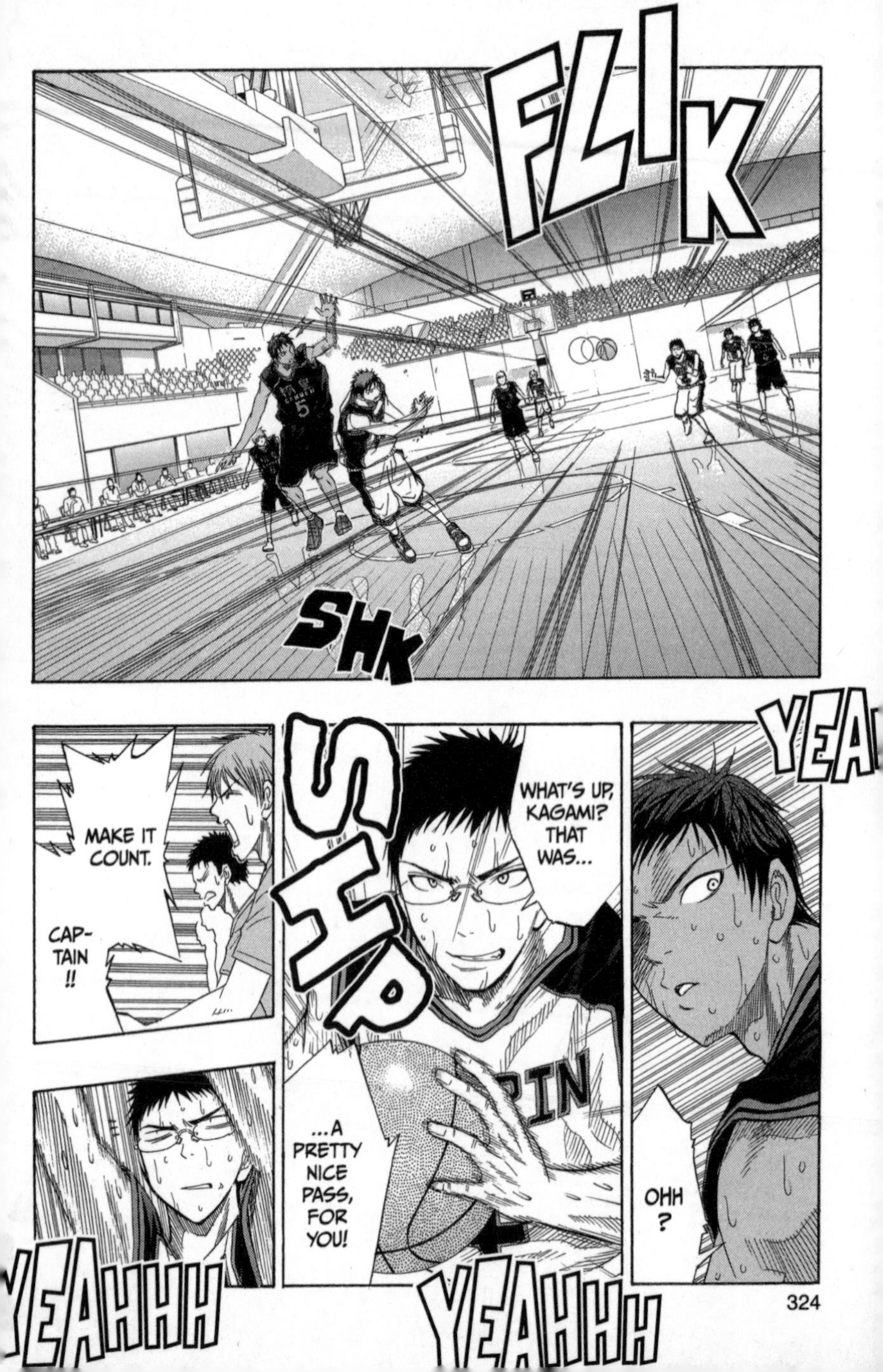
FLIK
SHK
YEA
OHH ?
SHP
WHAT'S UP, KAGAMI? THAT WAS...
...A PRETTY NICE PASS, FOR YOU!
MAKE IT COUNT.
CAP-TAIN !!
YEAHHH
YEAHHH

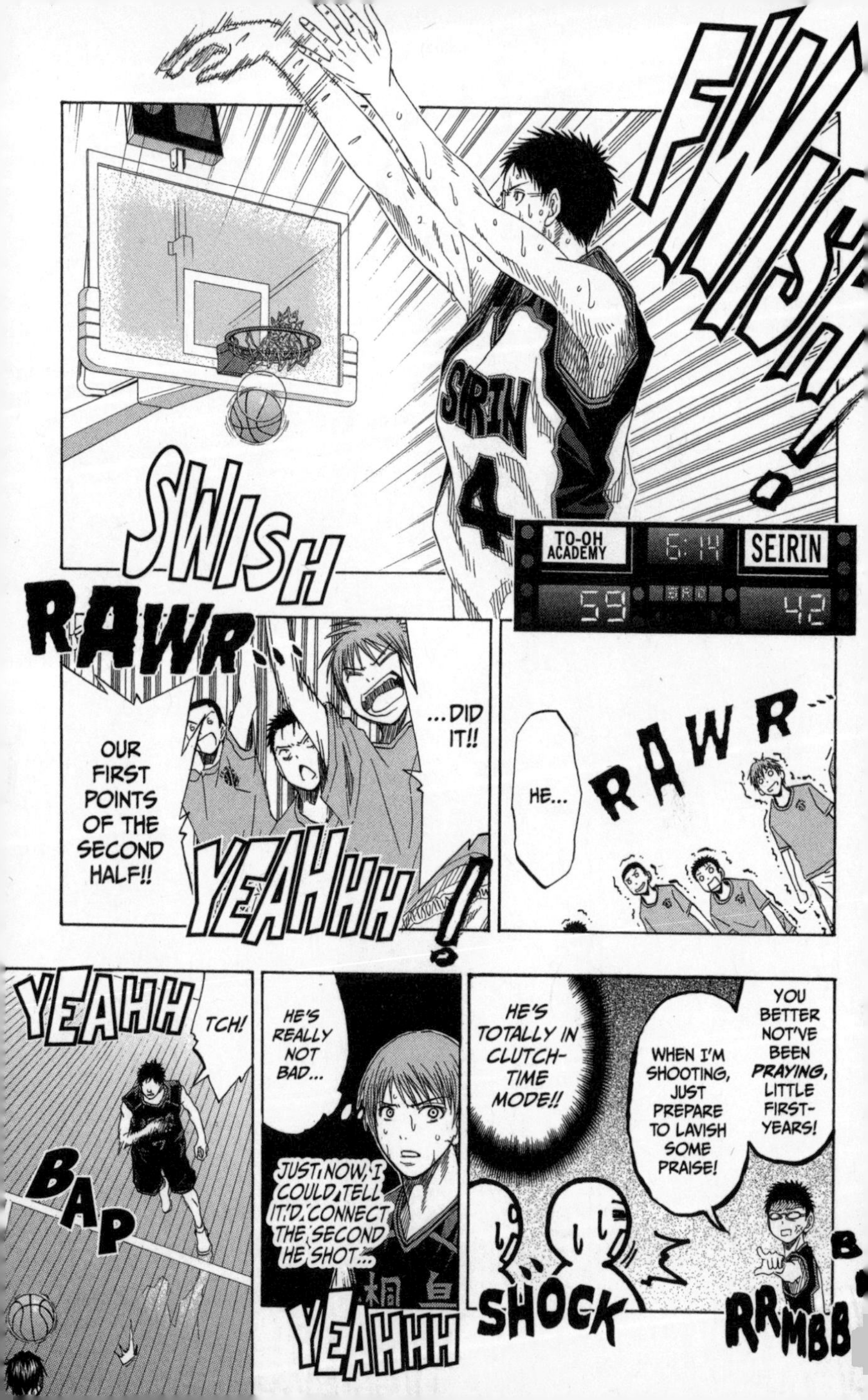
SWISH
TO-OH ACADEMY
6:14
SEIRIN
59
42
RAWR
HE...
RAWR
...DID IT!!
OUR FIRST POINTS OF THE SECOND HALF!!
YEAHHH!
YOU BETTER NOT'VE BEEN *PRAYING*, LITTLE FIRST-YEARS!
WHEN I'M SHOOTING, JUST PREPARE TO LAVISH SOME PRAISE!
HE'S TOTALLY IN CLUTCH-TIME MODE!!
SHOCK
RRMBB
HE'S REALLY NOT BAD...
JUST NOW, I COULD TELL IT'D CONNECT THE SECOND HE SHOT...
YEAHHH
YEAHH
TCH!
BAP

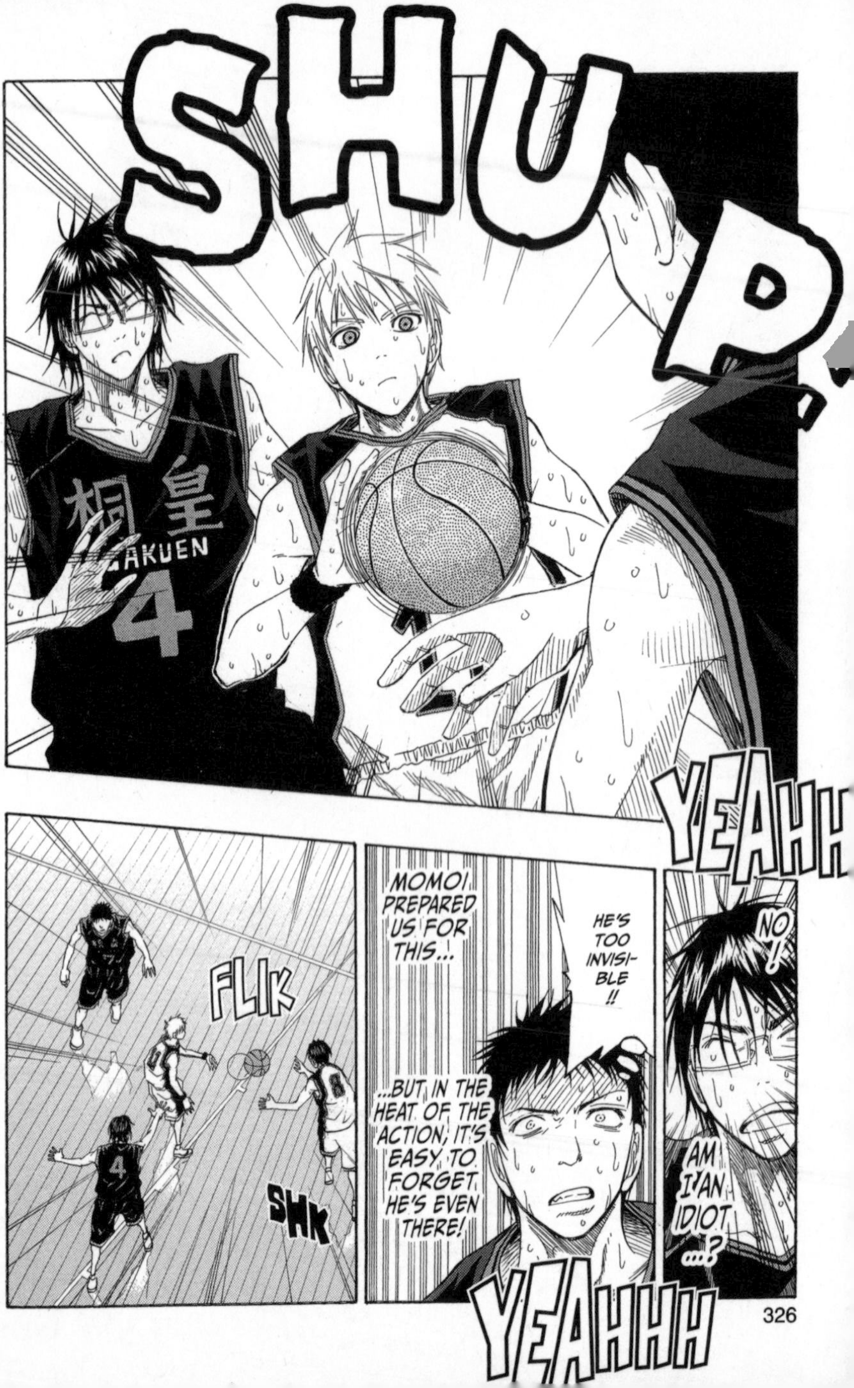

SHUP
桐皇
GAKUEN
YEAHH
NO!
AM I AN IDIOT...?
HE'S TOO INVISIBLE!!
MOMOI PREPARED US FOR THIS...
...BUT IN THE HEAT OF THE ACTION, IT'S EASY TO FORGET HE'S EVEN THERE!
YEAHHH
FLIK
SHK

YEAHHH

YEAHHH

TO-OH ACADEMY	6:11	SEIRIN
59	3RD	48

YEAHHH

SMACK

NICE!

WHOA, TWO IN A ROW!!

IT'S A WHOLE NEW GAME WITH KUROKO IN THERE!!

YEAHHH

YOU HAVEN'T CHANGED SINCE MIDDLE SCHOOL.

NOT ONE BIT...

SAME AS EVER, TETSU...

...WHEN TETSU'S INVOLVED.

IT REALLY IS DIFFERENT.

桐皇
GAKUEN

YEAHHH

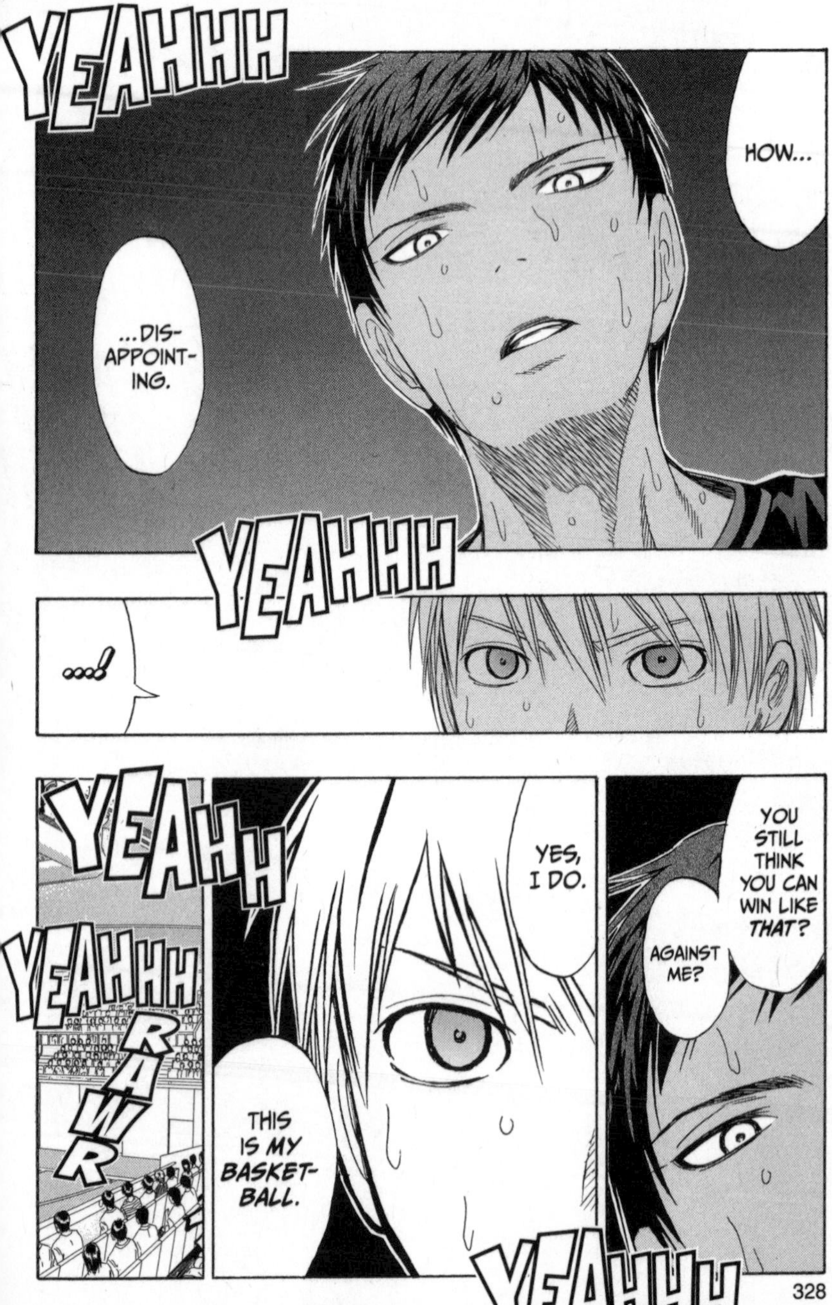
YEAHHH
HOW...
...DIS-APPOINTING.
YEAHHH
...!
YOU STILL THINK YOU CAN WIN LIKE THAT?
AGAINST ME?
YES, I DO.
THIS IS MY BASKETBALL.
YEAHH
YEAHHH
RAWR
YEAHHH

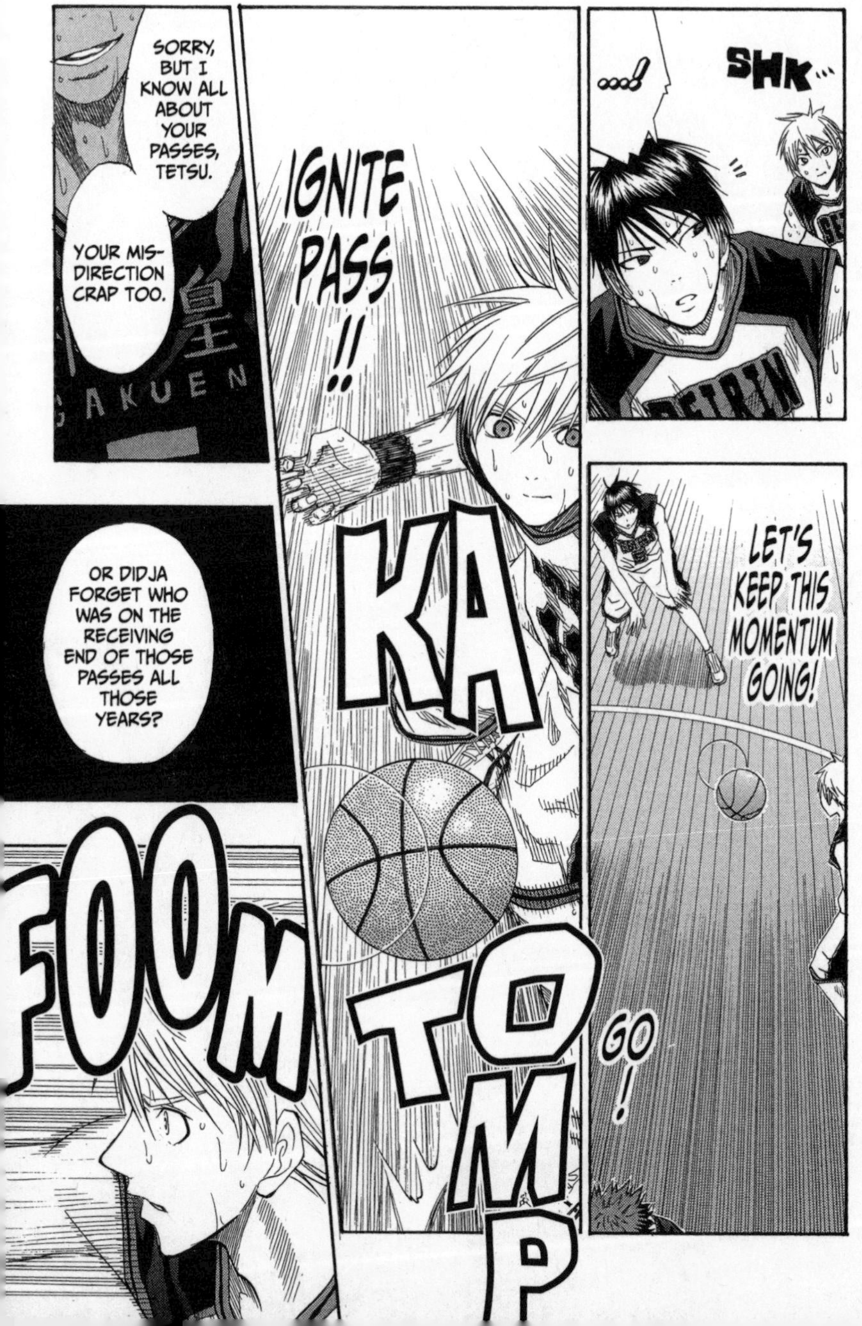
SHK...
...!
LET'S KEEP THIS MOMENTUM GOING!
GO!
IGNITE PASS!!
KA
TOMP
SORRY, BUT I KNOW ALL ABOUT YOUR PASSES, TETSU.
YOUR MIS-DIRECTION CRAP TOO.
OR DIDJA FORGET WHO WAS ON THE RECEIVING END OF THOSE PASSES ALL THOSE YEARS?
FOOM

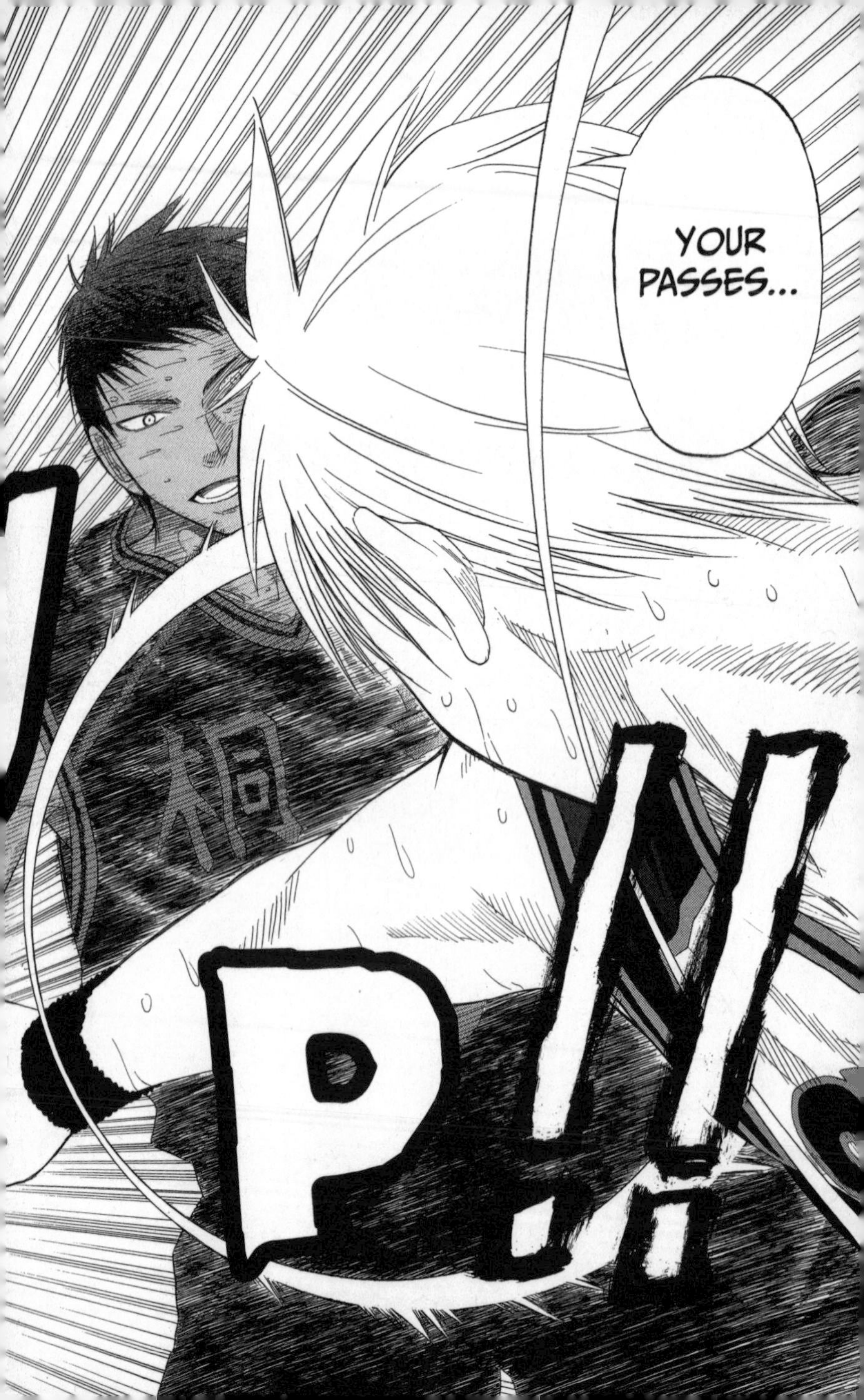
YOUR PASSES...
P!!

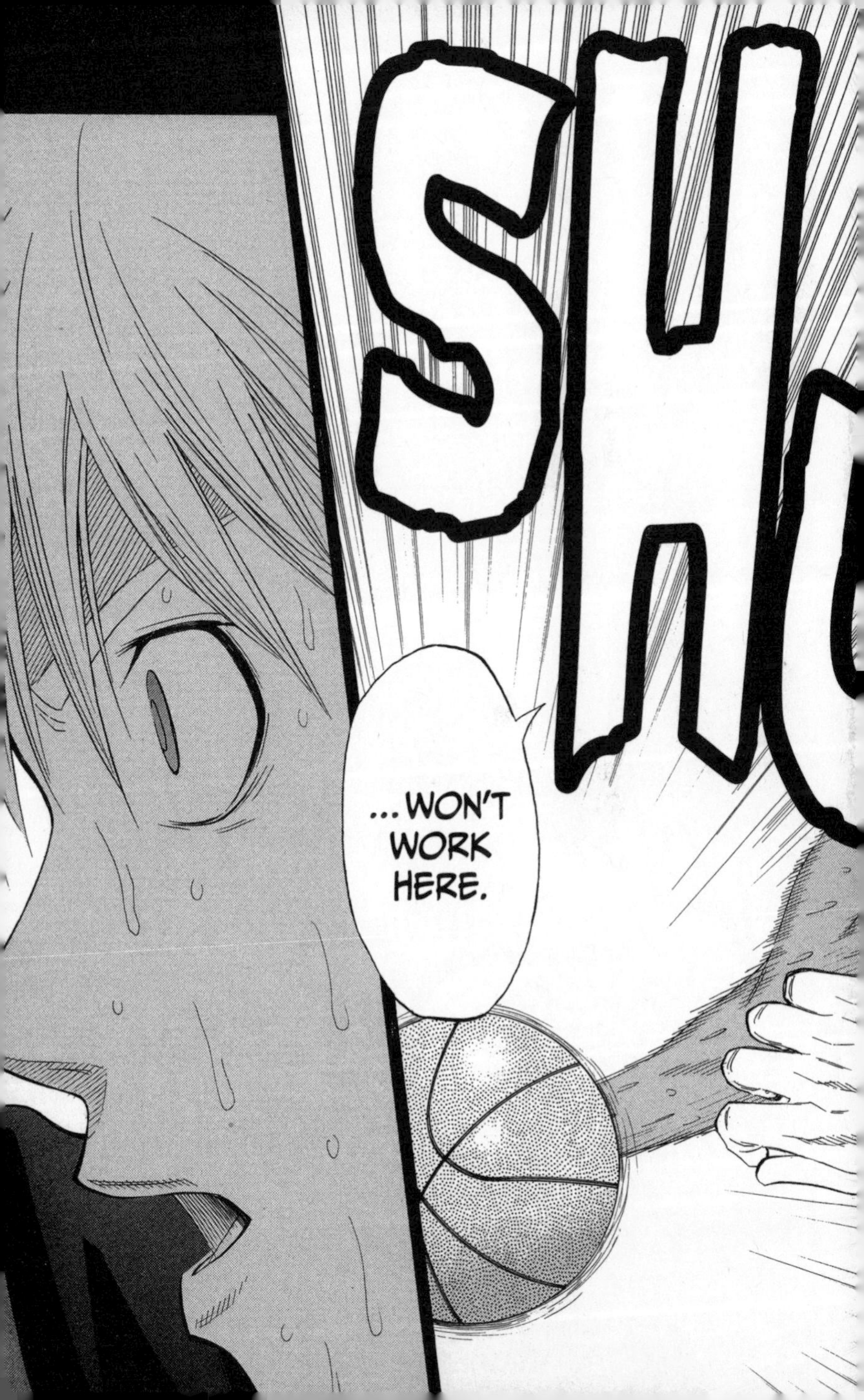
SH
...WON'T WORK HERE.

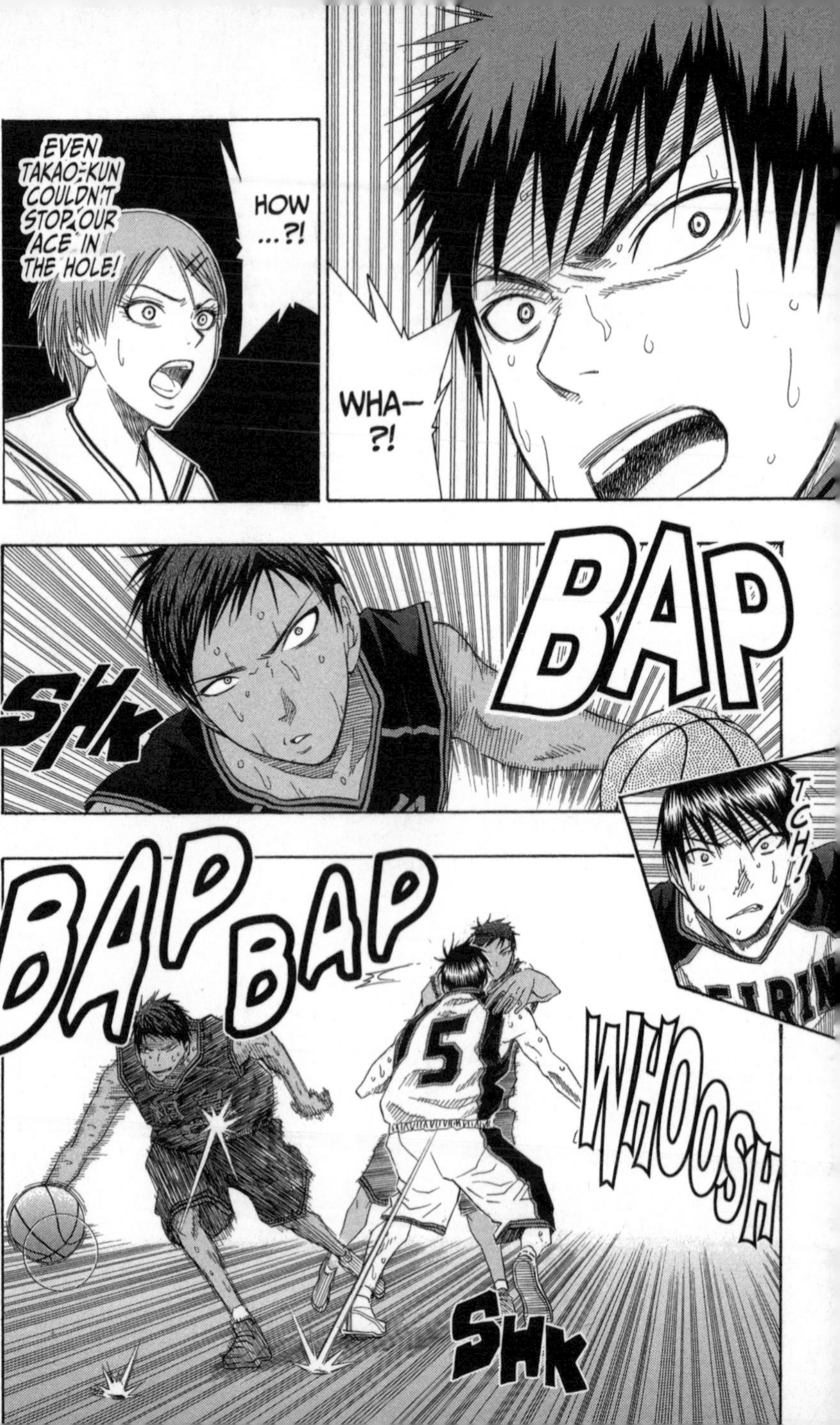
WHA—?!
HOW ...?!
EVEN TAKAO-KUN COULDN'T STOP OUR ACE IN THE HOLE!
BAP
SHK
TCH!
WHOOSH
BAP BAP
SHK

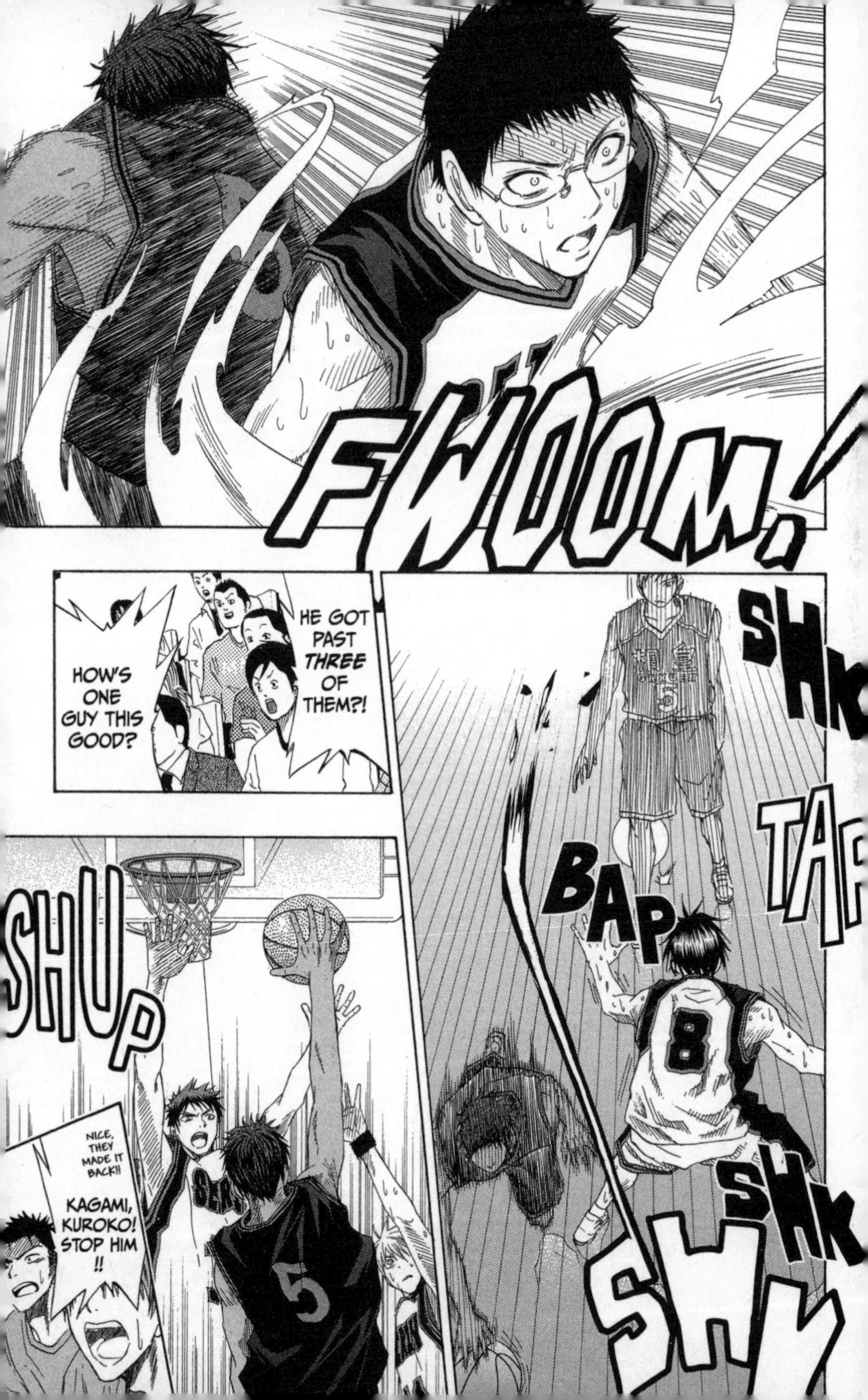
FWOOM!
SHK
TAP
BAP
SHK
SHK
HE GOT PAST THREE OF THEM?!
HOW'S ONE GUY THIS GOOD?
SHUP
NICE, THEY MADE IT BACK!!
KAGAMI, KUROKO! STOP HIM!!

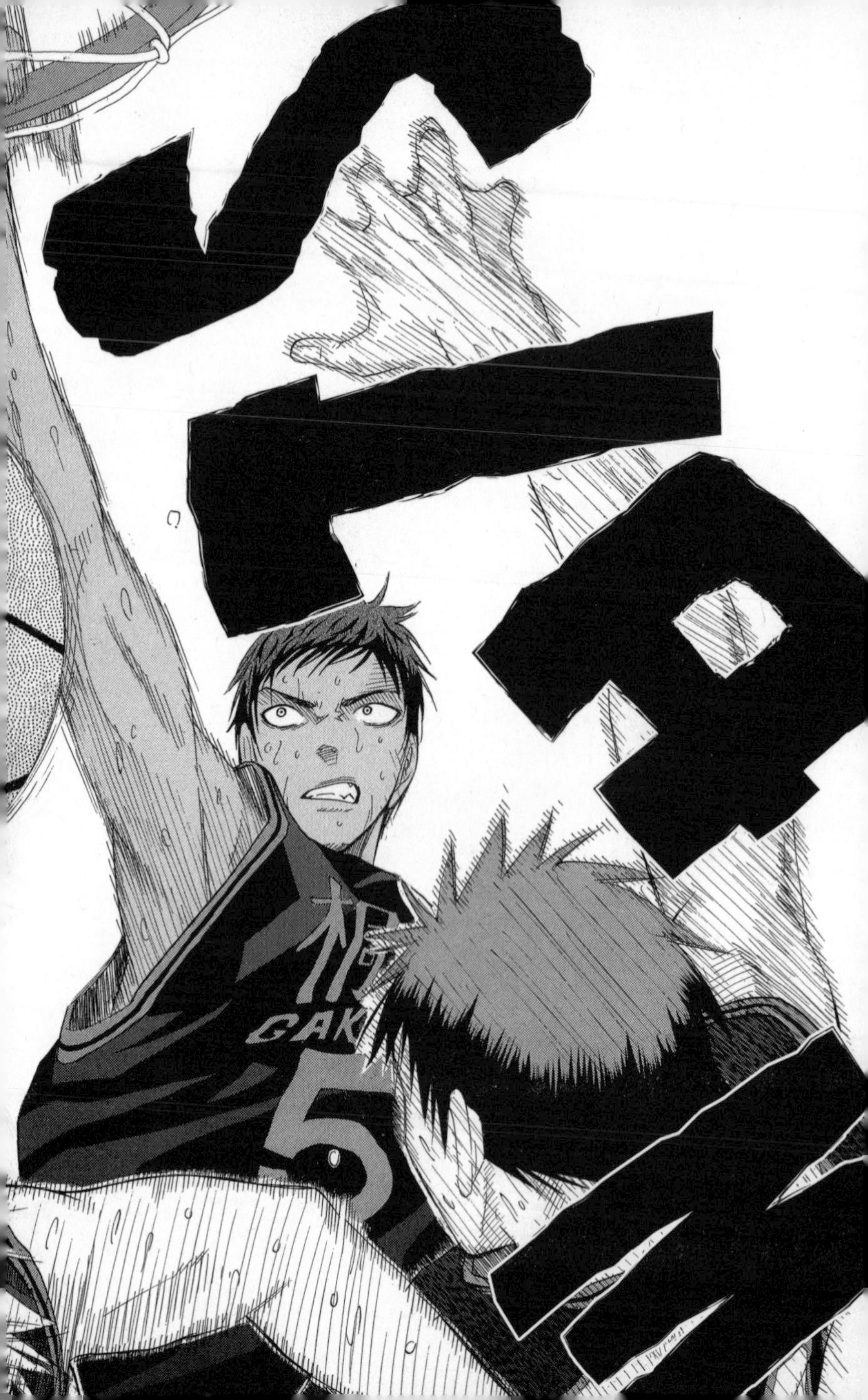

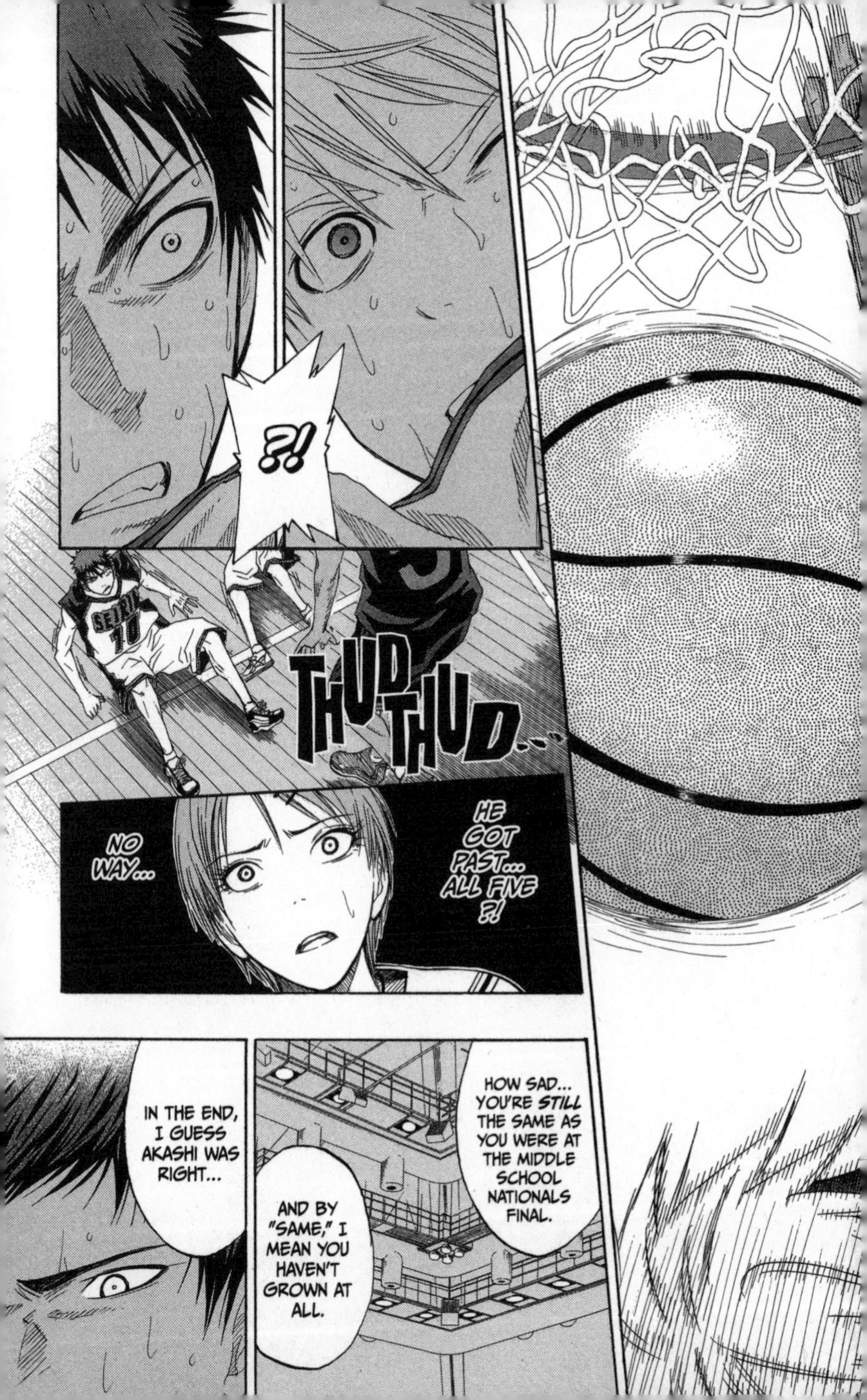
?!
THUD THUD...
HE GOT PAST... ALL FIVE ?!
NO WAY...
HOW SAD... YOU'RE *STILL* THE SAME AS YOU WERE AT THE MIDDLE SCHOOL NATIONALS FINAL.
AND BY "SAME," I MEAN YOU HAVEN'T GROWN AT ALL.
IN THE END, I GUESS AKASHI WAS RIGHT...

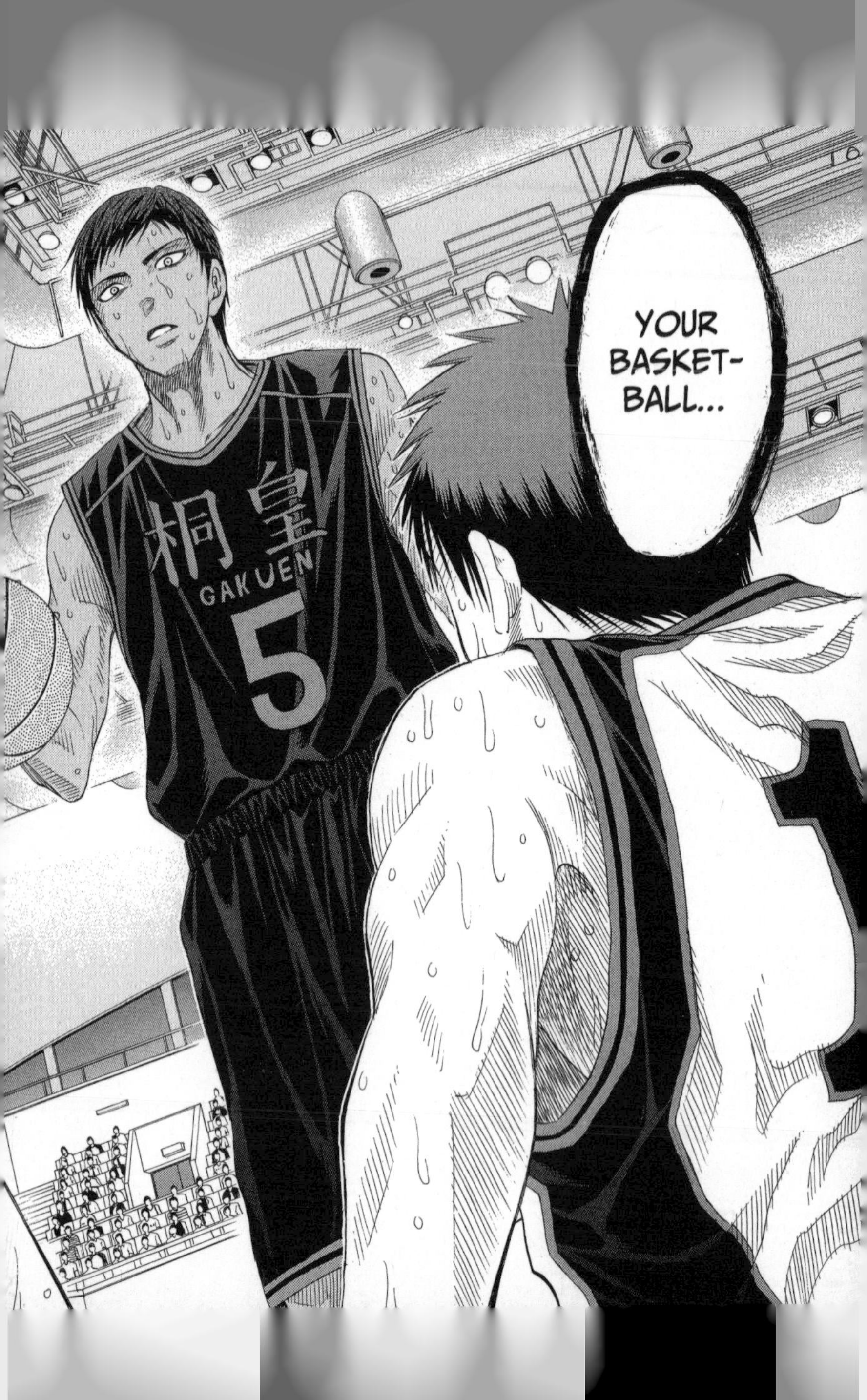
YOUR BASKET-BALL...

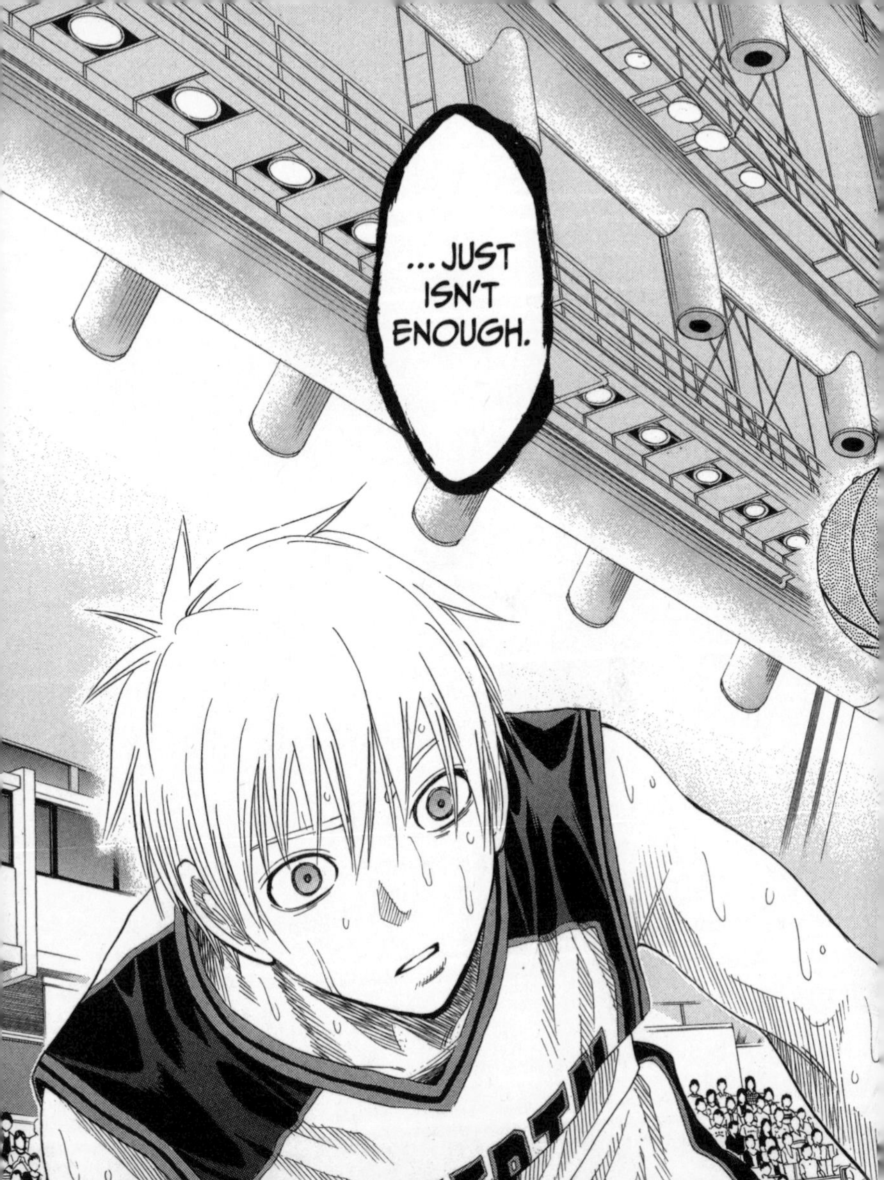
...JUST ISN'T ENOUGH.

KUROKO'S BASKETBALL BLOOPERS

TAKE 1

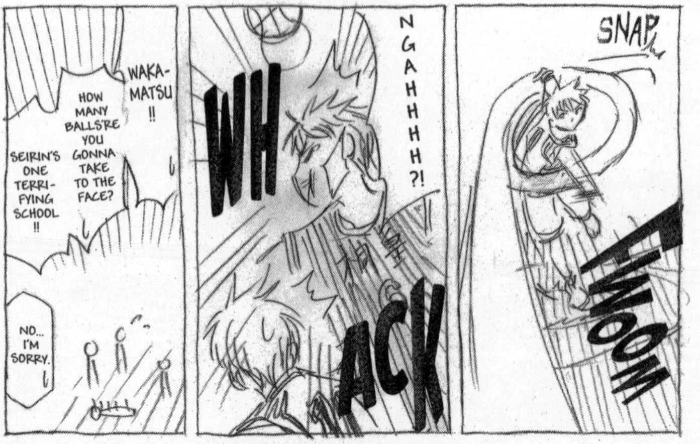
SNAP
FWOOM
NGAHHHHH?!
WH
ACK
WAKA-MATSU!!
HOW MANY BALLS'RE YOU GONNA TAKE TO THE FACE?
SEIRIN'S ONE TERRI-FYING SCHOOL!!
NO... I'M SORRY.

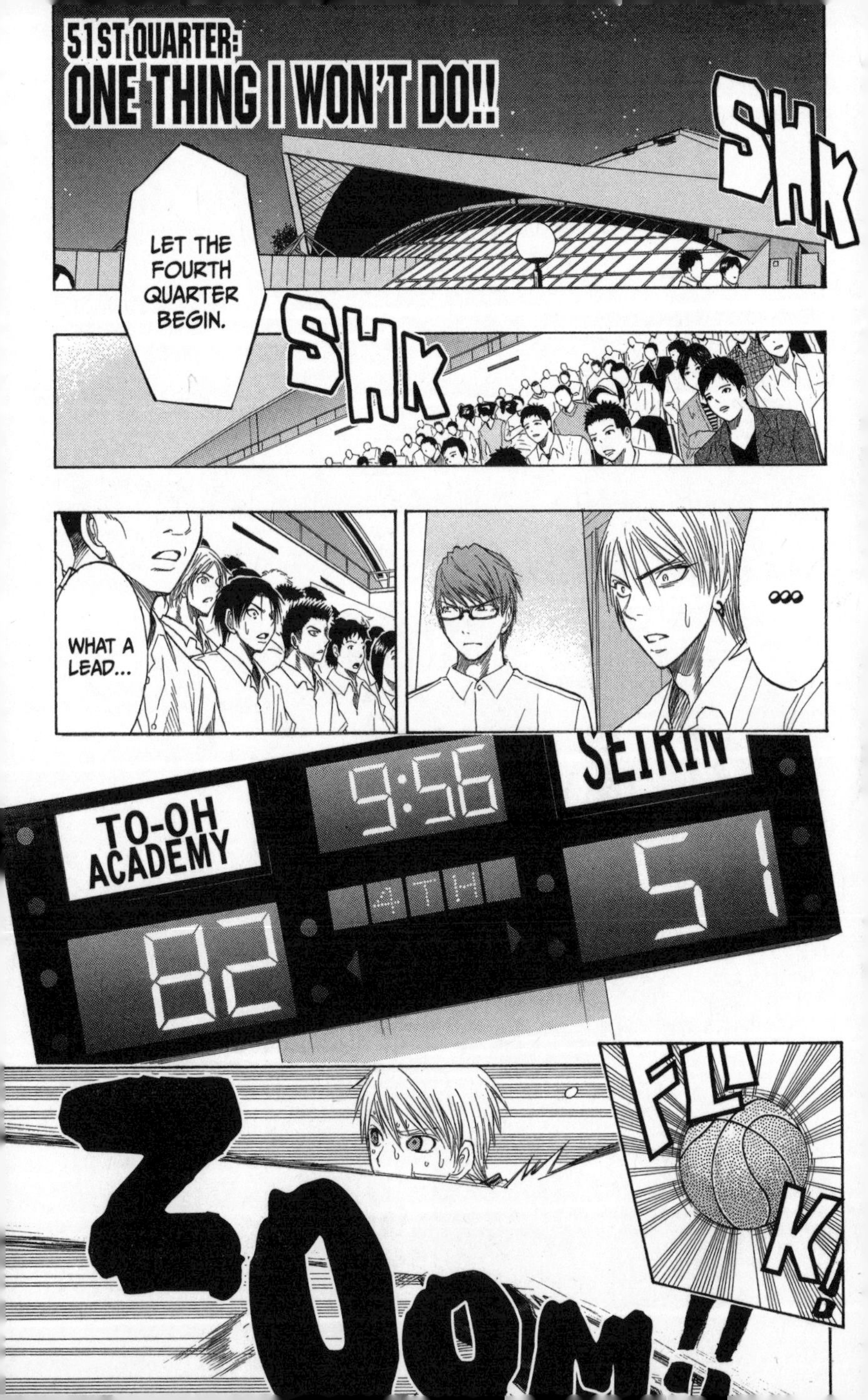
51ST QUARTER:
ONE THING I WON'T DO!!
SHK
LET THE FOURTH QUARTER BEGIN.
SHK
...
WHAT A LEAD...
SEIRIN
51
9:56
4TH
TO-OH ACADEMY
82
FLIK!
ZOOM!!

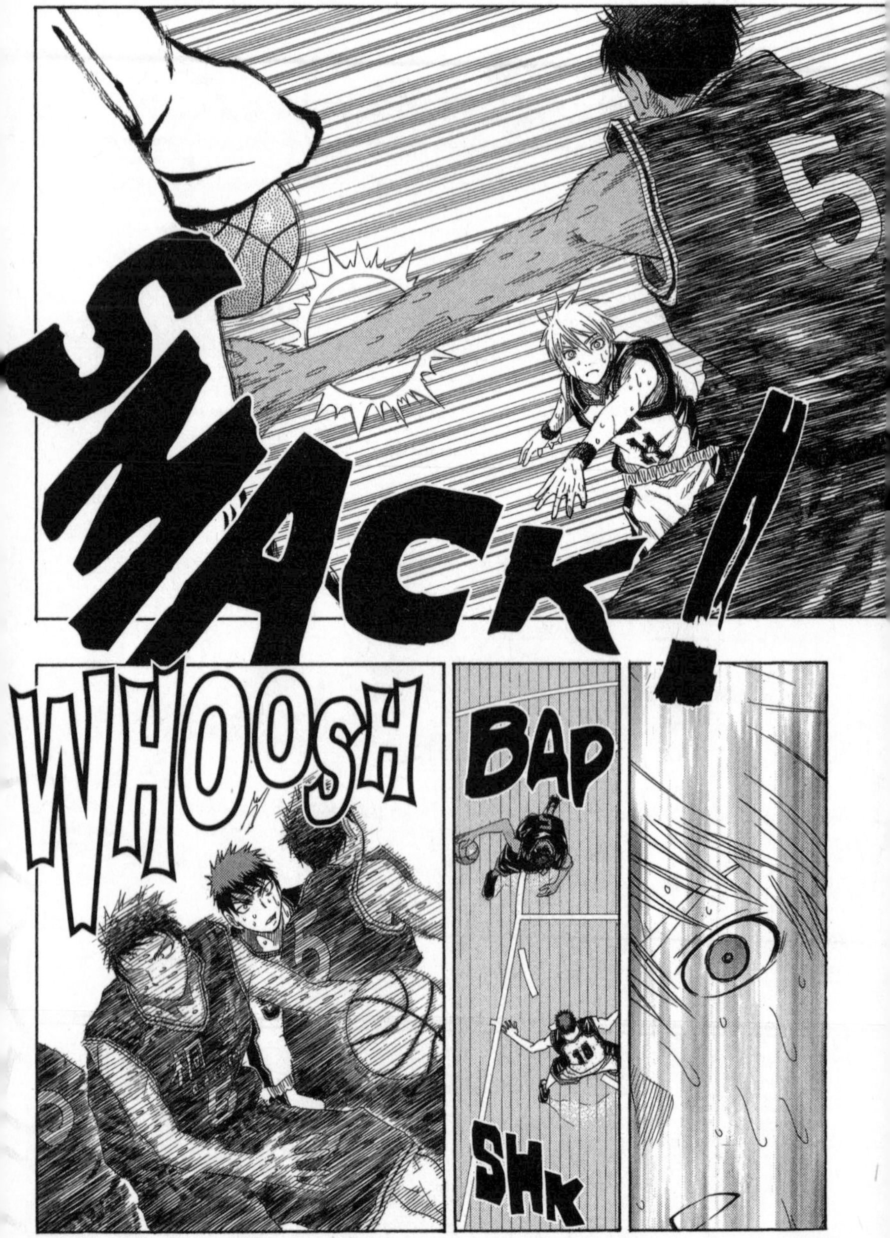
SMACK!!
BAP
SHK
WHOOSH

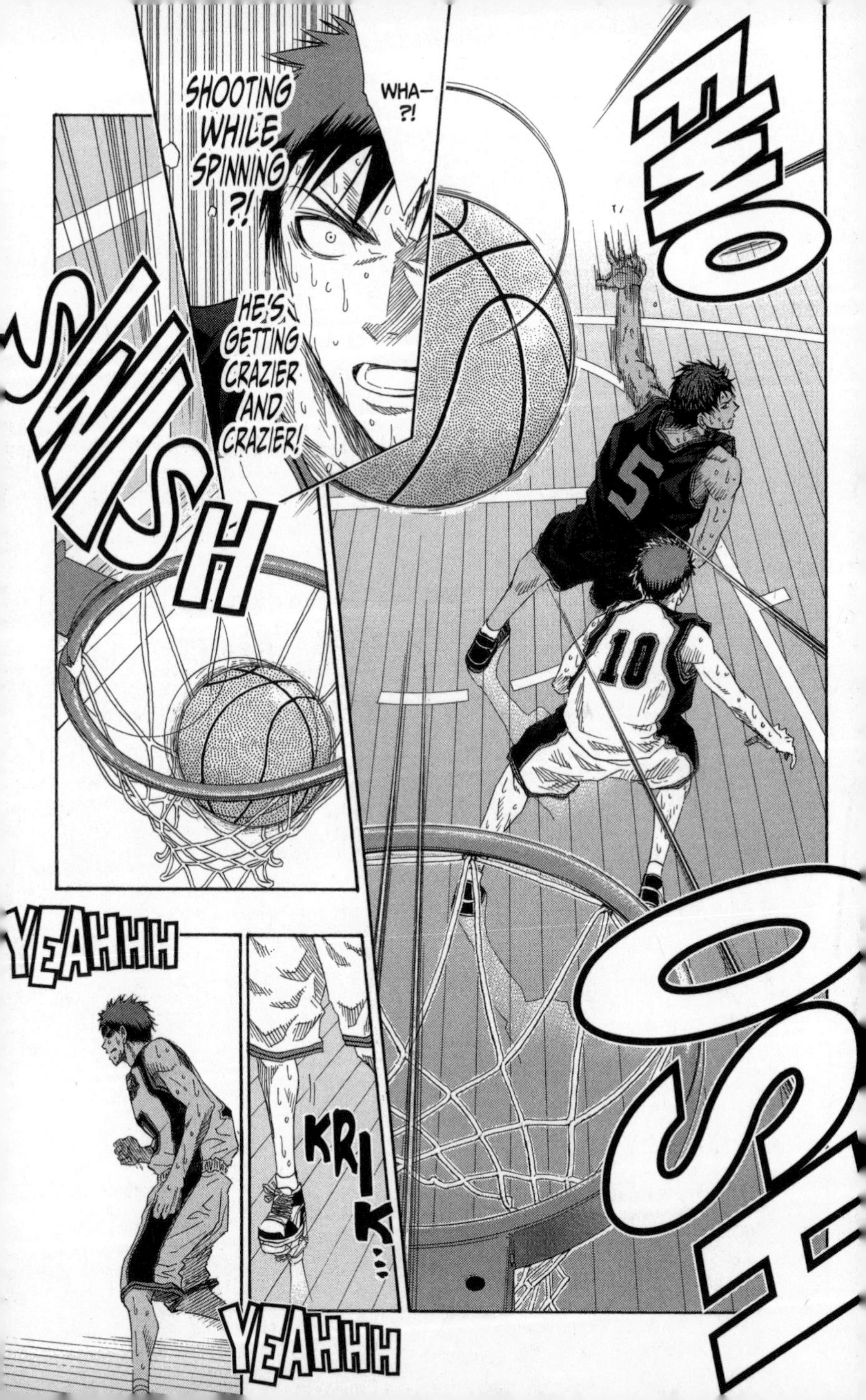
FWOOSH!
WHA—?!
SHOOTING WHILE SPINNING?!
HE'S GETTING CRAZIER AND CRAZIER!
SWISH
KRIK...
YEAHHH
YEAHHH

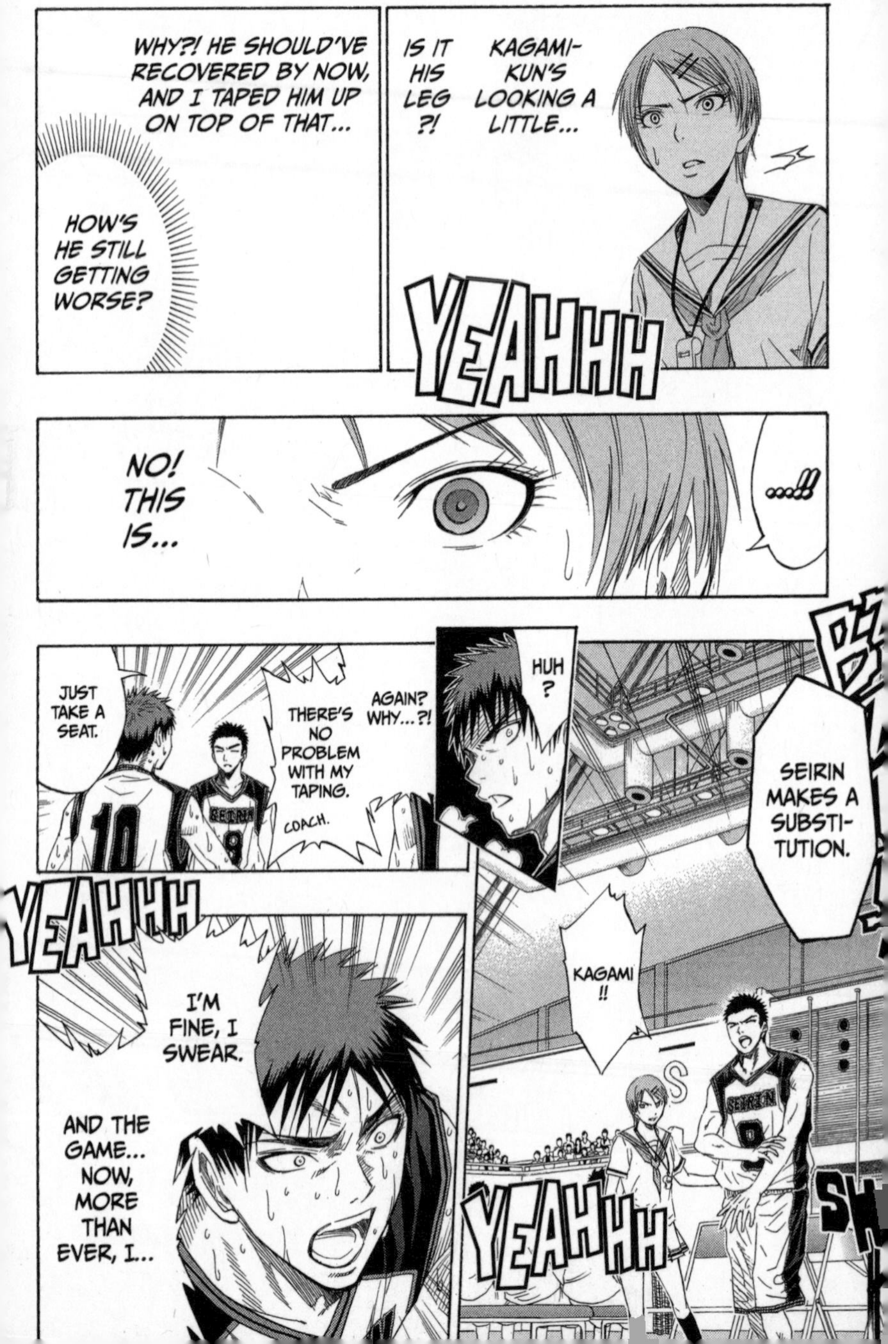
KAGAMI-KUN'S LOOKING A LITTLE...
IS IT HIS LEG ?!
YEAHHH
WHY?! HE SHOULD'VE RECOVERED BY NOW, AND I TAPED HIM UP ON TOP OF THAT...
HOW'S HE STILL GETTING WORSE?
...!!
NO! THIS IS...
SEIRIN MAKES A SUBSTITUTION.
KAGAMI !!
YEAHHH
HUH ?
AGAIN? WHY...?!
THERE'S NO PROBLEM WITH MY TAPING.
COACH.
JUST TAKE A SEAT.
YEAHHH
I'M FINE, I SWEAR.
AND THE GAME... NOW, MORE THAN EVER, I...

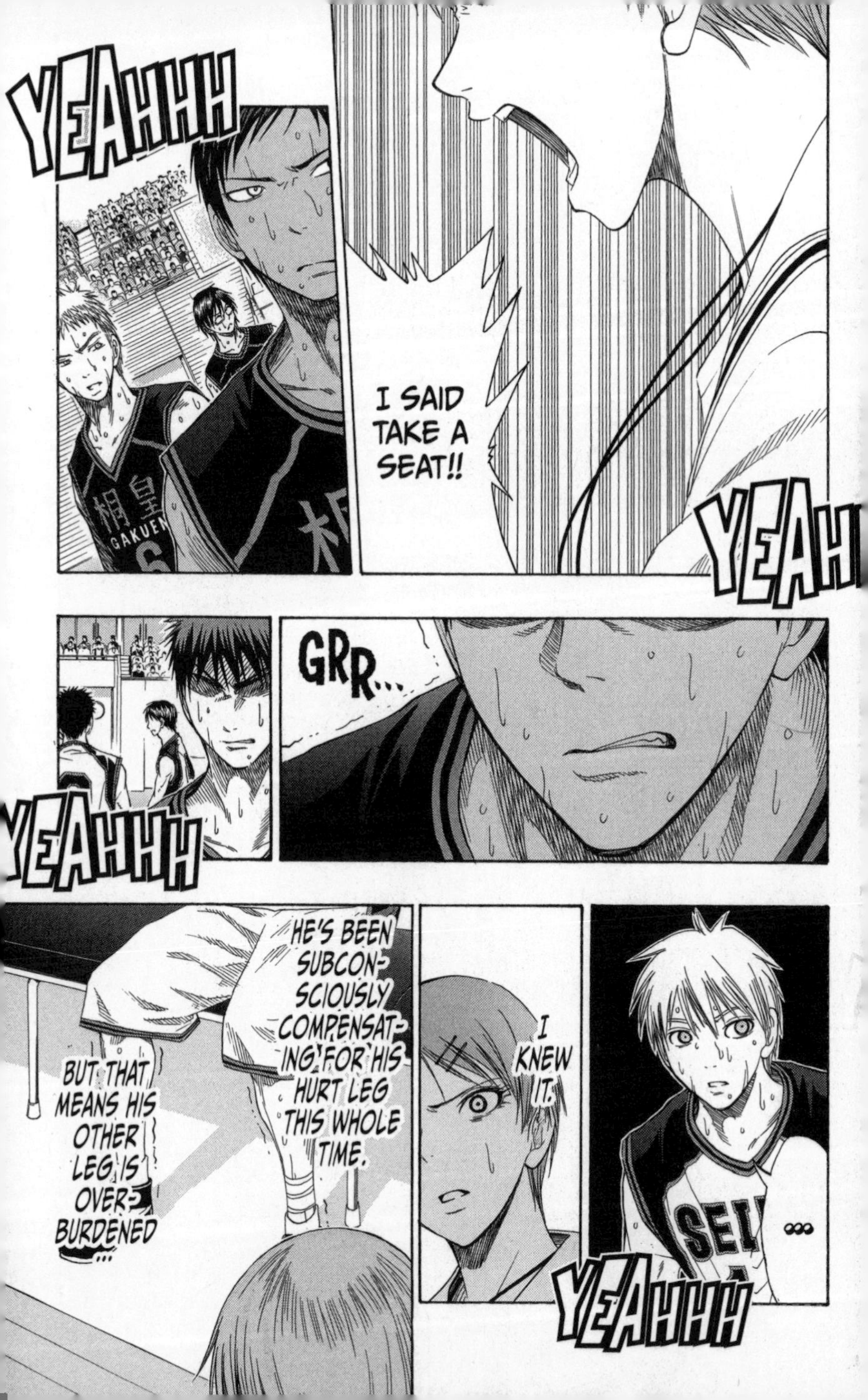
I SAID TAKE A SEAT!!
YEAH
YEAHHH
GRR...
YEAHHH
...
YEAHHH
I KNEW IT.
HE'S BEEN SUBCONSCIOUSLY COMPENSATING FOR HIS HURT LEG THIS WHOLE TIME.
BUT THAT MEANS HIS OTHER LEG IS OVERBURDENED...

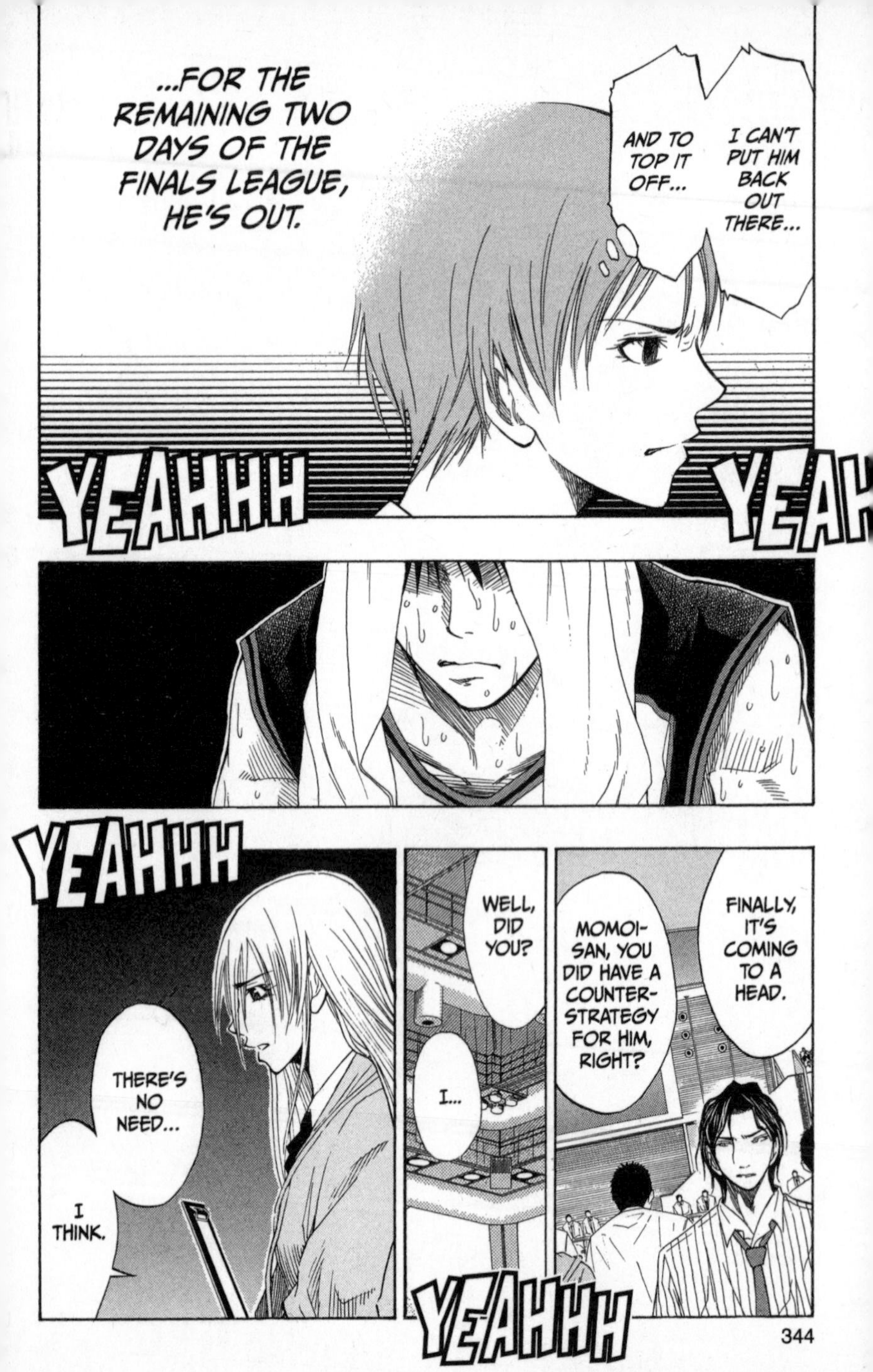
I CAN'T PUT HIM BACK OUT THERE...
AND TO TOP IT OFF...
...FOR THE REMAINING TWO DAYS OF THE FINALS LEAGUE, HE'S OUT.
YEAH
YEAHHH
YEAHHH
FINALLY, IT'S COMING TO A HEAD.
MOMOI-SAN, YOU DID HAVE A COUNTER-STRATEGY FOR HIM, RIGHT?
YEAHHH
WELL, DID YOU?
I...
THERE'S NO NEED...
I THINK.

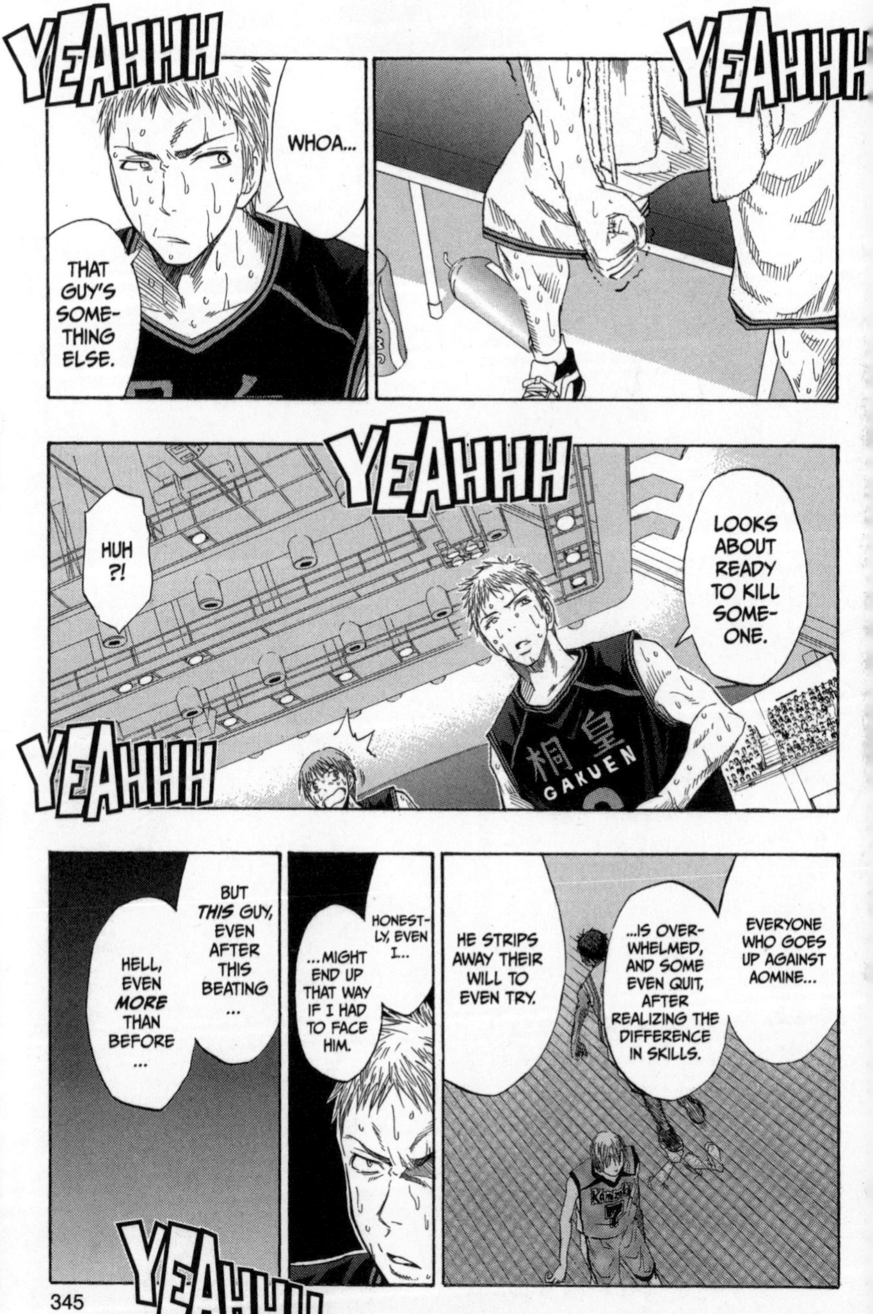
YEAHHH
YEAHHH
WHOA...
THAT GUY'S SOME-THING ELSE.
YEAHHH
LOOKS ABOUT READY TO KILL SOME-ONE.
HUH ?!
GAKUEN
YEAHHH
EVERYONE WHO GOES UP AGAINST AOMINE...
...IS OVER-WHELMED, AND SOME EVEN QUIT, AFTER REALIZING THE DIFFERENCE IN SKILLS.
HE STRIPS AWAY THEIR WILL TO EVEN TRY.
HONEST-LY, EVEN I...
...MIGHT END UP THAT WAY IF I HAD TO FACE HIM.
BUT *THIS* GUY, EVEN AFTER THIS BEATING...
HELL, EVEN *MORE* THAN BEFORE...
YEAHHH

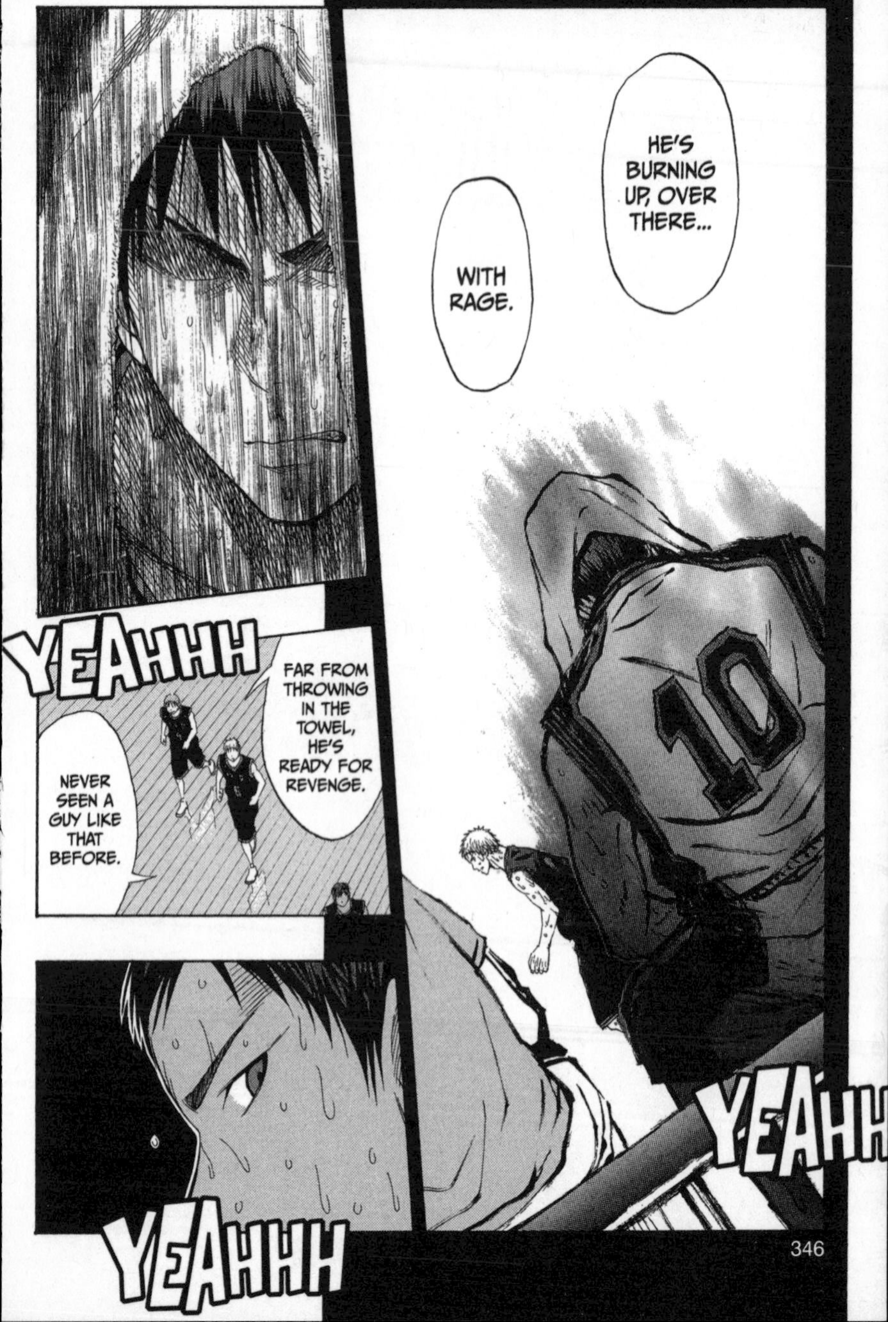

HE'S BURNING UP, OVER THERE...
WITH RAGE.
YEAHH
YEAHHH
FAR FROM THROWING IN THE TOWEL, HE'S READY FOR REVENGE.
NEVER SEEN A GUY LIKE THAT BEFORE.
YEAHHH

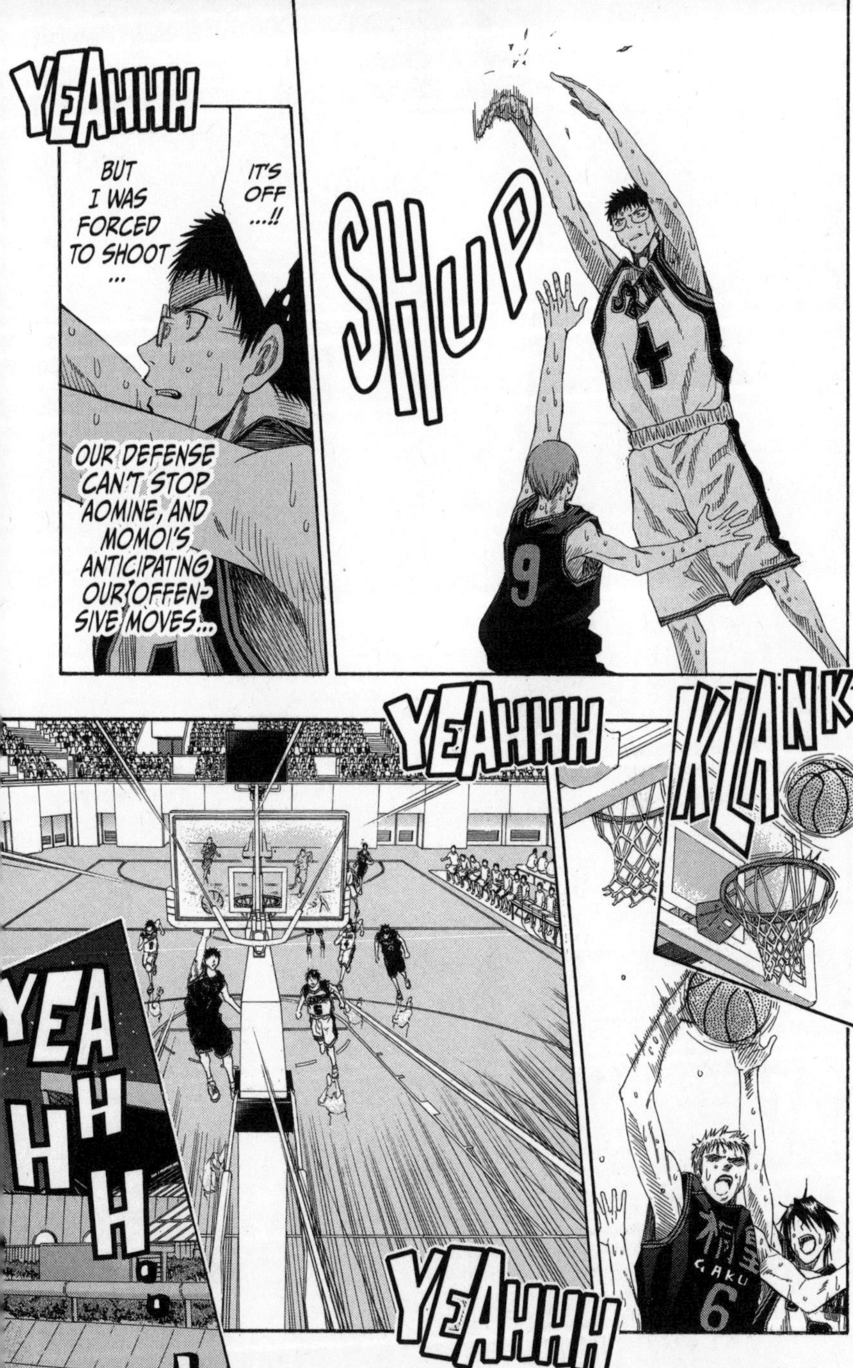
SHUP
YEAHHH
IT'S OFF ...!!
BUT I WAS FORCED TO SHOOT ...
OUR DEFENSE CAN'T STOP AOMINE, AND MOMOI'S ANTICIPATING OUR OFFEN-SIVE MOVES...
KLANK
YEAHHH
YEAHHH
YEAHHHHH

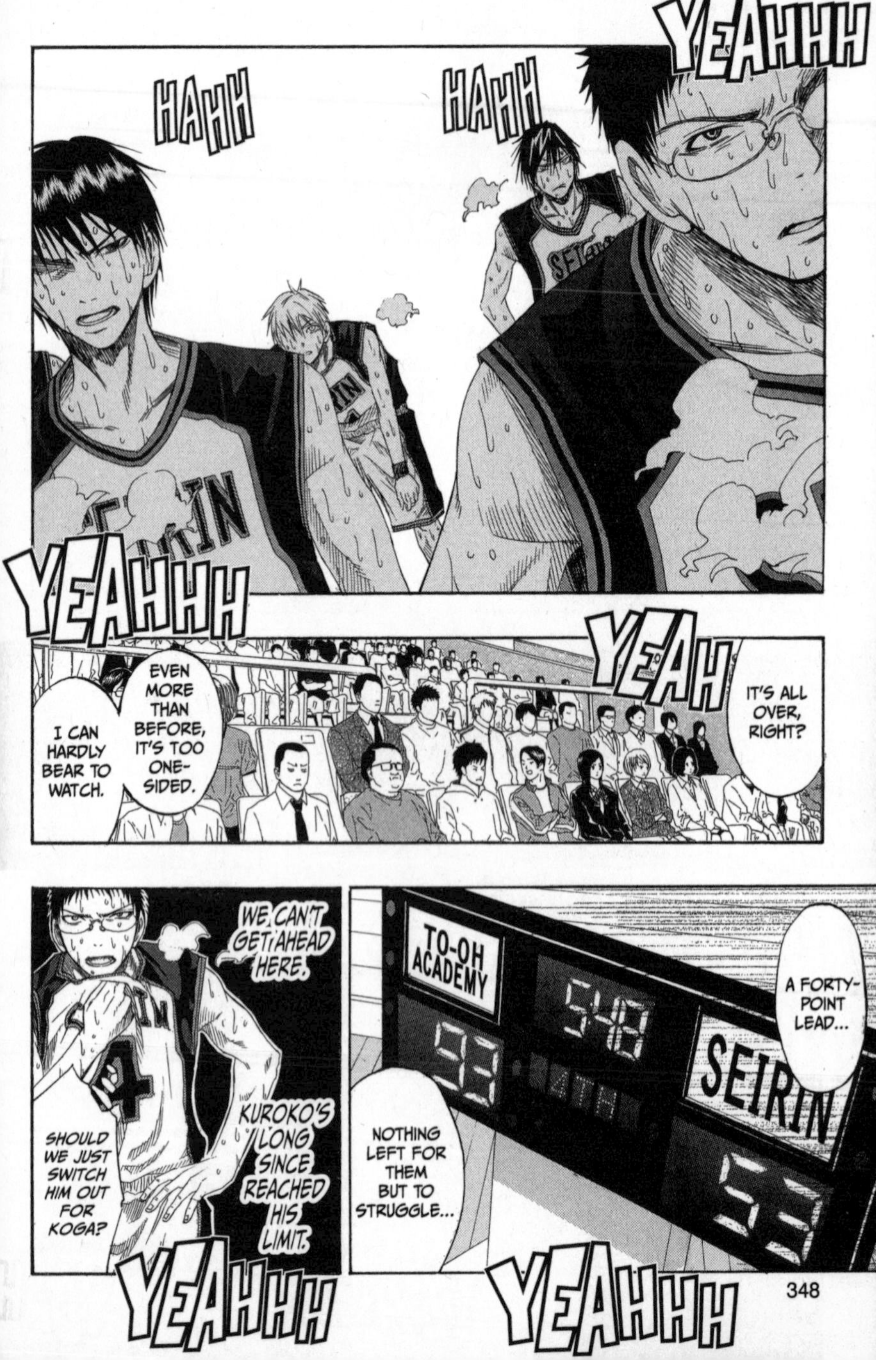
YEAHHH
HAHH
HAHH
YEAHHH
YEAH
IT'S ALL OVER, RIGHT?
EVEN MORE THAN BEFORE, IT'S TOO ONE-SIDED.
I CAN HARDLY BEAR TO WATCH.
TO-OH ACADEMY
SEIRIN
A FORTY-POINT LEAD...
NOTHING LEFT FOR THEM BUT TO STRUGGLE...
YEAHHH
WE CAN'T GET AHEAD HERE.
KUROKO'S LONG SINCE REACHED HIS LIMIT.
SHOULD WE JUST SWITCH HIM OUT FOR KOGA?
YEAHHH

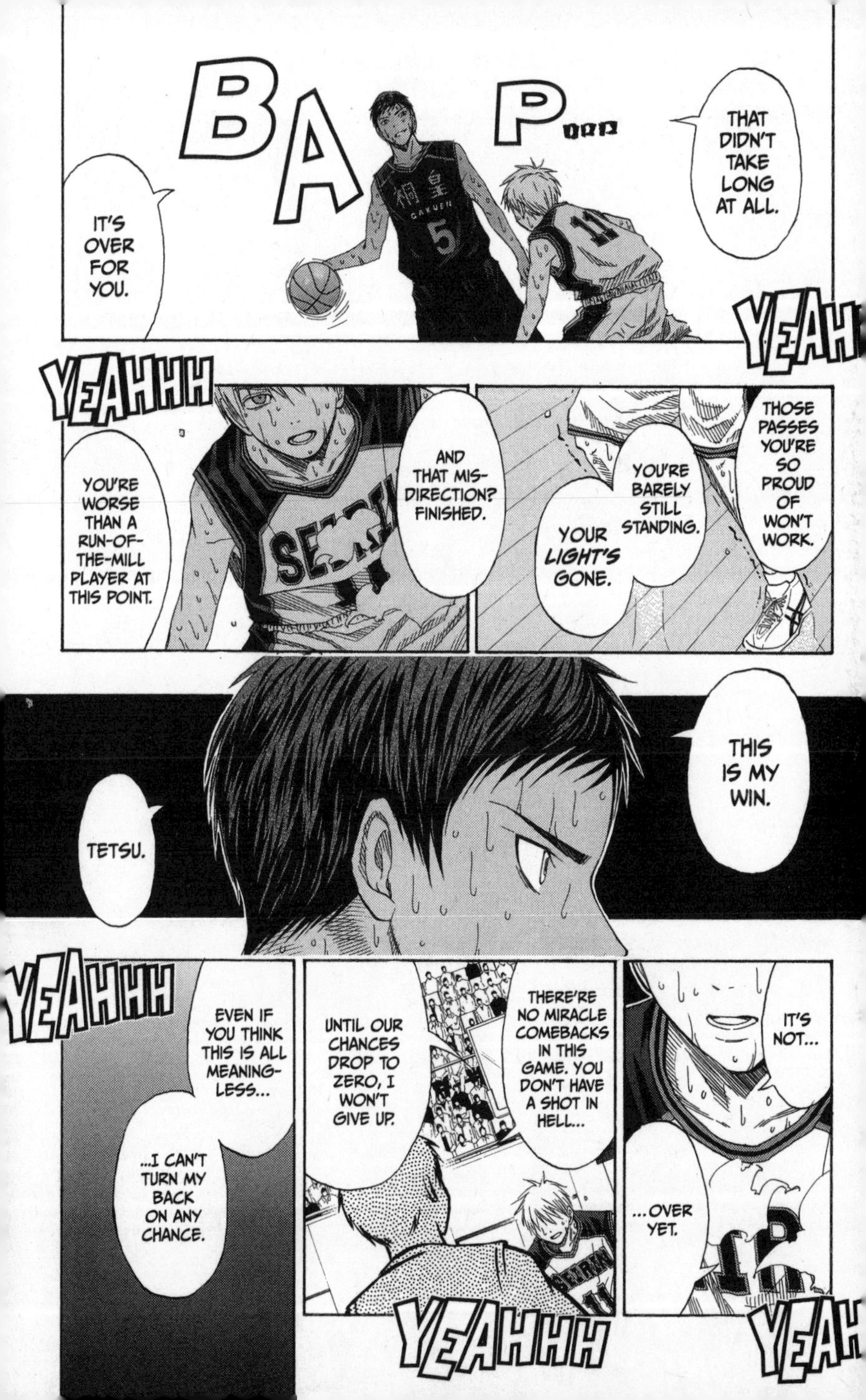
BAP
THAT DIDN'T TAKE LONG AT ALL.
IT'S OVER FOR YOU.
YEAH
THOSE PASSES YOU'RE SO PROUD OF WON'T WORK.
YOU'RE BARELY STILL STANDING.
YOUR LIGHT'S GONE.
AND THAT MIS-DIRECTION? FINISHED.
YOU'RE WORSE THAN A RUN-OF-THE-MILL PLAYER AT THIS POINT.
YEAHHH
THIS IS MY WIN.
TETSU.
IT'S NOT...
...OVER YET.
YEAH
THERE'RE NO MIRACLE COMEBACKS IN THIS GAME. YOU DON'T HAVE A SHOT IN HELL...
UNTIL OUR CHANCES DROP TO ZERO, I WON'T GIVE UP.
YEAHHH
EVEN IF YOU THINK THIS IS ALL MEANING-LESS...
...I CAN'T TURN MY BACK ON ANY CHANCE.
YEAHHH

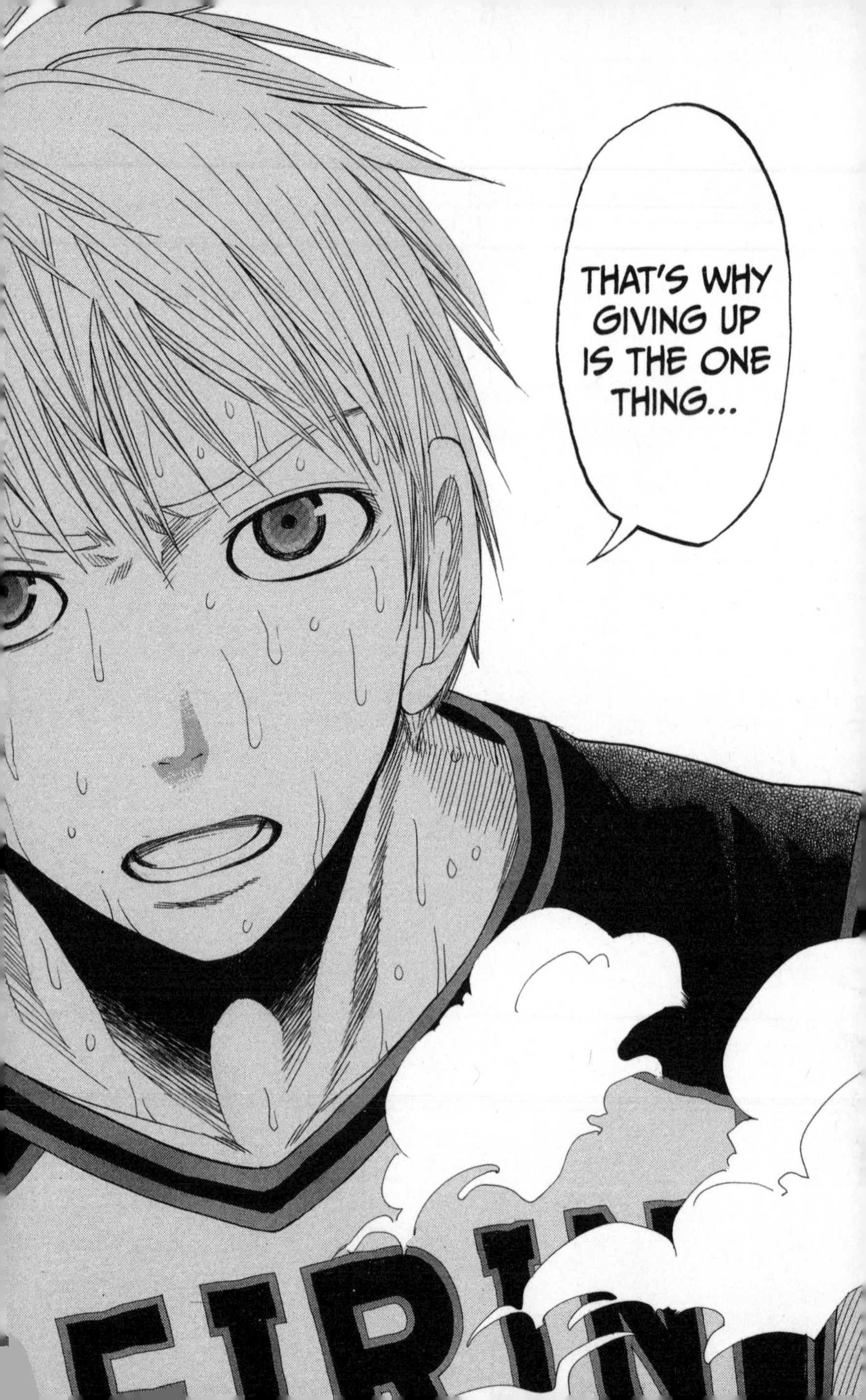
THAT'S WHY GIVING UP IS THE ONE THING...

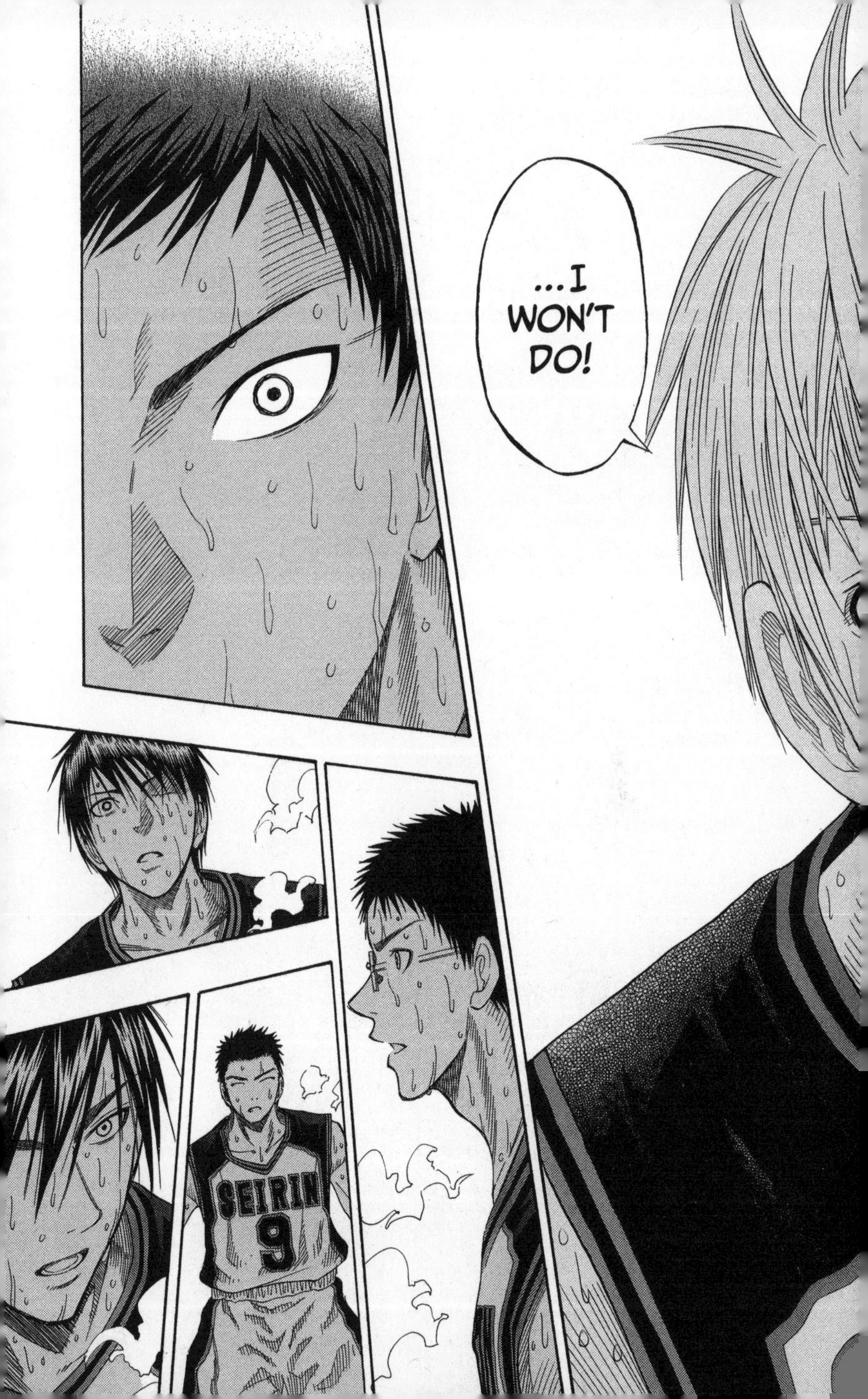
...I WON'T DO!
SEIRIN
9

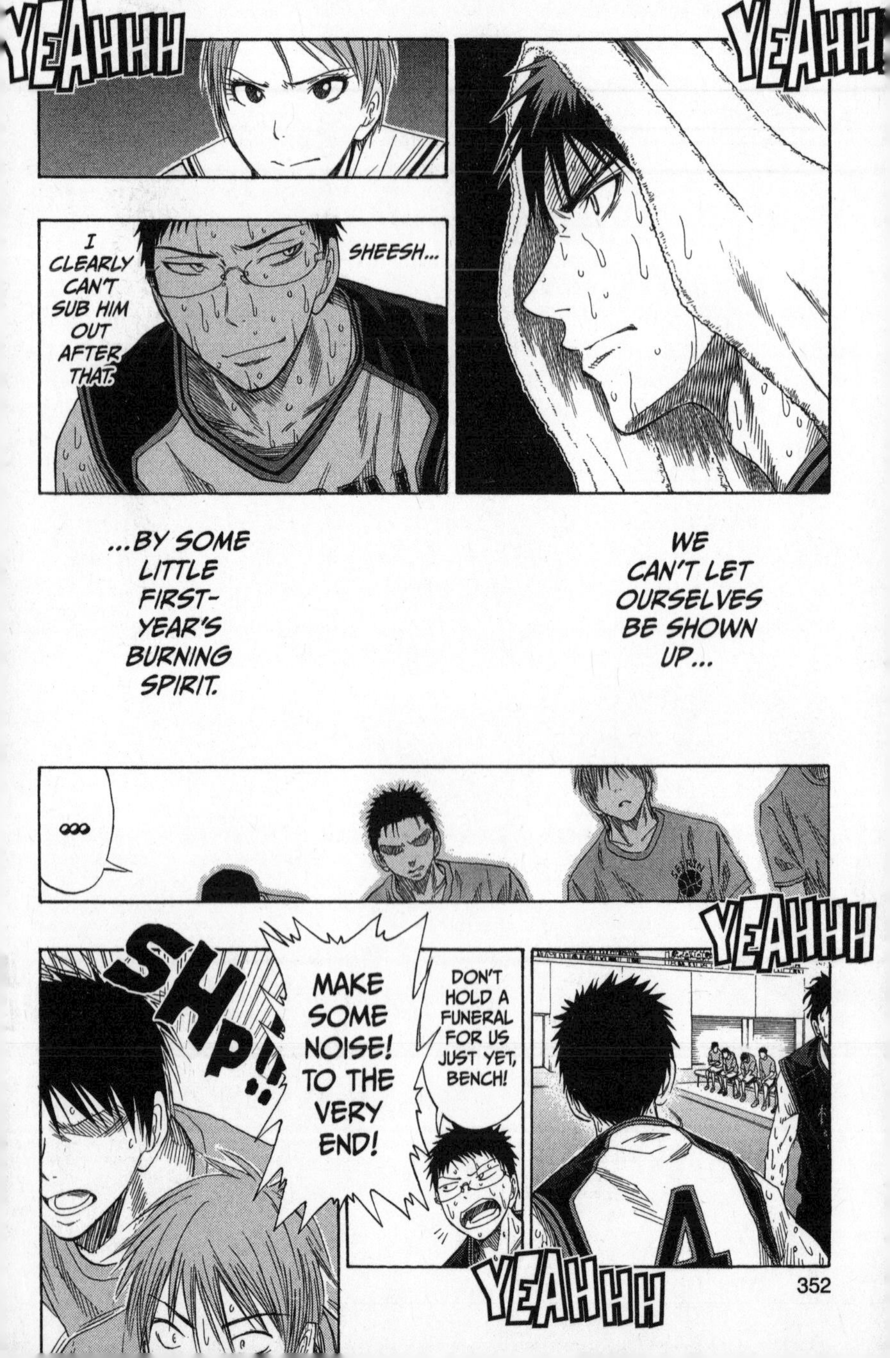

YEAHH
YEAHHH
SHEESH...
I CLEARLY CAN'T SUB HIM OUT AFTER THAT.
WE CAN'T LET OURSELVES BE SHOWN UP...
...BY SOME LITTLE FIRST-YEAR'S BURNING SPIRIT.
...
YEAHHH
DON'T HOLD A FUNERAL FOR US JUST YET, BENCH!
MAKE SOME NOISE! TO THE VERY END!
SHP!!
YEAHHH

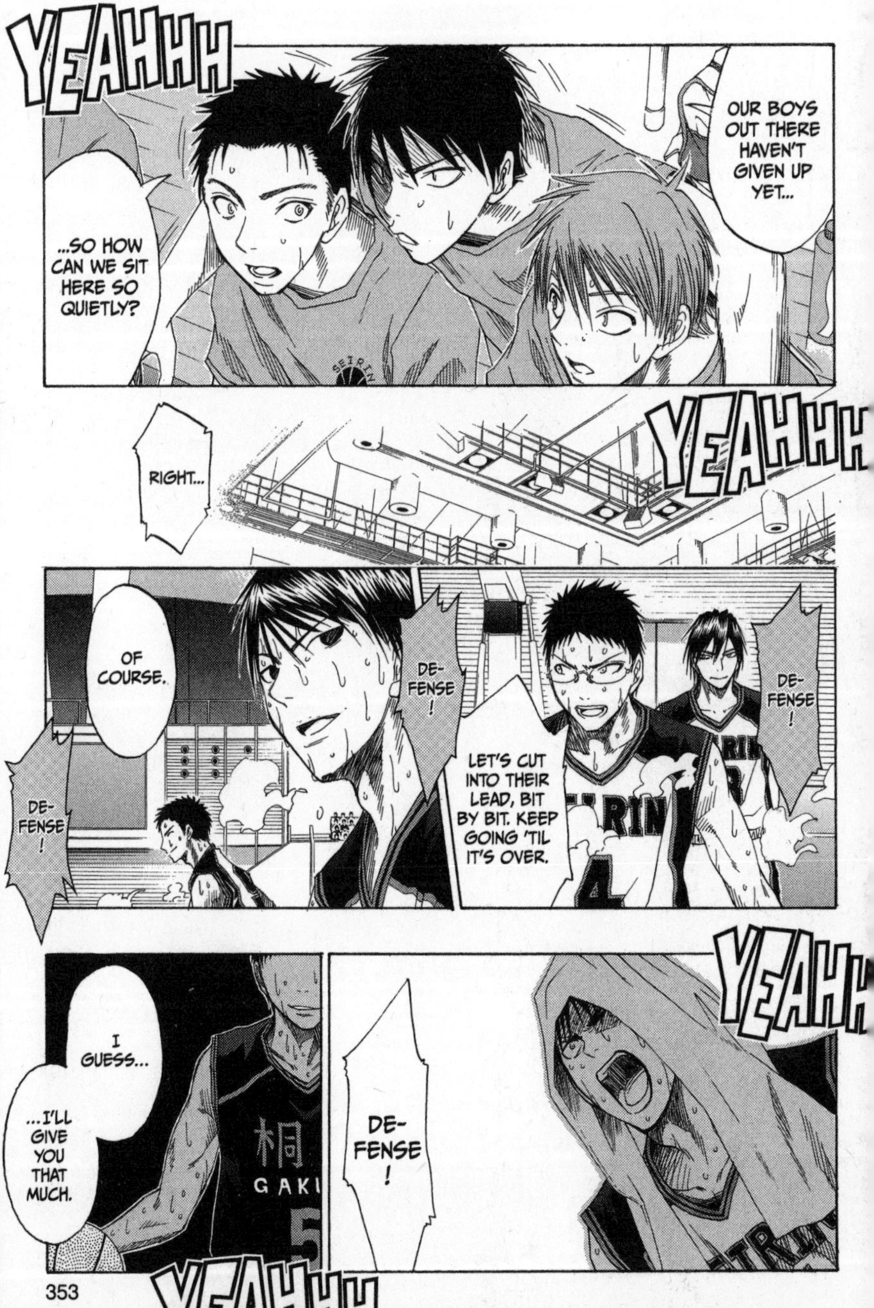
YEAHHH
OUR BOYS OUT THERE HAVEN'T GIVEN UP YET...
...SO HOW CAN WE SIT HERE SO QUIETLY?
YEAHHH
RIGHT...
DE-FENSE!
LET'S CUT INTO THEIR LEAD, BIT BY BIT. KEEP GOING 'TIL IT'S OVER.
DE-FENSE!
OF COURSE.
DE-FENSE!
YEAHH
DE-FENSE!
I GUESS...
...I'LL GIVE YOU THAT MUCH.
YEAHHH

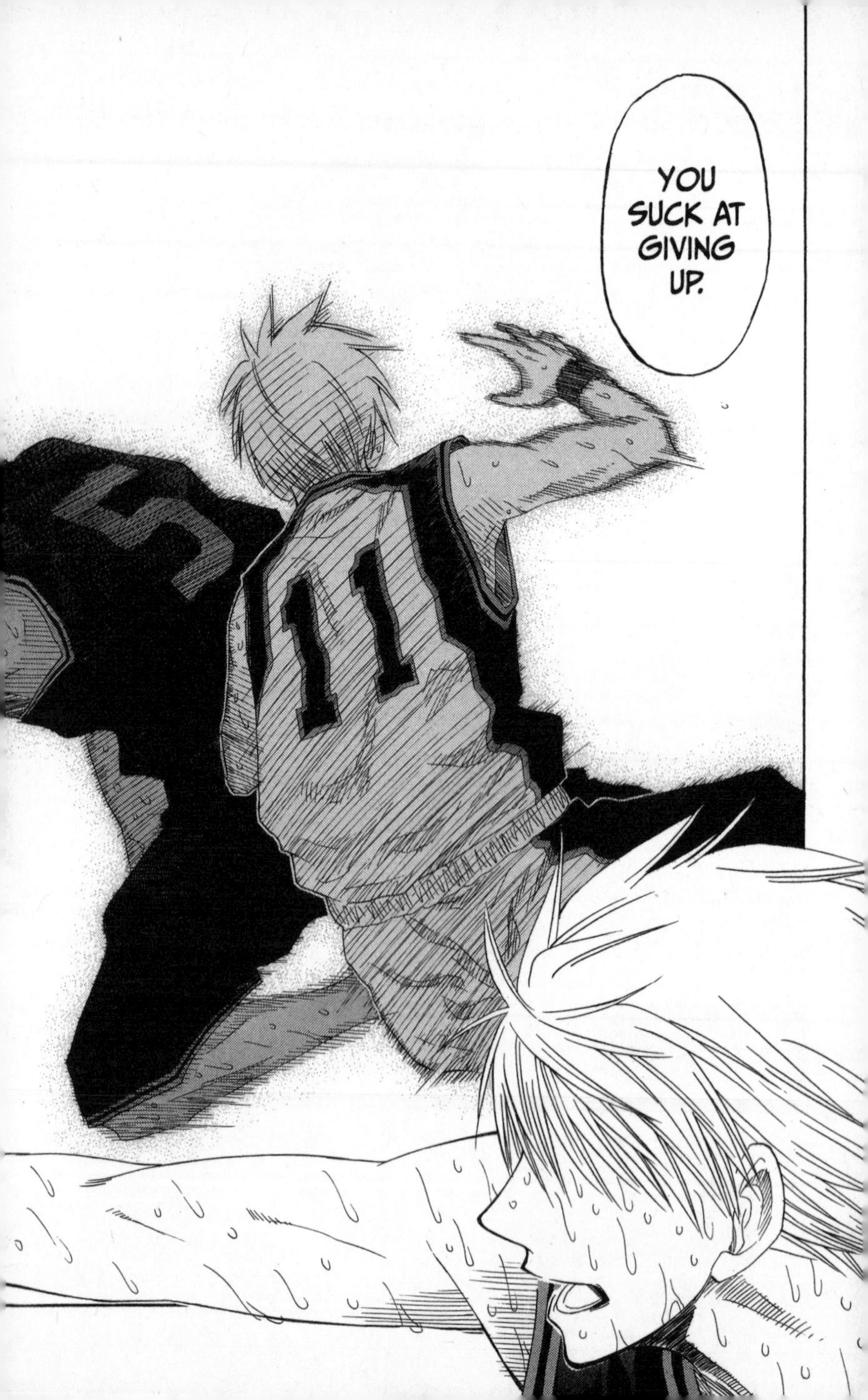
YOU SUCK AT GIVING UP.

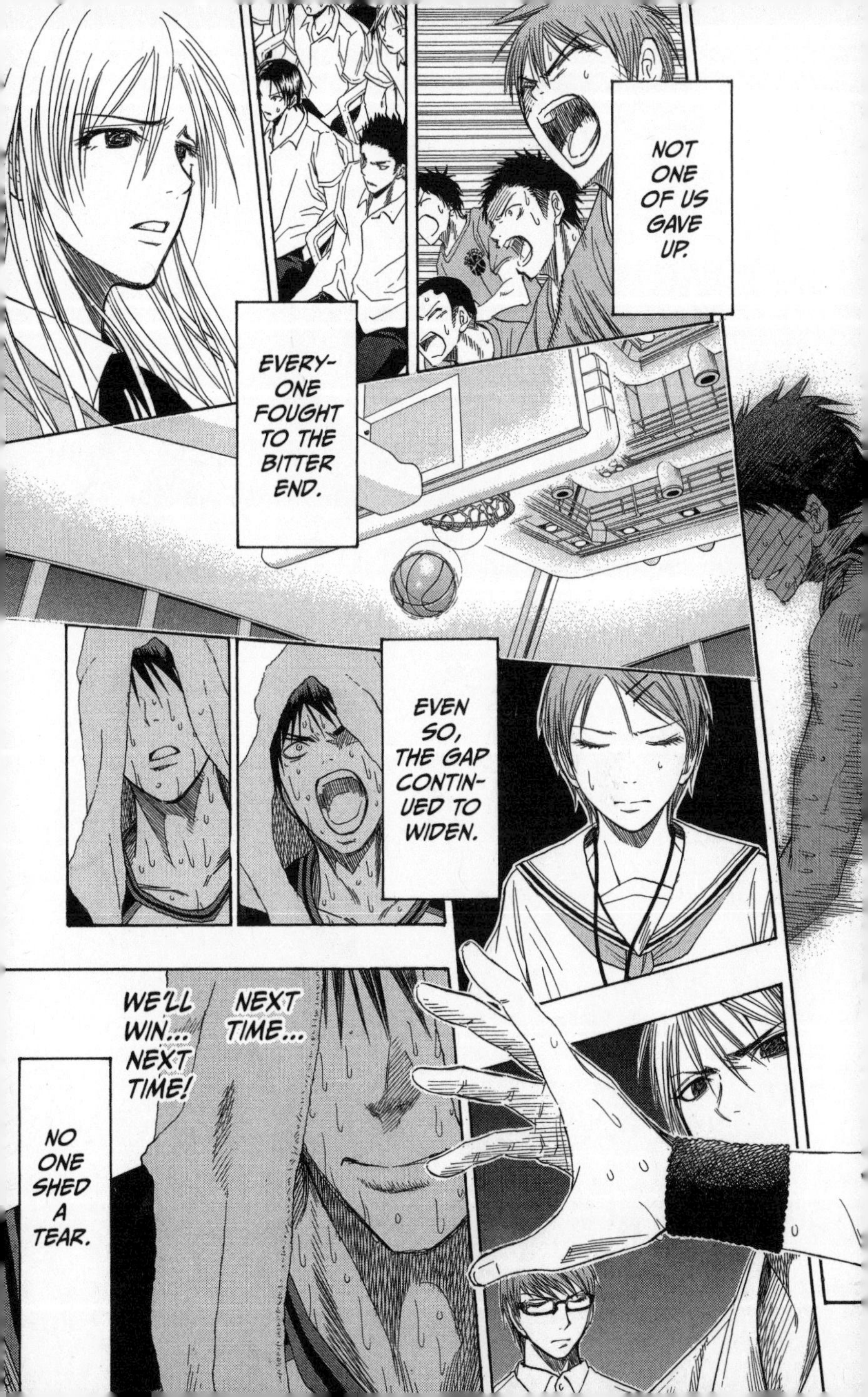
NOT ONE OF US GAVE UP.
EVERY-ONE FOUGHT TO THE BITTER END.
EVEN SO, THE GAP CONTIN-UED TO WIDEN.
NEXT TIME...
WE'LL WIN... NEXT TIME!
NO ONE SHED A TEAR.

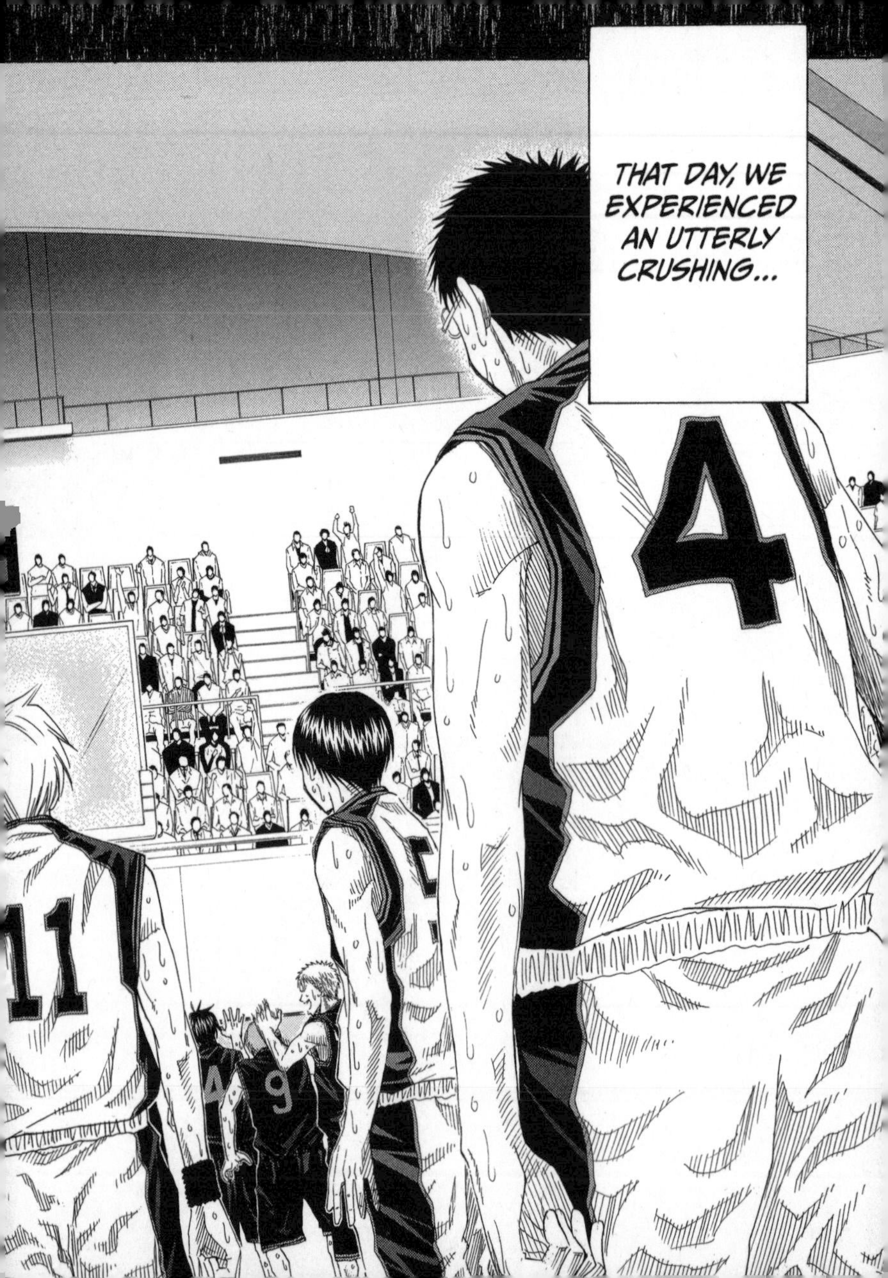
THAT DAY, WE EXPERIENCED AN UTTERLY CRUSHING...

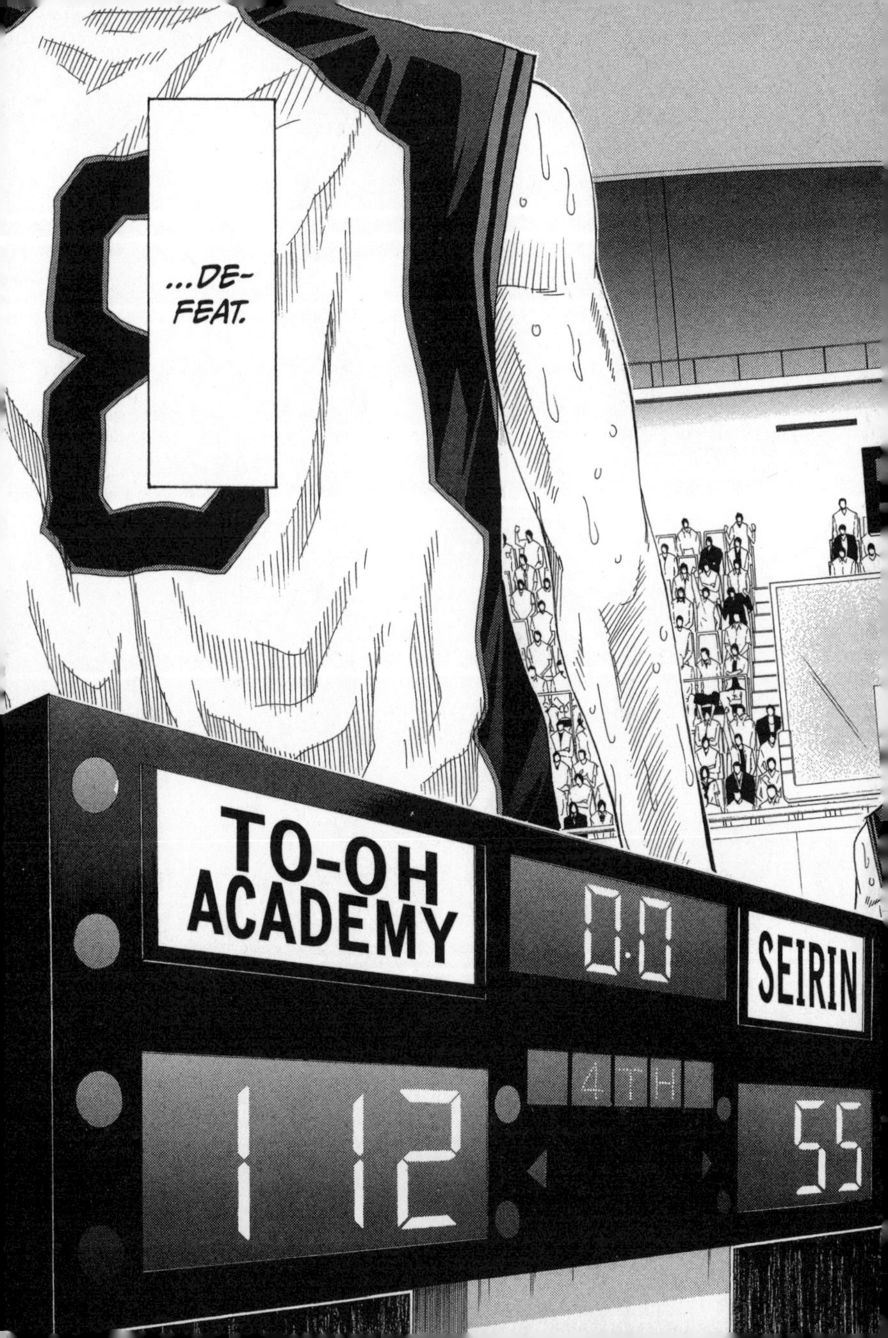
...DE-
FEAT.
TO-OH
ACADEMY
0.0
SEIRIN
4TH
112
55

NOTHING.

SORRY,
JUST
CAN'T DO
IT THIS
TIME...

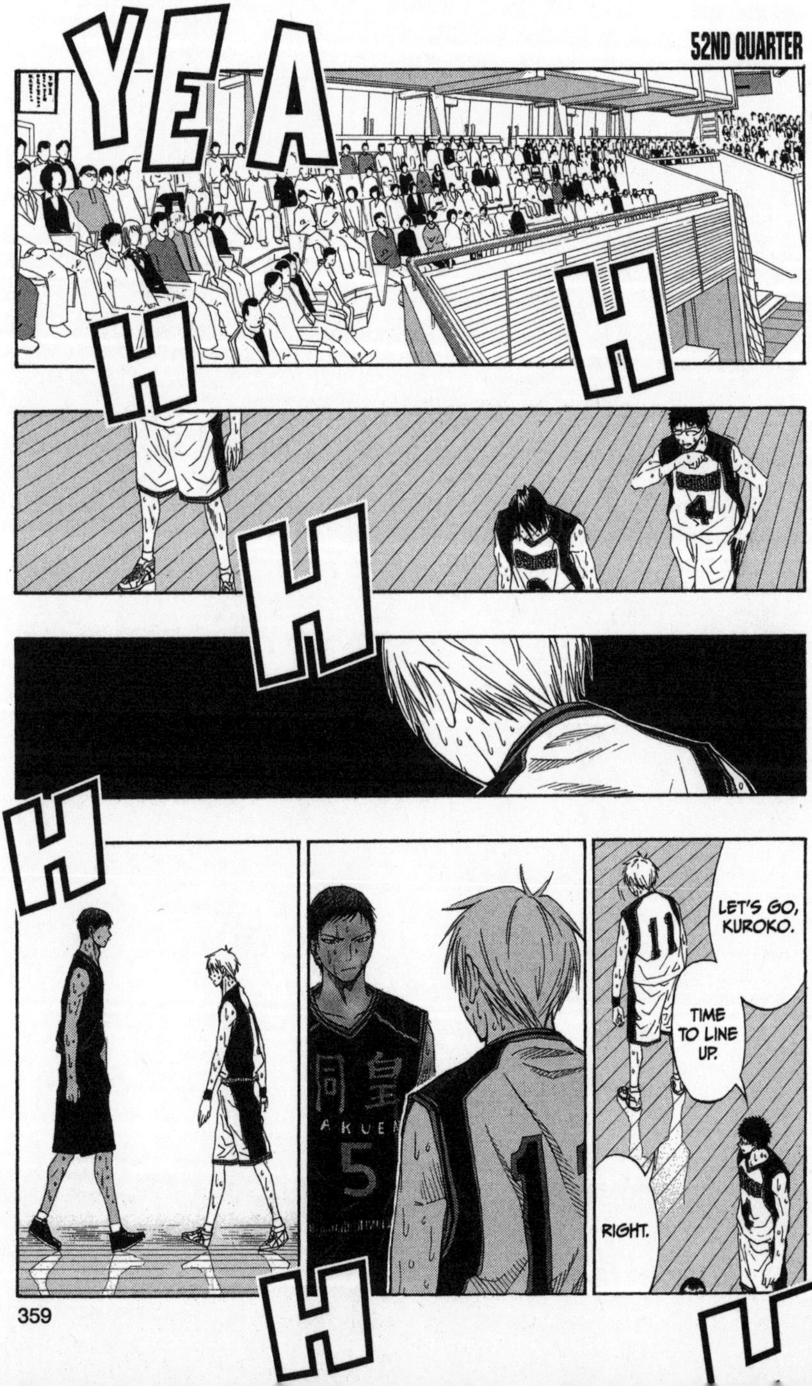
YEAHHHHHH
LET'S GO, KUROKO.
TIME TO LINE UP.
RIGHT.

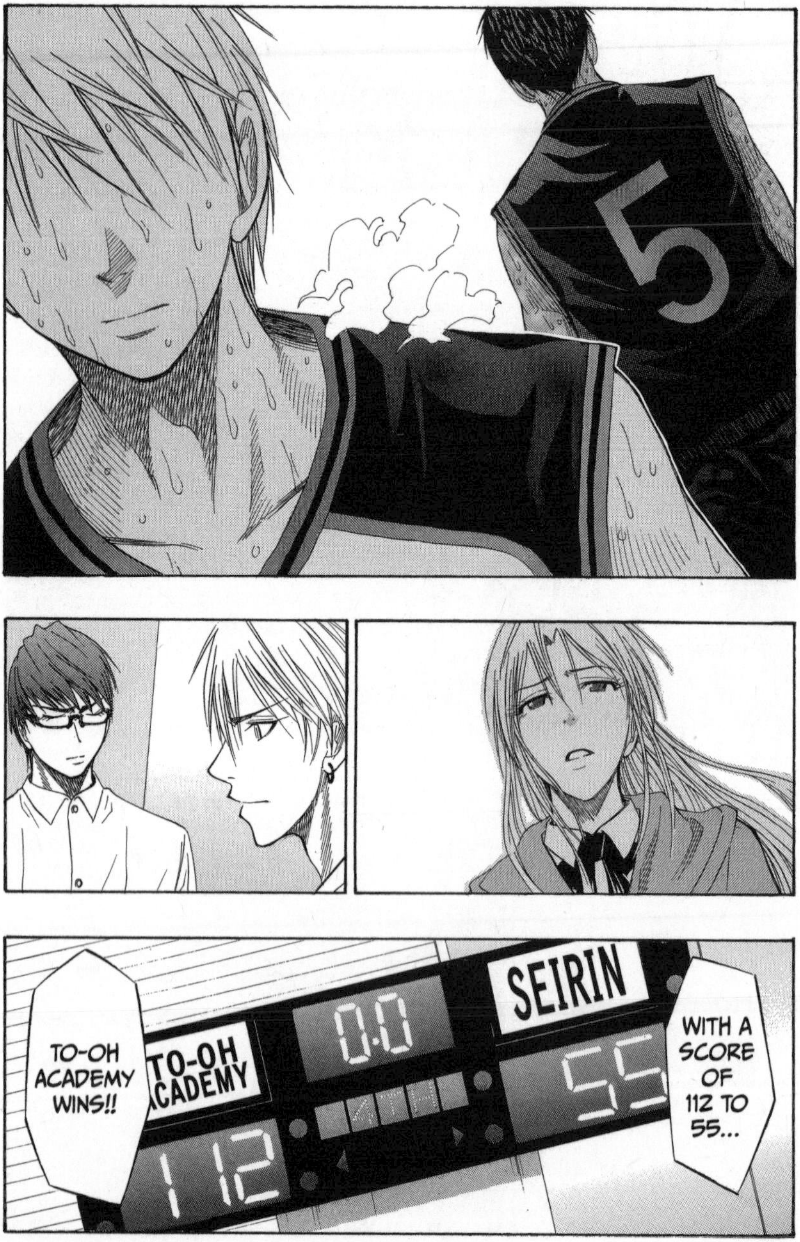
SEIRIN
WITH A SCORE OF 112 TO 55...
55
0.0
TO-OH ACADEMY
112
TO-OH ACADEMY WINS!!

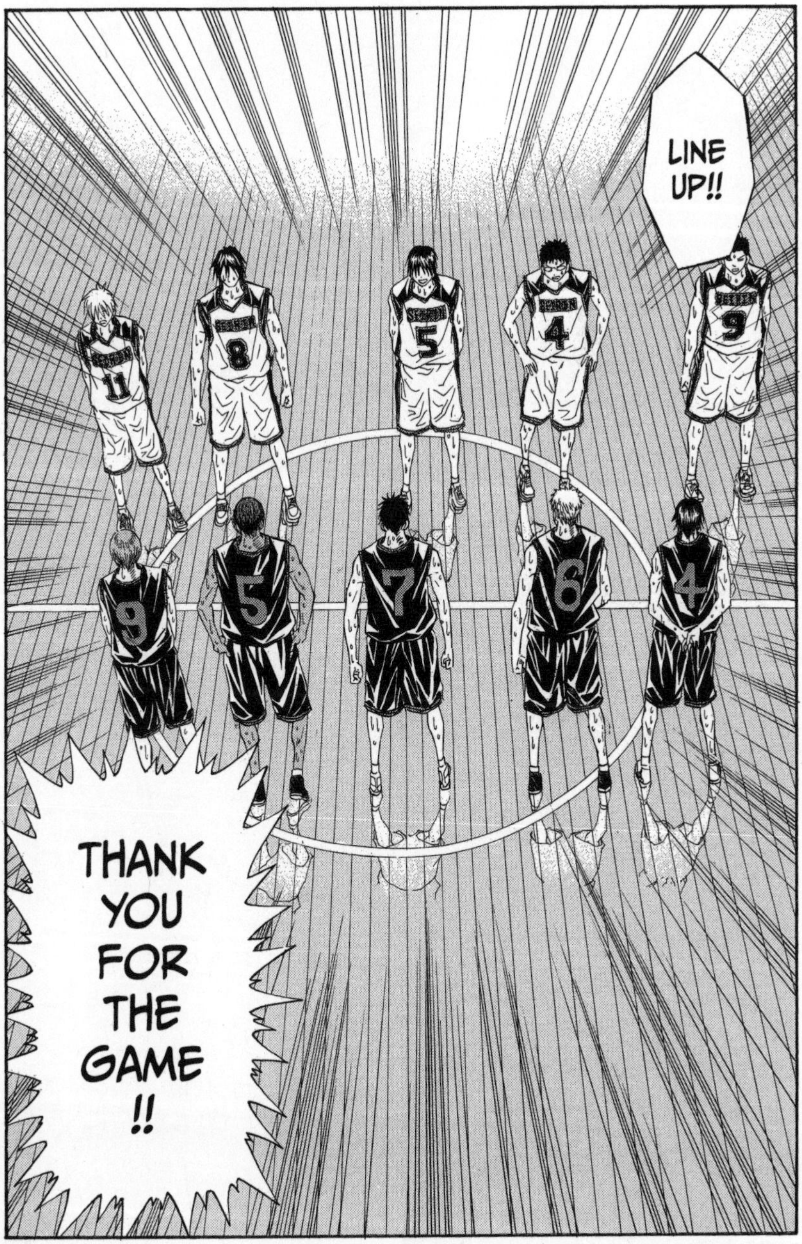
LINE UP!!
THANK YOU FOR THE GAME !!

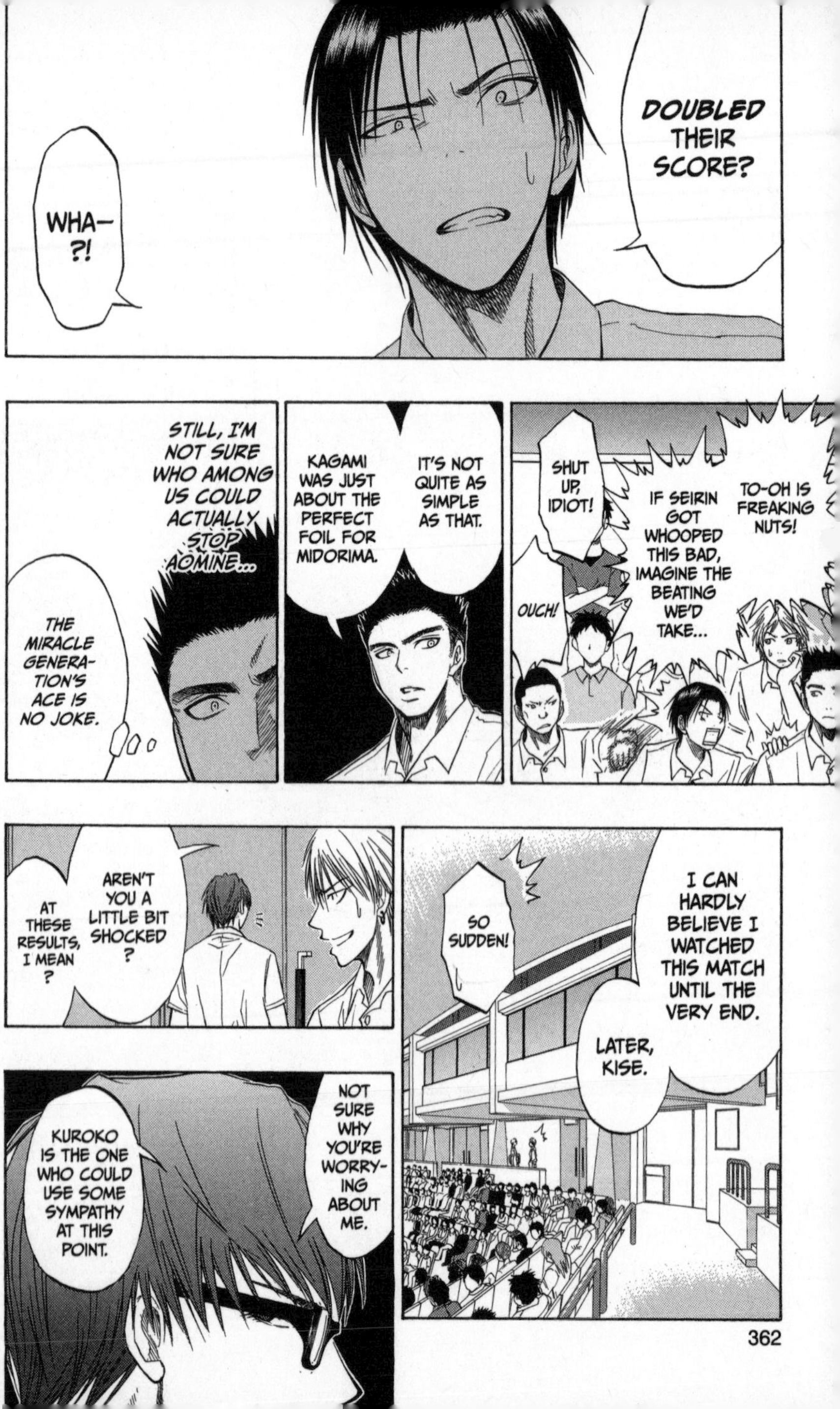
DOUBLED THEIR SCORE?
WHA— ?!
TO-OH IS FREAKING NUTS!
IF SEIRIN GOT WHOOPED THIS BAD, IMAGINE THE BEATING WE'D TAKE...
SHUT UP, IDIOT!
OUCH!
IT'S NOT QUITE AS SIMPLE AS THAT.
KAGAMI WAS JUST ABOUT THE PERFECT FOIL FOR MIDORIMA.
STILL, I'M NOT SURE WHO AMONG US COULD ACTUALLY STOP AOMINE...
THE MIRACLE GENERATION'S ACE IS NO JOKE.
I CAN HARDLY BELIEVE I WATCHED THIS MATCH UNTIL THE VERY END.
SO SUDDEN!
LATER, KISE.
AREN'T YOU A LITTLE BIT SHOCKED?
AT THESE RESULTS, I MEAN?
NOT SURE WHY YOU'RE WORRYING ABOUT ME.
KUROKO IS THE ONE WHO COULD USE SOME SYMPATHY AT THIS POINT.

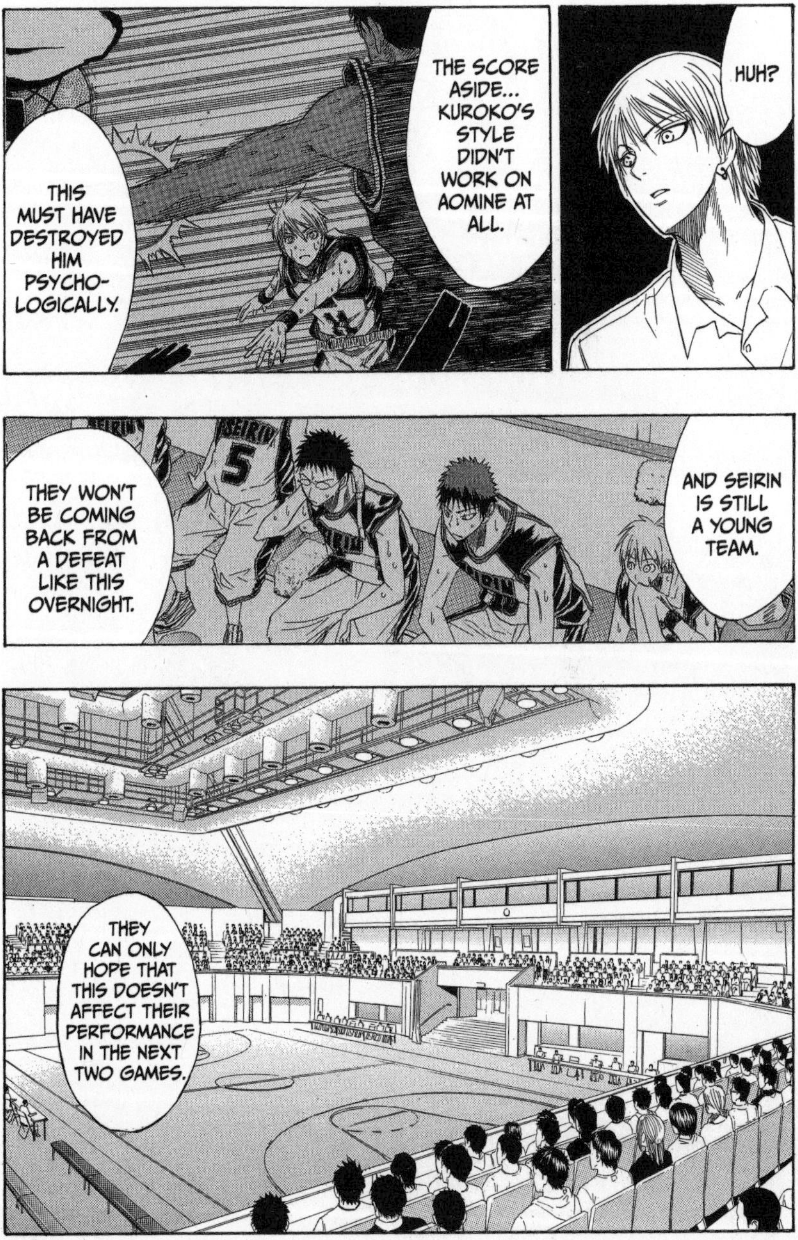
HUH?
THE SCORE ASIDE... KUROKO'S STYLE DIDN'T WORK ON AOMINE AT ALL.
THIS MUST HAVE DESTROYED HIM PSYCHO-LOGICALLY.
AND SEIRIN IS STILL A YOUNG TEAM.
THEY WON'T BE COMING BACK FROM A DEFEAT LIKE THIS OVERNIGHT.
THEY CAN ONLY HOPE THAT THIS DOESN'T AFFECT THEIR PERFORMANCE IN THE NEXT TWO GAMES.

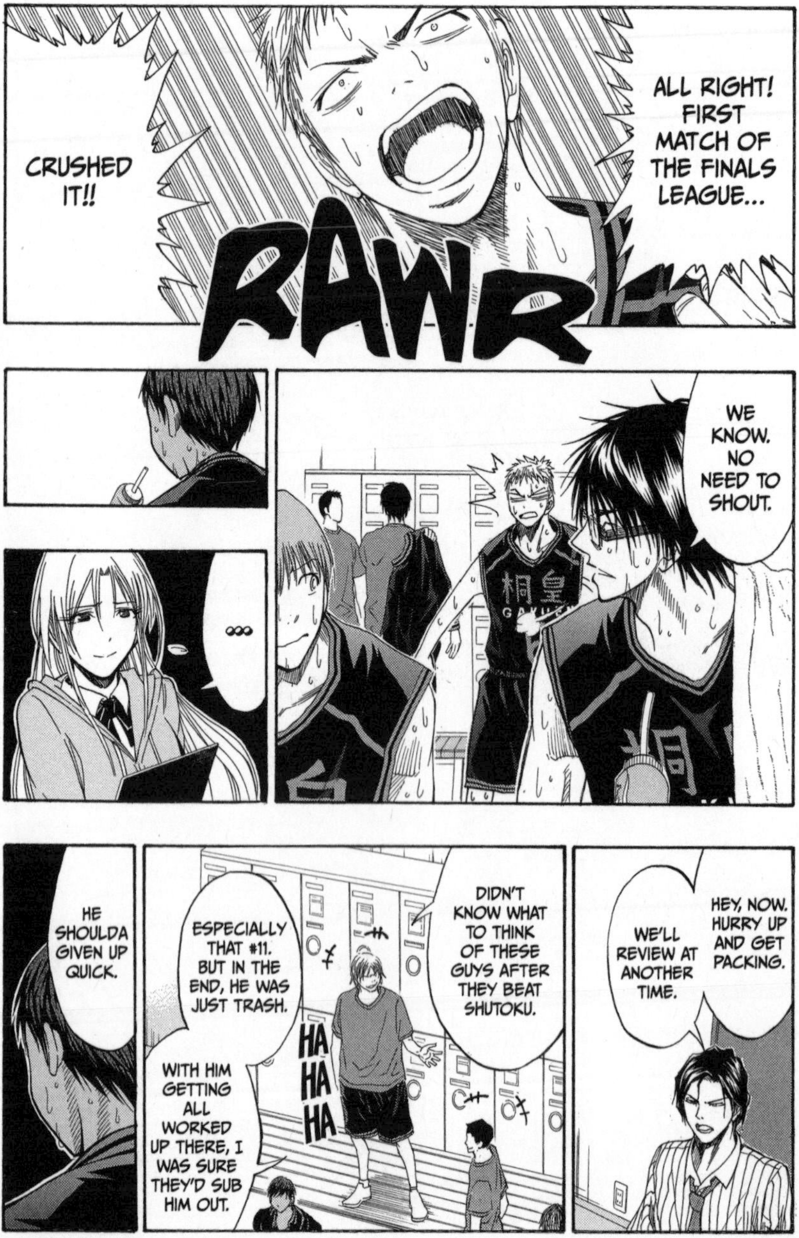
ALL RIGHT! FIRST MATCH OF THE FINALS LEAGUE...
CRUSHED IT!!
RAWR
WE KNOW. NO NEED TO SHOUT.
...
HEY, NOW. HURRY UP AND GET PACKING.
WE'LL REVIEW AT ANOTHER TIME.
DIDN'T KNOW WHAT TO THINK OF THESE GUYS AFTER THEY BEAT SHUTOKU.
ESPECIALLY THAT #11. BUT IN THE END, HE WAS JUST TRASH.
HA HA HA
WITH HIM GETTING ALL WORKED UP THERE, I WAS SURE THEY'D SUB HIM OUT.
HE SHOULDA GIVEN UP QUICK.

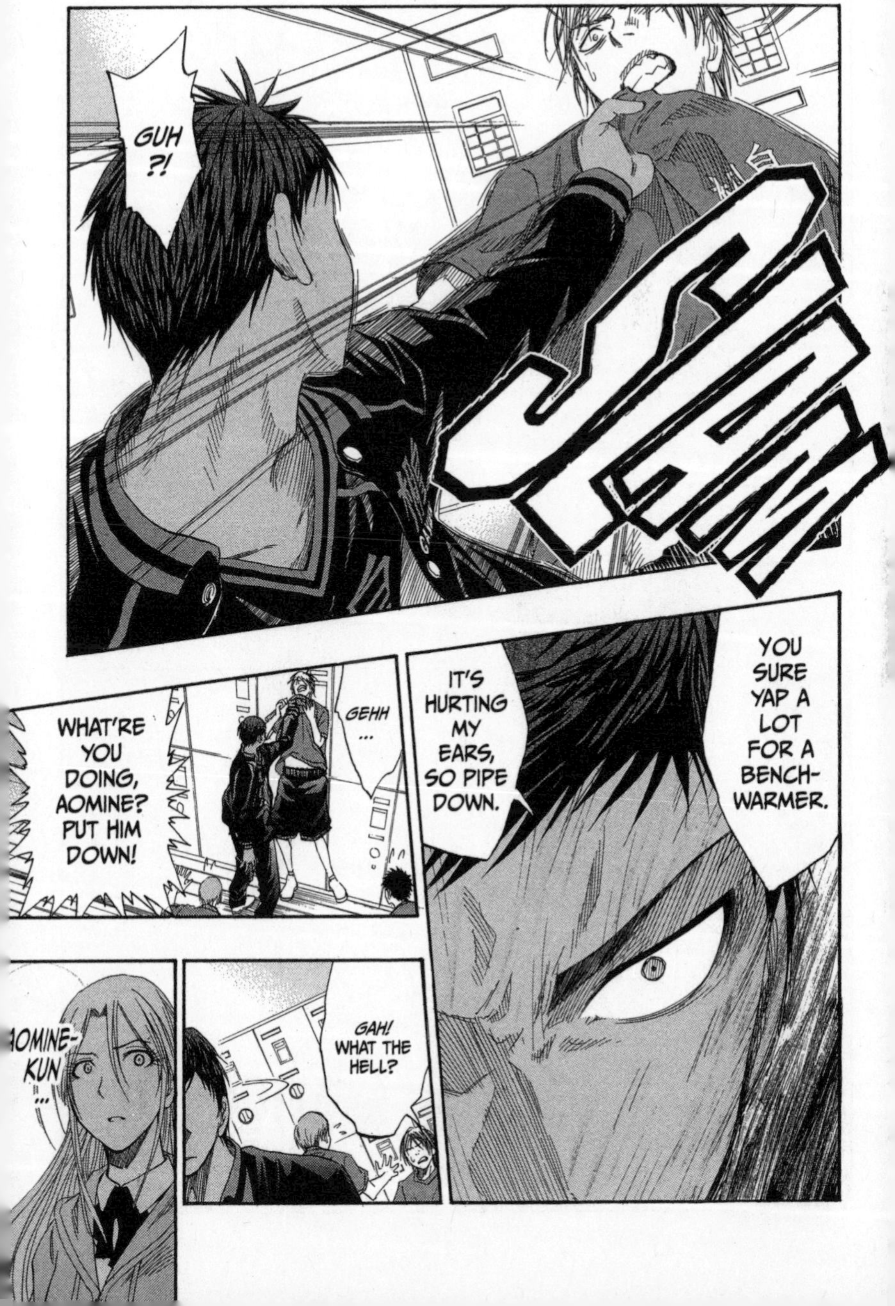
GUH ?!
YOU SURE YAP A LOT FOR A BENCH-WARMER.
IT'S HURTING MY EARS, SO PIPE DOWN.
GEHH ...
WHAT'RE YOU DOING, AOMINE? PUT HIM DOWN!
GAH! WHAT THE HELL?
AOMINE-KUN ...

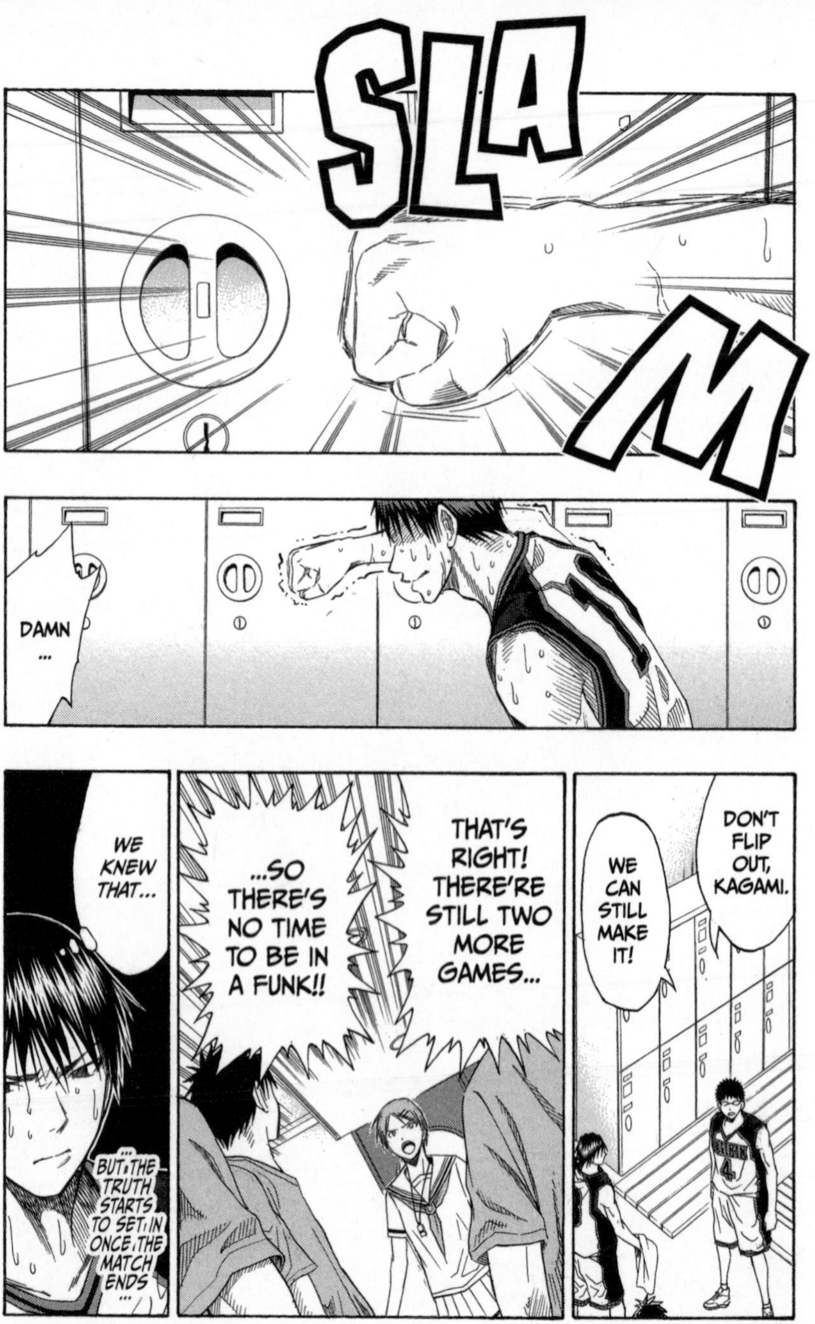
SLAM
DAMN ...
DON'T FLIP OUT, KAGAMI.
WE CAN STILL MAKE IT!
THAT'S RIGHT! THERE'RE STILL TWO MORE GAMES...
...SO THERE'S NO TIME TO BE IN A FUNK!!
WE KNEW THAT...
...BUT THE TRUTH STARTS TO SET IN ONCE THE MATCH ENDS...

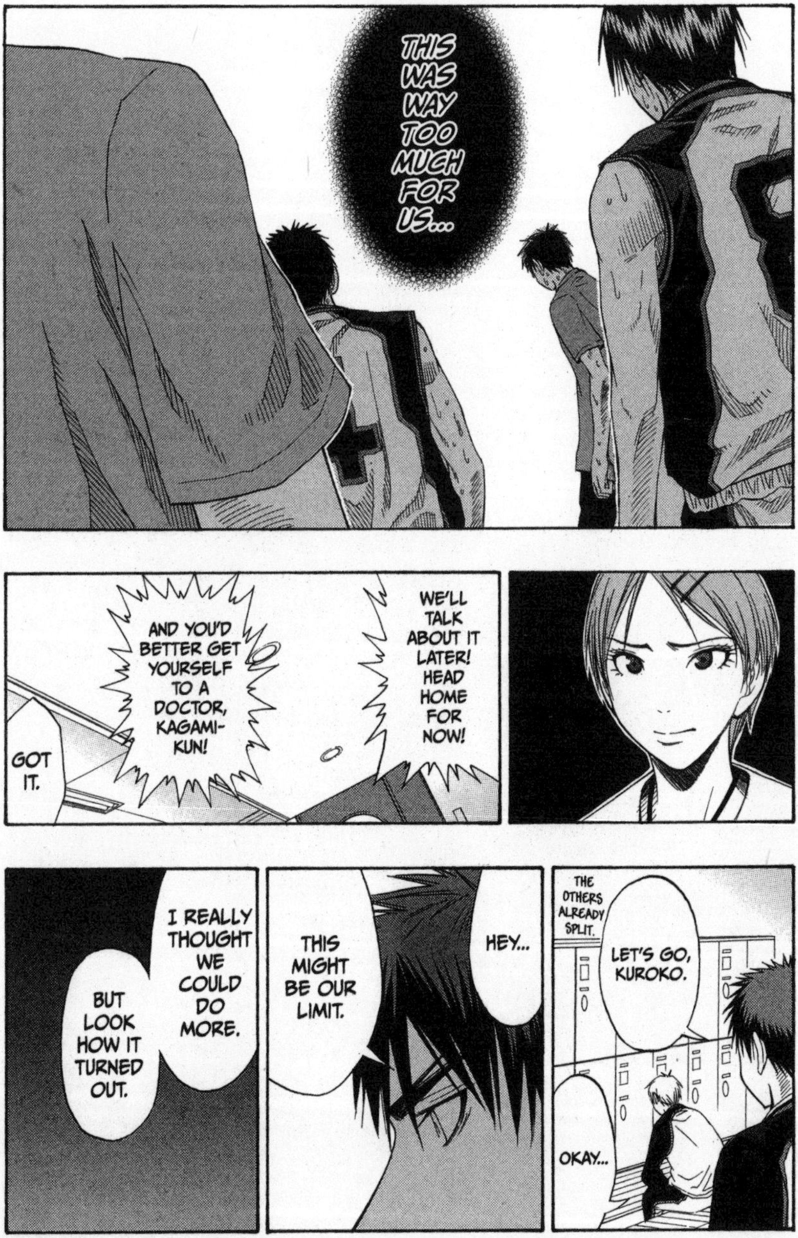
THIS WAS WAY TOO MUCH FOR US...
WE'LL TALK ABOUT IT LATER! HEAD HOME FOR NOW!
AND YOU'D BETTER GET YOURSELF TO A DOCTOR, KAGAMI-KUN!
GOT IT.
THE OTHERS ALREADY SPLIT.
LET'S GO, KUROKO.
OKAY...
HEY...
THIS MIGHT BE OUR LIMIT.
I REALLY THOUGHT WE COULD DO MORE.
BUT LOOK HOW IT TURNED OUT.

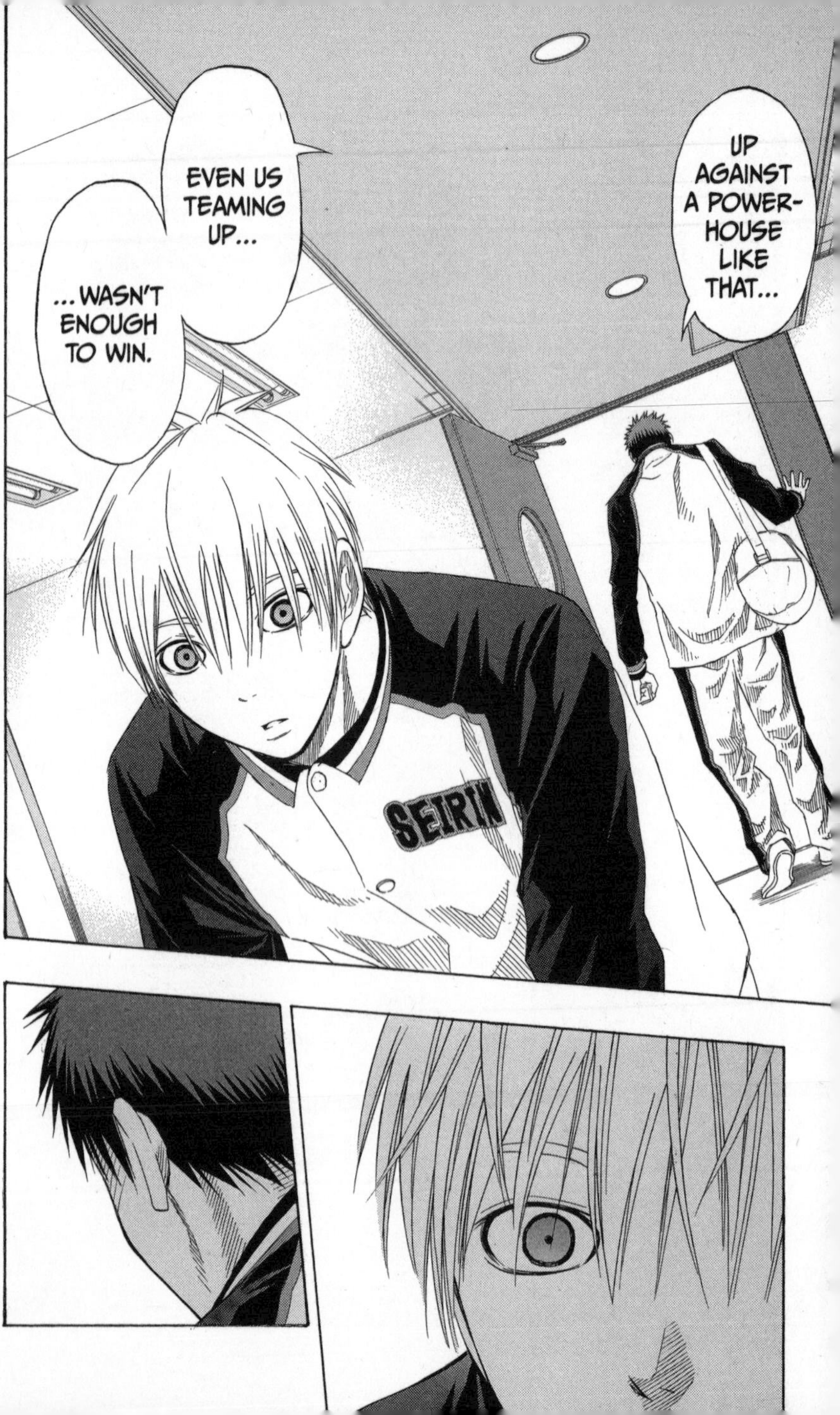
UP AGAINST A POWERHOUSE LIKE THAT...
EVEN US TEAMING UP...
...WASN'T ENOUGH TO WIN.
SEIRIN

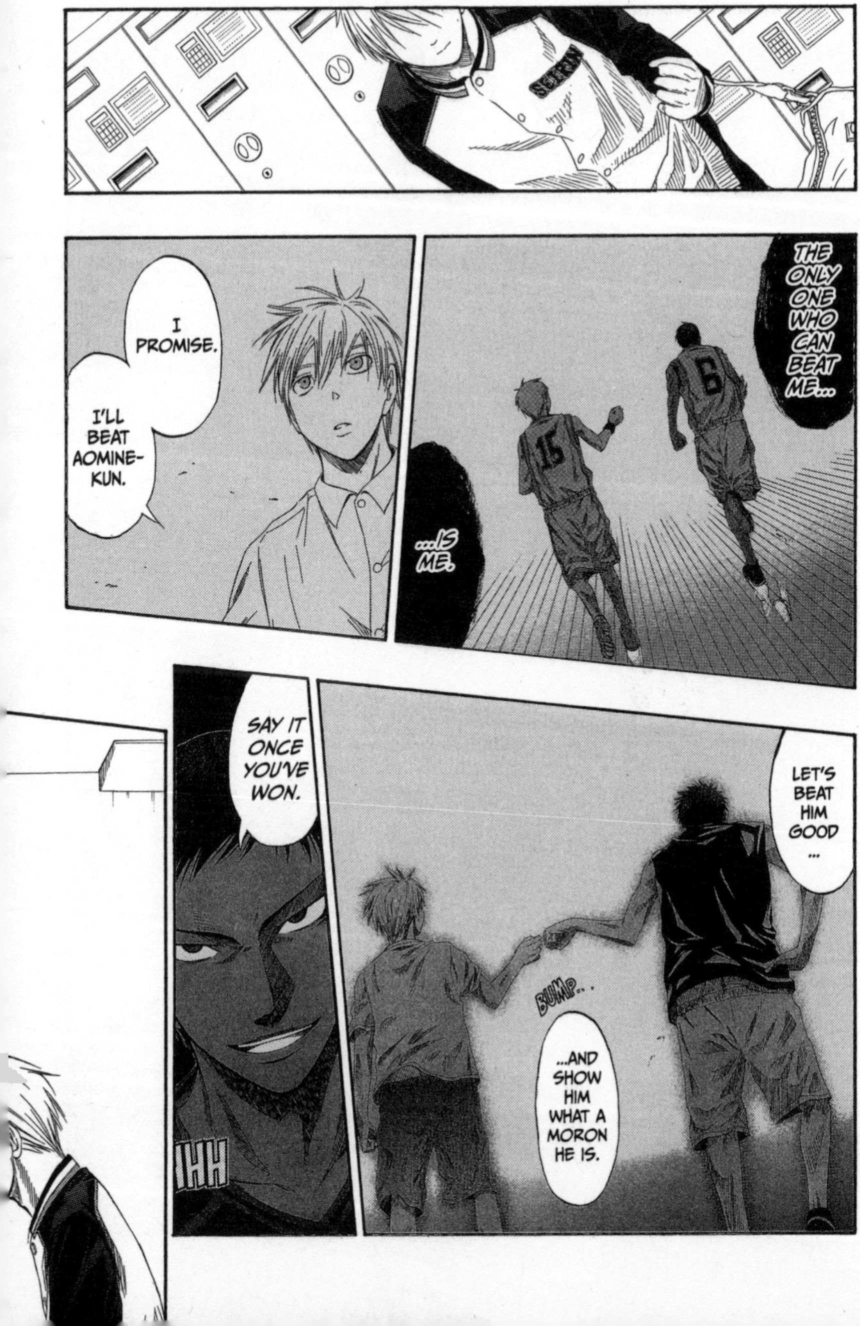
THE ONLY ONE WHO CAN BEAT ME...
...IS ME.
I PROMISE.
I'LL BEAT AOMINE-KUN.
LET'S BEAT HIM GOOD...
BUMP...
...AND SHOW HIM WHAT A MORON HE IS.
SAY IT ONCE YOU'VE WON.
HHH

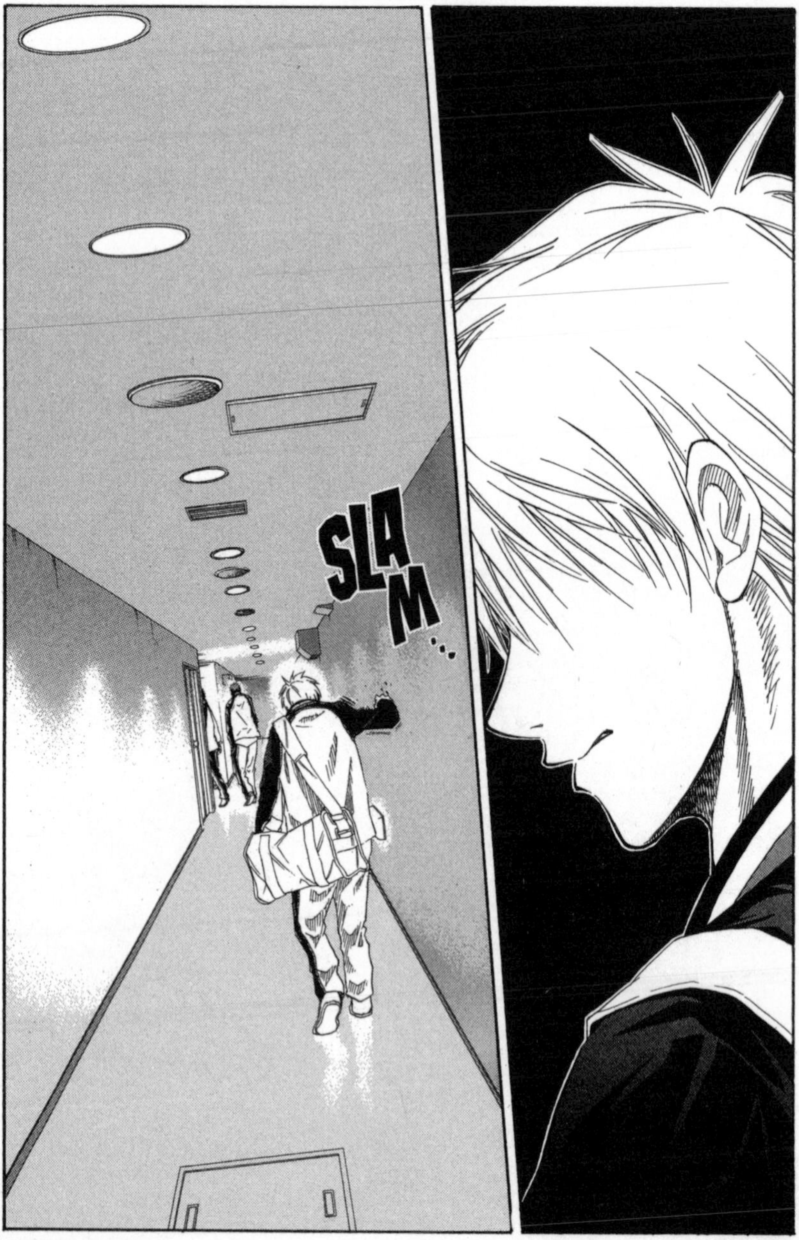
SLAM...

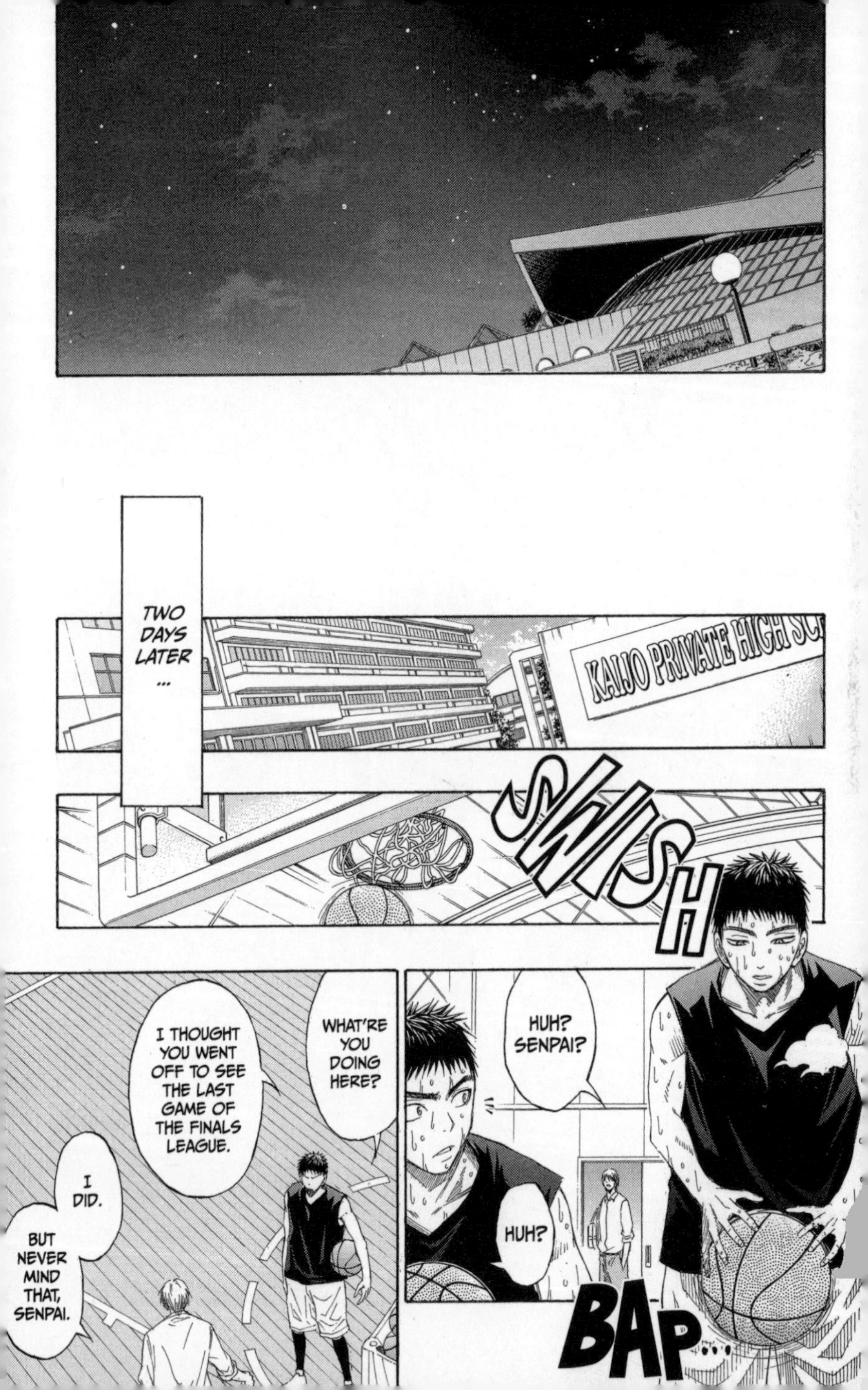
TWO DAYS LATER ...
KAIJO PRIVATE HIGH SC
SWISH
HUH? SENPAI?
HUH?
BAP
WHAT'RE YOU DOING HERE?
I THOUGHT YOU WENT OFF TO SEE THE LAST GAME OF THE FINALS LEAGUE.
I DID.
BUT NEVER MIND THAT, SENPAI.

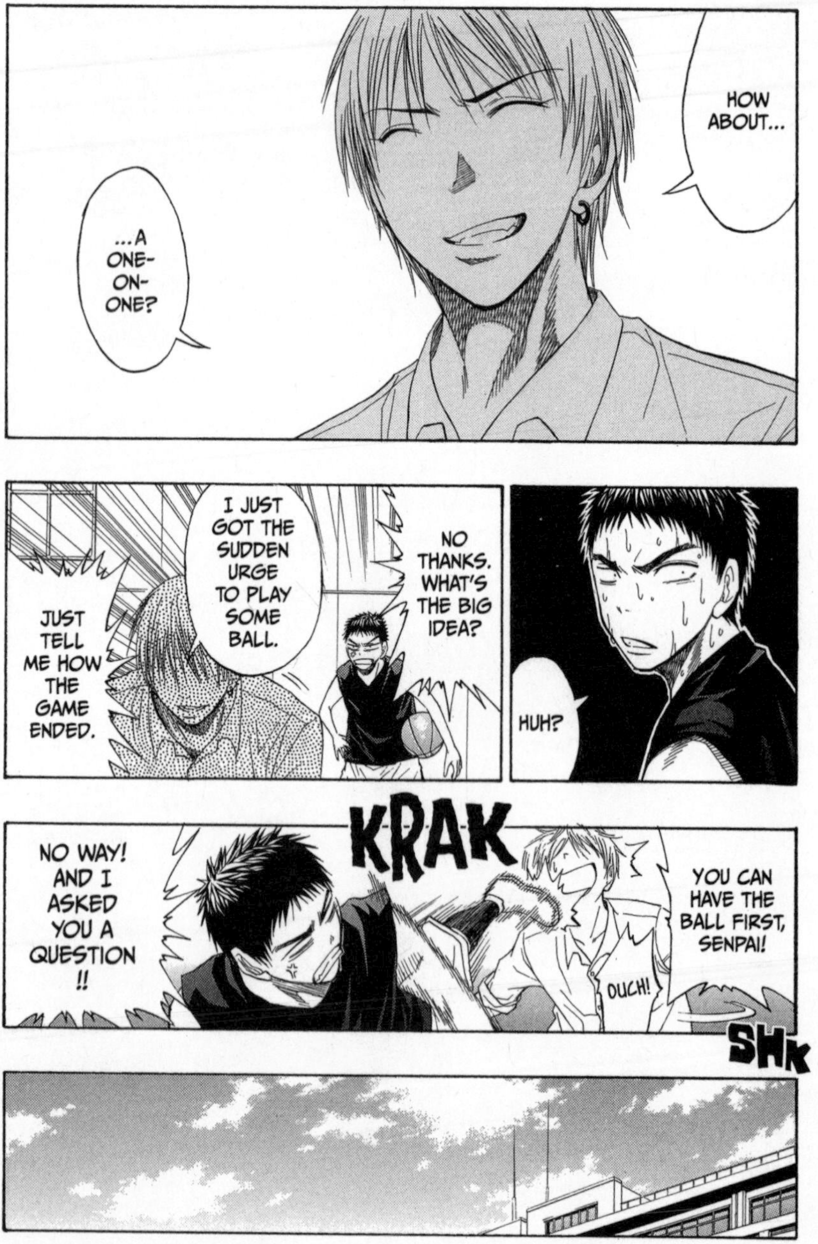
HOW ABOUT...
...A ONE-ON-ONE?
HUH?
NO THANKS. WHAT'S THE BIG IDEA?
I JUST GOT THE SUDDEN URGE TO PLAY SOME BALL.
JUST TELL ME HOW THE GAME ENDED.
YOU CAN HAVE THE BALL FIRST, SENPAI!
NO WAY! AND I ASKED YOU A QUESTION!!
KRAK
OUCH!
SHK!

NOT TO MENTION KUROKO'S SUDDEN DOWN-TURN.

KAGAMI-KUN HAD TO SIT OUT, WHICH MESSED UP THE TEAM'S CHEMISTRY.

HIS PASSES THAT HAD SAVED OUR BUTTS WHO KNOWS HOW MANY TIMES LOST THEIR EFFECTIVE-NESS. HE WAS A SHADOW OF HIS FORMER SELF.

BUT THE SCARS FROM OUR BATTLE AGAINST TO-OH RAN DEEP.

WE GAVE ALL WE HAD IN THE NEXT TWO GAMES.

OUR SECOND GAME WAS AGAINST MEISEI HIGH.

WE LOST BY A HAIR.

IN THIS SORRY STATE, WE FOUGHT TO THE VERY END.

SEIRIN 78   MEISEI 79

BUT NOT EVERY CHALLENGER CAN BE A WINNER.

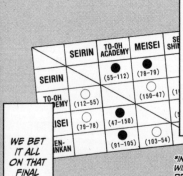

	SEIRIN	TO-OH ACADEMY	MEISEI	SE SHIN
SEIRIN		● (55–112)	● (78–79)	
TO-OH ADEMY	○ (112–55)		○ (150–47)	(1
MEISEI	○ (79–78)	● (47–150)		(5
EN-NKAN		● (91–105)	○ (103–54)	

WE BET IT ALL ON THAT FINAL GAME.

THE THIRD DAY SAW TO-OH ACADEMY'S THIRD WIN, AND IF SEIRIN COULD'VE PULLED OFF A WIN, THAT WOULD'VE MEANT THREE TEAMS WITH ONE WIN AND TWO LOSSES, GIVING US ONE LAST SHOT AT INTER-HIGH.

*IN THAT CASE, THE WINNERS WOULD BE DECIDED BY OVERALL POINTS SCORED.

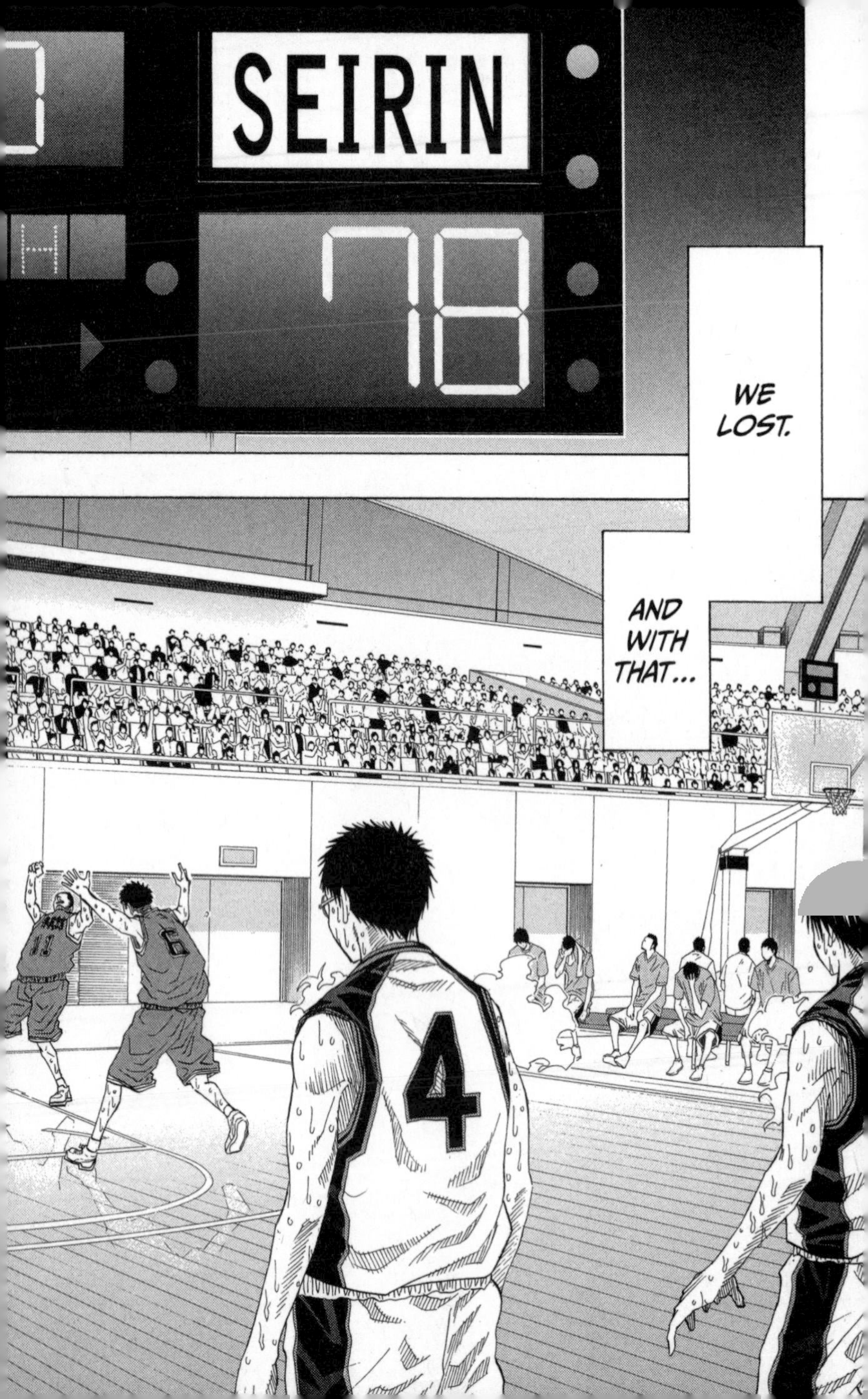
SEIRIN
78
WE LOST.
AND WITH THAT...

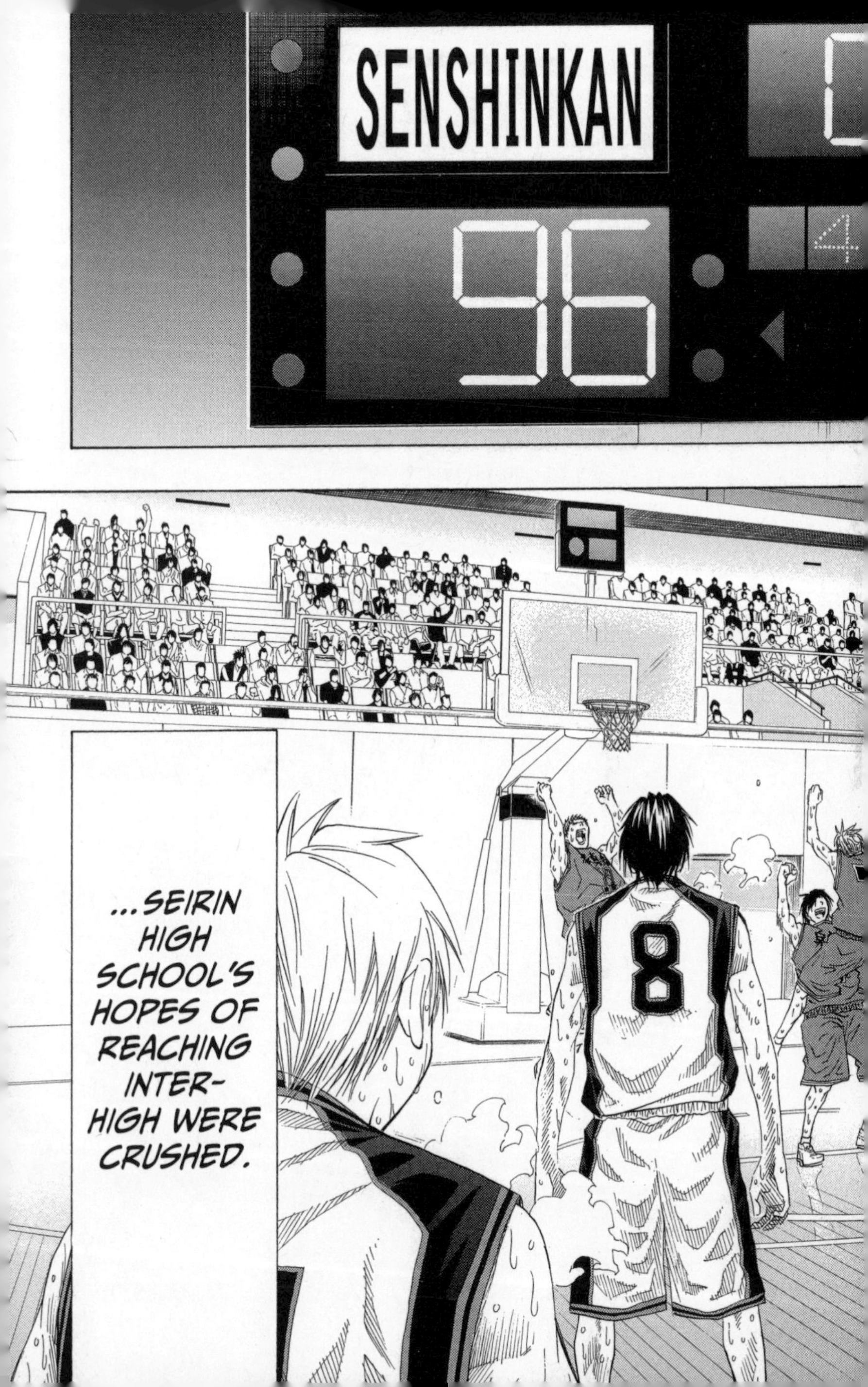
SENSHINKAN
96
...SEIRIN HIGH SCHOOL'S HOPES OF REACHING INTER-HIGH WERE CRUSHED.

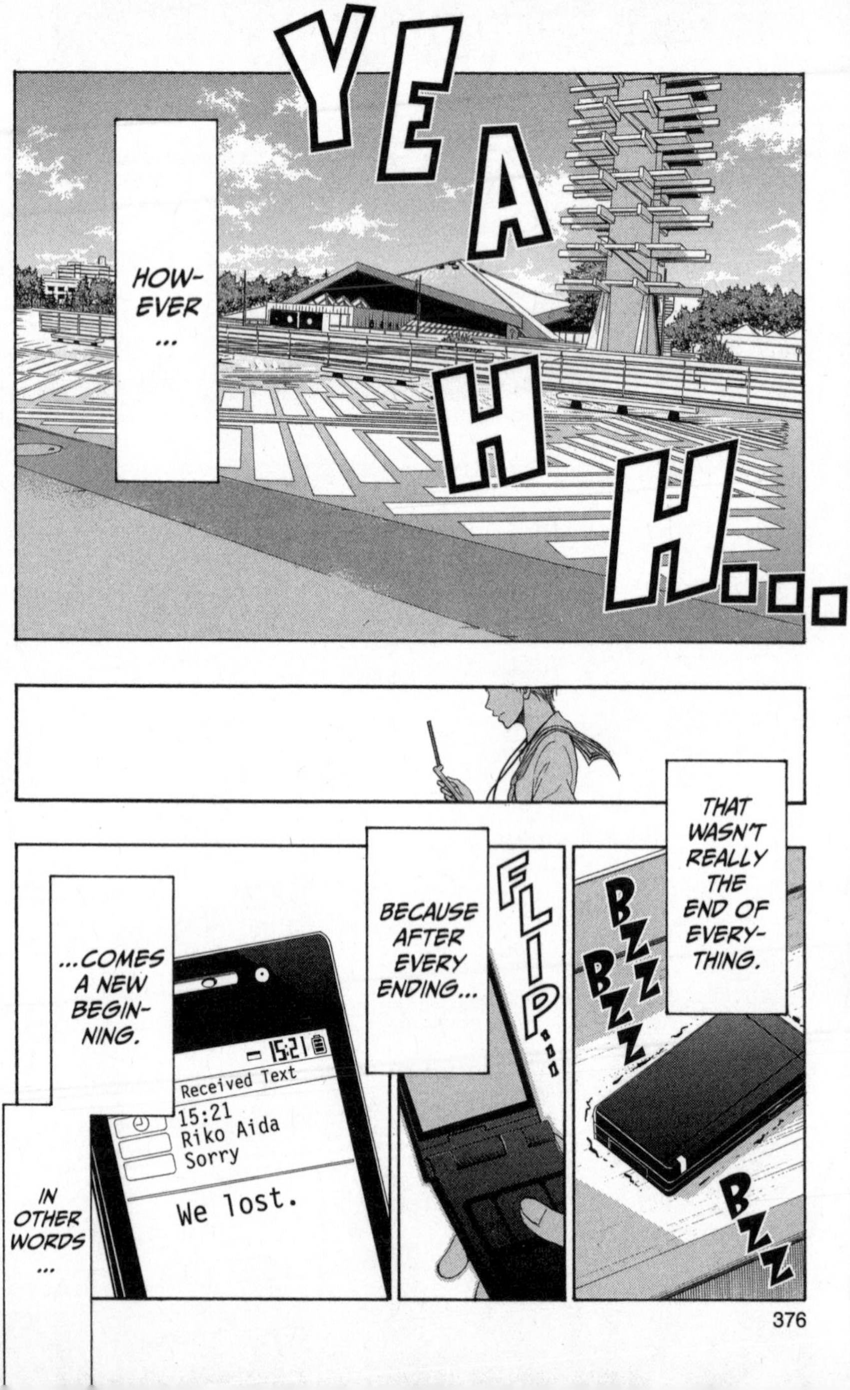
YEAHH...
HOW-EVER...
THAT WASN'T REALLY THE END OF EVERY-THING.
BZZ BZZ
BZZ
FLIP...
BECAUSE AFTER EVERY ENDING...
15:21
Received Text
15:21
Riko Aida
Sorry
We lost.
...COMES A NEW BEGIN-NING.
IN OTHER WORDS...

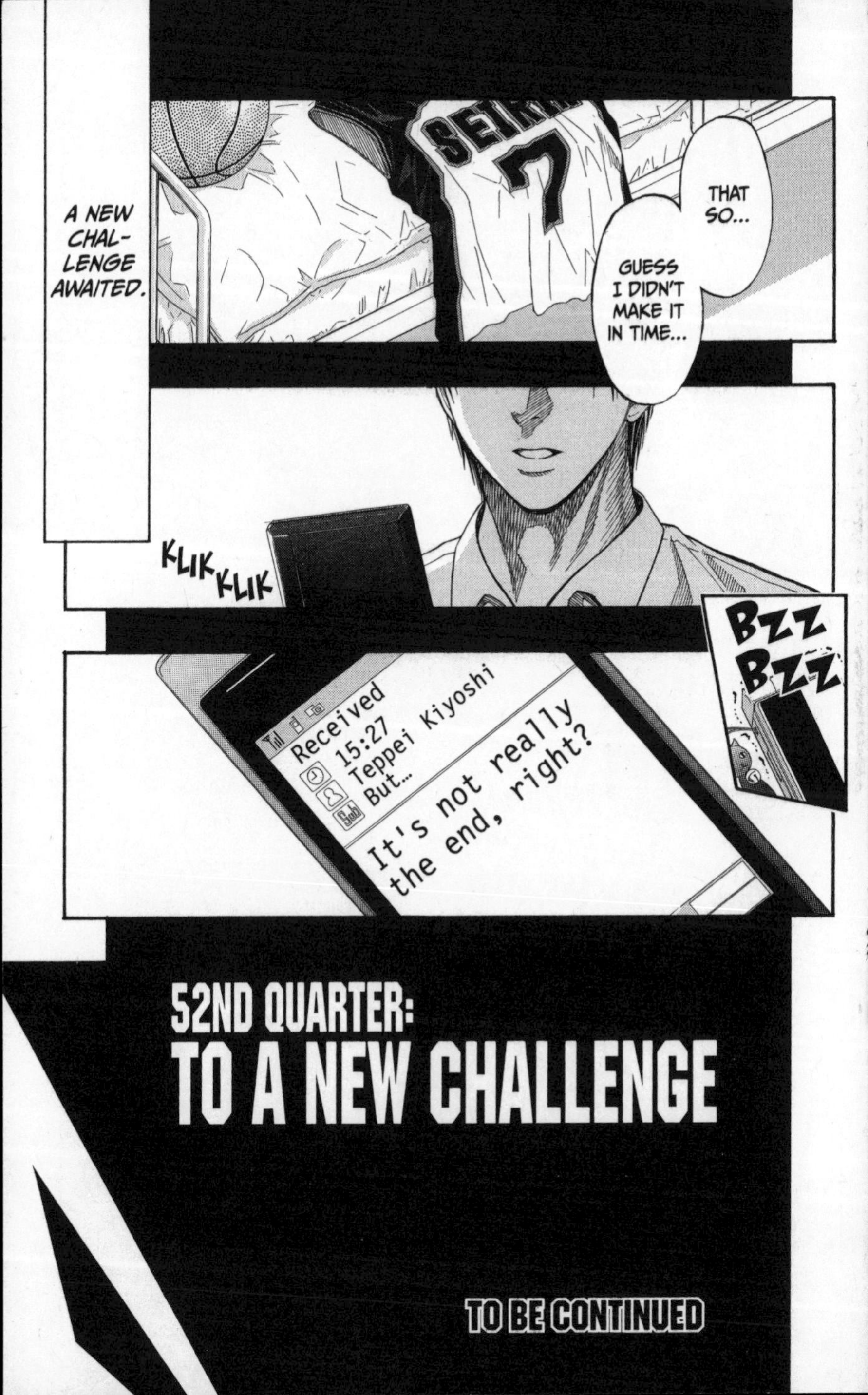

THAT SO...
GUESS I DIDN'T MAKE IT IN TIME...
A NEW CHALLENGE AWAITED.
SEIRIN 7
KLIK KLIK
BZZ BZZ
Received
15:27
Teppei Kiyoshi
But...
It's not really the end, right?
52ND QUARTER:
TO A NEW CHALLENGE
TO BE CONTINUED

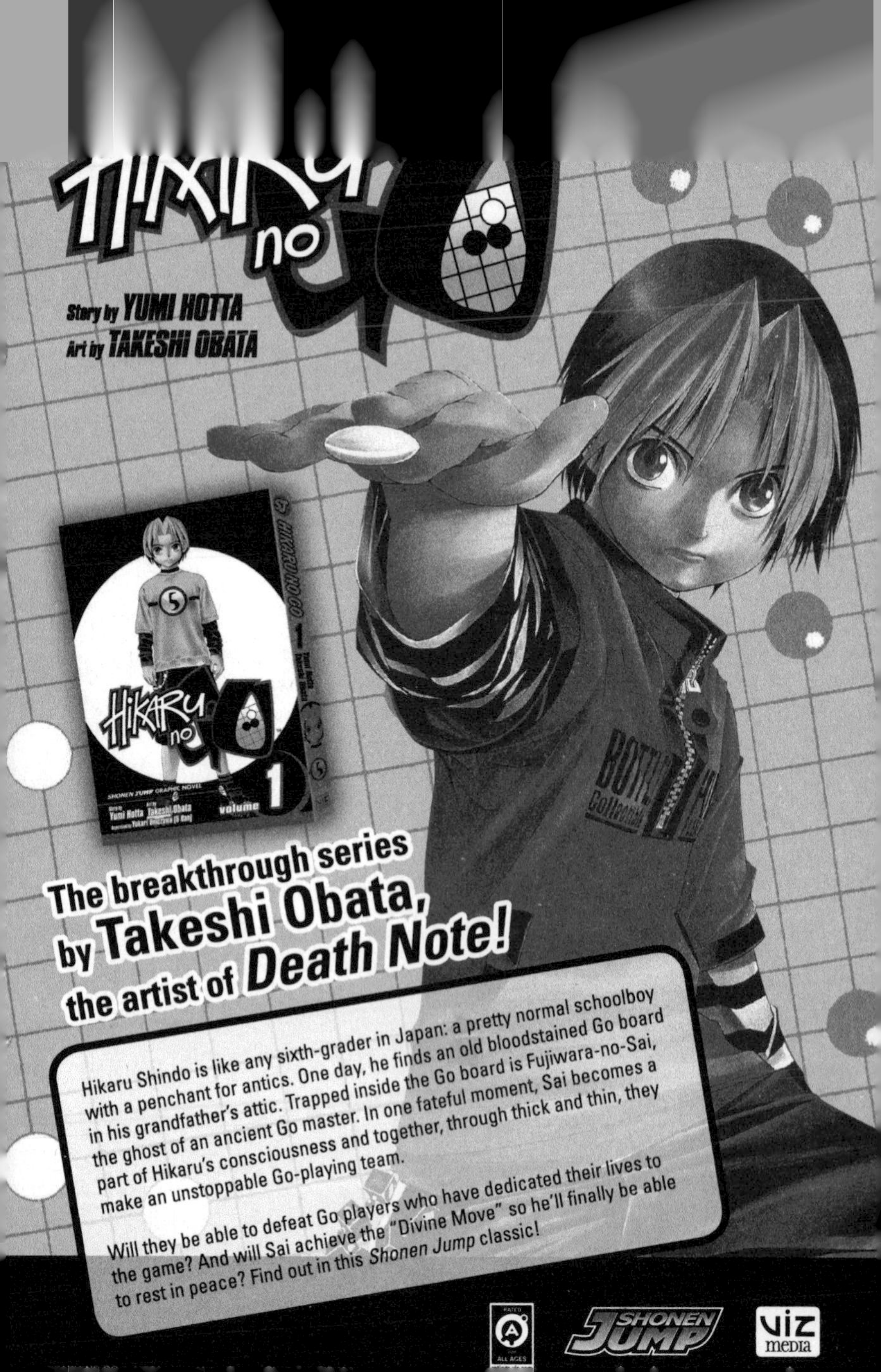
no
Story by YUMI HOTTA
Art by TAKESHI OBATA
HIKARU no
SHONEN JUMP GRAPHIC NOVEL
Yumi Hotta Takeshi Obata
volume 1
The breakthrough series by Takeshi Obata, the artist of *Death Note!*
Hikaru Shindo is like any sixth-grader in Japan: a pretty normal schoolboy with a penchant for antics. One day, he finds an old bloodstained Go board in his grandfather's attic. Trapped inside the Go board is Fujiwara-no-Sai, the ghost of an ancient Go master. In one fateful moment, Sai becomes a part of Hikaru's consciousness and together, through thick and thin, they make an unstoppable Go-playing team.
Will they be able to defeat Go players who have dedicated their lives to the game? And will Sai achieve the "Divine Move" so he'll finally be able to rest in peace? Find out in this *Shonen Jump* classic!
RATED A ALL AGES
SHONEN JUMP
VIZ media

★EYESHIELD 21

STORY BY RIICHIRO INAGAKI
ART BY YUSUKE MURATA

From the artist of *One-Punch Man!*

Wimpy Sena Kobayakawa has been running away from bullies all his life. But when the football gear comes on, things change—Sena's speed and uncanny ability to elude big bullies just might give him what it takes to become a great high school football hero! Catch all the bone-crushing action and slapstick comedy of Japan's hottest football manga!

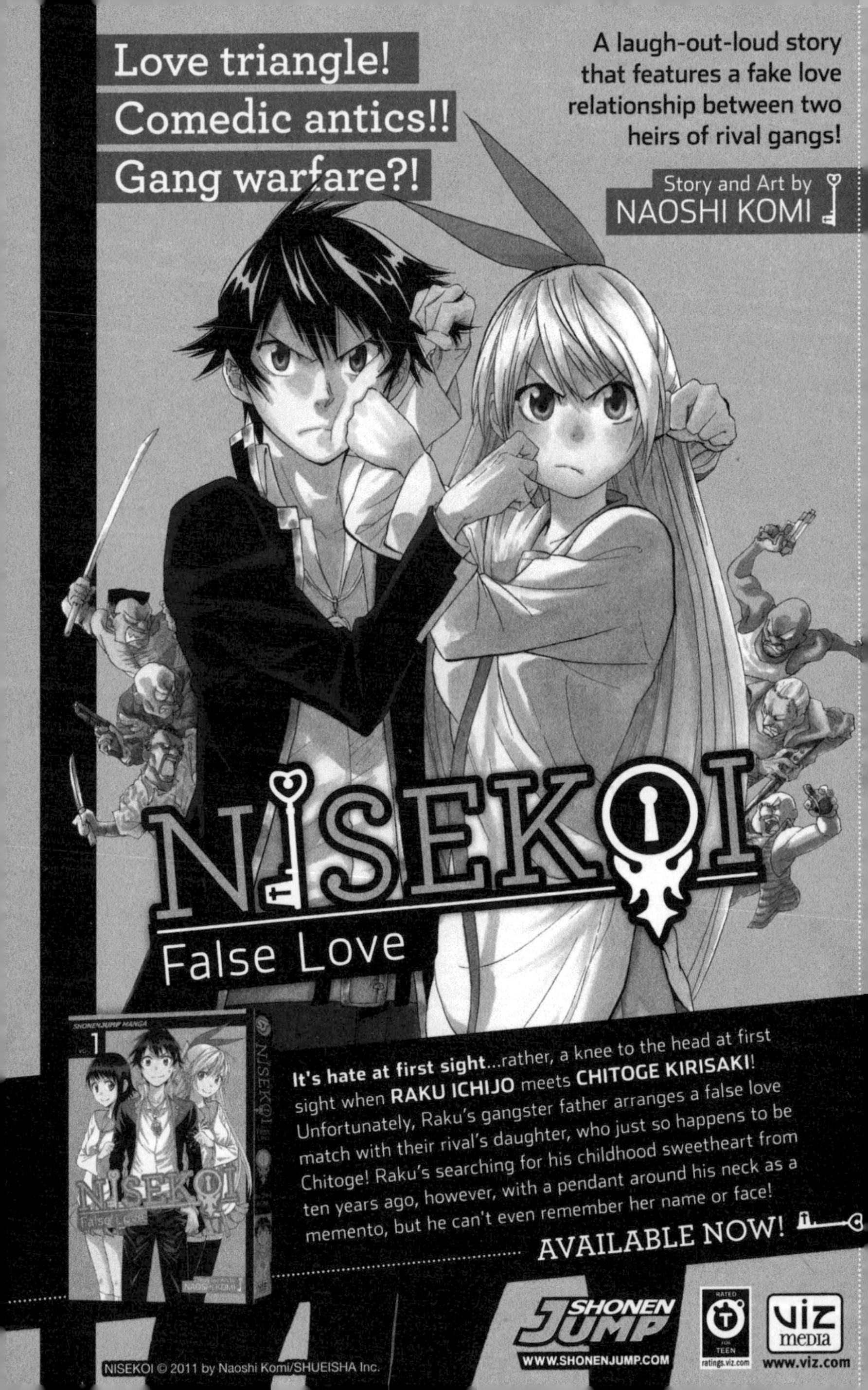
Love triangle!
Comedic antics!!
Gang warfare?!
A laugh-out-loud story that features a fake love relationship between two heirs of rival gangs!
Story and Art by
NAOSHI KOMI
NISEKOI
False Love
SHONEN JUMP MANGA
1
It's hate at first sight...rather, a knee to the head at first sight when RAKU ICHIJO meets CHITOGE KIRISAKI! Unfortunately, Raku's gangster father arranges a false love match with their rival's daughter, who just so happens to be Chitoge! Raku's searching for his childhood sweetheart from ten years ago, however, with a pendant around his neck as a memento, but he can't even remember her name or face!
AVAILABLE NOW!
SHONEN JUMP
WWW.SHONENJUMP.COM
RATED T FOR TEEN
ratings.viz.com
viz media
www.viz.com
NISEKOI © 2011 by Naoshi Komi/SHUEISHA Inc.

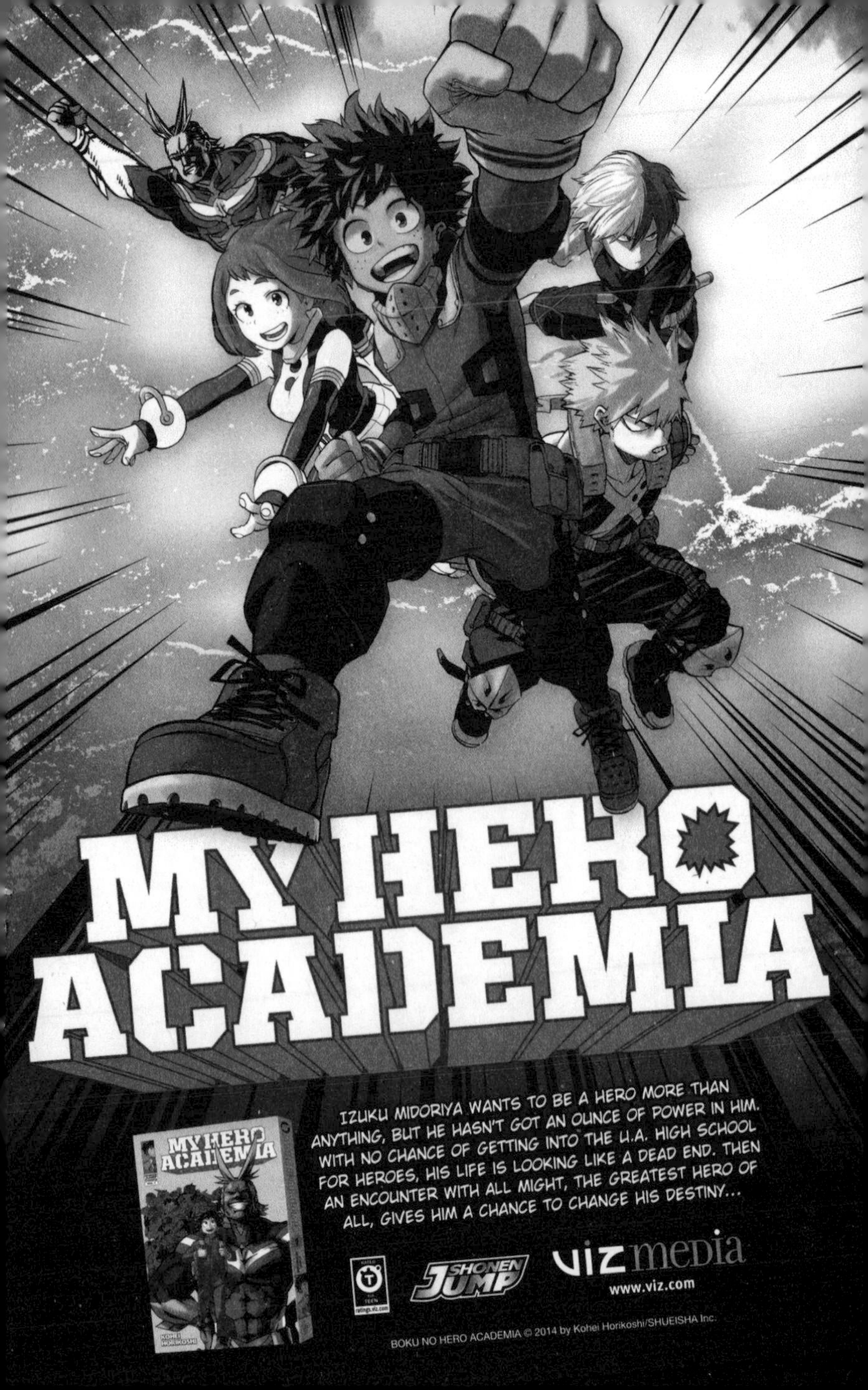
MY HERO ACADEMIA
IZUKU MIDORIYA WANTS TO BE A HERO MORE THAN ANYTHING, BUT HE HASN'T GOT AN OUNCE OF POWER IN HIM. WITH NO CHANCE OF GETTING INTO THE U.A. HIGH SCHOOL FOR HEROES, HIS LIFE IS LOOKING LIKE A DEAD END. THEN AN ENCOUNTER WITH ALL MIGHT, THE GREATEST HERO OF ALL, GIVES HIM A CHANCE TO CHANGE HIS DESTINY...
MY HERO ACADEMIA
KOHEI HORIKOSHI
SHONEN JUMP
viz media
www.viz.com
BOKU NO HERO ACADEMIA © 2014 by Kohei Horikoshi/SHUEISHA Inc.

COMING NEXT VOLUME

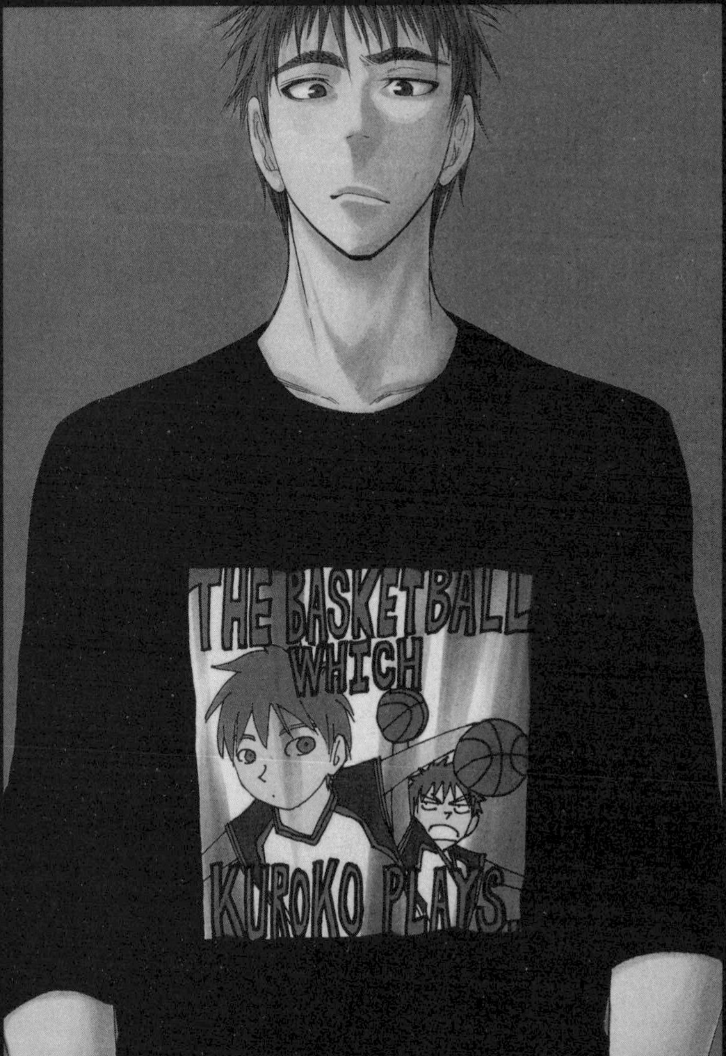
THE BASKETBALL WHICH
KUROKO PLAYS

Seirin's loss to To-oh Academy and Aomine has them feeling down
but all is not lost with a new tournament on the horizon and a

YOU'RE READING THE WRONG WAY!

KUROKO'S BASKETBALL reads from right to left, starting i upper-right corner. Japanese is read from right to left, me that action, sound effects and word-balloon order are compl reversed from English order.

1
2
1
3
4
2
5
6
3
7
8
4
9
5
142

FLIP IT OVER TO GET STARTED!

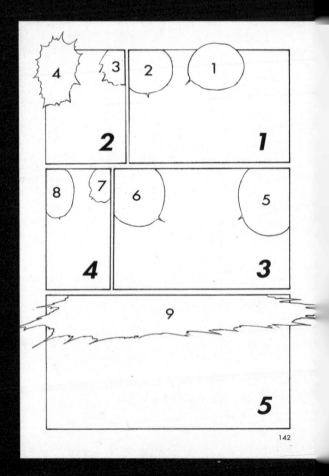